D1483648

CONCEPTS IN DATA STRUCTURES AND SOFTWARE DEVELOPMENT

A Text for the Second Course in Computer Science

Ron Larson
x 3635
NRH 6/07

CONCEPTS IN DATA STRUCTURES AND SOFTWARE DEVELOPMENT

A Text for the Second Course in Computer Science

G. Michael Schneider
Macalester College

Steven C. Bruell
University of Iowa

WEST PUBLISHING COMPANY
St. Paul New York Los Angeles San Francisco

COPYEDITING: Pam McMurry
TEXT DESIGN: Lucy Lesiak Design
TECHNICAL ILLUSTRATIONS: G&S Typesetters, Inc.
COMPOSITION: G&S Typesetters, Inc.
COVER DESIGN: David J. Farr, Imagesmythe, Inc.

Turbo Pascal is a registered trademark of Borland International, Inc.
Ada is a registered trademark of the United States Department of Defense.
Cray-2 is a registered trademark of Cray Research, Inc.
VAX is a registered trademark of Digital Equipment Corporation
Macintosh is a registered trademark of Apple Computer, Inc.

COPYRIGHT © 1991 By WEST PUBLISHING COMPANY
50 W. Kellogg Boulevard
P.O. Box 64526
St. Paul, MN 55164-1003

All rights reserved

Printed in the United States of America

98 97 96 95 94 93 92 91 8 7 6 5 4 3 2 1 0

Library of Congress Cataloging-in-Publication Data

Schneider, G. Michael.
Concepts in data structures and software development : a text for the second course in computer science / G. Michael Schneider, Steven C. Bruell.
p. cm.
Includes index.
ISBN 0-314-77460-2 (hard)
1. Data structures (Computer science) 2. Computer software—Development.
I. Bruell, Steven C. II. Title.
QA76.9.D35S36 1991
005.1—dc20

90-42783
CIP

I dedicate this book to my wife Ruthann, my children Benjamin and Rebecca, and my sister Karen.

G. Michael Schneider

To Sandy

Steven C. Bruell

ABOUT THE AUTHORS

G. Michael Schneider

G. Michael Schneider is currently Professor of computer science and Director of the computer science program at Macalester College in St. Paul, Minnesota, where he has been since 1982. Prior to that he was on the faculty of computer science at the University of Minnesota for eight years.

In addition to his research interests, he is the author of a number of best-selling college textbooks, including *Introduction to Programming and Problem Solving with Pascal, Advanced Programming and Problem Solving with Pascal* (with Steven C. Bruell), and *Principles of Computer Organization.* For the past ten years he has been extremely active in computer science education and curriculum development through membership in the ACM Special Interest Group in Computer Science Education (SIGCSE), the national Computer Science Accreditation Board (CSAB), and the Consortium of Liberal Arts Computer Science Programs (LACS). He has written and presented papers on a range of issues related to the undergraduate curriculum and the design and use of computer laboratories. He is the recipient of two recent National Science Foundation grants to create formal teaching and research laboratories and to study how they can be integrated into the undergraduate computer science curriculum.

Professor Schneider received his Ph.D. in computer science from the University of Wisconsin with a research specialization in computer networks, distributed systems, and parallel processing.

Steven C. Bruell

Steven C. Bruell received the B.A. degree in mathematics (with honors) from the University of Texas at Austin in 1973, and the M.S. and Ph.D. degrees in computer science from Purdue University, West Lafayette, Indiana, in 1975 and 1978, respectively.

He is currently an Associate Professor of computer science at the University of Iowa, Iowa City. His current research interests include distributed systems, parallel simulation, and computer performance evaluation. He has coauthored many papers and three books. He has been an ACM National Lecturer and is currently serving as the Associate Chair of the Computer Science Department.

CONTENTS

PREFACE

This book is intended for the second course in computer science, the course called CS 2 by the ACM in its curriculum recommendations. It assumes that the reader has completed a traditional first course that introduced programming in a high-level language, most likely Pascal. In this text we investigate the topics of data structures and software development.

The material is divided into two parts. Part I (chapters 2 through 11) covers abstract data types, data structures, recursion, and the analysis of algorithms. This section can be viewed as a study of "programming in the small" because it treats issues related to the construction of correct, efficient, and maintainable program units. Part II (chapters 12 through 15) addresses topics related to the software life cycle—specification, design, implementation, validation, and maintenance. This part can be viewed as a study of "programming in the large," since it looks at issues related to the construction of software systems made up of hundreds or thousands of individual units of the type discussed in Part I.

Pictorially, the organization of this book is:

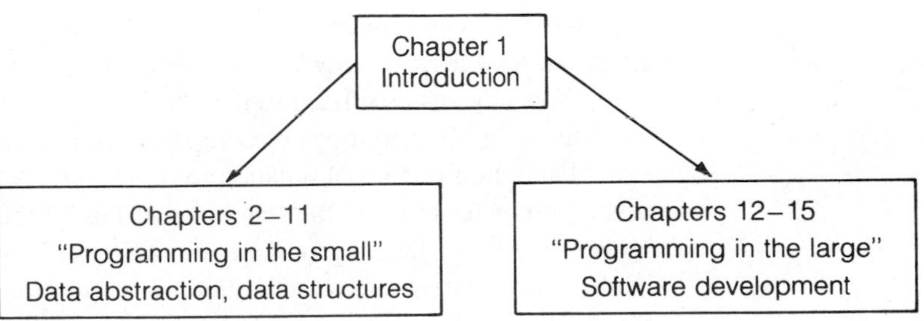

The placement of the discussion on software development following the data abstraction and data structures chapters does not imply that the material must be presented in that order. We have tried to keep these two sections independent from a teaching perspective, and the instructor who wishes to reverse the order of presentation and treat the material on software development first can do so without difficulty.

The material in Part I of this text is a continuation of ideas begun in CS 1. In that first course, students focused on the construction of correct, robust, and reliable program units through a study of algorithm design, structured programming, data types, elementary data structures, procedural abstraction, empirical testing, and programming style. In Part I we continue that investigation and present concepts that permit the design of program units with increased robustness, efficiency, shareability, and maintainability. The topics covered include the specification, design, and implementation of abstract data types (chapter 2) and advanced data structures such as stacks, queues, strings (chapters 3 and 4), trees (chapters 7 and 8), sets (chapter 9), and graphs (chapter 10). The topics of sorting and searching are woven throughout the chapters of Part I, but in chapter 11, we present a separate discussion on the important topic of external sorting and searching. In chapter 5, we introduce recursion so that the student can understand and utilize recursively defined data structures and feel comfortable using recursion as a general problem-solving paradigm. Finally, in chapter 6, we provide the mathematical tools needed for analyzing the time and space efficiency of algorithms, including sequential, recursive, and parallel algorithms.

When presenting the topic of data structures in Part I, we have been guided by and strongly influenced by the following four principles:

1. A student should first study a data structure in terms of its high-level behavior before becoming enmeshed in the details of its implementation. It is not that these implementation details are unimportant. However, the separation of the external and internal properties of a data structure allows us to look first at the formal properties of a data type, such as the nature of operations on objects of that type. Only after these fundamental properties are fully understood do we move on and look at how this structure can be implemented in a typical high-level language. The tool that allows us to create this conceptual separation is the abstract data type (abbreviated ADT), and it is the central theme of Part I. It is the method used to present the data structures studied in chapters 2 through 11. We first study a data structure as an abstract data type, concentrating only on its formal properties and its operations. Later we look at ways in which this structure can be implemented, and we investigate efficiency issues related to the choice of implementation.
2. One of the shortcomings of computer science has been a resistance to the widespread adoption of formal notation to represent key concepts. For example, in CS 1 it is common to describe the semantics of Pascal statements using natural language. However, natural language can be imprecise and highly ambiguous, and its use can lead to inconsistencies, misinterpretations, and incorrect implementations. Just as the freshman physics major learns to use calculus to express fundamental laws of physics, so must the CS student learn to use precise notation to express the "laws" of computer science. Therefore, to describe the behavior of operations on an abstract data type, we use the method of *axiomatic semantics,* which is a powerful, albeit complex, technique for describing the actions of operations on data objects. While this text contains only an introduction (with additional coverage coming in advanced courses in compilers and formal languages), it should make the student aware of the importance of precise and accurate notation. In addition to axiomatic semantics, we also use Big-O notation for the time and space analysis of algorithms (chapter 6), decision tables and finite state automata for the specification

of software (chapter 13), and a directed graph representation of program design documents (chapter 14).

3. There are many different data structures that can be covered in a CS 2 course, from arrays to AVL trees, from heaps to hash tables. Because of the large number of topics that can be studied, any treatment of this subject should initially provide an overall structure or classification scheme. If this classification is done well, the student will not view the subsequent discussion as a large and apparently unrelated collection of facts but as an organized and related body of knowledge. (The problem is identical to the one faced by a biologist teaching a first course. He or she first presents the well-known taxonomy of living organisms (kingdom, phylum, class, order, . . .) rather than immediately presenting a "Noah's Ark" of animal types. This latter approach would quickly collapse into chaos.) In chapter 3, before beginning our discussion of data structures, we present a taxonomy of data structures based on the following four classes: sets, linear types, hierarchical types, and graphs (Figure 3.1). We then show why all data structures, regardless of what properties they may possess, fall into one of these four classes, thus giving the student a much better idea of how these ideas fit together (the "big picture").

4. Finally, and most controversially, we made the decision not to use a specific high-level language to present our programming examples. Instead, we have chosen to use the pseudocode shown in Figure 2–16. While this pseudocode is closely related to a number of existing languages (especially Modula-2 and Ada), it provides these capabilities in a much more simplified manner. There will no doubt be those who ask why we did not select ———, where the missing word is the name of the individual's favorite language, such as Modula-2, Ada, Turbo Pascal, or C++. To completely and accurately describe the abstract data type capabilities of a "real" language, such as Ada packages, would take many pages of language- and system-specific information. This material would dwell on highly technical syntactic and semantic details such as semicolons, indentation, reserved words, and programming environments. But this approach is exactly opposite from what we stress in this book—that the ideas and concepts we are presenting are language-, system-, and vendor-independent, and that one can study them at a high level of abstraction without worrying about the specific language into which they will be translated (the very definition of abstraction!). This is not a book on advanced concepts in Modula-2 or Ada or ——— but a text on advanced concepts in computer science.

However, computer science is an applied as well as a theoretical discipline, and it is important for a student to implement the abstract ideas presented in a course. It is through this hands-on experience that a student can gain a deeper understanding of these concepts. To support this empirical experience, we have provided a series of language-specific supplements that are coordinated with the material in the text. These supplements describe an actual high-level programming language that can then be used to implement the examples, case studies, and homework assignments. Alternatively, an instructor could choose to provide this language- and system-related information through reference manuals, other texts, or locally prepared handouts. Regardless of the approach, however, it is important to send a message to the student that this is *not* just a language course or a programming course, but a course in computer science. The language that will ultimately be used, so important in CS 1, is more properly viewed in CS 2 as material supplementary to the central discussion.

Part II of the text, chapters 12 to 15, is an overview of the software life cycle. It focuses on those life cycle phases not stressed in the student's previous class work. Four chapters cannot possibly cover software development in great detail, and this text does not purport to replace a full semester course on the subject of software engineering. However, many students graduate in computer science without completing such a course and with little or no introduction to the life cycle of a software project. Part II of the text provides that needed introduction.

In chapter 12 we overview the eight stages in the software life cycle, from the initial rough problem statement to finished documentation and ongoing maintenance. Some of these eight stages may be inappropriate for extended discussion in a CS 2 course, for example, the feasibility study can require a knowledge of economics, accounting, and marketing as well as computer science. Some software development stages have been studied extensively in CS 1, namely coding and debugging. However, the remaining steps in the software life cycle are both highly appropriate to discuss and generally unfamiliar to students in a second course. They are presented in the next three chapters.

Chapter 13 discusses the topics of problem specification and the content of the problem specification document, including functional, error, and performance specifications. As we mentioned earlier, natural language is not the most precise way to express user needs. Therefore, in this chapter we look at two formal alternatives to natural language—decision tables and finite-state automata. These methods can provide the precision needed to develop high-quality specifications.

Chapter 14 treats the program design phase. Here we use the top-down problem-solving strategy called *divide and conquer* to select and specify the program units and data structures needed in our solution. The relationships between these program units will be expressed as a structure chart using a formal notation based on directed graphs. This chapter also describes the information contained in the program design document and presents guidelines for evaluating the quality of a proposed design.

Finally, chapter 15 looks at the two validation and verification (V & V) techniques called *empirical testing* and *formal verification*. We review the strengths and weaknesses of each of these approaches and conclude by describing a third method called *structured walkthroughs*. Regardless of which method is used, the goal of all V & V techniques is the same—to increase the confidence with which we can assert the correctness of each individual program unit as well as the correctness of the software system as a whole.

This is the outline of the text. As the preface clearly shows, it covers a good deal of material and ranges over many subject areas. However, its central themes can be clearly and simply stated: To improve the students' ability to specify, design, and solve real-world problems and to deepen their understanding and appreciation of the discipline of computer science.

Acknowledgments

I would like to thank the people who assisted me during the writing of this text. This certainly includes all the reviewers who read the initial drafts so carefully and made many helpful suggestions and comments. Their ideas were invaluable to me during the rewriting and revising of the manuscript. Alphabetically, these reviewers were

Douglas Bickerstaff
Eastern Washington University

Thomas E. Byther
University of Maine

Maurice Eggen
Trinity University

Henry Etlinger
Rochester Institute of Technology

Charles E. Frank
Northern Kentucky University

Michael Hennessy
University of Oregon

Lawrence A. Jehn
University of Dayton

Kenneth Modesitt
Western Kentucky University

William R. Nico
California State University at Hayward

Alex T. Prengel, Jr.
Brandeis University

C. Ray Russell
Virginia Commonwealth University

Paul S. Schnare
Eastern Kentucky University

Greg Scragg
State University of New York at Geneseo

Theodore Sjoerdsma
Washington and Lee University

Jeffrey Slomka
Southwest Texas State University

Greg Starling
University of Arkansas, Fayetteville

Stan Thomas
Wake Forest University

Susan R. Wallace
University of North Florida

A special thanks to Mr. David Sielaff who helped prepare and debug all the algorithms and code in the text and I am deeply grateful. Thanks also to Ms. Michelle Villinski who typed the original manuscript and did an outstanding job. Finally, I would like to thank the people at West Publishing who worked with me during the preparation and production of the book. They are professionals in every sense of the word, and they were a pleasure to work with: Mark Jacobsen, Denis Ralling, and, most of all, Jerry Westby, whom I consider to be not only my editor but also a good friend.

G. Michael Schneider
Macalester College

CHAPTER 1

AN INTRODUCTION TO ADVANCED PROGRAMMING CONCEPTS

CHAPTER OUTLINE

1.1 INTRODUCTION

This text is designed to be used in a second course in computer science. It assumes that the reader has completed an introductory programming course (or something equivalent) and knows how to code in a high-level procedural language, most likely Pascal. Because of limited time, first courses in programming usually address only a small part of the overall programming and problem-solving process—the concept of an algorithm, the syntax of Pascal, the translation of a few simple algorithms into Pascal, and methods for debugging and testing programs. These first courses teach important *introductory* concepts in programming and software development. We will now expand those initial ideas and introduce a wide range of *advanced* concepts that will allow us to solve larger and more interesting problems.

The text is divided into two parts. Part I, chapters 2 through 11, presents topics drawn from the areas of data abstraction and data representation, including the following:

- The concept of data abstraction
- The formal specification and implementation of abstract data types
- Advanced data structures, including linear, hierarchical, set, and graph structures
- Recursion
- Time and space analysis of algorithms
- Internal and external sorting techniques

Because first courses emphasize (some would say overemphasize) coding, students frequently develop the mistaken belief that computer science is identical to programming, which is identical to coding. This belief is, of course, untrue. In Part II, chapters 12 through 15, we will introduce a broader view of the overall programming process—the *software life cycle*—and you will see that the *software development* process involves a number of distinct steps from the initial problem statement to the finished solution. Although this process does include coding, it also involves many other important and intellectually demanding operations:

- Problem specification and validation
- Program design
- Data structure specification and design
- Algorithm specification and design
- Implementation (coding and debugging)
- Program testing, verification, and benchmarking
- Documentation
- Program maintenance

As this list indicates, a great deal of important preparatory work must be done before we arrive at the implementation stage, and much remains to be done after coding has been completed. The second part of the text will introduce you to the wealth of operations that go into the development of correct, maintainable, and efficient software.

1.2 PART I: ABSTRACT DATA TYPES AND ADVANCED DATA STRUCTURES

1.2.1 Abstract Data Types

The Random House Dictionary of the English Language defines *abstraction* as "the act of considering something as a general quality or characteristic, apart from any concrete realities, specific objects, or actual instance." For us, *abstraction* means studying a system from a high-level viewpoint, disregarding the enormous number of "messy" and "ugly" details that are involved in implementing that system and about which we may not be concerned at the present time.

Abstraction is a powerful programming tool that has already been introduced and widely used in most first courses in programming. For example, we can approach the concept of iteration (i.e., looping) in terms of a few simple and easily understood high-level language constructs (**While**, **Repeat**, and **For**) without regard for the complex machine-language compare and branch operations that must be carried out on the underlying hardware:

High-level abstraction: **For** *i* := 1 **To** *N*+1 **Do** *<statement>*

Low-level implementation:

```
        MOVL #1, R6
        MOVL N, R7
        INCL R7
Loop:   CMPL  R6, R7
        BGT   Done
        <statement>
        INCL  R6
        JMP   Loop
Done:
```

Most people would agree that this high-level abstraction is more understandable than the functionally equivalent but more detailed low-level implementation. This example illustrates *control abstraction*, an important feature of all high-level programming languages.

Similarly, we can simplify a long and highly complex set of operations by using the *procedure mechanism*, which allows us to give a name to a (potentially large) collection of declarations and statements:

High-level abstraction: **Procedure** *MatrixInvert(Matrix, N, NewMatrix);*
(Take a nonsingular N × N Matrix, invert it, and return the result in NewMatrix. *)*

Low-level implementation: *The hundreds of lines of declarations and code needed to implement the program*

Even though this routine may be hundreds of lines long and utilize totally unfamiliar algorithms, the high-level abstraction hides all these details from us. We can think of the operation of matrix inversion only in terms of the name MatrixInvert and its three formal parameters. This example illustrates *procedural abstraction*, a central theme of most introductory courses in programming. Together, control and proce-

Figure 1–1
Model of an Abstract Data Type

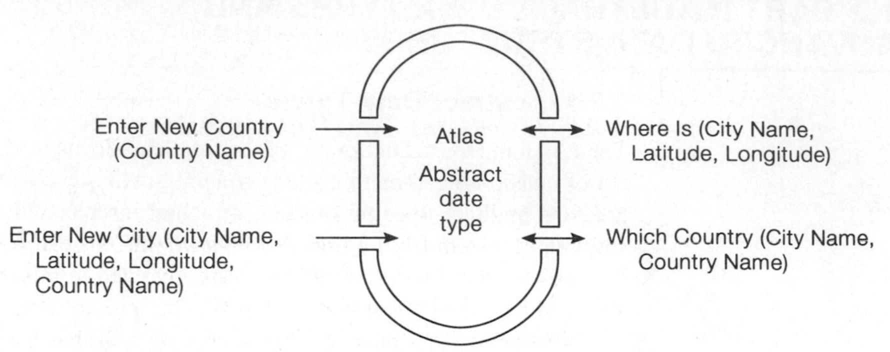

dural abstraction are two of the most important features provided by Pascal or, indeed, any high-level language, and they allow us to manage problems of enormous length and complexity effectively.

We now extend these ideas to the concept of *data abstraction*. Just as we were able to use the procedure MatrixInvert without being aware of its internal structure, we can design and use a data structure without knowing anything about its internal implementation. This process uses the concept of an *abstract data type*.

For example, suppose we have a data type called Atlas, which contains a list of countries and major cities in the world, along with their geographic location—latitude and longitude. We are allowed to perform the four operations illustrated in Figure 1–1 on this data structure: entering a new country into the Atlas, entering a new city into the Atlas along with its geographic coordinates and country, retrieving the geographic coordinates of a given city, and determining in which country a given city is located. To carry out these four operations, we do not need to know how Atlas has been implemented.

Figure 1–1 demonstrates how the internal details of an abstract data type such as Atlas are hidden from view; we are unaware of whether the actual data object is implemented internally as a file, an array, a linked list, or a record structure. Our access to the abstract data type is limited to the four operations shown in Figure 1–1, and no other manipulation of Atlas is possible. Not only does this simplify our understanding of Atlas' use, but it also protects Atlas from unauthorized or unexpected operations, such as moving a city!

A number of well-known programming languages (e.g., Modula-2, Ada, C++, and Turbo Pascal) allow abstract data types like the one shown in Figure 1–1 to be designed, implemented, and used as part of your programs. Together with control and procedural abstraction, data abstraction is one of the most important tools available to the software designer.

The concept of data abstraction is one of the fundamental and central themes of this text. We first introduce new data structures as abstract data types, concentrating on the properties of objects of this type and the operations allowed on these objects. Only then do we look "inside" these types and investigate the issues related to their implementation. This approach will allow us to avoid getting lost in detail before we understand what a data structure is and how it works.

Chapter 2 will introduce you to the concept of abstract data types, as well as teach you how to specify and design them formally.

1.2.2 Advanced Data Structures

In a first programming course, you utilize the data types and data structures provided directly in the language under study—for example, arrays, records, sets, files, and pointers, in the case of Pascal. However, there are many additional ways to organize, structure, and maintain data, and these other representations can lead to extremely fast and efficient algorithms.

For example, imagine a tree-like data structure that stores English words. Assume that each word in the collection can point to two other words. The left pointer points to words that come before it alphabetically, whereas the right pointer points to words that come after it alphabetically. This data structure is called a *binary search tree*; an example is shown in Figure 1–2.

A binary search tree can be a very efficient data structure for maintaining lists of words that must be searched frequently. For example, if the 12 words in Figure 1–2 were stored in random order in a one-dimensional array and searched sequentially, it would take on the average about six accesses to find any specific word, and it would take 12 accesses to discover that a word was not in the collection. Using the binary search tree of Figure 1–2, it would never take more than four accesses to locate a word or to determine that it was not there—four is simply the maximum distance from the top to the bottom of the tree. This three-fold improvement in efficiency comes not from our cleverness in coding, but rather from our ability to analyze the problem and select a better data representation.

The binary search tree is just one of the advanced data structures that we will introduce. We will devote six chapters to surveying a range of interesting new ways to represent and organize data. In chapters 3 and 4, we will look at these *linear structures:*

- Abstract arrays
- Strings
- Stacks
- Queues
- Priority queues
- Deques
- Linear lists

Figure 1–2
Example of a Binary Search Tree

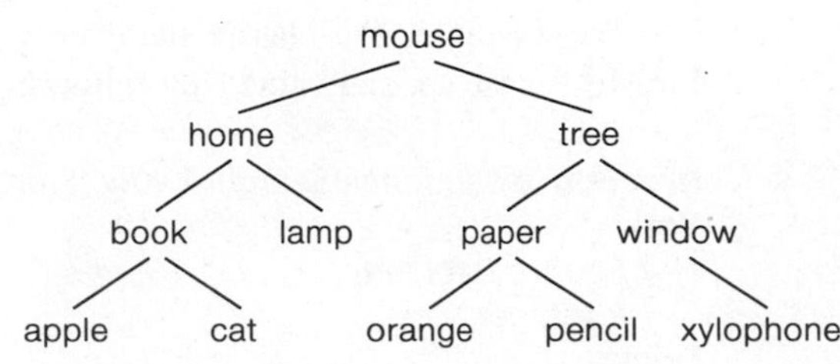

In chapters 7 and 8, we will consider the *hierarchical structures:*

- General trees
- Binary trees
- Binary search trees
- Balanced search trees
- Tries
- Heaps
- B-trees

In chapter 9, we will examine *set structures:*

- Sets
- Hash tables

In chapter 10, we will discuss *graphs:*

- Directed graphs
- Undirected graphs

For each of these data structures, we will study its formal properties as an abstract data type, as well as one or more techniques for its implementation.

Notice that virtually none of the data structures in the preceding lists are directly available in Pascal, C, Modula-2, or Ada, in contrast to such types as records, arrays, and integers. However, this will not be a problem. Just as the procedure mechanism can be viewed as a way of extending a language, so can abstract data types. Using the abstract data type mechanism, we can create these structures, implement them, put them into a data type library, and use them as though they were primitive constructs of our language. We are thus "freed" from the limitations of the relatively small collection of data structures available in a given programming language. Instead, we are able to use whatever data representations we wish to dream up and build! In later chapters, we will see many examples of this language extension capability.

1.2.3 Recursion

Iteration is one of the fundamental problem-solving techniques introduced in a first programming course. With *iteration*, we solve a problem by executing a series of statements sequentially, from beginning to end, until some condition has been satisfied. An alternative method of problem solving is *recursion*, in which we define a solution in terms of repeated invocations of the same solution; that is, we define a problem in terms of itself!

For example, the classic iterative approach to searching an array T[Start .. Finish] for the special value Key follows:

```
Procedure SequentialSearch(T, Key, Start, Finish);
Var
    Found: Boolean;
    i: Integer;
Begin
    Found := False;
    i := Start;
```

```
    While (i <= Finish) And (Not Found) Do
        If T[i] = Key Then
            Write ('Found');
            Found := True
        Else
            i := i + 1
End;
```

A recursive solution for the same problem would look like this:

```
Procedure SequentialSearch(T, Key, i, j);
Begin
    If i > j Then Return
    Else
        If T[i] = Key Then
            Write ('Found')
        Else
            SequentialSearch(T, Key, i+1, j)        (* A recursive call. *)
End;
```

The search would be initiated by the following procedure call:

```
    SequentialSearch(T, Key, Start, Finish)
```

Notice how the operation of searching the array from location T[i] to T[j] is defined in terms of the identical SequentialSearch procedure, but this time from location T[i + 1] to T[j].

Recursion is a powerful problem-solving tool, especially for data structures defined in an inherently recursive manner (e.g., the binary search tree mentioned in the previous section). Recursion can lead to some elegant and compact solutions to problems that would be difficult and cumbersome to implement iteratively. It can also lead to some highly inefficient programs that perform more poorly than do the corresponding iterative ones. Chapter 5 will introduce the concept of recursion, discuss the method's strengths and weaknesses, and show a number of examples of recursive algorithms.

Because recursion is frequently introduced after iteration, some students tend to view it as a specialized and rather arcane technique, well out of the mainstream of normal problem solving. This perception is absolutely untrue. Any problem that can be solved iteratively can be solved recursively, and a number of well-known and widely used languages (e.g., Prolog, SmallTalk, and LISP) use recursion as their primary looping control structure. For many problems that we will introduce, one of our first and most important design decisions will be whether to develop our solution iteratively or recursively. Recursion will be an important and widely used technique in our problem-solving tool kit.

1.2.4 The Analysis of Algorithms

In Section 1.2.2 and Figure 1–2, we showed a diagram of a binary search tree and said that this structure can provide a better method for searching a collection of words than the sequential search technique. However, that was an informal analysis that appealed only to our intuition, because we never defined exactly what we meant by the term *better*. For example, consider the following list of the 12 words stored in the tree structure of Figure 1–2:

apple
tree
mouse
home
book
.
.
.

If we searched sequentially for the word *apple*, we would find it on the very first look, but it would take four comparisons to find the word *apple* using the tree diagram of Figure 1–2. Does this invalidate our conclusion about the relative efficiency of the two techniques? Or should we recognize that this is simply a special case, not at all representative of the general behavior of these two algorithms?

The point is that we cannot rely on informal methods, intuition, or common sense to answer these questions. We need to develop formal techniques to analyze algorithms so that we can say unequivocally that for a given class of problems, algorithm A is superior (i.e., faster, more compact, or more robust) than algorithm B. This type of conclusion will allow us to make clear, informed decisions during algorithm selection and data structure design. Chapter 6 will develop such a formal technique, called *asymptotic analysis* and will provide examples of the analysis of iterative, recursive, and parallel algorithms.

This analysis will have a profound effect on the efficiency of the resulting software. As we will see in chapter 6, the efficiency of a program is affected most strongly by our choice of algorithms and data representation, not by the language in which we choose to code, the machine on which the code is run, or the ability and cleverness of the coder! Essentially, the "efficiency game" is won or lost once the solution method and data structures have been selected. The formal analysis techniques we will study in chapter 6 will give us the tools we need to make intelligent selections.

1.3 PART II: SOFTWARE DEVELOPMENT AND THE SOFTWARE LIFE CYCLE

1.3.1 Specification and Design

Part II of this text will address the *software life cycle*—the complete set of operations needed to develop a correct and efficient software system for solving a given problem. This life cycle is diagrammed in Figure 1–3.

Students are generally unfamiliar with the initial planning, specification, and design phases shown in Figure 1–3 because of the nature of software development in an academic environment. Since there are no custom hardware designs, budget-

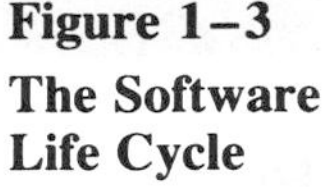

Figure 1–3
The Software Life Cycle

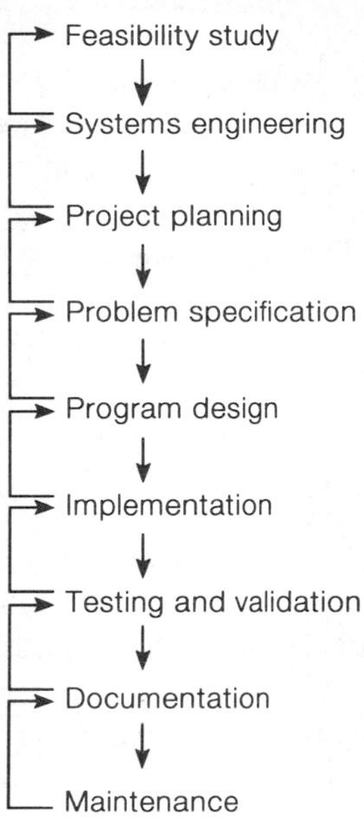

ing, scheduling, or personnel issues involved in student projects, students skip the feasibility study, systems engineering, and project planning phases. The instructor, not the student, is responsible for specifying the problem, and because these proj-ccts arc so simplc (typically 50 to 500 lines of code), students can (and frequently do) skip program design and go directly into implementation—that is, coding and debugging. After they have been tested and run correctly once, student projects are finished. They are not documented extensively and are rarely maintained.

This approach can give students a highly misleading impression of the software development process. It reinforces the incorrect impression that programming is equivalent to coding, and it leads to the mistaken belief that implementation is the most important and intellectually exciting aspect of programming. In reality, the most intellectually demanding parts of software development are the operations carried out prior to implementation—namely problem specification, where we formally specify the details of the problem we will solve, and program design, where we decompose that one large task into a collection of simple subtasks that solve our original problem.

Although many details of the software life cycle are beyond the scope of this book (they are usually covered in an upper-level course entitled "Software Engineering"), it is important for students to be introduced to the software development phases shown in Figure 1–3 and to realize the enormous amount of specification, design, and analysis work that must be done both prior to and after implementation. Chapter 12 will survey the life cycle of Figure 1–3 and will review the decisions that must be made at each stage in the software development process. Chapters 13 and 14 will introduce important issues that occur during the problem specification and program design stages.

1.3.2 Testing and Formal Verification

Once the problem has been specified and designed and the program has been implemented in some high-level language, we must verify the correctness of our solution. The terms *validation* and *verification* are not synonymous. In the *validation* process, we want to ensure that the detailed specifications of the problem are correct. In *verification*, we want to ensure that our implementation of the solution is correct. Informally, we can say that the goal of validation is making sure we solve the right problem, whereas the goal of verification is making sure we solve the problem right!

In computer science, the classic method of program verification is *empirical testing,* in which the finished program is run with a number of carefully chosen test cases. If the program works properly for these data sets, we conclude that it is correct and will work properly for all data, even those not tested.

Such a conclusion about the program's correctness is mathematically weak, and the program may still contain errors that went undetected during testing because of the method we used to select our test data. Testing has always been one of the problem areas in software development, and we have all endured the frustration of encountering a fatal bug in a program that was supposedly correct.

There is, however, a more powerful, albeit more complex, method, called *formal verification*. Instead of testing a program, we attempt to prove that it is correct. We treat a program P as a mathematical function $y = P(x)$, and we show that for every input x, the function (i.e., the program) produces the correct output y. Verification provides a stronger form of correctness than we can achieve using empirical testing, and it allows us to make assertions about the program's behavior for data sets not tested explicitly. We are able to make statements about the absence of errors, as well as about the presence of errors.

With the empirical testing method, we do the coding and testing phases in a sequential fashion, first writing the program and then testing what we wrote:

Coding → Testing

In contrast, with formal verification, we develop the proof of correctness in parallel with the code:

Coding →
Proof →

Thus, with formal verification, the programmer can no longer write code and allow someone else to prove it correct. He or she must be familiar with proof techniques and must develop them simultaneously with the writing of the code. Thus, the programmer must be knowledgeable about symbolic logic, proof methods, and discrete mathematics. It is unlikely, however, that formal verification will completely replace empirical testing in the near future. From a practical point of view, correctness proofs can be extremely complicated; they are sometimes as difficult to construct as is the program itself. Also, it has been shown theoretically that, although we may be able to prove the correctness of a specific program, we cannot, in general, prove the correctness of any arbitrary program. For these reasons, it is likely that formal verification and empirical testing will both continue to have their place in the software verification process.

We will introduce the principles of both empirical testing and formal verification in chapter 15, where we discuss the strengths and weaknesses of each technique.

1.4 CONCLUSION

We have now described what we mean by the phrase *advanced programming concepts*. We have chosen to exclude such activities as learning a second programming language, writing programs for different computers, or learning more Pascal syntax and programming tricks. The details of a specific programming language—so central to the discussion of the first course—will be much less important here, as we focus our studies on higher-level issues that are independent of any specific language or system. Our goal in this text is to improve your ability to specify, design, and implement high-quality software, regardless of what language or system you may choose for the implementation, and to deepen your understanding and appreciation of the discipline of computer science.

CHAPTER EXERCISES

1. Describe three additional operations that you might wish to perform on the Atlas abstract data type shown in Figure 1–1. For each operation, say whether you need to know the internal structure of Atlas to specify these new operations? Explain your answers.
2. Using the notation of Figure 1–1, design an abstract data type called WaitingLine, which represents people waiting in line for a movie. Specify the five most important operations you want to carry out on the waiting line. For each operation, say whether you need to know the internal structure of WaitingLine to specify it.
3. Assume we have a binary search tree of the type shown in Figure 1–2 and that it has 1,000 entries. What is the maximum number of words we would have to look at to find a given word or to determine that it is not there? What would be the maximum number if the words were stored in an array or file?
4. Describe one or two situations in your everyday life where you use the idea of abstraction to simplify large tasks that you need to perform.
5. Given the first n natural numbers 1, 2, . . . , n, set up a recursive solution to the problem of summing all n elements.
6. Look back over some previous Pascal programs that you either used or wrote and in which errors accidently remained in the final version. Describe the errors. Why did you not discover them? What was wrong with your plan for testing the program?
7. Do you agree or disagree with the following statements? Explain your answers.
   a. Empirical testing is an adequate testing technique, because all you need to do is to *exhaustively* test all possible cases.

b. Empirical testing will allow you to determine both the pr ence or absence of any errors in a program unit.
c. Empirical testing can prove the presence of errors, but not the absence of errors.

8. Interview one or two professional programmers (possibly at your local computer center) to find out what proportion of their time is spent on each of the phases listed in Figure 1–3. Compare the results of your interviews with an estimate of how much time you spent in each phase when you were writing programs for your first class in computer science.

PART I

ABSTRACT DATA TYPES, ADVANCED DATA STRUCTURES, RECURSION, AND THE ANALYSIS OF ALGORITHMS

In Part I of this text, chapters 2 through 11, we will study advanced techniques for building correct, efficient, robust, and maintainable program units. This subject can be termed a study of *programming in the small*, because the concepts presented concern the design, implementation, and analysis of high-quality program units rather than entire integrated software systems. This material is a continuation of ideas introduced in first programming courses. These first courses taught us how to decompose large problems into small ones and how to solve those separate problems using the tools of procedures, iterative and conditional control structures, and the data structures available in our language. We will now improve this strategy by presenting new and more powerful tools to assist in the problem-solving task.

Chapter 2 introduces the topic of data abstraction as a way to create secure, shareable, and maintainable library units. Chapters 3 and 4 and chapters 7 through 11 demonstrate how we can use this feature to design and implement advanced data structures and their associated algorithms. These new representations expand our limited data-structuring capabilities and allow us to create more efficient solutions to important problems in computer science. Since many data structures are defined recursively, chapter 5 discusses and offers numerous examples of this important concept. Finally, to demonstrate that we have indeed increased the efficiency of a program unit, chapter 6 describes and gives examples of a mathematical technique for the formal analysis of algorithms. These ideas are illustrated using case studies drawn from applications within the field of computer science.

We must remember that any realistic piece of software is composed not of one or two program units, but rather 100 or 200—or even 1,000 or 2,000—units. It is not sufficient to learn to design and implement individual program pieces correctly and elegantly. We must also be able to manage the task of developing, testing, and integrating an enormous number of these units into a correct and functioning solution to the overall problem. The task of managing the development of a large software system is called *programming in the large*; it is the central topic of Part II of this text.

CHAPTER 2

ABSTRACT DATA TYPES

CHAPTER OUTLINE

2.1 INTRODUCTION TO ABSTRACT DATA TYPES

One of the most powerful ideas in programming and problem solving is the concept of *abstraction*—the ability to view something as a high-level object while temporarily ignoring the enormous amount of underlying detail associated with that object. Another way to describe abstraction is to say that it means viewing something only in terms of its external appearance, without regard for its internal implementation. Without abstraction, we would be unable to manage or understand any large, complex system. (Imagine the president of General Motors being able to view the company not in terms of major divisions, but only in terms of every worker, every assembly line, every engine!)

First programming courses introduce one extremely powerful example of abstraction—*procedural abstraction*, which we mentioned briefly in chapter 1. Procedural abstraction says that any well-defined operation can be viewed as a single, nondecomposable named entity, even if, in reality, it may be implemented by an extremely complex sequence of lower-level operations. Using the procedure and function mechanisms of Pascal, Ada, or Modula-2, we can develop program units, get them working, and place them in a programming library. The following QuickSort procedure is an example of such a program unit:

```
Procedure QuickSort(List,N);    (* Use QuickSort to sort an array called List of
                                   length N, N >= 1, into ascending order. *)
```

We now treat this procedure and all the other procedures in our library as though they were part of the language. We use them only for *what* they do, without regard for the enormous amount of detail associated with *how* they work. For example, the code

```
For i :=1 To 100 Do
    Read(ExamScore[i])          (* Input 100 exam scores. *)
End;
QuickSort(ExamScore,100)        (* Sort them. *)
```

makes perfectly good sense, even if we are totally unfamiliar with the details and workings of the recursive QuickSort sorting algorithm. Its ability to hide the underlying details of the implementation of an algorithm makes the procedure mechanism one of the most important parts of any high-level programming language.

In this chapter, we extend the ideas of abstraction to data structuring, and we develop a concept called the *abstract data type*. To explain this idea, let us first consider the *data-type hierarchy* shown in Figure 2–1.

At the lowest level in the hierarchy is the hardware, which provides a programmer with very few interesting data types or data structures. (The study of the data types supported by the underlying hardware is part of the computer science course called "Principles of Computer Organization.") Typically, the only *hardware data types* directly implemented in the instruction set of a computer are signed and unsigned integers, reals, and characters.

The wealth of interesting data types that are part of most high-level languages—subranges, user-defined scalars, Boolean, arrays, records, sets, pointers—do not actually "exist" in the sense of being directly represented and manipulated by the

Figure 2–1
The Hierarchy of Data Types

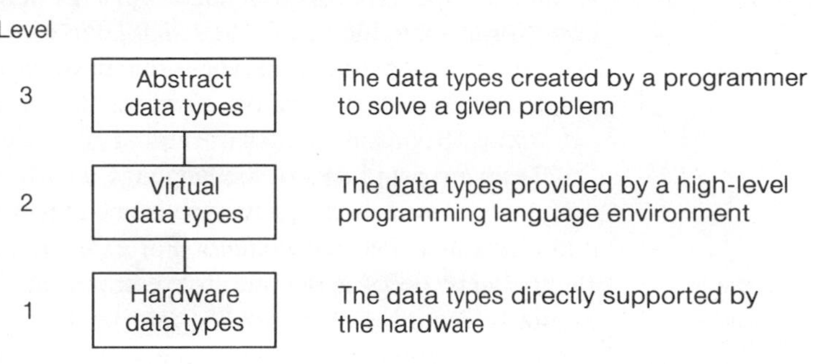
Level
3
Abstract data types
The data types created by a programmer to solve a given problem
2
Virtual data types
The data types provided by a high-level programming language environment
1
Hardware data types
The data types directly supported by the hardware

hardware. The language (actually the compiler) creates these *virtual data types*, also called *high-level–language data types*, from the available hardware facilities. For example, a compiler might implement the data type Boolean by mapping the logical values True and False onto the integer values −1 and +1. The compiler would convert all Boolean operations such as **Or** and **Not** to integer operations on the values −1 and +1. It appears to the programmer that these virtual data types exist as primitives of the machine, and the language lets you use them in your programs. It is the compiler's responsibility, not the programmer's, to worry about the messy details involved in translating these virtual data types into machine-language instructions and hardware data types. As programmers and problem solvers, we are no longer limited to what the hardware has to offer—instead, we are able to use whatever data structures the language designer chooses to provide.

We now carry that idea one step further. Why should we be constrained to use only those data types provided by the language? What if we wish to create a data representation that is not supported in our language? Why not use the same strategy? Why not think, design, and create using whatever data representation we want and worry later about the messy details involved in translating those ideas into a virtual data type supported by the underlying programming language? That is exactly what we do—these programmer-created data representations are called *abstract data types* (ADTs). They free us from the limits imposed by a given programming language, regardless of how interesting or how powerful that language might be. Data abstraction creates a conceptual separation between the programmer's high-level view of a data type and that data type's underlying implementation. We do not need to know how the data type is being implemented internally to use it properly.

We can define an abstract data type more formally:

> An *abstract data type* (ADT) is a data type defined only in terms of the operations that may be performed on objects of this type. Users are allowed to examine and manipulate objects using only these operations, and they are unaware of how the objects are implemented in the programming language.

To specify an ADT we must provide up to four pieces of information. The first is the *domain* of values of the ADT, that is, the set of values that may be assigned to variables of this type. Abstract data types (as well as virtual data types) come in two basic forms—atomic (also called *simple* or *scalar*) and structured.

An *atomic* abstract data type is one in which the domain of values is made up of nondecomposable or primitive *elements*. It is analogous to data types such as integers, reals, Booleans, and characters. The elements of these simple types (e.g., 1, 'a', True) are primitives of the language and cannot be decomposed further.

A *structured* abstract data type is one in which the values can be further divided into elements called *components*. For example, the five-element array [10, 8, −3, 17, 0] can be decomposed into five components, each of which is a simple integer. Similarly, records can be divided into fields, and files can be divided into blocks.

For structured ADTs, there are two additional pieces of information that we provide during design. First, we describe the properties of the *component elements* from which we will build the ADT. That is, we indicate from what type of objects (primitive or structured, virtual or abstract) the ADT is constructed. Second, we specify the nature of the *structural relationship* between component elements of the ADT. This relationship is extremely important and will be the basis for organizing and classifying the numerous data structures that we will study in the upcoming chapters. In the case of an array, for example, we need to describe the data type of the array elements, and the 1 : 1 mapping between subscripts and array elements.

Finally, whether the ADT is atomic or structured, we specify the *operations* that can be carried out on objects of this data type. This last step is the most important part of the overall ADT design process, because the operations that we provide with the ADT are the only ones we will be able to use. If we accidently (or intentionally) omit an operation that a user needs, it will not be possible to carry out that operation, and our data structure may not be very useful. (This situation would be analogous to a language that supported the integer data type but did not provide an integer addition operation!) We must always design ADTs that are *complete*—that is, the design must include all operations needed to utilize fully the capabilities of the ADT.

In summary, we need to provide the following four pieces of information for the specification and design of an abstract data type:

1. The *domain* of values
2. The data type of the *components* (for structured types only)
3. The *structural relationship* between components (for structured types only)
4. The *operations* on the ADT

Looking back over this discussion, we can see the two properties that make abstract data types so important and so useful. First, we have packaged a collection of data values together with the operations on those values. This packaging process is called *data encapsulation*, and it is exactly what a high-level language does with its own virtual data types. These languages package a collection of values (e.g., −Maxint .. +Maxint) with operations on those values (+, −, *, **Div**, >, <, sqr, . . .) and call the result a data type—integer, in this case. Now we will show how a user can build his or her own ADT package, plug it into a given program, and use it as though it were part of the language.

The second important property of ADTs is that the language does not allow the user of an ADT to be aware of, or to take advantage of, the internal implementation of this data structure. For example, Pascal does not allow its users to know whether

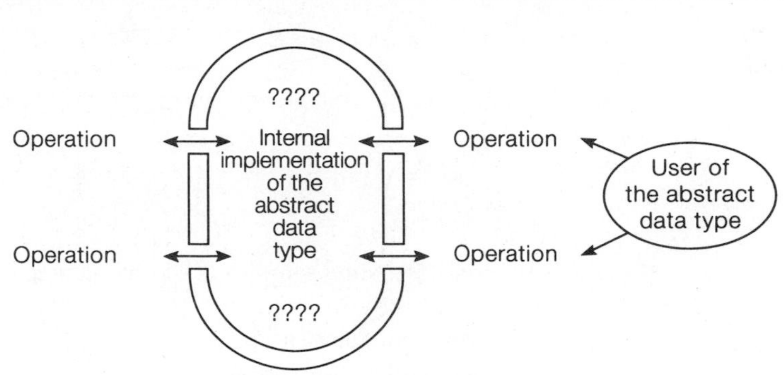

Figure 2–2
Pictorial Model of an Abstract Data Type

integers are stored using 16 or 32 bits, or whether they are represented in two's-complement or sign-magnitude notation. This masking of the internal implementation of a data type is called *information hiding*.

Together, data encapsulation and information hiding are two of the most fundamental properties of abstract data types; these properties are illustrated in Figure 2–2. Notice that the "wall" around the component values of the ADT hides their implementation from the user. The only way to access and manipulate these components is through the operations we provide—that is, through the "windows" in the wall.

In the next section, we present two examples of abstract data types that demonstrate and clarify the principles just described.

2.2 EXAMPLES OF ABSTRACT DATA TYPES

2.2.1 Water Tank: An Atomic Data Type

As our first example, we will create an abstract data type called Water Tank. This ADT is a high-level abstraction of a storage tank that can hold between 0 and 10,000 gallons of water, with each object of this data type representing a single tank, as shown in Figure 2–3. The tank is completely characterized by the amount of water it is holding.

The domain of this ADT will be the water level in the tank, which is simply a real number in the range 0.0 .. 10,000.0. Since this quantity is a single, nondecomposable value, this example is an atomic ADT. (Note, however, that a different design could lead to a structured ADT. For example, the tanks could be uniquely numbered and could be allowed to hold different types of liquids. Then, we would represent each water tank as a structured 3-tuple: [TankNumber, FluidType, CurrentLevel].)

For this atomic ADT, we do not need to worry about describing components or structural relationships. Instead, our only task will be to specify the operations that can be performed on the Water Tank ADT. As mentioned in section 2.1, this step is critically important in the design process, because the only way a user of our ADT can manipulate the objects he or she creates is via the operations that we provide. If we fail to include a necessary operation, the user will be unable to perform key tasks, and the ADT will be less useful than it could have been. Therefore, the design must be done carefully to ensure that all necessary operations are included.

Figure 2–3
Water Tank

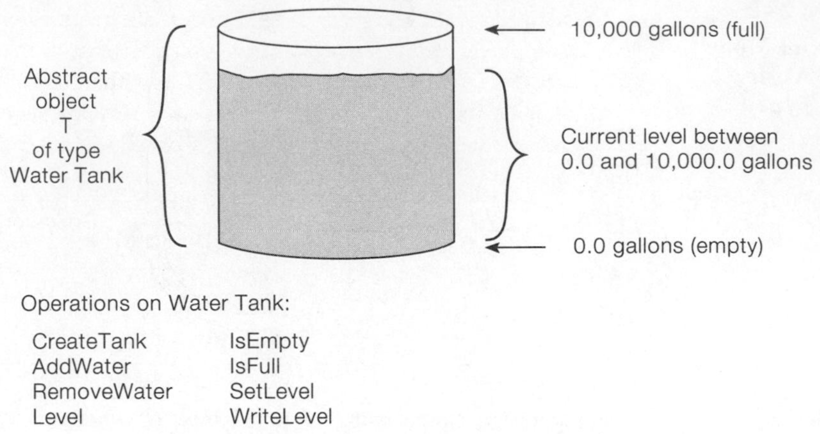

We will now describe five classes of operations on an ADT; we will usually include operators from each one for each ADT we create.

The first class of operations contains *creator* operations; it is the class of operations that creates and initializes new objects of this data type. If T is an object of our abstract data type, we symbolically represent creator operations as

creator: () → T

This notation implies that new objects of type T are being created where none existed before. Without creator operations, we would be unable to *instantiate* (bring into existence) new objects of an ADT. For Water Tank, the following creator function should suffice:

T := CreateTank()	*(* Create a new instance of a water tank T, which is empty; that is, it holds 0.0 gallons of water. *)*

The second class of operations includes *transformer* operations. These operations take an existing object of type T, perform some modification to it, and transform it into a new object also of type T. Symbolically,

transformer: T → T

For Water Tank, the transformations we want to perform involve adding water to a tank and removing water from a tank:

T := AddWater(T,G)	*(* Add G gallons of water to the amount in tank T. The new water level of T becomes (previous level + G). However, if (previous level + G) > 10,000.0, then the new level is set to 10,000.0. *)*
T := RemoveWater(T,G)	*(* Remove G gallons of water from the amount in tank T. The new water level of T becomes (previous level − G). However, if (previous level − G) < 0.0, then the new level is set to 0.0. *)*

The third class of operations is composed of *observer* operations. Typically, these operations observe an object of our abstract data type and return status information about the condition of that object. The object itself is left unchanged. Frequently, observer operations are *predicates*; that is, they are functions that return a Boolean value. However, they may also return other simple data types, such as integers or reals that describe various characteristics of the ADT. Symbolically, an observer operation can be represented in any of the following ways:

observer:	T → B	(Boolean)
	T → I	(Integer)
	T → R	(Real)

For our Water Tank, we might postulate three observer functions (although not all three are really necessary):

R := Level(T)	*(* Returns the current water level in tank T. The value will be a real number R in the range 0.0 <= R <=10,000.0. *)*
B := IsFull(T)	*(* This operation returns True if tank T is currently full (i.e., Level(T) = 10,000.0), and False otherwise. *)*
B := IsEmpty(T)	*(* This operation returns True if tank T is currently empty (i.e., Level(T) = 0.0), and False otherwise. *)*

The fourth class of operations consists of *type conversion* operations; they allow us to convert objects of other data types (e.g., integer, real, arrays) into objects that are members of our new abstract data type, T. Symbolically, a type conversion operation is represented as

type conversion:	I (integer)	→ T
	R (real)	→ T
	A (array)	→ T

For example, we may want the ability to convert an arbitrary real value R into a water level for a given water tank, T, regardless of its current level:

T := SetLevel(T,R)	*(* Reset the water level in tank T to the real value R, 0.0 <= R <= 10,000.0, regardless of the current value. *)*

The fifth and final class of operations is *input/output* (I/O). Most languages provide I/O operations only for simple data types of the language, such as integer, real, and character. They do not allow these operations to be applied to variables of arbitrary types. Unless we include an adequate set of I/O operations as part of our Water Tank ADT, we will not be able to input or output values of this type. Therefore, we might wish to include the following operation as part of our Water Tank ADT:

WriteLevel(T) (* *Write to the standard output file the current water level of tank T. The water level in T is unchanged by this operation.* *)

Our specification of the ADT called Water Tank is now complete, and the information about our design is summarized in Table 2–1.

Before we move on to the implementation phase and begin to build this ADT, we should review our design carefully. We must ask ourselves whether we have included all operations necessary to utilize this ADT fully. Is our design complete? For example, our set of I/O questions includes only output. We might want to include an input operation that has the following format:

ReadLevel(T) (* *Input a single real value in the range 0.0 .. 10,000.0, and set the level of tank T to that value, overwriting whatever value may have been stored in T previously.* *)

We might also want to include a second creator operation, which creates a full, rather than an empty, tank:

T := CreateFull() (* *Create a new tank T whose water level is 10,000.0.* *)

We should consider these and other operations carefully to see whether their inclusion would enhance the design and increase the power and flexibility of this ADT. The selection of the proper set of operations can be a most difficult task for the software designer.

2.2.2 Train: A Structured Data Type

For our second example, imagine that we are developing a program to manage the coupling and switching of trains within a large railroad switching yard. Rather than thinking of a train in terms of a specific virtual data type such as an array or record, it may be more convenient to view it as a structured ADT called Train made up of a collection of components called Engines and Boxcars. These components are primitive objects, since we will assume that Engines and Boxcars cannot be decomposed. Furthermore, Engines and Boxcars are themselves abstract data types, so we will not specify how they are implemented internally. An object of type Train will be an ordered sequence of one or more Engines followed by zero or more Boxcars.

A great many operations could be carried out on Trains. For the purposes of this example, we will describe only five:

T := CreateTrain (E) (* *Create a new Train T containing only Engine E.* *)

AddEngine(E,T) (* *Put Engine E at the head of Train T.* *)

AddBoxcar(B,T) (* *Add Boxcar B to the end of Train T.* *)

B := Compare(T1,T2) (* *True if Trains T1 and T2 have the same number of Engines and Boxcars; otherwise, False.* *)

l := Length(T) *(* Returns the total number of Engines and Boxcars in Train T. *)*

Obviously, this list is not complete. For example, we have not provided a means of creating either Engines or Boxcars. Similarly, we have not included the transformation operators needed to remove an Engine or a Boxcar from a Train. Exercise 8 at the end of the chapter asks you to complete the selection of the operations on this ADT. Table 2–1 summarizes the design of the ADT Train as far as we have gone.

When we have completed the specification of the ADT, we can create a solution to our railroad-switching problem using the abstract ADTs Trains, Engines, and Boxcars, and the operations defined on these types, instead of using lower-level objects such as arrays, records, and integers. Later, after the solution is complete, we can select an implementation for these abstract types. We may choose, for example, to implement the data type Train as a one-dimensional array of integers or as a singly linked list. The key point is that the programmer does not need to know how it is implemented, and it should not matter. In fact, it should not matter even if we change the internal implementation at some later time. The programmer has designed and created in terms of Trains, *not* in terms of arrays or linked lists, and the solution will be unaffected by whatever technique is ultimately used to implement these abstract objects.

Table 2–1 Summary of the Design of the Water Tank and Train ADTs

	Water Tank (Atomic ADT)	Train (Structured ADT)
a. Domain	A water level in the range 0.0 .. 10,000.0	A sequence of m or more Engines followed by n or more Boxcars, $m \geq 1$, $n \geq 0$; that is, objects of type Train can be described as 2-tuples (m, n) such that $m \geq 1$, $n \geq 0$.
b. Components		A Train is made up of primitive elements called Engines and Boxcars that are abstract, nondecomposable atomic objects.
c. Structural relationships		A Train is an ordered sequence of Engine and Boxcar objects, in which all the Engines precede all the Boxcars.
d. Operations		
Creators	CreateTank()	CreateTrain (E)
Transformers	AddWater(T,G) RemoveWater(T,G)	AddEngine(E,T) AddBoxcar(B,T)
Observers	Level(T) IsFull(T) IsEmpty(T)	Compare(T1,T2) Length(T)
Type Conversion	SetLevel(T,R)	
Input/output	WriteLevel(T)	

Standard Pascal does not support the concept of an abstract data type. The language cannot separate the notion of a data type declaration from that data type's implementation. In Pascal, the declaration

```
Type
    Train;
```

would not compile and would cause a syntax error. We must simultaneously declare a type name and its internal structure. For example,

```
Type
    Train = Array [1..100] Of (Engine, Boxcar);
```

Formally, we say that Pascal does not support the concept called *information hiding*—the ability to hide the details of the virtual data type used to construct an ADT—which we mentioned in the chapter introduction. However, ADTs and information hiding are supported by a number of modern programming languages, including Ada, Modula 2, C++, and recent versions of Turbo Pascal. In the next sections of this chapter, we discuss how to design and implement abstract data types in these languages.

Like procedural abstraction, data abstraction is one of the most powerful problem-solving tools available. It lets you create your own personal data representations and manipulate them with a set of complex operations, all the while hiding the welter of detail necessary to support these abstractions. The proper use of the data abstraction facility within a programming language helps us to construct correct software in an efficient manner and to build systems that are easy to maintain.

2.3 THE SYNTAX AND SEMANTICS OF ABSTRACT DATA TYPES

In the preceding section, our description of the operations on the Water Tank and Train abstract data types was informal and mathematically not very rigorous. We relied on a natural language (English, in our case) as the vehicle for describing the behavior of our operators. While easy to read, write, and understand, natural language suffers from one very severe problem—inexactness. The richness of the English language allows for multiple interpretations, shades of meaning, and ambiguities. Natural language does not have the precision needed to be used as a specification language for designing and implementing abstract data types.

For example, in the previous section we described the AddEngine function:

```
AddEngine(E,T)        (* Put Engine E at the head of Train T. *)
```

However, this description fails to say what type of object is *returned* by the function—does AddEngine return an object of type Train, type Engine, or something else? This information is important, because a nested call such as

```
Length(AddEngine(E,T))
```

would be legal if AddEngine returns an object of type Train but illegal if AddEngine returns an object of type Engine.

Similarly, if we look at the description of the operation Compare, we see the following

B := Compare(T1,T2) (* *True if Trains T1 and T2 have the same number of Engines and Boxcars; otherwise, False.* *)

The preceding comment is ambiguous. It could be interpreted to mean that the *total* number of objects contained in the trains (engines and boxcars together) must be the same $((T1_{engine} + T1_{boxcar}) = (T2_{engine} + T2_{boxcar}))$ or to mean that the two trains must have the same number of engines and the same number of boxcars $((T1_{engine} = T2_{engine})$ *and* $(T1_{boxcar} = T2_{boxcar}))$.

Such ambiguities can lead to serious design and implementation errors and can increase the cost of building and maintaining software. To avoid these problems, we need to use a more rigorous and precise notation to describe abstract data types. This notation should minimize ambiguities and lead to well-designed and clearly specified program units. We introduce such notation in the next two sections.

2.3.1 A Formal Syntax for Abstract Data Types

First, we develop a formal notation for the *syntax*, that is, the format, of the operations on an ADT. This syntax will describe *how* we use an operation, although it does not tell us *what* that operation does.

To define the syntax of a simple abstract data type in our notation, we first write out the name of the ADT. For example:

Define WaterTank

This statement simply means that the rules that follow will define the syntax of operations on an ADT called WaterTank. To describe the syntax of a structured abstract data type called TypeName and composed of component types $c_1, c_2, \ldots, c_n$ we use the notation

Define TypeName[$c_1, c_2, \ldots, c_n$]

which indicates that the rules that follow will define the syntax of operations on a structured ADT called TypeName, which will be constructed from component objects of type $c_1, c_2, \ldots, c_n$. For example,

Define Train[Engine,Boxcar]

Following the declaration of the name of the ADT, we provide a syntactic description of the operations on this ADT. To formally specify the syntax of an operation on an abstract data type, we provide three pieces of information:

1. The *name* of the operation.
2. The *data type* of the arguments to the operation.
3. The *data type* of the result returned by the operation.

We will use the following notation to describe the operations on an ADT:

OperationName(arg_1, arg_2, . . . , arg_n) : ReturnType

where OperationName is the name of the operation being defined; arg_1, arg_2, . . . , arg_n are the data types of the n input parameters; and ReturnType is the data type of the value that is returned as the result of this operation. (Note that in our notation we represent all operations as functions that return a single result. However, when these operations are implemented, they may be coded as either functions or procedures, whichever is more convenient.)

Using the Water Tank example of Table 2–1, the first operation, CreateTank, would be described as follows:

CreateTank() : WaterTank

This statement says the operation named CreateTank has no input parameters and returns as its value an object of type WaterTank.

The AddWater operation is

AddWater(WaterTank,Real) : WaterTank

which means that AddWater must be given two input parameters, the first of type WaterTank and the second of type Real (an amount of water). It returns a WaterTank as a result. By looking at these previous two syntactic descriptions, we can immediately determine that the following nested function calls

AddWater(CreateTank(), 500.0)

are syntactically valid and will produce a WaterTank as a result, even though we may not yet be sure what these two calls actually do. Similarly, we can show that the nested sequence

AddWater(CreateTank(), AddWater(CreateTank(), 500.0))

is invalid:

⇒ AddWater(T, AddWater(CreateTank(), 500.0))
⇒ AddWater(T, AddWater(T, 500.0))
⇒ AddWater(T, AddWater(T, R))
⇒ AddWater(T, T)   **error**

because the data types of the two parameters to the AddWater function violate the syntactic definition just given.

The syntactic definitions of all eight operations on the WaterTank ADT are given in Figure 2–4a.

We use the same notation to specify the syntax of the operations on our structured data type Train. The CreateTrain function is defined as

CreateTrain (Engine) : Train[Engine,Boxcar]

Figure 2–4
Examples of Formal Syntactic Notation

Define WaterTank

a. CreateTank() : WaterTank
b. AddWater(WaterTank,Real) : WaterTank
c. RemoveWater(WaterTank,Real) : WaterTank
d. Level(WaterTank) : Real
e. IsFull(WaterTank) : Boolean
f. IsEmpty(WaterTank) : Boolean
g. SetLevel(WaterTank, Real) : WaterTank
h. WriteLevel(WaterTank) : WaterTank

a. Syntax of the Abstract Data Type WaterTank

Define Train[Engine,Boxcar]

a. CreateTrain(Engine) : Train[Engine,Boxcar]
b. AddEngine(Engine,Train[Engine,Boxcar]) : Train[Engine,Boxcar]
c. AddBoxcar(Boxcar,Train[Engine,Boxcar]) : Train[Engine,Boxcar]
d. Compare(Train[Engine,Boxcar], Train[Engine,Boxcar]) : Boolean
e. Length(Train[Engine,Boxcar]) : Integer

b. Syntax of the Abstract Data Type Train

which says that CreateTrain takes as input an object of type Engine and returns a structured object of type Train. AddEngine is syntactically defined as

AddEngine(Engine,Train[Engine,Boxcar]) : Train[Engine,Boxcar]

This definition clarifies the ambiguity mentioned in the previous section, namely, what type of object does AddEngine return, an Engine or a Train? This rule clearly states that the operation returns an object of type Train. This example is a good demonstration of the increased precision we can achieve by using a formal notation to describe our syntax rather than an informal notation such as natural language.

A complete description of the syntax of the five operations on our structured ADT Train is given in Figure 2–4b. We will use this notation again when describing the syntax of abstract data types in later chapters.

2.3.2 Formal Semantics for Abstract Data Types

The notation CreateTank(): WaterTank describes only the mechanical aspects of how to use an operation correctly. It does not say anything at all about what that operation does. (This is analogous to describing how to spell a word in English. While the spelling is important, it does not tell you anything about the meaning of that word or help you to use it correctly in a sentence.) Such information is contained in the semantics of an operation. *Semantics* describe the actions of an operation and the effects that this operation has on other objects in the system.

There are a number of techniques for formally specifying the semantics of operations on an ADT, and this subject is an important area of research in computer science. It is also a very complex topic and our goal here will be only to introduce it, not to cover it in detail. Advanced courses in compiler construction, formal languages, and theoretical computer science will go into this interesting topic in greater depth.

The technique we will use to describe the behavior of an operation is called *axiomatic semantics*. An *axiom* is a universally accepted truth, a basic principle, or an invariant condition. To describe the semantics of ADTs, we specify the axioms that hold for our ADT operations, that is, we describe those conditions that are true for every application of these operations to objects of this data type. If done correctly, this set of axioms will characterize fully the behavior of our ADT operations.

For example, if we were describing the behavior of the addition operation on integers, we would start by listing the universal properties that the + operator obeys, for example,

$x + y = y + x$ (Commutativity axiom)

$(x + y) + z = x + (y + z)$ (Associativity axiom)

$x + 0 = x$ (Identity axiom)

These axioms state that the above equalities will always be true, regardless of which integer values we use to replace the symbols x, y, and z. These axioms, together with addition tables that define decimal integer addition, would allow us to characterize the behavior (i.e., the semantics) of the algebraic operation +.

We take the same approach when describing the semantics of ADT operations such as CreateTank, AddWater, Level, AddBoxcar, and so forth. By specifying the axioms that hold for these operations, we can describe the universal behavior of these operations in all situations. Some of our semantic definitions use what is called a *composition* of operations. Recall that if you have two functions, f and g, the interpretation of

$f(g(x))$

is that function g is first performed on the argument x, then the value returned by this function becomes the argument of the function f.

Let's begin by describing the semantics of the WaterTank operations listed in Figure 2–4a. We want the CreateTank() operation to produce an empty tank, one with a water level of 0.0. This statement is equivalent to saying that if we apply the Level function to any water tank produced by CreateTank, we will always get the real value 0.0. Formally, we write:

Level(CreateTank()) = 0.0

Thus, this statement is an axiom of our ADT since it is a true statement of the universal behavior of the CreateTank and Level operators. Similarly, the water tank produced by CreateTank is always empty and never full:

IsEmpty(CreateTank()) = True
IsFull(CreateTank()) = False

These last two axioms tell us how IsEmpty and IsFull behave when applied to the tank produced by CreateTank. But how do they behave when given an arbitrary water tank T? The answer is simple—if the water level of any arbitrary tank T is 0.0, it is empty, and if it is 10,000.0, it is full. We express these ideas in the following way:

If (Level(T) = 0.0) **Then**
  IsEmpty(T) = True
Else
  IsEmpty(T) = False

If (Level(T) = 10,000.0) **Then**
  IsFull(T) = True
Else
  IsFull(T) = False

Note that these last two axioms eliminate the need for the two rules

IsEmpty(CreateTank()) = True
IsFull(CreateTank()) = False

since they can be deduced from the two axioms shown above, as follows:

If (Level(T) = 0.0) **Then**
  IsEmpty(T) = True
Else
  IsEmpty(T) = False

Replacing T by CreateTank() we get

If (Level(CreateTank()) = 0.0) **Then**
  IsEmpty(CreateTank()) = True
Else
  IsEmpty(CreateTank()) = False

but we know that (Level(CreateTank()) = 0.0) is always True by an earlier axiom so

IsEmpty(CreateTank()) = True

Finally, we must describe how AddWater and RemoveWater behave. These two operations affect the water level in the tank by increasing or decreasing the current level by a real value. They also must handle the physical limitation of 10,000.0 gallons per tank, and the impossibility of negative gallons of water.

If (Level(T) + G) <= 10,000.0 **Then**
  Level(AddWater(T,G)) = Level(T) + G
Else
  Level(AddWater(T,G)) = 10,000.0

If (Level(T) − G) >= 0.0 **Then**
  Level(RemoveWater(T,G)) = Level(T) − G
Else
  Level(RemoveWater(T,G)) = 0.0

Figure 2–5
Formal Semantics of the Water Tank ADT

a. *Level(CreateTank()) = 0.0*
b. **If** *(Level(T) = 0.0)* **Then**
    IsEmpty(T) = True
  Else
    IsEmpty(T) = False
c. **If** *(Level(T) = 10,000.0)* **Then**
    IsFull(T) = True
  Else
    IsFull(T) = False
d. **If** *(Level(T) + G) <= 10,000.0* **Then**
    Level(AddWater(T,G)) = Level(T) + G
  Else
    Level(AddWater(T,G)) = 10,000.0
e. **If** *(Level(T) − G) >= 0.0* **Then**
    Level(RemoveWater(T,G)) = Level(T) − G
  Else
    Level(RemoveWater(T,G)) = 0.0
f. *Level(SetLevel(T,R)) = R*
g. *Level(WriteLevel(T)) = Level(T)*

The rule describing the behavior of the AddWater operation is an axiomatic encoding of the statement: If the current level of water in a tank T plus the amount that you want to add, G, is less than or equal to 10,000.0, then the new water level of tank T produced by the AddWater(T,G) operation is the previous water level plus G, otherwise the water level of tank T is the real value 10,000.0. However, the axiom is much more concise and direct. We leave it to you to determine the natural language meaning of the axiom describing the behavior of the RemoveWater operation.

The complete axiomatic semantics of the water tank operations are given in Figure 2–5.

The description of the semantics of the Train ADT follows in a similar way. To help you understand what these axioms are asserting about the operations, we will write out the natural language description of the behavior of an operation, followed by the axiomatic representation of that natural language statement. The axioms we will describe make use of four auxiliary functions that were not included in the previous section but that are needed to describe the behavior of Trains, Engines, and Boxcars. These four auxiliary functions are:

EngineLength(Train) : Integer	(* Returns the total number of Engines on the Train. *)
BoxcarLength(Train) : Integer	(* Returns the total number of Boxcars on the Train. *)
Front(Train) : Engine	(* Returns the Engine at the front of the Train. *)
Back(Train) : Boxcar	(* Returns the Boxcar at the end of the Train. *)

These last two operations are explicitly allowed because in our original description of the Train ADT we said that a Train was an *ordered sequence* of Engines and Boxcars (see the Structural relationships section of Table 2–1). Formally, this means that if a Train is not empty, it always has a first item (i.e., a front) and a last item (i.e., a back). We will discuss the formal properties of this type of ordered, or *linear*, data structure at much greater length in chapters 3 and 4. Here are the axiomatic semantics of our Train:

a. A newly created Train contains one Engine and no Boxcars.

   EngineLength(CreateTrain(E)) = 1
   BoxcarLength(CreateTrain(E)) = 0
   Front(CreateTrain(E)) = E

b. When we add a new Engine to a Train, it goes at the front of the Train and does not affect what is at the back.

   EngineLength(AddEngine(E,T)) = EngineLength(T) + 1
   Front(AddEngine(E,T)) = E
   Back(AddEngine(E,T)) = Back(T)

c. When we add a new Boxcar to a Train, it goes at the back of the Train and does not affect what is at the front.

   BoxcarLength(AddBoxcar(B,T)) = BoxcarLength(T) + 1
   Back(AddBoxcar(B,T)) = B
   Front(AddBoxcar(B,T)) = Front(T)

d. The overall length of a Train is the number of Engines plus the number of Boxcars on the Train.

   Length(T) = EngineLength(T) + BoxcarLength(T)

e. Adding a Boxcar to a Train does not affect the number of Engines, and vice-versa.

   EngineLength(AddBoxcar(B,T)) = EngineLength(T)
   BoxcarLength(AddEngine(E,T)) = BoxcarLength(T)

f. Two Trains are said to be identical if and only if they have the same number of Engines and Boxcars.

   If (EngineLength(T1) = EngineLength(T2)) **And**
   (BoxcarLength(T1) = BoxcarLength(T2))
   Then
   Compare(T1,T2) = True
   Else
   Compare(T1,T2) = False

Figure 2–6
Formal Semantics of the Train Abstract Data Type

a. *EngineLength(CreateTrain (E)) = 1*
b. *BoxcarLength(CreateTrain (E) = 0*
c. *Front(CreateTrain (E)) = E*
d. *EngineLength(AddEngine(E,T)) = EngineLength(T) + 1*
e. *Front(AddEngine(E,T)) = E*
f. *Back(AddEngine(E,T)) = Back(T)*
g. *BoxcarLength(AddBoxcar(B,T)) = BoxcarLength(T) + 1*
h. *Back(AddBoxcar(B,T)) = B*
i. *Front(AddBoxcar(B,T)) = Front(T)*
j. *Length(T) = EngineLength(T) + BoxcarLength(T)*
k. *EngineLength(AddBoxcar(B,T)) = EngineLength(T)*
l. *BoxcarLength(AddEngine(E,T)) = BoxcarLength(T)*
m. **If** *(EngineLength(T1) = EngineLength(T2))* **And** *(BoxcarLength(T1) = BoxcarLength(T2))*
Then
Compare(T1,T2) = True
Else
Compare(T1,T2) = False

The last axiom clears up the confusion we mentioned in Section 2.3 about the interpretation of the Compare function. It states that the meaning of the Compare function is to compare the number of engines and the number of boxcars and say that two trains are identical if and only if *both* values are the same. This axiom is a second demonstration of the increased precision that is available through the use of a formalized notational scheme.

The complete semantics of the five operations of the Train ADT are summarized in Figure 2–6. We will use this notation again to describe the semantics of the abstract data types introduced in the succeeding chapters.

These axioms allow us to determine unambiguously the behavior and meaning of any arbitrary sequence of Train operations. For example, let's analyze the effect of creating a new Train, adding a Boxcar, adding a second Engine, and applying the Length function. This sequence of operations can be expressed as:

$$\text{Length(AddEngine}(E_2,\ \text{AddBoxcar(B,CreateTrain}(E_1))))$$

Our analysis proceeds as follows (the axiom identifications refer to the letters in Figure 2–6):

$$\text{Length(AddEngine}(E_2,\ \text{AddBoxcar(B,CreateTrain}(E_1))))$$

$$= \text{Length(AddEngine}(E_2,\ \text{AddBoxcar}(B,T_1)))$$

where	$\text{EngineLength}(T_1) = 1$	axiom a
	$\text{BoxcarLength}(T_1) = 0$	axiom b
	$\text{Length}(T_1) = 1$	axiom j
	$\text{Front}(T_1) = E_1$	axiom c

= Length(AddEngine(E_2,T_2))

where	EngineLength(T_2) = 1	axiom k
	BoxcarLength(T_2) = 1	axiom g
	Length(T_2) = 2	axiom j
	Back(T_2) = B	axiom h
	Front(T_2) = E_1	axiom i

= Length(T_3)

where	EngineLength(T_3) = 2	axiom d
	BoxcarLength(T_3) = 1	axiom l
	Front(T_3) = E_2	axiom e
	Back(T_3) = B	axiom f

= 3 axiom j

Thus, we have produced a three-element Train with E_2 at the front and B at the back. We could do a similar analysis for any syntactically valid sequence of function calls to determine unambiguously the effect that those calls have on the arguments of the functions.

Another important point about axiomatic semantics is to remember that the behavior of our ADT operations is not predetermined. We *design* these operations, and within limits, we are free to have them behave in whatever way we feel is best for our particular needs. For example, if we wanted the Compare function to say that two trains are identical if the *total* number of objects were the same, regardless of the number of engines and boxcars, we could have expressed this axiomatically as:

If Length(T1) = Length(T2) **Then**
    Compare(T1,T2) = True
Else
    Compare(T1,T2) = False

Similarly, we could have created our water tanks full of water (instead of empty) by saying:

Level(CreateTank()) = 10,000.0
IsFull(CreateTank()) = True

Remember that an ADT is a programmer-created structure, and the programmer is free to select the behavior that is best suited to solving a given problem.

2.3.3 Pre- and Postconditions

There are two problems with the axiomatic semantics introduced in the previous section. First, not every operation is well defined under all conditions. We are familiar with this problem from operations on integer and real values:

a / b
sqrt(c)

In the first case, the divide operation is meaningless if $b = 0$. In the second, c must be nonnegative. In our Train example, we can see a similar problem in the following sequence:

Back(CreateTrain(E))

Back returns an object of type Boxcar—the Boxcar currently at the back of the Train. However, CreateTrain(E) produces a Train that has no Boxcars, so there is nothing for Back to return, and the function is undefined.

To solve this problem, we must include in our semantics a description of what starting conditions each operation expects before it is invoked in order to guarantee that the operation is well defined and can be carried out to completion. These starting conditions are called *preconditions* of the operation. The operations we have just discussed require the following preconditions:

Operation	*Precondition*
a / b	$b \neq 0$
sqrt(c)	$c >= 0$
Back(T)	BoxcarLength(T) > 0

In addition to the direct effect that an operation has in producing a result, it may also have indirect, or *side effects* on other objects within the system or its environment, and they can be difficult to describe using formal methods. These side effects, which usually involve the setting of error switches or I/O behavior, are frequently described using natural language. Together, the axiomatic description of the behavior of an operation along with the natural language description of any side effects of the operation are termed the *postconditions* of that operation.

For example, assume that we decided to maintain a global variable called Error that would be set to True if we attempted to apply the function Back(T) to a Train with no Boxcars. We might express this side effect in natural language as:

Back(T)	Precondition:	BoxcarLength(T) > 0
	Postcondition:	Error = True if precondition is not met, and Error = False otherwise.

Similarly, the WriteLevel(T) operation on Water Tanks has no direct affect on T or its water level. It is executed only for its side effect of displaying a value on a screen:

WriteLevel(T)	Precondition:	None
	Postcondition:	The water level in tank T is displayed on the screen in scientific notation.

These essential pre- and postconditions will usually be included in the semantic description of an abstract data type. We will see a number of examples in upcoming chapters.

In summary, to specify an ADT completely, you must provide the following six pieces of information:

1. The domain of values of the ADT
2. The component elements of a structured ADT
3. The relationship between the components of a structured ADT
4. The formal syntax of the operations
5. The formal semantics of the operations
6. The pre- and postconditions associated with those operations

In the next section we will show how to build these abstract structures using the facilities of some well-known high-level programming languages.

2.4 LANGUAGE SUPPORT FOR ABSTRACT DATA TYPES

The previous sections have stressed the fundamental importance of abstract data types as a tool for designing and building reliable, maintainable, and correct software. Therefore, a key question to ask is, What support do programming languages provide for data abstraction? Are the ideas of sections 2.1–2.3 simply a theoretical curiosity that one can study but cannot use, or do they constitute a real-world programming tool that is an important part of the software development process? The answer is the latter, and a number of well-known languages do support the ADT concept. In this section we look at what language constructs are needed to provide the data abstraction facilities described in this chapter. We first develop a language- and system-independent pseudocode for ADTs that we will use throughout the remainder of this text. We then show how this informal representation is typical of what is found in existing languages and can be easily mapped into the syntax of either Ada, Modula-2, C++, or Turbo Pascal.

We have chosen to use pseudocode rather than one of these languages to emphasize that the truly important concepts we are studying are data abstraction, encapsulation, and information hiding, *not* the syntax of a particular language. The use of pseudocode will allow us to concentrate on specifying, designing, and building ADTs, free of the extensive rules and restrictions associated with a particular real-world language and system.

2.4.1 Required Language Constructs

Four constructs are needed in a high-level programming language to support abstract data types.

1. The ability to separate the declaration of names of objects from their implementation and to place these two parts in different program units
2. The ability to restrict user access to the implementation unit
3. Separate compilation for the two program units that contain the declaration and implementation of objects
4. Statements that allow user access to the resources created in these units

When we create a new data type in Pascal, we declare not only its name but the details of its implementation as well. Such a declaration is called a *transparent type* declaration. For example,

```
Type
    Complex = Record
                  a : Real;
                  b : Real
              End;
```

This declaration creates a new type called Complex and also specifies that this type is implemented as a record structure with two real fields. If any other module uses this declaration and creates a variable of type Complex, it is free to use this knowledge of the implementation.

```
Var
        X, Y, Z : Complex;
    .
    .
    .
X.a := 1.0;        (* These are all legal operations *)
Y.a := 1.5;        (* because we know that Complex *)
X.b := 2.0;        (* is implemented as a record structure. *)
Y.b := 2.5;
Z.a := X.a + Y.a;
Z.b := X.b + Y.b
```

Furthermore, we cannot change this record-based implementation without having a profound impact on the users of the data type Complex. A change in the implementation of Complex would require a recoding of all program units that use this information.

However, we have said in earlier sections that we want to hide the implementation of an ADT from the user and have him or her access the structure only via the operations that we provide. Transparent type declarations do not provide this capability, which can be accomplished only by using another type declaration called an *opaque type*. Its syntax is simple:

```
Type
    Identifier;
```

This declaration names a data type, but it does not describe how that type is implemented. The details of implementation are separated from the declaration of the name of the object, making that information unavailable to the user. So, for example, if we make the following opaque type declaration,

```
Type
    Complex;        (* An opaque data type for representing complex numbers. *)
```

any other program unit that uses this data type will have access only to the type name Complex:

```
Var
    X,Y,Z     : Complex;        (* This is legal. *)
```

Any attempt to access the individual fields of X or Y, as in X.a, X.b, Y.a, or Y.b, would be flagged by the compiler as illegal. In fact, the user is unaware that we are using records to implement complex numbers—we might have chosen to implement Complex using an array, a pointer, or some other method.

How then is a user able to manipulate the opaque types that he or she has declared? Exactly as described in earlier sections—by using the operations provided with our abstract data type. For example, we might provide an operation called ComplexAdd to add two complex numbers and produce a complex result. If the user wishes to add complex numbers, he or she would not be allowed to do it directly, as in:

```
Z.a := X.a + Y.a;     or     Z[1] := X[1] + Y[1];
Z.b := X.b + Y.b             Z[2] := X[2] + Y[2]
```

Both of these are illegal operations on opaque types. Instead, the user is required to carry out the addition via the following operation:

```
Z := ComplexAdd(X,Y)          (* Z := X + Y *)
```

If we did not include ComplexAdd as part of our abstract data type package, then the user would have no way to carry out this function. This example illustrates why the design phase is so important—we must be sure to provide the complete set of operations a user will need.

The operations we provide for our opaque data types will be implemented as functions or procedures, and like an opaque type, they are also separated into two parts: the declaration of the procedure's name and calling sequence and the procedure body that shows how it is implemented internally. The header for the operation ComplexAdd would look like the following:

```
Procedure ComplexAdd(X : Complex; Y : Complex) : Complex;
```

This header is visible to the user, but the statements within the program unit are not. The user is unaware of how an operation is implemented and what algorithm is being used. He or she is only aware of its external interface—what input it requires and what output it produces.

In our pseudocode, an ADT will be implemented as two separate but matching compilation units called *modules*. One module contains the *visible* or *external* part of the ADT, and the other the *hidden* or *internal* part of the ADT.

The visible part, which we call the *external module,* contains the declarations for all objects we wish to make available to a user, including **Const** declarations, transparent and opaque **Type** declarations, **Var** declarations, and the headers of all procedures and functions that will operate on these objects. The notation we will use for our external module is:

```
External Module Name;
    Const declarations;
    Type declarations;        (* Both transparent and opaque *)
    Var declarations;
    Procedure headings;       (* Either procedures or functions *)
End Name.
```

Figure 2–7 shows an external module for the abstract data type called Complex (note that it is not complete, and we would need to add additional operations to make it a usable package). The external module in Figure 2–7 is a separate program unit that can be written, compiled, and stored in a program library. It contains everything a user needs to know about the resources available for the abstract data type Complex.

The second compilation unit needed to complete our abstract data type is called an *internal module* in our pseudocode. It has two responsibilities:

1. To specify the implementation of all opaque types contained in the matching external module
2. To specify the body of all procedures whose headings are contained in the matching external module

Whereas the external module specifies *what* resources are available, the internal module must specify *how* an abstract data type is implemented. However, these details are hidden from users who may access only the resources specified in the external module. Furthermore, any objects declared in the internal module are treated as local to that module and are also inaccessible. The notation we will use to specify our internal modules is shown on the top of the following page.

Figure 2–7
External Module for ComplexNumbers

```
(* External Module defining complex numbers and operations to manipulate them.
The data type and operations are discussed in section 2.4.1. *)
External Module ComplexNumbers;

Type
    Complex; (* The opaque data type *)

(* Perform complex addition X + Y *)
Procedure ComplexAdd ( X : Complex; Y : Complex ) : Complex;

(* Create a complex number A + Bi *)
Procedure CreateComplex ( A : Real; B : Real ) : Complex;

(* Write out the complex number X *)
Procedure WriteComplex ( X : Complex );

End ComplexNumbers.
```

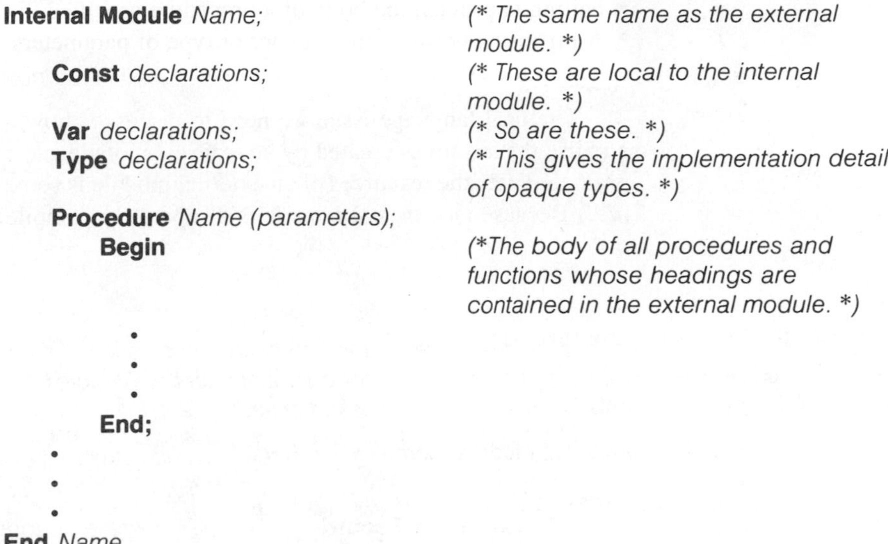

```
Internal Module Name;                  (* The same name as the external
                                          module. *)
    Const declarations;                (* These are local to the internal
                                          module. *)
    Var declarations;                  (* So are these. *)
    Type declarations;                 (* This gives the implementation details
                                          of opaque types. *)
    Procedure Name (parameters);
        Begin                          (*The body of all procedures and
                                          functions whose headings are
                                          contained in the external module. *)
            •
            •
            •
        End;
    •
    •
    •
End Name.
```

Figure 2–8 on the next page shows one possible internal module for the abstract data type Complex, whose external module was given in Figure 2–7.

The internal module in Figure 2–8 is also a separate program unit that can be written, compiled, and stored in a program library. Together this pair of external and internal modules creates a complete abstract data type package of the type described in sections 2.1–2.3.

An important service provided by a compiler that supports external and internal modules is *separate compilation*, that is, the compiler will ensure the syntactic consistency of declarations made in separate modules even though they may be compiled at different times. This consistency is necessary to insure the integrity and correctness of our ADT package. If, for example, an external module contained the following procedure header

```
Procedure Check (A : Integer) : Boolean;
```

but the corresponding internal module implemented that operation as follows

```
Procedure Check (X : Real; Y : Real) : Char;        (* The body of Check follows. *)
```

we would want to be warned of this mismatch and be allowed to fix it before anyone attempted to use this incorrect procedure. Some languages check for type consistency *within* a program unit, but not *between* compiled units—this level of type checking is insufficient for supporting ADTs whose definition is split between two separate program units.

Separate compilation will detect the following kinds of errors in the definition and implementation of an abstract data type:

- Failing to provide the implementation of an opaque type specified in the external module

- Failing to provide the body of a procedure specified in the external module
- A mismatch between the number or type of parameters for an operation specified in the external and internal modules

The final language issue we need to discuss is how a user program can access and use the resources created by an external module and stored in a library. (A program that uses the resources of an external module is sometimes called a *client module*.) Because an external module is a separately compiled unit independent of the

Figure 2–8
Internal Module for ComplexNumbers

```
(* This module contains the internal representation of the Complex data type, along
with the implementation for operations on the Complex data type. The data type
and operations are discussed in section 2.4.1. *)

Internal Module ComplexNumbers;

Type
        Complex = Record                    (* How the opaque type *)
                        a : Real;           (* has been implemented. *)
                        b : Real
                  End;

(* Complex addition X + Y. *)
Procedure ComplexAdd( X : Complex; Y : Complex )
    : Complex;
Var
        C : Complex;
Begin
        C.a := X.a + Y.a;       (* Add the real parts. *)
        C.b := X.b + Y.b;       (* Add the imaginary parts. *)
        Return C;
End ComplexAdd;

(* Create a complex number A + Bi. *)
Procedure CreateComplex( A: Real; B: Real )
    : Complex;
Var
        C : Complex;
Begin
        C.a := A;     (* Assign the real portion. *)
        C.b := B;     (* Assign the imaginary portion. *)
        Return C;
End CreateComplex;

(* Write out the complex number X. *)
Procedure WriteComplex( X : Complex );
Begin
        Write(X.a, '+', X.b, 'i');      (* Write the string A+Bi *)
End WriteComplex;

End ComplexNumbers.
```

user's program, we cannot use the scope rules of languages like Pascal or Modula-2 to pass objects into the user's program, as in the following:

```
Procedure A;
Var x, y : Integer;
    .
    .
    .
    Procedure B;
```

In this example, the variables x and y are available to Procedure B (as global variables) because of the placement of Procedure B within the scope of the declarations in Procedure A. This technique does not work with independent ADT library modules, and user programs that want to use an abstract data type must explicitly transfer them into their own program. The process of transferring resources from an external module into the user's own program is called *importing* resources. It is done by using a declaration of the form

```
Import ExternalModuleName;
```

This declaration says that all objects created in the specified external module (i.e., constants, opaque types, variables, procedure names) are to be made available for use within the program unit making the import declaration. This example is a *global import* declaration, since it makes all resources of the external module available to the user. Some languages also provide a *selective import* declaration of the form

From *ExternalModuleName* **Import**
    Object$_1$, *Object*$_2$, . . . , *Object*$_n$;

which simply allows you to pick and choose which objects you wish to import rather than having to automatically transfer them all.

Figure 2–9 shows a simple example of a program that imports the abstract data type Complex and three operations on that type. It uses those operations to create two complex numbers called X and Y, adds them to produce a new complex value Z, and writes out the value of Z, all the time blissfully unaware of how complex numbers are represented.

To execute the client module of Figure 2–9, we would first compile it and then link it with the proper external and internal modules. The syntax of the compile and link commands will depend on the specific language and operating system being used.

The sequence of compile and link operations that need to be carried out are summarized in Figure 2–10. This sequence is important to follow not only the first time, but any time a change is made to one of the modules in the program.

If a change is made to the user program, there is no need to recompile either the external or internal module; simply recompile the user's program and relink it with the external and internal modules of the abstract data type (steps C and D). If a change is made to an internal module, it is not necessary to recompile either the associated external module or the user program; simply recompile the new internal

Figure 2–9
A Program That Uses the Abstract Data Type Called Complex

```
(* Client module using ComplexNumbers, the abstract data type described in
section 2.4.1. *)
Module ComplexExample;

From ComplexNumbers Import
          Complex,              (* The abstract data type *)
          ComplexAdd,           (* Function to add complex numbers *)
          CreateComplex,        (* Function to create complex numbers *)
          WriteComplex;         (* Procedure to write complex numbers *)

Var
          X       : Complex;
          Y       : Complex;
          Z       : Complex;

Begin
          (* Create the complex value 1 + 2i. *)
          X := CreateComplex(1.0, 2.0);

          (* Create the complex value 3 + 4i. *)
          Y := CreateComplex(3.0, 4.0);

          (* Now add these two values and display the results. *)
          Z := ComplexAdd(X, Y);
          WriteComplex(Z);

End ComplexExample.
```

Figure 2–10
Order of Compilation of Modules

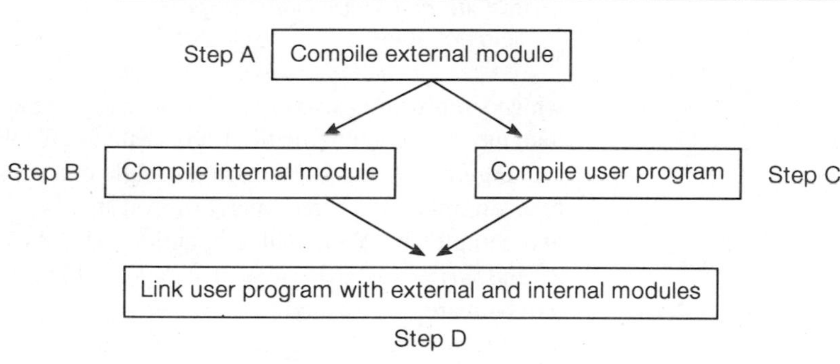

module and relink the new pieces (steps B and D). Because the details of the internal module are hidden from the user, the user's program cannot possibly be affected by a change in the internal module. However, if the external module is changed, we must go through the *entire* process of recompiling both the external and internal modules and every program that uses them (steps A, B, C, and D). Thus a change to an external module should be done only with reluctance. It is clear why adequate time must be put into the *initial* design of the ADT. Changes to the external module of an ADT cause the greatest amount of upheaval and change to the overall system.

If you fail to recompile the pieces of an abstract data type in the order shown in Figure 2–10, most programming languages that support abstract data types will generate an error message during the linking operation to the effect that you are using "incompatible" or "mismatched" modules. If you get this message, you will need to go back and recompile and relink the units in the correct order.

2.4.2 High-Level Language Implementation of the Water Tank Abstract Data Type

If the design of an abstract data type has been carried out according to the guidelines in sections 2.1 to 2.3, then the translation of the formal specifications of that ADT into an external module is straightforward and quite easy.

A comment describing the ADT, including its component elements and structure, should be included at the top of the external module. Next, the ADT is implemented as an opaque type, with each ADT operation implemented as a procedure header whose calling sequence matches the formal syntactic description. Any other resources (e.g., important constants) could also be included as declarations within the external module.

To make sure that the user clearly understands what each operation does, the semantic description of each operation should be included as a comment before each procedure heading. These specifications should unambiguously describe exactly what this operation does and what it produces. They can be written in either natural language or, better yet, a combination of natural language and the axiomatic semantics of each operation.

Figure 2–11 contains a definition module for the Water Tank ADT specified in Figures 2–4a and 2–5. We leave it as an exercise for the reader to design and code the external module for the Train ADT described in section 2.2.2. Similarly, we leave the selection of an internal representation for both Water Tank and Train and the coding of the internal modules as an exercise at the end of the chapter.

We recommend that you use the guidelines laid out in this section and the format shown in Figure 2–11 for all ADTs you create. The reason for our concern for format and presentation is that an external module is much more than just a program unit. It also serves as a formal specification document that must provide a clear and unambiguous statement of exactly how the operations on this ADT behave. It must contain all the information needed by a programmer to implement the corresponding internal module, and it must have all the information needed by a user to determine if this package provides the services that he or she needs. In a sense, the external module serves as a contract between the user and the designer describing what will be provided and exactly what it will do. It should therefore be a document that is precise, complete, and easy to interpret.

2.4.3 Data Abstraction Facilities in Existing Languages

The pseudocode introduced in section 2.4.1 is representative of what is available in a number of well-known and widely used languages, although it lacks the extensive details, options, and restrictions found in any realistic programming environment.

Figure 2–11
External Module for the Water Tank ADT

```
(*  This is the External Module for the abstract data type called WaterTank.
    The domain of the data type is a water level, which is a real value between
    0.0 and 10,000 gallons. The abstract data type WaterTank is described in
    sections 2.2.1 and 2.4.2.   *)
External Module WaterTankPackage;

Type
    WaterTank;          (* The abstract data type *)

(*  Procedure Create returns a newly created WaterTank
    whose water level is 0.0

        Precondition:  None
        Postcondition: Level(Create()) = 0.0   *)
Procedure Create() : WaterTank;

(*  Procedure AddWater, given a WaterTank T and a quantity of water G, returns T
    with G gallons added to it (with a maximum total of 10,000.0).

    Precondition:  T is a WaterTank
                   G is a real value in the range 0.0 <= G <= 10,000.0
    Postcondition: If Level(AddWater(T, G)) <= 10,000.0 Then
                       Level(AddWater(T, G)) = Level(T) + G
                   Else
                       Level(AddWater(T, G)) = 10,000.0 *)
Procedure AddWater( T : WaterTank; G : Real ) : WaterTank;

(*  Procedure RemoveWater, given a WaterTank T and a quantity of water G,
    returns T with G gallons removed from it (RemoveWater will return an
    empty WaterTank if T has less than G gallons in it.)

    Precondition:  T is a WaterTank
                   G is a real value in the range 0.0 <= G <= 10,000.0

    Postcondition: If Level(T) < G Then
                       Level(RemoveWater(T, G)) = 0.0
                   Else
                       Level(RemoveWater(T, G)) = Level(T) - G   *)
Procedure RemoveWater( T : WaterTank; G : Real ) : WaterTank;

(*  Procedure Level returns the current level of a WaterTank

    Precondition:  T is a WaterTank
    Postcondition: The water level of T is returned   *)
Procedure Level( T : WaterTank ) : Real;

(*  Procedure IsFull returns True if the WaterTank is full, False otherwise.

    Precondition:  T is a WaterTank
    Postcondition: If (Level(T) = 10,000) Then
                       IsFull(T) = True
                   Else
                       IsFull(T) = False   *)
Procedure IsFull( T : WaterTank ) : Boolean;
```

(continued)

Figure 2–11 (continued)

```
(*  Procedure IsEmpty returns True if the WaterTank is empty, False otherwise.

    Precondition:  T is a WaterTank
    Postcondition: If (Level(T) = 0) Then
                          IsEmpty(T) = True
                   Else
                          IsEmpty(T) = False   *)
Procedure IsEmpty( T : WaterTank ) : Boolean;

End WaterTankPackage.
```

In this section we briefly survey four languages that support, to at least some degree, the concept of data abstraction. We do not discuss these languages at length, but simply make you aware of their capabilities, similarities, and differences.

Modula-2

The language that most closely models our pseudocode is Modula-2. Created by Professor Nicklaus Wirth, the developer of Pascal, it was designed to extend the capabilities of Pascal in the areas of data abstraction, concurrency, and low-level machine access. In Modula-2, the description of an abstract data type is divided into two separately compilable units called a *definition module* and an *implementation module*. The definition module contains the declaration of transparent and opaque types, constants, variables, and procedure headers. All objects declared in the definition module are visible and can be imported into any other unit.

The implementation module contains the internal implementation of all opaque types as well as the body of all procedures whose headers were contained in the definition module. Figure 2–12 shows the Modula-2 representation of an ADT called Date, along with two operations called Tomorrow and WriteDate. Note the strong similarity between the definition and implementation modules of Modula-2 and our concept of external and internal modules.

Modula-2 uses an **Import** statement to access objects declared in other definition modules. Notice in Figure 2–12 that we imported two I/O routines called Write and WriteInt needed by the procedure WriteDate. These routines were imported from the system module called InOut, which is standard with every implementation. Modula-2 provides both a global and a selective import statement.

A major restriction on ADTs in Modula-2 is that the internal implementation of opaque types must be either a scalar type, such as integer or real, or a pointer variable. Structured types such as records or arrays are not allowed. This restriction allows the compiler to know exactly how much memory space to allocate for opaque types without having to know about the implementation of that opaque type (this information is in the implementation module and may be written and compiled at a different time). This restriction is not as severe as it may sound. It simply means that if you wish to implement an opaque type T using some structured type V, it will have to be implemented as a pointer to that structured type instead:

```
TYPE T = POINTER TO V;
```

Figure 2–12
Abstract Data Types in Modula-2

```
(*  Abstract data types in Modula-2 *)

DEFINITION MODULE DatePackage;

TYPE
    Date;          (* The abstract data type. *)

PROCEDURE Tomorrow(D: Date) : Date;
PROCEDURE WriteDate (D: Date);

END DatePackage;


IMPLEMENTATION MODULE DatePackage;

FROM InOut IMPORT Write, WriteInt;

TYPE Date = POINTER TO
                  RECORD
                      Month, Day, Year : INTEGER;
                  END;

PROCEDURE Tomorrow (D: Date) : Date;
BEGIN
        IF D^.Day = 31 THEN     (* We won't worry about 28-30 day months. *)
                D^.Day := 1
                D^.Month := D^.Month + 1
        ELSE
                D^.Day := D^.Day + 1
        ENDIF;
        IF D^.Month := 13 THEN      (* Must cycle the year. *)
                D^.Month := 1
                D^.Year := D^.Year + 1
        ENDIF;
        RETURN D
END Tomorrow;

PROCEDURE WriteDate(D:Date);
BEGIN
        WriteInt(D^.Month,2); Write('/');
        WriteInt(D^.Day,2) ; Write('/');
        WriteInt(D^.Year,2)
END WriteDate;

END DatePackage.
```

and any reference to an object X of type T will first need to dereference X, that is, go to the object being pointed at by X, using the dereference operator ^. In Modula-2, if T is a pointer to an object, then T^ is the object being pointed at. This approach is used in Figure 2–12 where the opaque type Date is implemented as a pointer to a record structure rather than as the record structure itself. All references to the fields of the variable D of type Date are dereferenced as D^, for example, D^.Day, D^.Month, and D^.Year. (Don't worry if you did not follow this. We will describe pointer operations extensively in chapter 3.)

Ada

Ada is a systems implementation language developed for use by the Defense Department in the early 1980s. It is intended to be the single language used for the implementation of all military systems and software. It is one of the largest and most complex languages ever developed, and it supports a wide range of new software concepts including data abstraction, parallelism, exception handling, generic program units and formal assertions. Its data abstraction capabilities are also similar to the pseudocode described in section 2.4.1.

In Ada, the units of data abstraction are called *packages*. The visible part of the ADT is placed in the *package header*, while the implementation details are placed in the *package body*. The Ada version of the ADT Date is shown in Figure 2–13.

Some of the major differences between Modula-2 and Ada are evident from Figure 2–13. Ada allows an opaque type, called a *private type*, to be implemented using any virtual data type in the language, not just pointers. Notice in Figure 2–13 that Date is implemented as a record structure rather than as a pointer to a record. However, this flexibility requires that the code describing the internal implementation of a private type be placed in a *private* (i.e., hidden) section of the package header rather than in the package body as in Modula-2. Thus the compiler has access to implementation details during compilation of the package header and can determine the proper amount of memory space needed by objects of the opaque type. One problem with this approach is that a change in the implementation of a

Figure 2–13
Abstract Data Types in Ada

```
(* Abstract data types in Ada *)

Package DatePackage is
          Type Date is private;
          Procedure Tommorrow(D : in Date) return Date;
          Procedure WriteDate(D : in Date);

Private
          Type Date is Record
                         month, day, year : Integer;
                    End;

End DatePackage.

With Text_IO; Use Text_IO;
Package Body DatePackage is
          Procedure Tomorrow(D : in Date) return Date;
               •
               •         (* Here is the body of Tomorrow. *)
               •
          End Tomorrow;

          Procedure WriteDate(D : in Date);
               •
               •         (* Here is the body of WriteDate. *)
               •
          End WriteDate;

End DatePackage.
```

private type requires recompilation of both the package header and the package body, rather than just the package body.

Ada supports only the global form of import statement, not the selective form available in Modula-2. The import statement in Ada is

```
With PackageName;
```

which imports all visible resources in the header unit of the specified PackageName. For example, the statement **With** Text_IO in Figure 2–13 would import all resources of the package Text_IO, including routines to read and write integer values, ReadInt and WriteInt.

The clause **Use** Text_IO of Figure 2–13 allows you to use those imported resources without having to qualify their names, that is, without having to write them in the form PackageName.ResourceName. Instead we can refer to them simply by ResourceName. Within the body of procedure WriteDate we can refer to the routine WriteInt rather than having to refer to it as Text_IO.WriteInt.

C++

The popular systems implementation language C does not support data abstraction, but the variant called C++ does. It implements ADTs using a concept called a *class*, borrowed from the language Simula-67. A class is a user-defined data structure that has both a private and a public part. In a sense, the class itself is the abstract data type. The private part contains the implementation of the data structure. The public part contains the ADT interface—the headers of all functions available to objects of this class. There is no equivalent in C++ to the internal module of section 2.4.1. The body of the functions are simply included anywhere within the definition of the program. Figure 2–14 shows the abstract data type Date implemented as a class in C++.

Since there could be a number of functions with the same name but located in different classes, we use the notation ClassName::FunctionName to indicate that what follows is the body of the function called FunctionName that was declared in the public section of the class called ClassName.

In C++ there is also no explicit import mechanism. To use a function that is a member of a class, we simply create an object of that class and then apply our functions to that object using the qualified naming syntax ClassName.FunctionName, as in

```
Date t                          // Assume t gets set to today's date
                                // Somewhere in the program
Void PrintTomorrowsDate()
{       t := t.Tomorrow();      // This changes t to tomorrow's date
        t.WriteDate();          // And this writes it out.
}
```

Turbo Pascal

Our final example of a language that provides data abstraction capabilities is Turbo Pascal. Standard Pascal does not support any aspect of data abstraction described in this chapter. (Support for data abstraction was one of the main reasons for the design

Figure 2–14
Abstract Data Types in C++

```
// Abstract data types in C++
class Date {                          // This is the private part
    int month, day, year;             // Date has three integer fields
public:                                   // This is the visible part
    Date Tomorrow ();
    Void WriteDate();                     // Void means the function does
                                          // not return a value
};
Date Date::Tomorrow()
{
        . . .          // Here is the body of Tomorrow
};
Void Date::WriteDate()
{
        . . .          // Here is the body of WriteDate
};
```

and development of Modula-2 as an extension to Pascal.) However, the more recent versions of Turbo Pascal do support some (although not all) of the concepts we have discussed. Specifically, these versions support the idea of encapsulation in which a data type is packaged with the operations on that data type and all resources are imported as a unit into a program. However, they do not fully support the concept of information hiding through the use of opaque data types. In Turbo Pascal, the declaration of a data type must include not only its name but its internal implementation as well.

The unit of encapsulation in Turbo Pascal is called a *unit*. It includes an *interface section* that contains the visible resources of the unit—**Const** declarations, **Var** declarations, transparent types, and procedure headers. The second part of the unit is the *implementation section*, which contains the body of all procedures included in the interface. These two pieces are not separately compilable, but are simply two parts of a single unit. To import the resources of a unit we include the statement

```
Uses UnitName;
```

in a program unit; this statement makes all the visible resources of UnitName available to that program unit. Turbo Pascal does not support the selective import option of Modula-2.

Figure 2–15 shows a Turbo Pascal implementation of the abstract data type Date.

Looking back at these examples, we can see a great deal of similarity in the concepts and capabilities of these four languages, although there are differences in the details of implementation. By using a simple and easy-to-understand pseudocode, rather than a specific language, we can concentrate on the important ideas of ADTs and advanced data structures without getting bogged down here in the syntax as well as in the system-dependent and vendor-dependent details. At this stage in

Figure 2–15
Abstract Data Types in Turbo Pascal

```
(* Abstract data types in Turbo Pascal *)
Unit DatePackage;
Interface
    Type Date = Record
                    month, day, year : Integer;
                End;
    Function Tomorrow (D: Date) : Date;
    Procedure WriteDate (D : Date);
Implementation
    Uses SomeUnit;        (* Assume we need the resources in this unit. *)
    Function Tomorrow (D : Date) : Date;
    Begin
        . . . (* Here is the body of Tomorrow. *)
    End;
    Procedure WriteDate (D : Date);
    Begin
        . . . (* Here is the body of WriteDate. *)
    End;
End.
```

our study of software development, concerns for the details of a given language are less important than concerns for such fundamental principles as procedural and data abstraction and data structure design.

However, the discussion in this section should familiarize those students who actually wish to implement and utilize ADTs with the capabilities of some existing and widely used languages. We encourage the interested reader to investigate the details of the ADT facilities of any of these four high-level programming languages, using either the language supplements that come with this text or other reference materials that he or she may be familiar with. The abstract data types that we will study in upcoming chapters can then be implemented and used.

Figure 2–16 summarizes the pseudocode notation that we will use to represent ADTs throughout the remainder of the text.

2.5 ADVANTAGES OF DATA ABSTRACTION

After spending a good deal of time learning how to specify, design, and build abstract data types, your natural question is, What advantages does it provide? What help do ADTs provide in constructing correct, efficient, and maintainable software? There are four advantages that we will describe.

The first advantage is *security* and *software integrity*. With an ADT, a user is allowed to perform only the operations that you, the designer, explicitly provide. You control access to all resources, helping to guarantee that no improper, illegal, or potentially dangerous operations can be carried out. For example, if the user of the Water Tank ADT of section 2.2.1 knew that it was implemented internally using a

Figure 2–16
Summary of Pseudocode for Abstract Data Types

External modules

```
External Module Module Name;
    Const declarations;
    Type declarations;        (* Both transparent and opaque types. *)
    Var declarations;
    Procedure headings;       (* Only the heading, not the code. *)
End ModuleName;
```

Opaque types

```
Type
    OpaqueTypeName;
```

Internal modules

```
Internal Module ModuleName;          (* Name must match external
                                        module. *)
    Const declarations;              (* These are local to the
                                        internal module. *)
    Var declarations;                (* So are these. *)
    Type declarations;               (* This is the implementation of
                                        opaque types. *)
    Procedure PName(parameters)      (* This is the description of the
        Begin                           procedures whose headings were
          .                             in the external module. It includes
          .                             the code. *)
          .
        End;
    (* The other procedures and functions would follow next. *)
    End ModuleName;
```

Import declarations

```
Import ModuleName;                   (* This is the global form of the
                                        import declaration. *)
From ModuleName Import               (* The selective form of the import
                                        declaration. *)
    Name, Name, . . . ;              (* The names are resources that can
                                        be imported. *)
```

pointer to a real variable, then he or she would be able to create an illegal value for the water level in tank T by saying

T^ := 10,001.0;   (* Put 10,001.0 gallons in T. This is impossible. *)

With the use of opaque types this operation is not possible, and full integrity can be maintained. We have essentially put a wall around the internal implementation, exactly as diagrammed in Figure 2–2.

A second advantage is *maintainability*. Software packages are used for long periods of time—5, 10, or 15 years is not atypical. During that time, these programs will almost certainly be modified (i.e., updated, fixed, changed, or extended)

many times. To keep maintenance costs low, we would like a change to affect as few modules in the system as possible. Specifically, we would like those modules not being changed to be unaffected by and unaware of the change. We take advantage of this all the time with procedural abstraction. For example, when you write the assignment statement

```
y := sin(x) - cos(x);
```

you do not care what algorithm is used to implement the two trigonometric functions. You do not even care if the algorithm changes, as long as it is correct. Your program is unaffected since it is independent of the underlying techniques being used.

The same situation exists with data abstraction. The external module is independent of the underlying implementation. Therefore, both the external module and all user modules are unaffected by changes made to the associated internal module. (In fact, if the internal module changes, the external and user modules do not have to be recompiled, just relinked to the new internal module.) This advantage greatly facilitates the maintenance operation and helps keep costs down over the life of the software.

Data abstraction also facilitates the *sharing* and *reusability* of software. By encapsulating a data type with its operations and by making that collection a separately compilable library unit, we make it easy for someone to import and use those resources in his or her own programs. During your studies you will likely import and use a large number of existing computational resources, such as string handling packages, graphics routines, I/O functions, and file handling packages. Code sharing can improve programmer productivity and keep software costs down.

The final advantage is the most nebulous, but perhaps the most important—the idea of *intellectual manageability*. We began this chapter by stating that procedural abstraction allows us to view a highly complex operation (our example was QuickSort) in terms of a clean, simple external interface—**Procedure** QuickSort(List,N). We did not need to understand the relatively complicated recursive QuickSort algorithm. An abstract data type gives us exactly the same advantage. We can view a complicated data structure (e.g., a Train) in terms of a clean, simple set of well-defined external operations (CreateTrain, Length, AddEngine, AddBoxcar). We do not have to be aware of the details of the implementation, which may run into dozens or even hundreds of lines of complicated code.

As programs get larger—as large as tens of thousands of lines in length—this ability to hide detail and concentrate on the "bigger picture" becomes critically important. Without it, it would become virtually impossible to implement any large software system correctly. That is why procedural abstraction and data abstraction are two of the most important and useful techniques in the software development process.

2.6 CONCLUSION

We have now shown how to specify, design, and build abstract data types and have discussed a number of reasons why they are such an important programming tool. In the succeeding chapters we will make extensive use of ADTs to build data structures such as lists, stacks, and trees, that are widely used in computer science.

Abstract data types have been included as a feature of virtually every important programming language developed in the last few years. In fact, one class of high-level languages has made the ADT the single most important feature of its entire design. These languages are called *object-oriented languages*, and the *object*, the fundamental concept of these languages, is virtually identical to what we have termed an ADT. (However, object-oriented languages also have other capabilities. Thus Modula-2 and Ada are not considered to be members of this class.) This group, which includes such languages as Smalltalk, Eiffel, Objective-C, C++, and Object Pascal, offers the possibility of significant improvements in programmer productivity, cost containment, and software maintainability. Many computer scientists believe that in the near future these languages will become one of the most important and widely used classes of languages in computer science. To make full use of their power and functionality, it will be essential for software developers to understand how to take advantage of the concept of data abstraction.

CHAPTER EXERCISES

1. In addition to control, procedures, and data abstraction, discuss other areas where a programming language provides you with a degree of abstraction, that is, areas where the compiler lets you think in terms of higher-level interfaces while hiding the underlying details.
2. Using the Pascal array type, give an example of
   a. a Transformer operation
   b. a Creator operation
   c. an Observer operation

   on arrays.
3. Write out the informal specification (i.e., domain, components, relationship, operators) for the following Pascal virtual data types.
   a. **Real**
   b. **Array** [1 .. 10] **Of** Integer;
4. Explain how something can be both a hardware data type, a virtual data type, and an abstract data type. Give an example.
5. Are the following atomic or structured data types? Give reasons for your answers.
   a. Files
   b. Pointers
   c. Sets
   d. Enumerated ordinal data types
6. Add the following operations to the Water Tank ADT. For each new operation, give the formal syntax, semantics, and pre- and postconditions for that operation.
   a. ReadLevel(T) (* As described in section 2.2.1. *)
   b. CreateFull(T) (* As described in section 2.2.1. *)
   c. EmptyOut(T) (* Set the water level of T back to 0.0 regardless of its current level. *)
   d. Transfer(T1,T2) (* Transfer all the water in tank T1 to tank T2, leaving tank T1 empty. *)

7. Propose additional operations for the Water Tank ADT beyond those listed in exercise 6. For each new operation give the syntax, semantics, and pre- and postconditions for that operation.
8. Finish the design of the Train ADT described in section 2.2.2. Add a sufficient number of operations so that we can do useful operations on Trains. For each operation, give the syntax, semantics, and pre- and postconditions for that operation.
9. Are the following composite operations syntactically valid or not? Give reasons for your response.
   a. IsEmpty(Level(CreateTank(),500.0))
   b. AddWater(CreateTank(),Level(RemoveWater(CreateTank(),1000.0)))
   c. Length(AddEngine(E,AddBoxcar(B,T)))
10. Using the formal notation shown in Figure 2–4, describe the syntax of the following Pascal operations on integers:
    a. +
    b. sqrt()
    c. >
    d. chr()
11. Using the formal notation shown in Figure 2–4, describe the syntax of the subscript operations on the following array type:

    X : **Array** *[1 .. 10]* **Of** *Real;*

12. Express informally (i.e., in English) what the following axioms state formally for operation X on the Water Tank ADT
    a. X(T) = **Not** (IsEmpty(T) **Or** IsFull(T))
    b. **If** (Level(T1) > Level(T2)) **Then**
          X(T1,T2) = T1
       Else
          X(T1,T2) = T2
13. Change the semantic rules of the Water Tank ADT in Figure 2–5 so that attempts either to put in more than 10,000 gallons of water or to remove more water than is currently stored in the tank are both treated as fatal errors.
14. Show the semantic analysis of the following sequences of operations. For each one, justify your analysis using the axioms in Figures 2–5 and 2-6.
    a. IsEmpty(RemoveWater(AddWater(CreateTank (),300.0),300.0))
    b. Back(AddEngine(E_1,AddBoxcar(B_1, AddBoxcar(B_2,CreateTank (E_2)))))
15. Explain in your own words why an **Import** statement is not needed in Pascal.
16. External modules are useful not only for building ADTs but for grouping together any collection of resources that you wish to treat as a single coherent package. Write an external module that collects together the following useful metric-to-English conversion constants:

    2.54 centimeters/inch
    3.79 liters/gallon
    28.35 grams/ounce
    0.3048 meter/foot

17. Explain why it is not possible for the compiler to support opaque types in Pascal.
18. What is wrong with the following two external modules?

External Module *M;*	**External Module** *N;*
From *N* **Import** *Y;*	**From** *M* **Import** *X;*
Procedure *X;*	**Procedure** *Y;*
Procedure *Z;*	**End** *N;*
End *M.*	

19. Write a client module that uses the complex number package of Figure 2–7 to add up and print out the following sum:

$$(3 + 2i) + (7 - i) + 8$$

20. Write a user module of the Water Tank ADT of Figure 2–11 that does the following operations:
    a. Creates a new tank T
    b. Inputs a real number G
    c. Adds G gallons to the tank
    d. Repeats steps b and c until the tank is full or would overflow and then stops
21. Write an external module for the Train ADT described in section 2.2.2.
22. Select an internal implementation for the opaque types Water Tank, Train, Engine, and Boxcar and code the internal modules of the two ADTs.
23. Design, formally specify, implement, and test an abstract data type called Matrix. Include the familiar set of matrix operations, including matrix addition, multiplication, transposition, and inversion. Follow all guidelines given in this chapter with respect to syntactic specifications, semantics, pre- and postconditions, and module design. Use any language that was discussed in this chapter or that provides support for ADTs.
24. Design, formally specify, implement, and test an abstract data type called Deck that models a deck of 52 playing cards. The operations you should include should be those that are needed in playing typical card games, such as shuffling the deck, cutting the deck, and dealing out *n* cards each to *m* players. Follow all guidelines given in this chapter with respect to syntactic specifications, semantics, pre- and postconditions, and module design. Use any language that was discussed in this chapter or that provides support for ADTs.
25. Design, formally specify, implement, and test an abstract data type called Thermostat. The operations you should include are creating a new thermostat with an initial temperature setting, raising and lowering the temperature, checking the temperature, and sounding an alarm if the temperature gets too low or too high. Follow all guidelines given in this chapter with respect to syntactic specifications, semantics, pre- and postconditions, and module design. Use any language that was discussed in this chapter or that provides support for ADTs.

26. Rewrite the internal module for complex numbers shown in Figure 2–8 so that it uses the following implementation:

```
Type
    Complex = Array [ 1 .. 2 ] of Real;
```

What effect will this change have on users of the complex number package?

CHAPTER 3

LINEAR DATA STRUCTURES AND THEIR ARRAY IMPLEMENTATION

CHAPTER OUTLINE

3.1 THE CLASSIFICATION OF DATA STRUCTURES

In this chapter we begin our study of advanced data structures and show how these structures can be implemented as abstract data types.

A *data type* is a collection of values along with a set of operations defined on those values. A *simple,* or *scalar, data type* is made up of values that cannot be decomposed; examples include such familiar Pascal types as integer, real, char, and Boolean, as well as the Water Tank ADT of chapter 2.[1] A *composite data type*, also called a *data structure*, is one in which the elements of the data type can be decomposed into either simple data types or other composite data types. Examples of composite types include the familiar array and record structures of Pascal (and most other programming languages) and the Train ADT introduced in chapter 2.

Data structures can be classified by the structural relationship between component elements.

Linear data structures have a 1:1 relationship between elements; that is, if the structure is non-empty, there will exist a first and last element, and each element (except the first and last) will have a unique predecessor element and a unique successor element. This structure is diagrammed in Figure 3–1a. Linear data structures will be introduced and discussed in this chapter and in chapter 4.

Hierarchical data structures have a 1:many relationship between elements; that is, each element of the data structure may have many successors, but it always has a single predecessor (see Figure 3–1b). Notice that as you move downward through the structure in Figure 3–1b, each node may point to many others. However, as you move up through the structure, each node (except the top one) is connected to a unique element. These hierarchical structures are called *trees*, and they are an extremely important data representation in computer science. Trees will be introduced and discussed in chapters 7 and 8.

The third class of composite data types are *graph structures*, the richest and most complex data representations. With graph structures there is a many:many relationship between elements. Any element can connect to or be connected to an arbitrary number of other elements in the structure (see Figure 3–1c). We will introduce graph structures in chapter 10.

The fourth and final class of data structures is the *set structure*. In a set, there is no direct relationship between individual elements. The only relationship they share is membership in the overall set structure, and the exact position or location of a given element within the structure is irrelevant. A set structure is diagrammed in Figure 3–1d. We will study sets and other forms of set structures such as tables and dictionaries in chapter 9.

These are the four classes of composite data types, or data structures, that we will study. Even though there are an enormous number and variety of data structures, they all fall into one of the four fundamental classes shown in Figure 3–1.

In the remainder of this chapter we introduce linear data structures and their array implementation.

[1] At a lower level of abstraction, these simple Pascal types *can* be further decomposed. For example, the integer value 5 could be viewed as a sequence of eight binary digits 00000101. However, at this higher level of abstraction we treat these simple types as nondecomposable.

Figure 3–1
Classification of Data Structures

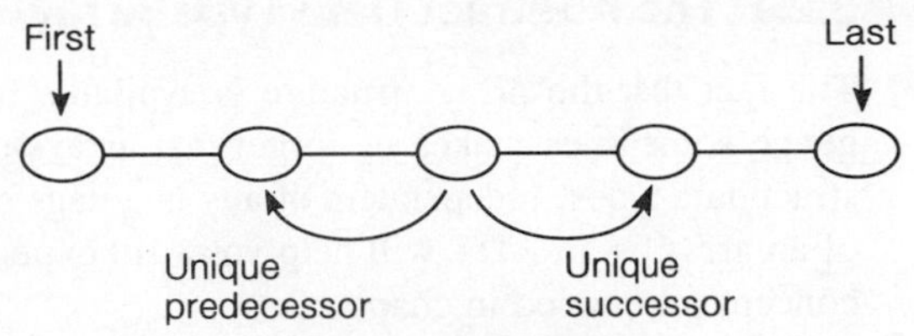

a. Linear structures

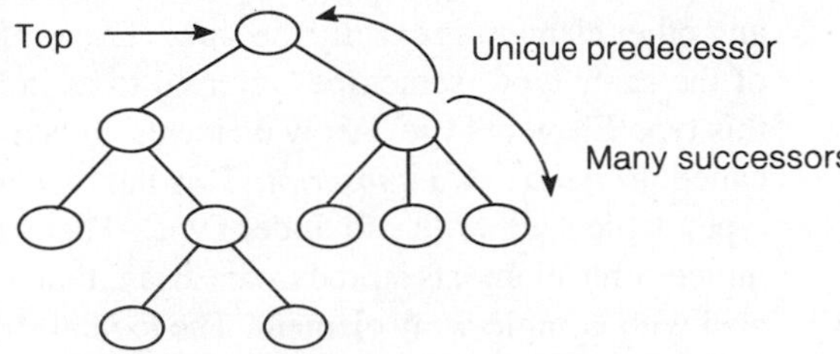

b. Hierarchical structures

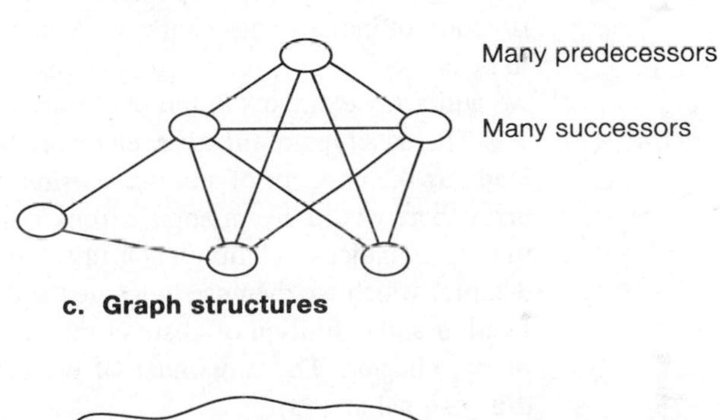

c. Graph structures

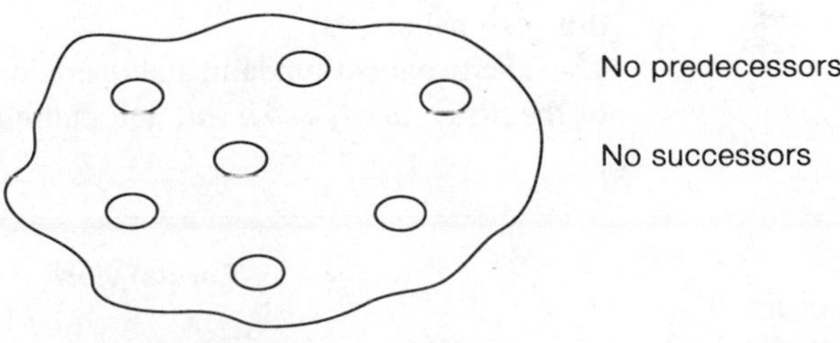

d. Set structures

3.2 ARRAYS

The simplest and best-known linear data structure is the *array*. The array is directly supported by most well-known programming languages, including Pascal, Ada, and Modula-2. In this section we study it as both an abstract and a virtual data type.

3.2.1 The Abstract Data Type Array

The fact that the array structure is available in virtually every programming language sometimes makes us forget that arrays can be described and studied as abstract data types, independent of any language or implementation. The specification of an array as an ADT will help you gain experience and confidence with the ADT concept introduced in chapter 2.

Formally, an array is a *linear*, *random-access* data structure. The term *random-access* means that it takes the same amount of time to access any element contained in the array; that is, the time required to fetch the first element, the last element, or any other element is exactly the same. Every element of an array must be a member of the same type, sometimes referred to as the *base type* of the array; we will call this type ElementType. Array elements are accessed by means of a unique identifier called an *index*, or a *subscript*. This index value must belong to some ordinal data type, which we will call IndexType. There exists a mapping function of array indices onto elements stored in the array, that is, each position in the array is associated with a single array element. The logical structure of an array is shown in Figure 3–2, along with the view of that array from a programming language perspective.

We see from Figure 3–2 that an array can be viewed formally as a three-tuple (I, E, f), where I is a set of indices, E is a set of array elements, and f is a mapping function of indices onto elements. When the array is initially created, it is assumed to be empty, $I = \{\}$. As we store elements into the array, we add indices to the set I, we add array elements to the set E, and we update the mapping function $f: I \rightarrow E$.

The data type of the array elements, ElementType, can itself be an array, which leads to the concept of *multidimensional array structures*. In a multidimensional array there would be a mapping from indices to three-tuples, $f: i \rightarrow (I, E, f)$, rather than from indices to individual array elements. We provide an index i and get back a 3-tuple, which we then use to locate the desired element. We leave the formal specification and definition of abstract multidimensional arrays as an exercise at the end of the chapter. The remainder of our discussion will be limited to abstract one-dimensional arrays.

The two most fundamental operations on arrays involve getting information out of the array, *array retrieval*, and putting information into the array, *array storage*.

Figure 3–2
Structure of an Array Abstract Data Type

Formal view of an array

$A = (I, E, f)$

Set of array elements $E = \{e_1, e_2, e_3, e_4, \ldots\}$

Mapping function f ↑ ↑ ↑ ↑

Set of array indices $I = \{i_1, i_2, i_3, i_4, \ldots\}$

Programming language view of an array

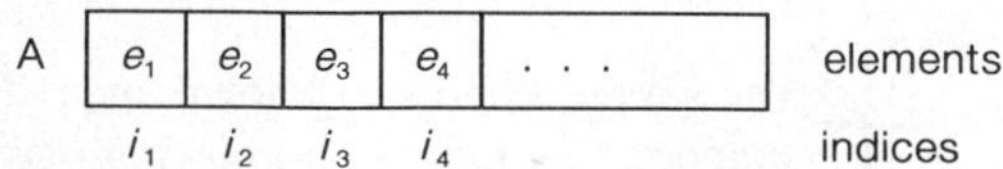

Both retrieval and storage are carried out using array indices. The calling sequence for these two operations is:

Element := Retrieve(A,i) — *(* Retrieve the element in array A associated with index value i. Retrieve: A,i → Element. *)*

A := Store(A,i,Element) — *(* Associate the specified element with index value i of A to produce a new array Store: A,i,Element→ A. *)*

The Retrieve operation is undefined if the index value *i* is not a member of the index set of A. Therefore, we need an additional function called Exists to tell us whether there exists an array element associated with a given index value:

Boolean := Exists(A,i) — *(* Exists is True if i is a member of the index set of A and False otherwise. *)*

We can use Exists to ensure that the Retrieve function operates properly at all times. The syntax and semantics of the ADT Array are summarized in Figure 3–3.

Figure 3–4 shows the external module for a one-dimensional Array ADT. As defined in Figure 3–4, the module describes an infinite capacity Array, since it does not include operations that check for index-out-of-bounds conditions. We leave it as an exercise to add this feature to both the formal semantics of Figure 3–3 and the external module of Figure 3–4.

Figure 3–3
Syntax and Semantics of the Array ADT

Syntax

Define Array[IndexType,ElementType]

```
    Create(): Array[IndexType,ElementType]
    Retrieve(Array[IndexType,ElementType],IndexType): ElementType
    Store(Array[IndexType,ElementType],IndexType,ElementType):
        Array[IndexType,ElementType]
    Exists(Array[IndexType,ElementType],IndexType): Boolean
```

Semantics

(A is an object of type Array
i is an object of type IndexType
e is an object of type ElementType)

a. A newly created Array is empty.

Exists(Create(), i) = False, for all i

b. When an object is stored in position i of an Array, that position is no longer empty.

Exists(Store(A, i, e), i) = True

c. When you retrieve a value from an Array location, the value returned by the Retrieve operation is the last value stored in that location. If nothing has been stored there, the Retrieve operation is undefined.

If Exists(A,i) **Then**
    Retrieve(Store(A, i, e), i) = e
Else
    Retrieve(A,i) is undefined

Figure 3–4
External Module for the Abstract Data Type Array

```
(* The following module defines the external specifications of
the abstract data type called Array which is discussed in
sections 3.2.1 and 3.2.2 and whose syntax and semantics are
given in Figure 3–3 *)

External Module AbstractArray;

Type
    Array;            (* The abstract data type *)
    ElementType;      (* The data type of the elements *)
    IndexType;        (* The data type of the index values *)

(*  Procedure Create returns a new, empty array.

    Precondition:  None
    Postcondition: Exists(Create(), i) = False for all i *)
Procedure Create() : Array;

(*  Procedure Retrieve, given an Array A and an index i, returns
    the element stored in A at position i, if it exists.

    Precondition:  Exists (A, i) = True
    Postcondition: If Exists(A, i) Then
                        Retrieve(Store(A, i, e), i) = e
                   Else
                        Retrieve(A, i) is undefined  *)
Procedure Retrieve( A : Array; i : IndexType ) : ElementType;

(*  Procedure Store stores element E in Array A at position i.

    Precondition:  A is an Array, i is an IndexType,
                   E is an ElementType
    Postcondition: Exists(Store(A, i, E), i) = True   *)
Procedure Store( A : Array; i : IndexType; E : ElementType): Array;

(*  Procedure Exists, for a given Array A and index i, returns
    True if there is an element stored at location i in A,
    False otherwise.

    Precondition:  A is an Array, i is an IndexType
    Postcondition: Returns True if there is an element in A
                   associated with index i.
                   Otherwise return False.   *)
Procedure Exists( A : Array; i : IndexType ) : Boolean;

End AbstractArray.
```

3.2.2 Implementation of Arrays

The array is one of the simplest virtual data types in Pascal, Ada, or Modula-2, where it is a high-level language implementation of the abstract data type described in Figure 3–3 (with the exception that the array size is fixed and finite).

To declare an array, we associate a name with it, define its permissible range of subscripts, and specify the type of its elements. For example, an array that con-

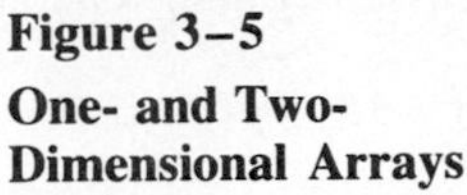

Figure 3–5
One- and Two-Dimensional Arrays

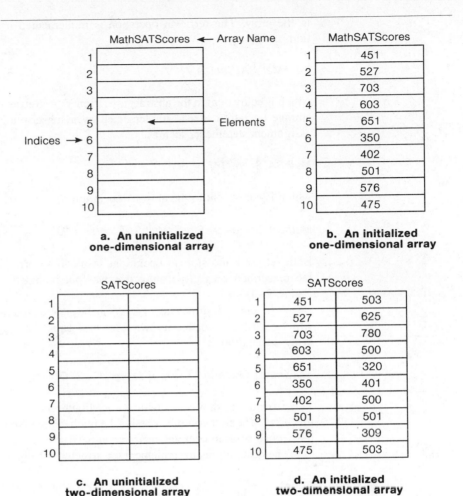

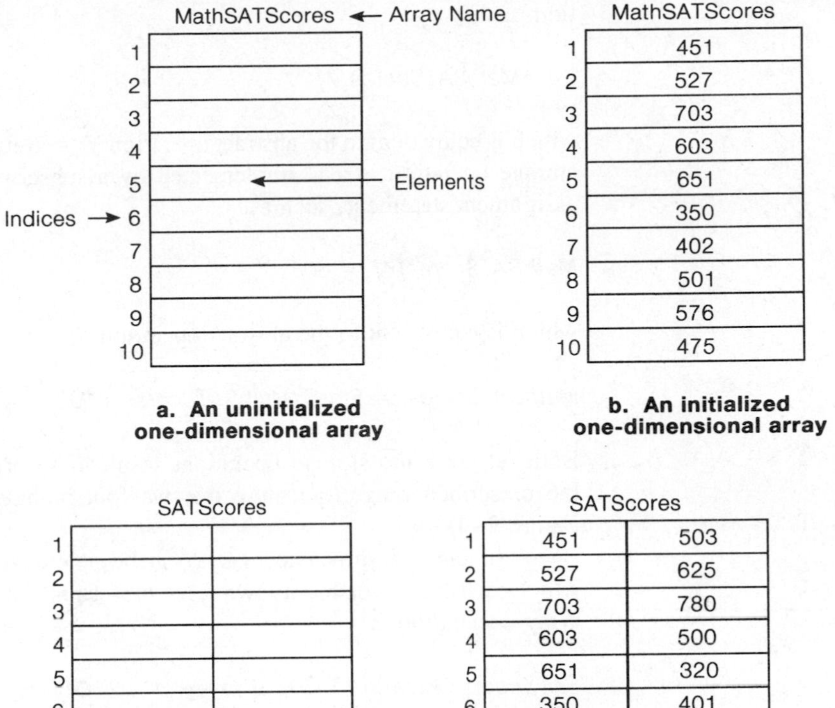

tains the mathematics SAT (Scholastic Aptitude Test) scores of 10 students (labeled 1, 2, . . . , 10) would be declared as follows:

MathSATScores : **Array** *[1 .. 10]* **Of** *Integer;*

Figure 3–5a helps us visualize this structure. Figure 3–5b represents the data structure after specific values (integers, in this case) have been stored in the array.

One advantage of arrays is that they allow programmers to store related elements in one place and refer to them by a single name. An array is a simple and convenient data structure for storing tabular information.

As we mentioned in the previous section, the two operations most commonly associated with Arrays are storage and retrieval. A storage operation enters a value into an array at the particular location defined by the *subscript* (i.e., the index i of Figure 3–2). A retrieval operation returns a value stored in a particular location in the array. The retrieval operation is implemented using a subscripting operation, as in

Y := MathSATScores[7]

which is equivalent to the abstract operation Y := Retrieve(MathSATScores,7). The storage operation is also implemented by a subscripting operation along with an assignment statement, such as

MathSATScores[4] := 603

which is equivalent to the abstract operation:

MathSATScores := Store (MathSATScores,4,603)

Both retrieval and storage operations result in an error if the subscript is outside the prescribed range (a feature that was not included in the external module of Figure 3–4).

A simple, one-dimensional array can be generalized to an *n*-dimensional array in which each dimension has its own set of subscripts. An example of a two-dimensional array declaration is

```
SATScores : Array [1 .. 10] of Array [1 .. 2] Of Integer;
```

This structure is shown in Figure 3–5c. Figure 3–5d represents an initialization of this array. The first column contains the mathematics SAT scores of the 10 students; the second column contains their verbal SAT scores.

The declarations to implement the structure of Figure 3–5c and d are

```
Const
    MaxStudents = 10;
Var
    SATScores : Array[1 .. MaxStudents] of Array [1 .. 2] Of Integer;
```

An understanding of how a computer actually stores data in memory can help programmers format data more efficiently. The basic problem is how to map any given data structure (e.g., a two-dimensional array) into a computer's memory, which can be visualized as a very large, one-dimensional array (see Figure 3–6). Notice that in the representation in Figure 3–6, the first word of memory has an index (actually an address) of 0. The number of words of memory is MemorySize, and therefore the last word in memory has the address value MemorySize-1. The value of MemorySize is usually a power of 2, since computers represent values internally in *binary*, the base-2 positional numbering system.

We now consider how one-dimensional and two-dimensional arrays can be mapped into the computer's memory. This mapping should (1) ensure that the retrieval of elements from the array is efficient, (2) ensure that the time to retrieve an item is essentially independent of location (the random-access property), and (3) determine the amount of memory needed to store the array.

Figure 3–6
Model of a Computer's Memory

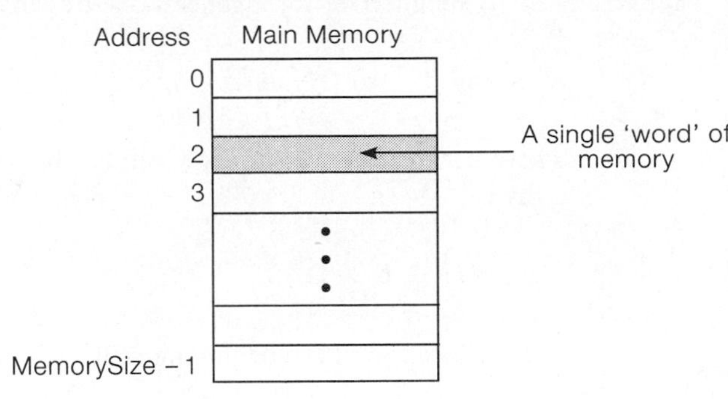

Determining how much memory to allocate for a one-dimensional array is simple. We assume for now that each element of the array of type ElementType requires one word of memory. The total number of words required to store an array declared as

Var
  Example : **Array** *[LowerBound .. UpperBound]* **Of** *ElementType;*

is

UpperBound − LowerBound + 1

For the one-dimensional array shown in Figure 3–5a and b, the number of words required is 10 − 1 + 1 = 10.

When an array A is stored in sequential memory words, the location in memory of the array element with subscript j is given by the following formula:

$$\text{loc}(A[j]) = \text{loc}(A[\text{LowerBound}]) + j - \text{LowerBound}$$

Once the location in memory of the LowerBound element is established, the location of all other elements is determined in relation to it.

The preceding formula applies only when each element of the array occupies one word of memory. However, it can easily be modified to accommodate elements of a base type requiring more than one word. If each object of type ElementType requires s words of storage, the total number of words needed to store the array becomes

$$s * (\text{UpperBound} - \text{LowerBound} + 1)$$

and the location of the jth element of the array becomes

$$\text{loc}(A[j]) = \text{loc}(A[\text{LowerBound}]) + [s * (j - \text{LowerBound})]$$

(We assume that loc(A[LowerBound]) refers to the address of the first of the s words of storage used to hold the first element of the array.)

To summarize, for a general one-dimensional array declared as follows:

A : **Array** *[*b .. u*]* **Of** *ElementType;*

where each element requires s words, the total number of words occupied by the array is

$$s * (u - b + 1)$$

and the location of the beginning of the jth element of the array is

$$\text{loc}(A[j]) = \text{loc}(A[b]) + [s * (j - b)]$$

Let us now consider how to map the two-dimensional array of Figure 3–5c and d into the one-dimensional memory of a computer. There are two ways to accomplish this mapping. The first is to store the first column of the array, followed by the second column, the third column, and so forth. This method is called *column-major ordering*. The second method stores one row after another; this system is called *row-major ordering*. Both of these methods are used in high-level languages. Figure 3–7 demonstrates these two techniques.

Again, let us initially assume that each object of type ElementType occupies one word of memory. To determine the location of the i, jth element of SATScores when the array is stored by columns, we establish the location of the first element of the array (loc(SATScores[1,1])). The location of the elements in the first column of SATScores[i,1] would be

$$\text{loc}(\text{SATScores}[i,1]) = \text{loc}(\text{SATScores}[1,1]) + (i - 1)$$

Since each column contains 10 elements, we simply add 10 to loc(SATScores[i,1]) to determine the location of SATScores[i,2]; that is,

$$\text{loc}(\text{SATScores}[i,2]) = \text{loc}(\text{SATScores}[1,1]) + (i - 1) + 10$$

From this discussion we should be able to write a formula that works to locate an item in any row i and column j.

$$\text{loc}(\text{SATScores}[i,j]) = \text{loc}(\text{SATScores}[1,1]) + (i - 1) + 10 * (j - 1)$$

For an arbitrary two-dimensional array declared as

A : **Array** *[1 ..* u_1*]* **of Array** *[1 ..* u_2*]* **Of** *ElementType;*

the formula for locating A[i,j], when the array is stored by columns and where objects of type ElementType require one word of storage, would be

$$\text{loc}(A[i,j]) = \text{loc}(A[1,1]) + (i - 1) + [u_1 * (j - 1)]$$

Figure 3–7 Two-Dimensional Array Stored by Columns and by Rows

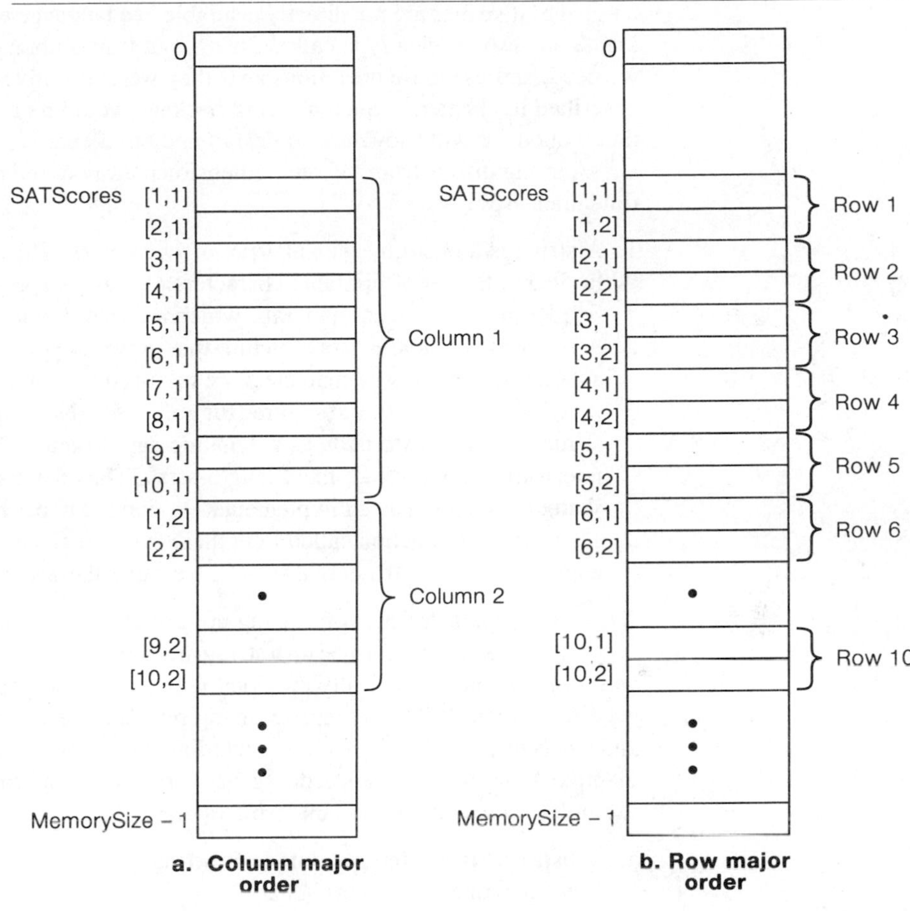

(It is interesting to note that this formula does not depend on the value of u_2, only the value u_1.) We leave the derivation of formulas for arrays declared as

A : **Array** *[*b$_1$ .. u$_1$*]* **of Array** *[*b$_2$ .. u$_2$*]* **Of** *ElementType;*
(Assume each element requires* s *words of memory. *)*

and higher-dimensional arrays as exercises.

Formulas of this type are called *array-mapping functions*. They are actually used by compilers to map multidimensional arrays onto the one-dimensional memory space of a computer and to implement the subscripting operation found in all high-level languages.

3.2.3 Strings

A *string* is a special type of linear one-dimensional array. It is an important data structure widely used in computer science for storing and manipulating textual data. A number of programming languages provide strings as a virtual data type of the language. If strings are not directly available in a language we are using, we can still create an abstract data type called String, put it in a library, import the operations we need, and use these operations as if they were primitives of the language, as we described in chapter 2. Such a String package would be a very useful tool, and in this section we will show how to design and build one.

A string differs from the one-dimensional array of the previous section in three fundamental ways:

1. A string is a one-dimensional array of *characters*. These characters are usually limited to the set of printable characters plus a few special *control characters* like Return, Line Feed, and Tab, which are useful in text-based applications.
2. A string is a *dynamic* data structure that grows in size as new characters are added and contracts as characters are removed, in contrast to the *static*, fixed-length view of an array structure (Figure 3–5). (Note, however, that while a string is viewed externally as a dynamic data structure, it may be implemented internally using a static, fixed-length array. Thus the maximum length of a string effectively has an implementation-defined upper bound.)
3. There exists a function called Length(s) that will always return the current length of string s. If Length(s) = 0, we call s the *empty string*.

These three characteristics of a string are illustrated in Figure 3–8.

The operations performed on a string are more extensive than the simple Retrieve and Store operations typically provided with an array structure. The operations that need to be included in a complete String package are those that create, transform, and analyze textual information, including the familiar types of character-based manipulations found in text editing or word processing programs. The following examples show some important string operators:

a. Substring(String, Integer, Integer): String
   Character(Integer, String): Char

   The function Substring(S, i, j) extracts a substring from the string S. The substring returned by the function consists of the j characters in S beginning at position i. The length of string S must be at least $(i + j - 1)$ characters or else the function is undefined. The function Character(n, S) returns the character located at integer position n of string S, $1 \leq n \leq$ Length(S).

Figure 3–8
Examples of Strings

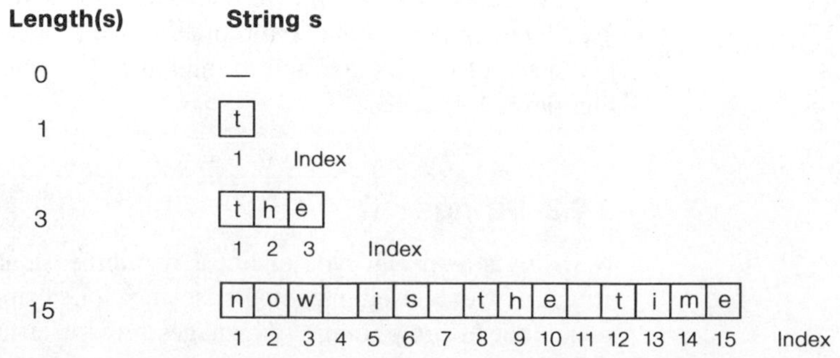

Length(s)	String s
0	—
1	[t] (Index: 1)
3	[t|h|e] (Index: 1 2 3)
15	[n|o|w| |i|s| |t|h|e| |t|i|m|e] (Index: 1 2 3 4 5 6 7 8 9 10 11 12 13 14 15)

Example: S = 'ABCDE' Substring(S,2,3) = 'BCD'
Character(4,S) = 'D'

b. Concatenate(String, String): String

Concatenate takes two input strings and produces a single output string by appending the second input string to the back of the first input string. The length of the resulting string is the sum of the lengths of the two individual strings. The axioms describing the behavior of Concatenate are:

Length(Concatenate(S_1, S_2)) = Length(S_1) + Length(S_2)

Character(i, Concatenate(S_1, S_2)) = Character(i, S_1) $1 \le i \le$ Length(S_1)

Character(i, Concatenate(S_1, S_2)) = Character(i − Length(S_1), S_2)
  Length(S_1) + $1 \le i \le$ Length(Concatenate(S_1, S_2)

Example: S_1 = 'ABC' S_2 = 'DEFGH'
Concatenate(S_1, S_2) = 'ABCDEFGH'

c. PatternMatch(String, String) : Integer

PatternMatch(S_1, S_2) takes a string S_1, and a string S_2, where Length(S_2) $\le$ Length(S_1), and determines if the string S_2 occurs anywhere within string S_1. If it does, PatternMatch returns the position i of the location of the beginning of the match in S_1. If string S_2 occurs more than once in S_1, PatternMatch returns the starting position of the first such match. If S_2 does not occur in S_1, PatternMatch returns a 0.

If Character(i, S_2) = Character($j + i - 1$, S_1), $1 \le i \le$ Length(S_2) **Then**
  PatternMatch(S_1, S_2) = j
Else
  PatternMatch(S_1, S_2) = 0

(Note that this axiom does not include the test to determine whether the match is the first match. This test has been left as an exercise.)

Example: S_1 = 'ABCDEFG' S_2 = 'CD'
  PatternMatch(S_1, S_2) = 3 (* The match begins at position 3 of S_1 *)

d. ChangeChar(String, Integer, Char) : String

The function ChangeChar(S, i, c) changes the character located in position i of string S to the character value c. It returns the newly created string as the result.

Character(i, ChangeChar(S, i, c)) = c

Example: ChangeChar('ABCDE', 2, 'X') = 'AXCDE'

Figure 3–9 shows an external module that creates the String ADT along with the six basic operations Length, Substring, Character, Concatenate, PatternMatch, and ChangeChar. Figure 3–10 shows a client module that imports these resources to implement a function called FindAndReplace(S_1, S_2, S_3), in which we locate all occurrences of substring S_2 within string S_1 and replace them with the substring S_3. So, for example, FindAndReplace('ABCDEABCDE', 'DE', 'ZZZ') would produce 'ABCZZZABCZZZ'. This very common operation is provided by virtually all text editors. It would allow you, for example, to replace every occurrence of the misspelling 'teh' in string S with the correct string 'the' by executing the command FindAndReplace(S, 'teh', 'the'). The function is easy to implement given the operations available with our String ADT.

Figure 3–9

External Module for the String Abstract Data Type

```
(* The following module defines the external specifications of the abstract data
type called String whose syntax and semantics are given in section 3.2.3 *)

External Module StringPackage;

Type
    String;          (* The abstract data type *)

(*  The procedure Length takes a string, S, and returns the number of
    characters in it.
        Precondition:  None
        Postcondition: Returns the number of characters in S   *)
Procedure Length( S : String ) : Integer;

(*  The procedure SubString extracts a substring from string S. The string
    returned by SubString will consist of the L characters in S starting
    at character position B.
        Precondition:  Length(S) >= B + L - 1
        Postcondition: If the precondition is not met then
                       SubString is undefined.   *)
Procedure SubString( S : String; B : Integer; L : Integer ) : String;

(*  The procedure Character returns the character at position i in string S.
        Precondition:  1 <= i <= Length(S)
        Postcondition: If the precondition is met, Character returns
                       the character at position i in S
                       otherwise, Character is undefined.   *)
Procedure Character( i : Integer; S : String ) : Char;

(*  The procedure Concatenate returns a string which consists of the
    string S1 followed by string S2.
        Precondition:  None
        Postcondition: Length(Concatenate(S1, S2)) =
                       Length(S1) + Length(S2)   *)
Procedure Concatenate( S1 : String; S2 : String ) : String;

(*  The procedure PatternMatch attempts to locate an occurrence of the
    string S2 within string S1. If it finds one or more matches, it
    returns the position of the first character of the first match.
    If it finds no matches, PatternMatch returns zero.
        Precondition:  None
        Postcondition: If Char(i, S2) = Char(j+i-1,S2) for
                                 1<= i <=Length(S2) Then
                           PatternMatch(S1, S2) = j
                       Else
                           PatternMatch(S1, S2) = 0   *)
Procedure PatternMatch( S1 : String; S2 : String ) : Integer;

(*  The procedure ChangeChar returns a string which is identical to
    the string S, except that the character at position i has been
    changed to the character c.
        Precondition:  1 <= i <= Length(S)
        Postcondition: If the precondition is met, Then
                       Char(i, ChangeChar(S, i, c)) = c
                       otherwise, ChangeChar is undefined.   *)
Procedure ChangeChar( S : String; i : Integer; c : Char ) : String;

End StringPackage.
```

Figure 3–10
Client Module to Implement the Find and Replace Operation

```
(* This module is a client program utilizing the resources provided
   by StringPackage. The function contained in this module is
   described in section 3.2.3. *)

Module StringExample;

From StringPackage Import
         String,                   (* The abstract data type *)
         PatternMatch,             (* Function locates patterns
                                       within string. *)
         Concatenate,              (* Function merges two strings. *)
         SubString,                (* Function extracts a portion
                                       of a string. *)
         Length;                   (* Function returns the length
                                       of a string. *)

(* Procedure FindAndReplace will search String S1 for all
   occurrences of String S2, replacing each with String S3 *)

Procedure FindAndReplace( S1 : String; S2 : String; S3 : String ) : String;
Var
    position : Integer;
    NewString : String;            (* This will contain the final string. *)
Begin
    NewString := ''
    position := PatternMatch(S1, S2);   (* Find the first occurrence
                                            of S2 in S1. *)
    While ( position <> 0 ) Do          (* Repeat this section as long as
                                            there are more occurrences
                                            of S2 in S1. *)
        NewString := Concatenate(NewString, Concatenate
                         (SubString(S1, 1, position - 1), S3));

        (* Add to the end of NewString all of the original
        string up to the occurrence of S1, followed by S3. *)

        S1 := SubString(S1, position + Length(S2), Length(S1) -
                  Length(S2) - position + 1);

        (* Replace S1 with portion of S1 which follows occurrence of S2. *)

        position := PatternMatch(S1, S2);  (* Find the next occurrence
                                               of S2 in S1. *)
    Endwhile;

    Return Concatenate(NewString, S1);

End FindAndReplace;

End StringExample.
```

There are many, many other operations on strings, and a complete and "full-blown" string-handling package would include additional operations not listed in Figure 3–9. We have included an exercise at the end of the chapter in which you will consider what additional operations might be included in the external module of Figure 3–9 and then specify and implement a complete ADT String package.

There are a number of different ways to implement strings internally. One of the most simple and straightforward is to use a record structure with two fields, the array of characters comprising the string and the string length.

```
Const
    MaxStringSize = . . . ;          (* The maximum string size. *)
Type
    String = Record
                 Size : 0 .. MaxStringLength;
                 S : Array[1 .. MaxStringLength] Of Char
             End;
Var
    x : String;
```

The characters of the string would be placed in x.S[1], x.S[2], . . . , and the length of x would be kept in x.Size. So, for example, to assign the value 'ABC' to the string x we would write:

```
x.S[1] := 'A';
x.S[2] := 'B';
x.S[3] := 'C';
x.Size := 3
```

Remember, however, that if String is implemented as an opaque data type, the user cannot directly code these four assignment statements. He or she would have to use an operation that we provide as part of our ADT package, such as SetString(x,'ABC').

Figure 3–11 shows the internal implementation of the two string procedures PatternMatch and Concatenate, using the record structure just described. The implementation of the operators Length, Character, SubString, and ChangeChar is left as an exercise.

3.3 STACKS

3.3.1 Formal Description

The array structure of section 3.2 is simple to deal with because it exists not only as an abstract data type but also as a virtual data type in most languages. In this section and the following one, we discuss two linear structures, the *stack* and *queue*, that do not exist as virtual types in either Pascal, Ada, or Modula-2. We can, however, implement them ourselves using the array structures of section 3.2.

Unlike the array, in which we can directly access all elements, a *stack* is a linear last-in/first-out (LIFO) data structure in which the only object we can access is the last one inserted. This element is called the *top* of the stack. In Figure 3–12a, for example, we see a stack containing three objects, X, Y, and Z. Only the top item, Z, can be accessed. Taking the top item off the stack is called *popping* the stack and produces the new stack shown in Figure 3–12b. Notice that the element Y has now become the top item of the stack. If we put a new item on top of the stack in Figure

Figure 3–11
Implementation of the Opaque Type String and the Procedures Substring and Concatenate

```
Internal Module StringPackage;
Const MaxStringSize = 100;
Type
    String = Record
                Size : 0 .. MaxStringSize;
                S    : Array [1 .. MaxStringSize] Of Char;
            End;

(*  The procedure PatternMatch attempts to locate an occurrence of the
    string S2 within string S1. If it finds one or more matches, it
    returns the position of the first character of the first match.
    If it finds no matches, PatternMatch returns zero. PatternMatch also
    returns zero if S2 is an empty string.   *)
Procedure PatternMatch( S1 : String; S2 : String) : Integer;
Var
    done    : Boolean;          (* Flag to exit inner loop *)
    end     : Boolean;          (* Flag to exit outer loop *)
    i       : Integer;          (* Index into first string *)
    j       : Integer;          (* Index into second string *)
    idx     : Integer;          (* Index of first char of match in first string *)
Begin
    If ((S2.Size = 0) Or (S1.Size < S2.Size)) Then
        Return 0;
        (* Can't search for an empty string, & the string being *)
        (* searched must be at least as large as the substring *)
    Endif;

    end := False;
    i := 1;

    While Not end Do
        If (Char(i, S1) = Char(1, S2)) Then
            (* We've matched the first character *)

            (* This loop tries to match the substring from the *)
            (* second character on with the first string. *)
            idx := i;
            j := 2;
            i := i + 1;
            done := False;
            While Not done Do
                If (j > S2.Size) Then
                    (* We've found a complete match! *)
                    done := True;
                    end := True;

                Elsif (Char(i, S1) <> Char(j, S2)) Then
            (* The characters don't match at this position, so it's not *)
            (* a complete match. Reset i and idx so matching can *)
            (* continue in the outer loop. *)
                    i := idx;
                    idx := 0;
                    done := True;
```

(continued)

Figure 3–11 (continued)

```
                Else
                                        (* So far, so good, but not done yet,
                                        so move on to next characters. *)
                    i := i + 1;
                    j := j + 1;
                Endif;
            Endwhile;
        Endif;

        If (i > (S1.Size - S2.Size)) Then
            (* Can't possibly match starting after this position *)
            end := True;
        Else
            i := i + 1;
        Endif;
    Endwhile;

    Return idx;
End PatternMatch;

(*  Concatenate returns a string which consists of S1 followed by S2. *)
Procedure Concatenate( S1 : String; S2 : String ) : String;
Var
    i, CharsToCopy          : Integer;
    NewString               : String;
Begin
    NewString.Size := 0;
    CharsToCopy := Length(S1);  (* The final string will contain all of
                                the characters from S1 *)
    For i := 1 To CharsToCopy Do
        (* Copy characters one at a time, keeping track of how many *)
        (* characters are copied. *)
        NewString.Size := NewString.Size + 1;
        NewString.S[NewString.Size] := S1.S[i];
    Endfor;

    (* We want to copy all of S2 into NewString *)
    CharsToCopy := Length(S2);
    If ((Length(S1) + CharsToCopy) > MaxStringSize) Then
        (* If the total length of S1 and S2 is greater than the *)
        (* maximum string length, only copy enough characters *)
        (* from S2 to the maximum string length. *)
        CharsToCopy := MaxStringSize - Length(S1);
    End;

    For i := 1 To CharsToCopy Do
        (* Copy characters we want from S2, keep track of how many *)
        NewString.Size := NewString.Size + 1;
        NewString.S[NewString.Size] := S2.S[i];
    Endfor;

    Return NewString;

End Concatenate;

End StringPackage.
```

Figure 3–12
The Stack Data Structure

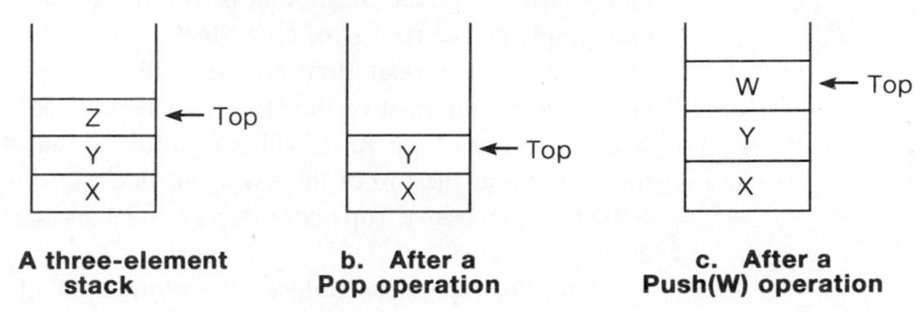

a. A three-element stack   b. After a Pop operation   c. After a Push(W) operation

3–12b, that item will become the new top and will produce the situation shown in Figure 3–12c. The process of adding a new element to the top of the stack is called *pushing* an element onto the stack. No element other than the top one can be accessed by a push or pop operation.

Let us proceed from this informal description of a Stack data structure to a more formal description of the operations that a stack user might require.

First, before any operations can be performed, a stack must be created. Since the user of the Stack module may require many different stacks in his or her program, we must be able to create new instances of the Stack data type dynamically by calling a Create operation. The Create operation does not require any parameters, and each call to it will result in a newly created and empty stack.

```
Stack := Create()
```

A user could establish another instance of an empty stack by issuing a second call on Create:

```
StackNumber2 := Create()
```

Clearly, the user can call on Create to generate any number of stacks (at least until memory runs out). Create will be our *creator* operation of the ADT called Stack.

The user of the Stack module might also find it useful to have a second operation that determines whether a stack is empty. Remember that the user does not know which virtual data structure will be chosen to implement the Stack, so an empty condition cannot be checked by seeing if Top = **Nil**, Top = 0, or any other test that depends on a knowledge of the implementation. The Empty operation will take a stack as an input parameter and return a Boolean result that is true if the stack is empty and false otherwise. It would be used like this:

```
If Empty(Stack) Then
    (* Do something for the case in which the stack is empty. *)
Else
    (* Do something for the case in which the stack is not empty. *)
End
```

A third operation in the same vein as Empty is Full. This operation is used to tell whether a stack is about to overflow. The Full operation takes a stack as an argument and returns a Boolean result that is true if the stack is full and false otherwise. Full and Empty are *observers* of type Stack.

The next two operations are Top and Pop. The Top operation permits us to inspect the top element of the stack. There will be times when we want to observe what is on top of the stack without removing that item. The Top operation returns the element at the top of the stack but does not alter the stack in any way (if you issue two successive Top operations on the same stack, the same element is returned each time).

The Pop operation reduces the number of elements on the stack by one by removing the top element and discarding it. It returns a new stack with one less element. The result of the Pop operation is a completely new stack, not the top element. The Pop operation is a *transformer* of type Stack, and the Top operation is an *observer* of type Stack.

The sixth and final operation on the stack is Push. It takes as arguments an element to be added to a stack and the stack to which the element is to be added. The result of the Push operation is a new stack with the specified element on top; hence the Push operation is another *transformer* of type Stack.

A complete description of the Stack ADT is given in Figure 3–13. The formal syntax of these operations is shown in Figure 3–14.

Figure 3–13
Description of the Stack Data Structure

1. Domain — A Stack is a structured abstract data type.
2. Component elements — A Stack is a collection of arbitrary elements referred to as StackElementType. They will not be further specified.
3. Structure — A Stack is a last-in/first-out linear collection of elements, in which the only element accessible is the last one that was inserted. This element is called the Top of the Stack.
4. Operations
   a. *Creators* — *Description*
      1. Create() — Create an empty Stack.
   b. *Transformers* — *Description*
      2. Push(E,S) — Add an element on the top of the Stack.
      3. Pop(S) — Remove the topmost element of the Stack to produce a new Stack.
   c. *Observers* — *Description*
      4. Empty(S) — True if the Stack is empty, false otherwise.
      5. Full(S) — True if the Stack is full, and false otherwise.
      6. Top(S) — Return the top element of the Stack and leave the Stack itself unchanged.

Figure 3–14
Formal Syntax of Operations on the Stack Data Type

Syntax:

Define Stack[Element]

1. Create() : Stack[Element]
2. Full(Stack[Element]) : Boolean
3. Empty(Stack[Element]) : Boolean
4. Top(Stack[Element]) : Element
5. Push(Element,Stack[Element]) : Stack[Element]
6. Pop(Stack[Element]) : Stack[Element]

Our next task is to describe the behavior of a Stack using the axiomatic semantics introduced in chapter 2. Let us start with the easy axioms first and work our way to the more complicated ones.

The semantic definition of the Empty operation is described by the following two rules:

Empty(Create()) = True

Empty(Push(X, S)) = False

The first axiom says that if we apply the Empty operation to a newly created Stack, the result is always true; that is, a newly created Stack will, by definition, be empty. The second statement says that if the Empty operation is applied to a nonempty Stack, the result is always false. Notice that you can guarantee that a stack is nonempty by simply pushing an element (X) onto an existing stack (S). These axioms are universal truths about the behavior of the Empty operation, regardless of the specific Stack S or the specific element X to which we are referring.

The semantic definition of the Full operation is given by the following two rules:

Full(Create()) = False

If Push(S, X) = 'Error' **Then**
    Full(S) = True
Else
    Full(S) = False

The first statement says that a newly created Stack will, by definition, never be full. The second statement says that the Full operation applied to an arbitrary Stack (S) will be true whenever adding one more element (X) to that Stack would result in an error condition (i.e., *stack overflow*); otherwise, the Full operation would be false.

The definition of the Top operation is

Top(Create()) = Null

Top(Push(X, S)) = X

The first statement says that if one attempts to inspect the top element of a newly created Stack, a special Null value is returned. (Null is some implementation-specific quantity. We will not concern ourselves with its internal value except to assume that it is of type StackElementType so that this axiom is consistent with the syntactic description in Figure 3–14. An exercise at the end of the chapter asks you to redefine the semantics so that this condition is treated as an error.) The second statement states that the top element of a Stack S is the element X, where X is the last element pushed onto the Stack. This last axiom represents the fundamental last-in/first-out property of a Stack—the value you get out is the last value you put in.

Finally, the Pop operation is defined as

Pop(Create()) = Create()

Pop(Push(X, S)) = S

Figure 3–15
Summary of the Axiomatic Semantics of Stack Operations

1. Empty(Create()) = True
2. Empty(Push(X, S)) = False
3. Full(Create()) = False
4. **If** Push(S, X) = 'Error' **Then**
   Full(S) = True
   Else
   Full(S) = False
5. Top(Create()) = Null
6. Top(Push(X, S)) = X
7. Pop(Create()) = Create()
8. Pop(Push(X, S)) = S

The first axiom says that if you try to apply the Pop operation to a newly created empty Stack, then this empty Stack will be returned as the result of the Pop operation. (As with the Top operation, you could also treat this condition as an error.) The second statement implies that if you push an element (X) onto a Stack (S) and then immediately pop that Stack, the result will be the original Stack (S) with which you started.

A summary of the semantic definitions of our Stack ADT operations is given in Figure 3–15.

To see how these semantic definitions can be applied, consider the following sequence:

S = Pop(Push(3, Push(4, Create())))

These operations create a new Stack, push the two values 4 and 3 onto the Stack (in that order), and then pop the top item off the Stack. To determine the contents of the Stack S created by this sequence, we can use the rules of Figure 3–15 and proceed as follows (the notation [x,y] means a stack whose top item is x and which contains the elements x and y):

S = Pop(Push(3, Push(4, Create())))	
S = Pop(Push(3, Push(4, [])))	(From rule 1)
S = Pop(Push(3, [4]))	(From rule 6)
S = Pop([3,4])	(From rule 6)
S = [4]	(From rule 8)

Thus, S is a one-item Stack whose top value is 4. We were able to determine this independent of whatever technique is used to implement the Stack. We can do the same analysis for any arbitrary sequence of Stack operations.

We should also mention that the axioms listed in Figure 3–15 are not fixed and unchangeable. As we said in chapter 2, an abstract data type is a programmer-created structure, and the programmer is free to design operations that behave in whatever way best fits his or her problem. For example, we could choose to describe a Stack of infinite capacity by changing rule 4 of Figure 3–15 to read: Full(S) = False. According to this new rule, it is not possible for any Stack S ever to be full. Similarly, we might wish to treat an attempt to pop from an empty Stack as a fatal error rather than have it return an empty Stack; if so, we could change rule 7 of Figure

3–15 to read: Pop(Create()) = 'Error'. Remember that the designer has total control over the semantic behavior of the operations when designing an ADT.

To complete the description of our ADT Stack, we must also include a description of what conditions each operation expects before it is invoked (the preconditions) and a description of any side effects on other objects (the postconditions). As we mentioned in chapter 2, these postconditions frequently involve the setting of error switches or other status variables affected by the operation. The four types of errors that are possible with a Stack structure are:

Error Type	*Meaning*
None	No error occurred during the last operation.
StackUnderFlow	A Pop operation was applied to an empty Stack.
StackOverFlow	A Push operation was applied to a full Stack.
TopOfEmptyStack	Attempt to return the top of empty Stack.

Given these four error types, the pre- and postconditions of our six Stack operations are as follows:

1. Create()
   Preconditions: None
   Postconditions: Error = None
2. Empty(S)
   Preconditions: None
   Postconditions: Error = None
3. Full(S)
   Preconditions: None
   Postconditions: Error = None
4. Top(S)
   Preconditions: Empty(S) = False
   Postconditions: Error = None if precondition is met
   Error = TopOfEmptyStack if precondition is not met
5. Push(S)
   Preconditions: Full(S) = False
   Postconditions: Error = None if precondition is met
   Error = StackOverFlow if precondition is not met
6. Pop(S)
   Preconditions: Empty(S) = False
   Postconditions: Error = None if precondition is met
   Error = StackUnderFlow if precondition is not met

The formal description of the last-in/first-out data structure called Stack is now complete. An external module to create this Stack ADT is shown in Figure 3–16.

3.3.2 Applications of Stacks

Like ADTs in general, stacks are not an academic curiosity of interest only in the classroom and on examinations. On the contrary, Stacks are used in a number of common problems in computer science. For example, whenever a procedure or function is called, the computer must save the address of the instruction imme-

Figure 3–16
External Module for the Stack ADT

```
(* The following module defines the external specifications
   to implement the abstract data type Stack described in
   Figures 3–13, 3–14 and 3–15   *)

External Module StackPackage;

From ElementModule Import
    StackElementType;     (* The data type of the component
                             elements stored on the stack   *)

Type
    (* The possible stack errors *)
    StackErrorTypes = (None, StackUnderFlow,
            StackOverFlow, TopOfEmptyStack);

    (* The abstract data type *)
    StackType;

Var
    (* A global error variable set by all the stack operations *)
    Error : StackErrorTypes;

(*  The procedure Create returns a newly created, empty stack.
        Precondition:  None
        Postcondition: Error = None,
                       and an empty stack is created   *)
Procedure Create() : StackType;

(*  The procedure Empty checks if the stack Stack is empty. If so, it
    returns True, otherwise it returns False.
        Precondition:  None
        Postcondition: Error = None
                       Empty(Create()) = True
                       Empty(Push(X, S)) = False   *)
Procedure Empty( Stack : StackType ) : Boolean;

(*  The procedure Full checks if the stack Stack is full. If so, it
    returns True, otherwise it returns False.
        Precondition:  None
        Postcondition: Error = None
                       Full(Create()) = False
                       If Push(X, S) = ERROR Then
                           Full(S) = True
                       Else
                           Full(S) = False   *)
Procedure Full( Stack : StackType ) : Boolean;

(*  The procedure Pop removes the top element from Stack.
        Precondition:  Empty(S) is False
        Postcondition: Error = None if precondition is met
                       Pop(Create()) = Create()
                       Pop(Push(X, S)) = S
                       Error = StackUnderFlow if precondition is not met   *)
Procedure Pop( Var Stack : StackType );
```

(continued)

Figure 3–16 (continued)

```
(*  The procedure Push adds Item to the top of Stack.
        Precondition:  Full(S) is False
        Postcondition: Error = None if precondition is met
                       Error = StackOverFlow if precondition is not met   *)
Procedure Push( Item : StackElementType; Var Stack : StackType );

(*  Precondition:  Empty(S) is False
    Postcondition: Error = None if precondition is met, and the most
                   recently inserted element is returned.
                   Error = StackUnderFlow is precondition is not met
                   Top(Create()) = Null
                   Top(Push(X, S)) = X   *)
Procedure Top( Stack : StackType ) : StackElementType;

End StackPackage.
```

Figure 3–17
Using a Stack to Implement Nested Procedure Calls

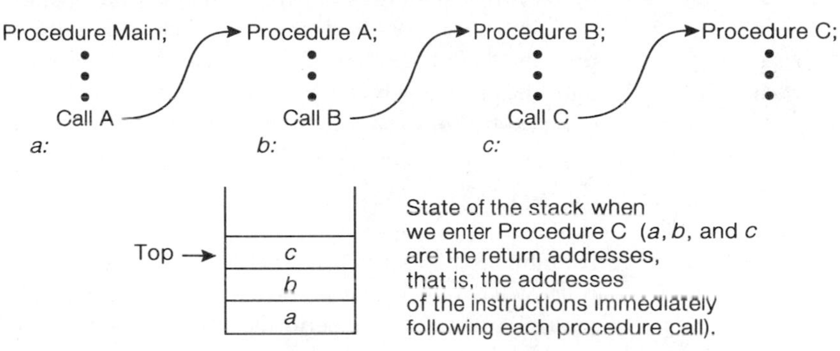

diately following the procedure invocation in order to return to that statement upon completion of the procedure. Stacks make this task very easy. When a procedure is called, the return address is pushed onto an execution-time Stack. After the procedure is completed, the return address is popped from the Stack, and control is transferred to that location.

Stacks are especially useful when several procedures are used in succession (procedure A calls procedure B, which calls procedure C, etc.). In this case, which is illustrated in Figure 3–17, the return addresses appear in the Stack in the reverse order in which the procedures were called (c, b, a). After each procedure is completed, its return address is popped from the Stack and control is returned to the address. In Figure 3–17, each procedure call pushes the address of the next statement onto the Stack, so that when we arrive at procedure C, the Stack is in the state shown. As each procedure finishes, it simply does a Pop operation, and execution continues at the address removed from the Stack. Control returns to each procedure at the correct time, in the reverse order of the calling sequence.

Stacks can also be used to convert expressions from infix notation to postfix notation. In an *infix* expression, the operators are located between the operands. In *postfix* notation, the operator immediately follows the operands. Examples of infix expressions are

$a * b$
$f * g - b$
$d / e * c + 2$

The corresponding postfix expressions (assuming Pascal precedence rules) are

$a\ b\ *$
$f\ g * b\ -$
$d\ e\ /\ c * 2\ +$

In a postfix expression an operation is always applied to its immediately preceding operands. Notice that the operands in a postfix expression occur in the same order as in the corresponding infix expression; only the position of the operators is changed.

Some operators (e.g., $+$, $-$, $*$, and /) require two operands. In a postfix expression these two operands immediately precede their operators. But, more important, the order in which the arithmetic operators are applied is explicit in the postfix expression. For example, the infix expression

$a + b * c$

is ambiguous. Does it mean $(a + b) * c$ or $a + (b * c)$? Without some additional rules, we cannot say. The *precedence rules* of Pascal and Modula-2 dictate that the multiplication $b * c$ is performed before the addition—we say that multiplication takes precedence over addition. The corresponding postfix expression is

$a\ b\ c * +$

and it contains no ambiguity. It is explicit that the multiplication operator applies to the immediately preceding two operands b and c. The addition operation is then applied to the operand a and the operand that results from the operation $b * c$. If we had meant to represent the expression $(a + b) * c$, we would have written it in postfix notation as $a\ b + c\ *$. With postfix notation it is never necessary to use grouping symbols such as brackets or parentheses to indicate the order of evaluation of an arithmetic expression.

We can convert an infix expression to a postfix expression by using a Stack to temporarily hold the operators that cannot be processed until their respective operands are available. The infix-to-postfix conversion algorithm operates as described in the following paragraphs.

We are given an input string representing an arithmetic expression in infix notation, for example,

input: a + b * c − d   (* This means (a + (b * c)) − d *)

We now begin to scan the input string from left to right. If the next symbol in the input is an operand (e.g., 'a'), it is placed directly in the output string without any further processing:

```
input: a + b * c − d        output: a
       ↑
```

If the next symbol in the input string is an operator (e.g., +), we must compare the precedence of that operator with the one currently on top of a Stack data structure called OperatorStack, which we created and initialized at the beginning of the algorithm. If that Stack is empty (as it now is) or if the precedence of the next operator in the input string is greater than the precedence of the one on top of OperatorStack, we push the operator from the input string onto OperatorStack and continue. Precedence is determined using a function called Precedence (in this example, we assume the standard precedence rules of Pascal).

Let us explain what is happening more intuitively. We are trying to locate the highest precedence operation in order to determine what to do next. As long as the operators being scanned are increasing in precedence, we will stack them and continue scanning the input stream.

```
input: a + b * c − d        output: a          OperatorStack: +
         ↑                                                    ↑
                                                             Top

input: a + b * c − d        output: a b
           ↑

input: a + b * c − d        output: a b        OperatorStack: + *
             ↑                                                  ↑
                                                               Top

input: a + b * c − d        output: a b c
               ↑
```

At this point we encounter the − operator, whose precedence is lower than that of the * operator, which is the one currently on top of the stack. We now pop operators from the Stack into the output string until either the Stack is empty or the precedence of the operator on top of the Stack is strictly greater than that of the current operator in the input string. In this example we would pop both the * and the + and place them in the output:

```
input: a + b * c − d        output: a b c * +      OperatorStack: empty
                 ↑
```

The scanning process continues until we come to the end of the input string, then any operators remaining on OperatorStack are popped into the output string and the algorithm terminates.

```
input: a + b * c − d     output: a b c * +        OperatorStack: −
                ↑                                               ↑
                                                               Top
input: a + b * c − d     output: a b c * + d
                  ↑
input: a + b * c − d     output: a b c * + d −    OperatorStack: empty
                    ↑
```

The algorithm has produced the output a b c * + d −, the correct postfix representation of our original infix input string (a + (b * c)) − d (the parentheses indicate the meaning of our original infix expression).

Figure 3–18 shows a module for converting an infix expression to a postfix one. It imports the resources of the Stack definition module of Figure 3–16 to solve the problem.

3.4 QUEUES

A *queue* is a linear first-in/first-out (FIFO) data structure in which all deletions are made at one end, called the *front* or *head* of the queue, and all insertions are made at the other end, called the *rear*, or *tail* of the queue. Unlike a stack, where we can access only the item most recently inserted, with a queue we can directly access only the item least recently inserted, that is, the oldest one.

Figure 3–19a shows a three-element queue containing the elements *a*, *b*, and *c*, added in that order; *a* is the element at the front of the queue, and *c* is the element at the rear. The only element that we can directly access right now is *a*. If we remove it, we have the situation shown in Figure 3–19b. If we then insert a new element *d* to the queue in Figure 3–19b, it must be placed at the rear of the queue, producing the new queue shown in Figure 3–19c.

Like Stacks, Queues are also a very important and widely used data structure in computer science. Their first-in/first-out structure models the behavior of a waiting line, and a Queue structure is used whenever we have a situation where objects are waiting to access resources. For example, a line of customers waiting to be serviced by a clerk at a bank is a Queue structure. Other examples drawn from the discipline of computer science might include processes waiting to obtain a processor or I/O requests queued up for service at a disk. (The latter example will be discussed in the case study at the end of the chapter.)

The seven fundamental operations on queues are similar in nature to those of a stack. First, we must be able to Create a new queue. The queue just created would be empty, and the front and rear pointers would be set to null.

The operation of inserting a new value at the rear of the queue is called Enqueue. It was shown in Figure 3–19c. Enqueue produces a new queue with the new item located at the rear and with a length one greater than the previous value. The operation of removing the value at the front of the queue is called Dequeue; it was shown in Figure 3–19b. Dequeue produces a new queue with the item that was previously at the front deleted and with a length one less than the previous value. Enqueue and Dequeue are the two transformer operations on queues.

Figure 3–18
Module for Infix to Postfix Conversion

```
(* The following module implements an algorithm to convert arithmetic
   expressions from infix form to postfix form. The algorithm is
   described in the text in section 3.3.2.  *)

Module InfixToPostfixPackage;

From StackPackage Import
        StackType,          (* The abstract data type Stack *)
        Create,             (* Function to create a new stack *)
        Empty,              (* Function to check if a stack is empty *)
        Pop,                (* Function to remove top element from
                               a stack *)
        Push,               (* Function to put an element on top of
                               a stack *)
        Top;                (* Function to return the top element of
                               a stack *)

From UserModule Import
        NextChar,           (* Function which returns the next character in
                               the expression, and takes one parameter, a
                               Boolean variable, which is set to True if the end
                               of the expression has been reached, False
                               otherwise. *)
        ErrorHandler;       (* Function that handles cases when things
                               go wrong with converting the expression (e.g.
                               invalid infix expression was provided as
                               input). *)

(*  The function Precedence returns an integral value for any operator
    passed to it, representing its precedence in an arithmetic
    expression. *)
Procedure Precedence( Op : Char ) : Integer;
Var
    p : Integer;
Begin
    Case Op Of

        '(' :
                p := 0 |
                            (* Open parenthesis means delay all pending
                               operators until after the close parenthesis. *)

        '+', '-', ')' :
                p := 1 |
                            (* Add, subtract, and close parenthesis all
                               have equal precedence. *)

        '*', '/' :
                p := 2 |
                            (* Multiplication and division have the highest
                               precedence. *)

    Endcase;

    Return p;
End Precedence;
```

(continued)

Figure 3–18 (continued)

```
(* This procedure, InfixToPostfix, uses the imported resources and the
      function Precedence to convert infix arithmetic expressions into
      postfix arithmetic expressions.   *)

Procedure InfixToPostfix;
Var
      OpStack      : StackType;      (* Stack to store operators pending
                                        processing *)
      c            : Char;           (* The symbol being processed *)
      Done         : Boolean;        (* Set to True when end of input
                                        is reached *)
Begin
      (* Set up some initial variables, and get the first character
            in the expression to begin processing. *)

      OpStack := Create();
      Done := False;
      c := NextChar(Done);

      (* The following loop is the main loop to process the expression.
            When this loop is finished, all of the operands will have been
            processed, and there will only be some operators left on the
            pending operator stack.   *)
      While Not Done Do

            Case c Of

                  'a' .. 'z', 'A' .. 'Z', '0' .. '9' :
                        Write(c) |
                  (* Simply output constants and variables immediately *)

                  '+', '−', '*', '/' :
                        While ((Not Empty(OpStack)) And
                              (Precedence(c)<=Precedence(Top(OpStack)))) Do

                              Write(Top(OpStack));
                              Pop(OpStack);
                        Endwhile;
                  (* Output all pending operators whose precedence is
                        greater than or equal to precedence of current
                        operator *)

                        Push(c, OpStack) |
                  (* Add current operator to stack of pending operators *)

                  '(' :
                        Push(c, OpStack) |
                  (* Put the open parenthesis on the stack, effectively
                        delaying all operators under it on stack *)

                  ')' :
                        While ((Not Empty(OpStack)) And
                              (Precedence(c)<=Precedence(Top(OpStack)))) Do

                              Write(Top(OpStack));
                              Pop(OpStack);
                        Endwhile;
```

(continued)

Figure 3–18 (continued)

```
        (* Output all operators up to previous open parenthesis *)
            If (Empty(OpStack) Or (Top(OpStack) <> '(')) Then
                ErrorHandler; (* There should have been an
                    open parenthesis left at top of stack *)
                Return;
            Endif;
            Pop(OpStack);
        (* Remove the matching open parenthesis from the stack *)

    Endcase;

    c := NextChar(Done);      (* Get next symbol in expression *)
Endwhile;

(* The following loop finishes outputing the operators left on the
    stack after the end of the expression has been reached. *)
While (Not Empty(OpStack)) Do
    If (Top(OpStack) = ')') Then
        Pop(OpStack);          (* Remove the close parenthesis *)
                               (* And the very next operator on the stack
                                   should be an open parenthesis *)
        If (Empty(OpStack) Or (Top(OpStack) <> '(')) Then
            ErrorHandler;
            Return;
        Endif;

    Elsif (Top(OpStack) = '(') Then
        (* There shouldn't be an open parenthesis left
            at the top of the stack *)
        ErrorHandler;
        Return;

    Else
                               (* Some other operator is left, so output it. *)
        Write(Top(OpStack));
    EndIf;

 (* Remove top of stack, so we can process next operator *)
    Pop(OpStack);
 Endwhile;

End InfixToPostfix;

End InfixToPostfixPackage.
```

Figure 3–19
The Queue Data Structure

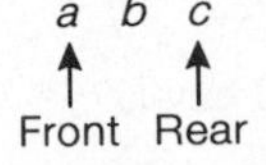

a. Original queue

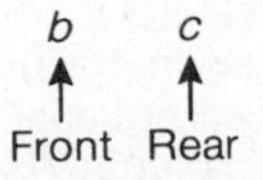

b. After removing one item (dequeue)

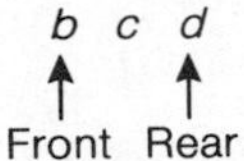

c. After inserting one item (enqueue)

There are four observer operations on queues. The operation called First returns a copy of the element at the front of the Queue, but like Top in the Stack module, it does not change the queue itself. This operation allows us to inspect the front element without having to remove it (it's like asking who is at the front of a line without requiring that person to get out of the line). Similarly, the operation called Last allows us to inspect the last item in the queue. The predicates Full and Empty operate exactly as their counterparts in the Stack package. Full is true if the Queue is full and false otherwise. Empty is true if the queue is empty and false otherwise.

Figure 3–20 summarizes the syntax and semantics of the seven queue operations we have just described. We leave it as an exercise for the reader to review each of the axioms shown in Figure 3–20 and describe informally what these axioms say formally about the behavior of the Queue data structure. Figure 3–21 shows an external module for the Queue abstract data type.

Figure 3–22 shows a client module of the Queue ADT given in Figure 3–21. It is a procedure called CheckLimit(Q, Max), which counts the number of elements in a Queue Q and if that size is greater than a specified upper limit, Max, it removes the last Size(Q) − Max items and discards them. For example, if Q were the six-element queue: *a b c d e f* and Max = 4, this procedure would return a new Queue Q = *a b c d* (the last two elements have been removed). This procedure could, for example, model the situation where we have placed a limit on the number of active processes

Figure 3–20
Syntax and Semantics of the Queue Data Type

Syntax:

Define Queue[Element]

1. Create() : Queue[Element]
2. Enqueue(Element,Queue[Element]) : Queue[Element]
3. Dequeue(Queue[Element]) : Queue[Element]
4. First(Queue[Element]) : Element
5. Last(Queue[Element]) : Element
6. Full(Queue[Element]) : Boolean
7. Empty(Queue[Element]) : Boolean

Semantics:

1. Empty(Create()) = True
2. Empty(Enqueue(X,Q)) = False
3. Full(Create()) = False
4. **If** Enqueue(X,Q) = 'Error' **Then**
   Full(Q) = True
   Else
   Full(Q) = False
5. **If Not** Empty(Q) **Then** First(Enqueue(X,Q)) = First (Q)
6. First(Enqueue(X,Create())) = X
7. First(Create()) is undefined
8. Last(Enqueue(X,Q)) = X
9. Last(Create()) is undefined
10. Dequeue(Create()) is undefined
11. Dequeue(Enqueue(X,Create())) = Create()
12. **If Not** Empty(Q) **Then**
    Dequeue(Enqueue(X,Q)) = Enqueue(X,Dequeue(Q))

Figure 3–21
External Module for the Queue Data Structure

```
(* The following is an external module to implement the
      abstract data type Queue described in Figure 3.20    *)

External Module QueuePackage;

From ElementModule Import
      QueueElementType;         (* The data type of the component elements
                                      stored in the queue *)

Type
      (* The possible queue errors *)
      QueueErrorTypes = (None, QueueUnderFlow,
               QueueOverFlow, FirstOfEmptyQueue);

      (* The opaque data type *)
      QueueType;

Var
      (* A global error variable set by all queue operations. *)
      Error : QueueErrorTypes;

(*    Precondition:  None
      Postcondition: Error = None, and an empty queue is created    *)
Procedure Create() : QueueType;

(*    Precondition:  Empty(Q) is False
      Postcondition: Error = None if the precondition is met,
                     and first element of queue is removed
                     Error = QueueUnderFlow if precondition is not met
      Dequeue(Create()) is undefined
      Dequeue(Enqueue(X, Create())) = Create()
      Dequeue(Enqueue(X, Q)) = Enqueue(X, Dequeue(Q))    *)
Procedure Dequeue( Var Queue : QueueType );

(*    Precondition:  None
      Postcondition: Error = None, return True if Queue is empty,
                     False otherwise
      Empty(Create()) = True
      Empty(Enqueue(X, Q)) = False    *)
Procedure Empty( Queue : QueueType ) : Boolean;

(*    Precondition:  Full(Q) is False
      Postcondition: Error=None if precondition is met, and an element
                     is added to the queue
                     Error=QueueOverFlow if precondition isn't met    *)
Procedure Enqueue( Item : QueueElementType; Var Queue : QueueType );

(*    Precondition:  Empty(Q) is False
      Postcondition: Error = None if precondition is met, and the first
                     element of the queue is returned
                     Error = FirstOfEmptyQueue if precondition isn't met
      First(Create()) is undefined
      First(Enqueue(X, Create)) = X
      First(Enqueue(X, Q)) = First(Q)    *)
Procedure First( Queue : QueueType ) : QueueElementType;
```

(continued)

Figure 3–21 (continued)

```
(*  Precondition:  None
    Postcondition: Error = None and return True if Queue is full,
                   False otherwise.
    Full(Create()) = False
    If (Enqueue(X, Q) = Error) Then
        Full(Q) = True
    Else
        Full(Q) = False   *)
Procedure Full( Queue : QueueType ) : Boolean;

End QueuePackage.
```

Figure 3–22 Client Module of Our Queue Abstract Data Type

```
(* The following module utilizes the Queue abstract data type
   to enforce a limit on the size of a queue. It imports
   the resources from the QueuePackage module   *)

Module CheckLimitModule;

From QueuePackage Import
        QueueType,      (* The abstract data type *)
        Create,         (* Function to create a new queue *)
        Dequeue,        (* Function to remove the head of a queue *)
        Empty,          (* Function to check if a queue has any elements *)
        Enqueue,        (* Function to add an element to tail of a queue *)
        First;          (* Function to examine the head of a queue *)

Procedure CheckLimit( Queue : QueueType; Max : Integer ) : QueueType;
Var
    Size            : Integer;
    NewQueue        : QueueType;
Begin
    Size := 0;
    NewQueue := Create();           (* Create the destination queue *)

    (* Repeat this as long as we are under the maximum queue *)
    (* length and we have more elements to copy. *)
    While ((Size < Max) And (Not Empty(Queue))) Do

        (* Transfer first item from original queue to new queue. *)
        NewQueue := Enqueue(First(Queue), NewQueue);

        Queue := Dequeue(Queue);    (* Remove item from original queue*)

        Size := Size + 1;           (* Increment size of the new queue *)

    Endwhile;

    Return NewQueue;                (* Return the queue with at most Max items *)
End CheckLimit;

End CheckLimitModule.
```

that are queued up waiting for a processor. In the exercises at the end of the chapter, there are additional programming exercises that use the Queue ADT of Figure 3–21.

We will briefly mention one more linear structure, the *deque* (pronounced "deck"), which stands for *double-ended queue*. With a deque, we can make insertions and deletions at either end of the queue, that is, at either the front or the rear of the queue.

```
   a  b  c  d
   ^        ^
(Front)  (Rear)
```

We could add a new item *e* either at the rear, as in a regular Queue (producing *a b c d e*) or before the front item (producing *e a b c d*). Similarly, we could choose to remove either the front item (producing *b c d*) or the rear item (producing *a b c*). Thus, the front and the rear of a deque are functionally equivalent.

We leave it as an exercise for you to design and write the external module for the Deque abstract data type.

3.5 ARRAY IMPLEMENTATION OF A STACK

A simple way to implement a stack is to use a one-dimensional array and a variable called Top pointing to the array position holding the top element of the stack. If our array indices begin at 1, then a Top value in the range 1 .. MaxStack will correspond to a nonempty stack, while a Top value of 0 means the stack is empty. The declarations for this array implementation are given below.

```
Const
    MaxStack = . . . ;        (* Maximum size of the stack *)
Type
    StackRecord = Record
                      Stack : Array [1 .. MaxStack] Of StackElementType;
                      Top : 0 .. MaxStack
                  End;
```

The implementation module for the Stack ADT using these declarations is shown in Figure 3–23.

There is one major problem caused by selecting an array to implement our stack—the size of the array is fixed (in this case, to the constant MaxStack). A better implementation would be one that allowed the stack to grow and/or contract to whatever size was desired, without the possibility of overflow (at least not until all of our memory has been used). This implementation is achievable using a linked list implementation of stacks, which will be introduced in the next chapter. This alternative implementation of a stack will also demonstrate how a change in the implementation has no effect whatever on either the corresponding definition module or the users of our Stack package—the data abstraction concept greatly facilitates and simplifies the maintenance task.

Figure 3–23
Array-Based Implementation of a Stack

```
(* This module contains the implementation for a Stack abstract
   data type using a one dimensional array, as described in
   section 3.5. The definitions for the Stack abstract data type
   are in Figure 3.16. *)

Internal Module StackPackage;

From ElementModule Import
   StackElementType;                    (* Data type to be stored in stack *)

Const
   MaxStack          = 50;

Type
   StackType         = Pointer To StackRecord;

   StackRecord       = Record
                          (* The actual data values in the stack *)
                          Stack : Array [1 .. MaxStack] Of StackElementType;
                          (* Array index of the top of stack *)
                          Top : 0 .. MaxStack;
                       End;

(* The procedure Create returns a new, empty stack *)
Procedure Create() : StackType;
Var
   NewStack : StackType;
Begin
   Error := None;
   New(NewStack);                       (* Allocate space for the new stack. *)
   NewStack^.Top := 0;                  (* There are no elements in the stack. *)
   Return NewStack;
End Create;

(* The procedure Empty returns True if Stack has no elements, False otherwise *)
Procedure Empty( Stack : StackType ) : Boolean;
Begin
   Error := None;
   Return Stack^.Top = 0;               (* The stack is empty if top is zero. *)
End Empty;

(* The procedure Full returns True if the stack is full, False otherwise. *)
Procedure Full( Stack : StackType ) : Boolean;
Begin
   Error := None;
   Return Stack^.Top = MaxStack;        (* The stack is full if all of the
                                           positions in the array are full. *)
End Full;
```

(continued)

Figure 3–23 (continued)

```
(* The procedure Pop removes the top element from Stack. *)
Procedure Pop( Var Stack : StackType );
Begin
    If Empty(Stack) Then
            (* Pop from an empty stack is illegal *)
        Error := StackUnderFlow;
    Else
        Error := None;                      (* There are elements to pop *)
        Stack^.Top := Stack^.Top − 1;       (* so remove the top one. *)
    Endif;
End Pop;

(* The procedure Push adds Item onto the top of Stack *)
Procedure Push( Item : StackElementType; Var Stack : StackType );
Begin
    If Full(Stack) Then
        Error := StackOverFlow;             (* Too many elements on stack *)
    Else
        Error := None;
        (* Make space in the stack for Item, and put it there *)
        Stack^.Top := Stack^.Top + 1;
        Stack^.Stack[Stack^.Top] := Item;
    Endif;
End Push;

(* The procedure Top returns the data in the top element of Stack *)
Procedure Top( Stack : StackType ) : StackElementType;
Begin
    If Empty(Stack) Then
        Error := TopOfEmptyStack;           (* There are no elements on Stack. *)
    Else
        Error := None;
        Return Stack^.Stack[Stack^.Top];
    Endif;
End Top;

End StackPackage.
```

3.6 ARRAY IMPLEMENTATION OF A QUEUE

We can also use an array to implement a Queue structure, but there is one problem that we must deal with carefully. If we start with an eight-element array and the queue shown in Figure 3–24a and we do the following four operations:

```
Dequeue(Q);
Dequeue(Q);
Enqueue(d,Q);
Enqueue(e,Q);
```

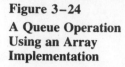

Figure 3–24
A Queue Operation Using an Array Implementation

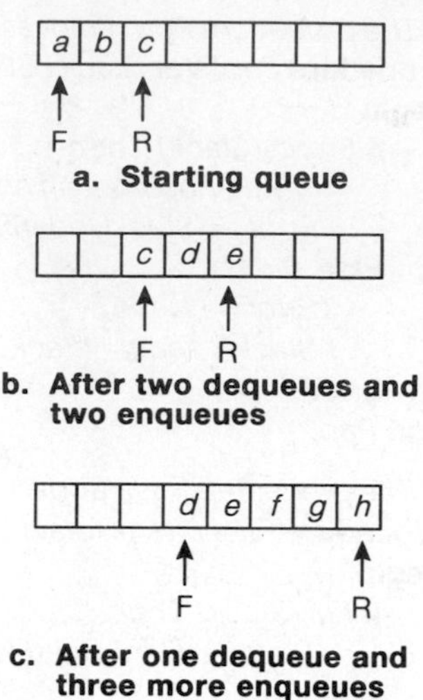

Figure 3–25
A Circular Array

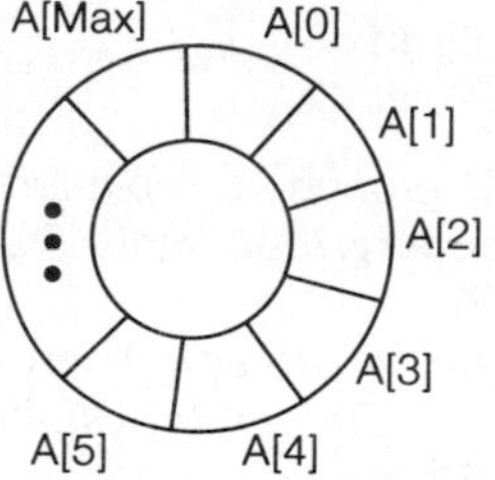

we get the queue shown in Figure 3–24b. Notice that the elements of the queue have "slid" to the right. This effect is sometimes called the "inchworm" effect; it is caused by taking elements from one end but adding them to the other, causing the queue to migrate to the right. If we now perform the following sequence of operations:

Dequeue(Q);
Enqueue(f,Q);
Enqueue(g,Q);
Enqueue(h,Q)

we have the queue shown in Figure 3–24c, and we have reached the end of the array, even though there are three empty slots remaining at the front of the queue.

How do we solve this problem? A good way to handle this situation is to view the array not as being indexed linearly from 0 to some maximum value Max but as a *circular array* or a *ring*, in which the first element A[0] follows immediately after the last one A[Max], as shown in Figure 3–25. We set up a circular array simply by incrementing the indices modulo the array size, so that the array element that is automatically accessed after Array[Max] is Array[0]. The declarations for this implementation are as follows.

```
Const
    MaxQueue = . . . ;          (* Maximum size of the queue *)

Type
    QueueRecord = Record
                      Queue: Array[0 .. MaxQueue] Of QueueElementType;
                      Front, Rear : 0 .. MaxQueue
                  End;
```

However, this solution leads to yet another problem—detecting the difference between an empty queue and a full queue. If we initialize an empty queue so that the front and rear pointers are both 0, we will not be able to distinguish between a queue with no elements and a queue with a single element—with a single element stored in location 0, both the front and the rear pointer would also have the value 0 (see Figure 3–26). However, if we initialize our queue so that Rear = Front − 1, we will not be able to tell the difference between an empty queue and a full queue—when the queue is full (i.e., all the elements of the circular array have values stored in them), the front pointer F will have some value N, and the rear pointer R will have the value $(N - 1)$ modulo MaxQueue—exactly the same condition as our empty queue. This situation is diagrammed in Figure 3–27.

Figure 3–26
Trying to Distinguish Between an Empty Queue and a Queue with One Element

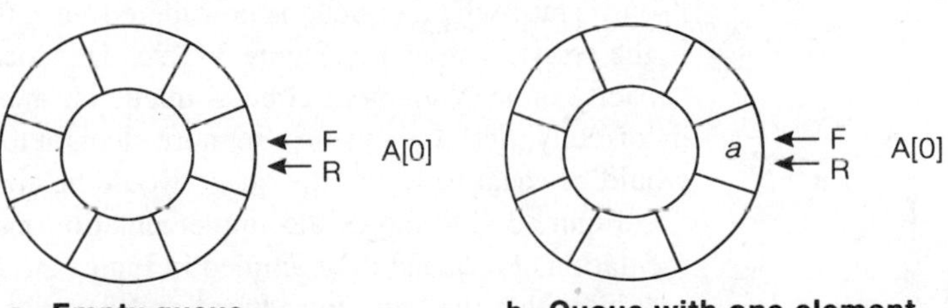

Figure 3–27
Trying to Distinguish Between an Empty Queue and a Full Queue

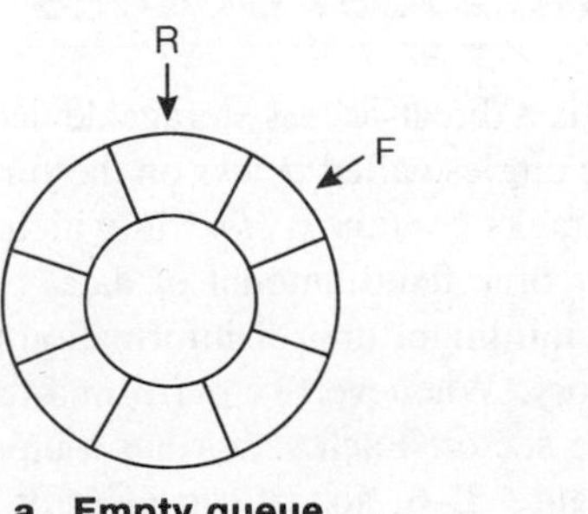

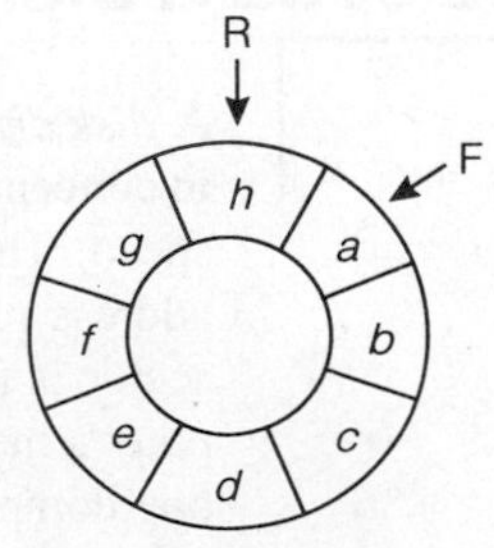

Figure 3–28
Actual Implementation of a Circular Queue

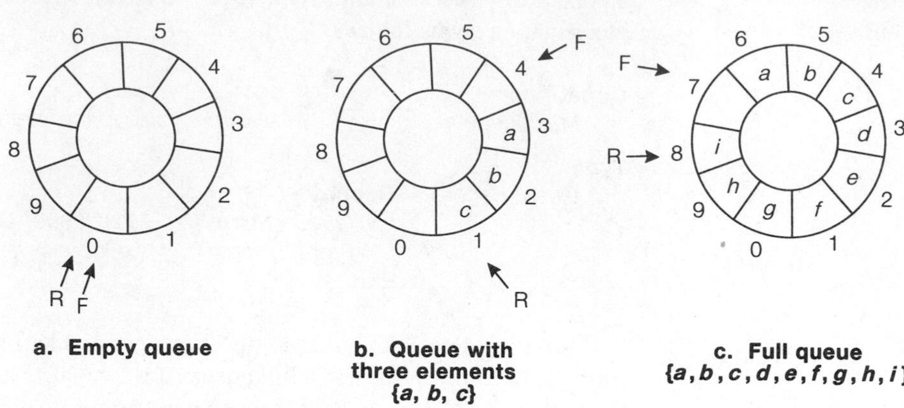

a. Empty queue

b. Queue with three elements {*a*, *b*, *c*}

c. Full queue {*a*,*b*,*c*,*d*,*e*,*f*,*g*,*h*,*i*}

There are a number of solutions to this problem. The solution we use employs the following conventions. A queue is empty whenever the Front and Rear pointers are equal to each other (e.g., Figure 3–28a). For a nonempty queue, the Front pointer will point to the element *in front of* the actual head of the queue rather than to the head element itself. The Rear pointer always points to the actual tail of the queue (see Figure 3–28b). With these conventions, a Full queue is detected if either (1) Rear is pointing to the UpperBound of the queue and Front is pointing to the LowerBound of the queue or (2) if the value of Rear is one greater than the value of Front. Thus, when a queue is considered Full, there is actually one empty location in the array, as shown in Figure 3–28c. This location is not usable, however, so the capacity of an N element circular queue is, in effect, only $N - 1$ elements. If we incorrectly tried to enqueue one more element to the queue of Figure 3–28c, then F would be equal to R and the queue would be considered empty!

Figure 3–29 shows the implementation module for the circular array implementation of a queue diagrammed in Figure 3–28.

Now that we have introduced and described these two linear data structures, let's see how they can be used to solve an important problem in computer science.

3.7 CASE STUDY: DISK REQUEST QUEUES

A *disk drive* is a direct-access storage device in which data is recorded magnetically in concentric circles called *tracks* on the surface of a thin metal disk rotating at high speed. The tracks contain *sectors* in which data is stored. Each sector contains an address plus some fixed amount of data, typically 256, 512, or 1,024 bytes. The sector is the minimum unit of information transfer between the disk and the computer's memory. Whenever we perform a read or write operation, we read or write one complete sector. Each sector has a unique address, like the memory structure shown in Figure 3–6, so we can identify and go directly to any specific sector. There is a single read/write head for the entire surface, and it can be moved in and out to position itself over any track; we can then read any sector on that track. The

Figure 3–29
Internal Module of the Queue ADT

```
(* This module implements a Queue abstract data type using a
    circular one-dimensional array, as described in section 3.6.
    The external specifications for the Queue abstract data type
    are in Figure 3.21. *)
Internal Module QueuePackage;
From ElementModule Import QueueElementType;
Const
    MaxQueue = 50;
Type
    QueueType        = Pointer To QueueRecord;
    QueueRecord      = Record
                          Queue : Array [0 .. MaxQueue] Of QueueElementType;
                          Front, Rear : 0 .. MaxQueue;
                       End;
(* Create returns a new, empty Queue *)
Procedure Create() : QueueType;
Var
    NewQueue : QueueType;
Begin
    Error := None;
    New(NewQueue);
    NewQueue^.Front := 0;    (* Front = Rear implies an empty queue. *)
    NewQueue^.Rear := 0;
    Return NewQueue;
End Create;
(* Dequeue removes the first item from Queue, setting error flags
    as appropriate. *)
Procedure Dequeue( Var Queue : QueueType );
Begin
    If (Empty(Queue)) Then
        (* Can't remove from an empty queue *)
        Error := QueueUnderFlow;
    Else
        Error := None;
        If (Queue^.Front = 0) Then
            Queue^.Front := MaxQueue;
        Else
            Queue^.Front := Queue^.Front - 1;
        Endif;
    Endif;
End Dequeue;
(* Empty returns True if there are no items in Queue, False otherwise *)
Procedure Empty( Queue : QueueType ) : Boolean;
Begin
    Error := None;
    Return Queue^.Front = Queue^.Rear;
End Empty;
```

(continued)

Figure 3–29 (continued)

```
(* Enqueue add Item to the rear of Queue, setting error flags as appropriate *)
Procedure Enqueue( Item : QueueElementType; Var Queue : QueueType );
Begin
    If (Full(Queue)) Then
        (* Can't add to a full queue *)
        Error := QueueOverFlow;
    Else
        Error := None;
        If (Queue^.Rear = 0) Then
            Queue^.Rear := MaxQueue;
        Else
            Queue^.Rear := Queue^.Rear - 1;
        Endif;
        Queue^.Queue[Queue^.Rear] := Item;
        Return Queue;
    Endif;
End Enqueue;

(* First returns the item in the Front of Queue, setting error flags
    as appropriate. *)
Procedure First( Queue : QueueType ) : QueueElementType;
Var
    Head : 0 .. MaxQueue;
Begin
    If (Empty(Queue)) Then
        (* An empty queue has no item at the front *)
        Error := FirstOfEmptyQueue;
    Else
        Error := None;
        If (Queue^.Front = 0) Then
            Head := MaxQueue;
        Else
            Head := Queue^.Front - 1;
        Endif;
        Return Queue^.Queue[Head];
    Endif;
End First;

(* Full returns True if there is no empty space in Queue, False otherwise *)
Procedure Full( Queue : QueueType ) : Boolean;
Begin
    Error := None;
    Return ((Queue^.Front + 1) Mod (MaxQueue + 1)) = Queue^.Rear;
End Full;

End QueuePackage.
```

Figure 3–30
Schematic of a Disk Drive

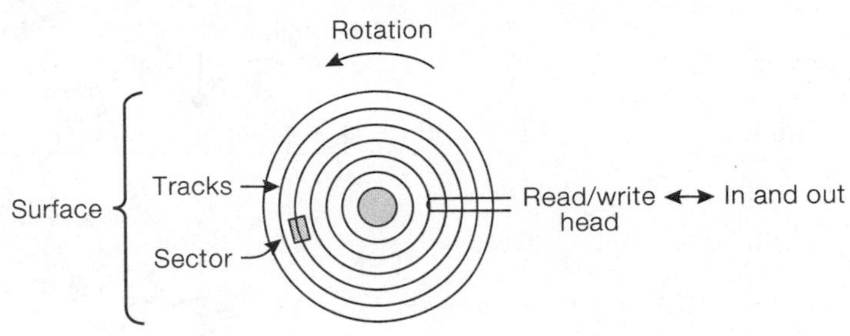

surface of a disk is diagrammed in Figure 3–30. You are probably familiar with this type of storage medium from your use of the floppy disks, hard disks, and optical disks found on virtually every workstation and PC.

The total time needed to fetch the data contained in any given sector on the surface of a disk is made up of three components:

1. The *seek time*. The time to position the read/write head over the correct track.
2. The *rotation time*. The time for the desired sector to rotate under the read/write head.
3. The *transfer time*. The time needed to read the data stored in that sector and transfer it into main memory.

Of these three components, the seek time is the largest, because it involves the relatively slow mechanical operation of moving an arm. Typically, the seek time of a disk is 10 to 50 milliseconds (thousandths of a second), which is about 10,000 times longer than the time it takes for a processor to execute a single machine language instruction. Because of this large delay, a good deal of effort goes into the design of *disk-scheduling* algorithms that minimize the in and out arm movement of the read/write head and thus maximize the overall throughput of the disk unit.

The worst possible scheduling policy (from the system's point of view) would be to simply service user requests in whatever order they arrive, without any consideration for the content of the request. For example, assume that our disk has 500 tracks and that we receive, in the order shown, the following four requests to read or write a sector from the specified track:

```
1, 499, 1, 499        (* the track numbers we want to read *)
```

If we service the requests in the order they arrive, we will be doing a great deal of arm motion (1 → 499 → 1 → 499), and the disk will not be used very efficiently. The majority of its time will be spent seeking data, not reading it. (This situation is analogous to a shopper in a grocery store who buys items in the order they are written on his or her grocery list, rather than the order that they appear in the aisles of the store!) If we were just a little bit clever, we would service both of the requests for track 1 before we moved the arm to track 499, and then we would handle both requests for track 499. This disk-scheduling policy is called *shortest seek time first* (SSTF), because the request that gets serviced is not necessarily the next one in line,

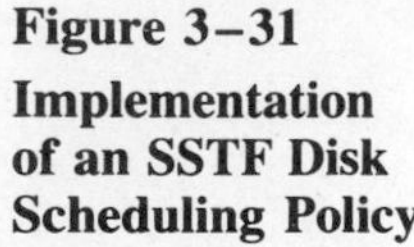

Figure 3–31
Implementation of an SSTF Disk Scheduling Policy

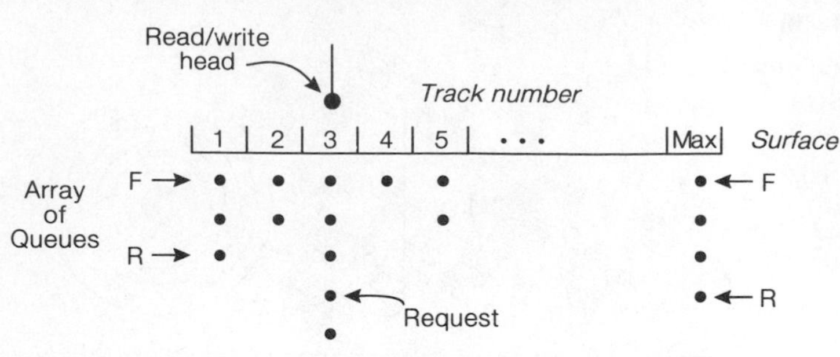

but the one which requests a track closest to the current location of the read/write head, that is, the one with the shortest seek time.

An easy way to implement an SSTF policy is to have an *array of queues*, one for each track on the surface of the disk. Assume that the tracks on our disk are numbered 1 to *Max*. When a request comes in to read or write a sector from track *N*, $1 \leq N \leq Max$, we place (i.e., enqueue) that request at the end of the Queue corresponding to track *N*, as shown in Figure 3–31. Now when the read/write head is positioned above track *i*, it will service all of the requests currently stored in the queue associated with track *i* before moving to the next track.

However, there is still one problem. If our only criterion is shortest seek time, then it is possible for the read/write head to remain over one part of the disk forever and never service requests on distant tracks. For example, assume that the read/write head is currently positioned over track 5 and there are a large number of requests for data on tracks 3, 4, 5, 6, and 99. The arm would remain in the region from track 3 to track 6 and would never get over to track 99 to service that user. The seek time out to that track would always be greater than the seek times to tracks 3 to 6. Thus, an SSTF policy without any modifications is inherently unfair in that it is theoretically possible for some requests never to be satisfied.

In order to ensure that all user requests get a reasonable level of service, we will make one small change to our algorithm. We will move the arm only in one direction at a time, moving first from track 1 up to *Max*, and then sweeping down from track *Max* back to track 1. This system is called a *one-directional SSTF policy*, or a *Sweep-SSTF algorithm*, and it ensures that all disk requests eventually do get service. We select the next request by taking the one with the shortest seek time, but only if it requests a track that lies in the direction that we are currently moving.

Figure 3–32 shows three procedures, Initialize, DiskRequest, and NextRequest, for Sweep SSTF scheduling. Initialize creates the array of empty queues, one for each track on the disk. DiskRequest(R,N) enqueues request R for track N if there is room for another request on that queue. If the queue is full (or if N is out of bounds), then the procedure sets a global error switch to the appropriate value and discards the request (we will assume that the operating system takes some appropriate corrective action). NextRequest(R) returns the next request to be serviced by the disk using the following one-directional SSTF scheduling algorithm:

1. If there is another request in the queue associated with the current track (specified by the global variable CurrentTrack), then dequeue that request and service it.

2. If the queue associated with the current track is empty, then move the arm in the direction indicated by the global variable Direction (either Up or Down) until you either find a nonempty queue or come to the end of the disk, at which time you reverse direction and repeat step 2 until all tracks have been checked.
3. If there are no requests in any queue, then the NextRequest procedure should set an appropriate flag indicating that all requests have been serviced and return.

The procedures in Figure 3–32 import the resources of the Queue ADT of Figure 3–21 to implement their solution. This ability to import resources from other modules is another example of the shareability and portability of software that is possible using ADTs.

Figure 3–32
Procedures to Implement a One-Directional Shortest Seek Time First Disk Scheduling Policy

```
Module SweepSSTFDiskScheduler;

From QueuePackage Import
    QueueType,          (* The abstract data type for queues *)
    QueueErrorTypes,    (* The kinds of errors queue operations can have *)
    Error,              (* Variable holding error result of queue operations *)
    Create,             (* Function to create a new, empty queue *)
    Enqueue,            (* Function to put a new item in a queue *)
    Dequeue,            (* Function to remove front item from a queue *)
    Front;              (* Function to return front item from a queue *)

Type
    (* These are the possible errors that can result from *)
    (* using the disk scheduler. *)
    DiskSchedErrorTypes = (None, IllegalTrack,
                           TooManyRequests, NoRequests);

Var
    (* The array of queues, one queue per track on the disk. *)
    RequestLists : Array [1 .. NumberOfTracks] Of QueueType;
    (* Global error flag for errors resulting from disk scheduling. *)
    DiskSchedError : DiskSchedErrorTypes;
    (* The current position of the disk head on the disk. *)
    CurrentTrack : 1 .. NumberOfTracks;
    (* Direction we are currently seeking in to find next request. *)
    Direction : (Up, Down);

(* Initialize creates the (empty) disk request queues so the disk scheduler
    can keep track of incoming disk requests. It is assumed that
    CurrentTrack and Direction are initialized elsewhere. *)
Procedure Initialize();
Var
    i : Integer;
Begin
    For i := 1 To NumberOfTracks Do
        RequestLists[i] := Create();
    Endif;
    DiskSchedError := None;
End Initialize;
```

(continued)

Figure 3–32 (continued)

```
(* DiskRequest takes a request, R, for track number N and places it on the
     correct queue. However, if there is no room left on that queue, an
     error message is returned. Also, if an invalid track number is
     specified, an error is returned. *)
Procedure DiskRequest( R : DiskRequest; N : Integer );
Begin

     If (N < 1) Or (N > NumberOfTracks) Then
          (* Invalid track number, so set error flag and return. *)
          DiskSchedError := IllegalTrack;
          Return;
     Endif;

     If (Full(RequestLists[N])) Then
          (* No room on appropriate queue, so set error flag and return. *)
          DiskSchedError := TooManyRequests;
          Return;
     Endif;

     (* Everything's fine if we make it here, so add the request to the *)
     (* queue, and indicate that there was no error. *)
     Enqueue(R, RequestLists[N]);
     DiskSchedError := None;

End DiskRequest;

(* NextRequest returns (in the variable parameter R) the next disk
     request that should be serviced. *)
Procedure NextRequest( Var R : DiskRequest);
Var
     HitOneEnd : Boolean; (* Flag to indicate that one end of *)
               (* the disk has been reached in the current search *)
Begin
     HitOneEnd := False;

     (* This loop keeps going until it finds a queue with a request in it. *)
     While (Empty(RequestLists[CurrentTrack])) Do

          If (Direction = Up) Then

               If (CurrentTrack = NumberOfTracks) Then
                    (* We've hit the top end of the disk. *)

                    If (HitOneEnd) Then
                         (* Already been at the bottom, so there *)
                         (* must not be any requests in the queues. *)
                         DiskSchedError := NoRequests;
                         Return;
                    Endif;

                    (* We haven't searched the whole disk yet, *)
                    (* so turn around and keep going. *)
                    HitOneEnd := True;
                    Direction := Down;
                    CurrentTrack := CurrentTrack - 1;
```

(continued)

Figure 3–32 (continued)

```
        Else
            (* Still somewhere in the middle of the disk, *)
            (* so keep moving up. *)
            CurrentTrack := CurrentTrack + 1;
        Endif;

    Else (* Direction = Down *)
        If (CurrentTrack = 1) Then
            (* We've hit the bottom end of the disk. *)
            If (HitOneEnd) Then
                (* Already been at the top, so there *)
                (* must not be any requests in the queues *)
                DiskSchedError := NoRequests;
                Return;
            Endif;
            (* We haven't searched the whole disk yet, *)
            (* so turn around and keep going. *)
            HitOneEnd := True;
            Direction := Up;
            CurrentTrack := CurrentTrack + 1;
        Else
            (* Still somewhere in the middle of the disk, *)
            (* so keep moving down. *)
            CurrentTrack := CurrentTrack - 1;
        Endif;

    Endif;
  Endwhile;

  (* We've found a request, so get it, and remove it from the queue. *)
  R := First(RequestLists[CurrentTrack]);
  Dequeue(RequestLists[CurrentTrack]);

End NextRequest;

End SweepSSTFDiskScheduler.
```

3.8 CONCLUSION

We have now introduced three of the many new advanced data structures we will study in this part of the text. These three, the String, the Stack, and the Queue, will be useful in a wide range of problems, as our examples on procedure linkage, infix expression conversion, and disk scheduling algorithms clearly demonstrated. We will see additional examples of their use in the exercises in this and later chapters.

The String, Stack, and Queue ADT packages shown in Figures 3–9, 3–16, and 3–21 are an important part of any software development library. By having these packages available, we have, in a sense, extended our high-level language so that these advanced data types appear to be as much a part of our language as arrays and records. For example, we are allowed to say:

```
Type    S : Stack;
        Q : Queue;
        T : String;
```

even though these ADTs are, of course, not part of the languages with which we are most familiar, such as Pascal and Modula-2. Reusability and language extensibility are just two of the many positive benefits that accrue from the intelligent use of data abstraction.

It is ironic that even though the Stack structure of section 3.3 is not part of most high-level languages, it is part of the hardware design of most processors. The Stack, along with its operations Push, Pop, and Top, is a hardware data type (see Figure 1–1) that is provided on most systems, such as the Motorola 680x0 and the Intel 80x86 family of processors, because many functions carried out by the hardware need the last-in/first-out properties of a Stack. Such functions include the procedure linkage idea described in Figure 3–17 and the processing of special system routines called *interrupts,* which handle special time-dependent hardware conditions like system errors, power failures, or clock updates. To process an interrupt we must save the current state of the system, process the special condition, and then restore the system to its most recently saved state. Thus the system state must be saved and restored using a stack. During your studies of computer organization and system architecture, you will encounter many more examples of hardware stack use, and it will be crucial for you to be familiar with this important data representation.

In the next chapter we will continue our discussion of linear data structures by introducing the idea of a list.

CHAPTER EXERCISES

1. Which of the four data structure classifications shown in Figure 3–1 do you think would be best suited to represent each of the following? Give reasons for your answers.
   a. A character string
   b. An organization chart of a corporation
   c. A waiting line
   d. A road map
   e. A railroad timetable
2. Which of the following are random-access data structures? Explain your answer.
   a. A record structure R with four fields a, b, c, d
   b. A file of integers (from Pascal)
   c. A dictionary alphabetized from A to Z
   d. A deque (a double-ended queue)
3. Given the following declaration

   ```
   A : Array [-10 .. 30] Of Real;
   ```

   and assuming that real values occupy 2 cells each and the array A begins at address 100, what is the address of the first cell of element A[0]? of element A[30]? Show your work.

4. Given the following declaration

```
B : Array [0 .. 10] of Array [-5 .. +5] Of Real;
```

and assuming that real values occupy 4 cells each and that the array B begins at address 300, what is the address of the first cell of element:
   a. B[7,−3] assuming column-major order
   b. B[8,5] assuming row-major order
5. Formally define an abstract two-dimensional array, and draw a picture (like Figure 3–2) to show the relationship between array elements and indices. Specify how the Retrieve and Store operations would operate on these two-dimensional structures.
6. Describe how we could implement the Boolean function Exists described in Section 3.2.1.
7. Using the external module for the ADT Array shown in Figure 3–4, describe how to implement the following code using the Array package operations Store and Retrieve rather than the built-in subscripting capabilities of Pascal:

```
For i := 1 To 100 Do
    a[i] := a[i] + 1;
    b[i] := b[i - 1] + b[i + 1]
End
```

8. Rewrite the external module of Figure 3–4 so that it defines an array with indices limited to the range 1 .. *N*. If either the Retrieve or Store operation attempts to access an index *i* outside the range 1 .. *N*, a global variable Error is set to true, and the array is unchanged. Otherwise, Error is set to false and the operation is carried out.
9. Derive the expression for the location of the *i,j*th element of an array created by the following declaration:

```
Var
    A : Array [b1 .. u1] of Array [b2 .. u2] Of ElementType;
```

Assume the array is stored in column-major order, and b_1, b_2, u_1, and u_2 are constants with the following restrictions:

$b_1 \leq u_1$ and $b_2 \leq u_2$

Also assume that each object of type ElementType requires *s* cells of storage.
10. Repeat exercise 9 assuming that the array A is stored in row-major order.
11. Generalize the results in exercises 9 and 10 to handle *n*-dimensional arrays, that is, arrays declared as

```
Var
    A : Array [b1 .. u1], [b2 .. u2], [b3 .. u3], . . . , [bn .. un] Of ElementType;
```

Again, assume that each object of type ElementType requires *s* cells of storage.

12. Given the string S = 'AABCDDXXX', what is the value of each of the following string operations, using the syntax and semantics specified in section 3.2.3
    a. Substring(S,5,4)
    b. Char(8,S)
    c. Char(10,S)
    d. Concatenate(S,'Hello')
    e. Concatenate(S,S)
    f. Length(Concatenate(S,S))
    g. PatternMatch(S,S)
    h. PatternMatch(S,'S')
    i. PatternMatch(S,'DX')
    j. ChangeChar(S,'C','Q')
    k. ChangeChar(S,PatternMatch(S,'D'),'E')
13. Specify the syntax and semantics of a string operation called ChangeString (S_1, S_2, S_3), which looks for the first occurrence of substring S_2 in string S_1 and replaces it with substring S_3.
14. PatternMatch locates the *first* occurrence of a substring within some text. However, it is sometimes more convenient to find the *next* occurrence by beginning not at the beginning of the string but at some value Start, $1 \leq \text{Start} \leq \text{Length(s)}$. Specify and implement a pattern-matching operation that behaves in this fashion.
15. Design and implement a complete and usable ADT String. Your package should include the operations listed in section 3.2.3, as well as any others that you think would be useful. Possibilities include:

CreateString	Create a new string whose length is 0.
ReadString	Input a string from the terminal.
WriteString	Print out a string on the terminal.
FirstCharacter	Return the first character of the string. Leave the string itself unchanged.

    The final decision on which operations to include is up to you. Justify your choices.
16. Implement the four remaining string operations—Length, Character, SubString, and ChangeChar—not shown in Figure 3–11 using the Record structure given in section 3.2.3.
17. Assume that we changed the implementation of our String data type to the following

```
Type
    String = Array [1 .. MaxStringLength + 1] Of Char;
```

    Instead of storing the length explicitly, we mark the end of the string using the control character CR (octal 15). Thus we would represent the three-character string 'ABC' by storing the four characters 'A' 'B' 'C' CR. Implement the routines Length, Substring, and Concatenate using this new internal representation. Did your external module change at all?

18. Given the following stack S:

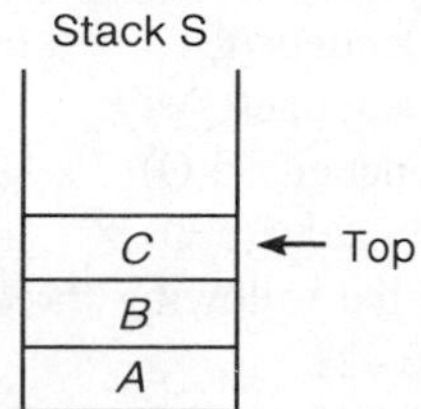

What would the stack look like after the following sequences (assume each sequence begins from the above state):

a. Push(D,S)

b. Push(D,S)
Push(E,S)

c. Pop(S)
Pop(S)
Push(D,S)
Pop(S)
Push(E,S)

d. Pop(S)
Pop(S)
Pop(S)
Pop(S)

e. Push(D,S)
Pop(S)
Push(E,S)

19. Add the following two operations to the Stack ADT shown in Figure 3–16.

a. Remove(S,N) Remove the top N elements off Stack S.

b. Size(T) Returns the total number of elements currently contained in Stack T. T is unchanged.

For each operation, give its syntax, semantics, and pre- and postconditions. Propose additional useful operations on the Stack data structure.

20. Assume that we added the Size function described in Exercise 19b to our Stack package and that we added the following semantic rules to our definition:

a. Size(Create()) = 0
b. **If** Full(T) **Then** Size(T) = 100
c. Size(Pop(T)) = Size(T) − 1
d. Size(Push(X,T)) = Size (T) + 1

Explain in simple English terms what each of these axioms says about the behavior of the Size operation.

21. Change the semantic rules of Figure 3–15 so that attempting to inspect the top of an empty stack or attempting to pop from an empty stack is treated as a fatal error. Rewrite the implementation module to support these changes.

22. Design an external module for the Deque ADT described in section 3.4. Then select an appropriate internal implementation and code the implementation module.

23. Propose solutions other than the one used in section 3.6 to the problem of distinguishing full and empty conditions in the ring implementation of queues.

24. Given the following six-element circular queue containing the three elements *a*, *b*, and *c*:

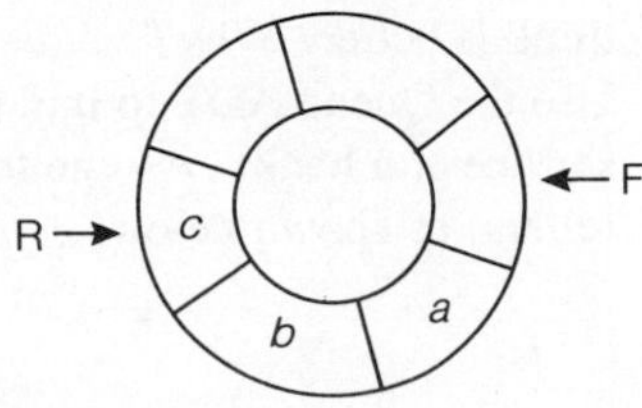

show what state the queue would be in after each of the following series of operations (assume each one starts from the above conditions):

a. Dequeue(Q)	b. Enqueue(d,Q)	c. Enqueue(d,Q)
Dequeue(Q)	Enqueue(e,Q)	Enqueue(e,Q)
Enqueue(d,Q)	Dequeue(Q)	Enqueue(f,Q)
Enqueue(e,Q)		

25. Add the following three operations to the Queue external module of Figure 3–21.

    a. Size(Q) — Returns the number of elements currently in queue Q.
    b. Remove(Q,N) — Removes the first N items from the front of queue Q.
    c. Cuts(Q,E,N) — Insert Element E into position N of the queue Q, rather than at the end.

    For each operation, give the syntax and semantics, and code the procedure in the implementation module. Propose additional useful operations on the Queue data structure.
26. Revise the disk-scheduling procedures in Figure 3–32 so that the disk arm is free to move in either direction, not just one. When choosing a request, it will select one from the queue that is closest to its current position, regardless of direction. What kind of behavior would you expect this type of scheduling policy to display?
27. A popular way to implement a pair of stacks is to allocate a single block of memory and have the two stacks start at opposite ends of the space and grow toward each other.

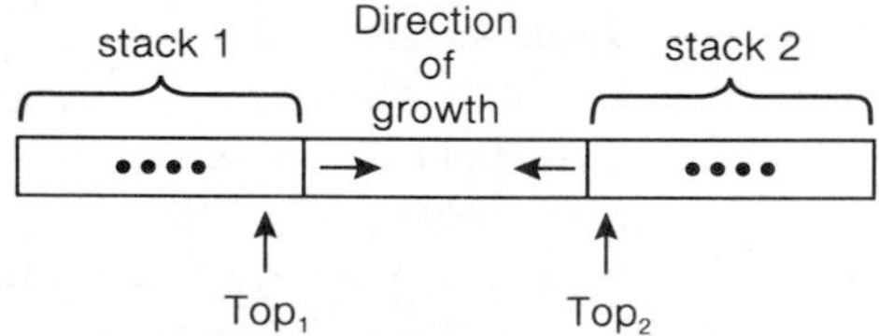

    Design a stack implementation using this principle. You may assume that you will never create more than two stacks. Be sure that your implementation detects the case when the two stacks meet.
28. As we have described the Pop operation, it effectively removes the top item of the stack and throws it away. An alternative form of the Pop operation is:

    Pop(Stack[Element]) : Element,Stack[Element]

    Pop now returns both the top element of the stack and a new stack with one less element. Change the external and implementation modules of the Stack ADT to carry out the Pop operation in this new way. Which form do you think is better? Why?
29. Use the Queue ADT to build a simulation model of customers waiting for service at a bank. Assume that we have a single queue of customers and k tellers, as shown below:

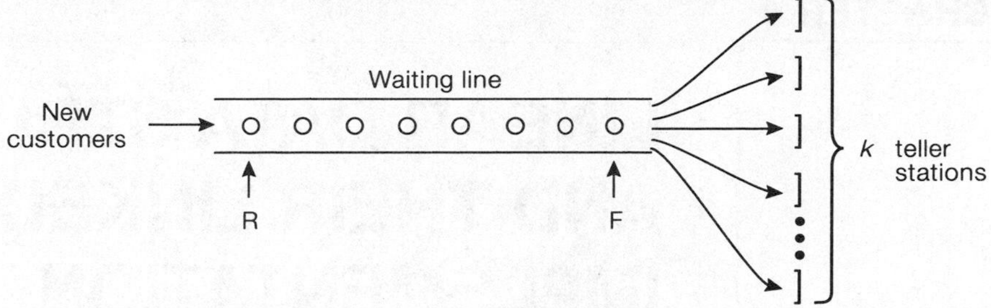

When a teller becomes available, the person at the front of the line is removed, served, and then departs from the bank. As new customers arrive, they go the end of the queue. Assume that new customers arrive randomly every 1 to 5 minutes and that it takes between 1 and 10 minutes to service each customer. Your program should determine the number of tellers needed (i.e., the value of *k*) to ensure that the average waiting time for customers in the waiting line is not more than two minutes.

CHAPTER 4

LINEAR DATA STRUCTURES AND THEIR LINKED LIST IMPLEMENTATION

CHAPTER OUTLINE

4.1 THE LINEAR LIST ABSTRACT DATA TYPE

4.1.1 Definition of a Linear List

In this section we introduce another linear data structure—a *Linear List*, sometimes just referred to as a *List*. A List is the most flexible of all linear structures. With an Array, for example, you can store or retrieve any element, but you need to know the index value of the desired element. The Stack, the Queue, and the Deque all place restrictions on where items can be inserted or deleted: Stacks may only insert/delete at one end; Queues may insert at one end and delete at the other; Deques may insert/delete at both ends but not in the middle. With a List, all these restrictions are removed, and stores, retrievals, insertions, and deletions may be done anywhere within the structure—beginning, middle, or end.

Formally, a Linear List is an ordered collection of zero, one, or more components called *nodes*. Each node contains an information field, which we abbreviate I, and some explicit way of identifying the unique successor of that node. (The data type of the information field is not important and, for now, will be left unspecified.) Finally, there will be some indication of which is the first node of the list. The pointer to the first node in the list is typically called the *head pointer*.

We typically represent a Linear List with the box diagram shown in Figure 4–1. The symbol Λ (capital lambda) is used to signify the end of the List. However, a word of caution goes with Figure 4–1: it is only a *logical*, or *conceptual*, view of a List, not an implementation model. The fact that we use arrows to connect nodes to each other by pointing to each one's successor does not imply that the only way to implement a List is by using pointer types. Although pointers can be useful for implementing Lists (and we will see many examples in later sections), they are certainly not the only way. In fact, in section 4.2.3 we develop an array-based implementation of Linear Lists that allows Lists to be used in languages that do not support pointer variables as virtual data types (e.g., FORTRAN, COBOL, and BASIC). Please keep in mind the distinction between the abstract data type called a *Linear List* and its implementation using pointers, which we call a *Linked List*.

Because the linear list is such a general structure, there are an enormous number of operations that we could select to include in a Linear List ADT package. The stack and the queue have well-defined operations—Push and Pop for the Stack and Enqueue and Dequeue for the Queue—but with lists it is not always obvious what operations we should include or exactly how they should behave. When selecting

Figure 4–1
Logical View of a Linear List

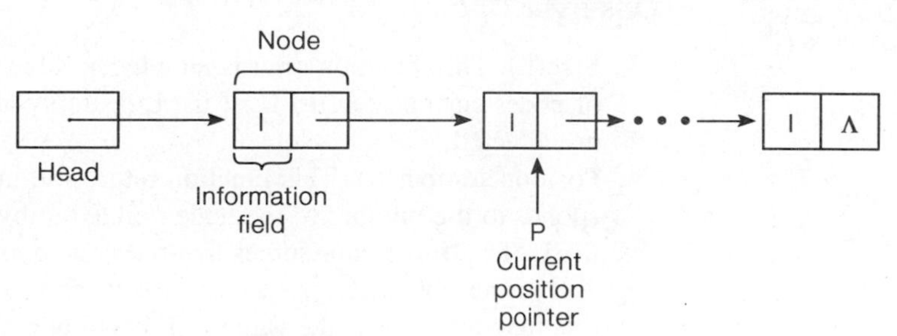

the operations for a List ADT, it is usually necessary to obtain additional information about how client modules will use the package so that those operations that are most useful for a particular application can be selected.

The operations that we have selected for inclusion in our list package are all based on the idea of a *current position pointer*. A current position pointer is simply a variable that points to the node on which we are currently working. For example, in the list in Figure 4–1, the current position pointer, P, is pointing to the second node, and any operation we perform will be done to that node. If we wish to work on another node, we must first perform an operation to move P. A position pointer value of null (represented in our diagrams by the symbol Λ) will be used to indicate either that P is not currently pointing to a node or that the list is empty. Most of the operations we describe in the next section involve either moving the current position pointer or performing operations on the node pointed to by the current position pointer.

4.1.2 Operations on Linear Lists

In this section we describe eleven operations on lists; we will use these operations throughout this chapter. To ensure that you understand the basic ideas behind lists, position indicators, and operations, our description of these operations will be informal and done in natural language. We leave it as an exercise to convert these informal descriptions into the formal syntactic and semantic notation introduced in chapter 2.

In the following description, L refers to an object of type List, I is an object of the data type stored in the information field of a node, and P is the current position pointer.

Create/Destroy Operations

1. L := Create(). This operation returns a new list of length 0, i.e., a List without any nodes. The value of P is set to null.
2. Destroy(L). This operation ends the existence of list L. No further references can be made to L, and all memory space previously allocated to L is returned to the system. P is no longer defined for this list. Destroy(L) is a procedure that does not return a value. It is executed only for the side effect it has on the list L.

Observer Operations

3. Size(L). This function returns an integer value that corresponds to the number of nodes currently in list L. If list L is empty, the function returns a 0. P is not affected.
4. PositionNumber(L). This function returns an integer value 0 .. N, that corresponds to the number of the node pointed to by the current position pointer of list L. This function assumes that the node pointed to by Head (see Figure 4–1) is numbered 1, its successor is numbered 2, and so forth. If L is empty, this function returns the value 0. P is not affected by this function.

Positioning Operations

These transformer operations move the current position pointer forward or backward but have no other effect on the nodes or their contents. In all cases they return an object of type List.

5. First(L). This operation moves the current position pointer so that it points to the first element of list L, that is, the node pointed to by Head in Figure 4–1. If L is empty, P is set to null.
6. Last(L). This operation moves the current position pointer so that it points to the last element of list L, that is, the node whose next field contains the value Λ (see Figure 4–1). If L is empty, P is set to null.
7. Next(L). This operation moves P so that it points to the successor of the node to which it is currently pointing. In a sense, P moves "forward" one node. If P is currently null or if it points to the last node in the list (which has no successor), it is set to null.

We will include these three positioning operations in our package. However, many more are possible, such as Previous(L), which moves P to its predecessor, Forward(L,*n*), which skips forward *n* nodes, or Backward(L,*n*), which moves backward *n* nodes. We leave the specification of these and other positioning operations as exercises.

Insert/Delete Operations

The insert/delete operations are also transformer operations of the ADT; they take an element of type List, modify it in some way, and return a new object of type List.

8. InsertFirst(L,I). This operation inserts a node containing the data value I as the first node of list L and sets the value of P to point to this new node. The size of the new list is one greater than the size of the old list (see Figure 4–2).
9. InsertAfter(L,I). This operation inserts a node containing the element I after

Figure 4–2
The List Operation InsertFirst(L,I)

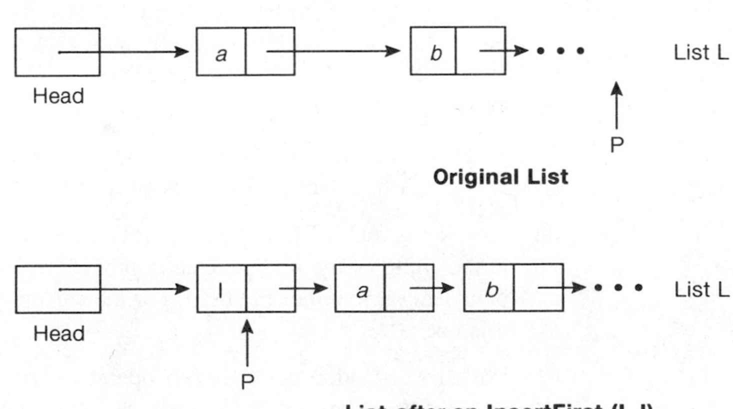

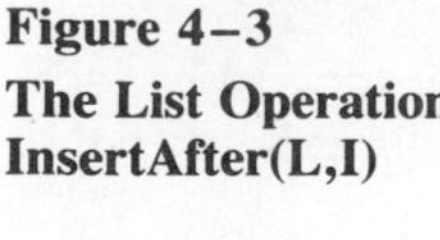

Figure 4–3
The List Operation InsertAfter(L,I)

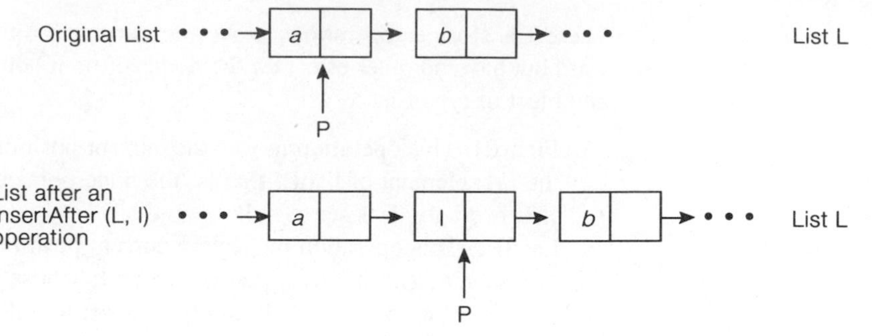

Figure 4–4
The List Operation Delete(L)

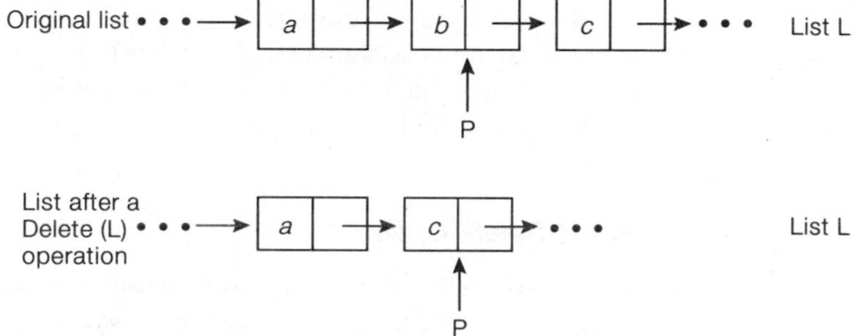

the node currently pointed to by P and sets P to point to the newly inserted node. If P is currently null, this operation is undefined (see Figure 4–3).

10. Delete(L). Delete(L) deletes the node currently pointed to by P, so the size of L is one less than its previous size. P is reset to point to the successor of the node just deleted, unless we delete the last node, in which case P is set to null (see Figure 4–4). If P is currently null, this operation is undefined.

Retrieval Operation

This operation retrieves the contents of the information field of a specific node from list L. It is an observer operation, since it does not modify the list in any way.

11. I := Retrieve(L). This operation sets the variable I to the value of the information field of the node currently pointed to by P. If P is null, this operation is undefined. Neither the list L nor the current position pointer are changed by this operation.

We have included these eleven operations in our Linear List ADT package. As we mentioned before, there are many other possible operations that could be selected; many of them are quite powerful and quite useful in certain applications.

These operations include:

InsertAtEnd(L,I)	Insert a node containing I at the end of the list L.
DeleteFirst(L)	Delete the first node of list L.
Concatenate(L1,L2)	Concatenate two lists (much like the string concatenate of section 3.2.3).
Sort(L)	Sort a List into order.
Split(L,N,L1,L2)	Split a list L into two separate lists L1 and L2 at position N. The first N elements are in L1. The remainder are in L2.
Find(L,I)	Find the first occurrence of element I in list L. Set P to point to the node containing this value.

We leave the description of these and other operations as exercises.

A complete external module for our Linear List ADT, including the eleven operations just described, is shown in Figure 4–5.

4.2 THE IMPLEMENTATION OF LINEAR LISTS

In chapter 3 we discussed arrays and their use in implementing stacks, queues, and strings. Although arrays are useful in many contexts, they are not appropriate in all situations. Specifically, a one-dimensional array is not a good way to implement a linear list, especially if frequent insertions or deletions are necessary. For example, if we use a one-dimensional array to represent the List containing the five elements 8, 13, 5, 101, 9, it might be depicted as shown in Figure 4–6a. If we now want to insert the value 24 between the values 8 and 13 (using, for example, our InsertAfter operation), there is no room unless we move elements A[2] through A[5] down one slot, as shown in Figure 4–6b. This reshuffling of elements can be a time-consuming operation. Similarly, if we delete the element 5, we have a "hole" (an empty space) in the array, and it must be removed by moving all succeeding elements up one slot, as shown in Figure 4–6c. (Note that even though this one-dimensional array implementation is not a good choice, we will see in section 4.2.3 that a multidimensional array can be used to store lists in an efficient way.)

This data movement problem is caused by storing *logically* consecutive elements of a linear list in *physically* consecutive memory locations. This use of consecutive storage locations is not necessary—the elements could be placed in any arbitrary locations in the array. However, assigning elements to arbitrary locations presents another problem: How do we preserve the logical ordering of the list structure in order to determine node successors? One solution is to include explicit pointers to the next element in the logical sequence. Then any element can be accessed by following the links, provided we know the location of the first element. Storing a linear list in this way reduces data movement during insertion and deletion operations.

These advantages are not free but come at a price. The price is the storage required to hold those explicit links and the processing time needed to maintain their correct values. We will discuss this efficiency trade-off in more detail in chapter 6.

Figure 4–5
External Module for the Linear List Abstract Data Type

```
(*  The following module contains the external specifications for
    the abstract data type List, with the operations discussed in
    section 4.1.    *)

External Module LinearListPackage;

From ElementModule Import Element;        (* Data type stored in the list *)

Type
    LinearListType;                       (* The abstract data type *)

(*  The procedure Create returns an empty linear list. The current position
    pointer P is set to Null.
        Precondition:  None
        Postcondition: Size(Create()) = 0   *)
Procedure Create() : LinearListType;

(*  The procedure Destroy deletes all of the nodes in the linear list
    L, and ends the existence of L so that any future references to
    L will be errors.
        Precondition:  None
        Postcondition: Any operation on L is an error   *)
Procedure Destroy( Var L : LinearListType );

(*  The procedure Size returns the number of nodes in linear list L.
        Precondition:  None
        Postcondition: The current size of L is returned   *)
Procedure Size( L : LinearListType ) : Integer;

(*  The procedure PositionNumber returns an integer corresponding to the
    location of node pointed to by the current position pointer P in the
    list L.
        Precondition:  P <> Null
        Postcondition: The current position in the list is returned for
                       a nonempty list L if the precondition is met.
                       If the precondition is not met, 0 is returned.   *)
Procedure PositionNumber( L : LinearListType ) : Integer;

(*  The procedure First sets the current position pointer P for L to the
    first element in the list L.
        Precondition:  Size(L) > 0
        Postcondition: If the precondition is met, P is set to point
                       to the first element of list L.
                       Otherwise, P is set to Null.   *)
Procedure First( Var L : LinearListType );

(*  The procedure Last sets the current position pointer for L to the
    last element in the list L.
        Precondition:  Size(L) > 0
        Postcondition: If the precondition is met, P is set to point
                       to the last element of list L.
                       Otherwise, P is set to Null.   *)
Procedure Last ( Var L : LinearListType );
```

(continued)

Figure 4–5 (continued)

```
(*  The procedure Next sets the current position pointer for L to the
    successor of the current element in the list L. If the node
    does not have a successor (P is Null or points to the last node),
    P is set to Null.
        Precondition:  P <> Null and PositionNumber(L) < Size(L)
        Postcondition: If the precondition is met, P is set to point to
                       the successor of the current element of list L.
                       Otherwise, P is set to Null.   *)
Procedure Next ( Var L : LinearListType );

(*  The procedure InsertFirst places element E at the front of list L.
        Precondition:  None
        Postcondition: Retrieve(InsertFirst(L,E)) = E   *)
Procedure InsertFirst ( Var L : LinearListType; E : Element );

(*  The procedure InsertAfter places element E immediately after the
    node pointed to by the current position pointer P in list L. P is
    set to point at the new node.
        Precondition:  P <> Null
        Postcondition: If the precondition is met:
                       Retrieve(InsertAfter(L, E)) = E
                       PositionNumber(InsertAfter(L, E)) =
                           PositionNumber(L, E) + 1
                       Otherwise InsertAfter(L, E) is undefined.   *)
Procedure InsertAfter ( Var L : LinearListType; E : Element );

(*  The procedure Delete removes the node pointed to by the current position
    pointer P from list L, and P is set to the successor of P. If P is
    Null when Delete is called, the result is undefined.
        Precondition:  P <> Null
        Postcondition: If the precondition is met:
                       Retrieve(Delete(L)) = Retrieve(Next(L))
                       Size(Delete(L)) = Size(L) - 1
                       Otherwise Delete(L) is undefined.   *)
Procedure Delete ( Var L : LinearListType );

(*  The procedure Retrieve returns the data stored at the node in list L
    pointed to by the current position pointer P. If P is Null the
    operation is undefined.
        Precondition:  P <> Null
        Postcondition: If the precondition is met:
                       The data at the current node is returned.
                       Otherwise Retrieve(L) is undefined.   *)
Procedure Retrieve ( L : LinearListType ) : Element;

End LinearListPackage.
```

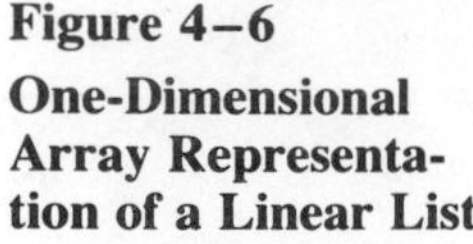

Figure 4–6
One-Dimensional Array Representation of a Linear List

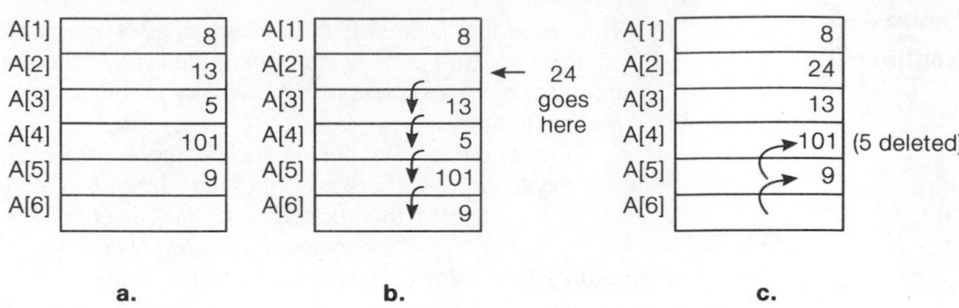

Figure 4–7
Linked-List Example

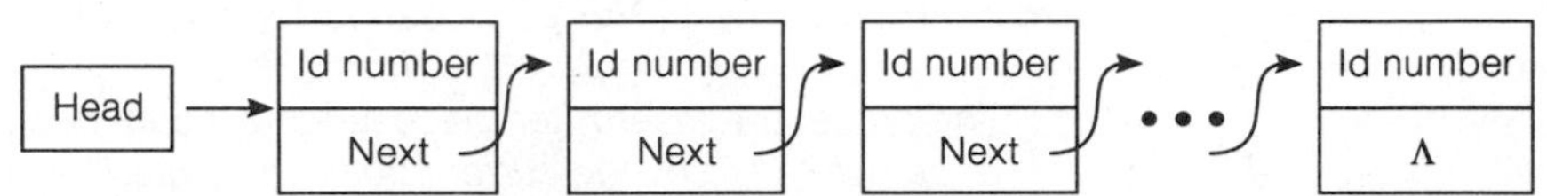

4.2.1 Pointers in High-Level Programming Languages

Storage locations for a linked list are created *dynamically* (i.e., while the program is executing). Usually, however, variables are declared and referenced *statically* by an identifier name. For example, the declaration

```
Var
    A : Integer;
    B : Real;
    C : Char;
```

creates three *static* variables. Each variable occupies a fixed and known set of memory locations.

Suppose we want to set up a linked list with nodes that contain two fields: a student identification number and a link field to point to the next node in the list, as shown in Figure 4–7. Such a list can be set up in any high-level language that supports the concept of *dynamic variables* (also called *pointer variables* and *reference variables*). Examples of languages that have this facility include Pascal, Modula-2, Ada, and C.

The first step in creating this linked list structure is to create a pointer data type called Student, using something like the following type declaration:

```
Student = POINTER TO StudentRecord;        (* Modula-2 *)
Student = ↑ StudentRecord;                 (* Pascal *)
StudentRecord *Student;                    (* C *)
Student is access StudentRecord;           (* Ada *)
```

We will use the first of these for our syntactic notation, although you should remember that all these declarations accomplish the identical function. This declaration defines Student to be a *pointer type*. Each variable of type Student will hold a pointer to an object of type StudentRecord. (Notice that StudentRecord has not yet been declared—here we have an exception to the rule that all identifiers must be declared before they are used.) For this simple example, we will let StudentRecord be a two-field **Record** type.

```
Type
    StudentRecord =
        Record
            IdNumber : Integer;
            Next : Student
        End; (* Of Record StudentRecord *)

    Student = Pointer To StudentRecord;
```

The IdNumber field will contain a student's identification number stored as an integer, and the Next field will contain an element of type Student, which is a pointer to the next node in the linked list. This node will be another object of type StudentRecord. This record declaration simply describes the layout of the data—it does not yet allocate any space.

In a linear list, each node (except the first) is referenced by a pointer from the previous node. But how do we reference the first item in the list? We create a special pointer variable called a *head* pointer, which points to the first element of our list. Once we have located the first item, we access all other nodes by following the pointer contained in the Next field of each node. To create this head node, we make the following variable declaration:

```
Var
    Head : Student;
```

in which we store a pointer to the first node. This **Var** declaration allocates a storage location for the variable Head. Its value is undefined, however, as it does not yet point to any storage location.

We now need a way to allocate space for the new nodes of our linked list. In Pascal we use a special system function called New. In Modula-2 the function is called ALLOCATE, and it is located in the system module. Ada uses the reserved word **new**. All languages which support dynamic variables will have similar functions. Regardless of what they are called, these predefined procedures dynamically allocate storage to individual pointer variables. That is, if we declare a pointer variable H as follows

```
Type
    PointerType = Pointer To X;
Var
    H : PointerType; (* H is a pointer variable pointing to objects of type X *)
```

then the Pascal procedure call New(H) will dynamically allocate sufficient space for one object of type X and put a pointer value into H to point to that new object, as shown in Figure 4–8. Memory allocation functions in C, Modula-2, and Ada work in a similar fashion.

Figure 4–8
The Predefined System Operation New

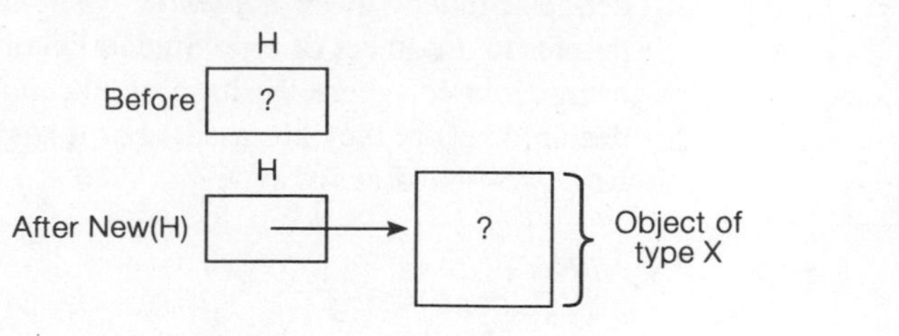

So, to create the first element of the linked list shown in Figure 4–7, we make the following procedure call:

New(Head)

which allocates space for a new node that is a two-field record of type StudentRecord and that is pointed to or *referenced* by Head.

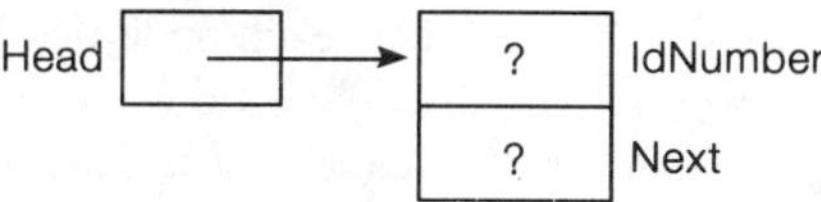

No values are stored in this new node yet. We can store a value into the IdNumber field of the newly created node by using the *dereferencing* operator, which we will denote by ^. If H is a pointer variable, then H^ is the object being pointed to by H. In this example, it is the first node of the list, so it is a record with two fields. To access the IdNumber field we use the standard dot notation for record structures:

Head^.IdNumber := 123456

Another question we must answer is, What value should we put in the Next field of the first node? We would like to use a value that means that there is currently no pointer value being stored in this field (i.e., something like the symbol Λ used in Figure 4–1). In Pascal and Modula-2 the reserved word **NIL** is used to indicate that the pointer field in the last node points to nothing. (In both Ada and C, the special word **Null** is used.) We can assign the constant value **Nil** to any *pointer* field, regardless of type. So the assignment statement

Head^.Next := **Nil**

results in the following condition

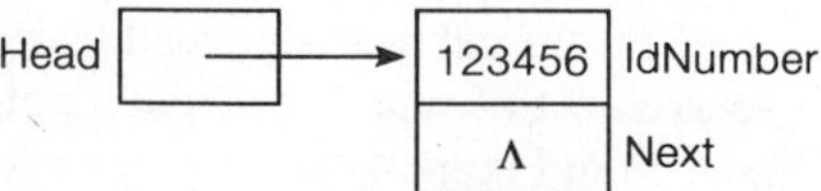

We can also use **Nil** to denote an empty list with no entries or nodes by simply assigning the value **Nil** to the head pointer itself.

```
Head := Nil        (* This creates an empty list. *)
```

The final pointer-related concept we introduce is a special system procedure called Dispose. If X is a pointer type pointing to object Y, then the procedure call Dispose(X) will return to the system all space currently allocated to Y and set X to the value **Nil**. In Modula-2 this function is called DEALLOCATE.

Dispose is a housekeeping function that lets you return memory space to the available space pool when you no longer need it, thus allowing yourself or others to use the space at some time in the future. The call to Dispose is not really required, but if you do not dispose of memory when you are finished with it, then it "sits around" unused in your address space and is unavailable for allocation for other needs. You may then run out of memory space and find that a program will not run when, in reality, memory space should be available. You should use Dispose with any problem in which you are doing a good deal of dynamic memory allocation and deallocation.

The ideas that we have just discussed are now combined into a simple program that creates a linked list of student ID numbers read from the standard input file. The program is shown in Figure 4–9.

Before you go on to the next section, trace through the program in Figure 4–9 to make sure that you understand the following five concepts related to pointers:

1. Pointer type declarations (**Pointer To**)
2. The dereferencing operator (^)
3. The New and Dispose procedures for memory allocation and deallocation
4. Head pointers
5. The special point value **Nil**

We will make extensive use of these ideas in the upcoming sections.

4.2.2 The Linked List Implementation of Linear List Operations

In this section we will see how we can use the pointer and linked list structures of section 4.2.1 to implement the Linear List ADT of Figure 4–5. We will not implement all eleven operations proposed for the package, but we will do enough examples to give you a good idea of how the other routines would be built. In all our examples, we will assume the declarations shown in Figure 4–10. Notice in our implementation that the role of the head pointer (the variable called List in Figure 4–10) has been expanded. Instead of simply pointing to the first node in the List, it now points to a record structure containing three fields—pointers to both the first and last nodes in the list and P, the current position pointer. This use of a *header record* rather than a simple header variable is a common practice in list implementations. We frequently wish to keep status information about a list (e.g., its size) as well as maintain additional pointers (e.g., Last). A good place to collect this global list information is in a header record pointed to by the head pointer. The header record then contains the pointer to the first node in the list.

Figure 4–9
Sample Program Using Linked Lists

```
(*  This module contains a program that demonstrates the use of
    pointers in creating and using linked lists, as described in
    section 4.2.1. All insertions and deletions are done
    at the front of the list.  *)

Module LinkedList;

Type
    Student              = Pointer To StudentRecord;
    StudentRecord        = Record
                                IdNumber      : Integer;
                                Next          : Student;
                           End;

Var
    Head    : Student;                 (* Pointer to the head of the linked list *)
    Node    : Student;                 (* Temporary pointer *)
    IdNum   : Integer;                 (* ID Number *)
    Done    : Boolean;

Begin
    Head := Nil;                       (* Initialize linked list to be empty *)
    Done := False;
    ReadInt(IdNum);                    (* Get first ID Number *)
    While (Not Done) Do
        New(Node);                     (* Create next node for list. *)
        Node^.IdNumber := IdNum;       (* Set ID Number for new node. *)
        Node^.Next := Head;            (* Place new node at beginning. *)
        Head := Node;                  (* of linked list. *)
        ReadInt(IdNum);                (* Get next ID Number. *)
        If IdNum = 99999
            Then Done := True          (* Stop on a 99999 *)
    Endwhile;

    (* Now the linked list is created, so we could process the data in it. *)

    (* We're done, so free the space used by the linked list. *)
    While (Head <> Nil) Do             (* As long a there are nodes left, *)
        Node := Head^.Next;            (* Save a pointer to the next node, *)
        Dispose(Head);                 (* Dispose the current node, *)
        Head := Node;                  (* Update head pointer to saved
                                       pointer. *)
    Endwhile;

End LinkedList.
```

Figure 4–11 depicts the linked list data structure created by the declarations in Figure 4–10. To avoid clutter, subsequent figures will show only the nodes from the bottom portion of Figure 4–11.

The first list operation we will implement is the insertion operation called InsertAfter. Its calling sequence is:

```
InsertAfter(Var L:LinearListType; Item : Element);
```

Figure 4–10
Declarations to Create a Linked Implementation of a Linear List

```
Type
    (* Data type of the information field of nodes in the list *)
    Element = Integer;

    (* Data type of the nodes in the list *)
    ListElementType = Pointer To ListElementRecord;
    ListElementRecord =                  (* This is the actual format of a node. *)
        Record
            Information     : Element;
            Next            : ListElementType;
        End;

    (* Data type for the Header record of the list *)
    LinearListType = Pointer To
        Record
            First   : ListElementType;     (* First node in the list *)
            Last    : ListElementType;     (* Last node in the list *)
            P       : ListElementType;     (* Current position pointer *)
        End;

(* This declaration allocates space for the pointer to the header record. *)
Var
    List : LinearListType;
```

Figure 4–11
Linked List Structure Created by the Declarations of Figure 4–10

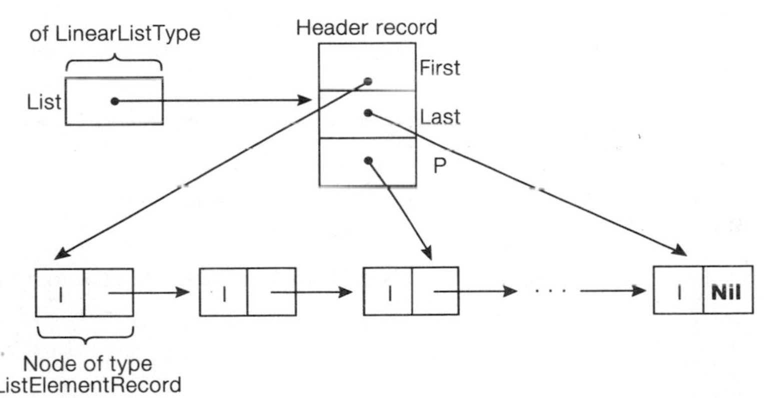

The operation begins from the following starting conditions:

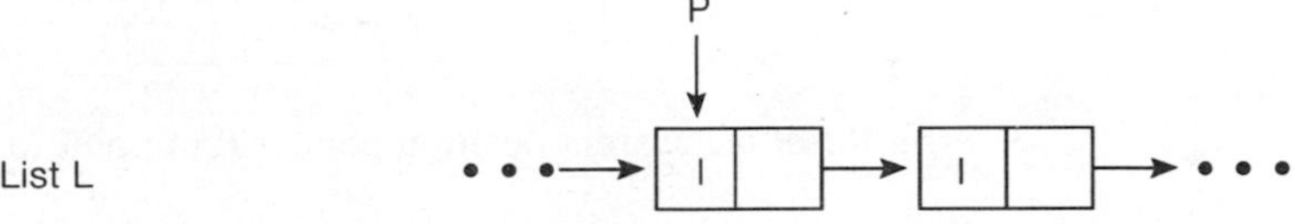

To insert the new information field called Item in its proper place (after the node pointed to by P), we carry out the following five steps. The diagram after each step shows what is happening to the list L.

1. Allocate space for a new node. Its reference variable will be named T (for Temporary).

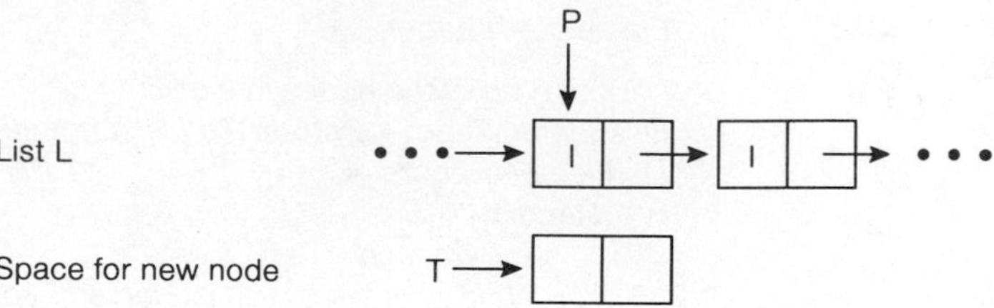

2. Set the Information field of T to the value Item.

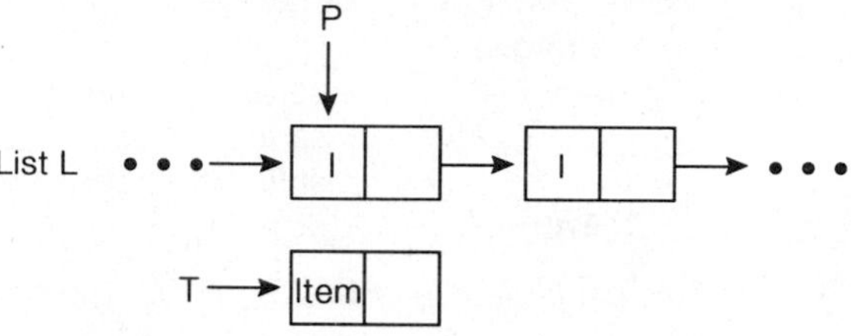

3. Set the Next field of the node pointed to by T to point to the successor of P. (Note: If we are adding the new node to the end of the list, the Next field will be **Nil** and we will also have to update the Last pointer in the header record.)

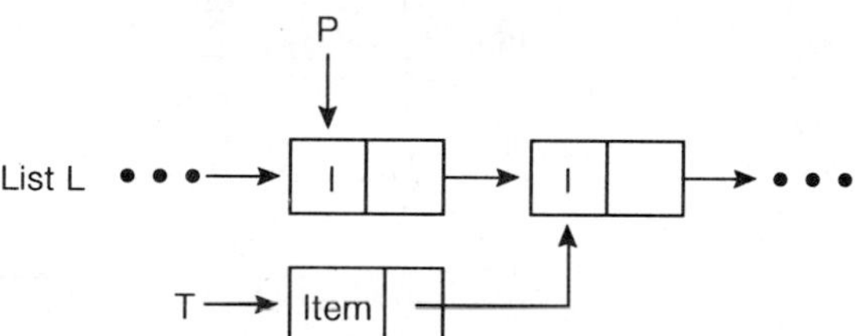

4. Reset the Next field of the node pointed to by P to point to the node pointed to by T.

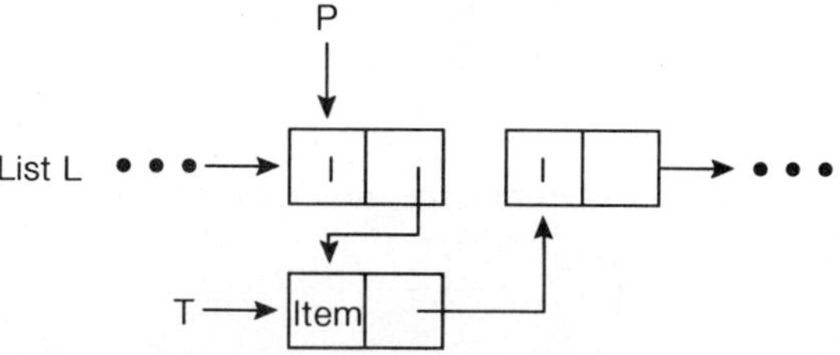

5. Reset the current position pointer P to point to the node pointed to by T.

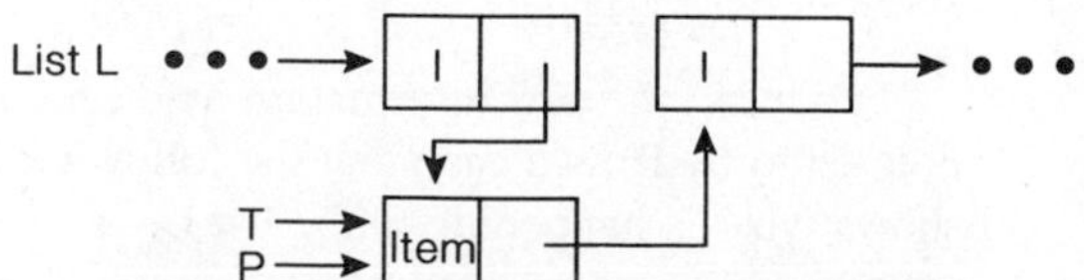

The InsertAfter procedure is now complete. We have added the new node in the proper spot and updated the value of P, the current position pointer. A complete procedure for implementing this algorithm is shown in Figure 4–12 (the comments in Figure 4–12 refer to the five steps we have just described).

As a second example we code the linear list procedure called Size. Its calling sequence is:

Procedure *Size (L: LinearListType) : Integer;*

This procedure counts how many nodes are currently contained in the list L. It must traverse the list, starting at First and continuing until the Next field of the current node has the value **Nil**. Each time it passes through a node, it adds one to a counter. When it has finished, it returns the value of the counter. The complete procedure is shown in Figure 4–13.

Figure 4–12
InsertAfter Procedure for Linked Lists

```
(* Insert element Item into list L immediately after the node pointed
   to by the current position pointer P. *)

Procedure InsertAfter ( Var L : LinearListType; Item : Element );
Var
    T : ListElementType;

Begin
    New(T);                          (* Step 1: Allocate space for new node. *)
    T^.Information := Item;          (* Step 2: Set information field of T. *)
    T^.Next := L^.P^.Next;           (* Step 3: Set next field of T. *)
    If (T^.Next = Nil) Then
        L^.Last := T;                (* If inserting at end, modify Last pointer. *)
    Endif;
    L^.P^.Next := T;                 (* Step 4: Set next field of P to point to T. *)
    L^.P := T;                       (* Step 5: Set P to point to T. *)
End InsertAfter;
```

Figure 4–13
Size Function for Linked Lists

```
(* Procedure Size counts and returns the number of nodes in list L. *)

Procedure Size( L : LinearListType ) : Integer;
Var
    Count   : Integer;
    Ptr     : ListElementType;

Begin
    Count := 0;                      (* Initialize Count of nodes to zero. *)
    Ptr := L^.First;                 (* Start at beginning of list. *)

    While (Ptr <> Nil) Do            (* Loop as long as there are more nodes. *)
        Count := Count + 1;          (* Count current element. *)
        Ptr := Ptr^.Next;            (* Move to next node. *)
    Endwhile;

    Return Count;                    (* Return final count of nodes in list. *)
End Size;
```

Two aspects of the Size procedure represent common pitfalls users may encounter when working with linked lists. The first is forgetting to consider the possibility of an *empty list* (i.e., L^.First = **Nil**). For example, the following code:

```
P := L^.First;
Repeat
    (* Some operation *)
    P := P^.Next
Until P = Nil;
```

will not work correctly if P is initially **Nil**. When we try to dereference P (on line 4), the program will halt with a fatal error. The dereferencing operation P^ is undefined if P = **Nil**. That is the reason why we used the **While** loop in the Size procedure of Figure 4–13. If P is initially **Nil**, the loop is never entered, and the procedure returns the correct value 0 for Count.

The second common problem when using linked lists is an *off-by-one error*. We will make this error if we attempt to look one node ahead of our current position before we check to see whether that successor actually exists. For example, suppose we were writing a fragment of code to check whether the information fields of two adjacent nodes were equal. That is, given the following conditions

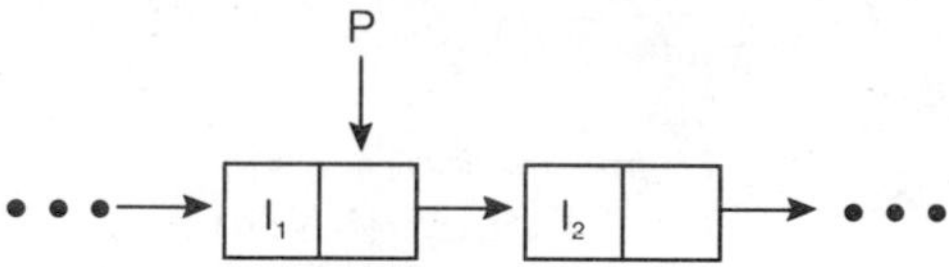

we want to know if $I_1 = I_2$. If we incorrectly write

```
If P^.Information = P^.Next^.Information Then . . .
```

we could be in trouble. This code will work properly only until we get to the end of the list. At that time the value of P^.Next is **Nil**, and our attempt to dereference it, P^.Next^, will cause a fatal error. Always make sure you check for a pointer value of **Nil** before you attempt to dereference a dynamic variable. (For a challenging problem, try writing a correct program that compares all adjacent nodes in a linked list.)

We will leave the coding of the remaining nine operations and the completion of the Linear List ADT implementation module as an exercise.

Our final comment about the Linear List package of Figure 4–5 is to note that it can be used in place of both the Stack and the Queue packages of chapter 3. The Push, Pop, Enqueue, and Dequeue operations can all be modeled using the list operations contained in the external module of Figure 4–5. For example, the stack operation Push(S,X), which puts X on top of stack S, is exactly the same as the list operation

```
InsertFirst(S,X)
```

The operation Pop(S) can be accomplished through the following two procedure calls:

```
First(S);
Delete(S)
```

Finally, the Enqueue(Q,X) operation, which places X at the end of queue Q, is equivalent to

```
Last(Q);
InsertAfter(Q,X)
```

We leave the specification of the other stack and queue operations in terms of our basic List operations as an exercise. A good List package provides a user with not only the operations necessary to manipulate a list but also the tools needed to build and manipulate stacks, queues, and deques as well.

Similarly, our linked list can, with minor changes, be used to implement the String ADT introduced in section 3.2.3. All we need to do to the declarations of Figure 4–10 is make the Information field a value of type Char (rather than Integer) and add a length field Length to the header record to keep track of the length of the string in characters. Given these changes, the five-character string 'Hello' could be represented as shown in Figure 4–14.

This implementation would be useful if we frequently insert or delete characters into or out of the string. Inserting or deleting using the one-dimensional array-based implementation would involve a good deal of shifting and compacting of information. However, as we mentioned earlier, there is a price to pay—namely, the space needed to store the pointer values in the node and the overhead required to keep the pointers current. We have included some exercises at the end of the chapter to implement string insertion/deletion operations using the linked list implementation shown in Figure 4–14.

Figure 4–14
Linked List Implementation of a String

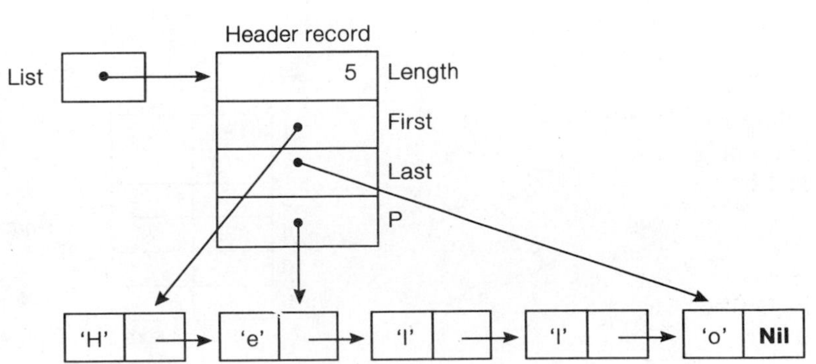

4.2.3 The Array Implementation of Linear List Operations

Even in a language that does not support pointer variables, the ADT List package shown in Figure 4–5 can still be implemented using a two-dimensional array. Each row of the array represents a single node, and the Next field is implemented as an integer value in the range 0 . . N to represent the row index of the next node (zero can be used as the equivalent of **Nil**). Thus, the following three-element linked list

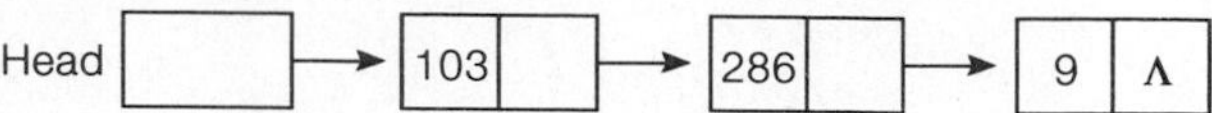

could be implemented in array form as shown in Figure 4–15. The Head pointer contains a 1, indicating that the first node of the list is contained in row 1 of the two-dimensional array. Row 1 contains the integer value 103 and a Next field of 4, indicating that the second node is located in row 4, and so forth. The last node of the list has a zero in the Next field to indicate that there are no more nodes in the list. The zero is analogous to **Nil** in the linked list implementation discussed earlier. The zero cannot be misinterpreted as a pointer since the rows of the array are numbered starting with a 1.

To use this method properly, we also need a way to indicate that a row of an array is empty and available for use (e.g., rows 3, 5, and 6 in Figure 4–15). Otherwise, we have no way of knowing whether a row is occupied when performing an insert operation. To keep track of free rows in the array we use an *available space list*, which is a linked list of nodes (i.e., rows of the array) that are available for use. The head of this linked list will be stored in a pointer called Available. The available cells will be linked together by the Next fields of the nodes. Thus we actually have two "intertwined" linear lists in our array structure—a list of data items beginning at Head and a list of available cells beginning at Available. When the value of Available becomes 0, we are out of memory and the table is full. Naturally, this available space list and the array structure will have to be properly initialized by the Create operator when the list is initially created.

The declarations needed to set up the two-dimensional array implementation just described are given at the top of the following page.

Figure 4–15
Array Implementation of a Linked List

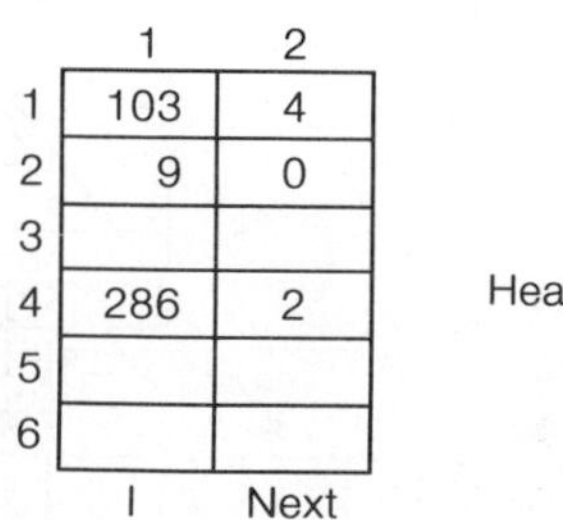

```
Const
    MaxListSize = 100;                       (* Maximum number of nodes *)

Type
    Element = Integer;                       (* Information field data type *)
    PointerIndex = 0 .. MaxListSize;
    (* This is the array-based linear list. *)
    LinearListType = Record
        A  : Array [1 .. MaxListSize] Of     (* The array of nodes *)
                Record
                Information  : Element;
                Next         : PointerIndex
                End;
        Available  : PointerIndex;           (* Head of the available space list *)
        First      : PointerIndex;           (* Pointer to the first node *)
        Last       : PointerIndex;           (* Pointer to the last node *)
        P          : PointerIndex            (* Current position pointer *)
                   End;                      (* of The LinearListType record *)
Var
    List  : LinearListType;
```

Figure 4–16 shows an example of this data structure applied to the three-node list of Figure 4–15. Notice the chaining together of the 97 available rows 3 → 5 → 6 → 7 → . . . → 99 → 100, beginning with the pointer Available. As space is needed for insertion operations, rows will be taken off the available space list. As delete operations free up rows, the newly freed cells will be added back to the available space list.

Figure 4–17 shows the array implementation of the list operation Delete(L), which deletes the node pointed to by the current position pointer. The space freed up by the operation is added to the available space list.

Figure 4–18 shows the array-based implementation of the list operation InsertFirst(L,I), which inserts a new node containing element I as the first node of list L. Notice that we must be careful to check for a special case—a full list. We can determine whether we have a full list by seeing if the available space list is

Figure 4–16
A Linear List Implemented Using an Array

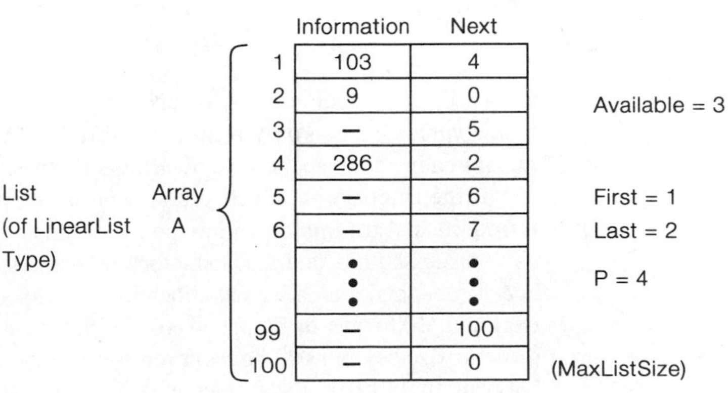

Figure 4–17
Array Implementation of the Delete Operation

```
(* The Delete procedure removes the element pointed to by the current
     position pointer P from the list L using the array implementation of lists *)
Procedure Delete ( Var L : LinearListType );
Var
     Ptr : PointerIndex;
Begin
     If (L.P = L.First) Then
          (* Delete the first element in the list. *)

          (* Set First pointer to second element. *)
          L.First := L.A[L.P].Next;

          If (L.P = L.Last) Then
               (* If this was the last element, set Last pointer to zero. *)
               L.Last := 0;
          Endif;
     Else
          (* Start searching for predecessor of the element. *)
          Ptr := L.First;

          While (L.A[Ptr].Next <> L.P) Do
               Ptr := L.A[Ptr].Next;
          Endwhile;

          (* Link predecessor to successor. *)
          L.A[Ptr].Next := L.A[L.P].Next;

          If (L.Last = L.P) Then
               L.Last := Ptr;
          Endif;
     Endif;

     Ptr := L.A[L.P].Next;            (* Save Index of successor element. *)
     L.A[L.P].Next := L.Available;    (* Add deleted item to available list. *)
     L.Available := L.P;
     L.P := Ptr;                      (* Set P to the successor of the deleted
                                         element. *)
End Delete;
```

empty, i.e., Available = 0. If we encounter this condition, we have no space to store a new value. We can only print a warning message and return. There is no way to dynamically add space to a static array structure.

If the language in which you are coding supports pointers, their use is the preferred method for implementing the Linear List ADT. The array implementation we have discussed has one unsatisfactory characteristic: the array is a static data type, and it must make an advance allocation of a fixed amount of space for the list, for example, 100 rows in Figure 4–16. With this array implementation, a list cannot grow in size beyond 100 nodes, even if memory space is available. Similarly, if our list contains only one or two elements, we are wasting an enormous amount of space, as our array declaration allocates 200 cells (100 rows x 2 columns) to the list, re-

Figure 4–18
Array Implementation of the InsertFirst Operation

```
(* The InsertFirst procedure puts Element E at the beginning of the
      Linear List L. *)

Procedure InsertFirst ( Var L : LinearListType; E : Element );
Begin
      If (L.Available = 0) Then
            Return;                     (* We should also issue a warning message or *)
                                        (* set an error flag here, since we could not *)
                                        (* insert the node due to the list being full. *)
      Endif;

      L.P := L.Available;               (* Get a node to hold the element being added. *)

      (* Remove allocated node from free list. *)
      L.Available := L.A[L.Available].Next;

      L.A[L.P].Information := E;        (* Set information field of new node. *)
      L.A[L.P].Next := L.First;         (* Link new node onto front of the list. *)
      L.First := L.P;                   (* Set First pointer to new node. *)

End InsertFirst;
```

Figure 4–19
Linked List Implementation of a Stack Structure

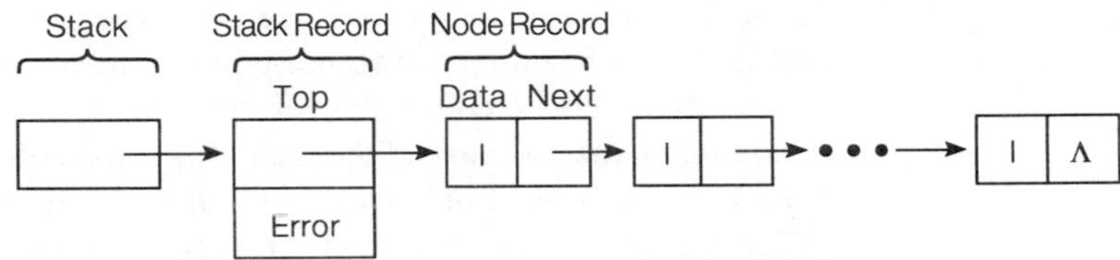

gardless of how much is actually in use; in Figure 4–16, for example, only 3 out of 100 rows are occupied. The linked list method, which only uses as much space as is needed, is generally more efficient, and in addition, our lists can grow as large as desired, as long as the memory allocation procedure New is able to find and return sufficient memory space.

4.3 LINKED LIST IMPLEMENTATION OF A STACK

In chapter 3 we saw how a stack can be implemented using an array. Sometimes it is better to implement a stack using a linked list. As mentioned earlier, the advantage of using linked lists is that we do not need to declare, in advance, a fixed maximum size for the stack. The stack can grow as long as memory is available within the system.

In our linked list implementation of a stack, we will use a head pointer that points to a header record containing two fields. The first field will be a pointer to the top element of the stack. The second field will store information about any errors that occur while carrying out operations on this stack. The structure of our stack is shown in Figure 4–19.

To create the structure shown in Figure 4–19, we first declare the following objects:

```
Type
    StackErrorTypes = (None, StackOverflow, StackUnderflow, TopOfEmptyStack);
    (* These are the declarations for the individual elements on the stack *)
    Node = Pointer To NodeRecord;
    NodeRecord =          (* This is the structure of a node in the stack. *)
        Record
            Data   : ElementType;
            Next   : Node;
        End; (* Of Record NodeRecord *)

    (* These are the declarations for the overall stack structure *)
    Stack = Pointer To StackRecord;
    StackRecord =
        Record
            Top    : Node;
            Error  : StackErrorTypes
        End; (* of Record StackRecord *)
Var
    S   : Stack;
```

These declarations define both Node and Stack to be pointer types. Stack, which is essentially the head pointer of the structure, points to a two-element record of type StackRecord. This record holds information about errors and a pointer called Top that points to the top entry of the stack. Each node of the stack will have two fields: a Data field and a Next field used to contain a pointer to the next node in the stack. When a stack is created, Top is set to **Nil**, Error is set to None, and there are no nodes in the linked list. These initial conditions are implemented within the Create function by the following operations:

```
New(S);                 (* Create a new stack S. *)
S^.Top := Nil;          (* Set Top to Nil. *)
S^.Error := None        (* and clear the error field. *)
```

and we are now ready to perform operations on our newly created stack structure.

For example, to push an item onto the top of the stack, we could use the procedure Push, shown in Figure 4–20.

Although correct, this linked list implementation of the Push operation does not handle the error condition called *stack overflow* in a very elegant manner. We cannot determine within our program whether the procedure New will be able to find enough space for the new node. In many languages there is no way to determine if all available space for new node creation has been exhausted. If we do run out of space, the procedure New will usually just "blow up" instead of returning an error flag; that is, a postmortem dump will be produced, and the program will halt. Thus, there may not be any way to allow us to set the variable Error to StackOverflow and continue on with the program.

A procedure to pop an element off the stack is shown in Figure 4–21. We leave it to you to complete the implementation module for our linked-list-based stack, including the operations Full, Empty, and Top.

Figure 4–20
Push Operation Using a Linked List Implementation of a Stack

```
(* Procedure Push puts an element on the top of the stack *)

Procedure Push ( Item : ElementType; Var S : Stack );
Var
     NewNode : Node;                (* Variable for the new stack node *)

Begin
     If (Full(S)) Then              (* There is no space left on stack *)
      S^.Error := StackOverFlow;    (* so set the error flag. *)
        Return;
     End;

     New(NewNode);                  (* Allocate space for the new node. *)
     NewNode^.Data := Item;         (* Put the data in the new node. *)
     NewNode^.Next := S^.Top;       (* Link it at the front of the list. *)
     S^.Top := NewNode;             (* Make the new node the Top of the Stack *)
     S^.Error := None;              (* and clear the error flag. *)

End Push;
```

Figure 4–21
Pop Operation Using Linked Lists

```
(* Procedure Pop removes the top element from the stack *)

Procedure Pop ( Var S : Stack );
Var
     Ptr : Node;
Begin
     If Empty(S) Then                     (* Can't Pop from an empty stack *)
        S^.Error := StackUnderFlow;       (* so set the error flag. *)
        Return;
     Endif;

     Ptr := S^.Top;                       (* We can Pop an element, so save
                                          pointer to top. *)
     S^.Top := S^.Top^.Next;              (* Move Top pointer to next element. *)
     Dispose(Ptr);                        (* Free space allocated to old top of
                                          stack *)
     S^.Error := None;                    (* and clear the error flag. *)

End Pop;
```

It is interesting to look back and review what we have done with the ADT called Stack. We have taken the external module of Figure 3–16 and looked at three different implementations of that module:

1. A one-dimensional array implementation (Figure 3–23)
2. An array-based linked list implementation (Figures 4–15, 4–16, 4–17, 4–18)
3. A pointer-based linked list implementation (Figures 4–19, 4–20, 4–21)

Each of these approaches has certain advantages and disadvantages, but the most important point to remember is that regardless of which technique we choose, the external module for the Stack data type *would not change*. The user is blissfully unaware of the myriad technical details concerning pointers, declarations, efficiency, or space. All he or she thinks about are the available resources and how to access and use them—this is the beauty of data abstraction.

4.4 LINKED LIST IMPLEMENTATION OF A QUEUE

Just as we did with the stack structure of section 4.3, we can also view a queue as a linked list, as shown in Figure 4–22.

It is much easier to implement a queue with the linked list representation than with the array representation, because with a list we do not have to worry about the "inchworm" effect described in section 3.6 and diagrammed in Figure 3–24. With a linked list there is never any problem distinguishing between an empty and a full queue, because with linked lists a queue can never be full (at least not until all available memory in the system has been exhausted). Therefore, we do not have to deal with problems such as circular arrays, compaction, or juggling elements. Virtually all applications that use queues prefer a linked list implementation over the array implementation described in chapter 3.

The linked list implementation of a queue is set up very much like the stack implementation shown in Figure 4–19, although we have changed the names of the field identifiers for clarity.

```
Type
    QueueErrorTypes = (None, QueueOverFlow, QueueUnderflow, QueueEmpty);
    (* Data type for the individual elements stored in the queue *)
    QueueNode = Pointer To QueueNodeRecord;
    QueueNode Record =
        Record
            Data   : QueueElementType;
            Next   : QueueNode
        End; (* Of Record QueueNodeRecord *)

    (* Data type for the overall queue structure *)
    Queue = Pointer To QueueRecord;
    QueueRecord =
        Record
            Front  : QueueNode; (* Front of the queue *)
            Rear   : QueueNode; (* Rear of the queue *)
            Error  : QueueErrorTypes
        End; (* Of Record QueueRecord *)
Var
    Q  : Queue
```

The Create function creates an empty queue by allocating space for a new queue record and setting its Front and Rear pointers to **Nil**.

```
New(Q);             (* Allocate space for a new Queue called Q. *)
Q^.Front := Nil;    (* Set both front and rear pointers to Nil to indicate the
                       queue is empty *)
Q^.Rear := Nil;
Q^.Error := None    (* and clear the error field. *)
```

Figure 4–22
Linked List Implementation of a Queue Structure

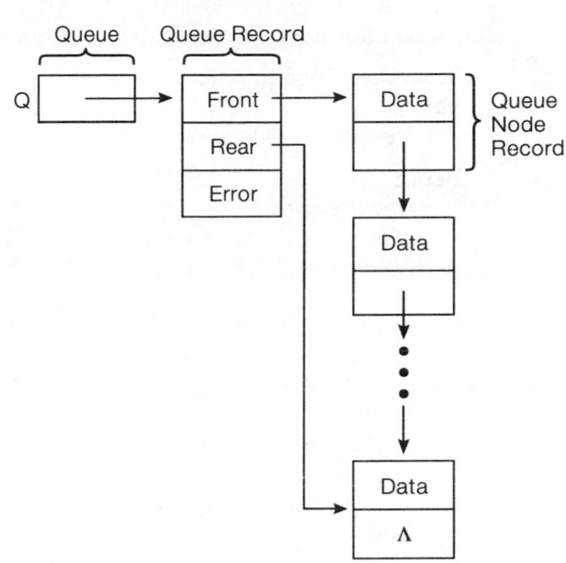

This empty queue has the form:

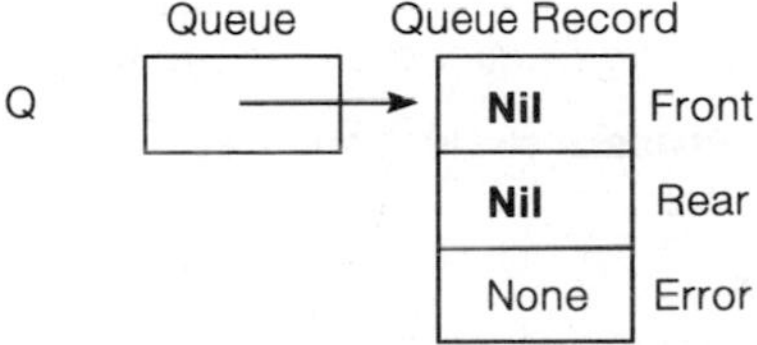

We are now ready to perform operations on our newly created queue data structure.

The procedure Enqueue, which adds a new element to the rear of the queue is shown in Figure 4–23.

Notice how simple and elegant this linked list solution is, especially when compared to the array implementation discussed in section 3.6. For example, there is no longer a need to check for a full queue condition (as we had to do with circular arrays) because, as mentioned earlier, we cannot have overflow until the memory in the entire computer system has been exhausted and the New procedure is unsuccessful. When that situation has been reached, we usually cannot recover anyway, so there is no need to check for it. Also notice that there is no need to maintain a separate available space list, as we had to do with the two-dimensional array implementation; the New and Dispose procedures provide that service for us automatically. Because of the simplicity and elegance of the resulting code, Queue structures are almost always implemented using linked lists of the type diagrammed in Figure 4–22.

The Dequeue procedure to delete the element at the front of the queue is shown in Figure 4–24. We leave it as an exercise to finish the linked list based implementation of a queue, including the operations Full, Empty, First, and Last.

Figure 4–23
Enqueue Operation Using Linked Lists

```
(* The Enqueue procedure will add an element to the end of a queue. *)

Procedure Enqueue ( Item : QueueElementType; Var Q : Queue );
Var
    NewNode : QueueNode;

Begin
    New(NewNode);                    (* Allocate space for the new node. *)
    NewNode^.Data := Item;           (* Set the data field. *)
    NewNode^.Next := Nil;            (* This node won't have a successor
                                     in the list. *)
    If (Empty(Q)) Then               (* This node will be only node in the list *)
        Q^.Front := NewNode;         (* so make it the first node *)
        Q^.Rear := NewNode;          (* and the last node. *)
    Else
        Q^.Rear^.Next := NewNode;    (* Otherwise, make it the successor *)
                                     (* to the current last node. *)
        Q^.Rear := NewNode;          (* Make new node the new last node *)
    Endif;
    Q^.Error := None;                (* and clear the error flag. *)

End Enqueue;
```

Figure 4–24
Dequeue Operation Using Linked Lists

```
(* The Dequeue procedure will remove the first element from a queue. *)

Procedure Dequeue ( Var Q : Queue );
Var
    Ptr : QueueNode;

Begin
    If (Empty(Q)) Then                 (* Can't Dequeue from an empty Queue,
        Q^.Error := QueueUnderFlow;    (* so set error flag and return, *)
        Return;                        (* doing nothing to the Queue. *)
    Endif;

    Ptr := Q^.Front;
    If (Q^.Front = Q^.Rear) Then       (* If we are removing the last node *)
        Q^.Front := Nil;               (* set the front pointer to Nil *)
        Q^.Rear := Nil;                (* and the rear pointer to NIL to *)
                                       (* indicate the Queue is now empty. *)
    Else
        Q^.Front := Q^.Front^.Next;    (* Otherwise, move front pointer *)
                                       (* to the next node in the Queue. *)
    Endif;
    Dispose(Ptr);                      (* Release the space allocated for *)
    Q^.Error := None                   (* the node and clear the error flag. *)

End Dequeue;
```

4.5 VARIATIONS ON THE LINKED LIST STRUCTURE

4.5.1 Circular Lists

Assume that we have a standard Linked List with the following structure

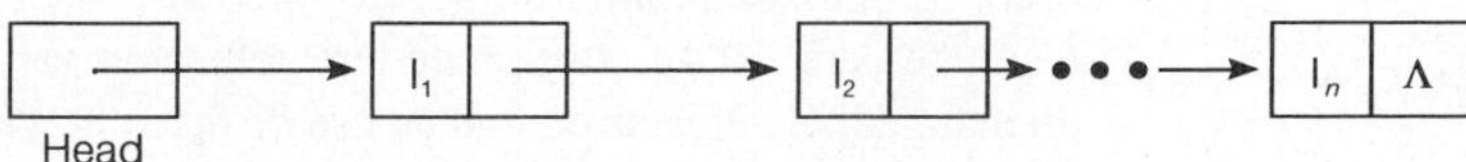

and we wish to search the list for a specific data value, I_k. The most efficient way to accomplish this is to begin at Head and search sequentially until we either find the value we are looking for or we come to the end of the list, i.e., P^.Next = **Nil**. In many situations this approach works well. However, there are also applications where this type of search can cause some serious problems.

Imagine that our list contained the names and identification of computational resources that could be allocated to a program, e.g., a list of laser printers. Each resource could be either "Free" or "InUse," and when a request is made by a program ("I need a laser printer"), we search through the list until we find one that is Free. We then mark it InUse and return the identification of that resource to the requesting program. The program is now the sole owner of that device and may use it until it is finished, at which time it voluntarily returns it and it is again marked Free.

If we always begin our search from the head of the list, it is obvious that the resources whose names appear near the front will be allocated much more often than those whose names appear nearer the back. If the resources were laser printers, then those whose names were closer to the front will have a much greater stress on their printing mechanism and internal components because of their heavier use. A fairer way to handle this problem would be to allocate resources in such a way that all devices in our linked list are allocated an equal percentage of the time.

A simple way to do that is to keep a pointer called StartSearch that tells us where we ended the last search. The next time a request comes in, we will begin our search not from the node pointed to by Head but from the node pointed to by StartSearch. Thus the starting point for our search will move circularly throughout the list, and in the long run, all nodes will be allocated on an approximately equal basis.

However, there is still one problem. We must be able to move through the entire list, including moving from the last node in the list back to the first. To facilitate this process, we will make one additional change to our standard linked list structure. Instead of marking the end of the list with a Next field value of **Nil**, we will have it point back to the first node in the list, thus producing a structure called a *circular list*, shown in Figure 4–25. The nice thing about the circular list structure of

Figure 4–25
General Structure of a Circular List

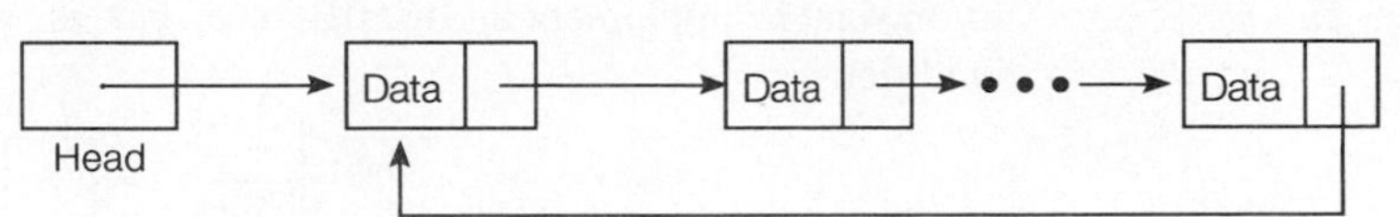

Figure 4–25 is that it allows you to traverse the entire list beginning at any node, rather than beginning only at the front.

Figure 4–26 shows an implementation of our resource allocation problem solved using a circular list. The procedure GetResource(L) begins its search for a free resource in list L at the node pointed to by StartSearch. If it finds a resource that is Free, it returns a pointer to that resource and updates the value of StartSearch. If all resources are InUse, the procedure returns a value of **Nil** and leaves StartSearch unchanged. GetResource makes use of the following declarations:

```
Type
    HeadPointer = Pointer To HeadRecord;
    HeadRecord = Record
        ListHead        : NodePointer;        (* The head of the list *)
        StartSearch     : NodePointer         (* Where to begin the
                                                 search *)
                 End;
    (* This describes a node in the list of available resources *)
    NodePointer = Pointer To NodeRecord;
    NodeRecord = Record
                      Data    : ResourcePointer;
                      Status  : (Free, InUse);
                      Next    : NodePointer
                 End; (* the NodeRecord *)
    ResourcePointer = Pointer To ResourceRecord; (* Detailed information about
                                                    the resource to be allocated.
                                                    Not shown here *)
    CircularList = HeadPointer;                  (* Simply to give it a more
                                                    descriptive name *)
Var
    List  : CircularList;
```

The procedure GetResource is shown in Figure 4–26. We leave the implementation of the related procedure called ReturnResource, which retrieves the resource and marks it as Free, as an exercise.

4.5.2 Doubly Linked Lists

The list structures we have discussed so far contain only one pointer field and generally look like the List diagrammed in Figure 4.1. This type of structure allows us to move through the list only in the "forward" direction and thus places some limitations on us. For example, if we are somewhere in the middle of a long list and need to look at a node three positions to the "left" of the current node, we would have to retraverse the list from the beginning to locate the node. As a second example, instead of implementing the InsertAfter operation shown in Figure 4–12, we might want to implement an InsertBefore. That is, we are given the following initial conditions

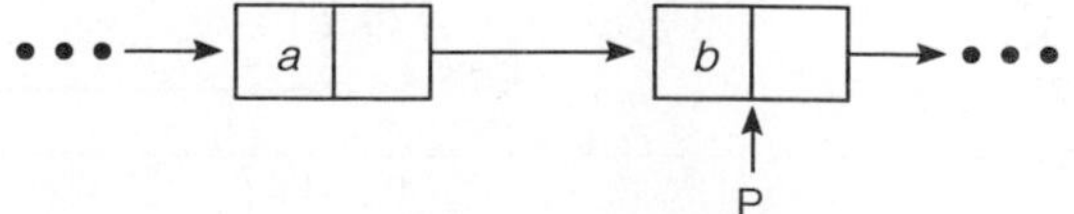

Figure 4–26
Implementation of the Procedure GetResource Using Circular Lists

```
(* The procedure GetResource searches a list of resources for one that
      is available. On finding one, it returns a pointer to it. If there
      are no available resources of the requested type, NIL is returned *)

Procedure GetResource( L : CircularList ) : ResourcePtr;
Var
      Ptr : NodePtr;
      Res : ResourcePtr;
Begin
      Ptr := L^.StartSearch;            (* Begin searching List at StartSearch *)

      If (Ptr = Nil) Then               (* There are no resources to allocate *)
            Return Nil;                 (* So return a Nil pointer. *)
      Endif;

      (* Loop as long we are looking at allocated resources and we have
            not gone through the entire list *)
      While (Ptr^.Status = InUse) And (Ptr^.Next <> L^.StartSearch) Do
            Ptr := Ptr^.Next;
      Endwhile;

      If (Ptr^.Status = Free) Then      (* We found an allocatable resource. *)
            Res := Ptr^.Data;           (* Set return value to available resource. *)
            Ptr^.Status := InUse;       (* Mark it allocated. *)
                                        (* Start search with next node next time. *)
            L^.StartSearch := Ptr^.Next;
      Else
            Res := Nil;                 (* No allocatable resources *)
      Endif;

      Return Res;

End GetResource;
```

Figure 4–27
Double Linked List with Both Forward and Backward Pointers

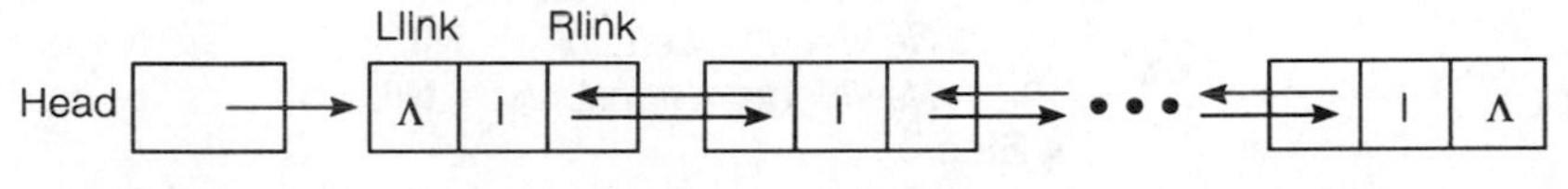

and we want to insert the new node *before* the node pointed at by P (between the two nodes containing the values *a* and *b*). Because our links point in only one direction, we have no way of locating the predecessor of P, except by traversing the entire list.

A solution to this problem is to design a data structure that includes both forward *and* backward links (called LLink and RLink), as shown in Figure 4–27. This structure is called a *doubly linked list*, and each node contains pointers to both its successor and its predecessor. Notice also that we now have two **Nil** pointers to indicate the two "ends" of the list. This type of data structure can be created quite easily using the following declaration:

```
Type
    NodePtr = Pointer To Node;
    Node = Record
                Data   : ElementType;          (* will leave unspecified *)
                LeftLink  : NodePtr;           (* pointer to the predecessor *)
                RightLink   : NodePtr          (* pointer to the successor *)
           End;

    HeadPtr = Pointer To HeadRecord;
    HeadRecord = Record
                    First: NodePtr;            (* first node in the list *)
                    CurrentPositionPtr   : NodePtr
                 End;
    DoublyLinkedList = HeadPtr;                (* more descriptive name *)
Var
    List   : DoublyLinkedList;
```

Figure 4–28 shows the implementation of the InsertBefore procedure, which was one of the examples that motivated the creation of both backward and forward point-

Figure 4–28
InsertBefore Procedure Using Doubly Linked Lists

```
(* The procedure InsertBefore will insert a node into a doubly linked list
    into the position immediately before the current node *)

Procedure InsertBefore ( Item : ElementType; Var L : DoublyLinkedList );
Var
    NewNode      : NodePtr;
    Prev         : NodePtr;

Begin
    New(NewNode);                         (* Allocate space for new node. *)
    NewNode^.Data := Item;                (* Set the data field in the new node. *)

    If (L^.First = Nil) Then              (* Inserting at the head of an
                                             empty list. *)
        L^.First := NewNode;              (* First element in list is new node. *)
        NewNode^.LeftLink := Nil;         (* Node has no node to its left *)
        NewNode^.RightLink := Nil;        (* or its right.*)
    Else
        (* Locate predecessor of current node. *)
        Prev := L^.CurrentPositionPtr^.LeftLink;
        If (Prev = Nil) Then              (* If it has none, then . . . *)
            L^.First := NewNode;          (* New node is at beginning of list. *)
        Else
            Prev^.RightLink := NewNode;   (* No, so set link from left.*)
        Endif;                            (* And from right. *)
        L^.CurrentPositionPtr^.LeftLink := NewNode;
        NewNode^.LeftLink := Prev;        (* Set node's links. *)
        NewNode^.RightLink := L^.CurrentPositionPtr;
    Endif;

    L^.CurrentPositionPtr := NewNode;     (* Set current position pointer to
                                             new node. *)

End InsertBefore;
```

Figure 4–29
A Circular Doubly Linked List

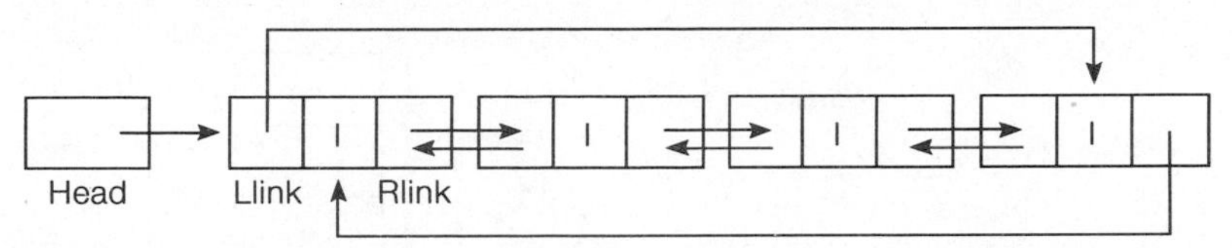

ers in a node. Although there are a number of special cases that must be checked (such as inserting before the first node), the basic logic of the procedure has been simplified because of the addition of the second pointer.

As a final example, we combine the ideas presented in the last two sections, circular lists and doubly linked lists, and describe a *circular doubly-linked list*, which has the structure depicted in Figure 4–29.

This data structure can be created using the declarations shown earlier for doubly linked lists. We would simply replace the two **Nil** values in Figure 4–27 with pointers back to the first and the last nodes in the list. The structure of Figure 4–29 would allow us to traverse the list efficiently in either the forward or backward direction, beginning from any arbitrary node. For certain types of applications, these added capabilities would be important enough to pay the twin prices of (1) the space needed for the increased number of pointers and (2) the time needed to maintain the proper values in all the pointer fields.

This last issue is quite crucial and cannot be overemphasized. Complex linked structures like those in Figures 4–25, 4–27 and 4–29 are powerful representational techniques, and they allow you to carry out certain operations quite efficiently. However, they are not "free"—they can consume a good deal of additional memory space and processor time. For example, in many systems an integer value requires two bytes of storage while a pointer value requires four bytes. Thus, if the nodes in Figure 4–29 each contained one integer and two pointers, only two of the ten bytes allocated to each node (20%) would be used to store information. The remaining 80% would be overhead needed to maintain the structure of the list. Whether the extra functionality is worth this cost is an important question that the programmer must answer when designing and implementing data structures.

4.6 CASE STUDY: A MEMORY MANAGER

One of the most important components of any multiuser operating system is the *memory manager*. It is the component that responds to requests for memory from other processes and returns memory to the available space pool when it has been freed up. This memory can be used for any number of needs, for example, newly created processes, dynamic data structures, or input/output buffers.

A memory manager works by keeping a collection of information called a *block descriptor record* for each *memory block* in the system, where a memory block is a set of contiguous memory cells treated as a single unit. These block descriptor records are linked to form a linear list of the type shown in Figure 4.1. The blocks are linked in order of increasing memory addresses. If, for example, our memory was currently in the following state

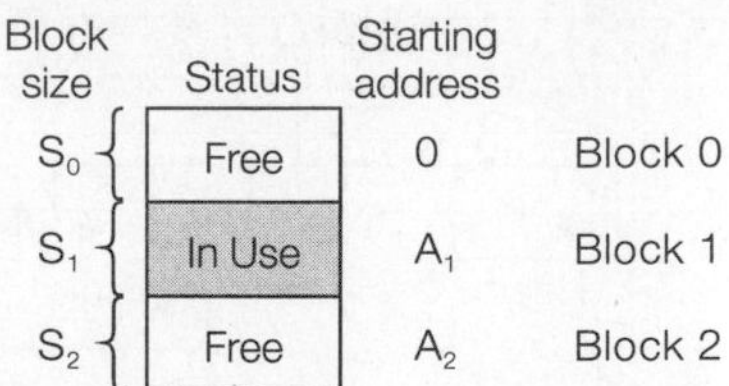

then our memory manager would maintain the following three-node list to describe the current state of memory:

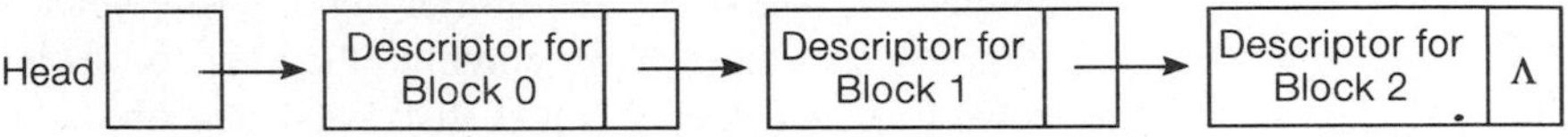

The descriptor information that is kept for each memory block will vary somewhat from operating system to operating system, but it will always contain at least the following three pieces of information:

a. Starting memory address of the block
b. Size of the block in memory cells
c. Status of the block (free or in use)

Other vital information such as the name of the process that owns the block and the time that the block was originally allocated will not be included in this case study, although it would certainly be an important part of any real-world memory manager system.

A more detailed picture of the block descriptor list structure maintained by the memory manager for our sample memory allocation might look like the following:

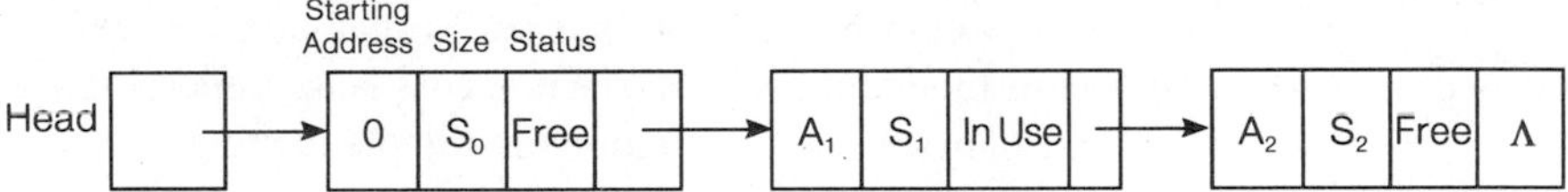

The memory manager provides its services through system procedures that are invoked either by other operating system routines or by user processes. The memory manager that we will describe responds to four types of requests called Initialize, Allocate, Free, and Map. (Again, a real memory manager might have many more request types and service facilities.)

The Initialize procedure initializes the block descriptor list by creating the head pointer and placing two nodes on that list. The first node describes the memory block permanently assigned to the core-resident *kernel* of the operating system (of which the memory manager is part). This block is assumed to begin at address 0 and occupy KernelSpace words. The remainder of memory, from address KernelSpace to address LastMemoryAddress, is one large block that is marked as free. Thus, the Initialize procedure will create the following structure:

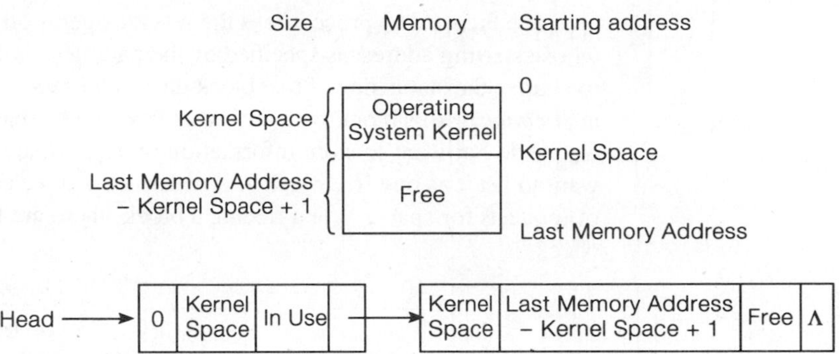

No other memory management operations are allowed until the Initialize call has been made.

The second memory manager procedure is called Allocate(N). A process makes a request to allocate a block of N contiguous memory cells. If the request can be satisfied, i.e., if there is a block of the required size or larger, then Allocate will return to the requesting program the address A of the first cell of the block and will mark locations A, A+1, . . . , A+N−1 as InUse.

When allocating memory space our memory manager uses what is called a *first fit* allocation method: when it searches sequentially for a free block on the linked list, it will stop when it finds the *first* free block whose size M is greater than or equal to N, where N is the size of the request. (An alternative algorithm called *best fit* looks for the block such that (M − N) is a minimum, that is, it finds the free block that comes closest in size to our request. This algorithm is left as an exercise.) When we find a free block of size M, we split it into two pieces—one block of size N which is allocated to the requesting process and is marked InUse, and a second block of size M − N, which is still Free (the "leftover" space). In order to ensure that we don't end up with very tiny and unusable free blocks (e.g., blocks with 1 or 2 cells), we assume the existence of a global constant called MinBlockSize. If the free space that remains after allocating a block is less than MinBlockSize, then we simply give the requesting process the entire M cells and assume there is no leftover space. The following illustration shows how Allocate works for a block of size 50:

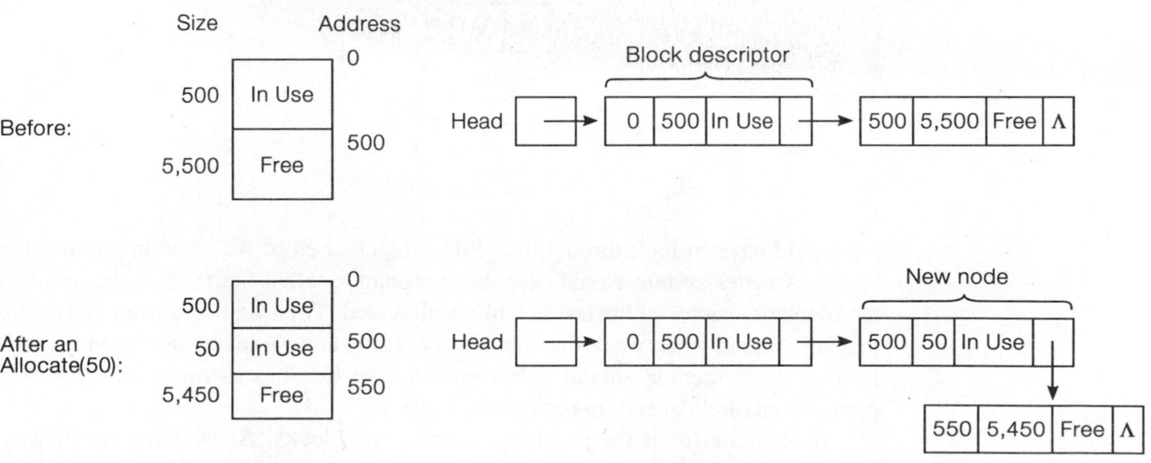

The Free(*addr*) procedure is the reverse operation of Allocate. It frees the block whose starting address is specified by the parameter *addr*. However, it is not enough to change the status flag of that block descriptor record from InUse to Free. We must also *coalesce* this block with any other free blocks that come before or after it. That is, we do not want to store information on two adjacent free blocks of size 50—we want to list it as one free block of size 100 so that we can satisfy the greatest number of requests for space. When freeing a block, there are four possibilities that we must check:

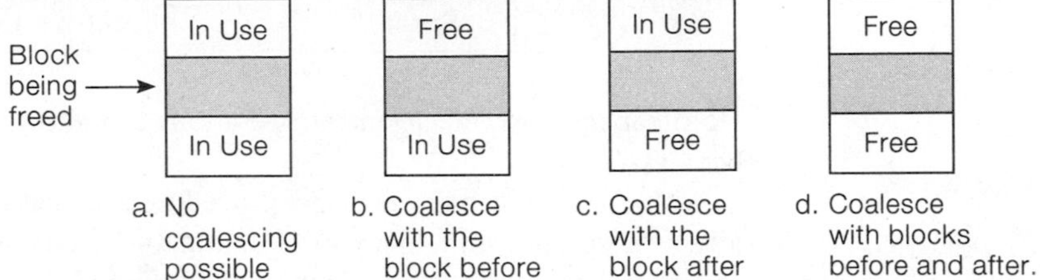

If cases *b* or *c* occur, then the nodes describing the two free blocks will be combined into a single node. In case d, three nodes will be combined into a single node. Our Free procedure must correctly handle all four of these cases.

Finally, the Map procedure displays a nicely formatted table showing the location of all memory blocks along with their status and the total percentage of memory currently in use.

When we design the List structure for this application, two concerns will influence our decision. First, we probably will not want to start from the head node each time we search for a free block. If we did, most of the InUse blocks would cluster near the beginning of the memory and our search would have to pass through these blocks before getting to the available space. This searching could slow down the Allocate process. For example, with the following memory allocation

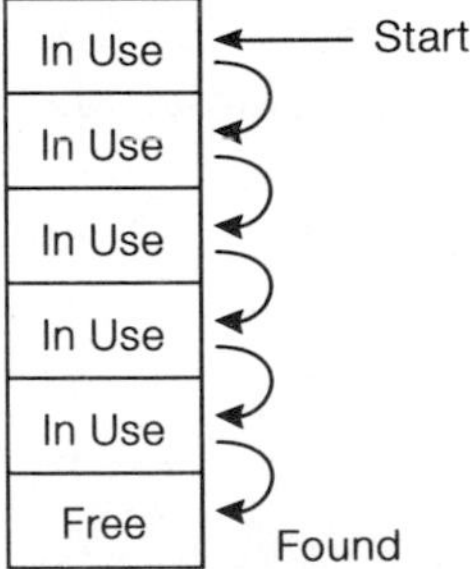

we would have to look through five InUse blocks before we came to the first Free block. A better system would be to have a pointer called StartSearch that points to the block descriptor of the last free block allocated. Then we begin from StartSearch instead of Head when we do an Allocate operation, and we search our list in a circular fashion. This method should help distribute the free blocks more evenly through memory and help speed up the search process.

A second issue is the problem of coalescing blocks. As we have mentioned, a block may be coalesced with one either before it or after it. Therefore, having pointers only in the forward direction will not be adequate—we would be able to find the memory block after the current one, but we would have great difficulty finding its predecessor. Instead, we need pointers to both the block immediately before and the block immediately after the current one.

These two issues lead us to the conclusion that our memory manager data structure should be a *doubly linked circular list* of the type discussed in section 4.5.2 and diagrammed in Figure 4–29. The declarations to create our block descriptor list is given below:

```
Const
    LastMemoryAddress = . . . ;          (* Set to the highest address in
                                            memory. *)
Type
    NodePtr  : Pointer To Node;
    HeadPtr  : Pointer To HeadRecord;
    (* This is the declaration of a node in the list. *)
    Node = Record
                 StartingAddress   : 0..LastMemoryAddress;
                 BlockSize   : Integer;
                 Status      : (Free, InUse);
                 NextBlock   : NodePtr;       (* successor *)
                 PreviousBlock   : NodePtr    (* predecessor *)
           End;

    (* This is the declaration for the header record of the list. *)
    HeadRecord = Record
                       First          : NodePtr;
                       StartSearch    : NodePtr;
                       CurrentPositionPointer   : NodePtr
                 End;
Var
    MemoryList   : HeadPtr;              (* The Head of the block *)
```

Figure 4–30 shows the implementation of the four procedures Initialize, Allocate, Free, and Map using the doubly linked circular list declarations just given. In addition to handling the memory management responsibilities, the procedure also detects the following three error conditions:

1. Illegal parameter to Allocate ($N > \text{MemorySize}$ or $N \leq 0$)
2. Insufficient free memory available to satisfy a request
3. Address of block being freed not currently allocated

If any of these conditions occur, the procedure sets a global error flag called Error and returns. We assume that this error condition will be handled by some other component of the operating system not shown here.

4.7 CONCLUSION

This completes our introduction to the class of linear data structures. We have seen and studied a number of different linear structures—Arrays, Strings, Stacks, Queues, Deques, Lists, Circular Lists, Doubly Linked Lists, and Circular Doubly

Figure 4–30
Memory Management Procedures

```
(*  The following module contains routines for managing the allocation of the
    memory of a computer system. Note that the following constants are assumed
    to be defined:
        LastMemoryAddress,
        MinBlockSize  *)
Module MemoryManager;
Type
    (* Memory addresses are represented as integers. *)
    AddressType = -1 .. LastMemoryAddress;
    (* Note that -1 is an illegal address and is only used to signal errors. *)

    (* The following are declarations for nodes in the list of memory block
    descriptors. Each node represents one block of either free or
    allocated memory. *)
    NodePtr = Pointer To Node;
    Node    = Record
                (* First address in the block *)
                StartingAddress : AddressType;
                (* The size in words of the block *)
                BlockSize : Integer;
                (* Whether or not the block has been allocated *)
                Status : (Free, InUse);
                NextBlock   : NodePtr;
                PreviousBlock  : NodePtr;
                  End;

    (* The following declarations describe the header node for the
    memory descriptor block Linked List. *)
    HeadPtr      = Pointer To HeadRecord;
    HeadRecord =
        Record
            First          : NodePtr;        (* The first node in the List *)
            StartSearch  : NodePtr;        (* Where, in the List, to start searching
                                               for the next free block *)
            CurrentPositionPointer : NodePtr;
        End;

    (* Possible errors resulting from operations of the memory manager *)
    MemoryErrorTypes = (None, IllegalParameter,
                NotEnoughMemory, BlockNotAlloc);

Var
    (* The head node for the Linked List describing memory *)
    MemoryList        : HeadPtr;
    Error             : MemoryErrorTypes;

(* The procedure Initialize sets up the Linked List describing memory.
KernelSpace words at the beginning of memory are reserved for the operating
system. No other calls to the memory manager can be made successfully until
Initialize has been called. *)
Procedure Initialize();
```

(continued)

Figure 4–30 (continued)

```
Var
    (* Pointer to the node for the operating system (O.S.) space *)
    KernelMemPtr   : NodePtr;
    (* Pointer to the node for the rest of memory *)
    FreeMemPtr     : NodePtr;

Begin
    New(KernelMemPtr);                      (* Allocate space for the two *)
    New(FreeMemPtr);                        (* nodes. *)

    KernelMemPtr^.StartingAddress := 0;     (* The O.S. space starts at
                                            address 0. *)
    KernelMemPtr^.BlockSize := KernelSpace; (* Reserve KernelSpace words. *)
    KernelMemPtr^.Status := InUse;          (* This space can never
                                            be freed. *)

    (* The free space starts just after the O.S. space. *)
    FreeMemPtr^.StartingAddress := KernelSpace;
    (* And takes up the rest of memory. *)
    FreeMemPtr^.BlockSize := LastMemoryAddress - KernelSpace;
    FreeMemPtr^.Status := Free;                 (* This space is available. *)

    KernelMemPtr^.NextBlock := FreeMemPtr;      (* Link nodes together *)
    KernelMemPtr^.PreviousBlock := FreeMemPtr;  (* in a Circular *)
    FreeMemPtr^.NextBlock := KernelMemPtr;      (* Doubly Linked List. *)
    FreeMemPtr^.PreviousBlock := KernelMemPtr;

    New(MemoryList);                            (* Allocate space for the
                                                header node. *)
    MemoryList^.First := KernelMemPtr;          (* O.S. space is at beginning
                                                of List. *)

    (* This is the only place to get memory. *)
    MemoryList^.StartSearch := FreeMemPtr;

    Error := None;
End Initialize;

(*  The procedure Allocate takes a parameter, Size, and attempts to find
    a free space in memory equal to, or larger than Size words. If it can
    find a suitable space, it allocates Size words and returns a pointer
    to the block. If there is no suitable space, it sets a global error
    flag and returns zero. Note that Allocate never leaves blocks of
    less than MinBlockSize words lying around.   *)
Procedure Allocate( Size : Integer ) : AddressType;
Var
    Ptr        : NodePtr;
    NewNode    : NodePtr;
    Addr       : AddressType;

Begin
    If (Size < 1) Or (Size > LastMemoryAddress) Then
        (* You can't allocate less than one word or more than
        the total amount of memory in the system. *)
        Error := IllegalParameter;
        Return;
    Endif;
```

(continued)

Figure 4–30 (continued)

```
(* Start searching for the next block where the last allocation left off.   *)
Ptr := MemoryList^.StartSearch;
While ((Ptr^.Status = InUse) Or (Ptr^.BlockSize < Size)) And
          (Ptr^.NextBlock <> MemoryList^.StartSearch) Do
      Ptr := Ptr^.NextBlock;
   Endwhile;

   If (Ptr^.Status = Free) And (Ptr^.BlockSize >= Size) Then
      (* We've found a free block that's large enough. *)

      If ((Ptr^.BlockSize - Size) < MinBlockSize) Then
            (* Just allocate the whole thing. *)
         Ptr^.Status := InUse;
         MemoryList^.StartSearch := Ptr;
      Else
      (* The free block is big enough, so just allocate part of it. *)
         New(NewNode);
         NewNode^.Status := Free;
         NewNode^.StartingAddress := Ptr^.StartingAddress + Size;
         NewNode^.BlockSize := Ptr^.BlockSize - Size;
         NewNode^.PreviousBlock := Ptr;
         NewNode^.NextBlock := Ptr^.NextBlock;
         Ptr^.NextBlock^.PreviousBlock := NewNode;
         Ptr^.NextBlock := Ptr;
         Ptr^.Status := InUse;
         Ptr^.BlockSize := Size;
         MemoryList^.StartSearch := NewNode;
      Endif;

      Addr := Ptr^.StartingAddress;
      Error := None;

   Else     (* There wasn't a free block that was large enough. *)
         Addr := -1;
         Error := NotEnoughMemory;
   Endif;

   Return Addr;
End Allocate;

(*   Procedure Free locates the memory block whose base address is zero, and
     returns it to the free pool. If there is not such memory block, Free
     sets the error flag and returns.   *)
Procedure Free ( Addr : AddressType );
Var
   FreePtr   : NodePtr;
   Ptr   : NodePtr;
Begin
   FreePtr := MemoryList^.Head^.Next;   (* Start searching for the block at
                                           the node following the kernel space
                                           (the kernel space cannot be freed). *)

   While (FreePtr^.StartingAddress <> Addr) And
            (FreePtr <> MemoryList^.Head) Do
      FreePtr := FreePtr^.Next;
   Endwhile;
```

(continued)

Figure 4–30 (continued)

```
If (FreePtr = MemoryList^.Head) Or (FreePtr^.Status = Free) Then
        Error := BlockNotAlloc;                (* The block referred to is not the base
                                                  address of a block, or the block has
                                                  not been allocated. *)
        Return;
    Endif;

    FreePtr^.Status := Free;                   (* Free the block. *)

    Ptr := FreePtr^.NextBlock;                 (* Check the next block. *)
    If (Ptr^.Status = Free) Then               (* If it is also free . . . *)
        FreePtr^.BlockSize := FreePtr^.BlockSize + Ptr^.BlockSize;
        FreePtr^.NextBlock := Ptr^.NextBlock;      (* Merge the two *)
        Ptr^.NextBlock^.PreviousBlock := FreePtr;  (* free blocks into *)
        Dispose(Ptr);                              (* one large free block *)
    Endif;

    Ptr := FreePtr^.PreviousBlock;                 (* Similarly, check the
                                                      previous block. *)
    If (Ptr^.Status = Free) Then                   (* If it is also free, Merge *)
        FreePtr^.BlockSize := FreePtr^.BlockSize + Ptr^.BlockSize;
        FreePtr^.PreviousBlock := Ptr^.PreviousBlock;
        Ptr^.PreviousBlock^.NextBlock := FreePtr;
        Dispose(Ptr);
    Endif;

End Free;

(*  Procedure Map displays the current state of the memory of the system.
    For each block of memory, it displays three columns of information:
        (1) the base address of the block;
        (2) the size of the block; and
        (3) whether the block is free or in use.  *)
Procedure Map();
Var
    Ptr : NodePtr;
Begin
    Ptr := MemoryList^.Head;        (* Start at the beginning of memory. *)

    Repeat
        (* Display the base address and size of current block,
            using ten columns for each number *)
        Write(Ptr^.StartingAddress : 10, Ptr^.BlockSize : 10);

        (* Display whether the block is free or in use. *)
        If (Ptr^.Status = Free) Then
            WriteLn('Free');
        Else
            WriteLn('In Use');
        Endif;

        Ptr := Ptr^.Next;           (* Move on to next block *)
                                    (* until we have gone through all of memory *)
    Until (Ptr = MemoryList^.Head);
End Map;

End MemoryManager.
```

Linked Lists—and we have investigated different ways to implement these structures, including array- and pointer-based techniques.

As was the case with stacks and queues, list structures are not just a textbook curiosity but a fundamentally important representation in computer science. In fact, they could be considered the most important linear structure because, as we showed in section 4.2.2, they can be used as building blocks to construct all other linear types. In programming languages such as LISP (an acronym for LISt Processing) and Prolog, the List is the *only* data structure available to the programmer. These languages do not support the familiar data structures that we have come to expect in every language, e.g, the array and the record. Instead, the LISP programmer must express the solution to a problem only in terms of list operations similar to those described in section 4.1.2.

For example, the following functions are all primitive operations in LISP, a language widely used for solving problems in artificial intelligence (L is a list):

Car(L)	This function returns the first element of the list L. If L = (1, 2, 3) then Car(L) is the value 1.
Cdr(L)	This function returns the list that remains after the first element has been removed. If L = (1, 2, 3) then Cdr(L) = (2, 3)
Cons(L1,L2)	This function places the items in L1 at the front of L2 to produce a new list. If L1 = (1, 2) and L2 = (3, 4) then Cons(L1, L2) = (1, 2, 3, 4)

These operations should look familiar to anyone who has read this chapter and studied the ideas that we have presented. For example, The Car(L) function of LISP produces the same result as the nested calls Retrieve(First(L)). Similarly, the list returned by the function Cdr(L) is identical to the one produced by the nested calls Delete(First(L)). Obviously, anyone planning on using LISP (or a similar language) needs to be familiar with and knowledgeable of the list data structure and the fundamental set of list operations.

CHAPTER EXERCISES

1. Is a linear list as defined in section 4.1.1 a random-access data structure? Justify your answer.
2. In section 4.1.2 we described the syntax and the semantics of our eleven list operations using natural language. Convert them to the formal syntactic and semantic notation introduced in chapter 2. You may wish to introduce some additional functions to help you describe the semantics.
3. Referring to the list operations given in the external module of Figure 4–5, propose some additional positioning, insertion, deletion, and retrieval operations that you think would be useful to include. For each new operation, give the syntax, semantics, and pre- and postconditions for that operation.
4. Referring to Figure 4–1, why would it be difficult to implement the following operation as part of the List package:

(* *Precondition:* *L is a nonempty list*
P is non-null
Postcondition: *L is unchanged*
P points to the predecessor of N. If P initially pointed to the first node of L, it is now set to null. *)
Procedure *Before(L : LinearListType);*

5. Assume that we have created a list L. Write a function called Find that imports the resources of the external module of Figure 4–5 to locate a specific element in the list. The calling sequence for Find is

   (* *Find will search through list L looking for the first occurrence of Item. The return value is the position number of the node where Item occurs. If Item does not occur anywhere in L, the function returns a 0.* *)
   Procedure *Find(L : LinearListType; Item : Element) : Integer;*

6. Write a procedure called Concatenate that merges two lists into a single list. The calling sequence is

   (* *Precondition:* *L1 is a list of length m, m ≥ 0*
   L2 is a list of length n, n ≥ 0
   Postcondition: *L1 is a list of length (m + n), with all the elements of L2 added after elements of L1. L2 becomes the empty list.* *)
   Procedure *Concatenate(***Var** *L1 : LinearListType;* **Var** *L2 : LinearListType);*

   Use the resources of the external module in Figure 4–5. The behavior of Concatenate is shown below.

Before concatenation

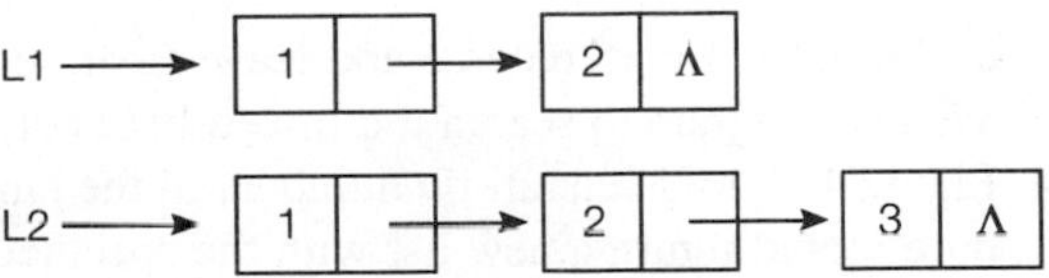

After concatenation

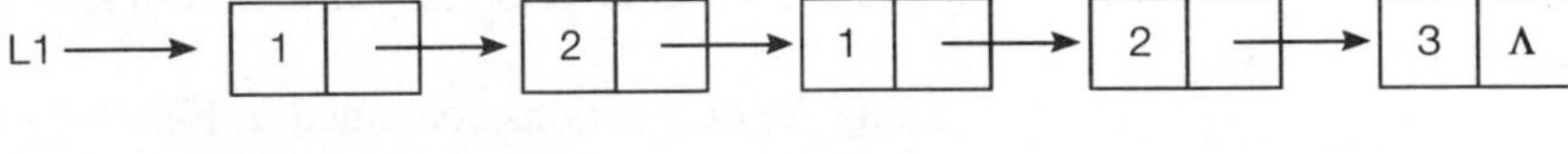

L2 **Nil**

7. Why do we need both an InsertFirst and an InsertAfter procedure in the Linear List package of Figure 4–5?
8. Why do we *not* need a procedure called InsertLast(L,I) that inserts a new node containing I as the last node of list L?
9. Assume that we implemented our linear list structure using the following one-dimensional array declaration:

```
Type
    LinearListType      = Array [1 .. 100] Of Element;
    Pointer             = 0 .. 100;
Var
    L       : LinearListType;
    P       : Pointer;      (* This is the current position pointer. *)
```

Using these declarations, implement the InsertAfter and Delete operations of Figure 4–5. Describe why it was cumbersome to use this array structure.

10. Assume that we had a pointer variable declared as

```
Type
    X = Pointer To Y;
    Y = Record
            A  : Integer;
            B  : Array [1 .. 3] Of Real;
            C  : X
        End;
Var
    Head  : X;
```

Show how to perform the following operations:

a. Generate a new record of type Y and put a pointer to it in Head.
b. Set the field A of the record to 0.
c. Set the field B of that record to 1.0, 1.0, 1.0.
d. Generate another new record that is linked to the first one. The values in the second record should be
   A = 3
   B = 2.0, 2.0, 2.0
   C = **Nil**
e. Dispose of both records and leave Head set to **Nil**.

11. Write a program to search the linked list of student ID numbers coded in Figure 4–9 to delete all ID numbers in the range [Low .. High]. The procedure should return a new list with the specified nodes removed. The calling sequence is

```
Procedure RemoveRange(Var List : Student; Low, High : Integer);
```

12. Using the declarations contained in Figure 4–10, write procedures to implement the nine operations in the linear list package that were not implemented in section 4.2.2. When all the modules are coded, write a client module to test your completed package.
13. Show how the following stack operations could be implemented in terms of the List operations of Figure 4–5.
   a. Pop(S,X)   (* This Pop saves the top element of S in X. *)
   b. Top(S,X)
   c. Full(S)
   d. Empty(S)

14. Show how the following queue operations can be implemented in terms of the List operations of Figure 4–5.
    a. Dequeue(Q,X) (* This Dequeue saves the first element of Q in X. *)
    b. First(Q,X)
    c. Full(Q)
    d. Empty(Q)
15. Given a list L of integers

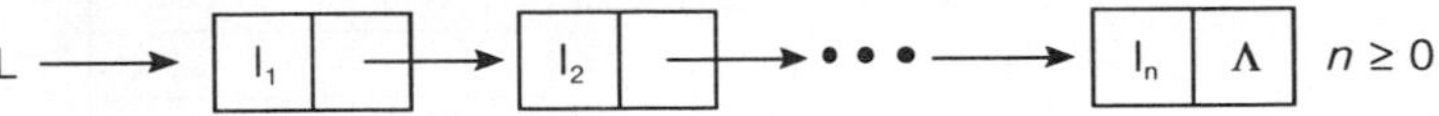

write a procedure called InOrder(L,Sw) that compares adjacent node values and ensures that the second value is greater than or equal to the first for all node pairs. That is, $I_k \leq I_{k+1}$, $k = 1, 2, \ldots, n-1$. If the list satisfies this condition, then set Sw = True; otherwise set Sw = False. Be very careful about both empty lists and attempting to dereference the **Nil** pointer.

16. Using the declarations given in Figure 4–10, write a procedure to *reverse* a list. That is, if L has the initial value

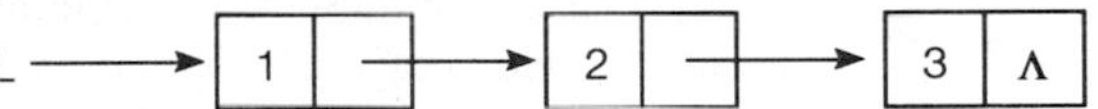

a call to Reverse should produce the new list

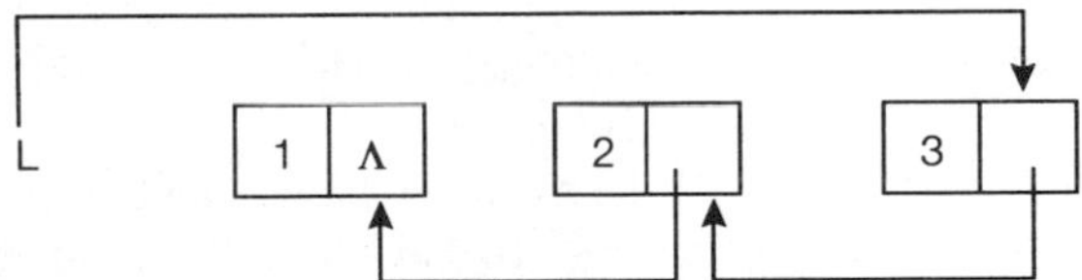

17. Using the declarations given in Figure 4–10, write a procedure to *sort* a list into ascending order. That is, if L has the initial value

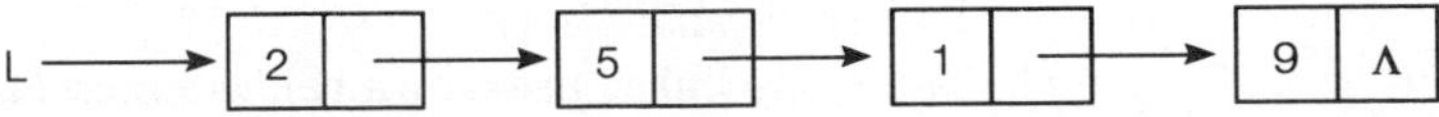

a call to Sort should produce the new list

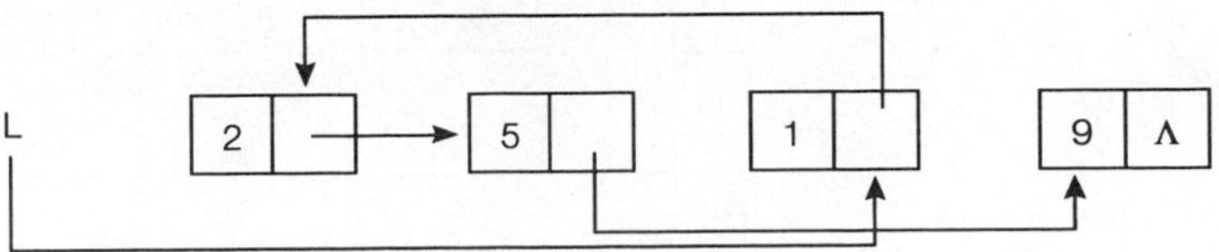

18. Draw the box diagram of the List represented by the following array:

1	2	8
2	9	0
3	15	6
4	12	2
5	-8	4
6	0	0
7	10	3
8	65	5

First = 1
Last = 2
Available =7

19. Using the array declarations in section 4.2.3, implement the following list operations using a two-dimensional array. Be sure to account for the possibility that the list is full.
    a. InsertAfter(L,I)
    b. Size(L)
    c. Retrieve(L)
20. Write the declarations to create the linked list implementation of a String abstract data type as shown in Figure 4–14. Then write procedures to implement the following string operations:
    a. PatternMatch(S_1, S_2, N). Return the index N of the first occurrence of substring S_2 in string S_1.
    b. FindAndReplace(S_1, S_2, S_3). Find the first occurrence of substring S_2 in string S_1 and replace that occurrence by substring S_3.
21. Why would the linked list implementation of a stack be preferred over the Array implementation? What would be a drawback of the linked list implementation?
22. Finish the implementation module for the stack whose external module is given in Figure 3–16 and whose Push and Pop routines are shown in Figures 4–20 and 4–21. To finish it, you will need to write the code for Create, Full, Empty, and Top.
23. Finish the implementation module for the queue whose external module is given in Figure 3–21 and whose Enqueue and Dequeue routines are shown in Figures 4–23 and 4–24. You will need to code the five routines Create, First, Last, Full, and Empty.
24. The singly linked list shown below represents a queue with separate Front and Rear pointers.

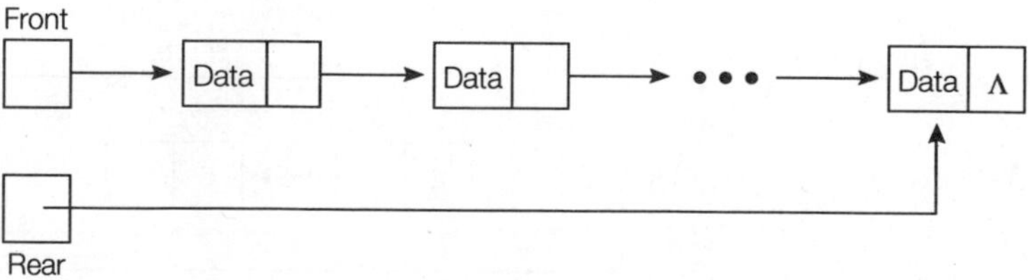

Show that only one of the pointers Front and Rear is necessary if the queue is represented as a singly linked circular list. Write a procedure to dequeue an element from a circular queue.

25. Write the procedure called ReturnResource, which frees the resources allocated by the GetResource procedure of Figure 4–26. ReturnResource(L,P) is given a list L and a pointer P to a node of L. ReturnResource sets the status field of that node back to Free.
26. Using the doubly linked list structure declarations described in section 4.5.2, write a procedure called Back(n), which moves you backward n nodes in the list. That is, you will move the current position pointer P to the nth predecessor of the current node. If there are not n predecessors of the current node (i.e., we encounter a **Nil** pointer), then reset P to **Nil**.
27. Repeat Exercise 26 using a circular doubly linked list. Now there is no problem with special cases and not having the proper number of predecessors. We simply move "left" n positions from our current location as specified by the current position pointer.
28. Recode the memory manager program so that it uses a *best fit* rather than a first fit algorithm. The best fit says that we search the entire list looking for the free block that most closely matches the size of the block being requested. That is, we find a block of size M, $M \geq N$, which minimizes the value $M - N$, where N is the size of the user request.
29. A classic example of the use of linked lists is the representation and manipulation of polynomials. A polynomial is a mathematical formula of the following form:

$A_nX^n + A_{n-1}X^{n-1} + \ldots + A_1X + A_0$ $\quad$ A_i are Real coefficients

This formula can be represented by a list using the node structure shown below. Each node will store the information about one nonzero term of the polynomial.

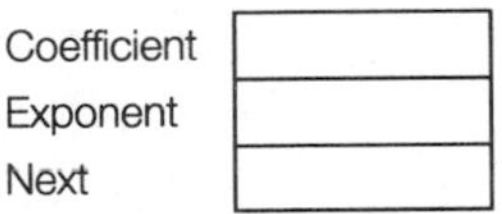

This method allows us to efficiently represent polynomials of arbitrarily large degree. For example, the polynomial

$5X^{20} + 2X - 5$

is a 20th degree polynomial, but it has only three nonzero terms. Its linked list representation will have only three nodes and would be represented as follows:

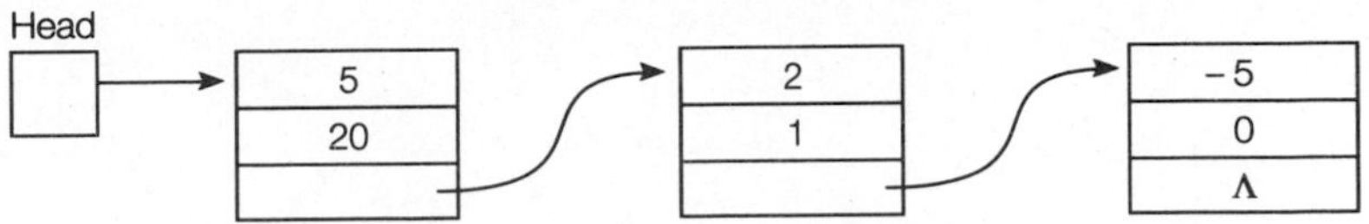

Write a polynomial external module. It should create an abstract data type called Poly and operations to Read, Write, Add, and Subtract polynomials. Now implement Poly using the linked list technique just described. Try out your package using the polynomials

$$A = X^5 + X^3 + X^2 - 5$$

$$B = 3X^4 + 2X^3 - X^2 - 6$$

for the following three problems:

a. $A + B$
b. $A - B$
c. $2A$

CHAPTER 5

RECURSION

CHAPTER OUTLINE

5.1 Introduction
5.2 The Basic Concepts of Recursive Algorithms
5.3 How Recursion is Implemented
5.4 Examples
    5.4.1 Sequential Search of a Linked List
    5.4.2 Reversing a Linked List
    5.4.3 Recursive Binary Search
    5.4.4 MergeSort
    5.4.5 QuickSort
    5.4.6 Finding a Path Through a Graph
5.5 Conclusion

5.1 INTRODUCTION

This chapter introduces *recursion*, a problem-solving technique often used in computer science. *Recursion* defines a problem in terms of itself. A recursive solution repeatedly divides a problem into smaller and simpler subproblems until a directly solvable subproblem is reached. Once we obtain the solution to that solvable subproblem, we feed it back into the next larger subproblem, thus obtaining its solution. This process continues until we ultimately solve the original problem. The following picture should help to clarify this idea.

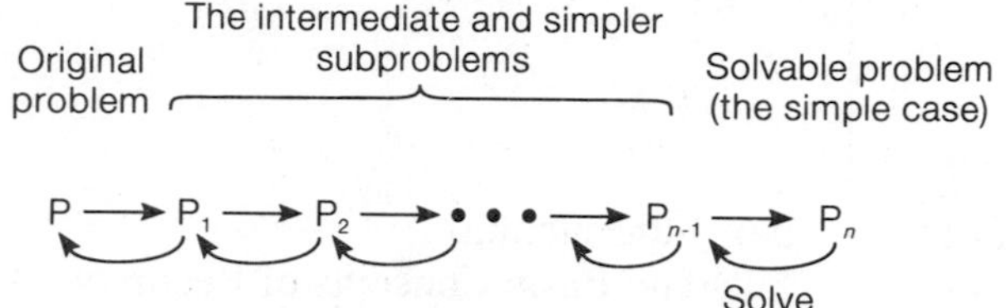

Our original problem P is redefined in terms of subproblem P_1, a simpler version of P. P_1, in turn, is redefined in terms of P_2, a simpler version of P_1. This simplification process continues until we reach P_n, which is a problem that is so simple it can be solved without further simplification. The solution to P_n is then fed back into problem P_{n-1} to solve it. That solution is fed back into $P_{n-2}, \ldots, P_2, P_1$ until we finally have solved our original problem P.

As an example, consider how you would define the term *ancestor*. Your parent is your ancestor, so is your grandparent, your great-grandparent, and so forth. But how do you write a good definition of this term without using either . . . or a phrase like "and so forth"? There is an elegant solution that uses the technique of recursion:

An ancestor is either your parent or an ancestor of your parent.

Notice that we have defined the problem in terms of a simpler version of itself. To determine if A is the ancestor of B, we need only determine if A is either the parent of B or the ancestor of the parent of B, a gap that is one generation smaller. How do we answer that new question? We repeat that same process and determine if A is either the grandparent of B or the ancestor of the grandparent of B, a gap that is two generations smaller. Eventually we will get an answer because A will be the parent of the person we are checking or we will come to the oldest person in the family tree.

Another example, more relevant to computer science, is the use of recursion to specify the syntax of programming languages. For example, in most high-level languages, an identifier is defined as any arbitrarily long sequence of letters or digits that begins with a letter. How do we express this definition in a formal manner? If we start by trying to exhaustively list all possible formats:

<Identifier> ::= <Letter>	(* <Letter> is any character A–Z or a–z. *)
<Identifier> ::= <Letter> <Letter>	(* ::= means "is defined as" *)
<Identifier> ::= <Letter> <Digit>	(* <Digit> is any character 0–9. *)

<Identifier> ::= <Letter> <Letter> <Letter>
<Identifier> ::= <Letter> <Letter> <Digit>

•
•
•

we quickly realize that this task is impossible because the length of an identifier is unbounded. Even if the length were finite, the number of combinations of letters and digits grows exponentially and even for small values is too large to exhaustively enumerate.

A simpler way to solve the problem is to use the concept of recursion. We are trying to describe an arbitrarily long string of letters and digits. Note that if we remove the first character from that string we are still left with a string of letters and digits, but one character shorter! This realization forms the basis of a recursive solution to our problem.

Rule 1: <Identifier> ::= <Letter> <LetterDigitString>

This rule says that an identifier is defined as a single letter (A–Z or a–z) followed by a syntactic construct called <LetterDigitString> which is just any string of letters and digits. Of course, that string can be empty (i.e., there can be one-letter identifiers), so we add this rule:

Rule 2: <LetterDigitString> ::= "empty" (* The empty string *)

<LetterDigitString> can also be any arbitrarily long string of letters or digits. This idea can be expressed by the following rules:

Rule 3: <LetterDigitString> ::= <Letter> <LetterDigitString>
Rule 4: <LetterDigitString> ::= <Digit > <LetterDigitString>
Rule 5: <Letter> ::= A | B | C | . . . | Z
Rule 6: <Digit> ::= 0 | 1 | 2 | . . . | 9

Rules 3 and 4 use the idea of recursion, since they define the construct <LetterDigit String> in terms of itself. They say that a <LetterDigitString> is something that can begin with a letter or a digit and what follows that first letter or digit must itself be a valid <LetterDigitString>.

For example, to show that the string B3XY57Z is a valid <LetterDigitString> we must show that B is a valid letter or digit (it is) and that what follows, 3XY57Z, is a valid <LetterDigitString>. To solve that problem we repeat the recursive operation. We show that 3 is a valid letter or digit (it is) and that XY57Z is a valid <LetterDigitString>. We keep repeating this process, and eventually reach a situation where we have only one character left, Z, that we must show is a <LetterDigit String>. We can show this without further use of recursion. We show that Z is a valid letter (it is), and we show that what is left, the empty string, is a valid <Letter DigitString> by Rule 2 above. This step of the problem is the "simple case" referred to earlier. We now take this solution and work backwards through our subproblems to produce the solution to our original problem. Recursion has allowed us to define a complex idea—an infinite length sequence of letters and digits—using only six simple rules.

This use of recursive definitions is an essential part of the formal definition of the syntax of programming languages, and it is just one example of why recursion is such an important problem-solving tool in computer science.

This approach to problem solving might seem strange at first. In fact, in everyday conversation we explicitly try to avoid recursion and are irritated when we encounter it. We call it a circular definition, as in

A circle is something that has a circular shape.

or

Where is Mr. Jones' office?
Next to Ms. Smith's.
Where is Ms. Smith's office?
Next to Mr. Jones'!

However, in computer science such "circular definitions," if expressed properly, can be quite handy, and a careful study of recursive algorithms will show you the usefulness, power, and simplicity of recursion. This topic is usually mentioned only briefly in a first course in computer science, and the student gains only a vague understanding of recursion. This brief treatment can lead to the incorrect assumption that recursion is a specialized and unimportant topic, but this idea is absolutely untrue—recursion is a vital and fundamental problem-solving paradigm.

The objective of this chapter is to provide a variety of examples along with explanations to make you more comfortable in your ability to design and understand recursion. Recursive algorithms are especially useful in manipulating data structures that are themselves defined recursively. We will see many examples of this in chapter 7 when we introduce the data structure called a *tree*.

5.2 THE BASIC CONCEPTS OF RECURSIVE ALGORITHMS

Our first example will introduce you to some fundamental concepts of recursive programming. It involves the computation of n factorial, denoted mathematically as $n!$ Most people have seen a recursive definition for this value. Consider the following (incorrect) definition:

$$n! = n * (n - 1)!$$

This definition says that we obtain the value of $n!$ by taking the number n and multiplying it by $(n - 1)!$ To obtain the value of $(n - 1)!$, we use the definition again, substituting $n - 1$ for n; that is,

$$(n - 1)! = (n - 1) * (n - 2)!$$

Suppose we want to evaluate 2!. Our definition would lead to the following result:

$$\begin{aligned} 2! &= 2 * (2 - 1)! \\ &= 2 * 1! \\ &= 2 * 1 * (1 - 1)! \\ &= 2 * 1 * 0! \\ &= 2 * 1 * 0 * (0 - 1)! \\ &= 2 * 1 * 0 * (-1)! \\ &= \ldots \end{aligned}$$

We can immediately identify two major problems. The first and most serious is that we did not provide a way to stop the recursion. The second problem is that with this definition of $n!$ we have generated a multiplicand of zero; thus, for $n > 0$, $n!$ will always evaluate to zero.

The first problem is common to all recursive algorithms: there must always be a mechanism to stop the recursion from continuing forever, just as with iterative algorithms there must always be a way to exit a **Repeat** or **While** loop. To create such a mechanism, we need to divide a recursive definition into two cases: a *base case* and a *general case*. The base case is the nonrecursive definition that terminates the recursion. (We referred to it as the "simple case" in the preceding section.) The general case is the recursive part of the solution definition. In our factorial example, the base case is

$$0! = 1$$

Once the base case is defined, the general case can be specified as

$$n! = n * (n - 1)!$$

Both of these definitions are essential to the recursive solution. However, there is still one more condition that we must consider before this definition is precise.

According to our definition, what would $(-1)!$ be?

$$\begin{aligned} -1! &= -1 * (-2)! \\ &= -1 * (-2) * (-3)! \\ &= \ldots \end{aligned}$$

Once again, we have fallen prey to *infinite recursion*—a recursive evaluation that never terminates. The appropriate action here is to define factorials only for non-negative integers by augmenting the general case with the condition that $n > 0$. Now we have a precise, recursive definition of $n!$, namely,

$$\begin{array}{lll} 0! = 1 & & \text{(* The base case *)} \\ n! = n * (n - 1)! & n > 0 & \text{(* The general case *)} \end{array}$$

We are now ready for the implementation of $n!$. First, we define the type NaturalNumbers to be

```
Type
    NaturalNumbers = [1 .. MaxInt];        (* MaxInt is the largest integer value *)
```

Figure 5–1
Recursive Factorial Function

```
Procedure NFactorial ( n : Integer ) : NaturalNumbers;
Begin
    If (n < 0) Then                     (* This procedure handles the
        ErrorHandler();                 condition of a negative parameter
    Elsif (n = 0) Then                  to NFactorial. *)
        Return 1                        (* A *)
    Else
        Return n * NFactorial( n – 1 ); (* B *)
    Endif;
End NFactorial;
```

Using this type definition we can define the recursive function NFactorial. It is shown in Figure 5–1.

To understand how recursion works, it will be instructive to trace the execution of this function when called with NFactorial(3). To make the tracing clearer, we have labeled the **Then** and **Else** parts of the **If** statement with (* A *) and (* B *), respectively. We refer to the first call to the NFactorial procedure as being at Level 1. The next (recursive) call will be at Level 2, and so on. Therefore, to evaluate NFactorial(3) we proceed as follows:

Level 1: NFactorial(3)		
	Return 3 * NFactorial(2)	from (* B *)
Level 2: NFactorial(2)		
	Return 2 * NFactorial(1)	from (* B *)
Level 3: NFactorial(1)		
	Return 1 * NFactorial(0)	from (* B *)
Level 4: NFactorial(0)		
	Return 1	from (* A *)

At this point in the evaluation we have reached our base case and can evaluate NFactorial(0) without another recursive call. Its value is 1. We now "unwind" the recursion, that is, we complete the computations for the previously generated subproblems by evaluating the problems in the reverse order from the order in which they were generated:

Level 4: NFactorial(0) = 1

Level 3: NFactorial(1) = 1 * NFactorial(0)
= 1 * 1
= 1

Level 2: NFactorial(2) = 2 * NFactorial(1)
= 2 * 1
= 2

$$\text{Level 1:} \quad \text{NFactorial(3)} = 3 * \text{NFactorial(2)}$$
$$= 3 * 2$$
$$= 6$$

and we get the proper answer that $3! = 6$.

As a second example of a recursive algorithm, consider how one could sum the first n natural numbers:

$$\sum_{i=1}^{n} i = 1 + 2 + 3 + \ldots + n, \qquad n > 0$$

A recursive solution to this problem is to add n to the sum of all terms up to and including $n - 1$, as in

$$\sum_{i=1}^{n} i = n + \sum_{i=1}^{n-1} i \qquad n > 0$$

This expression defines the sum of the first n natural numbers in terms of n and the sum of the first $n - 1$ natural numbers, producing a recursive definition of the problem. However, as we showed in our first example, a recursive definition must be composed of two parts, the general case and a base case that will terminate the recursion. In this example, the base case is simply the sum of the first n natural numbers when $n = 1$. Clearly that sum is 1. Hence, the complete specification of our problem is

$$\sum_{i=1}^{n} i = 1 \qquad n = 1 \qquad \text{(* The base case *)}$$

$$\sum_{i=1}^{n} i = n + \sum_{i=1}^{n-1} i \qquad n > 1 \qquad \text{(* The general case *)}$$

Figure 5–2 shows a recursive function to solve this problem. Before leaving this example, we must point out that although this problem has led to a simple recursive

Figure 5–2
Recursive Function to Compute the Sum of the First *n* Natural Numbers

```
Procedure SumOfFirstNNaturalNumbers ( n : NaturalNumbers );
Begin
    If (n = 1) Then
        Return 1
    Else
        Return n + SumOfFirstNNaturalNumbers( n − 1 );
    Endif;
End SumOfFirstNNaturalNumbers;
```

formulation, one should never really use it! The expression has a closed-form solution called *Gauss' formula*:

$$\sum_{i=1}^{n} i = \frac{[n(n+1)]}{2}$$

this situation raises the entire issue of *efficiency*. Recursive algorithms are frequently quite short and elegant, but they may not be the quickest in terms of execution time or the most compact in terms of memory space. In this example, Gauss' formula is a far faster method than our recursive algorithm. There is also a more efficient way to compute factorials than the recursive algorithm of Figure 5–1. It is the following simple iterative solution:

```
Procedure NFactorial ( n : Integer ) : NaturalNumbers;
Var
    Value   : NaturalNumbers;
    i       : Integer;
Begin
    If (n < 0) Then
        ErrorHandler();              (* This procedure handles the condition of
                                     a negative parameter to NFactorial *)
    Else
        Value := 1;
        For i := n To 1 By -1 Do
            Value := Value * i;      (* Here is the iterative section *)
        Endfor;
        Return Value;
    Endif;
End NFactorial;
```

We will discuss the topic of efficiency in much greater detail in the next section.

As these first two examples have shown us, all recursive algorithms must be formulated in terms of a recursive general case and a nonrecursive base case. Application of the general case simplifies the problem and moves it toward the base case that terminates the recursion. You then unwind the recursion and solve all the recursively generated intermediate problems in the reverse order from the order in which they were created.

5.3 HOW RECURSION IS IMPLEMENTED

In the previous section we mentioned that inefficiency is one possible drawback in the use of recursion. Let us see why that is the case.

Whenever a procedure is called, the run-time system dynamically allocates memory space for the arguments of that procedure and all the local constants and variables declared within it. Space is also allocated to store the return address. All of this information about a procedure is collected and placed in a data structure called an *activation record* (abbreviated AR). The AR itself is placed in a data

Figure 5–3
Activation Record Structure

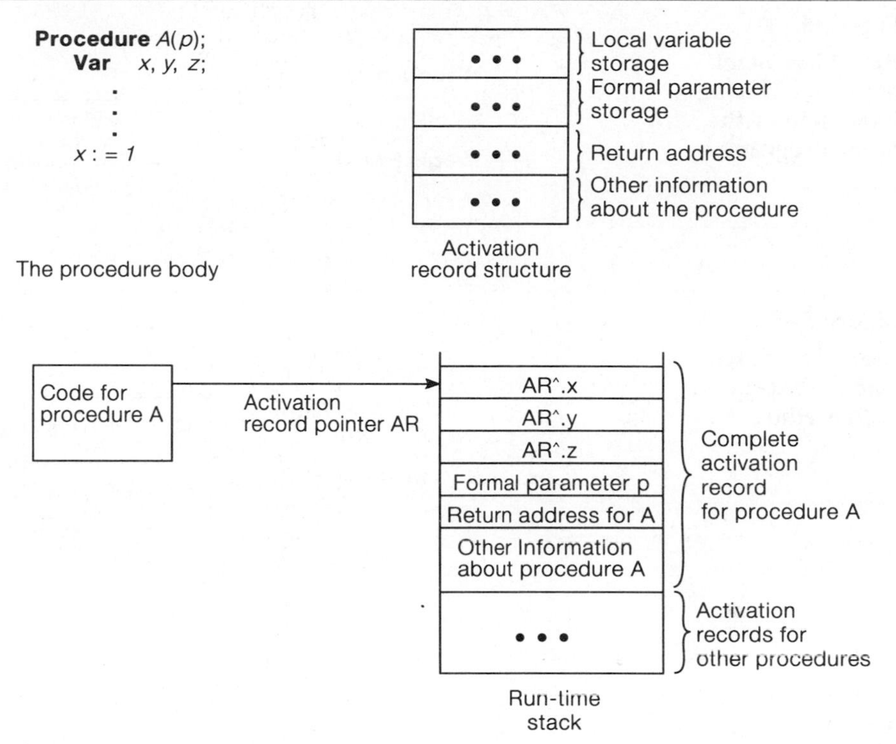

structure called the *run-time stack*. The run-time stack holds the activation record of every procedure that has been invoked but that has not yet been completed. For example, suppose a procedure references a local variable X, as in the assignment statement X := 1; when the code produced by the compiler is executed, it actually accesses the memory cell allocated for X within the current activation record of the procedure. Thus, the statement would effectively be compiled into AR^.X := 1 (see Figure 5–3).

The activation record of a procedure remains on the run-time stack until the procedure has been completed, at which time the record is released and the memory space is returned to the system. Since procedures are always exited in the reverse order from the order in which they are invoked, these activation records are kept on a stack structure of the type described in chapter 3. For example, when the Main program is executing the run-time stack contains only a single activation record, and it looks like Figure 5–4.

If Main then calls procedure A, we build an activation record for Procedure A and push it on top of the stack, as shown in Figure 5–5.

When procedure A has been completed, the activation record is popped off the stack, and its memory space returned to the system.

The size of an activation record can be quite large, depending on the number and type of parameters and on the number of local declarations within the procedure. For example, if a 1,000-element array is passed as a value parameter to a procedure, the activation record for that procedure would need to be large enough to

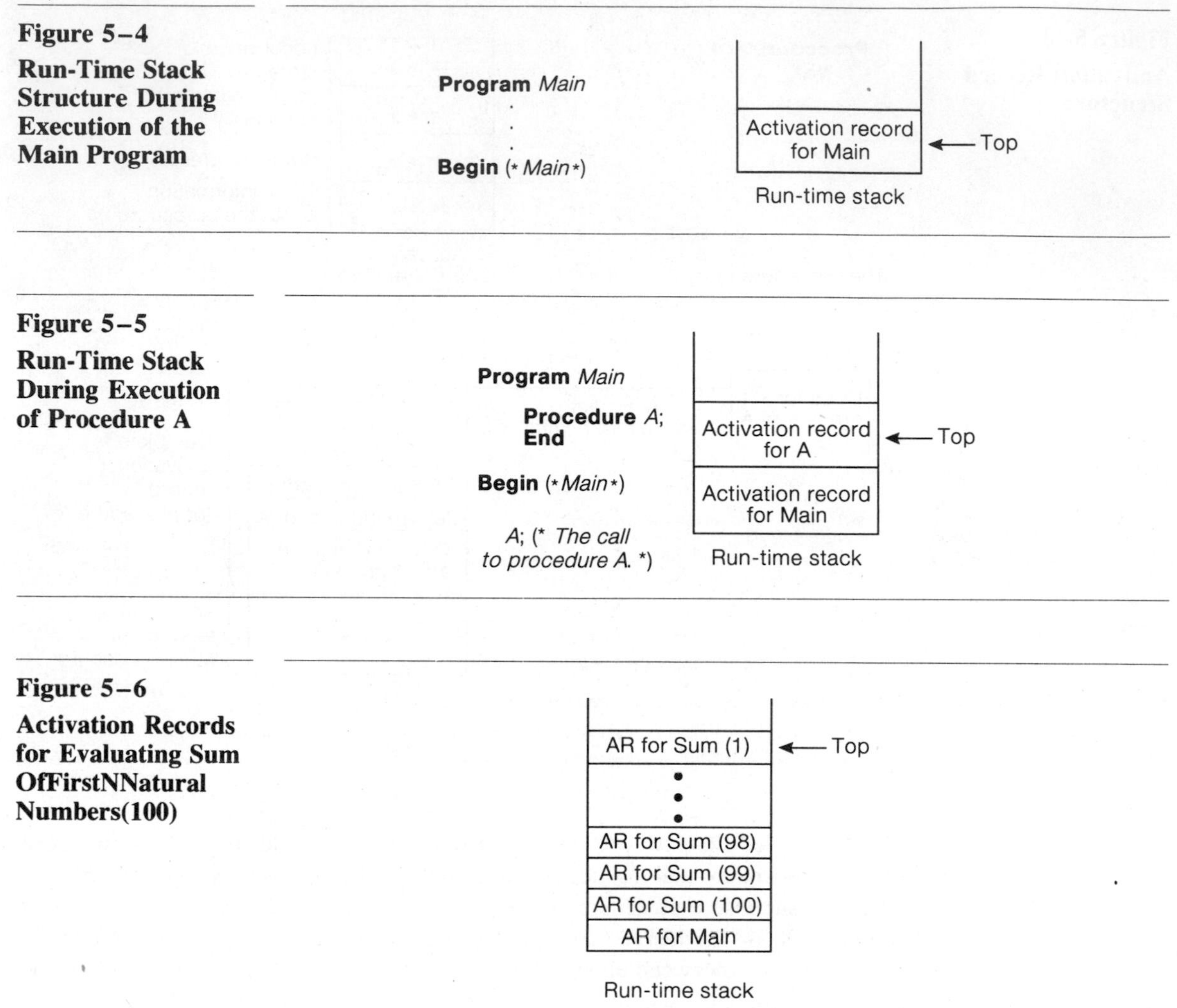

Figure 5–4 Run-Time Stack Structure During Execution of the Main Program

Figure 5–5 Run-Time Stack During Execution of Procedure A

Figure 5–6 Activation Records for Evaluating Sum OfFirstNNatural Numbers(100)

hold a copy of the entire array. Similarly, if the procedure creates dozens of local variables, the activation record will need to include space for all of them.

With iterative algorithms this is not usually a problem. The depth of procedure nesting (i.e., procedures invoked but not yet completed) is small, generally about 3 or 4 and rarely greater than 10 to 20. Thus, the number of activation records on the stack at any one time is not excessive. However, recursion is a different case altogether, since procedure activation is the primary iterative control structure. Every recursive call causes a new activation record to be created and placed on top of the run-time stack. For example, if we used the recursive function SumOfFirstNNaturalNumbers from Figure 5–2 to compute the value (1 + 2 + . . . + 100), the run-time stack would look like the one shown in Figure 5–6 when we reached the base case, Sum(1), and began to unwind the recursion.

As you can see from that figure, 100 copies of the activation record of the procedure SumOfFirstNNaturalNumbers were required to perform this computation. It is not uncommon when solving large problems recursively (e.g., 1 + 2 + . . . + 10,000) to run out of memory space building the activation records. It is also possible to exhaust the space allocated to the run-time stack and get a *stack overflow* error condition.

In addition to the potentially enormous space demands of recursive algorithms, there is also the issue of the time required to build the activation record when a procedure is invoked and return that space when it is completed. Procedure invocation involves a good deal of overhead, and it can be a time-consuming operation. Therefore, recursive algorithms that involve a great deal of procedure linkage can sometimes run more slowly than iterative algorithms that solve the same problem.

Recursion is an extremely powerful problem-solving technique. For certain classes of problems (especially those involving recursively defined data structures), it allows you to create highly elegant and compact solutions to complex problems. But, whenever you use recursion, you must be aware of the efficiency issues that we have discussed in this section. You should always evaluate whether an iterative algorithm (or some other technique) may be superior to recursion in a particular case.

5.4 EXAMPLES

The best way to become truly familiar and comfortable with recursion is not just to read about it but to see and study (and do!) a number of examples. In this section we present six recursive algorithms drawn from a range of areas of computer science including linked list operations, searching, sorting, and graph traversal. We will begin with some simple examples and build to include some interesting and complex functions. These examples will familiarize you with the steps involved in the design, development, and implementation of recursive procedures and functions.

5.4.1 Sequential Search of a Linked List

Our first example uses the Linked List data structure first introduced in chapter 4.

```
Type
    NodeRecord = Record
                     Data  : Integer;
                     Next  : Pointer To NodeRecord
                 End;

    List  : Pointer To NodeRecord;
```

We can picture this structure as

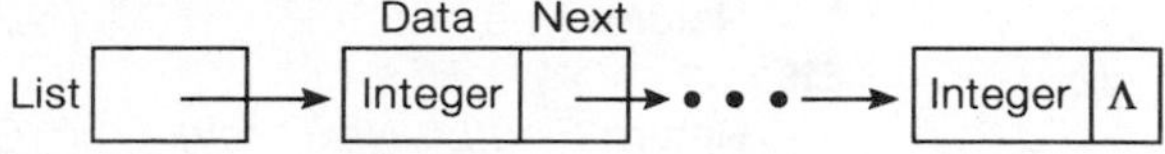

We want to design the recursive function

```
Function Find(L:List; Key:Integer) : Boolean;
```

which determines whether Key occurs anywhere within list L. If it does, we want the function to return the value True; otherwise we want it to return the value False.

Obviously Key could be the first item in the list, in which case the function returns True—this is the base case. But what do we do if Key is not the first item? The answer is simple: we search the list that remains after we remove the first item. This new list is simply the list returned by the nested function calls Delete(First(L)), where Delete and First are the functions included in the List ADT of chapter 4. This step is the general case. Informally, we can sketch out our recursive algorithm as follows:

```
Find(L,Key)
    If First(L) = Key Then                          (* Base case *)
        Return True
    Else
        Return (Find(Delete(First(L)), Key))        (* Recursive case *)
```

However, we are not finished. Our base case is applicable only if Key is found in the list. What if Key is not there? We will ultimately reach the end of the list and attempt to retrieve the value of First(L), but it does not exist, so the program will "blow up." Therefore we need a second base case that says we must return the value False if we reach the end of list L and have not found Key. The complete recursive definition of the function Find is

$$\text{Find(L,Key)} = \begin{cases} \text{True, if First(L) = Key} & \text{(* Base case 1 *)} \\ \text{False, if Next(L) = } \mathbf{Nil} & \text{(* Base case 2 *)} \\ \text{Find(Delete(First(L)), Key) otherwise} & \text{(* Recursive case *)} \end{cases}$$

The program to implement this recursive function is given in Figure 5–7.

We included this example primarily because it gives us a chance to apply recursion to the Linked List data structure described in chapter 4. However, the efficiency discussion in section 5–3 should warn us that recursion may not necessarily be the best way to solve this problem. There are two issues we must consider. The first issue is the potentially excessive number of activation records on the run-time stack (the situation diagrammed in Figure 5–6). If we have an *N*-item list and Key does

Figure 5–7
Recursive Search of a Linked List

```
Procedure Find( L : List; Key : Integer ) : Boolean;
Begin
    If (L = Nil) Then
        Return False;                  (* Base case 2 *)
    Endif;

    If (L^.Data = Key) Then
        Return True;                   (* Base case 1 *)
    Else
        Return Find(L^.Next, Key);     (* General case *)
    Endif;
End Find;
```

not occur until the Mth node, then we will have approximately M activation records on the run-time stack. If Key does not occur at all, we will have about N activation records on the stack. For realistic problems, M and N may be very large quantities, and the stack overflow situation discussed earlier could easily result.

Our recursive solution has a second problem—the requirement that we "unwind" our solution and solve all intermediate subproblems generated by our recursive approach. The following list shows the subproblems that will be generated by Find for a List containing N nodes with Key in position M:

Original Problem:	See if Key occurs anywhere in nodes 1 .. N of List.
Subproblem 1:	See if Key occurs anywhere in nodes 2 .. N of List.
Subproblem 2:	See if Key occurs anywhere in nodes 3 .. N of List.
•	
•	
•	
Subproblem (M−1):	See if Key occurs anywhere in nodes M .. N of List.

We have assumed that Key is the Mth item. At this point in the problem we will determine that Key does occur in the list (because it will be First(L)), and we will return the value True. We should be finished now, because the Key has been found. Because we are using recursion, however, we cannot quit. We must go back and solve all the intermediate problems that we generated. That is, we must return the value True for the $M - 2$ remaining subproblems, since if Key occurred in the portion of the sublist L[M .. N], it certainly occurred in sublists L[$M-1$ .. N], . . . , L[3 .. N], L[2 .. N], and finally, the original problem L[1 .. N]. The need to unwind the solutions is completely unnecessary in this case, and it leads to a relatively inefficient solution.

This type of recursion is called *tail recursion* because the recursive call occurs at the very end, or tail, of the problem; after the value of the recursive call has been determined, no further processing is done to that value except to pass it on to the next subproblem. Programs that use tail recursion can usually be implemented more efficiently using iteration, and in fact, some optimizing compilers automatically eliminate tail recursion (and replace it with iteration) when translating programs to machine language. For this problem an iterative approach, such as the following:

```
(* Assume that L initially points to the head of list L *)
Loop
    If L = Nil Then Return False;
    If L^.Data = Key Then Return True;
    L := L^.Next
End Loop
```

might work better on many systems.

5.4.2 Reversing a Linked List

In our first few examples there have been iterative solutions that are as good if not better than the recursive ones. In our next example, a recursive view of a problem leads to a very simple and elegant solution, while the corresponding iterative viewpoint may not give such clean and straightforward direction on how to design a solution.

Suppose we want to *reverse* a linked list. That is, given the list $1 \rightarrow 2 \rightarrow 3 \rightarrow 4$, we want to end up with a new list L* that contains $4 \rightarrow 3 \rightarrow 2 \rightarrow 1$. An iterative solution would be a bit messy and not at all obvious, and would involve a good deal of pointer juggling and **Nil** checking. (In fact, you might find it interesting to try to sketch out an iterative solution to this problem before reading on.)

In contrast, a recursive solution to the the list reversal problem is relatively easy to describe. Assume we start with the following four-element list L:

$$L = 1 \rightarrow 2 \rightarrow 3 \rightarrow 4$$

The result we want to produce is the list L* (for L reversed)

$$L^* = 4 \rightarrow 3 \rightarrow 2 \rightarrow 1$$

The first value in L* , 4, is the value previously located at the end of the original list L. Let's call this value Back(L). Our function Back takes a list L and returns the data value contained in the node at the end of list L. (If L is empty, then Back(L) is undefined.)

Back(L) : DataValue

Back(L) can be implemented quite easily using the List operations defined in chapter 4. It only involves retrieving the contents of the last node in list L.

Back(L) = Retrieve(Last(L))

The remainder of the reversed list L*, $3 \rightarrow 2 \rightarrow 1$, is simply the reverse of the list that remained after we removed the last item. Let us define a function called Rest(L) that returns a new list L′ that is the list L with the last node removed. Rest(L) is undefined if L is empty.

Rest(L) : L′

Rest will take a list L, remove the node Last(L), and return the list that remains. Using the List ADT operations presented in chapter 4, Rest(L) can be implemented quite simply as Delete(Last(L)). We can reverse the list L′ by using the Reverse function we are creating: Reverse(Rest(L)) which is just Reverse(Delete(Last(L))).

If we now concatenate these two pieces, we will have the desired list L*, which is L reversed. Pictorially,

L* = 4 ⟶ 3 ⟶ 2 ⟶ 1

Back(L) + Reverse (Rest(L))

(+ means concantenation)

The concatenation operation in the above diagram can be implemented using the procedure called InsertFirst from the List package of chapter 4. So we can now complete the definition of the general or recursive case of our Reverse function as follows:

Reverse(L) = Concatenate(Back(L),Reverse(Rest(L)))

or using only the operations from our List package:

Reverse(L) = InsertFirst(Retrieve(Last(L)), Reverse(Delete(Last(L))))

Recursion has led us to an elegant 1-line solution to a very difficult and tricky problem! Of course, this definition is not yet a complete program. We must also specify the base case that terminates the recursion. In this problem the base case is quite simple to describe; it would be reversing an empty list.

Reverse(L) = L if L is empty

5.4.3 Recursive Binary Search

The search algorithm of Figure 5–7 is an example of a *sequential search*. It involves looking at every item in a list or array in sequence (i.e., from X to Successor(X)) until we find what we want or we come to the end of the list. This technique is not very efficient, although if the items are in a totally random order we cannot do any better. A much improved approach, called a *binary search*, can be used if we know that the data items in the list are already sorted into ascending or descending order.

A binary search works by splitting the list we are searching, list L, into three pieces: the *middle item* L[middle], the *first part* of the list L[1 .. middle−1], and the *second part* of the list L[middle+1 .. *N*], as shown in Figure 5–8.

If the middle item L[middle] is equal to Key (the item we are looking for), then we have solved the problem. If they are not equal, we take advantage of the fact that we know the list is in sorted sequence. Let us assume that the elements of L are integers and that L is sorted into ascending sequence. If L[middle] > Key, we know that if Key is present, it must be in the first part of L, i.e., somewhere within L[1 .. middle−1]. If L[middle] < Key, we know that Key must occur in the second

Figure 5–8
The Splitting Operation in the Binary Search Process

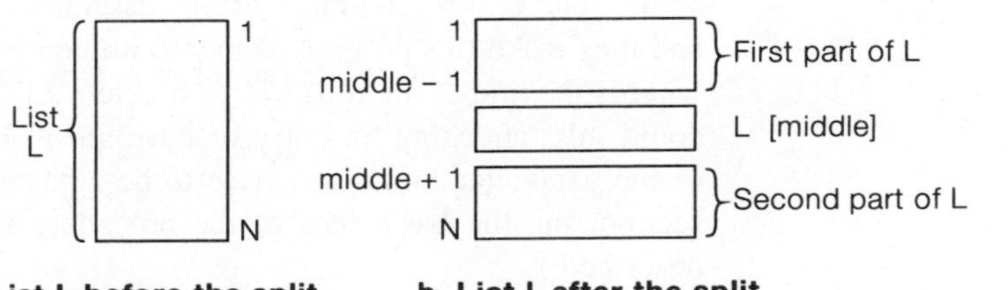

Figure 5–9
Recursive Binary Search

```
(* The Procedure BinarySearch searches the list L for an element Key
   in the range [Low .. Hi]. To call this procedure for the range [1 .. N]
   of the array L, invoke with:
      BinarySearch(L, 1, N, Key);   *)
Procedure BinarySearch( L : Array [1 .. N] Of Integer;
                        Low, Hi : Integer; Key : Integer ) : Boolean;
Var
   Mid : Integer;              (* This is the midpoint between Low and Hi. *)

Begin
   If (Low > Hi) Then
      (* The size of the list to search has become zero *)
      Return False;            (* so the element is not in the list. *)
   Endif;

   Mid := (Low + Hi) Div 2;    (* Calculate the midpoint. *)

   If (L[Mid] = Key) Then      (* Is this the correct element? *)
      Return True;             (* Yes, so return True. *)

   Elsif (L[Mid] < Key) Then   (* No, but it might be in upper half. *)
      Return BinarySearch(L, Mid+1, Hi, Key);

   Else                        (* L[Mid] > Key. It might be in lower half. *)
      Return BinarySearch(L, Low, Mid-1, Key);
   Endif;

End BinarySearch;
```

part of L, i.e., in L[middle+1 .. N]. In either case, we need to search only the proper half of the list.

The question now is, how do we search the first or second part of the list L? The answer is simple and, by now, not surprising—we use the binary search method just described! We simply invoke the binary search program with limits (1 .. middle−1) to search the first half of L or with limits (middle+1 .. N) to search the second half of L. This recursive call will repeat the splitting and comparing process diagrammed in Figure 5–8 until one of the following two base cases occurs: (1) we find what we are looking for and return the value True or (2) the length of the portion of the list we are searching becomes 0, in which case we return the value False.

A recursive binary search procedure that implements the method just described is shown in Figure 5–9. It assumes that the data are stored in an array rather than a list because of the difficulty of finding the middle item in a linked list. (There are some "picky" programming details associated with determining the middle item, and they make this program tricky to implement correctly. For example, if $N = 6$, what is the middle item of L[1 .. 6], item L[3] or L[4]? If we are not careful, we could miss checking an entry or have an off-by-one error. For this reason, some of the parameter limits will have to be adjusted from those we have given in this section, but the basic idea of the procedure BinarySearch is exactly as we have described.)

Unlike some of the examples from previous sections, efficiency is not a problem with the algorithm in Figure 5–9. Each time we do a splitting operation like the one

Figure 5–10
Model of the Divide and Conquer Technique

```
DivideAndConquer(Problem P)
    If P can be solved directly Then
        Return Solution(P)                        (* The base case *)
    Else
        Divide Problem P into subproblems P1 and P2
        S1 = DivideAndConquer(Problem P1)    (* S1 is the solution to P1 *)
        S2 = DivideAndConquer(Problem P2)    (* S2 is the solution to P2 *)
        Return (Merge(S1, S2))                    (* Merge combines the two partial
                                                     solutions *)
    End DivideAndConquer.
```

shown in Figure 5–8, we (roughly) halve the length of the list being searched. We repeat this until, in the worst case, the list is of length 0. The maximum number of recursive procedure calls required is $\log_2 N$, where N is the original list size. To search a list of length 1,000 would take no more than ten recursive calls ($2^{10} = 1{,}024$), and therefore our run-time stack would have no more than eleven activation records—ten recursive calls on BinarySearch plus the main program. Even a very large list of length 100,000 would require no more than seventeen recursive calls ($2^{17} = 128{,}000$). These are manageable numbers, and a recursive binary search of the type shown in Figure 5–9 is a popular and useful technique.

The binary search method we have just described is a good example of a powerful approach to problem-solving called *divide and conquer*. The basic idea behind divide and conquer is that if we do not know how to solve a given problem P, perhaps we can split P up (as we did in Figure 5–9) into two simpler problems, which we can call P_1 and P_2, solve each one of these smaller problems independently, and then *merge* or *join* these two solutions into the complete and final solution. This technique is modeled in Figure 5–10.

Notice that the divide-and-conquer method is inherently recursive as it calls itself for each of the two subproblems that it has generated. Also notice that, as with all recursion, we must have a base case to terminate the recursive process. The solution of the base case is specified by the **Then** clause of the **If** statement.

In the next section we will see an excellent example of this divide-and-conquer process applied to one of the most common problems in all of computer science—sorting.

5.4.4 MergeSort

Sorting is one of the most widely performed computer operations, and it occurs in a large number of applications. Teachers sort grades, scientists sort laboratory data, and business people sort payrolls; for the binary search method of Figure 5–9 to work correctly, the list L must be in sorted sequence.

There are many different sorting techniques available, and we will introduce and discuss a number of them in various places throughout this text. Here we introduce a recursive technique called MergeSort, which is based directly on the divide-and-conquer strategy outlined in Figure 5–10.

Figure 5–11
Outline of the MergeSort Technique

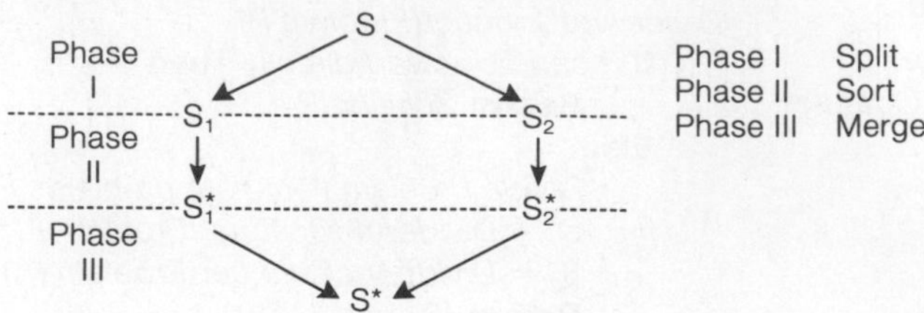

The basic idea behind MergeSort is to take a sequence S, split it into two approximately equal nonoverlapping subsequences, S_1 and S_2, and sort each one of those subsequences individually. After S_1 and S_2 have been sorted, we merge the two sorted sequences, called S_1^* and S_2^* into a single sorted sequence S*. This three-step MergeSort process is diagrammed in Figure 5–11.

To see how this method would work, assume S is the following sequence of integer values

$S = \{8, 1, 17, 19, 6, 18\}$

The split will produce the following two subsequences:

$S_1 = \{8, 1, 17\}$ $S_2 = \{19, 6, 18\}$ Phase I

We sort each subsequence, producing

$S_1^* = \{1, 8, 17\}$ $S_2^* = \{6, 18, 19\}$ Phase II

and now we implement a merge to produce

$S^* = \{1, 6, 8, 17, 18, 19\}$ Phase III

Phases I and III are quite straightforward and easy to understand. Therefore, the first question we must ask ourselves is how we implement Phase II, the sorting phase, which produces S_1^* and S_2^*. The answer is easy—we use MergeSort! We recursively call the MergeSort procedure twice, once with sequence S_1 and once with sequence S_2. These calls will result in execution of the entire split/sort/merge sequence for each of these two subsequences.

For example, the sequence $S_1 = \{8, 1, 17\}$ might be divided into the 2 sequences $S_{11} = \{8, 1\}$ and $S_{12} = \{17\}$. Notice that our sequences are getting smaller and our subproblems are getting simpler—the classic characteristic of recursion. The base case will simply be a request to sort a list with one element, like the sequence $S_{12} = \{17\}$. A one-element list is always sorted, so we simply return the list without having to make another recursive call. That is, $S_{12}^* = \{17\}$. The complete sequence of operations needed to sort our six-element sequence S would be:

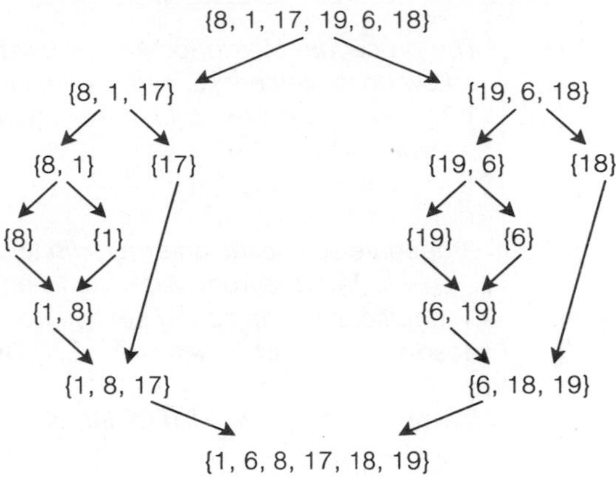

The basic logical structure of the MergeSort algorithm is sketched out below:

(Sort an N element sequence called S to produce the sorted sequence S*. *)*
MergeSort (S, N, S)*
If *N=1* **Then**
S is set equal to S and we return*
Else
Split S into two disjoint subsets S_1 and S_2, each with approximately N/2 elements *(*Phase I*)*
MergeSort (S_1, N/2, S_1)* *(* Phase II *)*
MergeSort (S_2, N/2, S_2)* *(* Phase II *)*
Join (S_1, S_2*, S*)* *(* Phase III *)*
End *MergeSort*

A procedure to implement this algorithm is given in Figure 5–12. MergeSort is a very efficient and very popular sorting technique that is widely used in computer science. It is the most complex recursive algorithm we have yet developed, and you should carefully review the program in Figure 5–12. It would also be a good idea to trace it with sample data sets to be sure that you fully understand it before continuing.

5.4.5 QuickSort

The MergeSort technique of the previous section is certainly popular, but it is not the most widely used sorting algorithm. That honor goes to an algorithm called QuickSort, first presented by Prof. C.A.R. Hoare of Oxford University in the mid-1960s and generally conceded to be, in terms of its average behavior and in some of its optimized variations, the fastest sorting algorithm yet developed.

The QuickSort algorithm selects one element from a sequence and refers to it as the *pivot*. The algorithm then splits the original sequence into two subsequences, in which all the elements in one subsequence are less than the pivot and all the elements in the other subsequence are greater than the pivot. These two subsequences may or may not be the same size. Ideally, about half the elements in the original

Figure 5–12
The MergeSort Procedure

```
(* The procedure MergeSort sorts the list L, beginning at element
   Low up to element Hi, into ascending order.
   To call this procedure for the entire range [1 .. N] of the array L,
   invoke with:
       MergeSort(L, 1, N);   *)

(* Procedure Join takes an array with two sorted subsections, from
   Low to Mid and from Mid+1 to Hi and merges the two subsections
   together into one sorted section from Low to Hi.   *)
Procedure Join( Var L : Array [1 .. N] Of Integer; Low, Hi, Mid : Integer );
Var
    Tmp : Array [Low .. Hi] Of Integer;   (* A temporary array for the sort *)
    Ins : Integer;                        (* Place in array Tmp to insert next
                                             sorted element *)
    Lpos: Integer;                        (* Place in lower portion of L to get next
                                             element *)
    Hpos: Integer;                        (* Place in upper portion of L to get next
                                             element *)
Begin
    Ins := Low;                           (* Index into temp array to put merged
                                             portions in *)
    Lpos := Low;                          (* Index into lower portion *)
    Hpos := Mid + 1;                      (* Index into upper portion *)

    (* Loop as long as there are elements left in both the lower
       and upper portions to be merged together. *)
    While (Lpos <= Mid) And (Hpos <= Hi) Do
        If (L[Lpos] < L[Hpos]) Then
            (* If current element from lower portion is smaller *)
            Tmp[Ins] := L[Lpos]; (* put it into the sorted array *)
            Lpos := Lpos + 1;
        Else
            (* Otherwise, use current element from upper portion *)
            Tmp[Ins] := L[Hpos];
            Hpos := Hpos + 1;
        Endif;
        Ins := Ins + 1;
    Endwhile;

(* Only one of the two following while loops will be executed. *)

    (* Copy left over elements from lower portion. *)
    While (Lpos <= Mid) Do
        Tmp[Ins] := L[Lpos];
        Lpos := Lpos + 1;
        Ins := Ins + 1;
    Endwhile;

    (* Or copy leftover elements from upper portion. *)
    While (Hpos <= Hi) Do
        Tmp[Ins] := L[Hpos];
        Hpos := Hpos + 1;
        Ins := Ins + 1;
    Endwhile;
```

(continued)

Figure 5–12 (continued)

```
(* Copy the temporary array with range [Low .. Hi] sorted back
            into the original array *)
    For Ins := Low To Hi Do
        L[Ins] := Tmp[Ins];
    Endfor;
End Join;

Procedure MergeSort( Var L : Array [1 .. N] Of Integer; Low, Hi : Integer );
Var
    Mid : Integer;                    (* The midpoint of the array *)
Begin
    If (Low < Hi) Then                (* We have a list larger than one
                                      to sort *)
        Mid := (Low + Hi) Div 2;      (* Find the midpoint *)
        MergeSort(L, Low, Mid);       (* Sort the bottom portion *)
        MergeSort(L, Mid + 1, Hi);    (* Sort the top portion *)
        Join(L, Low, Hi, Mid);        (* Put the two portions back together *)
    Endif;
End MergeSort;
```

sequence will be less than the pivot element and half will be greater. These two subsequences are then sorted, using the same algorithm recursively.

The idea behind partitioning the sequence around a pivot element is to make sure that after each partitioning operation the pivot element ends up in its correct position in the overall sorted sequence. Thus, once a pivot element is chosen and a partitioning operation performed, the pivot element is correctly placed within the final sequence; we need not consider that pivot element again.

If S_1 is the sequence of elements of S smaller than the pivot P and S_2 is the sequence of elements of S larger than the pivot P, then after we have partitioned about the pivot P, the structure of the sequence S will be:

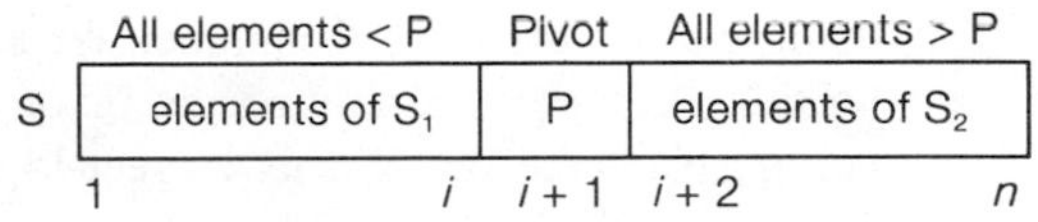

	All elements < P	Pivot	All elements > P
S	elements of S_1	P	elements of S_2
	1 $\quad$ i	$i+1$	$i+2$ $\quad$ n

We now have divided up the problem into two smaller problems—sorting S_1 and S_2. Also notice that even though the elements of these two subsequences will move around, they will always remain in the region of the sequence they currently occupy. That is, the elements of S_1 will remain in locations [1 .. i] and the elements of S_2 will remain in locations [i+2 .. N].

The high-level description of the recursive QuickSort algorithm is:

QuickSort(S[1 .. N])

1. Select a pivot element P from the set of elements of S.
2. Partition S into two subsequences, one containing elements less than the pivot in locations S[1 .. i] and one containing elements greater than the pivot in locations S[i+2 .. N]. The pivot will be located in S[i+1].

3. Call QuickSort[1 .. i].
4. Call QuickSort[i+2 .. N].

To illustrate the behavior of this algorithm, let us see how it acts with the following sequence S:

S = {7, 11, 3, 29, 2}

First we must choose the pivot element. For simplicity, we will select the first element of the sequence, 7, to be the pivot.

To implement the partitioning operation, we use two pointers called LeftPtr and RightPtr. The RightPtr scans the sequence backward from the rightmost element to the beginning of the sequence until we find an element that is less than or equal to the pivot element (2, in this case). The LeftPtr scans the sequence forward from the leftmost element to the end of the sequence until we find an element that is strictly greater than the pivot element (11, in this case). The elements found are then interchanged and the scan is continued until the two pointers cross, that is, LeftPtr ≥ RightPtr. The scan terminates at this point because we have now examined all elements in the sequence. At this point S contains the following:

S = {7, 2, 3, 29, 11}

When the scan terminates, we place the pivot element in its correct place in the overall sequence by interchanging the pivot with the last element in the subsequence of elements that are less than the pivot. In this example, we interchange the pivot element, 7, with 3. Now 7 is in the correct sorted place in S (the third element), and S contains the following:

```
        Subsequence 1  Pivot   Subsequence 2
           ⌐‾‾┴‾‾¬       ↓      ⌐‾‾┴‾‾¬
     S =  { 3,  2,       7,     29,  11}
```

We now recursively call QuickSort on the two subsequences {3, 2} and {29, 11}, using exactly the same technique. We select a pivot—let's say 3—and perform a partitioning operation around the pivot. This step produces no exchanges, so we simply place the pivot in its correct location by interchanging the 2 and the 3 to produce {2,3}. The value 3 is now correctly positioned, and we have created the two subsequences {2} and {}. However, we now have our base case, because a zero- and a one-element list are both sorted, by definition.

Figure 5–13 summarizes the sequence of steps needed to sort the five-element sequence S = {7, 11, 3, 29, 2} using the QuickSort algorithm.

Figure 5–14 contains a complete QuickSort procedure. It should be noted that the choice of a good pivot element is not as easy to determine as we have shown in the example. A good choice for a pivot would be a value that partitions the set into two subsets of roughly equal size.

In our diagrams we always selected the first number in the sequence as our pivot. However, if the sequence S is already in "almost" sorted order (or "almost" in reverse order)

S = {1, 2, 3, 4, 5, . . .}

Figure 5–13
Operation of the QuickSort Algorithm

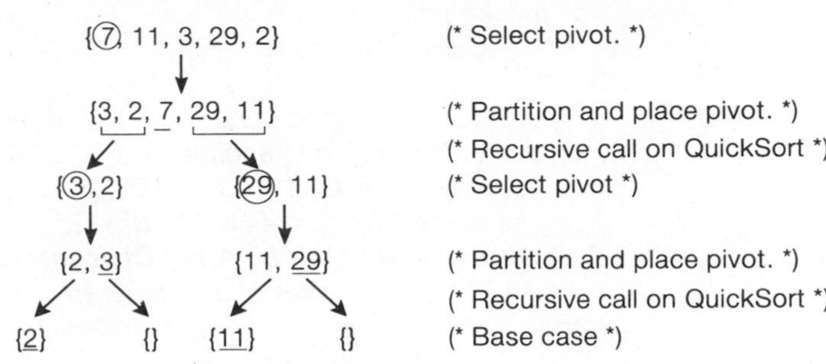

(The circled nodes are used as pivots. The underlined values are pivot elements placed in their correct location)

or

S = {99, 98, 97, 96, . . .}

then the first element of the sequence would be a very poor choice. It would partition the original N-element sequence into a subsequence with 0 elements and a subsequence with $(N-1)$ elements. If this situation happened repeatedly, approximately N (the number of elements in the sequence) recursive calls on QuickSort would be required to reach the base case, and the algorithm would be extremely inefficient.

A number of modifications to QuickSort have been proposed to solve this worst-case behavior. For example, instead of choosing the first element as the pivot, we could choose the ith element, where i is a random number in the range $[1 \, .. \, N]$, where N is the number of elements in the sequence. Alternatively, we could choose the median element of the first, the last, and the middle values of the current sequence. Another popular optimization technique is to use QuickSort until the individual subsequences we are sorting become small, say less than 25 or 50 elements, and then switch to a simple nonrecursive sorting method in order to reduce the overhead associated with recursion (see section 5.3).

These or similar modifications to QuickSort produce sorting algorithms that are quite fast for a wide range of data and that do not demonstrate the inefficient behavior just described. These optimized variations of QuickSort are among the most widely used sorting algorithms in computer science.

5.4.6 Finding a Path Through a Graph

Our final example will be the most substantive and complex algorithm we have developed so far. It involves searching for a path through a *Graph*—an abstract data structure that represents a set of nodes and a set of arcs connecting those nodes. (See Figure 3–1. We will have much more to say about Graph data structures in chapter 10.)

Figure 5–14
The QuickSort Algorithm

```
(* The procedure QuickSort sorts the list L, beginning at element
    Low up to element Hi, into ascending order.
    To call this procedure for the entire range [1 .. N] of the array L,
    invoke with:
        QuickSort(L, 1, N);   *)

(* The procedure Partition finds Mid, the correct, sorted position for the
    element L[Low] in L, and places it in L[Mid]. The array L is modified
    such that for all Low <= i < Mid, L[i] < L[Mid],
    and for all Mid < j <= Hi, L[Mid] < L[j].   *)
Procedure Partition( Var L : Array Of Integer; Low, Hi : Integer;
                     Var Mid : Integer );
Var
    LeftPtr      : Integer;
    RightPtr     : Integer;
    TmpNum       : Integer;
Begin
    LeftPtr := Low;
    RightPtr := Hi;

    While (LeftPtr < RightPtr) Do

    (* Search for the rightmost element greater than L[Low]. *)
        While (L[RightPtr] > L[Low]) Do
            RightPtr := RightPtr - 1;
        Endwhile;

    (* Search for the leftmost element less than L[Low] *)
        While (LeftPtr < RightPtr) And (L[LeftPtr] <= L[Low]) Do
            LeftPtr := LeftPtr + 1;
        Endwhile;

    (* If the pointers haven't crossed switch the values. *)
        If (LeftPtr < RightPtr) Then
            TmpNum := L[LeftPtr];
            L[LeftPtr] := L[RightPtr];
            L[RightPtr] := TmpNum;
        Endif;

    Endwhile;

    Mid := RightPtr;              (* The array is now correctly partitioned *)
    TmpNum := L[Mid];             (* so place pivot element into its position. *)
    L[Mid] := L[Low];
    L[Low] := TmpNum;

End Partition;

Procedure QuickSort(Var L : Array Of Integer; Low, Hi : Integer);
Var
    Mid : Integer;
Begin
    If (Low < Hi) Then
        Partition(L, Low, Hi, Mid);       (* Partition the whole array. *)
        QuickSort(L, Low, Mid - 1);       (* Sort the lower portion. *)
        QuickSort(L, Mid + 1, Hi);        (* Sort the upper portion. *)
    Endif;
End QuickSort;
```

Figure 5–15
Sample Graph Structure

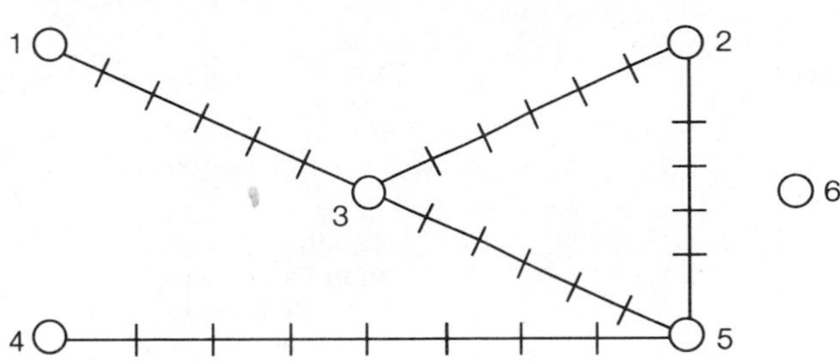

Figure 5–16
Two-Dimensional Array Representation of the Graph in Figure 5–15

	1	2	3	4	5	6
1	0	0	1	0	0	0
2	0	0	1	0	1	0
3	1	1	0	0	1	0
4	0	0	0	0	1	0
5	0	1	1	1	0	0
6	0	0	0	0	0	0

For example, suppose we have a diagram that shows the rail connections between six cities called 1, 2, 3, 4, 5, and 6, as shown in Figure 5–15. We can represent this graph internally using a 6 x 6 array that has a 1 in position (i,j) to indicate a direct connection from city i to city j and a 0 in position (i,j) to indicate no direct connection. The array representation for the example in Figure 5–15 is shown in Figure 5–16.

The problem now becomes: Given any two nodes $1 \leq i,j \leq 6$, is there a rail connection leading from city i to city j? (Note: In this example we do not care about finding the best, i.e., the shortest, path. We simply want to find any path. In chapter 10 we will look at the more difficult problem of finding the best route.) If we set $i = 1$ and $j = 4$, we can see from the previous picture that a possible answer is

$$1 \rightarrow 3 \rightarrow 5 \rightarrow 4$$

Another valid answer would be

$$1 \rightarrow 3 \rightarrow 2 \rightarrow 5 \rightarrow 4$$

If $i = 1$ and $j = 6$, then the correct response is

No Path Exists.

Essentially we want a function called Search(source, destination) that determines whether there is a path from the source node to the destination node. There is an elegant recursive solution based on the following principle: If I am currently located at node i and I am searching to see if I can reach node j (that is, I am executing

Figure 5–17
Recursive Search Process

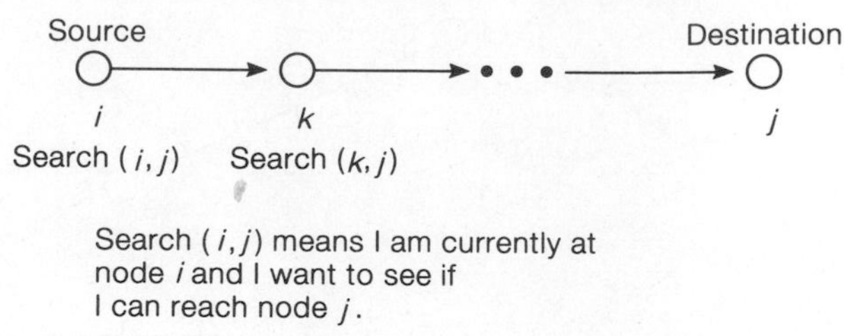

Search(i,j)), I can solve this problem by moving forward to node k (where k is any node directly connected to i) and seeing whether there is a path from node k to node j (that is, I execute the function call Search(k,j)). In essence I am asking if I have moved closer to my goal. This process is depicted in Figure 5–17.

This technique has three distinct base cases. One base case occurs when you reach the destination—then Search(j,j) will return True. A second base case occurs if a node has no exits and we cannot proceed—for this case Search(i,j) returns False.

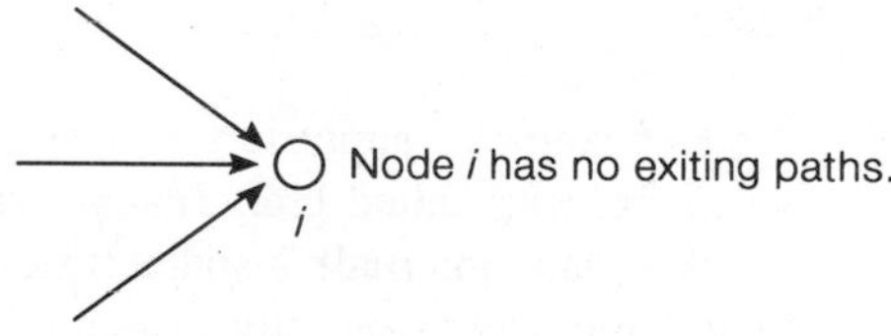

Finally, a third base case occurs if we come back to a node that we have already visited, that is, if we have completed a *cycle* (e.g., $2 \rightarrow 3 \rightarrow 5 \rightarrow 2$). In this case we are going in circles and obviously should abandon this path and try another one, so we simply return a False.

If we do not encounter one of our three base cases when we move forward one node, then we select our next node, move there, and recursively search for a path beginning from our new position. When we come to a node with n paths exiting from it: $k_1, k_2, \ldots, k_n$, we pick one of those as our candidate to search, say k_1. If k_1 turns out to produce a route to our goal, then we are finished. If it does not (i.e., if it produces a cycle or dead-ends), then we undo that last choice and try another path, say k_2.

A good data structure for saving the paths that we did not select is the Stack ADT of chapter 3. When we select one node out of n to move to, we can push the other ($n - 1$) nodes onto a stack.

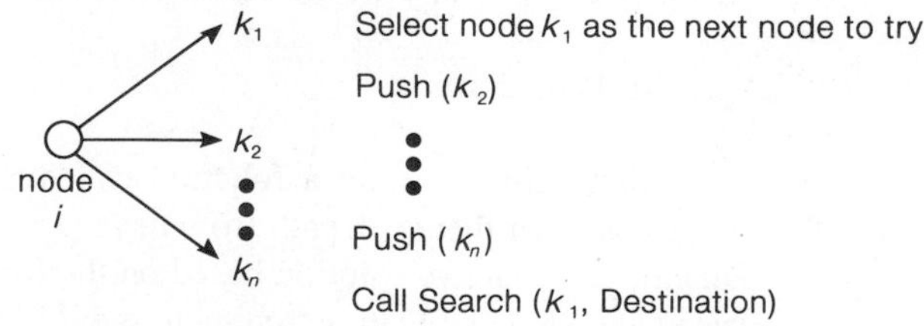

If our choice k_i turns out to be a dead end, we can move back to node i, pop the stack to produce a new path, and begin to follow it to see if that path will reach the goal, that is, we follow these steps:

Return to node i
Pop stack into X
Move to node X
Call Search(X,destination)

Given the following diagram, let's see how our algorithm might work to determine if there is a path from node 1 to node 4:

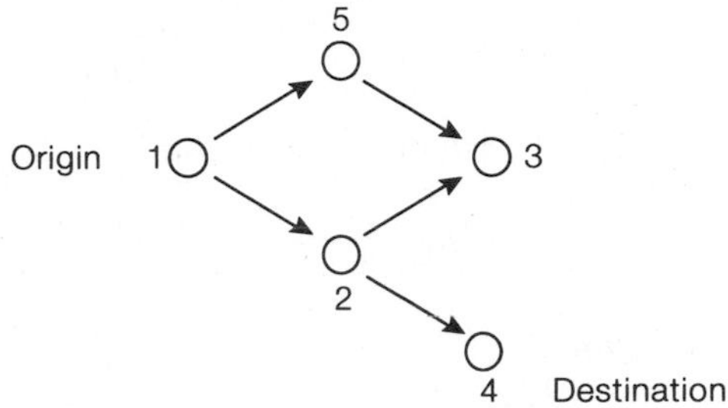

Search(1,4) (* See if there is a path from node 1 to node 4. *)
- Select a node to move to (say 2).
- Push the other alternative (node 5) onto the stack.
- Move to node 2 and recursively call Search(2,4).

Search(2,4)
- Select a node to move to (say 3).
- Push the other alternative (node 4) onto the stack.
- Move to node 3 and recursively call Search(3,4).

Search(3,4)
- Fail, because of base case 2—there is no exit from this node.
- Back up to the previous node, node 2, and redo Search(2,4).

Search(2,4)
- Pop the stack to get another alternative, node 4.
- Move to node 4 and recursively call Search (4,4).

Search(4,4)
- True. We have found the path. Print out node 4 and return.

Search(2,4)
- Print out node 2 and return.

Search(1,4)
- Print out node 1 and return.

Done

We have found a path and printed it out in the reverse order that it was discovered.

$4 \leftarrow 2 \leftarrow 1$

A recursive procedure to implement this graph search is shown in Figure 5–18. It imports the resources of the Stack abstract data type defined in chapter 3 to solve the

Figure 5–18

Recursive Procedure for Searching a Directed Graph

```
(* The procedure GraphSearch tries to find some path from node Source
   to node Dest in path G. If there is a path, it returns True, and
   the stack Path contains the sequence of nodes in the path such that
   Top(Path) = Source, Top(Pop(Path)) = next node in path toward Dest, etc.   *)
Module GraphPackage;

From StackPackage Import
        StackType,                  (* The abstract data type Stack *)
        Create,                     (* Function to create an empty
                                       stack *)
        Push,                       (* Function to add an element to the
                                       top of a stack *)
        Pop,                        (* Function to remove the element at
                                       the top of a stack *)
        Empty,                      (* Function to check if a stack has any
                                       elements *)
        Top;                        (* Function to return the top element
                                       from a stack *)

Const
    GSize = 6;                      (* A constant representing the graph
                                       size *)

Type
    GraphType = Array [1 .. GSize, 1 .. GSize] Of Integer;


Procedure GraphSearch( G : GraphType; Source, Dest : Integer;
                       Var Path : StackType) : Boolean;
Var
    i       : Integer;
    Exits   : StackType;
Begin
    If (Source = Dest) Then                (* Are we done ? *)
        Path := Push(Source, Create());    (* Yes, so place Dest in Path. *)
        Return True;
    Endif;                                 (* We arrive here if we are not done. *)

    Exits := Create();                     (* The stack to hold nodes in
                                              the path. *)

    i := 1;                                (* We're not done yet, so *)
    While (i <= GSize) Do                  (* find all possible next nodes. *)
        If (G[Source,i] = 1) Then
            Exits := Push(i, Exits);
        Endif;
        i := i + 1;
    Endwhile;
    For i := 1 To GSize Do                 (* Mark Source as being visited *)
        If (G[Source, i] = 1) Then
            G[Source, i] := -1;
        Endif;
    Endfor;
```

(continued)

Figure 5–18 (continued)

```
While (Not Empty(Exits)) Do
        (* Are there any possible next nodes left ? *)

        (* See if this possible next node leads to Dest. *)
        If (GraphSearch(G, Top(Exits), Dest, Path)) Then
            Path := Push(Source, Path);    (* Yes, so add Source to Path. *)
            Return True;
        Endif;

        Exits := Pop(Exits);              (* Go to next possible next node. *)

    Endwhile;

    Return False;                         (* No, no possible paths *)

End GraphSearch;

End GraphPackage.
```

problem. This use of the stack package is a good example of software reusability and the use of abstract data types to enhance programmer productivity. We will see many more such examples in later chapters.

5.5 CONCLUSION

As we mentioned at the beginning of the chapter, many students are uncomfortable and unfamiliar with the concept of recursion primarily because it is mentioned only briefly or sometimes not at all in a first course in computer science. For that reason it may be viewed as an arcane problem-solving technique that leads to some "cute" solutions but is rarely used, in essence, a computer science "parlor game." Another reason for its relative unfamiliarity is that many of the original high-level programming languages developed in the 1950s and 1960s did not support recursion; these languages include FORTRAN, COBOL, and BASIC, and they are still in widespread use today (although recent versions of these languages do support recursion).

However, this view of recursion is totally out of date, and virtually all new (or recently rediscovered) languages use recursion as their primary iterative control structure. Languages like Prolog (for logic programming), Smalltalk (for object-oriented programming), and LISP (for functional programming) do not contain the old, familiar **Repeat, While**, and **For** constructs, upon which we have all come to depend. Instead, iteration is implemented by means of recursive function calls exactly as we have described in this chapter. In the 21st century such "classic" procedural languages as Pascal, Modula-2, Ada, and FORTRAN may go the way of punched cards and paper tape to be replaced by one of the recursively oriented programming languages mentioned above. Even if this view is a bit extreme, recursion is a fundamentally important problem-solving paradigm that belongs in every modern programmer's tool kit.

CHAPTER EXERCISES

1. Write a recursive definition of the term *descendant*. Can you think of any other terms used in everyday life that could be defined recursively?
2. Give a recursive syntactic definition of an arbitrarily long sequence of digits in the range 0 to 9 separated by a + sign. That is, syntactic constructs of the form:

   1 + 8 + 7 + 3 + 0 + 5 + . . .

3. Explain why the circular definition

   Where is Mr. Jones' office?
   Next to Ms. Smith's.
   Where is Ms. Smith's office?
   Next to Mr. Jones'.

   violates the definition of recursion given in section 5.2.
4. Code both the recursive factorial procedure shown in Figure 5–1 and an iterative one. Run them both with $n = 10$ and $n = 20$ and measure how long it takes to compute the answer using the two different techniques. What does this tell you about the efficiency of the recursive factorial technique?
5. Write a recursive algorithm to make a copy of a linked list L. That is, the call

   Copy(L1, L2)

   will produce a new list L2 that is identical in content and structure to the list L1. L1 will not be affected by this procedure call.
6. Write a recursive algorithm to take an unsigned integer value I and print out the digits of I one character at a time, beginning with the leftmost digit. That is, given the call

   Print(I) (* where I = 123 *)

   we will print the value 1 and recursively call Print with the value 23 to print out the remaining digits. *Hint*: If I = 123, what is I **Div** 10? What is I **Mod** 10?
7. What is wrong with the structure of the following recursive function R?

```
Procedure R(n : Integer) : Integer;
Var
    T : Integer;
Begin
    T := 1 + R(n - 1);        (* The general case *)
    If n = 0 Then             (* The base case *)
        Return T
    End
End R;
```

   What happens when you execute the recursive call R(3)?

8. What would be the maximum number of activation records on the run-time stack when evaluating
   a. NFactorial(10) (Figure 5–1)
   b. SumOfFirstNNaturalNumbers(500) (Figure 5–2)
   c. Searching a 500-element list using BinarySearch (Figure 5–9)
9. Write a recursive procedure called CheckEqual that takes two linked lists, L1 and L2, and checks to see if the two lists are identical, that is, if they have the same number of nodes and if the information fields of each node (assumed to be integer) are equal. If the two lists are identical, the procedure returns the value True, otherwise it returns a False.
10. Write the recursive procedure Reverse(L) described in section 5.4.2. Use the technique that defines Reverse as

    Reverse(L) = Concatenate(Back(L),Reverse(Rest(L)))

11. We can recursively define sorting an array A as finding the biggest element in A, placing it at the beginning of A, and concatenating to it the result of sorting the remaining $N - 1$ items in the array. Algorithmically this is expressed as follows:

    Sort(A[i,j]) = Concatenate(Biggest(A[i,j]), Sort(A[i,j] − Biggest(A[i,j])))

    where the operation − means deletion of an element from the array (in this case, we delete the biggest element from array A). Write a sorting procedure based on this principle. This technique is called *ExchangeSort*. Comment on its efficiency.
12. A binomial coefficient is defined mathematically as

$$\binom{n}{m} = \frac{n!}{(n-m)!\,m!}$$

    It can also be recursively defined as

$$\binom{n}{1} = n$$

$$\binom{n}{n} = 1$$

$$\binom{n}{m} = \binom{n-1}{m-1} + \binom{n-1}{m} \qquad \text{for } n > m > 1$$

    Implement both methods and test them with a number of different values of n and m to see which one is more efficient for evaluating binomial coefficients.
13. Write a recursive function that counts the number of times a particular key occurs in a linked list L.

    Procedure CountKey(L:List; Key:Integer) : Integer;

14. Write a recursive procedure to find the greatest common divisor of two positive integers A and B. The GCD function is defined as

GCD(A,B) = B	if B ≤ A and A **Mod** B = 0
GCD(A,B) = GCD(B,A)	if A < B
GCD(A,B) = GCD(B, A **Mod** B)	otherwise

15. Trace the execution of the MergeSort procedure of Figure 5–12 on the following sequence:

    S = {1, 38, 17, 29, −2, 6, 20, 85}

    Show the recursive calls that would be generated at each stage and the sequence of merge operations that would be performed.
16. Trace the execution of QuickSort with the eight-element sequence shown in exercise 15. Assume that we select the first element in a sequence as the pivot. Show the recursive calls that would be generated at each stage in the solution.
17. Implement a modification of QuickSort (call it QuickSort1) that chooses as a pivot element a random value in the range [*i* . . *j*], where S[*i* . . *j*] is the part of the sequence being sorted. Try out your modification on a list of 500 elements that are 99% in sorted sequence. Compare the execution time to the time needed by the traditional QuickSort algorithm of Figure 5–14.
18. Implement a second modification of QuickSort (call it QuickSort2) that takes the improved version from exercise 17 and uses the following technique: The program uses QuickSort1 to sort subsequences until they have a length less than or equal to 50 elements. At this point the program switches to InsertionSort or BubbleSort and uses one of these simple nonrecursive algorithms to complete the task. Time all three programs (exercises 16, 17, and 18) on lists of length 5,000, both in random order and in sorted order, and discuss and explain your results. Try different size cutoff points (i.e., the point where you switch to the nonrecursive technique) to see if a value other than 50 would improve the overall behavior of this program.
19. Modify the graph search algorithm of Figure 5–18 so that in addition to telling you the path, it tells you how long the path is, in terms of the number of nodes along the path. The output would look something like:

    1 → 3 → 2 → 5 → 4   The path is of length 5.

CHAPTER 6

THE ANALYSIS OF ALGORITHMS

CHAPTER OUTLINE

6.1 INTRODUCTION

In this chapter we develop the mathematical tools needed to analyze the algorithms and data structures that we have already presented or that we will see in upcoming chapters. The analysis of algorithms is a critically important issue in computer science. The data structures that we have discussed (e.g., stacks, queues, linear lists) were introduced not just because they are mathematically interesting but because we claim that they allow us to develop more efficient algorithms for such tasks as insertion, deletion, searching, sorting, and pattern matching. But how do we formally show that this claim is valid? How do we demonstrate that algorithm X is superior to algorithm Y for a given application without relying on informal arguments, without getting misled by special cases, and without being influenced by the efficiency of the programming language used to encode the algorithm or the hardware used to run it?

For example, in the previous chapter we made the assertion that the binary search (Figure 5–9) is faster than a sequential search of an array. We made this argument informally, relying more on intuition than on a formal comparison of the properties of these two algorithms. But think about the possible counterarguments that could be used to refute our claim:

1. The item you are looking for might be in the first position of the array. In this case a sequential search would be faster than a binary search, since a sequential search begins looking at the first location of the array, while the binary search begins in the middle.
2. If the number of elements in the array is small, there really is no difference. For example, if there are 8 items in the array, then the sequential search will take on the average about $n/2$ or 4 looks, whereas the binary search will take approximately $\log_2(n) = \log_2 8 = 3$ looks. Virtually no difference at all.
3. If the sequential search is running on a Cray-Y/MP supercomputer and the binary search is running on a Macintosh SE/30, then the sequential search might run faster because of the enormous speed advantage of the Cray.
4. If the sequential search was coded by a team of professionals in optimized assembly language and the binary search was written by a first-year computer science student using interpreted BASIC, the sequential search might run faster.

Are any of these counterarguments valid? Do they negate our claim of superiority for the binary search? If they are not valid arguments, why not, and how do we formally refute them?

In this chapter we develop the mathematical methods needed to answer these questions. We introduce a technique called the *asymptotic analysis* of algorithms, which is the fundamental tool for evaluating the efficiency properties of algorithms; the results of asymptotic analysis are expressed in what is informally called *Big-O notation*.

6.2 THE ASYMPTOTIC ANALYSIS OF ALGORITHMS

It would seem that the most obvious way to measure the efficiency of an algorithm would be to run it using a specific set of data and measure how much processor time and memory space are needed to produce a correct solution. This process is called *benchmarking*. However, this test produces a measure of efficiency for only one particular case and would be inadequate to predict how the algorithm would perform using a different data set. An algorithm for finding a name in a telephone book by searching sequentially from A to Z might work well for a book with 50 entries, but it would be totally unacceptable for use with the Minneapolis city telephone directory. Benchmarking is a technique for seeing if a finished program meets certain timing specifications, but it is not an appropriate way to mathematically analyze the general properties of algorithms before we begin coding.

Instead, we need a way to formulate guidelines that will allow us to state that for any arbitrary data set, one particular method will probably be better than another. In the telephone-book example, a more helpful piece of information than the performance of the algorithm on a specific directory would be a general guideline such as "never use sequential lookup with a telephone book containing more than two hundred entries."

Specifically, we would like to associate a value n (the size of the problem) with either t (the processing time needed to get the solution) or s (the total memory space required by the solution). The value n is a measure of the size of the problem we are attempting to solve. For example, if we are searching or sorting a list, n would most likely be the number of items in the list. If we were performing arithmetic operations on an $r \times r$ array, the size of the problem would be r, the dimensions of the array. If we were enqueueing n objects in a queue, the size of the problem would be the number of elements currently in the queue.

The relationships between n, t, and s can sometimes be given in terms of explicit formulas:

$$t = f(n)$$

$$s = g(n)$$

If we had such a formula, it would allow us to plug in a value for n and determine exactly how many seconds it would take (or how many memory cells would be needed) to solve a problem of size n. Given that information for a number of different techniques, we could immediately select the algorithm that would run most quickly (or with the least memory) on a problem of size n.

However, such explicit formulas are rarely used. First, they are difficult to obtain because they rely on machine-dependent parameters that we may not know. Second, we usually do not want to use $f(n)$ and $g(n)$ to compute exact time or space requirements for specific data cases. Instead, we want a guideline for comparing and selecting algorithms for data sets of arbitrary size.

We can get this type of information by using *asymptotic analysis*, which is expressed using *Big-O notation*.

$t \approx O[f(n)]$ (* this is read "t is on the order of $f(n)$" *)

$s \approx O[g(n)]$ (* this is read "s is on the order of $g(n)$" *)

The function $f(n)$ is called the *time complexity* or *order* of the algorithm and $g(n)$ is called the *space complexity* of the algorithm.

Formally, asymptotic analysis states that there exist constants M and n^* such that if $t \approx O[f(n)]$, then $t \leq Mf(n)$ for all $n > n^*$. This formidable definition is not as difficult as it looks. It simply states that the computing time or space requirement of the algorithm grows no faster than a constant times the function $f(n)$. If the order of the algorithm were, for example, $O(n^3)$, then as the size of the problem doubled, the time needed to solve the problem would increase about eightfold (2^3).

For reasonably large problems we always want to select algorithms of the lowest order possible. If algorithm A is $O[f(n)]$ and algorithm B is $O[g(n)]$, then algorithm A is said to be of a *lower order* than B if $f(n) < g(n)$ for all n greater than some constant k. For example, $O(n^2)$ is lower-order than $O(n^3)$ because $n^2 < n^3$ for all $n > 1$. Similarly, $O(n^3)$ is a lower order than $O(2^n)$ because $n^3 < 2^n$ for all $n > 9$. Thus we would definitely want to select an $O(n^2)$ algorithm to solve a problem, instead of an $O(n^3)$ or $O(2^n)$ algorithm, if such an $O(n^2)$ algorithm existed.

If we always choose the lowest-order algorithm, we may not know exactly how much time or space is required to obtain a solution, but we will know that as the size of the problem increases, there is always a size (n^*) beyond which our lower-order method will take less time or space than a method of higher order. Furthermore, the gains become more significant as the problem gets bigger. Figure 6–1 shows this behavior for algorithms of order $O(n^2)$, $O(n^3)$, and $O(2^n)$. For small problems of size $n < n^*$, the choice of algorithm is not critical and in fact, the $O(n^3)$ or the $O(2^n)$ algorithm may be superior. However, when n finally becomes larger than n^*, the $O(n^2)$ algorithm will always be superior to the other two algorithms, and it becomes better and better as n increases.

This type of analysis provides the general guidelines we need, and thus O-notation is the fundamental technique for describing the efficiency properties of algorithms.

Table 6–1 lists some of the more common complexity classes that you will encounter along with some well-known algorithms that belong to each class. They are listed in ascending order from the lowest order algorithm to the highest. In the

Figure 6–1 Comparison of Three Complexity Measures $O(n^2)$, $O(n^3)$, and $O(2^n)$

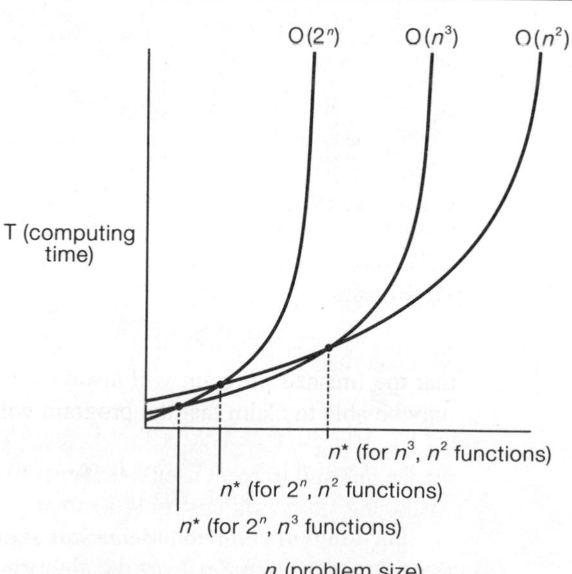

Table 6–1 Common Time Computational Complexities

Complexity	Comments	Examples
$O(1)$	*Constant-time* algorithm. Solution time is independent of problem size.	Extracting the (i,j)th element from an $(n \times n)$ array.
$O(\log_2 n)$	*Logarithmic time.*	Binary search.
$O(n)$	*Linear time.*	Sequential search, linear list traversal.
$O(n \log n)$	Theoretically optimal sorting time.	QuickSort, MergeSort.
$O(n^2)$	*Quadratic time.*	$n \times n$ matrix addition, simple pattern matching.
$O(n^3)$	*Cubic time.*	Matrix multiplication.
$O(k^n)$	*Exponential time.*	Finding a path through a graph.

next section we will learn how to work out the complexity of some well-known algorithms in computer science.

6.3 EXAMPLES OF TIME COMPLEXITY ANALYSIS

When analyzing an algorithm, there are three distinct conditions that we can investigate—the *best case*, the *average case*, or the *worst case* behavior of the algorithm.

We rarely make a best-case analysis, since the algorithm usually displays this optimal performance only under very unusual or special conditions. Remember, we are trying to develop general guidelines to describe the overall behavior of an algorithm, not its performance in rare and exceptional circumstances. For this reason we will not do any best-case analyses in this chapter. (An example of a best-case analysis would be looking for the name "AAA Auto Repair" in a telephone book using sequential search. The search would find the name on the very first look. However, this analysis would give us a very misleading picture of the typical behavior of the sequential search algorithm.)

It would seem then that the only condition that would be important would be the average-case behavior of an algorithm, which describes its average performance over the entire range of possible input, but this is not necessarily true. We usually design and implement software to meet strict performance specifications laid out by the user. If we select our key algorithms on the basis of only their average performance over a large range of data sets, we will not be in a strong position to assert that the finished program will always meet design specifications. Instead, we will only be able to claim that the program will usually be good enough. It may be that for certain "pathological" conditions the algorithm will display much worse performance and fail to meet user specifications. An average-case analysis will not warn us about such conditions; only a worst-case analysis can provide this information.

For example, both the MergeSort algorithm of section 5.4.4 and the QuickSort algorithm of section 5.4.5 are, on average, $O(n \log_2 n)$ in terms of running time for a list of length n. Both of these algorithms were coded in Pascal (along with a

Table 6–2 Run Times for Different Sorting Algorithms

A. TIME (IN SECONDS) FOR SORTING A RANDOMIZED LIST			
List Size:	500	2,500	10,000
MergeSort	0.8	8.1	39.8
QuickSort	0.3	1.3	5.3
SelectionSort	1.5	35.0	534.7

B. TIME (IN SECONDS) FOR SORTING ORDERED LISTS FOR $N = 2{,}500$			
	Random	In Order	Reverse Order
MergeSort	8.1	7.8	7.9
QuickSort	1.3	35.1	37.1
SelectionSort	35.0	34.4	35.3

simple $O(n^2)$ SelectionSort) and run using randomized arrays of 500, 2,500, and 10,000 integers. The results are shown in Table 6–2.

Although they are both $(n \log_2 n)$ techniques for the average case, QuickSort executes faster than MergeSort because of lower constant factors in its complexity function. (Also notice that at $N = 2{,}500$ and $N = 10{,}000$ both $(n \log_2 n)$ techniques are much better than the inefficient $O(n^2)$ SelectionSort, as we would expect.) Because of this behavior we would probably opt for QuickSort whenever sorting was part of a problem specification.

However, what if our specifications stated that we must be able to "sort *any* list of length 2,500 in 10 seconds or less." It still seems that there is no problem, since QuickSort is solving a problem of size 2,500 in 1.3 seconds. However, recall from our earlier discussion in chapter 5 that if the list is initially in almost sorted or almost reverse sorted order, the QuickSort algorithm rapidly degrades. In those cases the pivoting operation partitions the list not into the two equal halves we want but into two lists of lengths 0 and $N - 1$. In this worst case the behavior of QuickSort becomes $O(n^2)$ rather than $O(n \log_2 n)$.

We can see this behavior clearly in Table 6–2, in which we reran the case $N = 2{,}500$ with lists that were initially in perfect order and perfect reverse order. The times for MergeSort do not change markedly, as its worst case and average case behavior are about the same. But QuickSort "blew up" as we expected, taking over half-a-minute to solve the problem—longer than even the inefficient SelectionSort. Given our performance requirement that all data sets of length 2,500 be sorted in under ten seconds, we could not select QuickSort as our preferred sorting method.

However, if our performance requirements were changed to read "We must be able to sort *most* lists of length 2,500 items or less in under ten seconds," then we would probably choose QuickSort. The ordered data sets in Table 6–2 are quite rare and would not be expected to occur with any great frequency. The superior performance of QuickSort on the overwhelming majority of the data sets would, in this case, be the more important factor.

This example clearly shows that an in-depth analysis of an algorithm involves a study of both its average-case behavior under expected conditions and its worst-case behavior under the poorest conditions.

When analyzing an algorithm, we do not care about the behavior of every statement in the entire algorithm. Such detailed analysis would be too complicated and time-consuming. Besides, many parts of an algorithm are not executed very often, and an in-depth analysis of their individual behavior would not be important to determining the overall efficiency. For example, such infrequent operations as initialization and output are generally unimportant. Instead, we analyze only a single part of the algorithm called the *critical operation*, which is the operation in which the algorithm spends most of its time.

The critical operation can be a single operation, a single statement, or a group of statements; it has the following two characteristics:

1. It is an operation that is central to the function of the algorithm, and its behavior typifies the overall behavior of the algorithm.
2. It is inside the main loops of the algorithm, and therefore it is executed as often as any other part of the algorithm.

The critical operation can be said to be at the "heart" of the algorithm. The asymptotic method of analysis says that we can characterize the overall efficiency of an algorithm by looking at how many times the critical operation is executed as a function of the problem size. (If we are doing an average-case analysis, we consider the average number of times the critical operation is executed; if a worst-case analysis, the maximum number of times.) This value is called the *time complexity* or the *order* of the algorithm. Asymptotic analysis essentially says that the slowest part of the algorithm (the critical operation) dominates the overall completion time.

As an analogy, imagine that you had the job of delivering a gift to someone living in another city. The job involved the following three steps:

1. Wrap the gift.
2. Drive 1,000 miles to the destination city.
3. Deliver the package to the proper person.

The critical operation in which you would spend most of your time is step 2. The time it takes to perform this step will characterize the completion time of the entire job, and steps 1 and 3 can be ignored completely. Changing step 2 by flying instead of driving would have a profound impact on the overall completion time of the task, but taking a class to learn how to wrap packages more quickly would have no discernible effect.

Let us look at some specific examples. Figure 6–2 shows a simple sequential search procedure that looks at every item in an n-item list to locate a specific key. The critical operation in this look-up procedure is the comparison operation (L[i] = Key). This operation is the heart of the look-up procedure, and because it is inside the **While** loop, it is executed as often as any operation in the procedure. In the worst case (which occurs when Key is not in the list), this comparison will be carried out n times, so we would say that the sequential search algorithm of Figure 6–2 has a worst-case behavior of $O(n)$, that is, it has a *linear complexity* with respect to table size. If the list were to double in size, the worst-case time required to search it using this algorithm would also approximately double. (Note that we must say "approximately" rather than exactly because our computation does not account for the behavior of statements other than the critical operation.)

Linear-time algorithms are common in computer science. For example, the

Figure 6–2
Sequential Search Procedure

```
(* The procedure SequentialSearch looks through the array L[1 .. N] for an
   element Key. If it finds it, SequentialSearch returns the subscript
   of Key. Otherwise, it returns zero.   *)
Procedure SequentialSearch(L : ArrayType; N, Key : Integer) : Integer;
Var
    i : Integer;
Begin
    i := 1;
    While (i <= N) Do                (* Search the entire array *)
        If (L[i] = Key) Then         (* We've found the element *)
            Return i;                (* So return its position in the array *)
        Endif;
        i := i + 1;                  (* Otherwise move on to next element *)
    Endwhile;
    Return 0;                        (* Didn't find it *)
End SequentialSearch;
```

time it takes to count the number of nodes in a linked list (Figure 4–13) is linear with respect to the length of the list. Similarly, the time needed to sum up all of the elements in either a linked list or a one-dimensional array is a linear function of the list or array size.

In general, the structure of a linear-time algorithm will be something like

```
For i := 1 To N Do        (* A loop done N times *)
    S
End
```

where S is the critical operation being measured.

If the list we are searching is in sorted rather than random sequence, we can do much better than O(n) by using the binary search technique first introduced in section 5.4.3. Figure 6–3 shows an iterative version of the binary search algorithm.

The algorithm works by comparing the key we are searching for with the item located in the middle position of the list. If it matches, we have found our item. If not, we discard the half of the list that cannot contain the desired key and repeat the process. Eventually we will either find what we are looking for or we will discard the entire list. With each iteration through the **While** loop we halve the size of the list being searched—it will become 1/2, 1/4, 1/8, . . . of its original size. In the worst case (Key is not in the list), the process will continue until the portion of the list still under consideration has only one item, and we can then immediately determine whether Key is in the list. If we consider the comparison (L[Mid] = Key) to be our critical operation, then we can see that in the worst case, the maximum number of comparisons required by the binary search method will be the value k, where k is the first integer such that

$$2^k \geq n \text{ (the size of the list)}$$

Figure 6–3
Binary Search Procedure

```
(* The procedure BinarySearch searches the list L for an element Key
   in the range [Low .. Hi]. To call this procedure for the
   range [1 .. N] of the array L, invoke with:
      BinarySearch(L, 1, N, Key);   *)
Procedure BinarySearch( L : Array Of Integer;
                        Low, Hi : Integer; Key : Integer ) : Boolean;
Var
   Mid : Integer;                  (* This is the midpoint between Low and Hi. *)
Begin
   While (Low <= Hi) Do            (* Do we have elements left to search ? *)

      Mid := (Low + Hi) Div 2;     (* Calculate the midpoint. *)

      If (L[Mid] = Key) Then       (* Is this the correct element? *)
         Return True;              (* Yes, so return True. *)

      Elsif (L[Mid] < Key) Then    (* No, but maybe its in the upper half. *)
         Low := Mid + 1;

      Else                         (* L[Mid] > Key. In this case,
         Hi := Mid - 1;            maybe it's in the lower half. *)
      Endif;

   Endwhile;

   Return False;                   (* The item is not there *)
End BinarySearch;
```

Another way to write this is

$k = \lceil \log_2 n \rceil$ where $\lceil\ \rceil$ is the ceiling function, i.e., the smallest integer k such that $k \geq \log_2 n$

We can thus say that the time complexity, or order, of the binary search method is $O(\log_2 n)$. The time needed to find an element in a list using binary search is proportional to the logarithm (base 2) of the list size (rather than to the list size itself, as is the case with sequential search); thus this algorithm has a *logarithmic* complexity.

We can see that binary search is a lower-order algorithm than the $O(n)$ sequential search because the function $\log_2 n$ grows more slowly than n itself. From section 6.2, we know that there will exist a size n^* such that for all lists of size $n > n^*$, the binary search will always run faster than sequential search. We may not know the exact value of n^* (since it will depend on such things as hardware characteristics, programming style, and the language selected), but we can be certain that it exists. For example, it is possible that the binary search has a time complexity function of the form:

$$T_{bs} = 100 \log_2 n$$

while the complexity function of the sequential search is

$$T_{ss} = 4\ n$$

Table 6–3 Comparisons of O(*n*) and O(log₂*n*) Algorithm Performance

PROBLEM SIZE *n*	MAXIMUM NUMBER OF COMPARISONS	
	$O(n)$	$O(\log_2 n)$
10	10	4
100	100	7
1,000	1,000	10
50,000	50,000	16
800,000	800,000	20

Notice the larger constants in the formula for T_{bs}. They could result from such factors as the overhead from recursion or the time involved in completing operations other than the critical operation. For these time complexity functions and values of n up to roughly the point $n = 200$, the sequential search will execute more quickly, but past that point (the point we called n^*) the binary search becomes faster and will remain so for all problems of size $n > n^*$.

The larger the list (i.e., the greater the value of n), the more time is saved by using the binary search. For example, look at Table 6–3. We see that for small values of n the gains are not significant. However, as n gets bigger, the improvements can be monumental. A list with 800,000 items could require a maximum of 800,000 comparisons using sequential lookup, whereas the binary search will never need more than 20—an improvement factor of 40,000!

In general, the structure of an algorithm that displays logarithmic behavior is

```
X := N                 (* N is the original problem size. *)
Repeat
    •
    •
    •
    S;                 (* The critical operation *)
    X := X Div K       (* Reduce the problem to 1/Kth its original size, K > 1. *)
Until (X=0) Or the problem is solved
```

We can even improve on logarithmic behavior when performing a search operation. In chapter 9 we will present a technique called *hashing*, which can theoretically reduce the time needed to locate a specific key in a table to O(1). Such an algorithm is called a *constant-time* algorithm; O(1) means that we can locate any item in a fixed amount of time, independent of the size of the problem. Constant-time algorithms are obviously the best possible class of algorithm: regardless of how large a problem may get, the time required to solve it never increases!

Constant-time algorithms may initially seem like an impossibility, but in fact, they are common in computer science. For example, the time it takes to retrieve the [*i*,*j*th] element from an $n \times n$ array:

```
X := A[i,j]
```

is independent of the size of A. This array retrieval operation takes the same amount of time whether A is 5 × 5 or 500,000 × 500,000. The stack operations Push(X,S) and Pop(S) from chapter 3 both take a constant amount of time, independent of the size of the stack S. Similarly, the queue operations Enqueue and Dequeue and the linked-list procedure called InsertAfter (Figure 4–12) are all constant-time algorithms. The general model for a constant-time algorithm is extremely simple to diagram:

```
S          (* The critical operation *)
```

Recall from our earlier discussion of binary search that the list we are searching must first be sorted before we can apply the algorithm. One of the best-known sorting algorithms (although we will soon see that it is one of the least efficient) is the *bubble sort*, which is shown in Figure 6–4. The algorithm works by interchanging pairs of values that are out of order. After one complete pass through the list, the largest item will have been placed in its correct location (assuming ascending order). After making one pass through the list, we check to see if any exchanges were made. If not, the list is sorted. If at least one exchange was made, we must make another pass through the list. We repeat this process until no exchanges are made.

If we consider the critical operation to be the comparison operation (List[i] > List[$i + 1$]), then in the worst case we would have to make ($n - 1$) complete passes through the list, each time comparing the top j items, where $j = n, n - 1,$

Figure 6–4
Bubble-Sort Algorithm

```
(* The procedure BubbleSort sorts a list List[1 .. N] into ascending order. *)
Procedure BubbleSort(Var List : ArrayType; N : Integer);
Var
    i, j      : Integer;
    Done      : Boolean;
    Tmp       ; Integer;
Begin
    j := N;

    Repeat
        Done := True;           (* We're done if we go through the entire list
                                without moving any elements. *)
        j := j - 1;
        For i := 1 To j Do      (* Go though the list up to element j. *)
        (* Are these elements in the right place ? *)
            If (List[i] > List[i+1]) Then
                Done := False;  (* We're not done yet. *)
                Tmp := List[i];
                List[i] := List[i+1];
                List[i+1] := Tmp;
            Endif;

        Endfor;

    Until Done;
End BubbleSort;
```

$n - 2, \ldots, 2$. In the worst case, the total number of comparisons needed to sort the array would be

$$\sum_{j=2}^{n} j = \frac{n(n+1)}{2} - 1 = (1/2)\,n^2 + (1/2)\,n - 1$$

When analyzing algorithms and formulating Big-O notation, we generally do not care about the contributions of either constant factors or lower-order terms. For example, if our analysis of an algorithm leads to a time complexity polynomial of the form

$$an^k + bn^{k-1} + cn^{k-2} + \ldots$$

we would say that the algorithm is $O(n^k)$. The constant factor a will change only the location of the point n^* in Figure 6–1; it will not change either the shape of the curve or the conclusions that we reach about the algorithm's efficiency, and it can therefore be disregarded. Similarly, since we care about the behavior of the algorithm only as n becomes large, we disregard all lower-order items. As n becomes large, $n^k >> n^{k-1} >> n^{k-2} >> \ldots$, and the term containing n^k overwhelms the much smaller contribution made by lower-order terms.

However, because asymptotic analysis disregards constant factors and lower-order terms, we must be careful about the claims we make concerning the efficiency of one algorithm over another. For example, if algorithm A is $O(n)$ and algorithm B is $O(n^2)$, we cannot say that algorithm A is *always* superior to algorithm B, only that it will *eventually* be superior. For example, if the actual time complexity of A is a linear polynomial of the form $t = 1000n + 500$ and the actual time complexity of B is $t = 0.01n^2$, the quadratic algorithm would actually be faster for all problems up to size $n \approx 100{,}000$. Beyond that point, however, the inherent efficiency of the linear method starts to dominate. At a problem size of $n = 10{,}000{,}000$ the linear algorithm is already 100 times faster than the quadratic one!

With these two considerations, we can now say that the bubble sort of Figure 6–4, which requires $1/2n^2 + 1/2n - 1$ comparisons, is $O(n^2)$; it is an example of a *quadratic complexity* function. The typical structure of a quadratic algorithm is

```
For i := 1 To n Do          (* An outer loop done n times *)
    For j := 1 To n Do      (* An inner loop done n times *)
        S                   (* The critical operation *)
    End
End
```

Quadratic complexities are typical of a large class of simple sorting algorithms that are usually introduced in a first course in programming. This class includes not only bubble sort, but enumeration sort, copy sort, insertion sort, and selection sort. Analysis of these algorithms is left as an exercise for you at the end of the chapter. Other examples of quadratic algorithms include matrix addition and matrix transposition.

Recall that we introduced two other sorting algorithms, QuickSort and MergeSort, in chapter 5. Compared to the bubble sort, these algorithms display improved efficiency and a lower-order complexity; their running time is propor-

Table 6–4 Comparisons of $O(n^2)$ and $O(n \log_2 n)$ Algorithms

PROBLEM SIZE n	MAXIMUM NUMBER OF COMPARISONS NEEDED TO SORT A LIST $O(n^2)$	$O(n \log_2 n)$
10	100	33
100	10,000	670
1,000	1,000,000	10,000
50,000	2.5×10^9	780,000
800,000	6.4×10^{11}	1.6×10^7

tional not to n^2 but to the function $n \log_2 n$. (We will show how to determine the complexity of these recursive algorithms in section 6.5.) These algorithms are just two members of a class of fast and efficient sorting techniques whose time complexities are all $O(n \log_2 n)$. Other examples that we will see in upcoming chapters include TreeSort (chapter 7) and HeapSort (chapter 8).

Table 6–4 gives the maximum number of operations needed to sort lists of different sizes using these two classes of sorting techniques, $O(n^2)$ and $O(n \log_2 n)$. As with binary search, when n is small (e.g., $n < 100$), the differences between the behavior of the different classes of algorithms are small and the choice of which type of sorting method to use is relatively unimportant. As n gets large, however, the speed advantages of the $O(n \log_2 n)$ algorithms become more and more apparent. When sorting a list of 800,000 items, an $O(n \log_2 n)$ algorithm requires almost four orders of magnitude fewer comparisons to sort a list than the simpler but slower class of $O(n^2)$ methods.

Let's look at an example that will emphasize this point. Suppose we are going to run one program from each of the two classes of sorting algorithms listed in Table 6–4 and a third "compromise" $O(n^{1.5})$ algorithm on three quite different computers—a \$1000 Apple Macintosh, a \$100,000 VAX minicomputer, and a \$10,000,000 Cray-2 supercomputer. The Cray will run the inefficient $O(n^2)$ method, the VAX will execute the compromise $O(n^{1.5})$ algorithm, and the inexpensive Macintosh will be assigned the efficient $O(n \log_2 n)$ technique. Furthermore, let's assume that we can measure the performance capabilities of the three and develop exact formulas for the running times (in microseconds) of the algorithms on each machine. Assume these formulas are

$$t_1 = n^2 \qquad \text{(for the Cray-2)}$$
$$t_2 = 1{,}000\, n^{1.5} \qquad \text{(for the VAX)}$$
$$t_3 = 10{,}000\, n \log_2 n \qquad \text{(for the Macintosh)}$$

Notice how much larger the constants of proportionality are for the VAX and the Macintosh; the large constants reflect the fact that these computers are three to four orders of magnitude slower than the Cray-2. Table 6–5 shows the hypothetical results of running these three different classes of sorting algorithms on the three machines.

For small n (e.g., $n = 100$), the Cray-2 supercomputer's immense speed allows it to overcome the inefficient method it is using and it solves the problem 100 times

Table 6–5 Running Times for Three Different Algorithms on Three Different Computers

PROBLEM SIZE n	APPROXIMATE RUNNING TIME		
	Cray-2 $t = n^2$	VAX $t = 1{,}000\ n^{1.5}$	Macintosh $t = 10{,}000\ n \log_2 n$
100	0.01 sec	1 sec	7 sec
1,000	1 sec	31 sec	100 sec
10,000	1.7 min	17 min	22 min
100,000	3 hr	9 hr	5 hr
1,000,000	12 days	12 days	2 days
10,000,000	3 years	10 months	27 days

faster than the VAX and 700 times faster than the Macintosh. As n becomes larger, these differences gradually disappear as the inherent inefficiencies in the algorithms begin to overwhelm the abilities of the larger machines to keep up with the number of computations required. At $n = 100{,}000$, all three computers are taking roughly the same amount of time to solve the problem—on the order of a few hours. At $n = 10{,}000{,}000$, the efficiency of the $O(n \log_2 n)$ algorithm has become the dominant factor, and the Macintosh completes the sorting task 40 times faster than the Cray, a machine that costs 10,000 times more money and runs thousands of times faster! Simply recoding the $O(n^2)$ algorithm or buying more memory for the Cray may postpone the problem, but these improvements will not make the problem disappear. It is simply a characteristic of a lower-order algorithm that there will exist a point (about $n = 100{,}000$ in our example) beyond which the lower-order algorithm will always take less time to complete the task, regardless of the constants of proportionality.

As a final example, let us analyze the complexity of the well-known matrix multiplication operation, $C = A \times B$, defined as

$$C_{ij} = \sum_{k=1}^{n} (A_{ik} * B_{kj}) \qquad i = 1, \ldots, n;\ j = 1, \ldots, n$$

The critical operations in this example are the additions and multiplications needed to produce the result. If we assume that both A and B are $n \times n$ matrices, then the above formula shows that the determination of each separate element of the product matrix C will require $2n - 1$ operations—n multiplications and $(n - 1)$ additions. These $2n - 1$ operations must be repeated for each of the $n \times n$ positions in the resulting matrix C. Thus, the total number of operations required to obtain C is $n^2(2n - 1) = 2n^3 - n^2$. We could say that the complexity of matrix multiplication is $O(2n^3 - n^2)$. However, as we mentioned earlier, all we are interested in is the limiting or asymptotic behavior of the function. When n gets large the contribution of the n^2 term will be relatively insignificant compared to the value of n^3. Thus, we would say that the complexity of matrix multiplication as given by the previous formula is $O(n^3)$; it is a *cubic complexity* function. The general model of an algorithm with cubic complexity is

```
For i := 1 To n Do              (* Outermost loop done n times *)
    For j := 1 To n Do          (* Middle loop done n times *)
        For k := 1 To n Do      (* Inner loop done n times *)
            S                   (* The critical operation *)
        End
    End
End
```

(It is interesting to note that there is a faster algorithm for performing matrix multiplication. It is called Strassen's Matrix Multiplication Method, and its time complexity has been reduced to about $O(n^{2.81})$.)

Most of the time complexities we have seen so far have been of the form $O(n)$, $O(n^{1.5})$, $O(n^2)$, and $O(n^3)$. Algorithms with these types of time complexities are called *polynomial time algorithms* because their complexity functions are polynomial functions of relatively small degree. The computational demands of these algorithms are usually manageable, even for large problems, because their time and space needs do not grow unreasonably fast. However, not all algorithms are of this type. There is a second and very distinct group of methods called *exponential time algorithms*. Exponential algorithms typically display complexities of $O(2^n)$, $O(k^n)$, $O(n^n)$, or $O(n!)$. The time and space demands of these algorithms grow extremely fast, and they consume vast amounts of resources, even for small problems. In most cases it is not feasible to attempt to solve any problem of realistic size using an exponential algorithm, no matter how clever the programmer or how fast the computer.

Exponential algorithms are not just of academic interest. They occur frequently in several areas of computer science, applied mathematics, and operations research. In fact, an important area of computer science research has developed specifically to study this category of *computationally intractable* problems.

One example of such an algorithm is the traveling salesperson problem. In this problem, one of the most famous in computer science, we have a salesperson who must travel to *N* other cities, visiting each one only once, and end up back home. This travel circuit is called a *tour*. We want to know if it is possible to make a tour within a given mileage allowance, *k*; that is, the sum of all the distances traveled by the salesperson must be less than or equal to *k*. For example, given the following mileage chart, showing the distances between four cities A, B, C, and D

	A	B	C	D
A	—	500	100	800
B	500	—	900	150
C	100	900	—	600
D	800	150	600	—

and a mileage allowance of 1500 miles, an acceptable tour is possible starting at our home base A: A → C → D → B → A (length 1350 miles). If the mileage allowance were only 1000 miles, no acceptable tour would be possible.

No algorithm has yet been discovered that allows us to solve this problem in a reasonable (i.e., polynomial) time. For example, an exhaustive search of all possible tours would start from the premise that we could select any one of the N cities as the first one to visit. We could then select any one of the remaining $(N - 1)$ cities to visit next, then any of the remaining $(N - 2)$ cities, and so on. The total number of tours that we would need to examine to see if they fall within our mileage allowance would be

$$N \times (N - 1) \times (N - 2) \times \ldots \times 1 = N!$$

Thus the complexity of this "*brute force*," exhaustive search solution to the traveling salesman problem is $O(N!)$. Better algorithms have been developed, but they still display this characteristic explosive exponential growth that makes this problem unsolvable in the general case for anything except tiny values of N. If $N = 50$, a computer that could evaluate 1 billion tours per second would take approximately 1 million centuries to enumerate all possible tours! (The recursive path-finding algorithm in section 5.4.6 is another example of an exponential-time algorithm.)

As this example clearly shows, exponential time methods may be theoretically describable, but they are computationally impractical. In those cases where no known polynomial algorithm exists, we are usually limited to achieving approximations or "reasonable" rather than "optimal" solutions. Approximation algorithms of this type are called *heuristics*.

6.4 EXAMPLES OF SPACE COMPLEXITY ANALYSIS

In each of the examples in the previous section—searching, sorting, matrix multiplication, and the traveling salesman problem—we analyzed the *time complexity* of an algorithm. However, as we stated at the beginning of the chapter, memory space is also an important resource, and we can develop and analyze *space complexity* measures in a similar fashion. To analyze space complexity, we need to develop a formula that relates n, the problem size, to s, the the amount of memory space needed to solve the problem. For example, both the sequential and the binary search methods require a table large enough to hold all n items and are therefore $O(n)$ in terms of space complexity.

Memory space and computer time are usually inversely related; we can frequently reduce space requirements by increasing processing time or, conversely, reduce processing time by making more memory available. We refer to this situation as the *space-time trade-off*.

For example, when we store the elements of an $n \times n$ matrix using the following array declaration:

```
Var
    Matrix = Array [1 .. n, 1 .. n] Of Integer;
```

we obviously are using n^2 memory locations, and the space complexity of an algorithm using this declaration would be $O(n^2)$. But suppose most of the cells in this array are zero, as in

0	0	0	0	0	0
0	0	36	0	0	0
0	0	0	0	0	0
0	0	0	0	0	17
0	0	0	0	0	0
1	0	0	0	0	0

Such a structure is called a *sparse matrix*, and there are much more efficient ways to store the values of a sparse matrix. For example, we could create a $3 \times k$ data structure that stores only the row and column indices and the data values of the k nonzero elements. We could create this data structure using the following declaration:

```
Var
    Sparse              = Array [1 .. MaxNonZero] Of
        Record
            Row         : [1 .. n];
            Column      : [1 .. n];
            Value       : Integer
        End;
```

Now our previous sparse matrix, which contained only three nonzero values, would be stored as

Row	*Column*	*Value*
2	3	36
4	6	17
6	1	1

The space needs of this alternative representation are linear with respect to the number of nonzero values—that is, $O(k)$, where k is the number of nonzero entries—a significant improvement in space efficiency. With the previous $O(n^2)$ technique, a sparse matrix that increased in size from 10×10 to 100×100 would require an additional 9900 memory cells to store the additional values, even if many of them were zeros. Our new sparse matrix representation would require only three additional cells for each nonzero entry. If the 10×10 and 100×100 matrices contained the same number of nonzero elements, their space needs would be exactly the same, since the space complexity of the sparse representation is dependent not on the array dimensions, but only on the number of nonzero values.

In exchange for that reduction in space, however, we will generally have to spend additional time processing the data in this reduced representation. For example, printing the contents of a two-dimensional $n \times n$ matrix in the normal square form is a simple $O(n^2)$ operation if the matrix has been stored as a traditional two-dimensional array:

```
For i := 1 To n Do
    For j := 1 To n Do
        Write(A[i,j])       (* This is the critical operation. *)
    End;
    WriteLn
End
```

When the data are stored in our reduced representation, printing out the matrix is not so easy. For each $[i,j]$ position we print, we must first look up the row and column indices in the data structure to see whether that element is there. The algorithm will look something like

```
For i := 1 To n Do
    For j := 1 To n Do
        Value := Find(A,i,j);      (* See if the [i,j]th entry of A is in the
                                      reduced representation. If yes, Find return
                                      its value, if not Find returns 0. *)
        Write(Value)
    End;
    WriteLn
End
```

If the Find function searches the reduced data structure sequentially, it will take a maximum of $O(k)$ operations to determine if the $[i,j]$th entry is there, where k is the number of nonzero elements in the table. Since this operation will be done n^2 times, the overall printing operation now becomes a $O(kn^2)$ algorithm, compared to the $O(n^2)$ algorithm for traditional matrix storage. As we get more and more nonzero values (e.g., as k approaches n) this algorithm will degenerate into an $O(n^3)$ technique. We have saved on space at the expense of increasing the computational time needed to carry out operations on that data.

Similarly, inserting a nonzero value X into the $[i,j]$th position of the array, which used to be a simple $O(1)$ operation:

```
A[i,j] := X
```

is now an $O(k)$ operation in which we must first search the data structure to determine whether the entry is already there and, if it is not, add it in the proper place. This algorithm and its analysis are left as an exercise.

6.5 THE ANALYSIS OF RECURSIVE ALGORITHMS

The asymptotic or limiting behavior of algorithms is important for both the classic iterative techniques you are familiar with as well as for the recursive methods that were discussed in the previous chapter. However, the methods for analyzing these two types of algorithms differ dramatically. With iterative methods we study the looping structures of the program and count how many times a critical operation within that loop will be performed. So, for example, when we see

```
For i := 1 To n Do
    S;
```

it is easy to determine that S will be executed n times and that the algorithm must be $O(n)$ if S is the critical operation. We have used this basic approach in the first four sections of this chapter.

This technique does not work with recursive algorithms, however, because the fundamental control structure of recursive programs is not a loop but a recursive procedure call. For example, looking at the following code

```
Procedure Silly(n) : Integer;
    Var a,b : Integer;
Begin
    If n <= 1 Then
        Return 1
    Else
        a := Silly(n/2);
        b := Silly(n/2);
        Return (a + b)
    End If;
End Silly;
```

it is not obvious how to determine the number of times we will recursively call the procedure Silly as a function of the value of the parameter n. Determining complexity is no longer just a simple counting operation.

The technique that is used to analyze recursive algorithms uses a mathematical construct called a *recurrence relation*. These relations can be quite complex to solve, and in this section of the text we introduce you only briefly to this difficult but important topic. Other courses in discrete mathematics and computer science will discuss the topic in greater detail.

A recurrence relation is a formula of the form

$$T(n) = f(T(m)) \qquad m < n$$

which recursively describes the value of a function T with parameter n in terms of the same function T, but with a simpler (i.e., smaller) parameter value. When developing recurrence relations for recursive functions, we relate the number of times the critical operation is executed on a problem of size n to the number of times it is executed on the smaller subproblems generated by a recursive call. If $T(n)$ represents the number of times the critical operation is executed on a problem of size n, and if we recursively call the procedure for a smaller problem of size m, we need to determine the functional relationship between $T(n)$ and $T(m)$.

For example, looking back at the procedure Silly and assuming that the comparison $(n \leq 1)$ is the critical operation, we can see that when n is less than or equal to 1 the comparison will be done only once. For n greater than 1, we will make one comparison, and two recursive calls on problems that are half the size of the original. The number of comparisons that will be done for each of these calls is just $T(n/2)$. Therefore the total number of times the critical operation will be executed can be expressed as:

$$\begin{aligned} T(n) &= 2T(n/2) + 1 \qquad && n > 1 \\ &= 1 && n \leq 1 \end{aligned}$$

We solve this recurrence relation by using repeated substitution

$$T(n) = 2T(n/2) + 1$$

To get the value of T($n/2$) we substitute $n/2$ in the above formula and get

$$T(n/2) = 2T(n/4) + 1$$

substituting this value back into the first equation for T(n) gives

$$\begin{aligned} T(n) &= 2(2T(n/4) + 1) + 1 \\ &= 4T(n/4) + 3 \end{aligned}$$

Similar substitutions yield the following sequence of equalities:

$$\begin{aligned} T(n) &= 8T(n/8) + 7 \\ &= 16T(n/16) + 15 \\ &\bullet \\ &\bullet \\ &\bullet \\ &= 2^k T(n/2^k) + (2^k - 1) \end{aligned}$$

If we let $n = 2^k$ (that is, we assume the original problem size is some integral power of 2) we get

$$T(n) = nT(1) + n - 1$$

But we are given that T(1) = 1 in the original definition of the problem. Therefore,

$$\begin{aligned} T(n) &= (n * 1) + n - 1 \\ &= 2n - 1 \end{aligned}$$

and the total number of comparisons carried out by procedure Silly on a problem of size n is $2n - 1$, which is linear with respect to the parameter n, and the time complexity of algorithm Silly is O(n).

As a second example, let us analyze the Merge Sort algorithm of section 5.4.4. This algorithm splits the n-element list to be sorted into two lists of equal size, $n/2$. These lists are then sorted and merged to produce the final value. This recursive process continues until we have a list of only 1 item, which is returned directly.

The number of comparisons that must be made to sort a list of size n is given by the following recurrence relation:

$$\begin{aligned} T(n) &= 1 && \text{if } n = 1 \\ &= 2T(n/2) + f(n) && \text{if } n > 1 \end{aligned}$$

where f(n) is the complexity of the merge operation that joins the two sorted lists of size $n/2$ into a single sorted list of length n. The value of f(n) is easy to determine by simply looking at the following diagram:

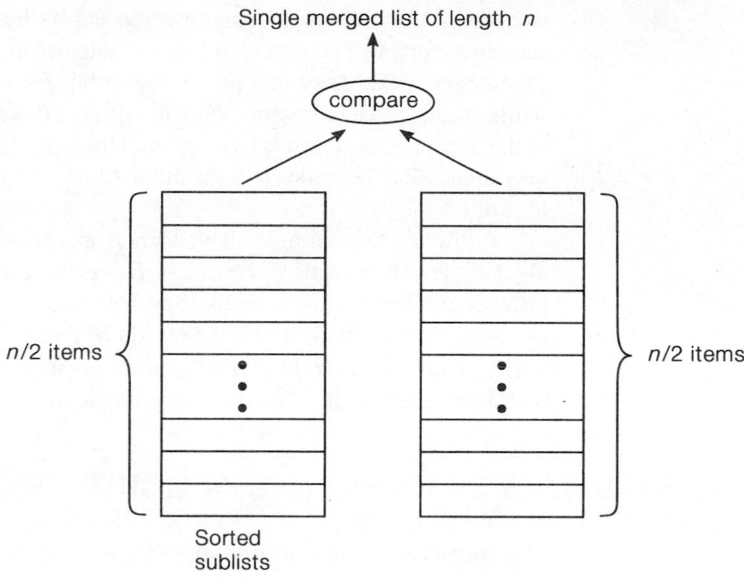

Every time we compare the top items of the two sublists, we select one item and move it to the final sorted list. Since there are a total of n items to be moved, the merge operation will obviously require $O(n)$ comparisons, so $f(n) = an$, where a is some constant value. Putting this value into our recurrence relation and using the technique of repeated substitutions yields

$$\begin{aligned} T(n) &= 2T(n/2) + an \\ &= 4T(n/4) + 2an \\ &= 8T(n/8) + 3an \\ &\quad\vdots \\ &= 2^kT(n/2^k) + kan \end{aligned}$$

Again we let the size of the list being sorted be $n = 2^k$. (If n is not an even multiple of 2^k, setting it to $\lceil 2^k \rceil$ will provide a reasonable approximation.)

$$\begin{aligned} &= nT(1) + an \log_2 n \qquad (\text{* but } T(1) = 1 \text{ *}) \\ &= n + an \log_2 n \end{aligned}$$

As we have done in previous asymptotic analyses, we are allowed to disregard both lower order terms (n) and constant values (a). Thus, the total number of comparisons T needed by MergeSort to sort a list of length n is

$$T(n) = O(n \log_2 n)$$

Thus we have a significant improvement over the $O(n^2)$ behavior of bubble sort (Figure 6–4). In fact, one of the major results of computational mathematics has been the proof that any sorting method that is based on comparing elements of a sequence must use at least $O(n \log_2 n)$ comparisons—sorting cannot be done faster. MergeSort is therefore an optimal algorithm for sorting lists of values, at least to within some constant factor. We will not go through the analysis of QuickSort, but in the average case it too is $O(n \log_2 n)$. However, in the worst case (an almost sorted list), QuickSort degrades to a quadratic $O(n^2)$ method, as was shown and discussed in Table 6–2.

As these two examples have shown, the time and space analysis of recursive algorithms can become exceedingly complex, even for very trivial problems like procedure Silly. For more realistic problems the analysis is quite difficult. The topic of recurrence relations and the analysis of recursive algorithms will be covered in much greater detail in advanced courses on such topics as algorithm design, computational complexity, and discrete mathematics.

6.6 THE ANALYSIS OF PARALLEL ALGORITHMS

The statement we just made—the fastest possible comparison-based sorting techniques are always at least $O(n \log_2 n)$—is really false! That statement is based on the assumption that we have only a single processor and therefore all statements of the sorting procedure must be executed in a strictly sequential order.

However, the rapidly decreasing cost of hardware has led to the development of *massively parallel computers*, systems with hundreds or even thousands of processors, all able to carry out independent operations simultaneously. This replication of processing elements can significantly reduce the time needed to solve a problem.

For example, with only one processor the following code

```
For i := 1 To N Do
    A[i] := 0;
```

represents a classic $O(n)$ **For** loop.

However, if we had N processors available instead of only one, this loop could effectively be "unwound" and reduced to O(1) by simply assigning each processor one of the N assignment statements and executing them all in parallel.

```
            ┌ A[1] := 0;      (* Processor 1 *)
Executed    │ A[2] := 0;      (* Processor 2 *)
in          ┤     •                 •
parallel    │     •                 •
            │     •                 •
            └ A[N] := 0;      (* Processor N *)
```

However, simply having N processors available does not mean that we can always take advantage of them to reduce the total time of some operations. (A commonly used analogy says that if one woman takes nine months to have a baby, the time can't be reduced to one month by assigning nine women to the job!) The following **For** loop,

```
For i := 2 To N
    A[i] := A[i - 1] + 1;
```

although similar in structure to the earlier one, cannot be unwound and carried out in parallel because of data dependencies between the operations:

```
A[2] := A[1] + 1
A[3] := A[2] + 1
    •
    •
    •
```

The second assignment statement cannot be started until the first one has been completed because it uses the value A[2] computed by the first statement. These statements are inherently sequential and cannot take advantage of parallelism.

One of the most rapidly growing areas of computer science is the design and analysis of *parallel algorithms* that can exploit the availability of multiple processing elements to reduce the overall running time of a problem. To demonstrate this possibility, we will design and develop a parallel sorting algorithm and compare it to some of the sequential techniques we discussed earlier.

The parallel sorting algorithm that we will develop is called the *enumeration sort*. It is an inefficient $O(n^2)$ method when executed sequentially, but it works reasonably well in a parallel environment and produces a significant increase in speed over sequential processing.

Given an array of n items A[1 .. n], enumeration sort works by determining the rank, r, of each item in the list. The rank of element A_i is defined as 1 + (the total number of elements in A smaller than A_i). For example, if there are 3 elements smaller than A_i, its rank would be 4, and it would belong in the fourth slot of our final sorted array. (Note: We are assuming that all n items of A are distinct and that we are sorting into ascending order.) If we were doing the ranking sequentially, it would require n looks to compare A_i against all A_j, $j = 1, \ldots, n$, and we would need to carry out all of these comparisons for all A_i, $i = 1, \ldots, n$, so a sequential enumeration sort is $O(n^2)$. As you will see, however, we can do much better in a parallel environment.

The algorithm proceeds in three stages:

Phase I	Comparison
Phase II	Summation
Phase III	Assignment

In Phase I we compare A_i against A_j for all $i, j = 1, \ldots, n$. If $A_i < A_j$ we output a 1. If $A_i > A_j$ we output a 0. (Remember, we are assuming that all A_i are distinct.) There are n^2 such comparisons to be performed. Let us assume that we have at least n^2 independent processors available to us; then all the comparisons can be done simultaneously since there are no data dependencies between the comparisons. We simply assign processor P_{ij} the job of comparing element A_i to element A_j as shown in Figure 6–5. All n^2 comparisons can be carried out in parallel, so the computing time of Phase I is O(1). (Note: We are disregarding any problems associated with doing n concurrent reads from the same memory location—we assume this is per-

Figure 6–5
The Parallel Comparison Phase

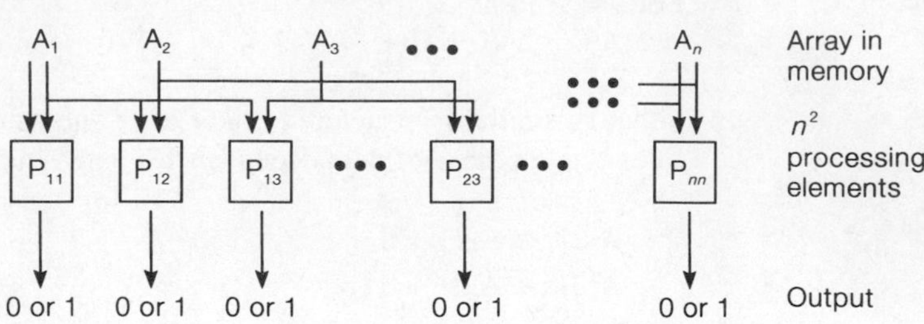

missible on our computer.) Each processor P_{ij} writes its result into location R_{ij} of a matrix called R. When the comparisons are completed, we will have created an $n \times n$ array R of 0s and 1s, where $R_{ij} = 0$ if $A_i > A_j$ and $R_{ij} = 1$ if $A_i < A_j$. For example, given A = (8, 3, 9, 5), we would end up with the following Boolean matrix R at the completion of Phase I.

$$R = \begin{bmatrix} 0 & 0 & 1 & 0 \\ 1 & 0 & 1 & 1 \\ 0 & 0 & 0 & 0 \\ 1 & 0 & 1 & 0 \end{bmatrix}$$

If we now sum up the values in each column of the array R, we will have the desired rank of each element in the array. The rank of element A_j is

$$\text{Rank}(A_j) = 1 + \sum_i R_{ij}$$

In this example the values for Rank would be: (3, 1, 4, 2). This rank array specifies the proper location of element A_j in the final sorted sequence. For example, the proper rank of the value 8 in A[1] is given by Rank[1], which is 3. In the final sorted array, (3, 5, 8, 9), the value 8 will be the third item.

How can we do this column addition operation efficiently and in a way that exploits the capabilities of parallelism? The answer is that we use a technique called *binary summation*: we simultaneously add up pairs of elements A[1] + A[2], A[3] + A[4], . . . , A[n − 1] + A[n]. The addition requires $n/2$ processors and again involves no data dependencies. When this first pairwise addition step has been completed, we take those results and add them together, a pair at a time. This pairwise summation process is repeated until we get the single value that is our desired result. This technique is diagrammed in Figure 6–6 for an eight-element array.

This process will require $n/2$ processors per column. (Actually we need this many processors only during the first step. After that we need only half as many processors for each succeeding step, so some processors will sit idle.) Since we have n columns in an array R, we will require $n * (n/2) = 1/2\ n^2$ processors, which we have assumed that we have available. Therefore we can do the addition operation shown in Figure 6–6 in parallel for each column of the array R. The time complexity of the algorithm that carries out this phase for one column will be $O(\log_2 n)$; it is determined in exactly the same way as we determined the complexity of the binary

Figure 6–6
The Parallel Addition Process

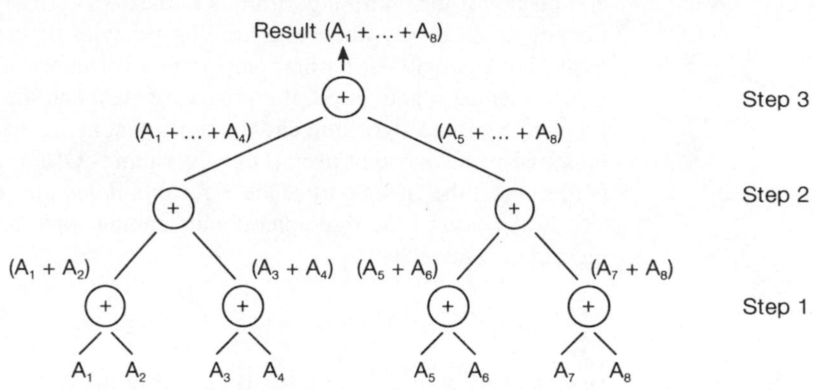

search algorithm, which also halves the size of the problem at each iteration. Since the operations on each column are going on simultaneously, the overall complexity of the summation operation for all n columns is also $O(\log_2 n)$.

Finally, we must place the data values in their proper order in the sorted array B[1 .. n]. However, once we have determined the value of Rank(j), $j = 1 .. n$, this operation is simple:

```
B[Rank(1)] := A[1]        (* Processor 1 *)
B[Rank(2)] := A[2]        (* Processor 2 *)
        •
        •
        •
B[Rank(n)] := A[n]        (* Processor n *)
```

These operations can all be done simultaneously by n processors, so the complexity of the assignment phase is O(1).

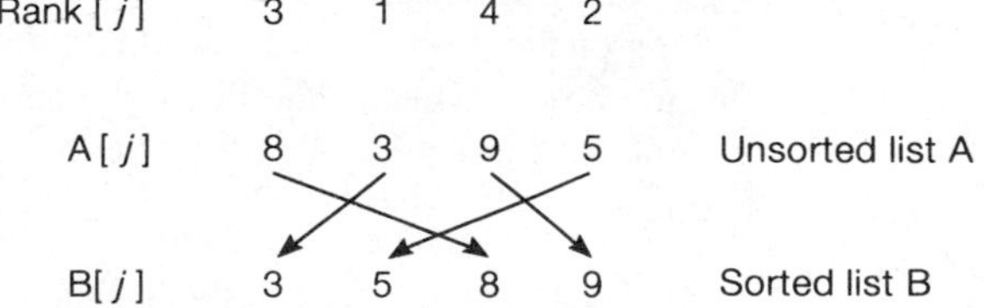

We now can complete our analysis of the parallel enumeration sort

	Phase	*Processors needed*	*Complexity*
I.	Comparison	n^2	O(1)
II.	Summation	$1/2n^2$	O(log n)
III.	Assignment	n	O(1)

If we are trying to determine the overall complexity of an algorithm that executes in two stages, where the first part is O(f(n)) and the second part is O(g(n)), then the complexity of the entire algorithm is O(max[f(n),g(n)]) because, as we have mentioned, we care only about the limiting behavior of the algorithm as n gets very large. For example, if the first part of an algorithm is O(n) and the second part is O(n^2), then as n gets large, the program will spend the majority of its time in the second part of the algorithm and the time spent in the first part would become negligible; we would say that overall the algorithm is O(n^2). Another way to phrase this is to say that the O(n^2) part of the algorithm *dominates* the O(n) part.

In the case of the three-phase enumeration sort, the overall complexity of the algorithm is given by:

$$O(\max[O(1),\ O(\log_2 n),\ O(1)]) = O(\log_2 n)$$

Here we have a significant improvement over the O(n^2) and O($n \log_2 n$) algorithms that we have studied. For example, referring back to Table 6–4, we see that for a sorting problem of size n = 50,000, an O(n^2) algorithm like bubble sort would require about 10^9 comparisons. To solve the problem with an O($n \log_2 n$) method like QuickSort would require about 10^6 comparisons. Our enumeration sort will require only that each processor do about $\log_2$ 100,000 = 17 comparisons, an improvement of almost eight orders of magnitude over bubble sort and five orders of magnitude over QuickSort. However, before we become too amazed at this efficiency, remember that to achieve this increase in speed we will need a computer with $(50{,}000)^2$ = 2.5 billion processors! Such a quantity of processors is many orders of magnitude beyond current capabilities. The largest parallel processors built so far have about 10^4 processors, and the typical parallel system has considerably fewer, usually on the order of 10^1 or 10^2 processing elements.

With parallel algorithms, a better measure of the overall efficiency of an algorithm would probably be the *processor-time product*, PT, also called the *cost* of the algorithm.

$$PT = (\text{number of processors used}) \times (\text{overall time complexity})$$

That is, it is not simply the time complexity that we should look at, but the number of processors it takes to achieve that time. (After all, with 2.5 billion processors all working on the problem, we would certainly expect to see an increase in speed! The question now is whether the increase justifies the extra resources.)

The processor-time product for the parallel enumeration sort using n^2 processors is:

$$PT = n^2 \times \log_2 n = O(n^2 \log_2 n)$$

When considered in these terms, the parallel enumeration sort is not even as good as our sequential, one-processor QuickSort technique of chapter 5. The processor-time product there is:

$$PT = 1 \times n \log_2 n = O(n \log_2 n)$$

There do exist a number of parallel sorting methods (e.g., a parallel version of MergeSort) that can sort n numbers in O($\log_2 n$) logarithmic time, as we did with

EnumerationSort, but with only a linear number of processors rather than a quadratic number. For these algorithms, the processor-time product would be

$$PT = n \times \log_2 n = O(n \log_2 n)$$

and the overall cost would be the same as the cost for sequential sorting using the best sequential algorithms such as QuickSort. It is therefore possible with parallelism to achieve an improvement in time complexity from $O(n \log_2 n)$ to $O(\log_2 n)$ for a comparable expenditure in resources; that is, given n times more processors, the program runs n times faster.

The topic of parallel computing systems and the design of parallel algorithms is becoming central to a study of computer science. This chapter has been only a brief introduction to this interesting and important subject. Future courses will investigate these ideas in much greater depth.

6.7 CONCLUSION

This chapter has been an introduction to the complexity analysis of iterative, recursive, and parallel algorithms. The central point to remember is the fundamental importance of algorithm behavior to the overall efficiency of the program. The selection of the best method is ultimately more important than the language used for the algorithm or the machine on which the program will be run.

CHAPTER EXERCISES

1. The most common computing times for algorithms are

   $O(1)$
   $O(\log_2 n)$
   $O(n)$
   $O(n \log_2 n)$
   $O(n^2)$
   $O(n^3)$
   $O(2^n)$

   Graph these time complexities in the range $1 \le n \le 128$ and compare their rates of growth. (Assume that the coefficients are 1 in all cases and that all lower-order terms are disregarded.) What is the difference between $O(n^2)$ and $O(2^n)$ for $n = 4, 8, 64$? At what point n^* do these time complexities become ordered in the sequence given above (that is, for any $n > n^*$, $O(1) < O(\log_2 n) < O(n) < O(n \log_2 n) < O(n^2) < O(n^3) < O(2^n)$)?
2. Time complexities generally have coefficients other than 1 and have lower-order terms that are not considered. For example, the actual time or space complexity of an $O(n^3)$ algorithm might be

   $(1/2)n^3 + 500n^2 - 1$

Nevertheless, it is still true that if f(n) is of a lower order than g(n), there will always be a point n^* such that for all $n > n^*$, O[f(n)] < O[g(n)]. For the following pairs of complexity functions, find the point n^* where the first function is always less than the second.

a. $(1/2)n^2 + (1/2)n - 1$ $\quad$ $(1/8)n^3$
b. $\log_2 n$ $\quad$ $10{,}000n$
c. $3n^3 + 50$ $\quad$ $(1/50)2^{n/2}$
d. 5×10^6 $\quad$ $(1/10{,}000)n$

3. Looking at the sequential search in Figure 6–2, why would it be inappropriate to let the critical operation be the assignment statement

   $i = 1;$

   in the first line of the program? If that were incorrectly called the critical operation, what would the time complexity of the procedure be?
4. In Figure 6–2, what operations, other than the comparison L[i] = Key, could properly be called the critical operation and produce a correct time complexity of O(n)?
5. What is the complexity of the following algorithmic structures with respect to problem size n? Assume that S is the critical operation and a is a constant greater than 1.

a.
```
For i := 1 To n Do
    For j := i To i Do
        S;
    End
End
```
b.
```
For i := 1 To n Do
    For j := 1 To a Do
        S
    End
End
```
c.
```
For i := 1 To a Do
    For j := 1 To a Do
        S
    End
End
```
d.
```
X := 1
Repeat
    S;
    X := X * a          (* a > 1 *)
Until X > n
```
e.
```
For i := 1 To n By a
    S
End
```

6. The function e^x can be approximated by using the following formula

$$e^x = 1 + x + \frac{x^2}{2!} + \frac{x^3}{3!} + \ldots + \frac{x^k}{k!}$$

What is the complexity of this evaluation as a function of k, the number of terms in the expansion? For the critical operation, use the number of arithmetic operations performed.

7. What starting conditions are necessary to produce the worst-case behavior of the bubble sort shown in Figure 6–4?
8. Is the following argument valid?

   An O(1) algorithm will be superior to an O(n^3) algorithm in every case.

   If valid, explain why. If invalid, give a counterexample.
9. The following is a description of a simple algorithm called *copy sort*, which sorts an array into ascending order. Copy sort searches an array A to find the smallest element, copies it to B[1], and "destroys" the original value in A by setting it to a very large value. The process of searching A, copying the value into the next cell of B, and destroying the value in A is repeated until the entire array A has been copied into array B in ascending order. What is the time complexity of this algorithm? What is the space complexity?
10. What is the time complexity of the matrix multiplication

    $$C = A \times B$$

    if A and B are no longer both $n \times n$, but A is $n \times p$ and B is $p \times m$?
11. What is the time complexity of matrix transposition for an $n \times n$ matrix? Transposition is defined as

    $$\text{Interchange}(A_{ij}, A_{ji}) \qquad i = 1, \ldots, n \qquad j = 1, \ldots, i - 1$$

    Sketch out an algorithm and analyze its complexity.
12. Assume that we have text containing n characters $T_1, \ldots, T_n$. We also have a pattern containing m characters $P_1, \ldots, P_m$ where $m \leq n$. We want to determine whether the pattern $P_1, \ldots, P_m$ occurs as a substring anywhere within the text T. Our method will be to line up P_1 with T_1 and compare up to the next m characters to see if they are all identical. If they all match, we have found our answer. If not, we stop the current comparison and "slide" the pattern forward, line up P_1 with T_2, and compare the next m characters. We continue in this way until we either find a match or know that no such match exists.

    Sketch an algorithm for this generalized *pattern-matching* process and determine its time complexity. Can you think of a more efficient way to do generalized pattern matching?
13. a. A polynomial

    $$P = a_n x^n + a_{n-1} x^{n-1} + \ldots + a_1 x + a_0$$

    can be evaluated in many different ways. The straightforward way is

    $$P = a_n * x * x * \ldots * x + a_{n-1} * \ldots * x + \ldots + a_0$$

Write a procedure to evaluate a polynomial with coefficients $a_0, \ldots, a_n$ at point x using this straightforward technique. Determine how many multiplications, additions, and assignments are required as a function of the degree, n, of the polynomial. What is the time complexity of this algorithm?

b. An alternative way to evaluate P is to factor the polynomial in the following manner (called *Horner's rule*):

$$P = (\ldots((a_n x + a_{n-1})x + a_{n-2})x + \ldots + a_1)x + a_0$$

Write a procedure to evaluate a polynomial with coefficients $a_0, \ldots, a_n$ at point x using Horner's rule. How many multiplications, additions, and assignments are required as a function of the degree, n? What is the time complexity of this algorithm?

14. In section 5.4.6 you were asked to determine for a given set of nodes and links whether there was a *path* between any two arbitrary nodes, i and j. You were given a matrix $M[i,j]$ that described the physical connections between nodes:

$M[i,j] = 1$ if there is a link from node i to node j.
$M[i,j] = 0$ if these is no link from node i to node j.

For example, if our connections are as shown below

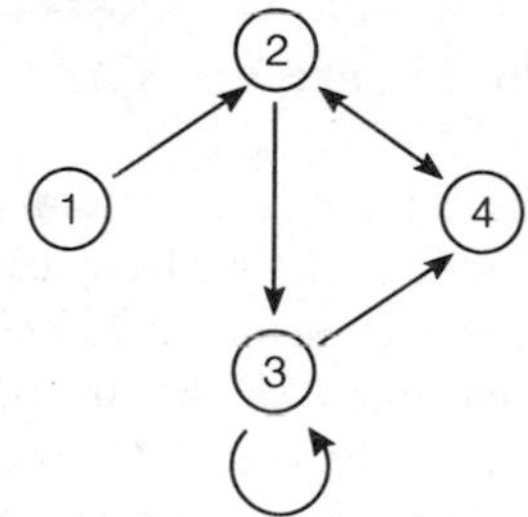

M would look like:

$$M = \begin{bmatrix} 0 & 1 & 0 & 0 \\ 0 & 0 & 1 & 1 \\ 0 & 0 & 1 & 1 \\ 0 & 1 & 0 & 0 \end{bmatrix}$$

There is a path from node 1 to node 3 ($1 \rightarrow 2 \rightarrow 3$) but no path from 4 to 1 or from 3 to 1. If you have not done so already, develop a procedure that, given M and some specific values for i and j, determines if there is a path from node i to node j. Determine the time complexity of your algorithm as a function of the number of nodes. Is your complexity polynomial or exponential?

15. In our example that showed the results of running three different sorting algorithms on three different computers, the time complexity of the algorithm

running on the Cray-2 was $t = n^2$. If we changed that to $t = 0.00001n^2$, would that change our conclusion? At what point (if any) would the Macintosh and Cray perform identically?

16. Imagine that we have an algorithm P whose time complexity we have analyzed and found to be $O(\log_2(\log_2 n))$. What would be the position of that complexity function in the ordered list of functions given in exercise 1?
17. Try to write the most efficient program to solve the following problem: You are given an array A of length n. The elements of A are signed integers. Your program should find the subscript values i and j such that the sum of the contiguous values $A[i] + A[i + 1] + \ldots + A[j - 1] + A[j]$ is the largest possible value. For example, given the following seven-element array:

	1	2	3	4	5	6	7
A	10	−18	−2	40	21	−5	16

your program would output the two values (4,7), since the largest sum of values in contiguous elements of the array is contained in A[4] through A[7] (the sum is 72). After writing the program, evaluate it for efficiency in terms of
a. Its time complexity (as a function of N).
b. Its space complexity.
Be careful with this problem, as there are many different ways to solve it with complexities running all the way from $O(n^3)$ down to $O(n)$.
18. Write a procedure called Insert to add a new value X to position $A[i,j]$, when A is stored in the sparse matrix representation shown in section 6.4. The calling sequence is

Insert(A, i, j, X)

Your procedure should look up the row and column indices (i,j) in the reduced representation of array A. If (i,j) is there, the procedure should change the value field to X. If it is not there, the procedure should add it so that the table is still sorted by row and column index. What is the time complexity of the Insert procedure?
19. If we wanted to store the complete contents of a text-oriented CRT screen with 80 columns and 24 rows, a straightforward approach would be to use the following structure:

```
Var
    Screen : Array [1 .. 24, 1 .. 80] Of Char;
```

This will require saving 1,920 characters. Design a data structure that saves the contents of a screen using less memory space. (Hint: What if most of the spaces are blank?) Using your data structure, write a procedure to display on a 24×80 screen the information that was saved. The characters should be placed in their proper position on the screen. What is the space complexity of your new representation? What is the time complexity of your procedure?

20. Can you write an O(1) algorithm to determine $n!$ for $1 \leq n \leq 15$?
21. A symmetric matrix is one in which $A_{ij} = A_{ji}$ for all i, j:

$$\begin{matrix} 1 & 8 & -13 & 4 \\ 8 & 70 & 82 & 2 \\ -13 & 82 & 0 & -6 \\ 4 & 2 & -6 & 99 \end{matrix}$$

    Develop a space-efficient representation for symmetric matrices that takes less than n^2 cells (assuming one integer value per cell). Now write a procedure to do matrix addition using your new representation. Does it take longer than addition using the traditional $n \times n$ representation?
22. Solve the following recurrence relation

$$T(n) = \begin{cases} 2T(n/2) + 2 & n > 2 \\ 1 & n = 2 \\ 0 & n = 1 \end{cases}$$

23. Design and analyze the parallel sorting algorithm called ShuffleSort. In this method we do a pairwise comparison of elements: A_1 and A_2, A_3 and A_4, A_5 and A_6, ... If the two elements compared are out of order we switch them. If they are in order, we leave them alone. We then compare A_2 and A_3, A_4 and A_5, A_6 and A_7, . . . and repeat these two levels of comparisons until no changes are made. Show how this sorting technique would work for the six-element list A:

    (17, 21, 10, 5, 3, 18)

    How many processors are needed for this problem? What is its time complexity?

CHAPTER 7

TREES AND BINARY TREES

CHAPTER OUTLINE

7.1 INTRODUCTION

In this chapter we will study a data structure that is quite different from the arrays, strings, stacks, and queues of chapter 3 and the lists of chapter 4. Those data structures are linear; that is, every nonempty example of these structures has a first and last element, and every element except the first and last has a unique successor and a unique predecessor element. Now we begin to look at the class of *hierarchical* data structures, which we first diagrammed in Figure 3–1b. Hierarchical structures are characterized by the fact that although every element has a single predecessor, it may have many successors. In computer science we call these hierarchical structures *trees*.

Such structures should be familiar to you from everyday life. For example, everybody has a family tree of the type shown in Figure 7–1. Sporting competitions, corporate management structures, and term paper outlines are often displayed in a tree-like manner as well.

Trees have many computer-related applications. One important use is in the construction of a *parse tree*, a tree structure that shows the grammatical relationships among the syntactic elements of a sentence. You may have been introduced to parse trees when you learned to diagram sentences in elementary school. For example, Figure 7–2 is a parse tree for the sentence, "The man bit the dog." When a

Figure 7–1
A Family Tree

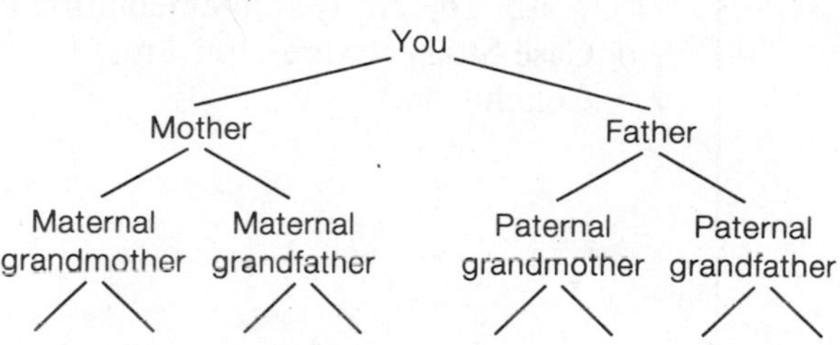

Figure 7–2
Sample of a Parse Tree

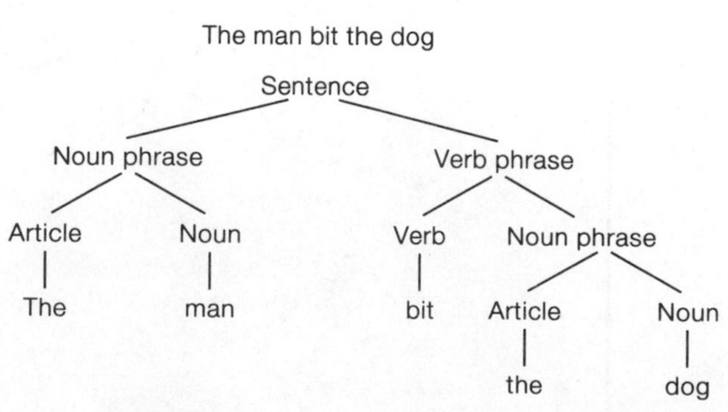

compiler parses a program to determine if it is syntactically correct, it also generates a parse tree.

Let's see how a compiler might check for the correctness of arithmetic expressions in a program. A four-rule grammar for writing simple arithmetic expressions in a language like Pascal or Modula-2 might look something like this:

Rule 1. <expression> ::= <term> { [+ | −] <term> }
Rule 2. <term> ::= <factor> { * <factor> }
Rule 3. <factor> ::= <letter> | (<expression>)
Rule 4. <letter> ::= **a** | **b** | **c**

Each of these four lines is a *rule* that defines part of the syntax of arithmetic expressions. The symbol ::= stands for "is defined as," and it means that the grammatical symbol on the left side of the ::= operator can be replaced by (or expanded into) the sequence of symbols on the right side. The braces {} mean zero or more repetitions of the information enclosed inside the braces, and | means selection of one and only one of the alternatives on either side of the |. Symbols set in **bold type** are *terminal* symbols, and they represent actual elements of the language being defined. Symbols set in <angle brackets> are called *nonterminal* symbols and represent intermediate grammatical constructs that are defined by other rules in the language. The syntax of every programming language is defined by a collection of rules of the type just shown; this collection of rules is the *grammar* of the language. The notation just described is called *Backus-Naur Form*, frequently abbreviated *BNF*. It is one of the most widely used methods for representing the grammar of high-level programming languages.

When you write an arithmetic expression as part of your program, e.g., $a * b + c$, the compiler uses the grammar of the selected language to try to construct a parse tree for that expression. If such a tree can be built, then the expression is syntactically legal in that language. If the compiler cannot build such a tree, then the expression is illegal.

The compiler starts with the nonterminal symbol that we have called <expression> (the construct that it is trying to validate), and it applies a rule of the grammar to expand this symbol into a sequence of one or more terminal and nonterminal symbols. For example, we can apply Rule 1 (and select the + alternative) to get:

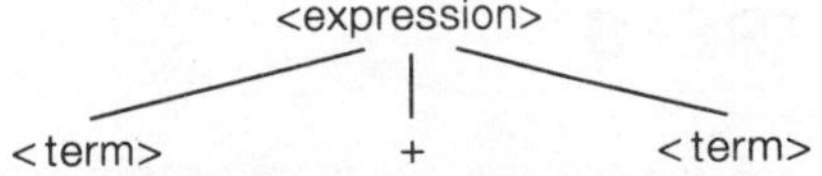

We repeat this process of using rules to expand the nonterminal grammatical symbols until we have either constructed the desired expression (i.e., we have generated all the terminal symbols in our expression) or we can go no further with the parse.

For example, given the expression $a * b + c$ and the four-rule grammar given earlier, a compiler could construct the valid parse tree shown in Figure 7–3, thereby proving that the expression $a * b + c$ is valid in our language. However, try as hard as it might, no compiler can construct a valid parse tree for the expression $a +$.

Figure 7–3
Parse Tree for
a* ∗ *b* + *c

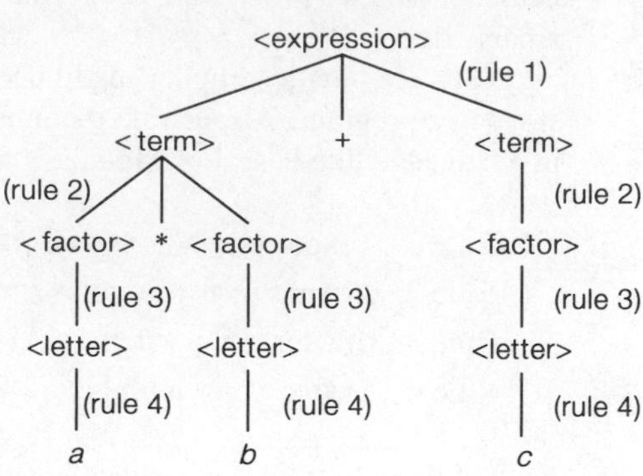

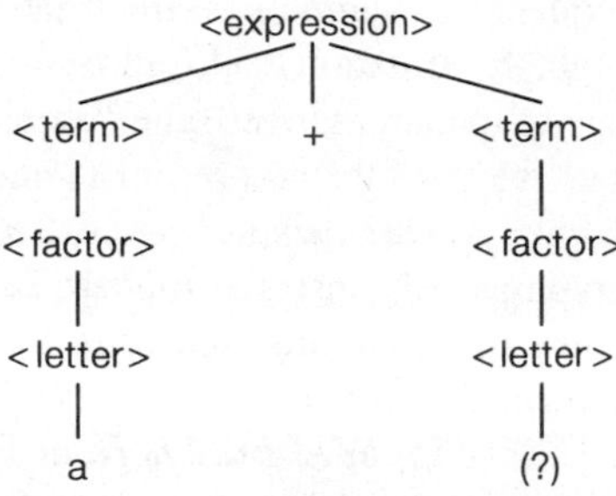

We are at a dead end here. We can build a parse tree for the expression a + <letter> where <letter> is either a, b, or c, but we cannot construct one for a + by itself. Because it cannot build a parse tree for the string a +, the compiler would reject the expression with an error message that says something like, "There is a missing term in this expression."

We will have much more to say about the use of tree structures for translating languages in the case study in section 7–4. Parsing is just one of many examples of the frequent use of hierarchical data structures throughout the field of computer science. We will see many more examples in upcoming chapters.

7.2 GENERAL TREES

A *general tree*, or more simply just a *tree*, has the following formal definition:

> *Definition*: A *tree* T is either empty or it is a finite set of one or more nodes such that there is a specially designated node $t \in T$ (called the *root* of T) and $T - \{t\}$ can be partitioned into zero, one, or more disjoint subsets T_1, T_2, . . . , T_n, each of which is itself a tree (called a *subtree* of T).

Notice that this definition is recursive: a tree T is defined in terms of structures T_1, T_2, . . . that are also trees. This recursive nature of a tree will result in many recur-

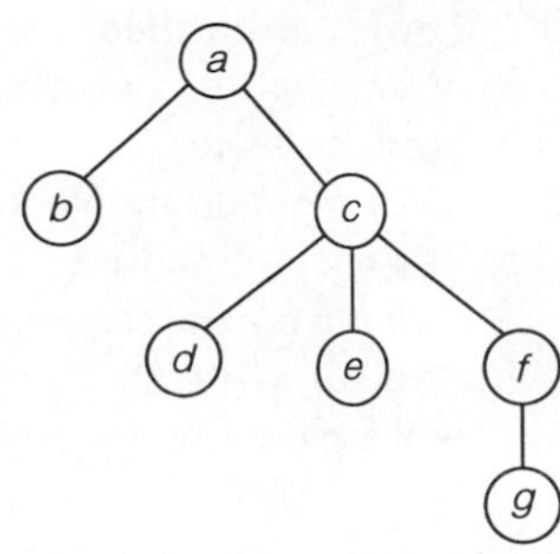

Figure 7–4
Sample Tree Structure

sive algorithms to implement the important operations on trees. We will have many opportunities to practice the recursive skills learned in the previous chapter!

The *nodes* are the components of the tree that store data. Each node contains a data element and zero, one, or more links to other nodes. The links are frequently called the *edges* or *arcs* of the trees. Our definition of a tree implies that every node of a tree is a root of some subtree contained in the whole tree. Let us consider this definition more carefully while looking at the tree shown in Figure 7–4. This tree is composed of seven nodes.

$$T = \{a, b, c, d, e, f, g\}$$

Its root is *a*, and it has two subtrees:

$$T_1 = \{b\} \qquad T_2 = \{c, d, e, f, g\}$$

The root of T_1 is *b*, which has no subtrees. The root of T_2 is *c*, and it has three subtrees $\{d\}$, $\{e\}$, and $\{f, g\}$.

In contrast, we cannot partition the structure

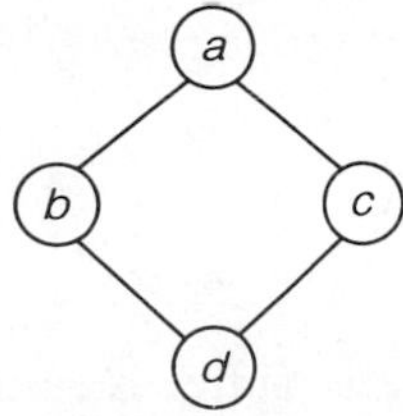

into a root and a collection of *disjoint* subtrees. If we had called *a* the root of our tree, then our subtrees would be $\{b, d, c\}$ and $\{c, d, b\}$, but they are not disjoint. This type of structure is a *graph*, not a tree, and it will be studied in detail in chapter 10.

The number of subtrees of a node is called the node's *degree*. Hence node *a* in Figure 7–4 is degree 2, node *b* is degree 0, and node *c* is degree 3. Nodes with no subtrees (*b, d, e, g* in Figure 7–4) are called *leaf nodes* or *terminal nodes*. All other nodes are called *nonterminal nodes*. In Figure 7–4, the nonterminal nodes are *a, c,* and *f*; they are also called *internal* or *branch nodes*.

In discussing trees we often use familial terms. For example, node *a* of Figure 7–4 is said to be the *parent* of nodes *b* and *c*, and nodes *b* and *c* are called the *children* of node *a*. Nodes that have the same parent are called *siblings*. In Figure 7–4 nodes *b* and *c* are siblings. So are *d, e,* and *f*.

A *path* is a unique sequence of nodes $n_1, n_2, n_3, \ldots, n_k$ such that either n_{i+1} is a child of n_i for $i = 1, 2, \ldots, k - 1$ (sometimes referred to as a *downward* path) or n_{i+1} is the parent of n_i for $i = 1, 2, \ldots, k - 1$ (sometimes referred to as an *upward* path). The *ancestors* of a node are all nodes that lie on the unique upward path from that node to the root of the tree. For example, in Figure 7–4 the ancestors of node *g* are $\{a, c, f\}$. The *descendants* of a node N are all nodes contained in the subtree of which N is the root. The *height* of a tree is defined as the length (in terms of the number of edges) of the longest path from any node N to the root of the tree. The height of the tree in Figure 7–4 is three, since the longest path from any node to the root is $\{a, c, f, g\}$, which contains three edges.

Finally, the *level* of a node is an integer value that measures the distance of a node from the root. We assign the root a level number of 0. The level number of any other node N in the tree is defined inductively as 1 + (level number of the parent of N). The height of a tree is just the maximum level number of any node in the tree.

With these terms we can state two important properties of tree structures that follow from the definition of a tree:

1. For every node N in a tree T there is a unique path from N to the root of the tree.
2. Every node N, except for the root, has a unique parent.

We can now understand why a structure such as the previous four-node graph is not a tree. The node *d* has two parents *b* and *c*, and there are two paths from *d* to the root, $\{d, b, a\}$ and $\{d, c, a\}$.

The type of tree that we have described is called a *general tree*. It is characterized by the fact that nodes can be of arbitrary degree, that is, they can have any number of children.

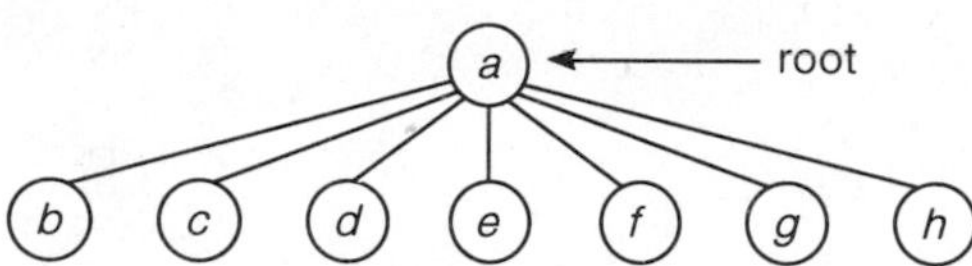

A general tree is easy to describe but it can be difficult to work with, and it is not widely used in computer science. To understand why, let us consider how we might implement this structure internally.

One possibility is to use a record structure with an array of from one to five pointer values (or **Nil**) to point to the children of this node. This record structure is shown in Figure 7–5, but it is unsatisfactory because a node in a general tree can have an *arbitrary* number of children, including values greater than 5. It will not do any good to change the constant 5 in Figure 7–5 to a larger number such as 10 or 15, because the node could have 11 or 16 children. In fact, for any static number, *N*, of pointers that we allocate for our node, we may find that we need *N* + 1. Thus, a

Figure 7–5
One Possible Implementation of a General Tree

```
Type
    Tree = Pointer To Node;
    Node =
        Record
            Data : Char;            (* Assume the data stored in the node
                                       is of type character *)
            Children : Array [ 1 .. 5 ] of Tree;
                                    (* Allow up to 5 children per node *)
        End;
Var
    Root : Tree;
```

general tree can be difficult to implement internally, although it is mathematically simple to work with.

There are other ways to internally represent general trees and avoid this problem. For example, instead of having the child pointers contained in the node itself, we could place them in a linked list. That is, we could create an array A where the element A[*i*] is the head of a linked list of all the children of node *i*. For example, to represent the following general tree:

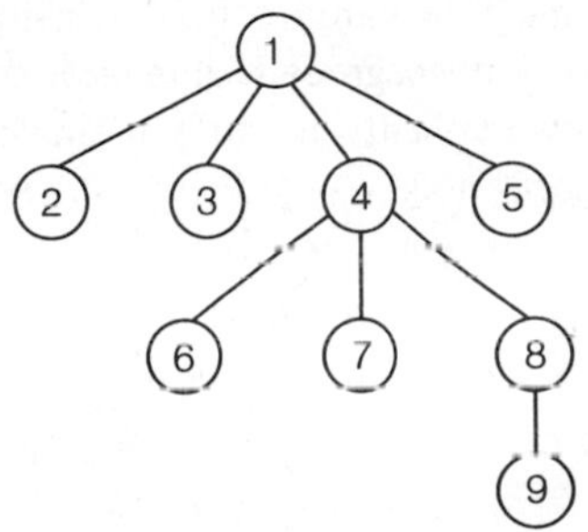

we would internally create the following structure:

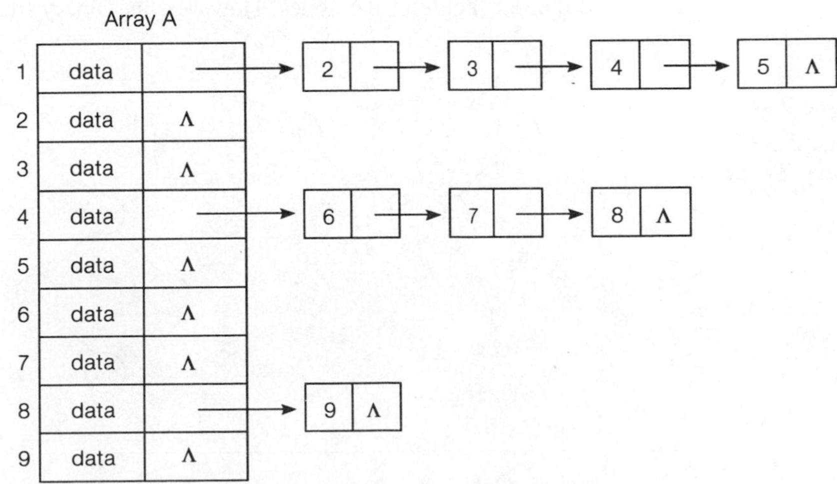

This structure would allow a node to have an arbitrarily large number of children. However, we would have the same problem we encountered in chapter 3 in the array implementation of stacks and queues. The size of the array A is fixed at compile time by the declaration

```
Var
    A : Array [1 .. MaxNodes] Of NodeRecords;
```

Now instead of being limited in the maximum number of children for one node, we are limited in the total number of nodes allowed in the entire tree. In addition, determining whether a node is a child of another node requires a slow sequential search of the linked list. We have not really solved our problem.

There is a better solution to this problem, and that is to restrict our use of trees to a special type of hierarchical structure called a *binary tree*. As we will see in the next section, binary trees are easy to implement and work with, and they have the useful property that any general tree can be represented as a binary tree.

7.3 BINARY TREES

7.3.1 Introduction

Binary trees are distinct from general trees in two important ways: Nodes in a binary tree have degrees less than or equal to 2 (i.e., they have at most two children), and they explicitly identify their children as being either the left or right child of the parent node.

> *Definition*: A *binary tree* is a finite set of nodes that is either empty or consists of a root and two disjoint binary trees called the *left* and *right subtrees*.

Some examples of binary trees are shown in Figure 7–6.

The binary trees of Figure 7–6a and b are structurally identical and differ only in the data fields of the nodes. However, the binary trees of Figure 7–6d and e are

Figure 7–6
Examples of Binary Trees

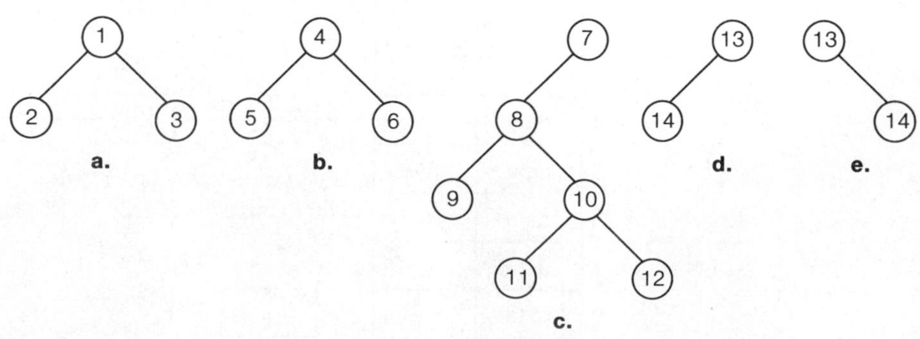

not structurally identical. The binary tree in d has an empty *right* subtree, whereas the one in e has an empty *left* subtree—this point is very important. A tree is identified not only by the data it contains but also by the position of the nodes within either the left or right subtree. When drawing a binary tree, be careful to indicate clearly whether a node is the right or left subtree of its parent. Diagrams such as

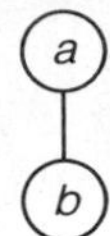

are ambiguous and can lead to confusion and possible error since it is not at all clear whether we mean

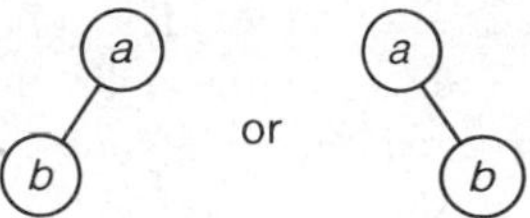

Binary trees are simply a specialization of the concept of a general tree introduced in section 7.2. However, because they are used (in computer science) much more frequently than general trees, we will, unless otherwise noted, use the term *tree* to refer to the special case of a binary tree as shown in Figure 7–6 rather than to the case of the general tree of Figure 7–4.

7.3.2 Operations on Binary Trees

To construct the external module of the abstract data type called Binary Tree, we must first select the operations we wish to perform on a binary tree. By far the most common operation on a binary tree is *tree traversal*. This operation starts at the root of the tree and visits every node in the tree exactly once; to "visit" means to process the data element contained in the node. (The exact nature of the processing depends on the specific application, and we will not concern ourselves with it here.)

There are a number of ways to visit each node. One method starts by visiting the root. Then we have a choice: we can traverse either the nodes in the left subtree or those in the right subtree. If we choose to traverse the left subtree first, we traverse it in the same way as the original tree. We visit the root (of the subtree) and then traverse all the nodes of the left subtree followed by all the nodes of the right subtree. This method is called a *preorder traversal*.

Let us see exactly what this means for the tree shown in Figure 7–7. This tree is a parse tree of the type first diagrammed in Figure 7–3. The three step algorithm for a preorder tree traversal is:

1. Visit the root: $(+)$.
2. Traverse the left subtree: $(* \ a \ b)$.
3. Traverse the right subtree: (c).

Figure 7–7
Sample Tree for Tree Traversal

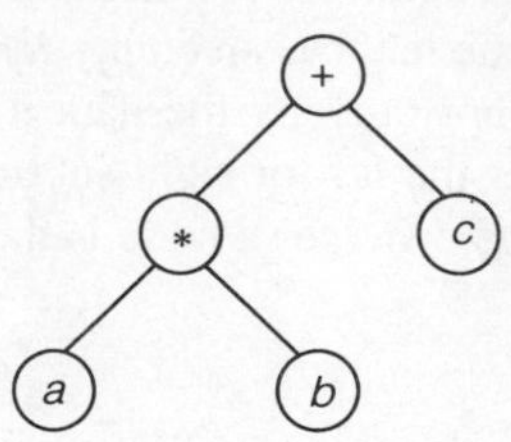

Steps 2 and 3 each involve traversing a subtree. We can visit each node of a subtree by simply reapplying all three steps recursively:

1. Visit the root: +.
2. Traverse the left subtree: (* *a b*).
   2.1 Visit the root: *.
   2.2 Traverse the left subtree: (*a*).
   2.3 Traverse the right subtree: (*b*).
3. Traverse the right subtree: (*c*).
   3.1 Visit the root: *c*.
   3.2 Traverse the left subtree: (empty).
   3.3 Traverse the right subtree: (empty).

When a subtree is empty as in steps 3.2 and 3.3, we have reached our base case and can go on to the next step. Therefore, our complete preorder traversal of the tree in Figure 7–7 is given by the following:

1. Visit the root: +.
2. Traverse the left subtree: (* *a b*).
   2.1 Visit the root: *.
   2.2 Traverse the left subtree: (*a*).
      2.2.1 Visit the root: *a*.
      2.2.2 Traverse the left subtree: (empty).
      2.2.3 Traverse the right subtree: (empty).
   2.3 Traverse the right subtree: (*b*).
      2.3.1 Visit the root: *b*.
      2.3.2 Traverse the left subtree: (empty).
      2.3.3 Traverse the right subtree: (empty).
3. Traverse the right subtree: (*c*).
   3.1 Visit the root: *c*.
   3.2 Traverse the left subtree: (empty).
   3.3 Traverse the right subtree: (empty).

This procedure may look complicated, but it is actually a very simple recursive algorithm. If R is the root of a binary tree, a preorder traversal algorithm for that tree is shown in Figure 7–8. The base case specifies what to do when an empty binary tree is passed into the procedure; as you can see, the procedure simply returns. The general or recursive case is to visit the root, traverse the nodes in the left subtree, then traverse the nodes in the right subtree. Recursion has led us to an elegant ten-line solution to a complex data structure problem.

Figure 7–8
Preorder Tree Traversal Algorithm

```
Procedure PreOrderTraversal(R)
Begin
    If R is empty Then
        Return
    Else
        Visit the Root R
        PreOrderTraversal(Left Subtree of R)
        PreOrderTraversal(Right Subtree of R)
    End
End PreOrderTraversal
```

There are a number of other ways to traverse a tree. The traversal scheme we have just described, preorder traversal, walks through the tree using the following method:

1. Visit the root.
2. Traverse the left subtree.
3. Traverse the right subtree.

Other traversal methods can be arrived at by permuting the order of these operations. Two permutations of interest are the *postorder traversal*:

1. Traverse the left subtree.
2. Traverse the right subtree.
3. Visit the root.

and the *inorder traversal*:

1. Traverse the left subtree.
2. Visit the root.
3. Traverse the right subtree.

There is a natural correspondence between the preorder, postorder, and inorder traversals of a tree and the prefix, postfix, and infix forms of an arithmetic expression. Using the tree in Figure 7–7 and assuming that "visit the root" means to output the contents of the data field of that node, we would produce the following:

Prefix expression for a * b + c:	+*abc	(* Operators precede operands *)
Preorder traversal of tree:	+*abc	
Postfix expression for a * b + c:	ab*c+	(* Operators follow operands *)
Postorder traversal of tree:	ab*c+	
Infix expression for a * b + c:	a*b+c	(* Operators between operands *)
Inorder traversal of tree:	a*b+c	

We will use this correspondence in the case study at the end of this chapter. The recursive algorithms for postorder and inorder traversal are given in Figure 7–9.

Figure 7–9
Postorder and Inorder Tree Traversal Algorithms

```
Procedure PostOrder Traversal(R)
Begin
    If R is empty Then
        Return
    Else
        PostOrder Traversal (Left Subtree of R)
        PostOrder Traversal (Right Subtree of R)
        Visit the Root R
    End
End PostOrder Traversal

Procedure InOrder Traversal(R)
Begin
    If R is empty Then
        Return
    Else
        InOrder Traversal (Left Subtree of R)
        Visit the Root R
        InOrder Traversal (Right Subtree of R)
    End
End InOrder Traversal
```

Figure 7–10
Aid to Remembering Tree Traversal Methods

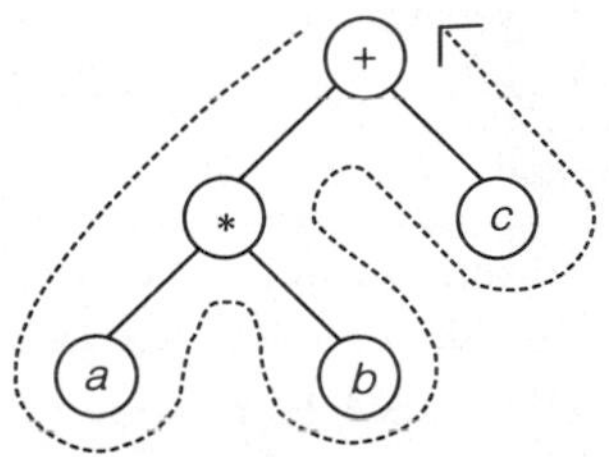

Notice that in each of the three methods the left subtrees are traversed before the right subtrees. This observation and the pattern in Figure 7–10 can be used as an aid in remembering the steps of the traversal methods. For a preorder traversal, we visit a node as we pass to its left, tracing out the tree, i.e., as the dotted line in Figure 7–10 passes to the left of the node going in a downward direction. Hence the nodes will be visited in the following order: $+*abc$. For a postorder traversal we visit a node as the dotted line passes it on its right going up; hence the nodes will be visited in the following order: $ab*c+$. Finally, for an inorder traversal we visit a node as we pass underneath it; hence the nodes will be visited in the order: $a*b+c$.

In addition to traversal, there are many other operations that can be carried out on trees. As was the case for the linear list structure in chapter 3, there is no universal agreement on exactly what operations should be included in the external module of the Binary Tree abstract data type. We need to know more about how the package will be used to know exactly what set of operations should be included or omitted. In the remainder of this section we will describe some typical and widely used operations on trees. We also propose a number of additional possibilities in the exercises at the end of the chapter.

We obviously need to be able to create new binary trees. Since a binary tree can be empty, we will have our create operation, called CreateBinaryTree, generate an empty tree T of the form:

T Λ

Our two transformer operations on binary trees will be called Insert and Delete. The operation Insert will create a new node containing a specified data value and insert that new node into the binary tree in a specified location. To work properly, Insert needs three values:

1. A pointer to the node where the insertion will take place (or a null if we are inserting the root node into an empty tree).
2. A value that tells whether the new node should be inserted as a left or right subtree of this node.
3. The data value to be inserted into the new node.

The precondition on Insert would be that the position where we are inserting the new node is unoccupied. For example, given the following tree

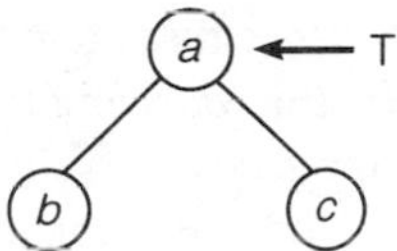

this call on the procedure Insert

Insert (pointer to node b, left, data value 'd')

would produce the new tree shown below:

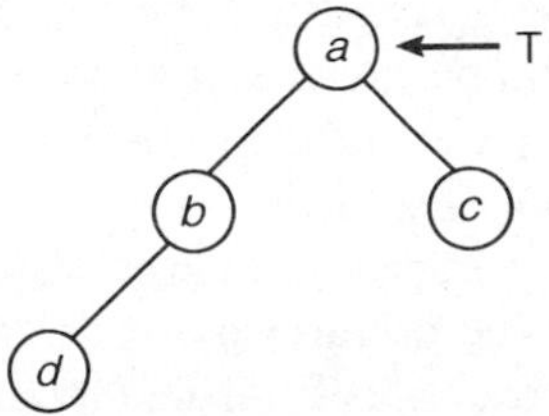

Notice that we have created a new node containing the data value *d* and have inserted that new node as the left child of node *b*, the node pointed to by the first parameter. Insert will return a pointer to the newly inserted node and will initialize the left and right branches of the new node to empty.

Insert is the operation we use to build binary trees. We start with an empty tree (created by a CreateBinaryTree operation) and insert new nodes, one by one, into their proper positions in the tree. A variation of this operation is InsertSubTree, which allows us to insert a complete subtree rather than a single node. The specification of this operation is left as an exercise.

The Delete operation removes nodes from a binary tree. Note, however, that we cannot delete individual nodes from a tree unless they are leaf nodes. We must delete the entire subtree of which the specified node is the root. For example, given the tree

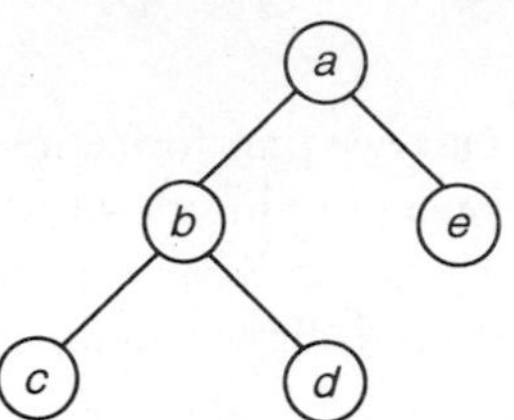

deleting node *b* would effectively delete the entire subtree of which node *b* is the root (the tree $\{b, c, d\}$). When completed, Delete returns a pointer to the parent of the node just deleted (*a*, in this case). (It is possible to describe an operation that deletes a single node, but it would involve not only the deletion of a node but reconstruction of the tree as well.)

The last three operations we will introduce are observer operations on binary trees. The Compare operation is given pointers to two binary trees, and it determines whether these two trees are the same; to be identical, the two trees must have the same structures and the data values in each node must be the same. The operator returns the Boolean value True if the two trees are identical and False otherwise.

The Find operation is given a pointer to the root of a tree and a key value of the same type as the values contained in the nodes. Find locates the node in the tree where that value occurs, and then it returns a pointer to that node and sets the parameter Found to True. If the key does not occur anywhere in the tree, it sets the parameter Found to False.

Finally, the Move operation allows you to move through a tree either up to the parent of a given node or down to the left or right child of that node. Move takes a tree, a pointer to a node in a tree, and a parameter that has one of the following three values: Left, Right, or Up. Move will move you to the left child, the right child, or the parent of that node, respectively, and set the parameter Success to True. If that parent or child node does not exist, Move sets the parameter Success to the value False.

A complete external module for the abstract data type Binary Tree, including the nine operations just described, is shown in Figure 7–11. This module imports two resources from another module called UserModule, which must be provided by the user of this package. The two resources are DataElementType (the data type of the elements to be stored in the nodes of the tree) and Equal (a Boolean function that determines if its two arguments of type DataElementType are equal).

Again, we stress that the external module of Figure 7–11 is not intended to be viewed as complete. Many other operations on binary trees are possible, and the exercises at the end of the chapter ask you to propose other useful operations, specify their syntax and semantics, and then add them to the external module of Figure 7–11.

Figure 7–11
External Module for a Binary Tree Abstract Data Type

```
(*  The following module contains the external specifications for the
    abstract data type Binary Tree, as described in Section 7.3   *)
External Module BinaryTreePackage;

From UserModule Import
        DataElementType,             (* The type of data stored in tree *)
        Equal;                       (* A function to tell if two DataElementType
                                          objects are equal. *)

Type
    DirectionType = (Left, Right, Up); (* Possible directions to move in a binary
                                          tree *)

    TreeType;                        (* The opaque type of the ADT binary tree *)

(*  Precondition:  None
    Postcondition: Returns True if Tree1 and Tree2 have the same
                       structure, and identical data values in identical locations.
                   Returns False otherwise.                                    *)
Procedure Compare(Tree1 : TreeType; Tree2 : TreeType) : Boolean;

(*  Precondition:  None
    Postcondition: A new, empty binary tree is returned                        *)
Procedure CreateBinaryTree() : TreeType;

(*  Precondition:  CurrentNode is a node in Tree
    Postcondition: If the precondition is met, the entire subtree in Tree
                       with root CurrentNode is removed.
                   Otherwise, Tree is unchanged.                               *)
Procedure Delete(Var Tree : TreeType; CurrentNode : TreeType);

(*  Precondition:  None
    Postcondition: All nodes in Tree are visited in an inorder traversal.
                       (i.e. Left subtree, root, right subtree)                *)
Procedure Inorder(Tree : TreeType);

(*  Precondition:  CurrentNode is either:     (1) a valid node in a binary tree
                                       or     (2) Nil
                   Additionally, for precondition (1), Direction must be
                       either Right or Left (cannot be Up).
    Postcondition: If precondition (1) is met:
                       a new node with data value NewNode is created, and
                       placed in the tree as the Direction child of CurrentNode.
                   If precondition (2) is met:
                       a new node with data value NewNode is created,
                       and becomes the root node of the tree.
                   Otherwise, the result is undefined.                         *)
Procedure Insert(Var CurrentNode : TreeType; Direction : DirectionType;
                     NewNode : DataElementType);
```

(continued)

Figure 7–11 (continued)

```
(*  Precondition:   None
    Postcondition:  If Key is the data value associated with a node in Tree,
                           Found is set to True, and the node is returned.
                    Note that if there are more than one node with the data value
                           Key, Find will return one of those nodes.
                    If no node has Key as its data value, Found is set to False
                           and Nil is returned.                                  *)
Procedure Find(Tree : TreeType; Key : DataElementType;
                           Var Found : Boolean) : TreeType;

(*  Precondition:   CurrentNode must be a valid node in Tree, and there is a node
                           in Direction from CurrentNode in Tree.
    Postcondition:  If preconditions are met, Success is set to True, and the node
                           in Direction from CurrentNode is returned.
                    Otherwise, Success is set to False, and the return value of
                           Move is undefined.                                    *)
Procedure Move(Tree : TreeType; CurrentNode : TreeType;
               Direction: DirectionType; Var Success : Boolean) : TreeType;

(*  Precondition:   None
    Postcondition:  All nodes in Tree are visited in a preorder traversal.
                           (i.e. Root, left subtree, right subtree)              *)
Procedure Preorder(Tree : TreeType);

(*  Precondition:   None
    Postcondition:  All nodes in Tree are visited in a postorder traversal.
                           (i.e. Left subtree, right subtree, root)              *)
Procedure Postorder(Tree : TreeType);

End BinaryTreePackage.
```

7.3.3 The Binary Tree Representation of General Trees

We have covered the subject of binary trees in depth because of an important principle—every general tree can be represented as a binary tree. Recall that a node in a binary tree has at most two link fields: one that points to the left subtree of that node and one that points to the right subtree. We can use these two links in the following manner to convert any general tree into a binary tree.

a. Use the left pointer of a node in the binary tree to point to the "oldest" (i.e., the leftmost) child of a node in the general tree; the left pointer will have the value null if a node has no children.
b. Use the right pointer of a node in the binary tree to point to the "next" sibling (i.e., the first one to the right) of a node in the general tree; the right pointer will have the value null if a node has no siblings to its right.

As an example, we will convert the following general tree

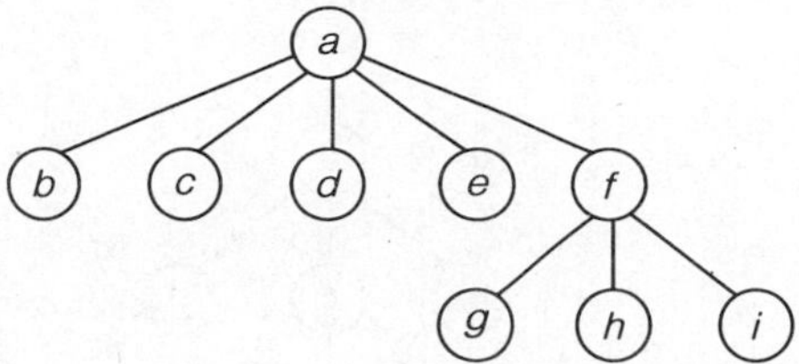

to a binary tree. The oldest child of node a is node b. So we use the left pointer of node a to point to node b. Since node a has no siblings its right pointer will be set to null. The right pointers of b, c, d, and e will point to their next (i.e., right) siblings, c, d, e, and f, respectively, while f, which has no next sibling, has its right pointer set to null. The left pointers of b, c, d, and e are null because they have no children. This process is now repeated with node f. Its oldest child is g. The right pointer of g points to its next sibling h, h points to i, and the right pointer of i is null. Therefore, the final binary tree representation of the above nine-node general tree is

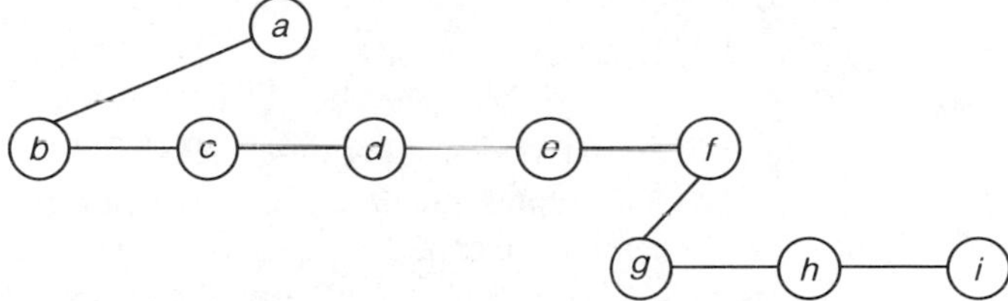

This structure may not look much like a binary tree, but it is, and it will look more like one if we just redraw it in the more traditional top-down format:

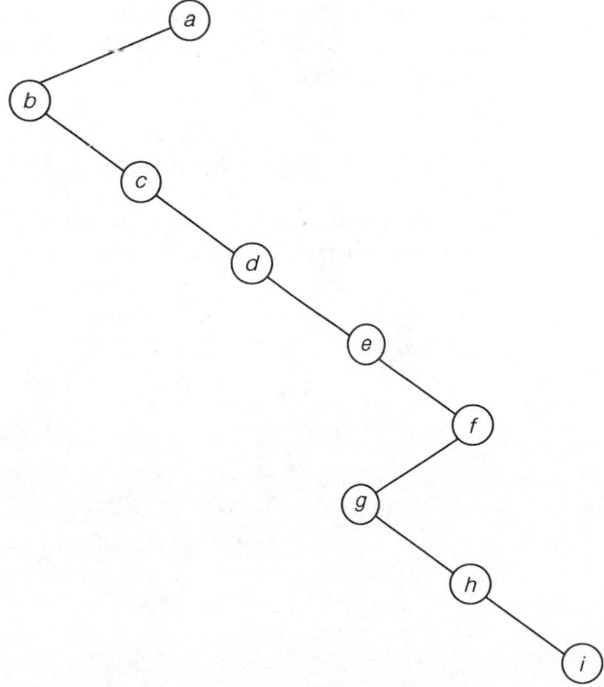

Figure 7–12
General Tree Transformed into a Binary Tree

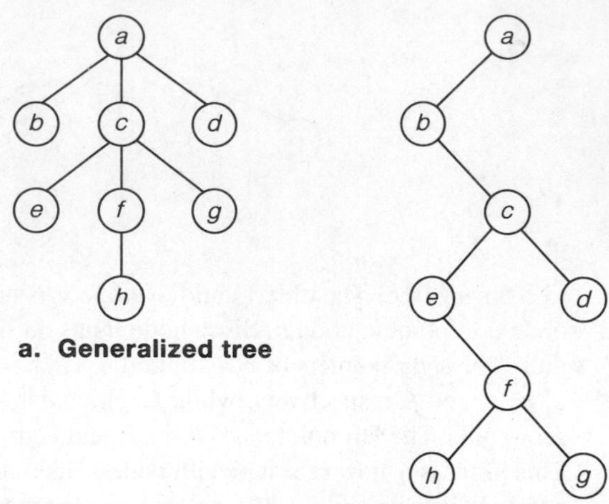

a. Generalized tree

b. Binary representation using the left child / right sibling representation

This conversion algorithm, called the *left child/right sibling representation*, allows us to represent a tree of arbitrary degree using only two links per node. Thus, any general tree can be converted to a binary tree in order to use the ADT operations listed in Figure 7–11. Furthermore, the structure of the original tree can be recovered from its binary tree representation. This convertibility is what makes the Binary Tree such an important abstract data type to study and a Binary Tree external module such an important software package to have available.

Figure 7–12 shows another example of this conversion algorithm applied to a general tree of degree 3. We have included additional examples in the exercises at the end of the chapter.

7.3.4 The Linked List Implementation of Binary Trees

To build the internal module for the Binary Tree package of Figure 7–11, we must select an internal representation for the nodes of the tree. A good way to represent a node of a binary tree is to use a pointer variable for both the left and right subtree pointers. This representation is shown in Figure 7–13. Using this implementation, the binary tree

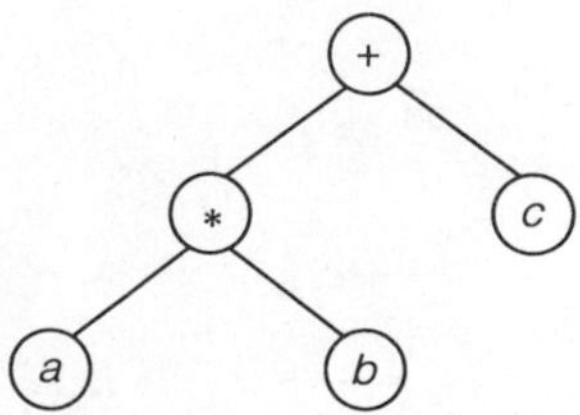

Figure 7–13
Possible Implementation of a Node in a Binary Tree

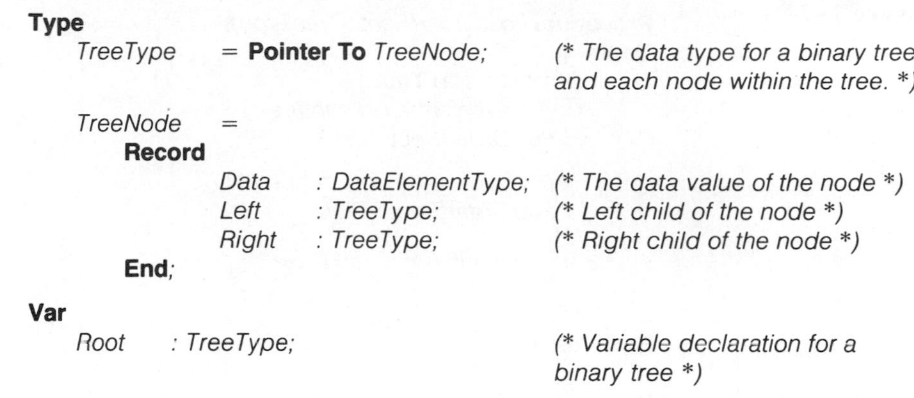

```
Type
    TreeType    = Pointer To TreeNode;      (* The data type for a binary tree,
                                               and each node within the tree. *)
    TreeNode    =
        Record
            Data    : DataElementType;      (* The data value of the node *)
            Left    : TreeType;             (* Left child of the node *)
            Right   : TreeType;             (* Right child of the node *)
        End;
Var
    Root    : TreeType;                     (* Variable declaration for a
                                               binary tree *)
```

would be represented internally as:

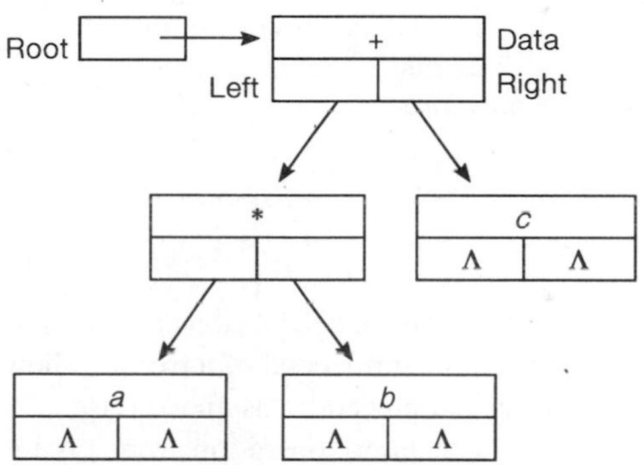

This pointer-based implementation is a convenient representation because it does not require us to know in advance how large the tree will be. Every time we want to add a new node, we simply use the New function described in chapter 3 to allocate adequate space.

```
Type
    TreeType = Pointer To TreeNode;
Var
    T : TreeType;
        •
        •
        •
New(T);         (* Generate space for a new node *)
```

Figure 7–14

Procedures for Postorder and Inorder Traversal of a Binary Tree

```
Procedure PostOrder(Root : TreeType);
Begin
    If (Root <> Nil) Then
        (* Traverse the left subtree *)
        PostOrder(Root^.Left);

        (* Traverse the right subtree *)
        PostOrder(Root^.Right);

        (* Visit the root *)
        Visit(Root);
    Endif;
End Postorder;

Procedure InOrder(Root : TreeType);
Begin
    If (Root <> Nil) Then
        (* Traverse the left subtree *)
        InOrder(Root^.Left);

        (* Visit the root *)
        Visit(Root);

        (* Traverse the right subtree *)
        InOrder(Root^.Right);
    Endif;
End Inorder;
```

Given the declarations in Figure 7–13, the body of the procedures for postorder and inorder traversal of a tree are shown in Figure 7–14. We will leave the preorder traversal procedure as an exercise.

The Insert operation from Figure 7–11 must first create the new node to be added and then insert it into the tree in the proper location. It must also check that the current pointer in that location is **Nil**. If it is not, then there is an error—we have violated the operation's preconditions by trying to add a new node to a location that is already occupied. The procedure that implements the operation must decide how to handle that situation. Our procedure simply overwrites the current pointer value with the new node being inserted. Another possibility is to set a global error flag to indicate this error condition.

The Insert procedure just described is shown in Figure 7–15.

We leave the implementation of the remaining operations contained in the Binary Tree external module of Figure 7–11 as exercises.

Although the declarations of Figure 7–13 are the most common technique for implementing binary trees using pointers, they are by no means the only way. For example, with the declarations in Figure 7–13, the operation of moving down the tree is easy, but moving up the tree is much more difficult, because there is no pointer from a child back to its parent. To locate a parent, we must essentially traverse the entire tree from its root. If moving up a tree from the leaves toward the root

Figure 7–15
Insert Procedure for Binary Trees

```
(*  Precondition: CurrentNode is either: (1) a valid node in a binary tree
                                  or (2) Nil
                          Additionally, for precondition (1), Direction must be
                              either Right or Left (cannot be Up).
    Postcondition:        If precondition (1) is met:
                              a new node with data value NewNode is created,
                              and placed in the tree as the Direction child of
                              CurrentNode.
                          If precondition (2) is met:
                              a new node with data value NewNode is created,
                              and becomes the root node of the tree.
                          Otherwise, the result is undefined.                    *)
Procedure Insert(Var CurrentNode : TreeType; Direction : DirectionType;
                                  NewNode : DataElementType);
Var
    Node : TreeType;
Begin
    New(Node);                       (* Allocate space for the new node *)
    Node^.Data := NewNode;           (* Set data value *)
    Node^.Left := Nil;               (* The new node has no children *)
    Node^.Right := Nil;

    If (CurrentNode = Nil) Then      (* Make new root node for the tree *)
                                     (* Note that in this case, Direction is
                                          ignored. *)
        CurrentNode := Node;

    Else                             (* Insert Node within the tree *)
        If (Direction = Left) Then   (* Add node as the left child *)
            CurrentNode^.Left := Node;

        Elsif (Direction = Right) Then (* Add node as the right child *)
            CurrentNode^.Right := Node;

        Else                         (* Direction = Up, an illegal option *)
            Dispose(Node);
        Endif;

    Endif;
End Insert;
```

is a common occurrence, we might wish to add an Up pointer field to each node to point to the parent of that node. (The Up pointer of the root would be **Nil**.)

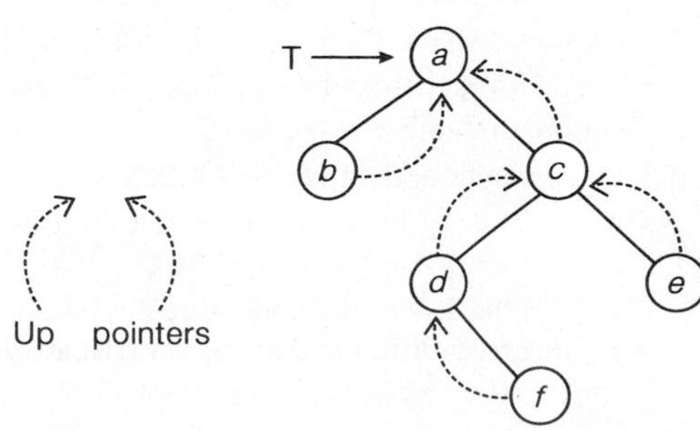

This representation will facilitate operations such as Move(T, CurrentNode, Up, Success), which moves you to the parent of CurrentNode in the tree T. However, the price you pay for this capability is a 50% increase in the number of pointers in each tree node, from two to three. For large trees this increased space requirement could be significant.

7.3.5 The Array Implementation of Binary Trees

Although the pointer-based implementation of trees shown in Figure 7–13 is probably the most efficient representation, it is certainly not the only one. If we were working in a language that did not support dynamic variables (e.g., languages such as BASIC, FORTRAN, or COBOL), we could still implement a tree structure using a two-dimensional array. (We demonstrated this technique in section 4.2.3 where we implemented a linked list.) We would construct a two-dimensional $k \times 3$ array in which each row of the array corresponds to a node in the binary tree. The first column of the array holds the data stored in the node, the second column holds a pointer to the left subtree, and the third column holds a pointer to the right subtree.[1] Thus, the following tree

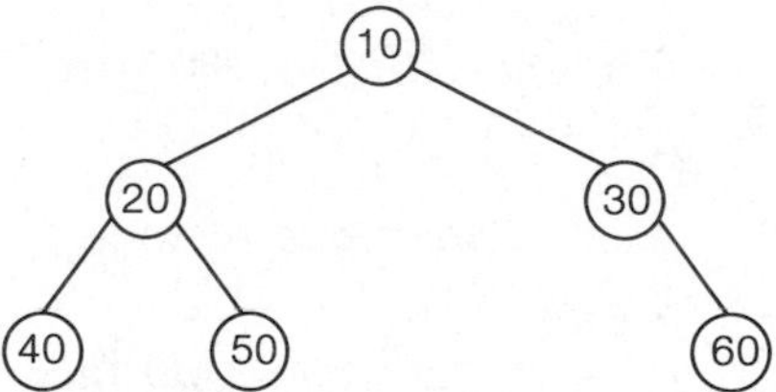

could be encoded as shown in Figure 7–16 (where 0 represents a null pointer and – indicates that a row is not currently in use). The root of the tree (the integer value 10) is stored in the fourth row of the array. The root of the left subtree is in row 2, and the root of the right subtree is stored in row 6. The rest of the tree is stored in similar fashion.

To indicate that a row of the array is not being used, we have used the notation – in Figure 7–16. We could implement that concept using the available space list technique first introduced in section 4.2.3 and Figure 4–16. A variable called Available would be the head of a linked list of unused rows in our array. These elements would be linked by either the left or right pointer fields of the nodes and would be initialized by the operation CreateBinaryTree. Figure 7–17 shows the declarations needed to set up this array-based implementation of a binary tree using available space lists, assuming that the data field of the nodes is of type Integer.

Although the declarations in Figure 7–17 are useful for languages that do not support dynamic variables, this array implementation suffers from the same problems mentioned in section 4.2.3 with respect to linked lists. We must know in advance exactly how much space to allocate for tree storage, for example, 100 nodes

[1] If the data in the node were not integers, we would need to use an array of records to avoid mixing different data types in the array.

Figure 7–16
Encoding of Sample Binary Tree Using Arrays

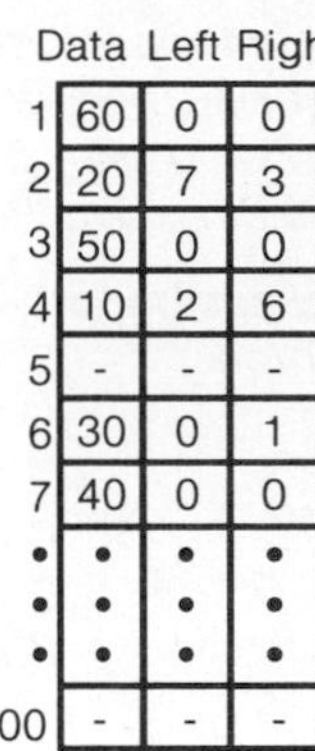

	Data	Left	Right
1	60	0	0
2	20	7	3
3	50	0	0
4	10	2	6
5	-	-	-
6	30	0	1
7	40	0	0
•	•	•	•
•	•	•	•
•	•	•	•
100	-	-	-

Root = 4

Figure 7–17
Declarations to Create an Array-Based Binary Tree Structure

```
Const
    MaxSize = . . . ;                    (* Some constant, the maximum number *)
                                         (* of nodes in the tree. *)

Type
    TreeType =
        Record
                                         (* The data and the two child indexes for
                                         the tree *)
            Tree      : Array [1 .. MaxSize], (Data,Left,Right) Of Integer;
            Root      : [0 .. MaxSize];  (* Index of the root node *)
            Available : [0 .. MaxSize];  (* Index of first free slot *)
        End;

Var
    BinaryTree : TreeType;               (* A binary tree variable declaration *)
```

for the tree encoded in Figure 7–16. If we try to insert 101 nodes into that tree, we overflow and get a fatal error, even if space is available elsewhere. Furthermore, if we have a very small number of nodes stored in the tree, a great deal of space is wasted, as all 100 × 3 cells in the array will be statically allocated to this data structure. The unused space cannot be used by other data structures or by the system. Because of these problems, the pointer-based implementation of section 7.3.4 and Figure 7–13 is definitely preferred.

Figure 7–18 shows the implementation of the Find procedure of Figure 7–11 using the $k \times 3$ array implementation just discussed. We have intentionally written it in a nonrecursive fashion using a stack and Push and Pop operations. Notice how much more complex this procedure is than the recursive algorithms of Figures 7–14 and 7–15. In a sense we have had to "invent" recursion ourselves using the stack mechanism. Recursive techniques can greatly simplify most tree-based algorithms.

Figure 7–18
Nonrecursive Find Algorithm Using an Array Implementation

```
(* This module contains the implementation of the function Find for a
      binary tree using the array based representation discussed in
      Section 7.3.5 and using the declarations shown in Figure 7.17   *)
Internal Module BinaryTreePackage;

From StackPackage Import
        StackType,          (* The ADT for a stack *)
        Create,             (* Function to make a new stack *)
        Empty,              (* Function to check if a stack has any elements in it *)
        Push,               (* Function to put a new element on a stack *)
        Pop,                (* Function to remove the top element from a stack *)
        Top;                (* Function to examine the top element on a stack *)

(*    Precondition: None
      Postcondition:    If Key is the data value associated with a node in Tree,
                           Found is set to True, and the node is returned.
                           Note that if there are more than one node with the
                           data value Key, Find will return one of those nodes.
                        If no node has Key as its data value, Found is set to
                           False, and Nil is returned.                        *)
Procedure Find(Tree : TreeType; Key : DataElementType;
                        Var Found : Boolean) : TreeType;
Var
      Stack     : StackType;
      Done      : Boolean;
      CurIndex  : Integer;
Begin
      Found := False;
      Done := False;
      Stack := Create();

      CurIndex := Tree.Root;                  (* Start searching at the root *)

      If (CurIndex = 0) Then
      (* The tree is empty, so we're done, but unsuccessful *)
            Done := True;
      Endif;

      While (Not Done) Do

            If (Tree.Tree[CurIndex, Data] = Key) Then
                  Found := True;              (* We've found it, *)
                  Done := True;               (* So stop searching *)

            Else
            (* If this node has a right child, push it on the stack (save for later) *)
                  If (Tree.Tree[CurIndex,Right] <> 0) Then
                        Push(Tree.Tree[CurIndex, Right], Stack);
                  Endif;
```

(continued)

Figure 7–18 (continued)

```
          (* If this node has a left child, try it next *)
              If (Tree.Tree[CurIndex,Left] <> 0) Then
                  CurIndex := Tree.Tree[CurIndex, Left];
          (* Otherwise, try searching the previously stacked right children *)
              Else
                  If (Empty(Stack)) Then       (* There aren't any more, *)
                      Done := True;            (* So we can stop searching *)

          (* There are more right children, so try the next one *)
                  Else
                      CurIndex := Top(Stack);
                      Pop(Stack);
                  Endif;
              Endif;
          Endif;
      Endwhile;

      (* If Found is True, CurIndex contains the index of the node where Key
          was found. Otherwise, it has the index of the node last searched. *)
      Return CurIndex;
  End Find;

  End BinaryTreePackage.
```

7.4 CASE STUDY: EXPRESSION TREES

In section 7.1 we discussed the role of tree structures in parsing statements in high-level programming languages. Figure 7–3 showed a parse tree produced by a compiler to determine the syntactic correctness of an arithmetic expression. The process of building a parse tree from a grammar is extremely complex and will not be discussed here. In this section we will discuss a much simpler but still important tree structure that is also used in the process of compiling programming languages and generating machine-language code. This tree is a form of binary tree called an *expression tree*, or a *syntax tree*. An expression tree is really a condensed and simplified parse tree. It is an intermediate form of representation that can be used in the translation of high-level languages to machine language.

In an expression tree, the root of any subtree is an operator of the language. The left child of that subtree is the left operand of the operator at the root, and the right child of that subtree is the right operand. (Note: If the operator is unary, then the single operand is in the left subtree and the right subtree is empty.) The expression 1 + 2, for example, would be represented as the tree

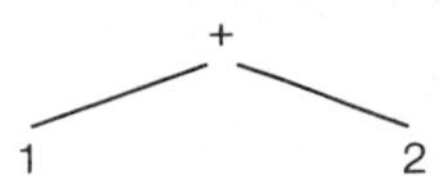

The expression tree for 1 + 2 − 3 (assuming left to right evaluation) is

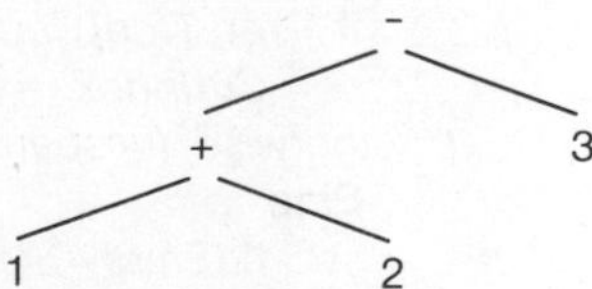

which says that the right operand of the operator − is 3, and the left operand is the result of evaluating the expression (1 + 2). The expression tree for 1 + 2 * 3 would depend on whether the + or * operator has higher precedence. If multiplication has higher precedence, then we would have:

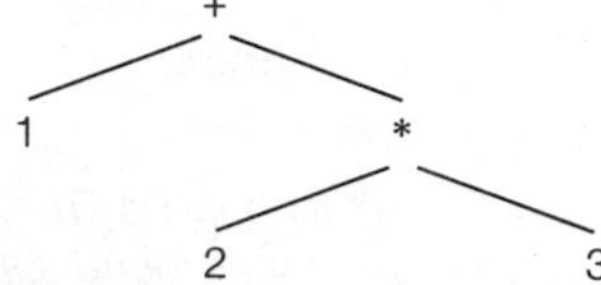

A higher precedence for addition would produce:

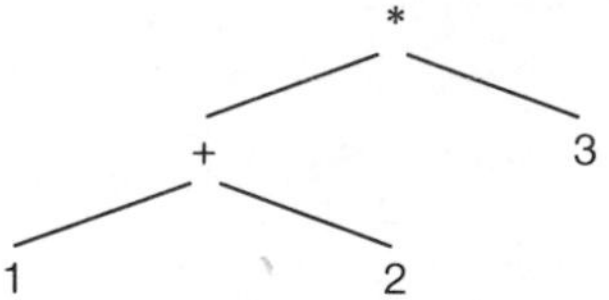

Notice that an expression tree always has operands as leaf nodes and operators as internal or branch nodes. A final and longer example is shown in Figure 7–19. It assumes the standard operator precedence rules of Pascal.

Figure 7–19
An Expression Tree

(-a + (b * (c / d)) + e) > 0

a. The expression in Pascal

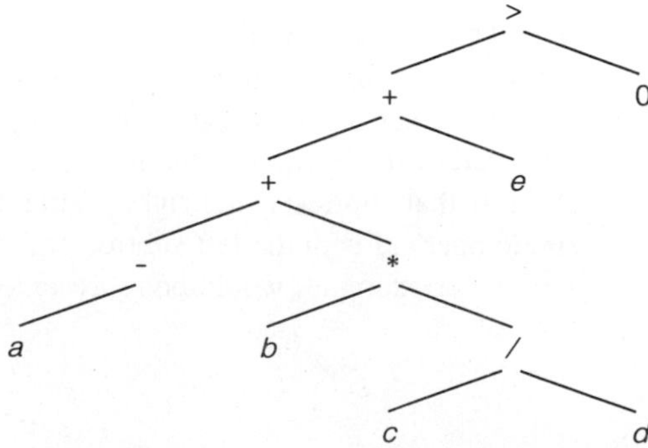

b. The corresponding expression tree

Expression trees can represent more than just arithmetic expressions. They can also represent a wide range of high-level language constructs, including assignment statements, **If/Then/Else** statements, and looping primitives. For example, the assignment statement var := expr can be represented as an expression tree with the following structure:

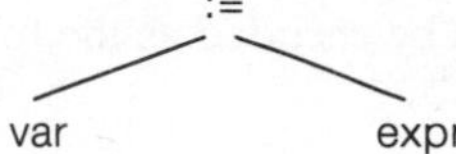

Where var is a variable and expr is an expression tree of the type we have just discussed. The assignment statement a := x + (y * z) would become:

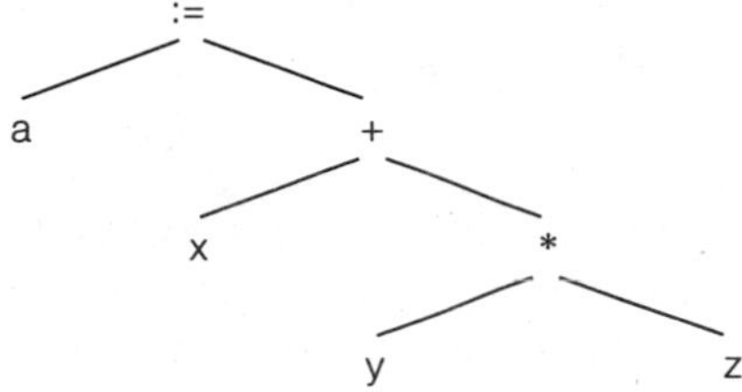

Similarly, the conditional statement

If Boolean **Then** statement

can be encoded using **If** as the root operator, the Boolean expression as the left subtree and the statement to be executed (assume for now that there is only one) as the right subtree:

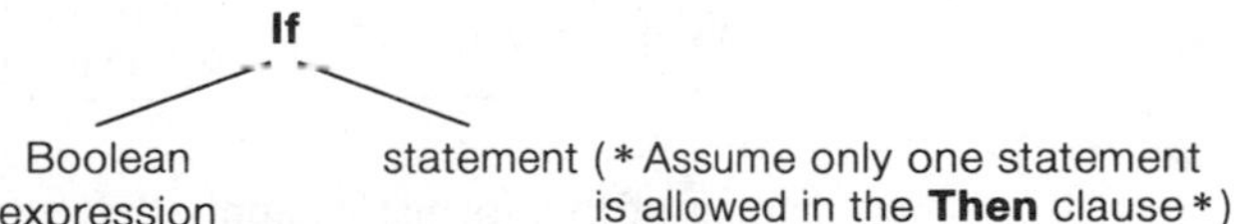

The following conditional statement

If a = b **Then** c := (d + e) + f

would become the expression tree:

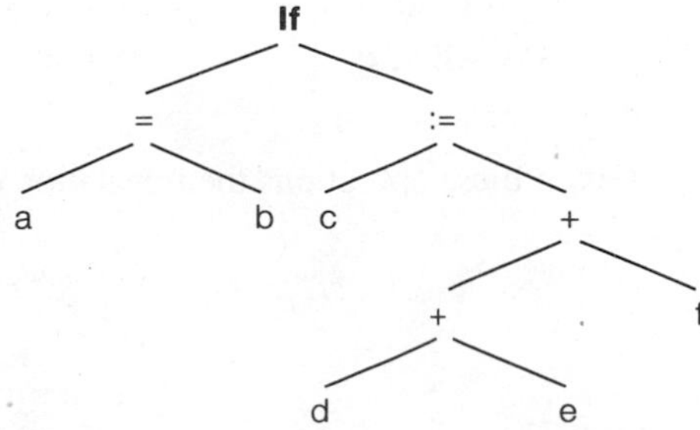

The nested conditional structure

If a = 0 **Then**
  If b = 0 **Then**
    c := 1

would be encoded as the following expression tree:

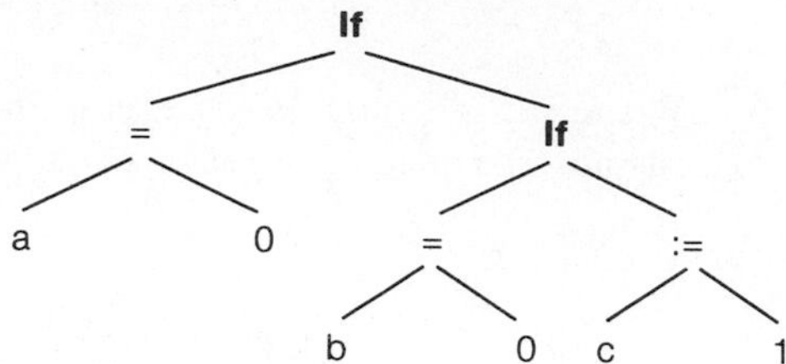

We leave it to you to work out the details of the expression tree representation of more complex statement types including multiple-statement **Then** clauses, the **If/Then/Else** statement, and **While** loops.

One useful feature of an expression tree representation of a high-level language statement is that it is easy for a compiler to generate correct machine language code from that expression tree. The compiler begins at the leaves of the tree and generates machine instructions corresponding to each operator/operand/operand subtree; it continues until the root is reached. The exact nature of the generated machine code will, or course, depend on the target machine selected. For this case study we will assume that our target machine has three address instructions of the form

operation code	left operand address	right operand address	result address

The meaning of this format is: apply the operation code to the two values stored in the left operand address and the right operand address and place the answer in the result address. The typical operations that exist at the machine language level are:

Operation	*Meaning*
ADD a, b, c	c := a + b
MULT a, b, c	c := a * b
DIVIDE a, b, c	c := a **DIV** b
SUBTRACT a, b, c	c := a − b
STORE a, c	c := a (* This operation has no right operand *)

Given these operations the translation of the following expression tree:

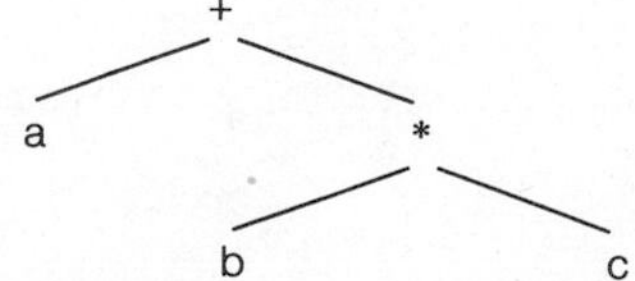

into low-level machine code would produce

```
MULT    b, c, Temp1            (* b * c → Temp1 *)
ADD     a, Temp1, Result       (* a + Temp1 → Result *)
```

The first instruction is the machine-language translation of this subtree:

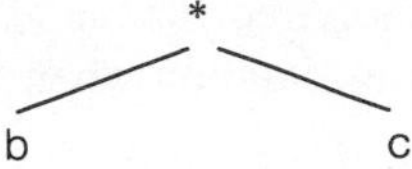

The result of the multiplication b * c is stored in a temporary memory location called Temp1. The second machine-language instruction is the translation of the following subtree:

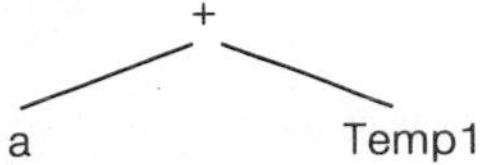

with the result of the entire expression placed in the memory location called Result.

A second example of code generation using an assignment statement is shown in Figure 7–20.

We have seen how easy it is for a compiler to generate machine language code if it has the corresponding expression tree representation of the high-level language statement. In this case study our goal is to show you how to build an expression tree of the type shown in Figure 7–20b from the original high-level language statements shown in Figure 7–20a. We will not discuss any further how to generate the code shown in Figure 7–20c; we leave that issue for future courses in compiler design.

Figure 7–20
Using Expression Trees to Compile Statements

a := (x **DIV** y) -z

a. High-level statement

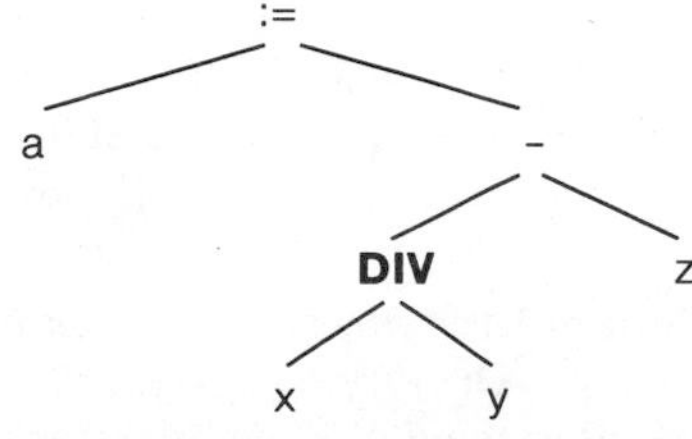

b. Expression tree

```
DIVIDE      x, y, Temp1         (* Temp1 := x div y *)
SUBTRACT    Temp1, z, Temp2     (* Temp2 := Temp1 - z *)
STORE       Temp2, a            (* a := Temp2 *)
```

c. General machine code

The algorithm for expression tree construction uses the Stack data structure introduced in chapter 3. We will use two stacks: the *operand* stack will hold operands and the *operator* stack will hold operators. Both are initially empty.

When we encounter an operand in the statement that we are examining, we push it on the operand stack; when we encounter an operator and the operator stack is empty, we push it on the operator stack. For example, if we were building the expression tree for the arithmetic expression $a + b * c - d$, we would have the following situation when we reach the $*$ operator.

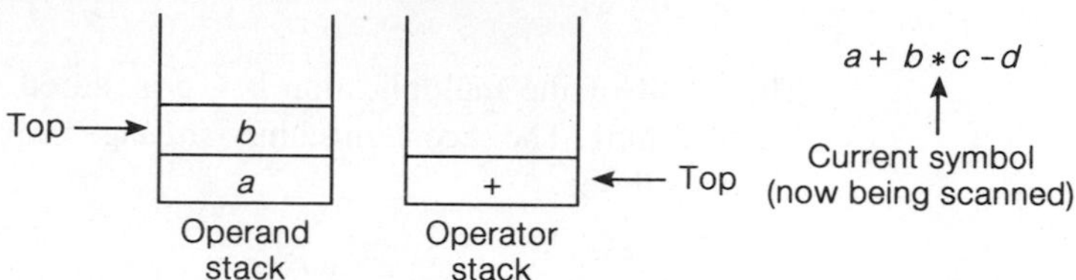

Notice that the operand stack holds the two operands a and b. The operator stack holds the operator $+$ because that stack was empty when the $+$ was encountered. At the point shown in the diagram we are deciding how to handle the $*$ operator. Whether we choose to stack it depends on the precedence of the $*$ operator and the precedence of the operator on top of the operator stack ($+$). If the precedence of the symbol being scanned is strictly greater than the precedence of the symbol on top of the operator stack, then we want to continue scanning our statement to obtain the right operand of the higher precedence operator. In this case we will assume that the precedence of multiplication is greater than the precedence of either addition or subtraction. Therefore, we push the operator $*$ onto the operator stack. After two more steps we reach the following situation:

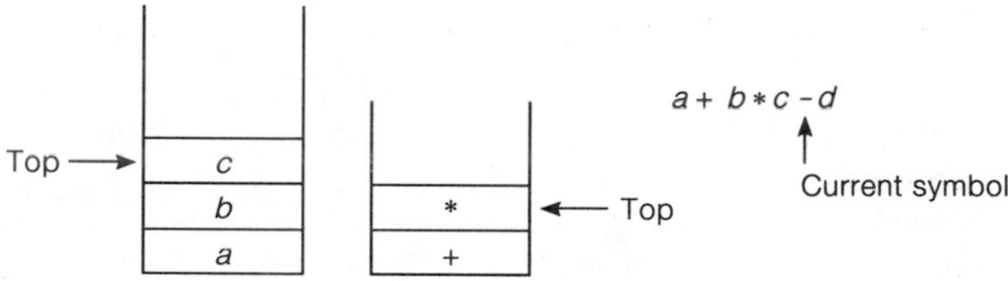

We now have the case where the precedence of the operator being scanned, $-$, is less than the precedence of the operator on top of the operator stack, $*$, so we now begin to build our expression tree by executing the following loop:

Repeat Until *(Precedence(CurrentSymbol) > Precedence(Top(OperatorStack)))*
  Or *(Empty(OperatorStack))*
  Pop the top of the operator stack and make it the root of a new binary tree.
  Pop the top of the operand stack and make it the right child of the root.
  Pop the top of the operand stack and make it the left child of the root.
  Push a pointer to this newly constructed tree on top of the operand stack.
End *of the Repeat Loop*

This loop builds a binary tree from the operator on top of the operator stack and the two operands on top of the operand stack. After one iteration of this loop we have the following condition:

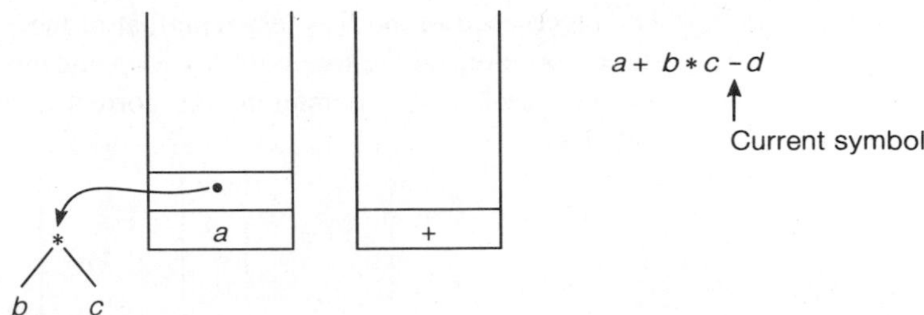

Notice that we have constructed a tree with $*$ as the root and b and c as the two children. A pointer to this tree has been placed on top of the operand stack. The operator that was previously on top of the operator stack, the $*$, has been popped, and $+$ is now on top. If we assume that the precedence of the subtraction operator $-$ is equal to the precedence of the $+$ now on top of the operator stack, then we repeat the loop one more time, because the loop termination condition is that the precedence of the current input symbol is strictly greater than the precedence of the symbol on top of the operator stack. After the second iteration through the loop we will have:

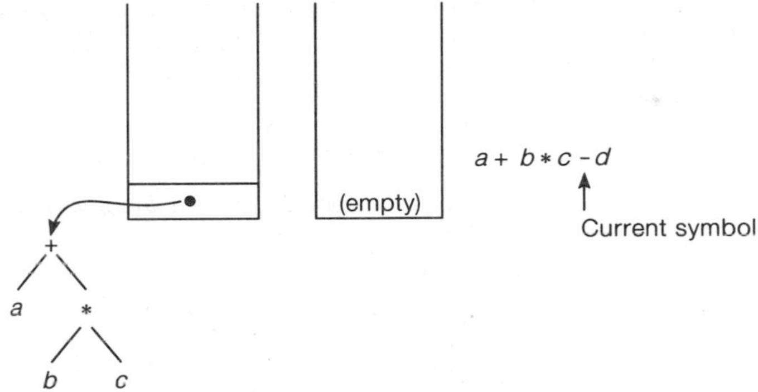

Since the operator stack is now empty, we stop execution of the loop and continue scanning the input stream. We now push the two symbols $-$ and d onto the operator and operand stacks, respectively. We will assume that there is a special *end marker* symbol at the end of every statement being analyzed, and we will, furthermore, assume that the precedence of the end marker is less than the precedence of any other operator in our language. When we reach this end marker (indicated by a $ in the diagram), we have the following state:

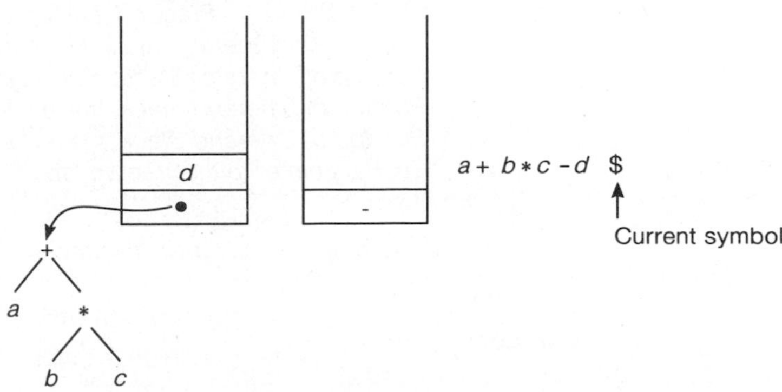

The precedence of the $ is less than that of the − currently on top of the operator stack, so we repeat the tree building loop one more time and end up with an empty operator stack and a pointer to the correct expression tree on top of the operand stack.

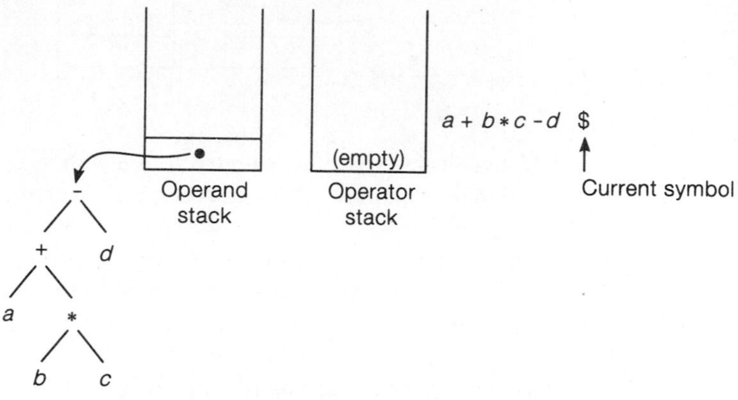

Figure 7–21

Algorithm for Construction of an Expression Tree

```
(* The following algorithm describes the process of generating an
     expression tree from an arithmetic expression.  *)
Procedure CreateExpressionTree

Create an empty Operator Stack
Create an empty Operand Stack

(* This is the main loop to process incoming symbols and generate an
expression tree from them.  *)
Repeat Until (CurrentSymbol = '$')

    GetNextSymbol(CurrentSymbol)

    If (CurrentSymbol is an Operand) Then
        Push(CurrentSymbol, Operand Stack)

    Elsif (Operator Stack is empty) Then
        Push(CurrentSymbol, Operator Stack)

    Elsif (Precedence(CurrentSymbol) > Precedence(Top of Operator Stack)) Then
        Push(CurrentSymbol, Operator Stack)

    Else

        Repeat Until (Precedence(CurrentSymbol) >
                              Precedence(Top of Operator Stack))
                  Or (Operator Stack is empty)
            Pop top of Operator Stack, make it the root of a new binary tree
            Pop top of Operand Stack, make it the right child of the root
            Pop top of Operand Stack, make it the left child of the root
            Push a pointer to this tree on top of the operand stack
        End Loop

        Push(CurrentSymbol, Operator Stack)

    Endif

End Loop
```

The complete algorithm for the construction of an expression tree using the technique just described is shown in Figure 7–21. This algorithm assumes the existence of a function called Precedence(op), which returns a scalar value giving the precedence of the operator specified in the argument. When the algorithm is finished, a pointer to the desired expression tree is left on top of the operand stack.

A procedure to implement this algorithm is given in Figure 7–22. It imports the resources of the Stack module of Figure 3–16 to aid in the solution of the problem. Here is yet another example of software reusability and the use of abstract data types to enhance programmer productivity.

Figure 7–22
Procedure to Build Expression Trees

```
(*  The following module contains the code for a function to create
    expression trees, as described in the case study in chapter 7.   *)
Module ExpressionTrees;

From StackPackage Import
        StackType,          (* The opaque data type *)
        Create,             (* Function to make a new stack *)
        Top,                (* Function to examine the top of a stack *)
        Pop,                (* Function to remove the top element of a stack *)
        Push,               (* Function to add a new element to a stack *)
        Empty;              (* Function to check whether a stack is full *)

From SymbolModule Import
        SymbolType,         (* The ADT representing operators & operands *)
        GetNextSymbol,      (* Function to return next symbol in the string *)
        IsOperator,         (* Function returns True iff parameter is an operator *)
        IsOperand,          (* Function returns True iff parameter is an operand *)
        Precedence;         (* Function returns precedence value of an operator *)

Type
    TreeType  = Pointer To Tree; (* The expression tree type *)
    Tree      = Record
                (* Symbol contained in the node *)
                    Value: SymbolType;
                (* Children of the node *)
                    Left   : TreeType;
                    Right  : TreeType;
                End;

(* This function uses the imported functions to create and return an
    expression tree from the symbols returned by GetNextSymbol.   *)
Procedure ExpressionTree : TreeType;
Var
        (* The current symbol being processed *)
    Sym           : SymbolType;
        (* Temporary variable for expression tree nodes *)
    Node          : TreeType;
        (* Stack to hold operators waiting to be processed *)
    OperatorStack : StackType;
        (* Stack to hold operands of the expression *)
    OperandStack  : StackType;
```

(continued)

Figure 7–22 (continued)

```
Begin
    OperatorStack := Create();
    OperandStack := Create();

    Repeat
        Sym := GetNextSymbol();

    (* For operands, create a leaf node and place on the operand stack. *)
        If (IsOperand(Sym)) Then
            New(Node);
            Node^.Value := Sym;
            Node^.Left := Nil;
            Node^.Right := Nil;
            Push(Node, OperandStack);

        Else (* IsOperator(Sym) *)

        (* This loop pops all operators on the operator stack whose
            precedence is greater than or equal to the current
            operator's precedence, and makes operands out of them.   *)
            While (Not Empty(OperatorStack)) And
                (Precedence(Sym) <= Precedence(Top(OperatorStack))) Do

                Node := Top(OperatorStack);
                Pop(OperatorStack);
                Node^.Right := Top(OperandStack);
                Pop(OperandStack);
                Node^.Left := Top(OperandStack);
                Pop(OperandStack);
                Push(Node, OperandStack);
            Endwhile;

        (* Finally, create a new node for the current operator. *)
            New(Node);
            Node^.Value := Sym;
            Node^.Left := Nil;
            Node^.Right := Nil;
            Push(Node, OperatorStack);

        Endif;
    Until (Sym = '$');

    Return Top(OperandStack);

End ExpressionTree;

End ExpressionTrees.
```

7.5 CONCLUSION

This chapter has introduced the fundamental properties of both general and binary trees. However, we are a long way from exhausting this important and fascinating area of study. Just as the binary tree can be considered a specialization of the general tree, so can we specialize the concept of a binary tree into other interesting and useful hierarchical structures such as binary search trees, balanced search trees, and indexed search trees.

In the next chapter we continue our study of hierarchical data structures by looking at some of these special purpose tree structures that are used to solve problems in such areas as searching, sorting, and finding minimum and maximum values.

CHAPTER EXERCISES

1. Given the tree

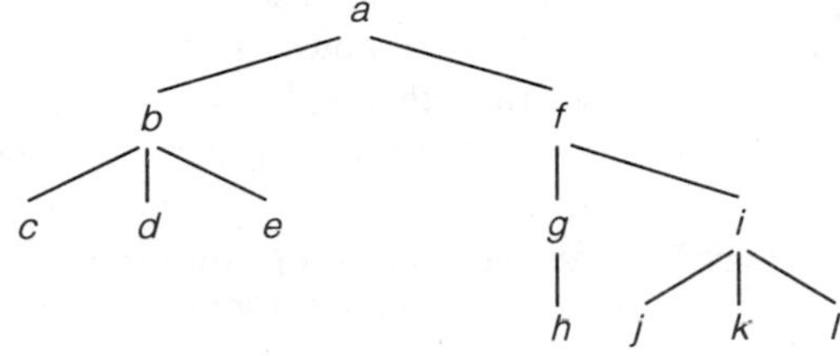

answer the following questions:
   a. What are the terminal nodes?
   b. What are the nonterminal nodes?
   c. What is the root of the tree?
   d. What is the degree of node a, node b, node c?
   e. What are the siblings of node c, node i?
   f. What are the ancestors of node h, node l?
   g. What are the descendants of node f?
   h. What is the level of node c?
   i. What is the height of the tree?
2. Given a single elimination sporting tournament with 64 teams (like the NCAA Basketball Championship)
   a. What is the height of the tournament tree?
   b. What is the degree of each internal node?
   c. What does the root of the tree represent?
3. Show the parse tree for the expression

   $a + (b + c * d)$

   using the four-rule grammar given in section 7.1.
4. Which of the following are trees?

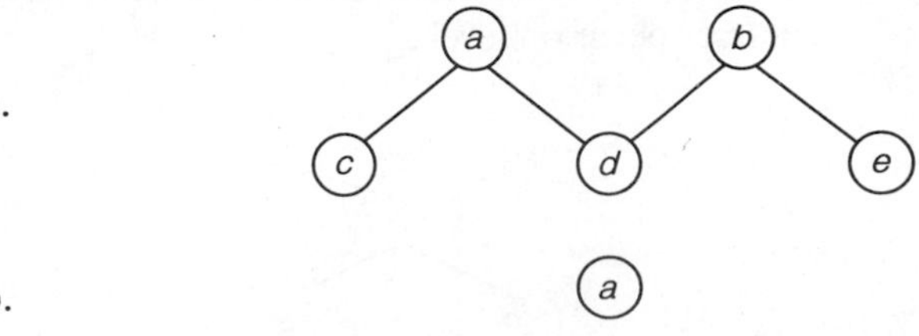

c.

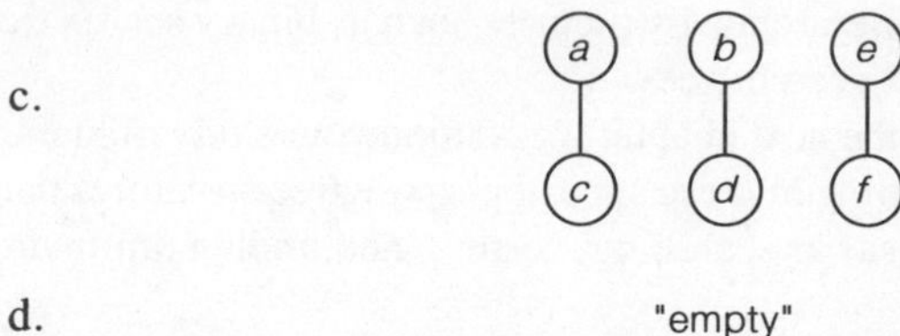

d. "empty"

5. Using the record structure of Figure 7–5, show how you would add a new child (call it node *m*) to node *f* in the tree shown in exercise 1. Node *m* itself has no children. Assume you start with a pointer called Root that points to *a*, the root of the tree.
6. Using the record structure of Figure 7–5, show how you would delete node *b* from the tree shown in exercise 1, along with the entire subtree of which *b* is the root, that is, {*c, d, e*}. (Do not worry about returning the space to the system.) Assume you start with a pointer called Root that points to *a*, the root of the tree.
7. Write the declarations for the array representation of general trees of the type shown in section 7.2. Given those declarations, write a procedure to find a specific data element in the tree

   Procedure Find (A, DataValue, Found)

   where:

   A is the array representation of a tree.
   DataValue is the value we are searching for.
   Found is True if there exists a node containing this value and False otherwise.

8. Given the binary tree

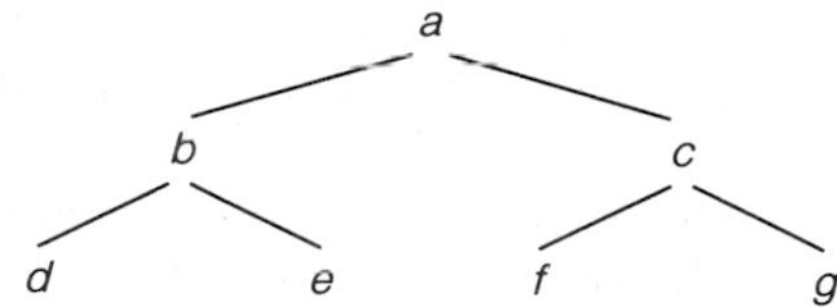

   we say that node *a* is at level 0, nodes *b* and *c* are at level 1, and nodes *d, e, f,* and *g* are at level 2. Sketch an algorithm that visits the nodes of a tree in a *level order* traversal. That is, it visits all the nodes on level *i* before visiting nodes at level *i* + 1. In this example we would visit the nodes in the order *a, b, c, d, e, f, g*. Assume that you are given R, a pointer to the root of the tree.
9. A binary tree is said to be *full* if all terminal nodes occur on the same level and each internal node has exactly two children. For example, the following binary tree is full because all internal nodes have two children and all empty subtrees occur on level 2.

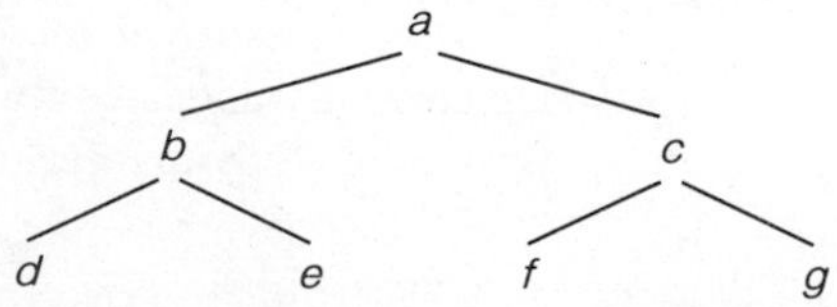

Design an algorithm that is given a pointer to the root of a tree and determine whether that tree is full.

10. What is the relationship between N, the total number of nodes in a full binary tree, and i, the level number on which the terminal nodes occur?
11. How many different ways would there be to traverse a tree structure in addition to the ones mentioned in this chapter, assuming we always complete the traversal of one subtree before starting on another? Show what each of your traversals would produce when it traverses the tree shown below.

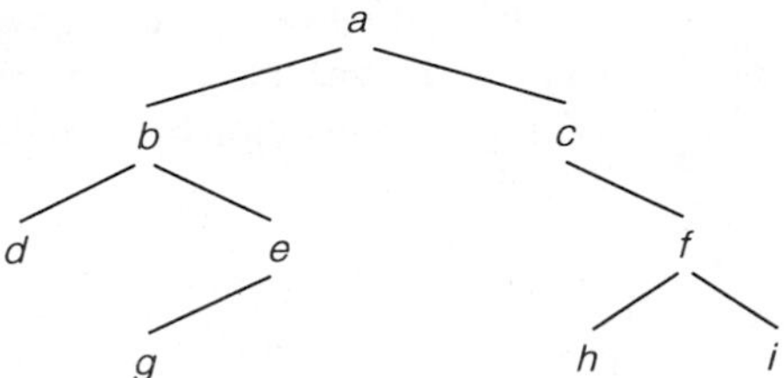

12. Modify the Preorder traversal algorithm of Figure 7–8 so that in addition to visiting the nodes it also counts how many nodes the tree contains.
13. Modify the Inorder traversal algorithm of Figure 7–9 so that you visit only those nodes with data fields greater than 0. (Assume that each node contains integer data values.)
14. Given the following binary tree

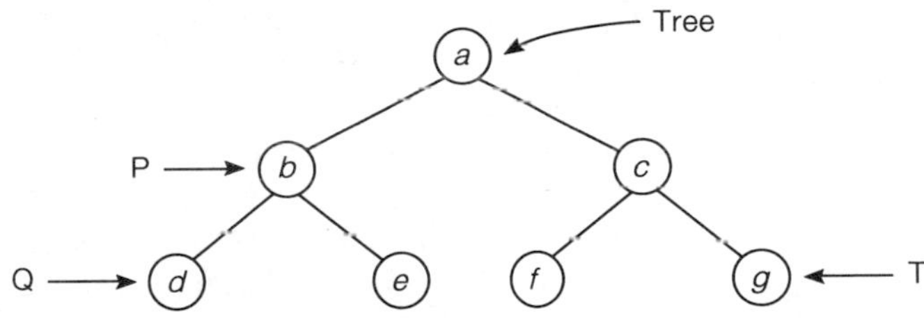

diagram the tree that will result from each of the following operations. (Assume that each operation begins with the tree shown above.)

a. Insert (T, Right, 'h')
b. Insert (Tree, Left, 'h')
c. Delete (Tree, P)
d. Ptr := Find (Tree, 'd', Found)
e. Ptr := Find (Tree, 'x', Found)
f. Ptr := Move (Tree, P, Up, Success)
g. Ptr := Move (Tree, P, Left, Success)
h. Ptr := Move (Tree, Q, Right, Success)

15. Specify the syntax and semantics for the following operations on binary trees, and then add them to the external module of Figure 7–11.
    a. A procedure Destroy that ends the existence of a tree T and returns all space currently allocated to T to the system.
    b. A procedure Copy that makes an identical copy of a tree T and returns the root of the copy.
    c. A procedure Update that changes the data field of a given node in a tree T.

d. A function Empty that is True if the tree pointed to is empty and False otherwise.
e. A procedure InsertSubtree(P, Direction, S). P is a pointer to a node in a tree, Direction is (Left,Right) and S is a pointer to the root of a tree. The procedure adds the tree pointed to by S to the node pointed to by P in the orientation specified by Direction.
f. A procedure Delete(T) that is given T, a pointer to a subtree, and that deletes only the node pointed to by T, not the entire subtree rooted at that node. The procedure takes a leaf node from another part of the tree and moves it into the place previously occupied by the deleted node.

16. Convert the tree shown below into a binary tree using the left child/right sibling representation described in section 7.3.3. What is the height of your resulting binary tree?

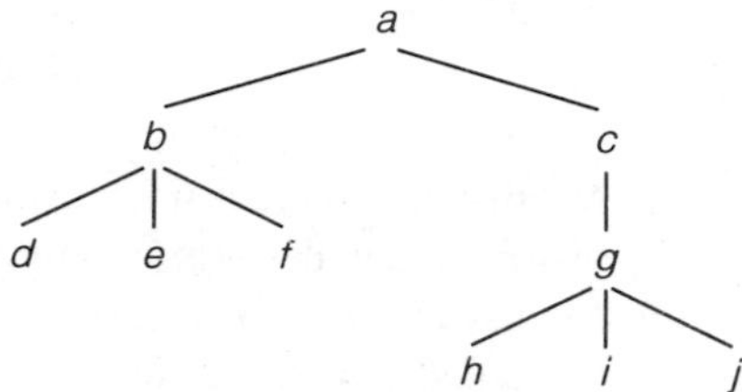

17. Complete the internal module of the abstract data type Binary Tree whose external module is shown in Figure 7–11. Use the declarations given in Figure 7–13 and write procedures for Compare, CreateBinaryTree, Delete, Find, Move, and Preorder.
18. Rewrite the Insert procedure of Figure 7–15 so that if the indicated insertion location is occupied, the procedure attempts to add the node as the other child. If that position is also occupied, it prompts the user to see whether or not they want to overwrite the information or suspend the operation.
19. Write procedures to implement the six new binary tree operations proposed in exercise 15. Use the pointer-based declaration given in Figure 7–13.
20. Show what the following tree would look like when stored in the $k \times 3$ two-dimensional array representation of Figures 7–16 and 7–17.

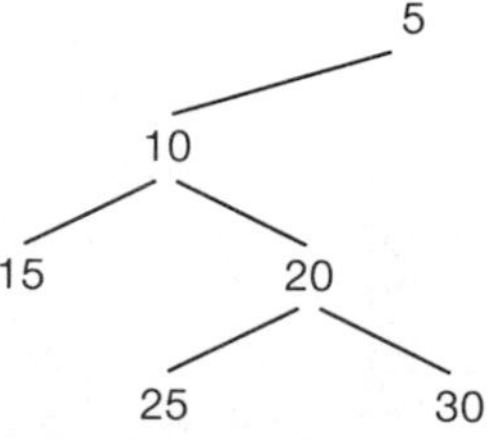

21. Using the two-dimensional array representation from exercise 20 and Figure 7–17, write the procedure Delete, which deletes a subtree of a tree.
22. Show the expression tree for the following
    a. $a + b * c - d * e$
    b. $c := 1 + (-x + \text{sqrt}\ (y/z))$
    c. **If** $a > b + c$ **Then** $d := -(e/f/g)$

23. Describe possible expression tree representations for the following Pascal statements and give examples
    a. **If/Then/Else**
    b. **While/Do**
    c. **Case/End**

CHAPTER 8

SPECIAL-PURPOSE TREE STRUCTURES

CHAPTER OUTLINE

8.1 INTRODUCTION

In chapter 7 we studied general-purpose tree structures in which few (if any) restrictions were placed on the data that could be stored in a node. In this chapter we will look at some *special-purpose* tree structures that either restrict the type of data placed in a node or specify relationships that must hold between the data value stored in the root of the tree and the data values stored in the left and right subtrees of that root. These special-purpose trees can be used for the efficient solution of problems in such areas as searching, sorting, finding maxima and minima, pattern matching, and data storage.

8.2 BINARY SEARCH TREES

8.2.1 Definition

A *binary search tree*, frequently abbreviated BST, is a special form of the binary tree discussed in chapter 7; it is particularly useful in computer science for carrying out search operations.

> *Definition*: A *binary search tree* is a binary tree in which one of the data values in each node is a special scalar value called a *key*. Every key value in the left subtree of a root node is less than the key value stored in that root, and every key value stored in the right subtree of a root node is greater than the key value stored in that root.

If there is more than one data value stored in a node of a BST (e.g., if it is a **Record** structure), then one field must be designated as the key value that is used to order the nodes in the tree. It is usually assumed that the keys in a BST are unique and duplicates are not allowed, and we will make this assumption in all the examples in this chapter. Figure 8–1 is an example of a binary search tree. Notice that every node in the left subtree of the root, {19, 23, 25}, is less than the value stored in the root, 31, and every node in the right subtree, {35, 38, 39, 40}, is greater than the root value 31. Similarly, looking at the subtrees of the root, we see that this ordering property holds for every node in the tree. In the tree whose root is 38, every value in

Figure 8–1
A Binary Search Tree

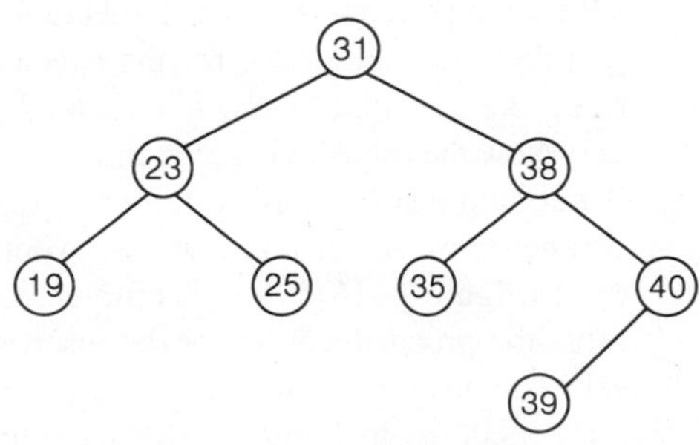

the left subtree, {35}, is less than 38, and every value in the right subtree, {39, 40}, is greater than 38.

The external module for a Binary Search Tree is similar to the binary tree package shown in Figure 7–11; it is listed in Figure 8–2. It imports the data type of the objects stored in the nodes, called BSTElementType, from another program unit called UserModule. The only restriction on this data type is that it must be a scalar that can be ordered by the relation $<$. That is, if a and b are both values of BSTElementType, then it must be possible to determine whether $a < b$; this property will be used when we code the internal module for this abstract data type.

8.2.2 Using Binary Search Trees In Searching Operations

There are two major differences between the binary search tree operations in Figure 8–2 and the binary tree operations of Figure 7–11. First, the Insert procedure must guarantee that the addition of a new node to an existing BST maintains the binary search tree property, and second, the Find procedure should exploit this property when trying to locate a given key within a BST.

When inserting a new node into a binary search tree, we are not given the location of the insertion (as we were with the binary tree Insert procedure of Figure 7–15). Instead, we are given only the value to be inserted and a pointer to the root of the binary search tree. The Insert operation itself must determine the new value's proper location in the tree by comparing the data value to be inserted, V, to the key value contained in the node, N. If $V < N$, then we follow the left branch of the node and repeat the process. If $V > N$, then we follow the right branch of the node and repeat the process. This comparison process continues until one of two things happens:

1. $V = N$. In this case the data value to be inserted is already contained in the tree. Since we have assumed that we do not want to store duplicate values the procedure just returns. Under other circumstances this case could be considered an error or treated as an update operation in which some node values will be modified.
2. The child pointer is Nil. We have now found the correct location to insert the new node.

Figure 8–3 shows an example in which four comparisons are needed to correctly place a new value in a binary search tree.

A procedure to implement this Insert operation is shown in Figure 8–4. It assumes the pointer-based implementation for binary trees given in Figure 7–13. Notice that we must check for the special case Root = **Nil**, because a binary search tree, like a regular binary tree, can be empty.

Now the important question is, What are the advantages of a binary search tree? What gain justifies paying the price of maintaining the binary search tree property whenever we insert a new node? After all, the Insert procedure for regular binary trees (Figure 7–15) is a very efficient O(1) operation since it does not have to determine the proper location for the insertion.

The answer to this question lies in the speed and efficiency of the Find procedure specified in Figure 8–2. Searching a data structure (e.g., a table, a list, or a

Figure 8–2
External Module for Binary Search Tree

```
(*  The following module contains the external specifications for the
    abstract data type Binary Search Tree, as described in section 8.2       *)
External Module BinarySearchTree;

From UserModule Import
        BSTElementType;      (* The type of data stored in the BST.          *)

Type
        (* The opaque type of the ADT Binary Search Tree.                    *)
    TreeType;

(*  Precondition: None
    Postcondition:    A new, empty binary search tree is returned.           *)
Procedure CreateBinarySearchTree() : TreeType;

(*  Precondition: CurrentNode is a node in Tree
    Postcondition:    If the precondition is met, the entire subtree in Tree
                          with root CurrentNode is removed.
                      Otherwise, Tree is unchanged.                          *)
Procedure Delete(Var Tree : TreeType; CurrentNode : TreeType);

(*  Precondition: None
    Postcondition:    All nodes in Tree are visited in an inorder traversal.
                          (i.e. Left subtree, root, right subtree)           *)
Procedure Inorder(Tree : TreeType);

(*  Precondition: None
    Postcondition:    A new node with data value NewNode is created, and
                          placed in Tree in the appropriate place to maintain
                          the binary search tree properties.                 *)
Procedure Insert(Var Tree : TreeType; NewNode : BSTElementType);

(*  Precondition: None
    Postcondition:    If Key is the data value associated with a node in Tree,
                          Found is set to True, and the node is returned.
                      If no node has Key as its data value, Found is set to
                          False, and Nil is returned.                        *)
Procedure Find(Tree : TreeType; Key : BSTElementType;
                          Var Found : Boolean) : TreeType;

(*  Precondition: None
    Postcondition:    All nodes in Tree are visited in a preorder traversal.
                              (i.e. Root, left subtree, right subtree)       *)
Procedure Preorder(Tree : TreeType);

(*  Precondition: None
    Postcondition:    All nodes in Tree are visited in a postorder traversal.
                              (i.e. Left subtree, right subtree, root)       *)
Procedure Postorder(Tree : TreeType);

End BinaryTree.
```

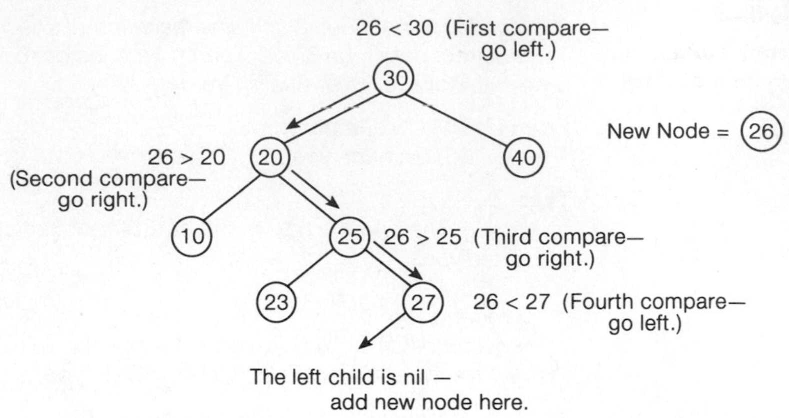

Figure 8–3
Placement of a New Node in a Binary Search Tree

Figure 8–4
Insert Procedure for Binary Search Trees

```
(*  Precondition: None
    Postcondition:    A new node with data value NewNode is created, and
                      placed in Tree in the appropriate place to maintain
                      the binary search tree properties.   *)
Procedure Insert(Var Tree : TreeType; NewNode : BSTElementType);
Begin
    If (Tree = Nil) Then          (* We have reached the place to insert *)
        New(Tree);
        Tree^.Data := NewNode;
        Tree^.Left := Nil;
        Tree^.Right := Nil;
    Else                          (* Keep searching for the place to insert *)
        If (NewNode < Tree^.Data) Then
            Insert(Tree^.Left, NewNode);
        Elsif (NewNode > Tree^.Data) Then
            Insert(Tree^.Right, NewNode);
        Endif;
    Endif;
End Insert;
```

record) to locate a particular value is one of the most common operations in computer science. When we sequentially search an unordered table containing N items looking for a special key, we will have to look at $N/2$ items, on the average, until we find the item we want. In the worst case, we may have to look at all N items in the table. Therefore sequential search is O(N) and can be very slow for large values of N (as we discussed in section 6.3 and Figure 6–2).

However, with a binary search tree we never have to look at more than H items, where H is the *height* of the binary search tree, that is, the distance to the leaf node

Figure 8–5
Height (H) of a Binary Search Tree

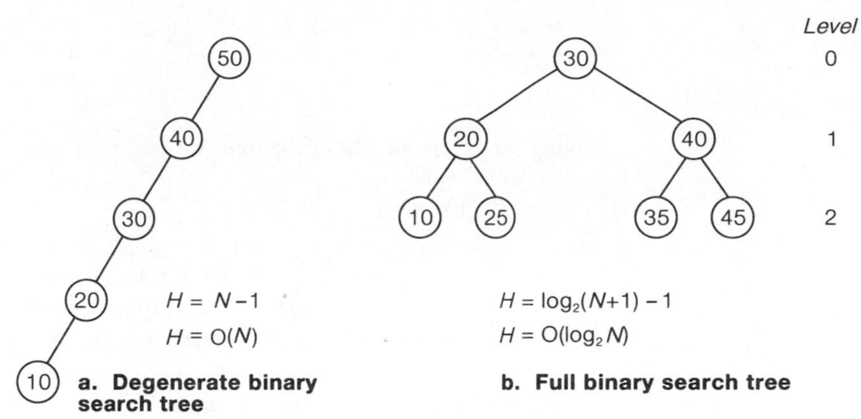

that is farthest from the root. For example, in Figure 8–3 we traveled from the root node to a leaf node looking for the place to insert the value 26 and thus examined four nodes, which is exactly equal to the value of H, the height of the tree. The Find operation on a binary search tree is therefore O(H). The next questions are, What is H? and is it always the case that $H < N$? More specifically, can we perform the Find operation with a lower order complexity than $O(N)$?

Figure 8–5 shows the two possible extremes of the binary search tree structure. In Figure 8–5a we see what is called a *degenerate binary search tree*—one of the two child pointers of every nonterminal node is equal to **Nil**. In this degenerate BST, $H - N - 1$, where N is the number of nodes in the tree; we have gained nothing since the BST has effectively become a linear list, and the Find operation is O(N). (In fact, our efficiency is actually worse, because we have to allocate a good deal of space for unused pointers.)

In Figure 8–5b we see the other extreme, called a *full binary search tree*. A full binary search tree is one in which all leaf nodes are on the same level and all nonleaf nodes have a degree of 2. Let us see how many nodes N are in a full binary search tree of height H. We will first count the number of nodes on each level in the tree and then add up these values.

	Level	*Number of Nodes on This Level*
(Root)	0	1
	1	2
	2	4
	3	8
	•	•
	•	•
	•	•
	i	2^i

The number of nodes at level i in a full binary search tree is just 2^i, so the total number of nodes N in the tree of Figure 8–5b is

$$N = \sum_{i=0}^{H} 2^i = 2^0 + 2^1 + 2^2 + \ldots + 2^H$$
$$= 2^{H+1} - 1$$

Solving for H, the height of the tree, we get

$$H = \log_2(N + 1) - 1 = O(\log_2 N)$$

Thus the maximum distance from the root to any one of the leaves in a full binary search tree (as in Figure 8–5b) is a logarithmic function of N, the number of nodes in the tree, rather than a linear function as in Figure 8–5a. Therefore the Find operation will be $O(\log_2 N)$.

If our BST looks more like the one in Figure 8–5b than the one in Figure 8–5a, we have gained a significant advantage in searching time. We will be able to locate any item in our tree in at most $O(\log_2 N)$ accesses, rather than the O(N) accesses in a sequential search of a linear data structure. For large values of N, $\log_2 N << N$. For example, if $N = 1000$ nodes, we will be able to locate any node in the binary search tree with $\log_2 1000 \approx 10$ searches—an improvement of two orders of magnitude over the 1,000 looks that could be required in a sequential search! The enormous increase in speed of the Find operation is the primary advantage of the BST data structure.

Figure 8–6 shows an implementation of the Find procedure to locate keys in a binary search tree. You might find it interesting to write a sequential search procedure too, and time both procedures for identical values of N to see the increased time efficiency that is possible using this new data structure.

The final question we must answer is, If we construct a binary search tree with any arbitrary and random sequence of N scalar values, will its height H be closer to N (Figure 8–5a) or to $\log_2 N$ (Figure 8–5b)? Will its final shape be closer to degenerate or to full? Another way to phrase this question is to ask whether a binary search tree built from a random sequence of values will or will not be *balanced*. Informally, we define a balanced tree containing N nodes as one whose height is very close to the theoretical minimum of $H = \log_2 (N + 1) - 1$. This definition is not precise since we have not defined what we mean by "close to." For some special tree structures, the term *balanced* is given a much more precise meaning. Here we simply mean that if the shape of the tree is approximately that of Figure 8–5b, it is considered well balanced.

For example, given the sequence {20, 17, 25, 22, 13, 30} the Insert procedure will construct the following six node tree:

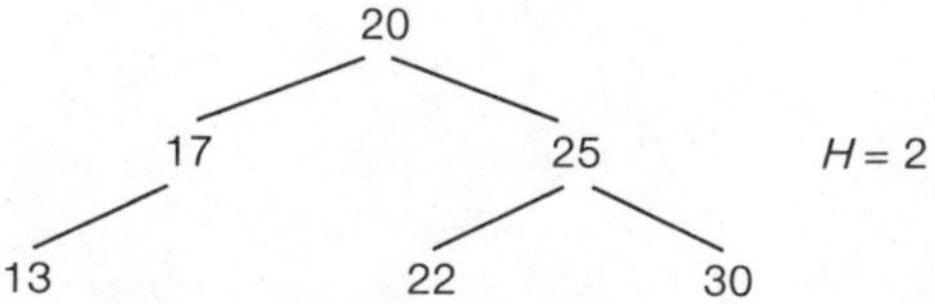

this tree is balanced because its height H is 2, which is the theoretical minimum.

Figure 8–6
Find Procedure for Binary Search Tree

```
(*   Precondition: None
     Postcondition:    If Key is the data value associated with a node in Tree,
                            Found is set to True, and the node is returned.
                       If no node has Key as its data value, Found is set to
                            False, and Nil is returned.   *)
Procedure Find(Tree : TreeType; Key : BSTElementType;
                       Var Found : Boolean) : TreeType;
Begin
     If (Tree = Nil) Then
               (* We have reached the bottom of the tree, Key is not there. *)
          Found := False;
          Return Nil;

     Elsif (Key = Tree^.Data) Then
               (* Key is there, we've found it. *)
          Found := True;
          Return Tree;

     Elsif (Key < Tree^.Data) Then
          (* Haven't found key yet, but it may be in the left subtree. *)
          Return(Find(Tree^.Left, Key, Found));

     Else (* Key > Tree^.Data *)
          (* Haven't found key yet, but it may be in the right subtree. *)
          Return(Find(Tree^.Right, Key, Found));
     Endif;

End Find;
```

However, if the same six values were presented in the following order {30, 13, 17, 20, 25, 22} we would end up with:

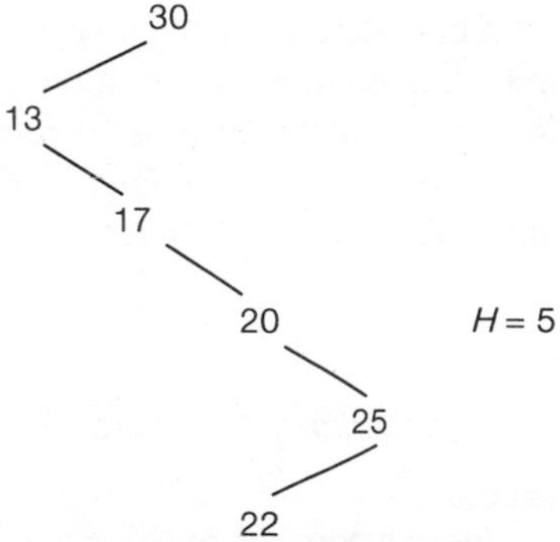

which is a degenerate tree whose height H is 5, which is $O(N)$. Are these two cases equally likely? If not, which type of structure can we expect to observe? We will not solve this complex mathematical problem here. Instead, we simply state the result: a binary search tree constructed from a random sequence of scalar values will look more like Figure 8–5b than Figure 8–5a, and it will be reasonably well balanced; its height H will satisfy the relationship $H = O(\log_2 N)$. Thus, for searching arbitrary lists of values, the binary search tree *is* an efficient data structure in which items anywhere in the tree can be located in approximately logarithmic time. (However, remember that these results apply to arbitrary and random sequences of values. There are certain specific patterns that in the worst case can produce degenerate trees that look like Figure 8–5a, and then the BST is less useful.)

8.2.3 TreeSort

In addition to efficient and rapid searching, a second application of binary search trees is in sorting a list of values into ascending or descending order. Suppose that we have already constructed a binary search tree like the following one:

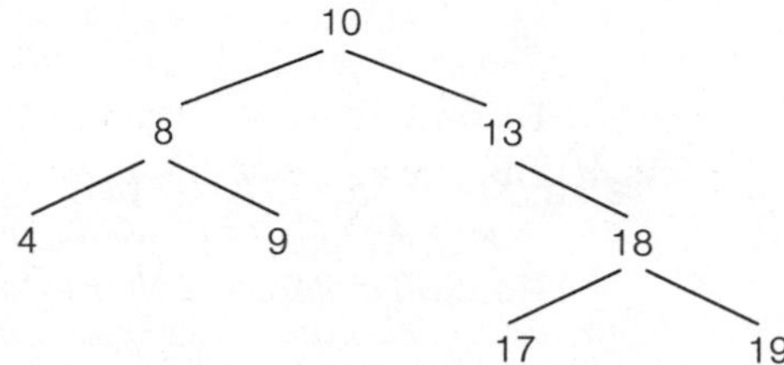

If we now execute an inorder traversal of this tree, printing out each node as we visit it (as shown in Figure 7–14), we get the following output:

4, 8, 9, 10, 13, 17, 18, 19

which lists values in ascending order. This observation is the basis for a very simple sorting algorithm called *TreeSort* , which is shown in Figure 8–7. This algorithm uses a number of operations from the BinarySearchTree external module of Figure 8–2.

Let us determine the time complexity of the algorithm in Figure 8–7. The insert procedure is called N times, once for each input value. To perform the insert operation, we must travel from the root of the tree to the leaf node where we will do the actual insertion, as pictured in Figure 8–3. We have already shown that this distance, H, is $O(\log_2 N)$ for the average case. Therefore, the time complexity for

Figure 8–7
The TreeSort Algorithm

```
T := CreateBinarySearchTree()    (* Create an empty BST. *)

Repeat                           (* Phase I *)
    Input a number, N            (* Build a BST. *)
    Insert(T, N)
Until no more input

                                 (* Phase II *)
Inorder(T)                       (* Now traverse the BST using
                                      an inorder traversal. *)
```

Table 8–1 Time Study of Four O(N log$_2$ N) Sorting Algorithms (all times in seconds)

	LIST SIZE N = 2,500		
Algorithm	Random Order	Sorted Order	Reverse Order
MergeSort	8.1	7.8	7.9
QuickSort	1.3	35.1	37.1
Tree Sort	2.1	30.7	30.2
Heap Sort	1.9	1.8	2.6

building the N node BST, one node at a time is N times the complexity of a single insertion, or O(N log$_2$$N$).

The inorder traversal of the tree that we have just constructed involves visiting every node in the tree exactly once. Since there are N nodes in the tree, the inorder traversal operation is O(N). Therefore, the overall complexity of the TreeSort algorithm of Figure 8–7 is Max (O(N log$_2$$N$), O($N$)) = O($N$ log$_2$$N$), which is the same complexity as both MergeSort and QuickSort (introduced in Section 5.4).

Remember, however, that this analysis looked only at the average case behavior. In the worst case, the binary search tree degenerates into the linear structure of Figure 8–5a, and the Insert procedure becomes O(N) rather than O(log$_2$$N$). Since we must repeat this insertion process N times, the complexity of insertion becomes O(N^2), and the overall complexity of tree sort is Max (O(N^2), O(N)) = O(N^2), an inefficient quadratic-time algorithm. Table 8–1 shows the performance of the TreeSort algorithm on lists of length N = 2,500 in random order, correct order, and reverse order (exactly the same performance test we applied to MergeSort and QuickSort in Table 6–2, from which the data for these two algorithms is repeated). The last two cases (correct order and reverse order) produce a degenerate tree like the one diagrammed in Figure 8–5a.

Notice that for the list of numbers in random order, the sorting time for TreeSort is generally comparable to that of the other two O(N log$_2$$N$) algorithms that we have measured, MergeSort and QuickSort. However, when the lists are initially in either sorted or reverse sequence, the performance degrades dramatically and the sort takes over 30 seconds, about 15 times longer than the average case. Because of this extremely poor worst case behavior, TreeSort is not as widely used as either QuickSort or MergeSort. It also suffers from a space complexity problem, requiring storage for 2N pointer fields as well as for the N key values.

In section 8.4 we will introduce another tree-based sorting method called HeapSort, which suffers neither a worst-case time problem nor a space problem. Along with QuickSort, this method is one of the most popular sorting algorithms in computer science.

8.3 INDEXED SEARCH TREES

There is a special form of search tree, the *indexed search tree*, that has some very interesting properties; it is also called a *trie* (pronounced "try").

In a binary search tree we use the entire key to determine in which direction to move through the tree. For example:

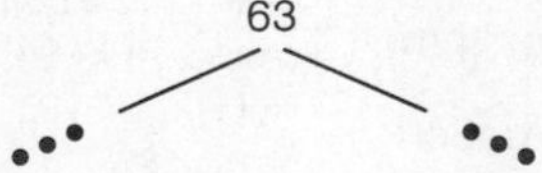

If our key value is 58 we move to the left; if it is 102, we move to the right. Since these are the only two possibilities (remember that if the key value is 63, we have found what we want and we stop), we always know in which direction to move.

However, sometimes the key for which we are searching cannot be viewed as a single primitive object but must be thought of as a composite object made up of a sequence of individual components c_i, each drawn from a set of values $V = \{v_1, v_2, \ldots, v_m\}$ as in

$$\text{key} = c_1 c_2 c_3 \ldots c_n \qquad \text{where } c_i \in V \qquad i = 1, \ldots, n$$

In a trie, the individual components c_i of the key (rather than the entire key) are used to build the individual nodes and traverse the tree. The data field of a particular node (if it exists) represents a concatenation of all the elements along the path from the root to that given node.

Assume that the set of possible values V for the component elements of the keys, c_i, $i = 1, \ldots, n$, has m members, $V = \{v_1, v_2, \ldots v_m\}$. Then each node in the trie will contain $m + 1$ fields—one data field and m pointer fields, as shown in Figure 8–8.

The basic idea behind a trie is that if we reach a node by following a particular sequence of pointers $v_{i_1}\ v_{i_2}\ v_{i_3} \ldots v_{i_k}$, then the node that we reach represents the key value

$$\text{key} = c_1 c_2 c_3 \ldots c_k \qquad \text{where } c_1 = v_{i_1},\ c_2 = v_{i_2},\ \ldots,\ c_k = v_{i_k}$$

If that key is actually to be stored in the tree, then we indicate that by the value stored in the Data field. If this key is not considered part of the tree, then the Data field will be set to Null.

We search the trie for the key $c_1 c_2 c_3 \ldots c_n$ in the following way:

Trie Search Algorithm:

1. Set $i = 1$, and set P to point to the root of the trie structure.
2. Remove component c_i from the key, c_i = some v_j for $j = 1, \ldots, m$.

Figure 8–8
Trie Node Structure

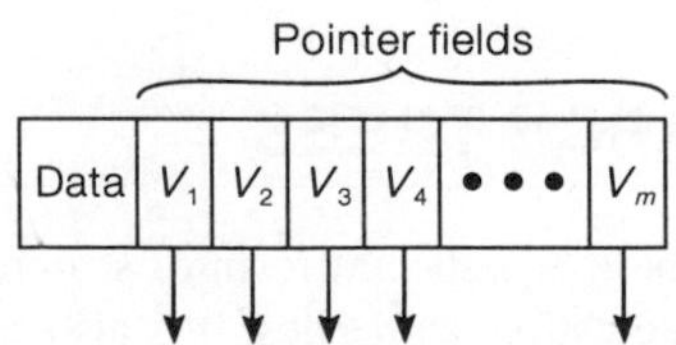

3. If the v_j pointer field of node P is **Nil**, then the key is not in the tree. We terminate the algorithm and report that the key was not found.
4. If the v_j pointer field of node P is not **Nil**, then we follow it by setting $P = v_j$.
5. $i := i + 1$. If $i \leq n$, where n is the number of individual components in the key, then we go back to step 2. If $i > n$, we have located the correct node in the trie, and we go to step 6.
6. If the Data field of the node pointed at by P is null, then the key is not in the trie and we can report that the key was not found. Otherwise, the key is in the trie and the Data field contains the desired value we are looking for. We report that the key was found.

Looking at this algorithm, we see that every node N in a trie corresponds to some valid prefix value $c_1c_2c_3 \ldots c_i$. If that prefix is a complete key, then the Data field of node N will hold a non-null value corresponding to that key. If the prefix is not a complete key, then the Data field will be null. Furthermore, if $c_1c_2c_3 \ldots c_i\, c_{i+1}$ is also a valid prefix for $c_{i+1} = v_j$ then the v_j pointer in node N will be non-null and will point to the node in the tree corresponding to the prefix $c_1c_2c_3 \ldots c_i\, c_{i+1}$. If $c_1c_2c_3 \ldots c_i\, c_{i+1}$, for $c_{i+1} = v_k$, is not a valid prefix of any key, then the v_k pointer in node N will be **Nil**.

Let us illustrate this idea with a simple example—Morse code. The keys will be a finite sequence of dots and dashes, so the value set V is just {•,–}. We will use the data field of a node to store the English letter corresponding to the sequence of dots and dashes used to reach that node. The data field will be null if the sequence is not part of the code set. In addition to the data field, each node will have two pointers corresponding to the two values • and –. A partial trie for the letters E, I, S, A, T, N, D, M, and O is shown in Figure 8–9.

Searching the tree in Figure 8–9 is quite easy. For example, given a key containing a sequence of dots and dashes, $c_1\ c_2 \ldots c_n$, and beginning at the root, we simply strip off each component of the key one element at a time, and follow the dot or dash pointer from the current node. After we have done this for all n symbols, we will have reached the node that represents the key. Whether it corresponds to a valid key for our trie depends strictly on the value stored in the data field. If the data field is null, then this sequence of dots and dashes is not a valid Morse code symbol. If the data field is non-null, it is a valid sequence and the data field contains the English letter equivalent. Furthermore, if we ever encounter a Null pointer as we are traversing the trie, we also know that this sequence of dots and dashes is not a valid Morse code symbol.

Figure 8–9
Partial Trie Structure for Representing Morse Code

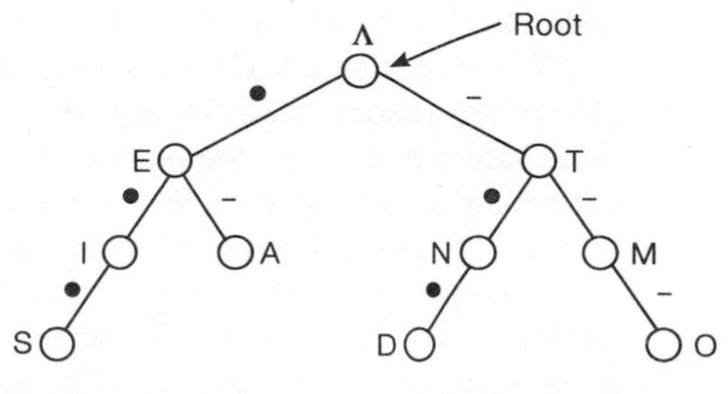

We can illustrate each of these cases using the trie structure of Figure 8–9. The sequence ••• will bring us to a node with a non-null data field, S, so this is a valid key. The empty sequence (" ") brings us to a node in the trie (the root node), but its data field is null (indicated by the symbol Λ in Figure 8–9), so it is not a valid key. Finally the sequence •–• will cause us to encounter a null pointer when we try to follow the • pointer on the last symbol, so this sequence is also not a valid key.

Insertion into a trie is similar to the search procedure just described. We must examine separately each component element of the key we wish to insert into the trie structure. There are three distinct cases that can occur during insertion, and we will again illustrate them using the trie in Figure 8–9. Case 1 occurs when the node corresponding to the new key already exists in the structure. Then all we need to do is set the data field to the desired value. This case would occur if we wished, for example, to reassign the sequence –– from the current value (M) to some other letter (we would just change the data value in that node from M to its new value). This case would also occur if we wanted to assign a new value to a node currently containing a null.

Case 2 occurs if the prefix for the new key already occurs in the structure. That is, if we wish to insert a new key $v_1, v_2, \ldots, v_n$, and the node corresponding to the prefix $v_1, v_2, \ldots, v_{n-1}$ already exists. All we need to do is create a new trie node, set its data field to the desired value, set all m pointer values in that node to Λ, and finally, set the v_n pointer of the prefix node $v_1, v_2, \ldots, v_{n-1}$ to point to this new node. This case would occur if we added the symbol –•– (K) to the trie of Figure 8–9, since the prefix node corresponding to –• (N) is already there.

The final case occurs when we wish to add the key $v_1, v_2, \ldots, v_n$ to the trie and the prefix $v_1, v_2, \ldots, v_{n-1}$ is not in the trie. Now we must add not only the final data node, we must also add one or more *intermediate* or *dummy* nodes in order to create a complete path to our data. If the new key is $v_1, v_2, \ldots, v_n$ and the longest prefix of that key that is currently a node in the trie is $v_1, v_2, \ldots, v_i$, $i < n - 1$, then we will have to add $n - i - 1$ dummy nodes $v_{i+1}, v_{i+2}, \ldots, v_{n-1}$. Each of these nodes will have a null data field and a single non-null pointer value pointing to the next dummy node in the prefix. This case would occur if we tried to add the key –––••, which is the code for the digit 8. In addition to the final data node, we also need one intermediate node corresponding to the prefix –––•, which is not currently in the tree. This example is shown in Figure 8–10.

The deletion process for a trie also has three cases—deleting an interior node (e.g., E in Figure 8–10), deleting a leaf node (e.g., S), and deleting a leaf node connected to the trie by only intermediate nodes (e.g., 8). When deleting an interior node, we cannot delete the node itself and reclaim the space, because the node represents not only a data value (e.g., E in Figure 8–10) but also a valid prefix for other nodes (e.g., I, S, and A). Instead, we simply reset the data value field to null.

When deleting a leaf node such as S, A, or D, we can delete the node and dispose of its memory space, because these leaf nodes are not acting as a prefix for any other values in the trie. We must also remember to reset the appropriate pointer of the parent of that node to **Nil**. For example, if we were to delete the D node of Figure 8–10, we must also reset the • pointer of its parent (N) to **Nil**.

Finally, when deleting a node like the 8, we delete not only the leaf but also all intermediate nodes as well, since they no longer serve as prefixes of any valid data items in the trie. We can determine that a node is no longer a prefix by noting

Figure 8–10
Adding An Intermediate Node to a Trie

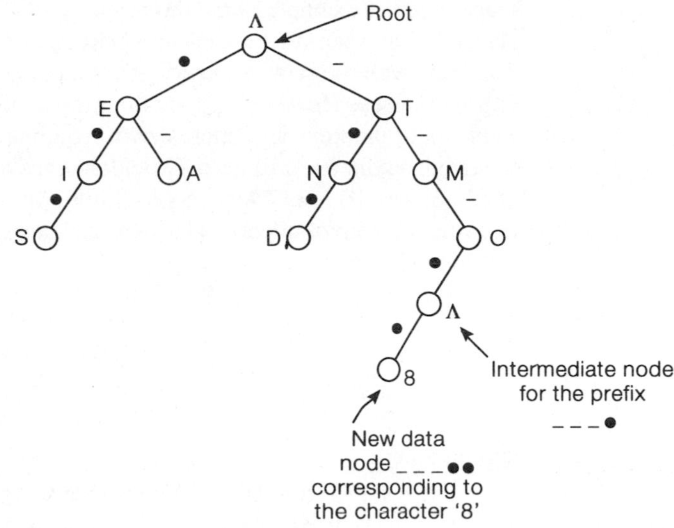

Figure 8–11
Trie Structure for Some English Language Words

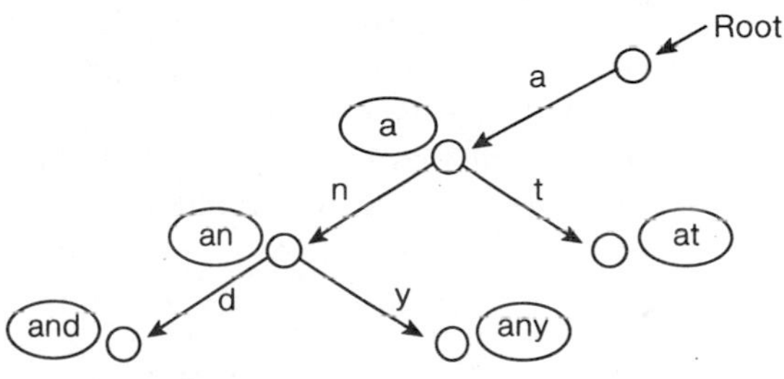

whether every one of the pointer values in the node is **Nil** as well as its data field. For example, after deleting the value 8 in Figure 8–10 and clearing the • pointer of its parent, every field within that parent node would have the value **Nil**, so that node could be deleted.

We leave the complete specification of the trie deletion algorithm as an exercise.

The major advantage of a trie is that the number of operations needed to find a key within the data structure is proportional to the length of the key being searched, not the number of nodes in the trie. If we have a dictionary of 100,000 English words stored as a binary search tree, then the number of comparisons needed to find a key in the dictionary will be $O(\log_2 100{,}000) \approx 17$, as we learned in section 8.2.2. However, if the dictionary is represented as a trie, the number of comparisons needed to locate a specific key would be equal to the average length of an English word, which is about five characters, a reduction of about 70%. For this reason, trie structures are widely used in textual application such as editors, thesauruses, and spelling checkers. Figure 8–11 shows a trie for the five English words *a*, *an*, *at*, *and*, and *any*.

However, the price for this time reduction can be very high in terms of memory space (another example of the time-space tradeoff discussed in section 6.4). At first glance it may seem that a trie is an extremely efficient representation, since words that begin with the same sequence of letters (e.g., *an, and, any*) share a common set of prefix nodes. However, this first impression is not correct. Since the component elements of the keys are letters drawn from the vocabulary V = {A, B, . . . , Z}, each node in the trie will need 27 fields—one data field and 26 pointers, rather than the 2 pointers {•,–} of Morse code. (Furthermore, this analysis does not even consider the problem of upper- and lowercase letters or special symbols). The trie nodes will look like this:

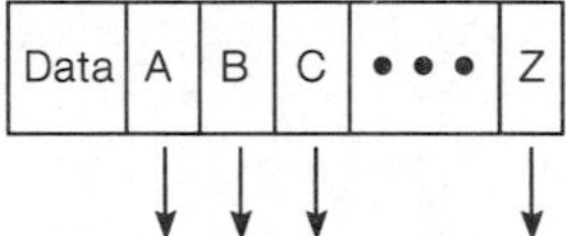

If we need to store 50,000 English words in our trie, we will have 50,000 data nodes and a much larger number of intermediate nodes, which will be required because they are valid prefixes of other English words (e.g., *c, co, com, comp*, . . . to store the word *computer*). Each of these nodes has 26 pointers and each pointer will be about four bytes long. When we add the space needed for intermediate nodes and data fields, we would probably find that we need billions of bytes of memory, greatly exceeding our available capacity. Hence it is usually infeasible to store a *complete trie* data structure, that is, one that includes all *n* components of a key. However, as we shall see in the case study at the end of this chapter, a *partial trie*, when used in conjunction with other data structures, can be useful in representing and managing collections of textual data.

8.4 HEAPS

8.4.1 Definition

A *heap* is a binary tree that satisfies the following two conditions:

1. The data value stored in any node is less than or equal to the value in any of that node's children. There is no restriction about orderings within the left or right subtrees, only between a parent and its children. Therefore, the value stored in the root of a heap is always the smallest value in the heap. (Note: We could just as easily define a heap where the value in a node is greater than or equal to the value stored in any of its children. In that case all algorithms in this section would simply change the $<$ operator to a $>$.) This condition is called the *ordering* property of heaps.
2. A heap must be a *complete* binary tree. A complete binary tree is a binary tree with *i* levels and where all leaves are located only on level *i* and level *i*-1. In addition, the leaves on level *i* must be as far to the left as possible. This condition is called the *structuring* property of heaps.

Figure 8–12 gives examples of complete binary trees as well as those that violate this constraint.

Figure 8–12
Valid and Invalid Complete Binary Trees

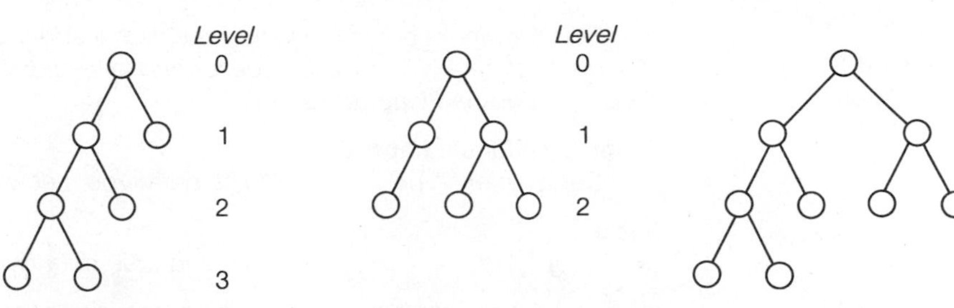

a. Not a complete binary tree because leaves occur on levels 1, 2, and 3 rather than just on levels 2 and 3.

b. Not a complete binary tree because the leaves on level 2 do not occur as far to the left as possible.

c. A complete binary tree.

Informally, we can say that you will produce a valid heap structure when you insert new nodes by moving across level i in a strictly left-to-right fashion until it is full and only then beginning to insert new nodes on level $i + 1$, again in a strictly left--to-right fashion.

The tree in Figure 8–12a violates the requirement that all of the leaves be located on two levels—it has leaf nodes at levels 1, 2, and 3. In Figure 8–12b the left-to-right property is violated—the leaf nodes on level 2 are not as far to the left as possible. Figure 8–12c shows a tree that meets the structure property of heaps.

We will provide four operations to support our Heap abstract data type. The syntax of these four operations is summarized below.

Define Heap[ElementType]
  CreateHeap() : Heap
  Insert(Heap, ElementType) : Heap
  GetSmallest(Heap) : ElementType, Heap
  Empty(Heap) : Boolean

Like all of our create functions, the creator operation, CreateHeap will return a new empty Heap structure.

The two transformer operations allowed on a Heap structure are inserting a new value into the heap and retrieving the smallest value stored in the heap (i.e., removing the root). The Insert procedure must ensure that the operation maintains both the ordering and the structuring properties that we just described. In addition, the retrieval procedure, called GetSmallest, will also have to rebuild the tree structure, since we are removing the root and all nonempty trees must, by definition, have a root! We will see how to carry out both of these operations in the next section.

The only observer operation on a Heap structure is the Boolean function Empty, which returns true if the heap is empty and false otherwise.

An external module for the Heap structure is shown in Figure 8–13. It includes the four basic heap operations that we have just described—CreateHeap, Insert, GetSmallest, and Empty.

Figure 8–13
External Module for a Heap

```
(*   The following module contains the external specifications for the
     abstract data type Heap, as described in section 8.4.                    *)
External Module HeapPackage;

From UserModule Import
     DataElementType;         (* The data type that will be stored in the heap. *)

Type
     HeapType;                (* The opaque data type itself *)

          (* The possible errors resulting from an operation on a heap.        *)
     HeapErrorType          = (None, HeapOverFlow, HeapUnderFlow);

Var
     Error : HeapErrorType;   (* A global variable, set by all heap functions,
                                    reflecting its success or failure.         *)

(*   Precondition: None
     Postcondition:     A new, empty heap is returned.                         *)
Procedure CreateHeap() : Heap;

(*   Precondition: None
     Postcondition:     If there are any elements in Heap, False is returned,
                        Otherwise, True is returned.                           *)
Procedure Empty( Heap : HeapType ) : Boolean;

(*   Precondition: Full(Heap) = False
     Postcondition:     If precondition is met, Error = None and the element
                             NewNode is placed in the proper position in Heap,
                             maintaining the heap properties.
                        Otherwise, Error = HeapOverFlow and Heap is unchanged.
Procedure Insert( Var Heap : HeapType; NewNode : DataElementType );

(*   Precondition: Empty(Heap) = False
     Postcondition:     If the precondition is met, Error = None and the smallest
                             element in Heap is returned.
                        Otherwise, Error = HeapUnderFlow and the return value
                             is undefined.                                     *)
Procedure GetSmallest( Var Heap : HeapType ) : DataElementType;

End HeapPackage.
```

A heap is a balanced binary tree that is particularly useful in solving three classes of problems:

1. Finding a minimum or maximum value in a collection of scalar values
2. Sorting a collection of scalar values into either ascending or descending order
3. Implementing another important data structure called a *priority queue*

We will see examples of all three of these important applications later in this chapter.

8.4.2 Implementation of Heaps Using Arrays

One of the major problems with tree structures is the need to allocate space for all their pointers, as we discussed when we saw that the trie structure for English words would need 26 pointer fields per node. A pointer is simply a memory address. Since most computers support primary memories of about 2^{16} to 2^{32} bytes, pointer fields in a node will typically require two, three, or even four bytes each, thus consuming a good deal of memory space.

However, we can take advantage of the restricted structure of a heap to produce an extremely space-efficient one-dimensional array representation that requires no pointers at all. We will store the elements of our heap in a one-dimensional array in left-to-right level order; that is, we will store all of the nodes on level i in a left-to-right order before we store the nodes on level $i + 1$. This one-dimensional array representation of a heap, called a *heapform*, is diagrammed in Figure 8–14. We do not need to use pointers in our array-based representation of a heap because the parent, children, and siblings of a given node in our array are all in a fixed and known position of the array relative to that node.

The root of the heap is always in position 1 of the array (since it is the only node on level 1), and for any node stored in array location i, $1 \le i \le N$, the location in the array of the parent, left child, right child, and sibling of that node are given by the following expressions:

Parent(i) = i **div** 2	if (i **div** 2) $\geq$ 1 else i has no parent
LeftChild(i) = $2i$	if $2i \leq N$ else i has no left child
RightChild(i) = $2i + 1$	if $2i + 1 \leq N$ else i has no right child
Sibling(i)	
if odd(i) then $i - 1$	if $i > 1$ else i has no sibling
if even (i) then $i + 1$	if $i < N$ else i has no sibling

We can use these formulas to recover the hierarchical relationships present in the tree representation of heaps shown in Figure 8–14a.

For example, let us look at node x_4 of Figure 8–14 whose index in the array X is

Figure 8–14
Tree and Array Representations of a Heap

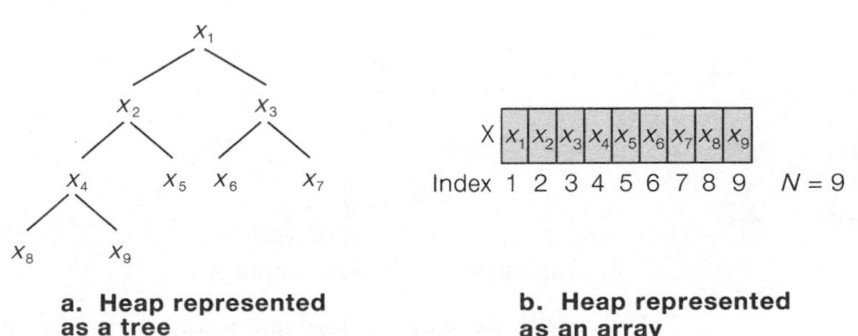

a. Heap represented as a tree

b. Heap represented as an array

$i = 4$. (that is, $X[4] = x_4$). We can reconstruct the tree-based relationships as follows:

Parent = 4 **div** 2 = 2	The node in X[2] is the parent of x_4
LeftChild = 2 * 4 = 8	The node in X[8] is the left child of x_4
RightChild = 2 * 4 + 1 = 9	The node in X[9] is the right child of x_4
Sibling = 4 + 1 = 5	The node in X[5] is the sibling of x_4.

As a second example, let us look at the node x_7 which is in the seventh position of the array X.

Parent = 7 **div** 2 = 3 The parent of x_7 will be in X[3].
LeftChild = 2 * 7 = 14, but 14 > 9, so x_7 has no left child.
RightChild = (2 * 7) + 1 = 15, but 15 > 9 so x_7 has no right child.
Sibling = 7 − 1 = 6 The sibling of x_7 will be in X[6]

Given the following array declarations to create a heapform:

```
Const
    MaxHeapSize = . . . ; (* Maximum allowable size of the heap *)
Type
    HeapType = Array [1 .. MaxHeapSize] of DataElementType;
Var
    Heap : HeapType;
    N    : 0 .. MaxHeapSize; (* Number of elements in the heap *)
```

we can now describe the internal implementation of the two basic heap transformer operations, Insert and GetSmallest.

To insert a value into a heap, we initially place it into the unique location that will maintain the structuring property of heaps. This location is the left-most unoccupied slot on level i or the first slot on level $i + 1$ if level i is full. In either case, this location always corresponds to element $X[N + 1]$ in the heapform array X, where N is the number of nodes stored in the heap prior to the insertion operation. This process is illustrated in Figure 8–15a and 8–15b.

However, referring to our example in Figure 8–15b, it may be the case that $x_6 < x_3$, and thus the placement of this node violates the ordering property of heaps. If so, then we simply interchange the child and parent that are out of order, as shown

Figure 8–15
The Insert Operation on Heaps

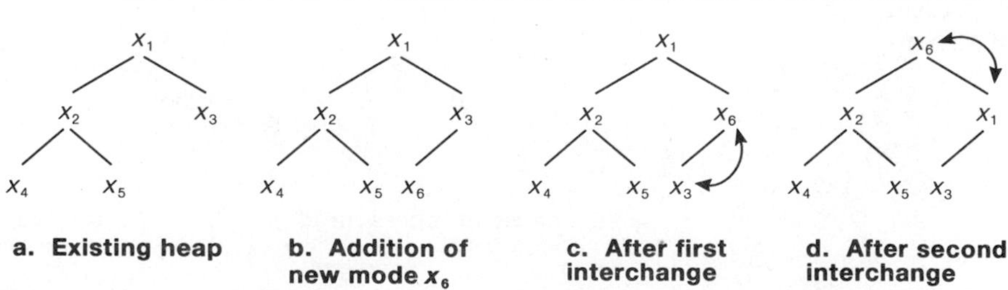

in Figure 8–15c. Now we know that x_3 and x_6 are in the proper order, but x_1 and x_6 may not be. If not, then we repeat the interchange of child and parent one more time (Figure 8–15d). We continue this interchange process until we have either found the correct location for the new value or, as was the case here, we reached the root of the heap. Still referring to Figure 8–15d, we know that x_6 and x_1 are in order because they were explicitly compared, but what about x_6 and its left child x_2? Are they in the proper order? We know that $x_1 < x_2$ because we assumed that Figure 8–15a was a valid heap and x_1 was its root, so x_1 was less than any other node in the heap. We know that $x_6 < x_1$, therefore $x_6 < x_2$ and the new node is in its correct location within the heap. This result proves that the swapping operation just described restores the ordering property of heaps.

The algorithm for the heap insertion just described is given in Figure 8–16. Looking at that algorithm we see that in the worst case we may have to exchange values with every node above the new one, starting from a leaf and working our way up to the root. Since a heap is, by definition, a balanced tree, its height will be $O(\log_2 N)$, where N is the number of nodes in the heap. Therefore, the maximum number of times we must do the interchange operation in the loop in Figure 8–16 is $O(\log_2 N)$, which is therefore the time complexity of the Insert procedure.

The GetSmallest operation works in a similar fashion. We remove the heap's smallest element which, by definition, is always located at the root. To reconstruct

Figure 8–16
The Heap Insertion Algorithm

```
(* This is the algorithm to insert a new value X into a Heap of size N. *)
Insert(Heap, N, X)
    If Full(Heap) Then                  (* Can't insert into a full heap *)
        Error := HeapOverFlow
        Exit
    Endif

    N := N + 1
    Heap[N] := X                        (* Add the new element in position N+1 *)
    Child := N

    Loop                                (* and rebuild the heap. *)
        If Child = 1 Then               (* We have reached the root. *)
            Exit
        Endif

        Parent := Child Div 2           (* Find the parent of Child. *)

                                        (* Out of order. *)
        If Heap[Child] > Heap[Parent] Then
            Interchange(Heap[Child], Heap[Parent])      (* So switch them *)
            Child := Parent                             (* and repeat. *)
        Else
            Exit                        (* In order, we are done. *)
        Endif

    Endloop

    End of the Insert Algorithm.
```

Figure 8–17
GetSmallest Operation on Heaps

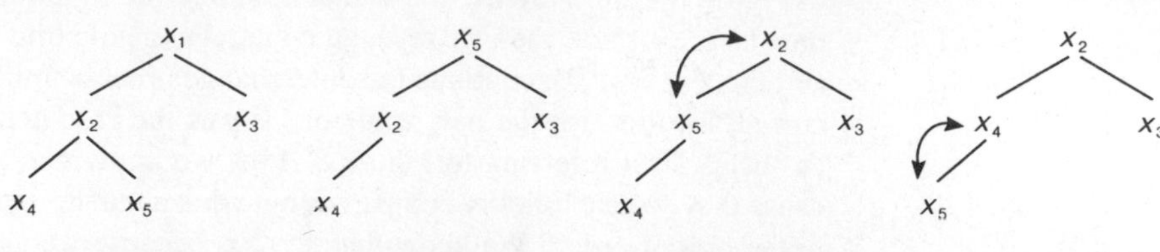

a. Existing heap **b. Removal of root and shifting of last element into the root position** **c. After one interchange with its smaller child** **d. After the second interchange**

Figure 8–18
The GetSmallest Procedure

```
(* An algorithm to return the Smallest value stored in a Heap of size N *)
GetSmallest ( Heap, N, Smallest )

    Smallest := Heap[1]          (* Smallest value is always the root. *)
    Heap[1] := Heap[N]           (* Bring last value to root position *)
    N := N − 1                   (* The heap has decreased in size by 1. *)
    Parent := 1

    Loop                         (* Here is the loop to rebuild the heap. *)
        Leftchild := 2 * Parent
        Rightchild := (2 * Parent) + 1

        If Leftchild > N Then    (* No children, we have reached a leaf *)
            Exit                 (* and we are done. *)
        Endif

        If Rightchild > N Then   (* Only 1 child *)

                                 (* Out of order *)
            If Heap[Parent] > Heap[Leftchild] Then
                Interchange(Heap[Parent], Heap[Leftchild])
                Parent := Leftchild          (* so interchange *)
            Else
                Exit             (* In order, so we are done rebuilding. *)
            Endif

        Else                     (* We have 2 children *)

                                 (* Interchange with the smaller of the two
                                 children *)
            If Heap[Parent] > Min( Heap[Leftchild], Heap[Rightchild]) Then
                Interchange(Heap[Parent],
                        Min(Heap[Leftchild], Heap[Rightchild]))

                Parent := Index(Min( Heap[Leftchild], Heap[Rightchild] ))
            Else
                Exit
            Endif

        Endif

    Endloop

    End of the GetSmallest Algorithm
```

the tree we need to move a new value into the root position, and the only node that can get moved and still maintain the structuring property of the heap is the "last" one, i.e., the right-most node on the lowest level i. The heap will now have $N - 1$ elements rather than N. This process is illustrated in Figure 8–17a and b. As we did in the insert operation, we must now determine the correct location for the new value that was placed at the root. Referring to Figure 8–17b, if ($x_5 < x_2$) and ($x_5 < x_3$) then this node is already in the correct location. If not, we interchange x_5 with the smaller of its one or two children, as shown in Figure 8-17c (where we assumed that x_2 was the smaller value). We repeat this downward interchange process until we have either migrated x_5 to its correct location or reached a leaf node. At this point x_5 will be in its correct location (the proof is left as an exercise).

A GetSmallest procedure for heap structures is shown in Figure 8–18. The maximum number of times we must interchange a node with its smallest child is equal to the height of the heap, which we have already showed was $O(\log_2 N)$. Thus, the worst case time complexity of the GetSmallest operation of Figure 8–18 is also $O(\log_2 N)$.

8.4.3 Applications of Heaps

HeapSort

One of the most important uses of heaps is as a basis for implementing a popular and widely used sorting algorithm called *HeapSort*.

Suppose we have a sequence of n integer values $\{i_1, i_2, \ldots, i_n\}$ that we wish to sort into ascending order. HeapSort proceeds in two phases, the *building phase* and the *removing phase*. During the building phase, we construct a heap structure containing these n integer elements by first creating an empty heap and then inserting the elements from the sequence one at a time, using the Insert procedure described in the previous section. Phase I can be summarized as follows:

Phase I. The Building Phase of HeapSort

```
H := CreateHeap ();
For k := 1 To n Do
    Insert (H, i_k); (* i_k are the elements to be sorted. *)
```

This heap building process is illustrated in Figure 8–19 for the set {11, 5, 13, 6, 1}. (Although the illustration shows a tree for clarity, the values will be stored internally as a heapform array of the type described in the previous section.) Once we have built the heap, it is a simple matter to obtain the list in sorted order. We simply remove the root (which, by definition, is the smallest value), print it out, and rebuild the heap, which now contains one fewer item. This step uses the GetSmallest routine described in the previous section. The removing phase of HeapSort can be summarized as follows:

Phase II. The Removing Phase of HeapSort

```
For k := n Down To 1 Do
    Smallest := GetSmallest (H);
    Print (Smallest)
```

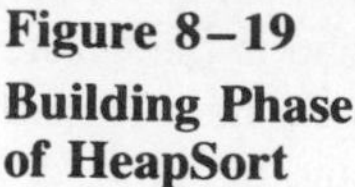

Figure 8–19 Building Phase of HeapSort

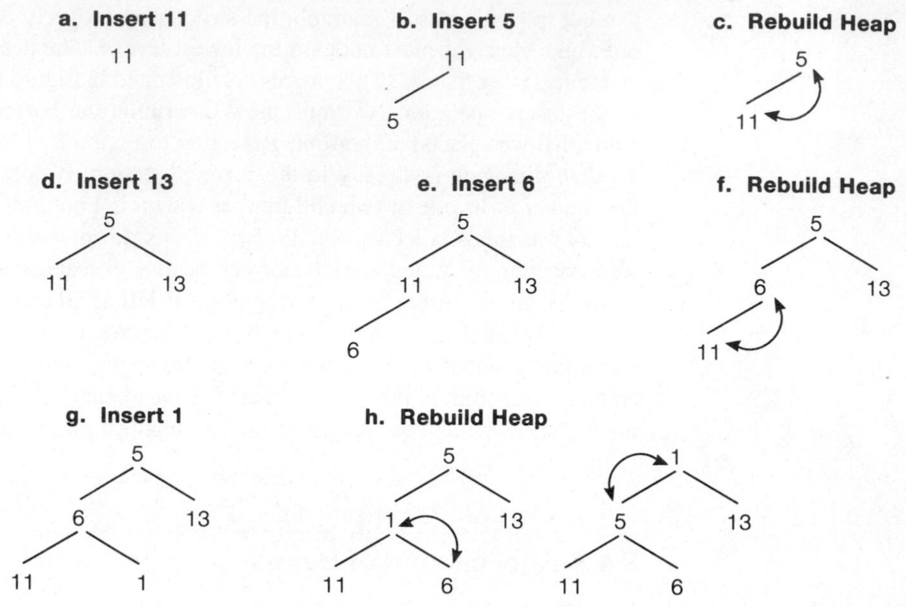

Figure 8–20 Removing Phase of HeapSort

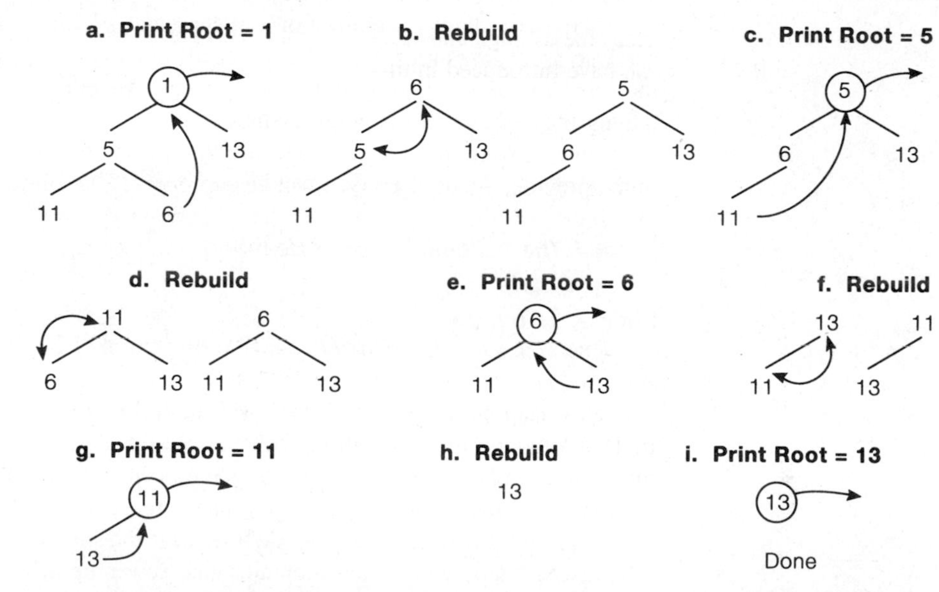

This process of removing the smallest item and rebuilding the heap is diagrammed in Figure 8–20 for the heap built in Figure 8–19.

As we showed in the previous section, both Insert and GetSmallest are $O(\log_2 N)$. In HeapSort these two operations are encased inside loop structures that are repeated n times, where n is the number of elements to be sorted, so both phases of

Table 8–2 Average and Worst-Case Complexity of Six Sorting Algorithms

	Average Case	Worst Case	
Bubble Sort	$O(n^2)$	$O(n^2)$	
Merge Sort	$O(n \log n)$	$O(n \log n)$	
QuickSort	$O(n \log n)$	$O(n^2)$	
Enumeration Sort	$O(\log n)$	$O(\log n)$	(* with n^2 processors *)
Tree Sort	$O(n \log n)$	$O(n^2)$	
Heap Sort	$O(n \log n)$	$O(n \log n)$	

the algorithm—building and removing—are $O(n \log_2 n)$. The overall time complexity of HeapSort is therefore $O(n \log_2 n)$, and this behavior is demonstrated in both the average and the worst case. Therefore, HeapSort (like MergeSort) is an excellent sorting algorithm to use in cases where we must guarantee efficient performance under all possible conditions. We timed HeapSort on a list of 2,500 values in random sequence, in sorted sequence, and in reverse sequence, repeating exactly the test that we had run previously on our other $O(n \log_2 n)$ sorting techniques, MergeSort, QuickSort, and TreeSort. The complete set of results for all four techniques is summarized in Table 8–1.

Notice how both TreeSort and QuickSort degrade in performance when presented with ordered data, but MergeSort and HeapSort do not. Table 8–2 summarizes the average and worst case time complexity for the six sorting algorithms that we have introduced in this text.

Priority Queues

The second heap application we will discuss is its use in the implementation of a data structure called a *priority queue*. We have already introduced the queue (a first-in/first-out linear data structure) in chapter 3, where we discussed two fundamental operations on queues:

Enqueue (Q, Object)	Put the specified Object at the rear of the queue Q.
Dequeue (Q, Object)	Remove the item at the front of the queue Q and store it in the specified Object.

In a "traditional" queue structure we keep all objects in time-ordered sequence; thus time can be viewed as a priority mechanism—the earlier your time of arrival, the higher your priority and the closer you are to the front of the queue.

In a priority queue we are no longer restricted to using only time as the implicit priority field. Instead, we allow the user to specify the priority of an object explicitly by modifying the enqueue and dequeue operations as follows:

PQEnqueue (PQ, Object, P)	Put the Object in priority queue PQ with priority P.

Table 8–3 Examples of Priority Queues in Computer Science

Queue of	Waiting for	Priority Ordering (High to Low)
a. processes	a processor	real-time processes interactive processes background batch processes
b. processors	disk service	swapping operations for the system input/output operations for the user on the current track input/output operations for the user on other tracks
c. processors	bus access	interrupt signals memory access for I/O operations instruction execution
d. users	terminals	undergraduate students graduate students faculty the Dean

PQDequeue (PQ, Object, P) Remove the item with the highest priority from the priority queue PQ. Place it in Object and place its priority value in P.

Priority queues are an important data structure in computer science because they model a number of situations that occur frequently in the design of computer systems. In these designs, time alone is insufficient to describe the needs of the system. We need the ability to prioritize requests and indicate that some needs are more important and must be serviced ahead of others, regardless of the time at which they arrive. Some examples of this are shown in Table 8–3.

In all of the situations in Table 8–3, using a simple time-ordered queue structure would lead to inefficient system behavior. For example, a *real-time* process is one that must be completed within a specified time span for its results to be useful—it must be given a processor as soon as one is available, regardless of what other processes are currently waiting in the queue. For example, a process controlling the setting of the wing flaps on a commercial airliner obviously cannot be delayed for any significant length of time. In contrast, an *interactive* process such as a word processing program needs a reasonable level of service so that the user does not become irritated, but it is not as time-critical as a real-time job. Finally, a *background* batch job has virtually no time constraints and can wait as long as needed for a processor. A nice way to implement these various levels of urgency is simply to assign priorities to the different classes of processes as follows

Class	*Priority*
Real-time	1 (highest)
Interactive	2
Background	3 (lowest)

Now when we remove a request from the queue using PQDequeue, we will always take a priority 1 process (real-time) before any others, if there is one in the queue. Only when all priority 1 requests have been satisfied will we begin to service priority 2 jobs.

We now need to select a data structure and algorithms that will allow us to implement the PQEnqueue and PQDequeue operations on priority queues efficiently. If we select either a linked list or an array implementation of queues (as we described in chapters 3 and 4), there are two possible strategies for coding these procedures:

a. Keep the queue in sorted order by priority field as we do each PQEnqueue operation. Then the PQDequeue operation simply removes the front element of the queue. The enqueue operation will be slow because we have to maintain the sorted sequence of priorities, but the dequeue operation will be extremely fast.

   PQEnqueue $= O(N)$ PQDequeue $= O(1)$

b. Have PQEnqueue place each new element at the end of the priority queue regardless of its priority. When we wish to dequeue an element, however, we will need to search the entire priority queue for the value with the highest priority. Now the enqueue operation will be fast, but the dequeue procedure will be slow as we must search the entire unordered queue.

   PQEnqueue $= O(1)$ PQDequeue $= O(N)$

In both cases we can get efficient constant time behavior for one operation only at the expense of spending linear time on the other.

However, there is a third possible strategy—implementing our priority queue internally as a heap structure of the type described in the previous two sections. We implement the operation PQEnqueue (PQ, Object, P) as the heap insertion operation Insert (Heap, Object, P), using the priority field P as the key field of the heap. This operation takes $O(\log N)$ time, as we showed in the previous section. Our PQDequeue (PQ, Object, P) function becomes the heap operation GetSmallest (Heap, Object, P), which removes the object with the smallest value of P (i.e., the highest priority) and rebuilds the heap. This also takes $O(\log N)$ time.

The result is that we have traded an implementation (arrays or linked lists) that demonstrates one extremely good ($O(1)$) and one extremely poor ($O(N)$) time complexity on the two priority queue operations for an implementation (heaps) that demonstrates reasonably good ($O(\log N)$) behavior for both. This trade-off is worthwhile, and thus heaps are an efficient structure for storing lists of objects ordered by an explicit priority field and retrieved in order of the smallest (or largest) value in that field.

8.5 CASE STUDY: A SPELLING CHECKER

Almost everyone reading this text has used a word processing package, and one of the most popular features of modern word processors is certainly a *spelling checker*. The concept behind a spelling checker is quite simple. The program contains a dictionary of English language words, typically 50,000 to 100,000 entries. The spelling checker compares each word in our newly created text against the words stored in the dictionary to see if the individual words in our document are there. If a word is there, it assumes that the word is correctly spelled (although it may be misspelled but match another word in the dictionary, such as *then* misspelled as *them*; a spelling checker cannot detect this type of error). If a word from the document is not in the dictionary, the spelling checker informs the user and asks if it is a misspelling or simply a word not in its dictionary. Most spelling checkers also allow users to add special-purpose words to the dictionary to customize it to their own needs. (Other facilities, such as suggesting the correct spelling of a misspelled word, will not be discussed here.)

A spelling checker must perform not only correctly but also reasonably quickly in order to be a useful tool, so we will add the following performance specifications to our functional description:

Memory Capacity:	1 Mbyte (the entire dictionary must fit in this memory)
Dictionary Size:	50,000 words
Shortest word:	1 character
Longest word:	14 characters
Average word:	5 characters
Time:	Must be able to spell-check one page of text (approximately 300 words) in less than one second.

Our purpose in this case study will be to design a data structure to store the dictionary entries and to ensure that our proposed structure can meet both the memory space and the timing constraints imposed by the performance specifications.

One of the most important principles in software development (or indeed any field) is that you should not create a complicated solution to a problem if a simple and straightforward solution will work just fine. In programming, unnecessary complexity can add a good deal to the overall cost of a piece of software. Therefore, let us first examine the behavior of the simplest data representation—the static array structure described in chapter 3 with a sequential search to locate items in the array. If this elementary data structure and algorithm work satisfactorily, we won't have to look any further.

```
Const
    MaxWordSize       = 14;
    MaxDictionarySize = 51000 (* Allow 1,000 user-added words. *);
Var
    Words             : Array [1 .. MaxWordSize] Of Char;
    Dictionary        : Array [1 .. MaxDictionarySize] Of Words;
```

The space occupied by these declarations is 51,000 words $\times$ 14 char/word = 714,000 bytes, which may be too large to fit in our 1 Mbyte memory, since we also need memory space to hold the spell-check program, our text, and portions of the operating system. This space requirement could be a problem, and we will probably want to investigate ways to reduce the size of the dictionary.

To evaluate the time required to check the spelling of a single word, let us assume that it takes approximately 3 μsec ($\mu\text{sec} = 10^{-6}$ sec) to compare a single character in our text against a single character in the dictionary. This estimate is probably a little large for just a compare step, but it also includes an allowance for the overhead involved in indexing through the arrays, incrementing loop counters, and checking for completion. Furthermore, when making a "ball park" estimate, it is better to be extra cautious than unduly optimistic (better to be pleasantly surprised by unanticipated efficiency than shocked by unexpected delays!).

Using the sequential search algorithm of Figure 6–2, we will on the average have to examine half the entries in the dictionary—about 25, 000 words—to locate each word. We will have to compare about two or three characters in each word (since we can stop scanning as soon as we find a mismatch), and each compare will take about 3 μseconds.

$$\begin{aligned} &25{,}000 \text{ words} * 2.5 \text{ char/word} * 3 * 10^{-6} \text{ sec/char} \\ &\qquad = 0.19 \text{ seconds to check one word} \\ &300 \text{ words/page} * 0.19 \text{ sec/word} = 57 \text{ seconds to check one full page of text} \\ &\qquad \approx 1 \text{ minute} \end{aligned}$$

This method will exceed our timing specification by a factor of about 60. Even if some of our estimates are excessive by a factor of 2 or 3 or even 10, we will probably not be able to meet the timing requirement given in the problem specifications. We will need to find a better method than an array and sequential search. In this case simplicity was not a virtue.

Using a linked list implementation as described in chapter 4 might be a way to help reduce our use of resources and should be considered. Instead of allocating space for the longest possible word (14 characters), we only need to allow space for the average length word (5 characters). Our linked list dictionary might have the following structure:

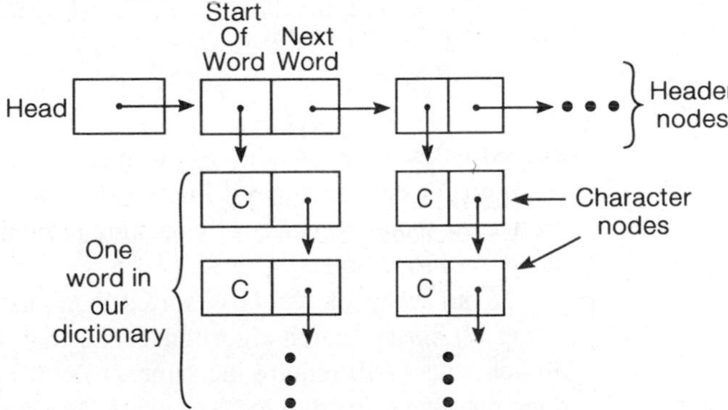

Our dictionary contains a linked list of header nodes, with each header node containing two links. The StartOfWord link points to a linked list of characters comprising a word. The NextWord link points to the header node for the next word in the dictionary. The declarations to create this linked list structure are:

```
Type
    CharNode        = Record
                          CharValue   : Char;
                          NextChar    : Pointer To CharNode
                      End;
    HeaderNode      = Record
                          StartOfWord : Pointer To CharNode;
                          NextWord    : Pointer To HeaderNode
                      End;
Var
    Head            : Pointer To HeaderNode;
```

Unfortunately, a closer investigation shows us that this linked list implementation has gained us nothing. We still will have to spend almost one minute doing a sequential search of the linked list, and surprisingly, there is no reduction in memory space. Instead of an array of 14 characters per word, we have one header node and one linked list with (on the average) 5 character nodes per word. The header node contains two pointer variables, and each character node holds one character and one pointer. (A pointer is simply a memory address, and it must be large enough to allow us to store all possible addresses. If our memory has a maximum of 2^n bytes of storage, then our pointer field must be at least n bits wide. With our 1 Mbyte (2^{20}) memory we would need at least three 8-bit bytes (3 bytes $\times$ 8 bits/byte = 24 bits) to address all of memory, so in the following computations we will assume 3-byte pointer fields.) Each header node will occupy 6 bytes and each character node 4 bytes. Since there are 50,000 words averaging 5 characters in length, the total data structure size is

$$
\begin{aligned}
&\text{50,000 header nodes} + \text{250,000 character nodes} \\
&= 50{,}000 * (6 \text{ bytes}) + 250{,}000 * (4 \text{ bytes}) \\
&= 300 \text{ K} + 1{,}000 \text{ K} \\
&= 1.3 \text{ Mbytes}
\end{aligned}
$$

exceeding the total capacity of our memory and requiring almost double the space required for the array-based implementation. So much for linked lists! (We could reduce the total space needs by packing more than one character per character node, as we will show later.)

If our array of words is sorted in alphabetical order then we could use the O(log N) binary search algorithm rather than the O(N) sequential search. This approach would still require the same 714K of memory, but it might significantly reduce the time needed to locate a word. As we saw in chapter 6, the number of comparisons needed to locate a word using binary search is a logarithmic function of the size of the sorted table. If we assume that we still need to look at approximately two to three characters per word, the time to check a full page of text is

$$(\log_2 50{,}000) \text{ words} \times 2.5 \text{ char/word} \times 3 \times 10^{-6} \text{ sec/char} \times 300 \text{ words/page} \approx .04 \text{ seconds}$$

This method looks good from a timing point of view. Instead of failing to meet our specifications by a factor of 60, we have bettered them by a factor of about 25. However, remember that the binary search method requires the dictionary to be sorted into alphabetical order. The original 50,000 words can be presorted before they are delivered, but when the user adds new words, we will have to resort the dictionary before we can search it.

If we use one of the $O(N \log_2 N)$ sorting methods discussed in this text, such as HeapSort from section 8.4.3, then we will need to look at approximately $(50{,}000 \log_2 50{,}000)$ words. Each step involves looking at enough characters in that word to properly determine its position. If we assume that, on the average, we must look at two to three characters in each word and each examination of a character still takes 3 μseconds, the sort operation will take roughly

$$(50{,}000 \log_2 50{,}000) \text{ words} * 2.5 \text{ char/word} * 3 \times 10^{-6} \text{ sec/char} \approx 12 \text{ seconds}$$

which is not too bad. It now appears that we have at least one method that meets our specifications, although it requires a significant portion of the available memory (714K) and requires about 12 seconds to rebuild the dictionary whenever new words are added to the list.

But our analysis must go deeper, or we might find that the program's performance is significantly worse than we had predicted. If we casually select either the QuickSort algorithm described in section 5.4.5 or the binary tree–based TreeSort of section 8.2.3, we could be in serious trouble. The average or expected behavior of these two methods is indeed $O(N \log_2 N)$. However, if we look at Table 8–2, we see that the worst case behavior for both degrades to $O(N^2)$. This degradation occurs when the list to be sorted starts out in almost sorted order. An almost sorted list may once have seemed like a highly unusual occurrence, but that is exactly what we have with our newly expanded dictionary! The 50,000 presorted words would be in correct alphabetical sequence, while the new words to be added, probably only a few dozen or a few hundred, would be out of order. Thus the list we are sorting would be almost in order, and both QuickSort and TreeSort would degenerate into approximately quadratic-time $O(N^2)$ algorithms.

A rough estimate of the time it would take to sort a list of 50,000 items using an $O(N^2)$ algorithm and the same conditions assumed earlier is

$$(50{,}000)^2 * 2.5 * 3 \times 10^{-6} = 18{,}750 \text{ seconds}$$

and instead of taking about 12 seconds to create the newly sorted dictionary it could take about five hours! (Imagine the screams and hollers from the user community!) Essentially this excessive time requirement would eliminate any possibility of a user ever modifying the existing dictionary and thus our functional specifications would not be satisfied. We must therefore be very careful to choose a sorting algorithm that displays not just $O(N \log_2 N)$ average case behavior but also $O(N \log_2 N)$ behavior under the extreme conditions we have just described. The HeapSort method introduced in section 8.4.3 would be an excellent choice in this situation because of its good worst-case behavior. Alternatively, one of the modifications to QuickSort discussed in the exercises at the end of chapter 5 might also be suitable to our needs.

Another possibility for representing our dictionary is to build a binary search tree in which each node contains a single word, as in

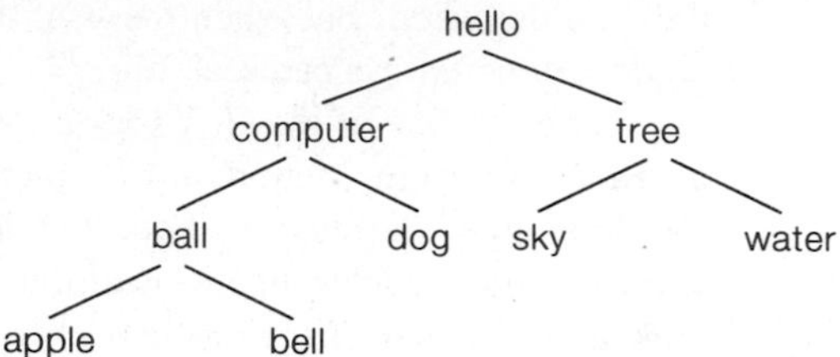

Certainly adding new words to the dictionary will not cause the kind of problems that occurred with a binary search of an array. We know from section 8.2 that insertion into a binary search tree is an O(log N) operation. With 50,000 words it will take a check of at most ($\log_2 50{,}000$) $\approx$ 16 words to locate the correct place to insert the new word (assuming the tree is reasonably balanced). Similarly, finding a word in the BST is a logarithmic operation, and the time required will be comparable to the time for a binary search of an array. We did this computation earlier and saw that it takes about 0.04 second, which is well within our timing specifications. The major problem we will have with a binary search tree data structure is the memory space required for all the pointers. If we use an array of fourteen characters to store the word, then each node of the BST will have one data field and two pointers and will look like this:

14	3	3	Bytes
Word	Left child	Right child	Node

Each node in the tree uses 20 bytes of storage. There will be 50,000 nodes, one for each word, so the total space needed for the binary search tree is $50{,}000 * 20 = 1$ Mbyte. Again, this space requirement exceeds the memory capacity, so this method is not an acceptable representation.

The next data structure we will examine is the indexed search tree introduced in section 8.3. We have already learned that the number of pointers in a trie node make it unfeasible to build a complete trie. Instead, we will construct a two-level trie, in which only the first two letters of each word are kept in the trie. The data field of each of the second level trie nodes will point to the head of a linked list of all words that begin with those two letters (see Figure 8–21). To access a word such as *computer*, we index into the trie using the first two letters of the word, *c* and *o*. The data field of the *co* node points to the head of a linked list of all words beginning with the two-character sequence *co*. We now search sequentially through that list for the remaining six characters *mputer*.

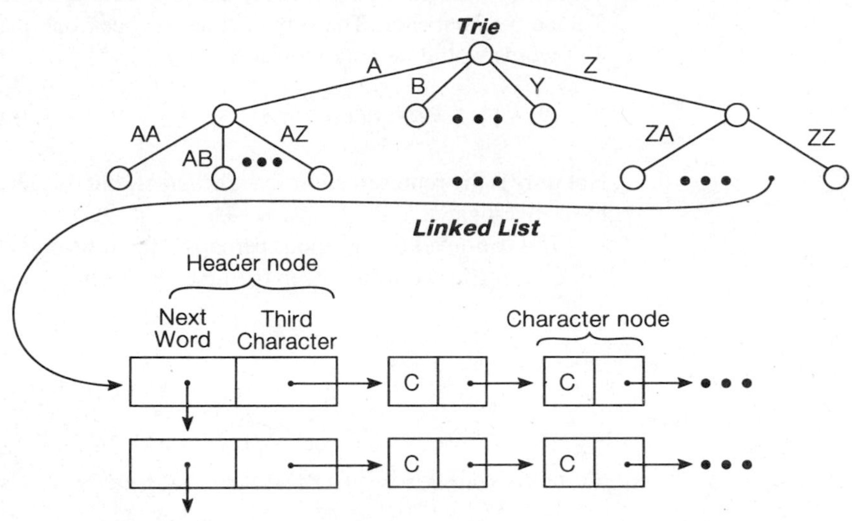

Figure 8–21
Two-Level Trie Structure for a Dictionary

The two-level tric will have 1 + 26 + 676 = 703 nodes, each with a 1-byte data field and 26 three-byte pointers. (There will actually be fewer nodes, since there are many character pairs that do not start any English words, e.g., *JX*, and those nodes will not need to be in the trie. In addition, we should have a blank pointer field for 1- and 2- character words. We have omitted this level of detail for clarity.) This two-level trie structure will require

$$703\ (1 + 26 * 3) \approx 56\ \text{K}$$

The linked list of characters will still store the complete set of 50,000 words, but on the average it will store only three characters per word instead of five, since the first two characters of the word are located in the trie. Also, each of the 676 trie leaf nodes requires one head node containing two pointers: a NextWord pointer that points to the next word beginning with that same two-character sequence and a ThirdCharacter pointer that points to the 3rd, 4th, 5th, . . . characters of this word. Each head node occupies six bytes, and each character node requires four. The total amount of space required by the head nodes and the linked list is

$$676 \text{ head nodes} + (50{,}000 * 3) \text{ character nodes}$$
$$676\ (6) + (50{,}000 * 3 * 4) \approx 604\ \text{K}$$

Thus the total space needs for the data structure shown in Figure 8–21 are only 56K + 604K ≈ 660 K (54,000 less than our previous best).

We also need to consider the time requirement of the two-level trie. We will have to make two access to the trie and then do a sequential search of about half of the 50,000/676 words per list, although this number will be highly uneven (many more words start with Sh or Te than with Xy). For each word we will need to look at about two and a half characters, and we have assumed that a comparison takes 3 μsec per character. The overall time to check one page of text containing about 300 words would be approximately:

$$(2 + [1/2 * (50{,}000/676) * 2.5]) * 3 * 10^{-6} * 300 \approx 0.08 \text{ seconds}$$

Not only is the representation space efficient, but this method is one of the fastest we have investigated.

If a two-level trie is good, perhaps a three-level trie would be even better. In a three-level trie we would keep the first three letters in the trie rather than just two:

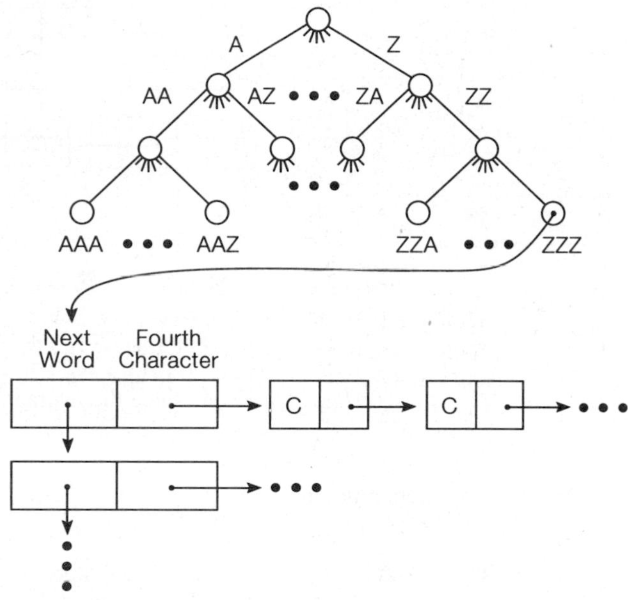

Now there are (1 + 26 + 676 + 17,576) = 18,279 nodes in the trie. Since each node has one data field and 26 pointers, 18,279 * (1+ 26 * 3) = 1.4 Mbytes will be required just for the trie itself, not even considering the space required for the remaining characters in the linked list. So, although the two-level trie worked quite well, the three-level structure would be totally unacceptable.

We will investigate one final improvement called *packing*—placing more than one character of a word in each character node. If we store one character and one pointer in each node as we have done so far, then 75% of the space of the node (three bytes out of four) is overhead (i.e., pointers) and is not being used to represent textual information. If we instead store two characters per node, this overhead would be reduced to 60% (three bytes out of five), and at three characters per node, it is 50% (three bytes out of six). If the word is not long enough to fill out the node, then we will pad the node with blanks that will be disregarded by the spelling checker. If we assume a two-level trie and a linked list containing three characters per node, then our packed trie structure looks something like

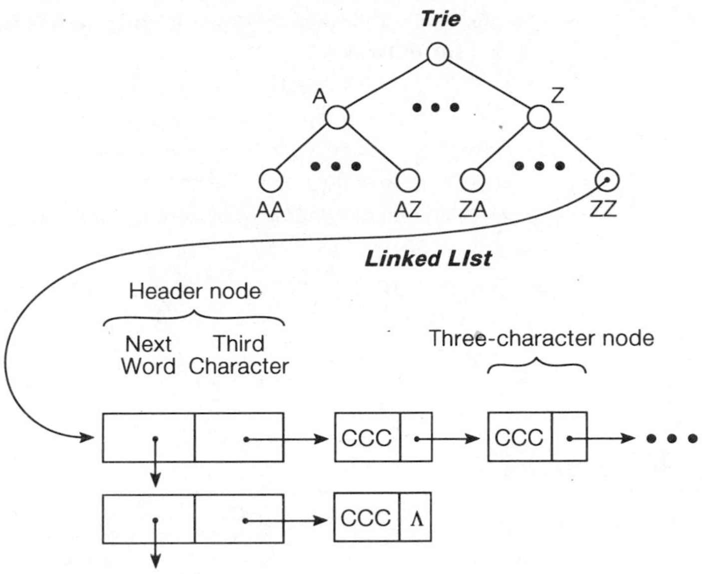

The trie component is identical to the one in Figure 8–21, and it requires the same amount of memory space, about 56 K. The linked list still has one 6-byte header node per trie leaf. However, since the average length of a word stored in the linked list is three characters, we require an average of only one three-character node per word. The size of each three-character node is six bytes (three bytes for the three characters plus one three-byte pointer). Thus the total space needed for our packed two-level trie is:

$$
\begin{aligned}
&\text{space for the two-level trie} + 676 \text{ head nodes} + 50{,}000 \text{ three-character nodes}\\
&\quad = 56\text{ K} + 676\,(6) + 50{,}000\,(6)\\
&\quad \approx 56\text{ K} + 4\text{ K} + 300\text{ K}\\
&\quad \approx 360\text{ K}
\end{aligned}
$$

We have reduced our memory space needs from about 660 K to 360 K, a reduction of about 45%! The time to access a word from our new structure will actually be a little faster than for the regular trie of Figure 8–21 because on the average we need to access only one character node rather than three. However, since the spell-checking time of the regular trie was already 12 times faster than specification, this is not an issue.

Table 8–4 summarizes the time and space needs of the seven data structures we have considered in this case study. The time value represents the time needed to spell-check one page of text, and the space is the total bytes of memory needed to store all of the 50,000 dictionary entries.

Table 8–4 Time and Space Requirements for Various Dictionary Data Structures

	Time (sec)	Space
Array and Sequential Search	57	714 K
Linked List and Sequential Search	57	1.3 M
Array and Binary Search (plus sorting time of 12 seconds)	.04	714 K
Binary Search Tree	.04	1 M
Two-Level Trie	.08	660 K
Three-Level Trie	—	>1.4 M
Two-Level Packed Trie	.08	360 K

8.6 CONCLUSION

Looking back at Table 8–4 we see how important good data structure design is to the success of a software development project. Different choices for the algorithms and data structures of our dictionary have led to time improvements of three orders of magnitude—from 57 seconds to 0.04 seconds—and space reduction of over one million bytes from the best case to the worst. Improvements of this magnitude can essentially convert an unusable program into a workable and even elegant piece of software. Of course, there are many data representations for our dictionary other than those discussed here, and the exercises at the end of the chapter ask you to investigate additional approaches and think about ways to improve even further on what we have done.

When designing and building programs, we must be sure to spend adequate time on *both* the structure of the program (i.e., the decomposition and modularity) and the abstract data types and internal representations of all major data structures. These latter decisions can be fundamental to the success or failure of a project.

Too often we forget that computer science is both a theoretical and an applied discipline. While the mathematician may be concerned only with proving conclusively that a certain solution exists, the computer scientist is concerned with both the existence of that solution *and* the development of an efficient algorithm for producing the answer. A method that can be formally shown to produce the correct result within 10,000 years would be of very little interest.

Therefore, the ability to do good approximations (sometimes jokingly called *back-of-the-envelope* calculations) is an important part of software development in particular and computer science in general. When choosing an algorithm or data structure to solve a problem, carry out time and space approximations as we did in this case study to see if you are close to meeting the performance specifications of the problem. If you are off by a factor of 10, 20, or more, then fine-tuning the finished program will not help, and you should probably investigate alternative solutions. If you exceed specifications by that amount, perhaps a less efficient but simpler and less costly technique could be considered. The point is that before you invest a good deal of your time and effort designing and implementing a solution, you should spend a little time trying to determine whether the solution will solve the problem in an adequate and timely way.

In the next chapter we will investigate yet another way to organize data and search it efficiently using a totally different class of data structure—sets and hash tables.

CHAPTER EXERCISES

1. Show the binary search tree that results from inserting the following values in the order given, beginning from an empty tree:
   a. 38, 65, 27, 29, 81, 70, 14, 53, 12, 20
   b. 81, 73, 70, 52, 51, 40, 42, 38, 35, 20
   What do these two cases say about the structure of the binary search tree as a function of the order of the input data?
2. Given the following specification of a Boolean function:

   ```
   (* Precondition:   T is a pointer to the root of an arbitrary binary tree.
      Postcondition:  BST is set to True if the tree pointed to by T is a binary
                          search tree, otherwise BST is False *)

   Procedure TreeCheck (T : TreeType; Var BST : Boolean);
   ```

   Implement the procedure TreeCheck using the declarations given in Figure 7–13.
3. Show that a full binary search tree with n internal, nonleaf nodes has exactly $n + 1$ leaf nodes.
4. Show that if we delete a node in a binary search tree and replace it by its successor in an inorder traversal, then the tree that remains is still a binary search tree. Does this situation also occur when either the preorder or postorder traversal successor is used as the replacement?
5. Implement a function to determine the height of an arbitrary binary tree. The specifications are:

   ```
   (* Precondition:   T is a pointer to the root of an arbitrary binary tree.
      Postcondition:  The function returns the height of the tree pointed to by T.
                          If T is empty, the function returns a -1. *)

   Procedure TreeHeightCheck (T : TreeType) : Integer;
   ```

   Assume the tree is constructed from the declarations shown in Figure 7–13. In addition, the procedure should determine whether the tree pointed to by T is relatively balanced. For this problem assume that the tree is considered relatively balanced if its height is within 30% of its theoretical minimum. For example, if the tree has 100 nodes, its minimum height would be the smallest integer greater than or equal to $(\log_2 101) - 1$ which is 6; therefore, the tree would be said to be balanced if its height is less than or equal to $6 + (.3) * 6 \approx 8$.
6. A binary search tree with 255 nodes would have a minimum height of 7 if the tree is full (Figure 8–5b). The maximum height would be 255 if the tree is completely degenerate, (Figure 8–5a). Write a program to generate 100 distinct sequences of exactly 255 random integers, build a binary search tree

from each sequence, and determine the height, H, of each BST using the procedure you wrote for exercise 5. Use this data to see if the expected height of a BST built from an arbitrary sequence of values is closer to ($\log_2 N$) than it is to N. How close to ($\log_2 N$) was your average?

7. How could we print out the nodes of a binary search tree in descending rather than ascending order?
8. Show what the trie structure would look like if we store the following ten English words using the trie structure of section 8.3.

ten	the
tent	them
pen	then
penny	thin
pin	think

9. Sketch out the Delete algorithm for a trie structure using the three cases specified in section 8.3.
10. Implement the external module for a Trie structure with operations CreateTrie, Insert, Delete, and Find. Assume that the trie is an opaque type but the keys are transparent and are a sequence of up to Max uppercase alphabetic characters.

```
Var
    DataField : Array [1 .. Max] Of ['A'. .'Z'];
```

11. Write the implementation module for the Trie ADT described in exercise 10 assuming the following declarations:

```
Type Trie = Pointer To TrieNode;

    TrieNode = Record
                    Data : DataField (* Pointer to a data record *)
                    Ptr  : Array ['A' .. 'Z'] Of Trie
               End;
```

12. Show the final heap structure (as a tree) when we build a heap from the following seven integers.

    S = {20, 19, 17, 23, 18, 22, 15}

    Show how that heap would be stored internally as a heapform.
13. State whether each of the following trees is a complete binary tree. If not, explain why.

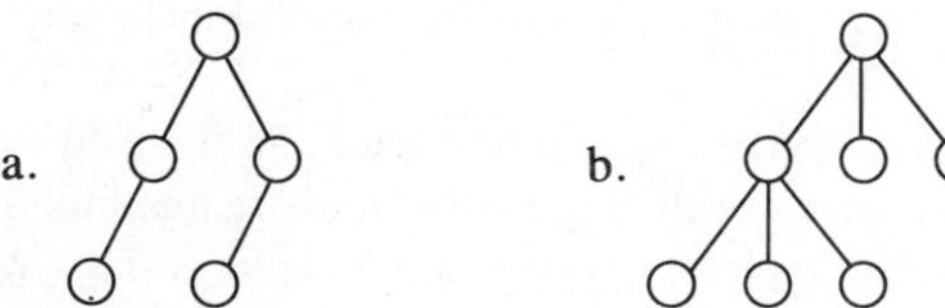

c. d.

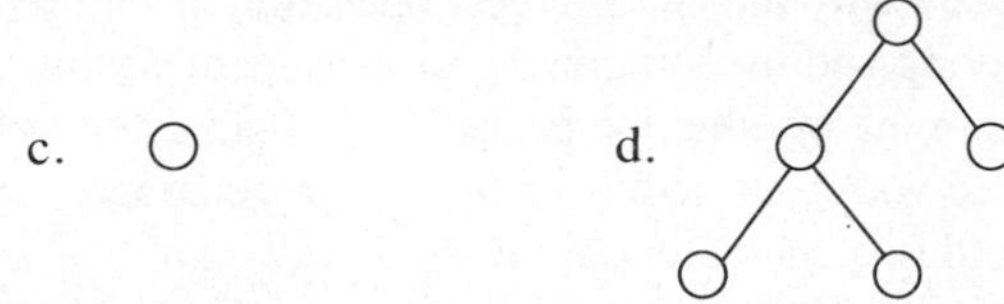

14. Develop a procedure to determine whether a node in an N-node heap stored as a heapform does or does not have a first cousin. Two nodes are first cousins if they have the same grandparent but different parents. Looking at Figure 8–14a, each of the following pairs of nodes are first cousins: (x_4, x_6) (x_5, x_6) (x_4, x_7) and (x_5, x_7). None of the other nodes stand in this relationship. Write a procedure that is given a node number i, where $1 \leq i \leq N$, and returns the node number j, $1 \leq j \leq N$, of any first cousin of i; it should return a 0 if i has no first cousin.

```
Procedure FirstCousin (H : HeapType; N : Integer; i : NodeNumber;
    Var j : NodeNumber);
```

15. Write a procedure

```
Procedure HeapCheck (H : Heapform; N : Integer; Var OK : Boolean);
```

that takes an N-element heap stored internally as a heapform and returns OK := True if the ordering property is satisfied for heap H and returns False otherwise. The definition of the data type heapform is

```
Type
    Heapform : Array [1 .. Max] Of Integer;
```

16. What would the heap below look like after completing each of the following four operations in sequence (i.e., do operation b on the heap produced by operation a, and so forth)?

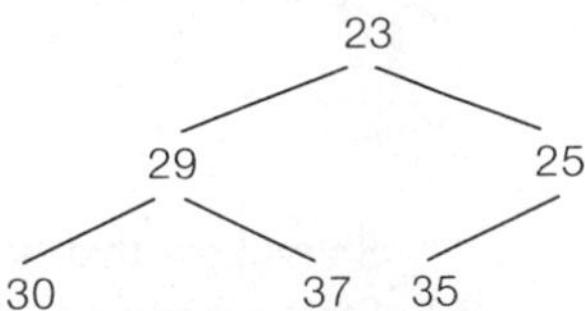

a. Insert a 26
b. Insert a 22
c. Delete the smallest value
d. Delete the smallest value

17. Implement the HeapSort algorithm shown in Figures 8–19 and 8–20. Explain why HeapSort is still an O(N $\log_2 N$) algorithm in the worst case.

18. Explain why the GetSmallest operation in Figure 8–17 maintains both the ordering and the structuring properties of heaps.
19. Determine whether the packed trie of our case study would be more efficiently stored with four or five characters per character node rather than three. How would two characters per node work?
20. Analyze and discuss the following string-oriented representation of our dictionary. It is a character array S with a special, nonalphabetic character (e.g., @) to mark the end of one word and the beginning of the next:

We also have a 26-element index table that gives the subscript in S where words beginning with A, B, . . . begin:

Index Table

A	1	(Words beginning with A start in S[1].)
B	1,014	(Words beginning with B start in S[1,014].)
⋮	⋮	⋮

To find a word such as *computer*, we index into the table with the letter *c*, and sequentially search for the word beginning at that point and continuing until we either find it or come to a word that is alphabetically greater than *computer*.

What are the time and space needs of this method? Would it meet our performance specifications? Are there any other problem areas with this representation? Can you improve even further on this string-based technique?

CHAPTER 9

SETS AND SEARCH TABLES

CHAPTER OUTLINE

9.1 SETS

9.1.1 Definition and Operations

We have now looked at two of the four classes of composite data structures illustrated in Figure 3–1—linear (chapters 3 and 4) and hierarchical (chapters 7 and 8). In this and the succeeding chapter we will introduce the two remaining classes—sets (chapter 9) and graphs (chapter 10).

Formally, a *set* is a collection of objects that has the following two properties:

1. There are no duplicates in the collection.
2. The order of the objects within the collection is irrelevant.

When a set is dealt with mathematically, there are usually no restrictions placed on the type of objects that can be members of the set—set elements can be either primitive or composite, i.e., other sets. In addition, a single set may mix objects of different data types—numbers, characters, or user-defined scalars—and the size of the set may be infinite. Thus, from a formal point of view the following collection S

S = {1, apple, {red, white, blue}, 3.8, {}, 'z'}

would be a perfectly valid set structure.

However, implementing this highly generalized definition of a set within a programming language can be quite difficult. so most programming languages (Modula-2 and Pascal included) place the following three restrictions on the definition of a set simply to facilitate their implementation of a set data structure:

1. The components of a set must be of identical type. This type is called the *base type* of the set.
2. The base type must be an ordinal data type—typically integers, Boolean, characters, or user-defined ordinals. Sets of arrays, records, or other sets are not allowed.
3. The maximal size or *cardinality* of a set is restricted to a small value that is related to the memory architecture of the particular computer. Values of 16, 32, 64, or 256 are the most common. This size restriction can frequently exclude some of the most popular uses of sets, such as sets of characters.

Thus, the computer scientist's definition of a set (and the one that we will use in this text) is quite different from and not as general as the mathematician's definition of a set. By our definition, the collection S shown above would not be acceptable, since it mixes objects of different types and includes both primitive and structured components. However, the set $S' = \{1, 7, 13, -8, 105, 99\}$ would be legal, because it is made up of a small number of objects all drawn from the same ordinal base type, integer.

One of the most important points in the definition of a set is that the order of elements within a set is irrelevant. The set $S'' = \{7, 99, 13, -8, 105, 1\}$ is equivalent to the set S' above, even though the numbers in the two sets appear in different sequence. This lack of ordering is the fundamental difference between sets and the class of linear and hierarchical structures that we have previously studied. In those two classes there were explicit ordering relations between component elements. With linear structures there are First, Last, Successor, and Predecessor relationships. If the set S' were a linear structure and we asked for the successor of 7, we would get 13, but with S'' we would get 99. Thus S' and S'' would not be considered identical linear structures. In a hierarchical structure there are Root, Parent, and Child ordering relationships.

In a set, none of these element-to-element mappings exist. Asking what element is the successor of 13 in set S′ or which object is First(S′) makes no sense, since the order of objects in S′ is immaterial. The objects in a set are unrelated to each other except by their common membership in this collection of objects. When developing an external module for a Set abstract data type, we must be careful to avoid describing any type of function that imposes an explicit ordering on the component objects, i.e., functions such as NextObject, FirstObject or Neighboring-Object would violate the fundamental definition of set structures.

The operations performed on sets are, like the stack and queue operations of chapter 3, well known and highly standardized, regardless of the underlying application; therefore, it is quite easy to specify an external module for our Set abstract data type. This situation is quite different from the one we encounter with some of the other structures such as the string and the binary tree, in which there is a wide range of operations to choose from, and the selection of appropriate ones is highly application-dependent.

The single creator operator for sets is called *CreateSet*:

CreateSet() : Set

which produces a set S containing 0 objects. This set is called the *empty set*.

There will be five transformer operations in our external module. The *Insert* operation adds a new element E to a set S to produce a new set. If the element to be added is already a member of the set, nothing is done since duplicates are not allowed; this attempted insertion is not considered an error. The *Delete* operation removes an element E from a set S. If E is not a member of the set, then nothing is done and the function completes. This attempt is also not considered an error. Syntactically,

Insert(Set,Element) : Set
Delete(Set,Element) : Set

There are three transformer operations that combine two sets to produce a new set. The *Union* operation, usually written $S_1 \cup S_2$, builds a new set S_3 whose members include all objects that are members of either set S_1 or set S_2 (eliminating duplicates). The *Intersection* operation, usually written $S_1 \cap S_2$, builds a new set S_3 whose members are only those objects that belong to both set S_1 and set S_2. Finally, the *Difference* operator, $S_1 - S_2$, builds a set S_3 whose members include only those objects that are members of set S_1 but not members of set S_2. The behavior of these set generator operations is shown pictorially in Figure 9–1 using a notation called a Venn Diagram. The shaded areas of the circles represent the elements included in the new set S_3. The syntax of these three operations is:

Union(Set, Set) : Set
Intersection(Set, Set) : Set
Difference(Set, Set) : Set

The three observer operations on sets are called Empty, Member, and Subset:

Empty (Set) : Boolean
Member(Set, Element) : Boolean
Subset(Set, Set) : Boolean

Figure 9–1
Venn Diagram of the Three Basic Transformer Operators on Sets

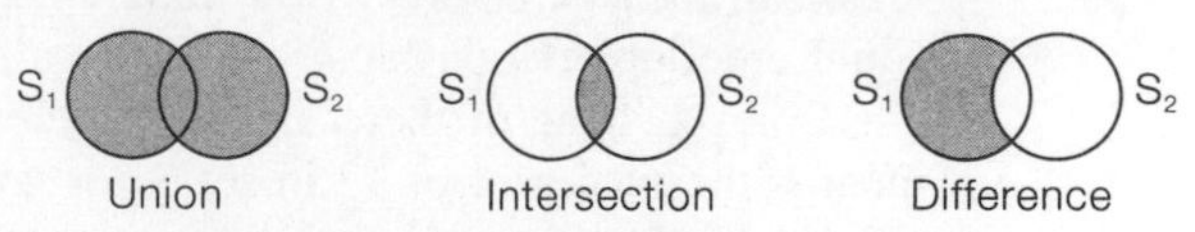

S_3 is the shaded part of each diagram

Empty is True if set is the empty set, i.e., it has no members, and False otherwise. *Member* is True if the element is currently a member of the set and False otherwise. Finally, *Subset* is True every object in the first set is also a member of the second set; otherwise the function returns False.

Examples

Assume S = {1, 2, 3, 4}   T = {3, 4, 5, 6}   U = {2, 3}   V = {.}

```
Insert (S,6)        = {1, 2, 3, 4, 6}
Insert (S,4)        = {1, 2, 3, 4}
Delete (T,3)        = {4, 5, 6}
Delete (T,2)        = {3, 4, 5, 6}
Union (S,T)         = {1, 2, 3, 4, 5, 6}
Intersection (S,T)  = {3, 4}
Difference (S,U)    = {1, 4}
Difference (U,S)    = {}
Empty (V)           = True
Member (T,2)        = False
Subset (U,S)        = True
Subset (S,T)        = False
```

The complete specification of the syntax and semantics of these operations is given in Figure 9–2. The external module for the set ADT is shown in Figure 9–3.

9.1.2 Implementation

There are some standard and well-known ways to implement sets in high-level programming languages. For example, we could store the elements of the set in an array structure

```
Const
    Max = . . . ; (* The cardinality of the base type of the set *)
Type
    SetType = Pointer To Record
                    Size : 0 .. Max;
                    Data : Array [1 .. Max] Of BaseType;
              End;
Var
    S : SetType;
```

Figure 9–2
Formal Syntax and Semantics of Sets

Syntax:

Define Set[Element]

a. CreateSet() : Set
b. Insert(Set, Element) : Set
c. Delete(Set, Element) : Set
d. Union(Set, Set) : Set
e. Intersection(Set, Set) : Set
f. Difference(Set, Set) : Set
g. Empty(Set) : Boolean
h. Member(Set, Element) : Boolean
i. Subset(Set, Set): Boolean

Semantics:

a. Empty (CreateSet()) = True
b. Member (Insert(S,E),E) = True
c. Empty (Insert (S,E)) = False
d. Member (Delete(S,E),E) = False
e. Empty (Delete(Insert(CreateSet(),E),E)) = True
f. **If** Member (S_1,E) **Or** Member (S_2,E) **Then**
    Member (Union(S_1,S_2),E) = True
  Else
    Member (Union(S_1,S_2),E) = False
g. **If** Member (S_1,E) **And** Member (S_2,E) **Then**
    Member (Intersection(S_1,S_2),E) = True
  Else
    Member (Intersection(S_1,S_2),E) = False
h. **If** Member (S_1,E) **And** (not Member (S_2,E)) **Then**
    Member (Difference(S_1,S_2),E) = True
  Else
    Member (Difference(S_1,S_2),E) = False
i. **If** (Empty(Difference(S_1,S_2))) **Then**
    Subset(S_1,S_2) = True
  Else
    Subset(S_1,S_2) = False

where Max is the maximum allowable size of the set and BaseType is the data type of the elements of the set . Using these declarations the set S = {10, 13, 41, −8, 22, 17} might be stored as

S^. Data[1]	41
S^. Data[2]	10
S^. Data[3]	-8
S^. Data[4]	13
S^. Data[5]	17
S^. Data[6]	22

S^. Size = 6

Notice that the internal order of storage in the array need not match the order in which the elements are written out in the language, since order is immaterial.

Figure 9–3
Definition Module of the Set ADT

```
(* The following module contains the external specifications for the Set
     abstract data type, as described in section 9.1. The formal syntax
     and semantics for the operations on Sets are given in Figure 9.2.           *)
External Module SetPackage;

From UserModule Import
        DataElementType;           (* The data type to be stored in the set.*)

Type
     SetType:                          (* The abstract data type for sets.   *)

(*   Precondition: None
     Postcondition:     A new, empty set is returned.
                               Empty(CreateSet())=True                               *)
Procedure CreateSet() : SetType;

(*   Precondition: None
     Postcondition:     After calling Insert, Set is guaranteed to contain Element.
                               Member(Insert(S, E), E) = True
                               Empty(Insert(S, E)) = False                           *)
Procedure Insert ( Var Set : SetType; Element : DataElementType );

(*   Precondition: None
     Postcondition:     After calling Delete, Set is guaranteed to not
                               contain Element.
                        Member(Delete(S, E), E) = False
                        Empty(Delete(Insert(Create(), E), E)) = True                 *)
Procedure Delete( Var Set : SetType; Element : DataElementType );

(*   Precondition: None
     Postcondition:     Union returns a set which contains only those elements
                               which are either in Set1, or in Set2, or in both.
                        If Member(S1, E) Or Member(S2, E) Then
                               Member(Union(S1, S2), E) = True
                        Else
                               Member(Union(S1, S2), E) = False                      *)
Procedure Union( Set1 : SetType; Set 2 : SetType ) : SetType;

(*   Precondition: None
     Postcondition:     Intersection returns a set which contains only those
                               elements which are in both Set1 and Set2.
                        If Member(S1, E) And Member(S2, E) Then
                               Member(Intersection(S1, S2), E) = True
                        Else
                               Member(Intersection(S1, S2), E) = False               *)
Procedure Intersection( Set1 : SetType; Set2 : SetType ) : SetType;

(*   Precondition: None
     Postcondition:     Difference returns a set which contains only those
                               elements which are in Set1 but not in Set2.
                        If Member(S1, E) And (Not Member(S2, E)) Then
                               Member(Difference(S1, S2)) = True
                        Else
                                    Member(Difference(S1, S2)) = False               *)
Procedure Difference( Set1 : SetType; Set2 : SetType ) : SetType;
```

(continued)

Figure 9–3 (continued)

```
(*  Precondition: None
    Postcondition:   Empty returns True if Set contains no elements.
                     Otherwise, Empty returns False.                     *)
Procedure Empty( Set : SetType ) : Boolean;

(*  Precondition: None
    Postcondition:   Member returns True if Element is a member of Set.
                     Otherwise, Member returns False.                    *)
Procedure Member( Set : SetType; Element : DataElementType ) : Boolean;

(*  Precondition: None
    Postcondition:   Subset returns True if every element which is a member
                         of Set1 is also a member of Set2.
                     Otherwise, Subset returns False.
                     If Empty(Difference(S1, S2)) Then
                         Subset(S1, S2) = True
                     Else
                         Subset(S1, S2) = False                          *)
Procedure Subset( Set1 : SetType; Set2 : SetType ) : Boolean;

End SetPackage.
```

Using these declarations, the operations we introduced in the previous section would translate into sequential searches of the array to see if an element is a member of the set. For example, Figure 9–4 shows the array-based implementation of the intersection operation $S_3 :=$ Intersection(S_1, S_2). For each element stored in set S_1, we scan the array S_2 to see if it is there as well. If so, we place it in the new set S_3; if not, we omit it. If S_1 and S_2 are unordered and if they each have N members, then the time complexity of the Intersection procedure of Figure 9–4 is $O(N^2)$. The time complexity may be a little better if both S_1 and S_2 are ordered. This is left as an exercise.

Similar behavior is observed if we choose a linked list implementation in place of the array.

In the previous section we made three assumptions about the base type of a set, namely that all objects in the set belong to this one base type, that it is a simple rather than a composite type, and that its cardinality is small, typically related to the word size of the memory of the computer. If we make one additional assumption about the nature of the base type, we can produce an extremely efficient internal representation of sets called a *bit vector representation.* The assumption we must make is that the elements of the base type can be uniquely mapped onto the integer values [0 .. $N - 1$], where N is the cardinality of the base type of the set. More formally, we say that there exists a one-to-one function f:

f: E → I   E is an element of the base type.
              I is an integer in the range [0 .. $N - 1$].

such that if $E_1 \neq E_2$, $f(E_1) \neq f(E_2)$.

Figure 9–4
Array-Based Implementation of Intersect

```
(*  Precondition: None
    Postcondition:   Intersection returns a set which contains only those
                         elements which are in both Set1 and Set2.
                     If Member(S1, E) And Member(S2, E) Then
                         Member(Intersection(S1, S2), E) = True
                     Else
                         Member(Intersection(S1, S2), E) = False   *)
Procedure Intersection( Set1 : SetType; Set2 : SetType ) : SetType;
Var
    NewSet      : SetType;
    i           : Integer;
Begin
    NewSet := CreateSet();                    (* This is the new set we will create *)

    For i := 1 To Set1^.Size Do               (* For each element in Set1 *)
                                              (* If it's also in Set2, *)
        If (Member(Set2, Set1^.Data[i])) Then
                                              (* Add it to NewSet. *)
            NewSet^.Size := NewSet^.Size + 1;
            NewSet^.Data[NewSet^.Size] := Set1^.Data[i];
        Endif;
    Endfor;

    Return NewSet;
End Intersection;
```

Any of the Pascal ordinal types—integer, character, Boolean, or enumerated scalars—is a good example of a base type that meets this criterion. In these cases the mapping function f is simply the standard function Ord(x) which returns the internal integer value of any ordinal variable x.

If such a function exists, then to represent a set S of length N we simply create an array of length N, with each array element being one of two values, Yes or No, corresponding to whether the unique element that maps to this location is or is not a member of the set. The declaration to set up this bit vector array are:

```
Type
    SetType = Array [0 .. N - 1] Of (Yes,No);

Var
    S : SetType;
```

Given this implementation, it is very easy to implement the operations on sets described in the previous section. For example, to insert a new value e into set S, we simply set the array element S[$f(e)$] to the value Yes. To delete that element we set S[$f(e)$] to No. To determine whether e is a member of S, we examine the location S[$f(e)$] to see if it is a Yes or a No. These are all extremely efficient O(1) operations. For example, if we were creating sets representing the days of the week Monday,

Tuesday, . . . , Sunday, then the Ord function by itself will perform the proper mapping

Ord(Monday) = 0
Ord(Tuesday) = 1
•
•
•
Ord(Sunday) = 6

and the bit vector representation of the set S = {Monday, Wednesday, Friday} would be

S:	Yes	No	Yes	No	Yes	No	No
	S[0] Monday	S[1] Tuesday	S[2] Wednesday	S[3] Thursday	S[4] Friday	S[5] Saturday	S[6] Sunday

To determine whether Tuesday is a member of the set, we would examine

S[Ord(Tuesday)] = S[1]

which has the value No, indicating it is not a member of the set. To delete Friday, we would set

S[Ord(Friday)] = S[4]

to the value No.

As a second example, if the base type of our set were the lowercase alphabetical values ['a' .. 'z'], which have the ordinal values 97 to 122, the mapping function f would be

$f(e) = \text{Ord}(e) - 97$

To see if the letter 'c' is a member of a set S, we first apply the function f to the letter 'c' as follows:

$$\begin{aligned} f(\text{'c'}) &= \text{Ord}(\text{'c'}) - 97 \\ &= 99 - 97 \\ &= 2 \end{aligned}$$

Therefore, to determine the membership of the letter 'c' in the set S we check the value of S[2] to see if it is a Yes or a No.

The set generator operations Union, Intersection, and Difference can be implemented using a simple **For** loop structure of complexity O(N). For example, set intersection can be defined as follows:

```
For i := 0 To N-1 Do
    If (S1[i] = Yes) And (S2[i] = Yes) Then
        S3[i] := Yes
    Else
        S3[i] := No
End For
```

This loop is a much more efficient implementation of Intersection than the array or linked list technique which required $O(N^2)$ comparisons. Simple **For** loop structures can also be used to implement the Union and Difference functions in $O(N)$ time.

The complete bit vector implementation module for the Set abstract data type of Figure 9–3 is shown in Figure 9–5. We have used a pointer to the array to implement the abstract data type. This will allow us to instantiate new sets in the CreateSet function using the procedure New.

Figure 9–5
Bit Vector Implementation of the Set ADT

```
(* The following module contains the internal code for the Set abstract
    data type, using bit vectors as described in Section 9.1.2.
    The external specifications for the operations on Sets are given
    in Figure 9.3. *)
Internal Module SetPackage;

From UserModule Import
    (* The data type stored in the set. *)
        DataElementType,
    (* The number of distinct values DataElementType has. *)
        MaxElement,
    (* The mapping function from DataElementType → [0 .. MaxElement−1] *)
        Ord;

Type
        (* The Set abstract data type itself. *)
    SetType        = Pointer To Array [0 .. MaxElement−1] Of (Yes, No);

(*  Precondition: None
    Postcondition:    A new, empty set is returned.
                          Empty(CreateSet()) = True   *)
Procedure CreateSet() : SetType;
Var
    NewSet        : SetType;
    i             : Integer;
Begin
    New(NewSet);            (* Allocate space for the new set *)

    For i := 0 To (MaxElement − 1) Do
        NewSet^[i] := No; (* Mark each member as not being in the set. *)
    Endfor;

    Return NewSet;
End CreateSet;
```

(continued)

Figure 9–5 (continued)

```
(*  Precondition: None
    Postcondition:    After calling Insert, Set is guaranteed to contain Element.
                          Member(Insert(S, E), E) = True
                          Empty(Insert(S, E)) = False                              *)
Procedure Insert( Var Set : SetType; Element : DataElementType );
Begin
    Set^[Ord(Element)] := Yes;
End Insert;

(*  Precondition: None
    Postcondition:    After calling Delete, Set is guaranteed to not
                          contain Element.
                      Member(Delete(S, E), E) = False
                      Empty(Delete(Insert(Create(), E), E)) = True                 *)
Procedure Delete( Var Set : SetType; Element : DataElementType );
Begin
    Set^[Ord(Element)] := No;
End Delete;

(*  Precondition: None
    Postcondition:    Union returns a set which contains only those elements
                          which are either in Set1, or in Set2, or in both.
                      If Member(S1, E) Or Member(S2, E) Then
                          Member(Union(S1, S2), E) = True
                      Else
                          Member(Union(S1, S2), E) = False   *)
Procedure Union( Set1 : SetType; Set2 : SetType ) : SetType;
Var
    i           : Integer;
    NewSet      : SetType;
Begin
    New(NewSet);

    For i := 0 To (MaxSize - 1) Do
        If ((Set1^[i] = Yes) Or (Set2^[i] = Yes)) Then
            NewSet^[i] := Yes;
        Endif;
    Endfor;

    Return NewSet;
End Union;

(*  Precondition: None
    Postcondition:    Intersection returns a set which contains only those
                          elements which are in both Set1 and Set2.
                      If Member(S1, E) And Member(S2, E) Then
                          Member(Intersection(S1, S2), E) = True
                      Else
                          Member(Intersection(S1, S2), E) = False                  *)
Procedure Intersection( Set1 : SetType; Set2 : SetType ) : SetType;
Var
    i           : Integer;
    NewSet      : SetType;
```

(continued)

Figure 9–5 (continued)

```
Begin
    New(NewSet);

    For i := 0 To (MaxSize - 1) Do
        If ((Set1^[i] = Yes) And (Set2^[i] = Yes)) Then
            NewSet^[i] := Yes;
        Endif;
    Endfor;

    Return NewSet;
End Intersection;

(*  Precondition: None
    Postcondition:    Difference returns a set which contains only those
                          elements which are in Set1 but not in Set2.
                      If Member(S1, E) And (Not Member(S2, E)) Then
                          Member(Difference(S1, S2)) = True
                      Else
                          Member(Difference(S1, S2)) = False              *)
Procedure Difference( Set1 : SetType; Set2 : SetType ) : SetType;
Var
    i           : Integer;
    NewSet      : SetType;
Begin
    New(NewSet);

    For i := 0 To (MaxSize - 1) Do
        If ((Set1^[i] = Yes) And (Set2^[i] = No)) Then
            NewSet^[i] := Yes;
        Endif;
    Endfor;

    Return NewSet;
End Difference;

(*  Precondition: None
    Postcondition:    Empty returns True if Set contains no elements.
                      Otherwise, Empty returns False.   *)
Procedure Empty( Set : SetType ) : Boolean;
Var
    i           : Integer;
Begin
    i := 0;

    While (i < MaxElement) Do          (* Look through each element of the set, *)
        If (Set^[i] = Yes) Then        (* Until we find one which is there. *)
            (* If any element is in the set, it is not empty. *)
            Return False;
        Endif;
        i := i + 1;
    Endwhile;

    Return True;                       (* No elements were found in the set. *)
End Empty;
```

(continued)

Figure 9–5
(continued)

```
(*  Precondition: None
    Postcondition:    Member returns True if Element is a member of Set.
                      Otherwise, Member returns False.                        *)
Procedure Member( Set : SetType; Element : DataElementType ) : Boolean;
Begin
    Return Set^[Ord(Element)];
End Member;

(*  Precondition: None
    Postcondition:    Subset returns True if every element which is a member
                          of Set1 is also a member of Set2.
                      Otherwise, Subset returns False.
                      If Empty(Difference(S1, S2)) Then
                          Subset(S1, S2) = True
                      Else
                          Subset(S1, S2) = False                              *)
Procedure Subset( Set1 : SetType; Set2 : SetType ) : Boolean;
Begin
    Return Empty(Difference(Set1, Set2));
End Subset;

End SetPackage.
```

It might be instructive to "drop down" one more level of abstraction (see Figure 2–1) to see how this bit vector array itself can be efficiently implemented within the memory of a computer system.

Since we are using only two values (Yes, No) to indicate membership in a set, each bit vector array element will require only a single binary digit, with a zero representing No and a one representing Yes. Thus the bit vector array can be implemented internally as a sequence of binary digits from consecutive memory cells. If the cardinality N of the set base type is an even multiple of the word size M of our computer, i.e., $N = kM$, then each bit vector array will require exactly k consecutive memory cells. Figure 9–6 shows the internal implementation of a set variable S using a word size of $M = 8$ bits and a base type size of $N = 16$. Since N = 2M, we will need two memory words per set variable.

```
Var
    S : Set Of ['A' .. 'P'];     (* Assume M = 8, N = 16, Then k = 2 *)
                                 (* We only go up to 'P' because our base type is
                                 limited to 16 elements in this example. *)
```

Since the internal ordinal value of the capital letters 'A', 'B', 'C', . . . is 65, 66, 67, . . . the mapping function is $f(e) = \text{Ord}(e) - 65$. Given this representation, we can see that it is quite easy to convert the subscript, i, of the bit vector array S into a word address W, $0 \le W < k$, and a bit number B within that word $0 \le B < M$. Looking at Figure 9–6, we see that the proper values for W and B are given by the following expressions.

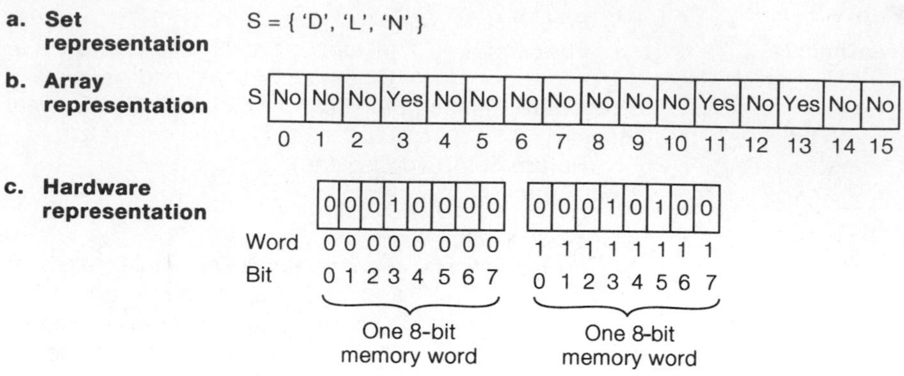

Figure 9–6
Internal Hardware Representation of a Set Variable Represented as a Bit Vector

a. Set representation S = { 'D', 'L', 'N' }

b. Array representation

S	No	No	No	Yes	No	No	No	No	No	No	No	Yes	No	Yes	No	No
	0	1	2	3	4	5	6	7	8	9	10	11	12	13	14	15

c. Hardware representation

	0	0	0	1	0	0	0	0	0	0	0	1	0	1	0	0
Word	0	0	0	0	0	0	0	0	1	1	1	1	1	1	1	1
Bit	0	1	2	3	4	5	6	7	0	1	2	3	4	5	6	7

One 8-bit memory word — One 8-bit memory word

$$W = f(e) \textbf{ Div } M \qquad \text{(* } M \text{ is the word size of our computer. *)}$$
$$B = f(e) \textbf{ Mod } M$$

For example, given the set variable S := {'D', 'L', 'N'} from Figure 9–6, let's insert the value 'K' into the set S, that is, let's carry out the operation Insert (S, 'K'). We first determine the correct placement of the value 'K' in the bit vector using the mapping function

$$\begin{aligned} f(\text{'K'}) &= \text{Ord}(\text{'K'}) - 65 \\ &= 75 - 65 \\ &= 10 \end{aligned}$$

which says that S[10] is the unique location in the array S corresponding to membership of the value 'K' in our set. Our final step will be to determine the proper word and bit position in memory corresponding to element 10 of the array.

$$W = 10 \textbf{ Div } 8 = 1$$
$$B = 10 \textbf{ Mod } 8 = 2$$

We would then set bit position 2 of word number 1 to the binary value 1. This last step is what ultimately implements the original Insert operation.

The point of this discussion has been to reinforce a fundamentally important idea raised at the beginning of the text and diagrammed in Figure 2–1—the concept of a *hierarchy of data types*. The increasing levels of the hierarchy provide a higher-level, machine-independent view of a data type while simultaneously hiding the details of the implementation of that data type in terms of the underlying software and hardware.

At the highest levels of abstraction we are allowed to view a set as an abstract data type without worrying about how it is implemented in our programming language. We simply use these objects as if they were part of our programming language, as in

```
Var
    S : Set;          (* The data types Set and Element are imported from our
    E : Element;      external module. *)
```

We manipulate these abstract objects using the collection of operations provided by the external module of Figure 9–3. Again we do not worry at all about how these operations carry out their tasks.

```
From SetModule Import
    Member,
    Insert;
        •
        •
        •
If Member (S,E) Then          (* See if it is in the set. *)
    WriteString ('It is there.')
Else
    Insert (S,E)              (* If not, then add it. *)
```

This viewpoint is that of a *user* of the set module. The user would simply want to know what resources were available, how they are used (i.e., their syntax), and what they do (i.e., their semantics).

At the next level of abstraction, the virtual data type level, we are concerned with how our abstract data type would be implemented in some high-level programming language. In this section we considered three possibles techniques, arrays, linked lists, and bit vectors, and for reasons of space and time efficiency we selected the latter method. Now we view a set as an *N*-element array of user-defined values Yes and No—certainly a much more detailed viewpoint than our previous one.

```
Type
    Set = Array [0 .. 25] Of (Yes,No);
    Element = ['A' .. 'Z'];
```

We manipulate these virtual data types using the operations provided with the language, e.g., subscripting, assignment, and standard ordinal functions such as Ord:

```
Var
    S : Set;
    E : Element;
•
•
•
i := Ord(E) – 65;
If S[i] = Yes Then
    WriteString ('It is there.')
Else
    S[i] := Yes
```

This viewpoint is that of the *coder* of the internal module of the abstract data type.

Finally, at the lowest level, the hardware level, we must worry about how to map programming constructs such as arrays and subscripts onto the memory and processor architecture of our computer system. As we showed earlier, we now must view a set data structure as a sequence of bytes of memory, each containing eight binary digits.

```
Set:      .Byte 0     (* Four bytes hold 32 bits, so we will be able to *)
          .Byte 0     (* represent a set with up to 32 elements. *)
          .Byte 0
          .Byte 0
Element:  .Byte 65    (* This is the character A. *)
             •
             •
             •
```

Now the compiler must translate our virtual high-level operations into the instructions available in the instruction set of our processor. For example, if our program were running on a MicroVax II workstation, the Member(Set,Element) operation might become

```
SUB   #65,Element,R0      (* f(e) = Ord(E) -65 *)
DIV   #8,R0,R1            (* W = f(E) Div M *)
REM   #8,R0,R2            (* B = f(E) Mod M *)
MOVB  #80,TEMP
ASL   TEMP,TEMP,R3        (* Get a one in bit position B. *)
BIT   R3,Set(R1)          (* Test that bit to see if it is a Yes. *)
BEQ   No                  (* Its a No. *)
JMP   Yes                 (* Its a Yes. *)
```

Don't worry if you do not understand this code; it is included only to make you aware of the complexity of low-level detail and to help you appreciate how nice it is to work at levels well above the machine's instruction set. However, this detail is necessary for those working at the level of the compiler writer or a computer designer.

Thus, whether you choose to view a set as a formal mathematical structure, an array, or a sequence of binary digits ultimately depends on your own needs as a user, a programmer, or a compiler writer. The idea behind a hierarchy of abstractions is that once you choose a point of view, all inappropriate and unnecessary lower-level detail is hidden from you and will not clutter up your solution.

9.2 SEARCH TABLES

9.2.1 Definition and Operations

Sets are an important concept in formal mathematics, and they are studied extensively in the branch of mathematics called set theory. However, the set structure described in section 9.1 is not an important or widely used data type in the field of computer science. (This fact can be easily confirmed by looking at the frequency of use of the **Set** type, which is supported in both Pascal and Modula-2. It is very low compared to the use of other composite types such as arrays or records.) Restricting the base type of a set to ordinal values and limiting the size of a set to unrealistically small values such as 16 or 32 have combined to give the set structure an extremely limited use.

That does not mean, however, that sets are not a useful data type in software development. With a few small changes to the definition given in section 9.1, we can produce one of the most important data structures in computer science, one that is based directly on the set diagram shown in Figure 3–1d. This new structure is called a *search table*.

Let us make the following three additional modifications to our definition of the set data structure:

1. Instead of limiting our set components to ordinals, let us assume that they are 2-tuples of the form (k_i, v_i) where k is called the *key field* and v is called the *value field*. We will place no artificially low limits on the number of 2-tuples that can appear in a set S, although it must, of course, be finite.

   $$S = \{(k_0, v_0), (k_1, v_1), \ldots, (k_n, v_n)\}$$

   The k_i are objects of type KeyType and the v_i are objects of type ValueType. Neither KeyType nor ValueType need be limited to primitive types—they can be any composite data type. The k_i must be unique within the set, but the v_i need not be.
2. We will no longer concern ourselves with the operations Union, Intersection, and Difference. The operations we will require are Create, Insert, Delete, and Member. The only things that we will do to our Search Table data structure is place tuples in the table (Insert), take tuples out of the table (Delete), and locate tuples in the table (Member).
3. The syntax of the operations on a search table will be changed slightly to reflect the differences in the structure of the component elements. The syntax of the operations on this Search Table data structure are shown in Figure 9–7.

What we have described in Figure 9–7 is an example of a *direct-access* data structure, in which all data values in the structure are associated at insertion time with a unique identifier called a *key* and are stored as the tuple (key, data value). All subsequent accesses to this data value are done via its key, rather than by the location of that value within the data structure, as was the case with such structures as arrays (A[*i*]), stacks (Top), and queues (Front, Back). Since the key is stored directly in the tuple, the order of the 2-tuples within the search table is immaterial in terms of determining membership. In addition, since the keys must be unique, each 2-tuple will be unique and there will be no duplication within the search table. Together, these two characteristics show that a search table of the form we have just described satisfies the definition of a set structure.

Rather than being of extremely limited use, a search table is a useful and important data structure. The type of keyed access that it provides models a large number of situations encountered in real life, for example

Figure 9–7
Syntax and Semantics of a Search Table Data Structure

Syntax:

Define SearchTable[Key,Value]

1. Create() : T

   Produce a new search table T that is empty. T = {}, that is, T has no tuples stored in it.
2. Insert(T_1, K, V) : T_2

   Produce a new search table T_2 that contains all the tuples from T_1 and that has the tuple (K,V), if it was not contained in T_1. If T_1 has a 2-tuple of the form (K,X), where X is any value, then instead of adding the tuple (K,V) to T_2, we replace the value field X in the existing 2-tuple by the new value V.
3. Delete(T_1, K) : T_2

   Look in T_1 for a 2-tuple of the form (K,X), where X is any value, and if it is found, remove that 2-tuple from the search table to produce a new search table T_2. If no such tuple exists then simply return the original table unchanged.
4. Member(T, K) : V

   Look in T for a 2-tuple of the form (K,V), and if it is found, return the value field V associated with the key K. If K is not found, then we return the special value Null in V.

Semantics:

1. Member(Create(), K) = Null
2. Member(Delete(T, K), K) = Null
3. Member(Insert(T, K, V), K) = V
4. Delete(Insert(T, K, V), K) = T
5. Member(Insert(Insert(T, K, V_1), K, V_2), K) = V_2
6. Delete(Create(), K) = Create()
7. Delete(Insert(Create(), K_1, V), K_2) = Insert(Create(), K_1, V)

Key Field	*Value Field*
Student ID No.	(Name, Major, GPA, Year)
Social Sec. No.	(Number, Address, Amount)
Part No.	(Part Name, Supplier, Amount on Hand)
License Plate No.	(Owner, Make, Year, Color, Fees Paid)
Process No.	(Process Name, Process State, Owner, Resources Used)

In all of these examples we want to provide a key value and retrieve the data located in the value field of that key (or learn that the key is not there). This process is identical to the Member operation that we defined in Figure 9–7.

An external module for the SearchTable data type just described is given in Figure 9–8 (the Member function has been renamed Retrieve for clarity). In the next section we will learn how to implement this table structure efficiently, and we will give some examples of its use.

9.2.2 Implementation Using Arrays and Linked Lists

As with the set structure of section 9.1.2, there are a number of quite simple and straightforward ways to implement a search table. However, as we will see, they demonstrate inefficient and generally unacceptable performance.

Figure 9–8
External Module for the Search Table

```
(* The following module contains the external specifications for the
     abstract data type Search Table as described in Section 9.2.1.
     The formal syntax and semantics for the Search Table are given
     in Figure 9.7.                                                    *)
External Module SearchTablePackage;

From UserModule Import
          KeyType,          (* The key values of items in the search table *)
          ValueType;        (* The actual values stored in the search table *)

Type
     SearchTableType;       (* The abstract data type *)

(*   Precondition: None
     Postcondition:    Create returns a new, empty Search Table.       *)
Procedure Create() : SearchTableType;

(*   Precondition: None
     Postcondition:    Insert adds the tuple (Key, Value) to Table, such that
                            any tuple already in Table of the form (Key, Val)
                            is replaced.                                *)
Procedure Insert( Var Table : SearchTableType;
                              Key : KeyType; Value : ValueType );

(*   Precondition: None
     Postcondition:    Delete removes the tuple of the form (Key, Value) from
                            Table.
                       If there is no such tuple, Table is unchanged.  *)
Procedure Delete( Var Table : SearchTableType; Key : KeyType );

(*   Precondition: None
     Postcondition:    Retrieves searches Table for a tuple of the form
                            (Key, Value), and returns Value. If no such
                            tuple exists in Table, the result is undefined.  *)
Procedure Retrieve( Table : SearchTableType; Key : KeyType ) : ValueType;

End SearchTablePackage.
```

The most obvious method for implementing a search table would be to store the table as an array of records, each record holding a single (key,value) 2-tuple. The declarations needed to create this array-based implementation are shown below.

```
Const
     Max = . . . ;          (* Maximum size of the array *)

Type
     DataRecord = Record
          Key : KeyType;
          Value : ValueType
                    End;
     SearchTableType = Array [0 .. Max] Of DataRecord;

Var
     SearchTable : SearchTableType;
```

Table 9–1 Time Complexities of Array and Linked List

	Array or Linked List Implementation-Unsorted	Array Implementation-Sorted	Binary Search Tree
Insert	O(1)	O(*N*)	O($\log_2 N$)
Delete	O(*N*)	O(*N*)	O($\log_2 N$)
Retrieve	O(*N*)	O($\log_2 N$)	O($\log_2 N$)

We have two choices about how to maintain information in the search table. We can keep the array in sorted order by key values. When we do an insertion, this system will require us to search the array to find the correct place to insert the value and keep the list sorted. This operation is O(*N*). However, keeping the array in sorted sequence will facilitate the Retrieve operation and will allow us to use the efficient O($\log_2 N$) binary search technique to locate a key and retrieve the value field. Alternatively, we could choose to keep the array in unsorted order and simply place values at the end of the array in O(1) time, but then our Retrieve operation would be sequential and would be O(*N*).

A linked list implementation does not fare any better. Insertions can be done in O(1) time by linking new items to the head of the list, but both deletions and retrievals require O(*N*) time because they must search the entire list to retrieve the desired value. The linked list also requires a good deal of memory space for the pointer fields in each node.

Another possibility for implementing our search table is the binary search tree discussed in chapter 8. If we assume that the tree is reasonably well balanced, then the insertions, deletions, and retrievals from the tree will all be O($\log_2 N$).

The time complexities of these various techniques are summarized in Table 9–1. It appears that we have the same problem we encountered when discussing binary search trees. Either we expend extra time during insertions to keep the search table in a given order and thus have very fast retrieval, or we spend virtually no time at all during the insertion phase but pay for it dearly in terms of slower retrievals and deletions. Alternatively, we can get reasonable logarithmic behavior for all three operations. Which method should we choose?

The answer is none of the above! There is an alternative implementation of search tables that demonstrates none of these problems or trade-offs. Its time complexity (under optimal conditions) for the three primary operations on search tables is

Insert: O(1)
Delete: O(1)
Retrieve: O(1)

You can't do any better than this! This method is called *hashing*, and it is by far the most popular method for building and maintaining search tables.

9.2.3 Hashing

The *hashing* method of search table management works by storing (key,value) pairs in an array A[1 .. *N*]. We transform the key that we are looking for into a number called a *hash value*, which can be used as an array index to access the search table directly. That is, given a key, we apply a *hash function* to the key to obtain an index value x in the range [1 .. N].

$$x = h(\text{key}) \qquad 1 \leq x \leq N$$

We use the index value x (not the key) to retrieve the 2-tuple (key,value) from the array, because, as we learned in Chapter 3, once you know the index x of the value you want, the retrieval operation on an array A, Retrieve(A, x, value) takes O(1) time.

Formally, we can say that a *hash table* T is a random-access data structure T[1 .. N] of (key, value) tuples in which a value field is accessed by an index value i which is determined by a mapping function h that is applied to the key field during insertion and retrieval operations. This structure is diagrammed in Figure 9–9.

As an example of a hashing function, suppose we are using names as our key values. We could develop a hash function by associating a number with each letter in the name, with the letter a having the value 1, the letter b the value 2, and so on. If the letters of the name are designated $c_1, c_2, \ldots, c_k$, and the function pos maps the letters $a, b, c, \ldots$ into the integers 1, 2, 3, . . . , then the hash function h would be

$$h = \sum_{i=1}^{k} \text{pos}(c_i)$$

Let's see how this function would work. Suppose we have a table of size 50 in which the keys are people's names. We would like each name stored in the table to hash to a value between 1 and 50, corresponding to the location in the table where the name and data values of that person will be stored. The function could be as simple as adding up the values for each letter in the key and taking that sum modulo 50. This process would generate a value between 0 and 49, so we would then add 1 to obtain a value in the correct range. Figure 9–10 shows the computation of the hash value for the name *smith*.

The key *smith* hashed to location 20, so we could go directly to the 20th element of the array, A[20], which would contain the desired record, that is, the record whose key field A[20].Key contains 'smith' and whose value field A[20].Value contains the desired information about Mr. or Ms. Smith.

Figure 9–9
Logical Structure of a Hash Table

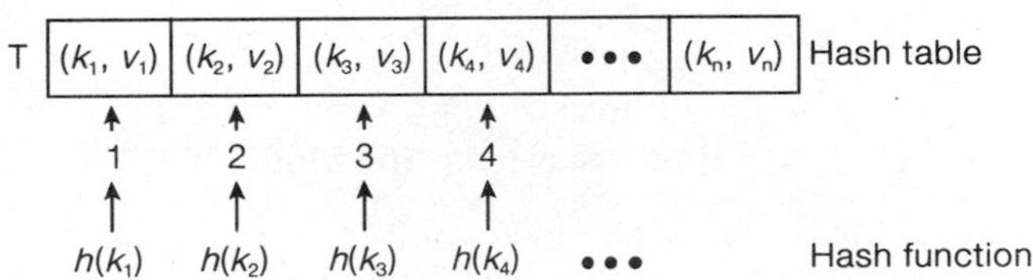

Figure 9–10
Computation of the Hash Value for 'smith'

Letter		Value
s	=	19
m	=	13
i	=	9
t	=	20
h	=	8
Total	=	69

Hash value = (69 **Mod** 50) + 1

= 20

If the hashing method always worked as described, then insertion in a hashed search tree would be an O(1) operation and would be given by the following algorithm:

```
Insert (T,key,value) :   x := h(key)
                         T[x].Key := key
                         T[x].Value := value
                         Return T
```

Retrieval would also be O(1):

```
Retrieve (T,key) :   x := h(key)
                     Return T[x].Value
```

Compared to the time complexities given in Table 9–1, we can see quite clearly that this technique appears to be far superior to the array and linked list implementations of section 9.2.2. Unfortunately, the solution to our problem is not that simple.

A *perfect hash function* has the property that if x and y are distinct keys, then $h(x)$ will not equal $h(y)$. Unfortunately, in almost all cases perfect hash functions are extremely difficult to create. The hash functions used in actual programs have the property that for $x \neq y$, they sometimes produce $h(x) = h(y)$. The situation when two distinct keys hash to the same location is called a *collision*. For example, using the hash function described above, the key *posen* hashes to the same value as the key *smith*.

Letter		*Value*
p	=	16
o	=	15
s	=	19
e	=	5
n	=	14
Total	=	69
Hash value	=	(69 **Mod** 50) + 1
	=	20

Collisions like this are unavoidable because the domain of possible keys can be very large, typically much larger than our table size. If our keys are people's names and we assume that names can contain up to fifteen letters, then the total number of possible keys is 26^{15}, a monstrously large value. It would be impossible to create a table large enough to guarantee that there would be no collisions. (Besides, it would be horribly wasteful of space, since most slots would be unused.)

How do we deal with this problem? There are two things that we can do: First, we try to minimize the number of collisions that occur, and second, we develop a procedure to deal with the collisions that do occur.

To minimize the number of collisions, we need to choose the best possible hashing function, which we define as a hashing function that has the following two characteristics:

1. It does not take a lot of time. The hashing function will have to be executed at least once for every insertion and retrieval operation, so a complex and time-consuming function could slow down the method considerably.
2. It scatters the keys *uniformly* over the N indices, [1 .. N], of the hash table array. That is, for any arbitrary key we want the probability of that key hashing to location i of the hash table to be uniform for all slots i.

   $$\text{Prob}\ (h(\text{key}) = i) = 1/N \text{ for all } i\ ,\ 1 \le i \le N$$

   A uniform distribution will minimize the number of keys hashing to the same location i, and reduce the number of collisions that do occur. (For this reason, hashing functions are also called *scatter functions*.)

An example of a very poor hashing function would be

$$h(\text{key}) = [2 * \text{key}]\ \textbf{Mod}\ N$$

This function will map keys into only the even-numbered locations 0, 2, 4, 6, . . . , completely disregarding the odd-numbered locations and effectively doubling the number of collisions we generate.

The study of the mathematical properties of hashing functions is quite complex and beyond the scope of this text. We leave it to other courses in function theory and numerical analysis to discuss this subject. We will simply state that the *multiplicative congruency* method is one of the classes of hashing functions that work quite well for typical table sizes and keys. With this method we treat the key as if it were an unsigned integer value (regardless of its data type) and compute the following value for a hash table with indices in the range [1 .. N].

$$h(\text{key}) = [(a * \text{key})\ \textbf{Mod}\ N] + 1 \qquad N \text{ is prime, } a \text{ is positive, odd, and prime}$$

For a reasonable choice of constants a and N, this type of function will produce reasonably well-scattered integer values in the range [1 .. N]. You can use this function (or something similar) to implement the hashing exercises at the end of the chapter.

Even with a well-designed hashing function we will still encounter the situation in which two or more distinct keys hash to the same slot. There are two fundamental ways to handle these collisions—*open addressing* and *chaining*.

Open Addressing

In open addressing, the keys and values are stored within the array structure itself.

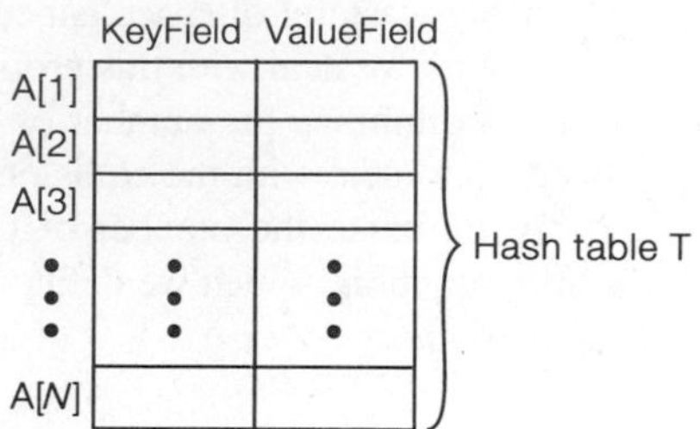

If the key field of the location we hash to is occupied, we search sequentially through the table looking for an empty location. Thus, if $x = h(\text{key})$ and location x is full, we search locations $x + 1, x + 2, x + 3, \ldots$. The search is done modulo the table size, so that after looking at the last item in the table we "wrap around" and continue the search from the top of the table. The retrieval operation works in a similar fashion. If $x = h(\text{key})$ and T[x].KeyField ≠ key, then we search sequentially through the table until we either find the desired key or we come to an empty slot. When we locate an empty slot, we know that the key is not in the table, because if it were, it would have been stored in this location.

The algorithms for inserting and retrieving values in a search table using hashing and open addressing are given in Figure 9–11. The actual encoding of these two algorithms is left as an exercise.

One minor problem with open addressing is that we frequently get long chains of occupied cells followed by long chains of empty cells because we search sequentially for an available slot. If cell x is occupied, the new value will be inserted in cell $x + 1$. Then if a key value hashes to either cell x or $x + 1$, it will be placed in cell $x + 2$, and so their is a greater probability of a value being stored in cell $x + 2$ than in other unoccupied cells, and we begin to build chains of occupied slots. These long chains of full cells degrade performance, as we are required to make longer and longer searches for an available location. If the empty slots were more evenly distributed throughout the table, our searches would be shorter.

A small but important modification to open addressing is to search our table not in increments of one cell but in increments of c cells, where c is a value that is greater than one and relatively prime (i.e., shares no common factor) with the table size N. To implement this idea we simply modify the increment step in our algorithms in Figure 9–11 to read

$$\text{NextCellToSearch} = [(x + k * c)\ \textbf{Mod}\ \text{N}] + 1 \qquad k = 0, 1, 2, 3, \ldots, N - 1$$

For example, assume our table size is $N = 10$ and c, the increment size, is 3. If our key value hashed originally to location 5 and found it full, the order in which the cells would now be searched is

8, 1, 4, 7, 10, 3, 6, 9, 2

rather than in a sequential fashion 6, 7, 8, 9, 10, 1, ...

Figure 9–11
Open Addressing Hash Algorithms

```
(* Algorithms for inserting and retreiving values from a hash table using the
technique called open addressing. *)

Insert ( T, Key, Value )

    x := h(Key)
    If (T[x] is empty) Then
        T[x].KeyField := Key
        T[x].ValueField := Value
    Else
        Repeat
            x := ((x + 1) Mod N) + 1    (* N is the table size *)
            If (T[x] is empty) Then
                T[x].KeyField := Key
                T[x].ValueField := Value
            Endif
        Until (an empty slot has been found) Or
                (the entire table has been searched)
    Endif

    Return T
End of Insert

Retrieve ( T, Key )

    x := h(key)
    If T[x].KeyField = Key Then
        Return T[x].ValueField
    Else
        Repeat
            x := ((x + 1) Mod N) + 1
            If T[x].KeyField = Key Then
                Return T[x].ValueField
            Endif
        Until (T[x] is empty) Or (the entire table has been searched)
        Return "Not found"         (* This is the case where the key is not found *)
    Endif
End of Retrieve
```

This technique is much better at scattering values uniformly throughout the table and distributing empty slots more evenly. Open addressing with a step size $c > 1$ is a popular form of hashing.

Looking at the algorithms in Figure 9–11 we see that in the best case, a retrieval using open addressing requires only one comparison to locate the key and is thus an O(1) algorithm. In the worst case, we may have to search the entire table to discover whether a key value is present; hashing then degenerates to an $O(N)$ sequential search. In the average case, the number of comparisons required for a successful retrieval using open addressing depends on how many entries are stored in the table. As the table becomes filled, the chance of a collision increases. If we denote the fraction of the table cells in use by ρ, the *load factor*, then the likelihood of having a collision is ρ and the likelihood of finding an empty slot is $1 - \rho$. The probability of having exactly m collisions during one search of a hash table is given by the following formulas, where $\rho = k/N$, k is the number of occupied cells, N is the table size, and $0 \leq \rho \leq 1$:

Probability of exactly 0 collisions $= (1 - \rho)$
Probability of exactly 1 collision $= \rho(1 - \rho)$ (* This is just the probability of first having a collision then finding an empty slot *)
Probability of exactly 2 collisions $= \rho^2(1 - \rho)$ (* This is just the probability of having exactly two collisions then finding an empty slot *)

•

•

•

Probability of exactly i collisions $= \rho^i (1 - \rho)$

The expected number of collisions C that we will encounter when looking for a key in a hash table with load factor ρ is given by the product of i, the number of collisions, times the probability of having exactly i collisions, summed over all values of i:

$$C = \sum_{i=1}^{n} i\, \rho^i(1 - \rho)$$

$$= \rho/(1 - \rho)$$

The total number of comparisons we must perform to find a key in our hash table is just C + 1, the C collisions followed by the one successful comparison

$$C + 1 = \rho\,/(1 - \rho) + 1 = [1/(1 - \rho)]$$

and the time complexity of the retrieval operation on a hash table using open addressing is $O(1/(1 - \rho))$.

For example, if our table is half full ($\rho = 0.5$), we will require on the average $1/(1 - 1/2) = 2$ comparisons to retrieve a key. Let's compare this method with a sequential or binary search applied to a table with 100,000 elements. These methods will require on the average about 50,000 and 17 searches, respectively. Even if our table is 80% full ($\rho = 0.8$), hashing will require on the average only $1/(1 - 0.8)$, or five searches—a vast improvement.

However, we must be aware that this speed is coming at the expense of a great deal of wasted space (another example of the time-space trade-off first discussed in Chapter 6). If our table is of size $N = 100{,}000$, then at 50% occupancy we are leaving 50,000 cells unused. At 80% occupancy, we are leaving 20,000 cells unused. Hashing with open addressing is a reasonable search technique to use only if we have sufficient memory space to leave at least 5 to 10% of our table vacant.

We can see the time-space trade-off for the hashing method quite clearly if we look at how many comparisons it will take to retrieve a value from a hash table of size $N = 100$ with load factors ranging from $\rho = 0.1$ to $\rho = 0.99$.

ρ	*Number of Comparisons*	
0.1	1.11	O(1)
0.2	1.25	
0.3	1.43	
0.4	1.67	
0.5	2	
0.6	2.5	
0.7	3.33	
0.8	5	$O(\log_2 N)$
0.9	10	
0.95	20	
0.98	50	$O(N)$
0.99	100	

We can see that for a relatively empty table (say $\rho < 0.5$) the number of searches needed to insert or retrieve a value from our search table is small, and hashing is approximately an O(1) operation. At around $\rho = 0.8$, the performance of hashing begins to degrade and becomes comparable to an $O(\log_2 N)$ binary search, which needs, on the average, $\log_2 100 \approx 7$ comparisons for a table of size $N = 100$. At $\rho = 0.98$, hashing has degraded almost to a linear search, and it requires the same number of comparisons, namely $N/2 = 50$. Thus, to get the best behavior from the open addressing hashing method, we should keep the load factor $\rho < 0.8$. If the occupancy increases much beyond that point, we begin to lose much of the improved efficiency that the hashing method can deliver.

Chaining

Chaining, the second method of collision resolution, is quite different in structure. The N elements of the hash table are used to store not the key values themselves, but only the head pointer of a chain of all keys that hashed to that location. That is, the element T[i] is the head pointer of a linked list containing all key values such that $i = h(\text{key})$. For example, if our hash table were of length 5, and the keys a and b hashed to 2, c hashed to 4, and d, e, and f hashed to 5, then our table would look like:

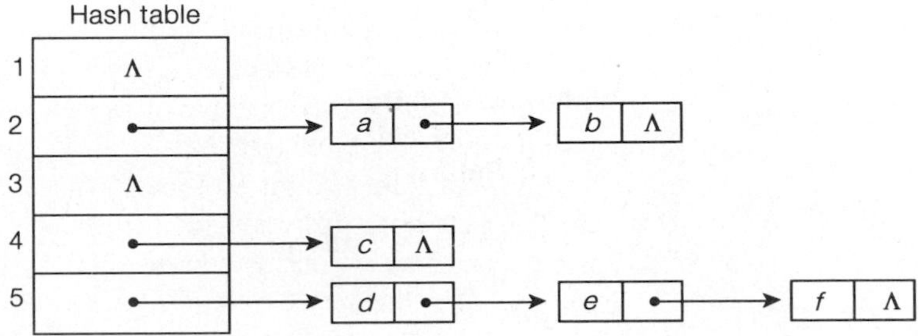

The declarations needed to set up this linked list structure are

```
Const
     Max = . . . ; (* Maximum size of our hash table *)
Type
     HashTableType = Array [1 .. Max] Of NodePointers;
     NodePointers  = Pointer To NodeRecords;
     NodeRecords = Record
                          KeyField : KeyType;
                          ValueField : ValueType;
                          NextField : NodePointers
                   End;
Var
     T : HashTableType;
```

Chaining thus facilitates the problem of handling collisions when inserting a new value in the table. Regardless of how many keys hash to the same location, we always carry out the same operation—add that new key to the head of the linked list pointed to by the value in the corresponding hash table location. For retrieval, we do a sequential search through the linked list, beginning with the node pointed to by T[i], where $i = h$(key). The algorithms for hashing using chaining are given in Figure 9–12.

One nice feature of chaining is that we can store more than N keys in the table, where N is the table size. (In the previous example we stored six keys, $a, \ldots, f$, in

Figure 9–12
Hashing Algorithms Using Chaining

```
(* Algorithms for inserting and retrieving from a hash table using the technique
called chaining. *)

Insert ( T, Key, Value )

     x := h(Key)
     Search linked list beginning at T[x]
     If Key is not there Then
          New(Node)
          Node^.KeyField := Key
          Node^.ValueField := Value
          Node^.NextField := T[x]
          T[x] := Node
          Return T
End of Insert

Retrieve ( T, Key )

     x := h(key)
     p := T[x]
     While p <> Nil Do
          If p^.KeyField = Key Then
               Return p^.ValueField
          Else
               p := p^.NextField
          Endif
     Endwhile
     Return p (* This is the case where the value is not found *)
End of Retrieve
```

a table of size $N = 5$.) On the average, each linked list in our hash table will be of length k/N, where k is the total number of keys stored in the table and N is the table size.

The time required to insert a value into our search table using chaining is the total time for the following three steps:

1. Accessing the head pointer stored in the hash table location T[i].
2. Searching the entire list pointed to by this head pointer to ensure that the value being inserted is not already there (remember, no duplicates are allowed).
3. If the value being inserted is not there, inserting the new value at the head of the list.

Steps 1 and 3 take only one operation, while step 2 takes k/N, the average size of each linked list in the hash table. Thus, insertion in a chained hash table takes about $2 + k/N$ operations and is $O(k/N)$.

Similarly, retrieval takes one access to the head element of the linked list, followed by a search of, on the average, half the list before we find the desired key. Retrieval in a chained hash table thus requires about $1 + k/2N$, operations and is also $O(k/N)$.

Knowing an approximate value for k, the number of keys we will store in the table, we can adjust the table size N to give us an acceptable level of performance with the minimum amount of wasted space. For example, if we wanted to store $k =$ 1000 keys in a hash table using chaining, then a table size of $N = 10$ will cause us to have linked lists of length approximately 100, requiring an average of 50 comparisons per retrieval—very poor. A table size of $N = 50$ will produce an average search length of 10, which is comparable with the length of a binary search ($\log_2 1000 \approx 10$). Finally, a table size of $N = 250$ will produce an average of two searches per retrieval, which is comparable with the number of searches in an open addressing scheme and a load factor of $\rho = 0.5$.

Again, it is interesting to note that this increase in speed is obtained at the expense of extra memory space. In this case the extra space is needed for the pointers in both the hash table and the nodes of the linked lists. If k, the number of keys, is 1000 and N, the table size, is 250 (and assuming that each integer and each pointer takes one cell), then the chaining method would require $(250 + 2 * 1000) = 2250$ cells. The open addressing method with $\rho = 0.5$ requires only 2000 cells, roughly 12% less space. However, both hashing methods use at least double the amount of space needed by either a sequential or a binary search, which is just the 1000 cells needed to store the data values themselves.

We leave the implementation of the chaining collision-resolution algorithm of Figure 9–12 as an exercise.

As a conclusion to our discussion on hashing, let us see what would happens if we use this method to store the 50,000 word spelling checker dictionary we discussed in chapter 8. If we use the open addressing method for collision resolution, we know that performance is highly dependent on the load factor of the table. For occupancy rates $\rho > 0.8$ performance will degrade to logarithmic. For $\rho > 0.98$ hashing will approximate linear behavior, which we already know is unacceptable for meeting performance specifications. Unfortunately space was already tight in our example array at 714K. Leaving 20% of our hash table vacant would require a memory allocation of $714K/0.80 \cong 890$ Kbyte of memory, which would probably exceed the capacity of our system. Even 10% vacant space would still require an additional 71K. In this example, the space demands of open address hashing are probably excessive.

Instead of open addressing, we could use a chaining scheme with an array of M pointers and about $50{,}000/M$ dictionary words per linked list.

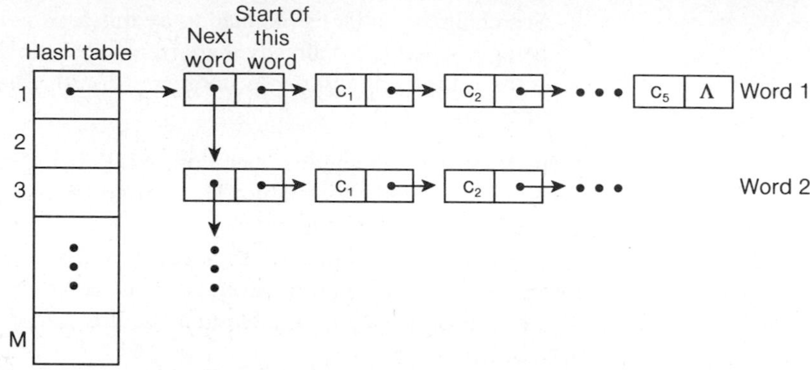

Our access time will consist of one access to the M-element hash table, followed by a search of about half of the $(50{,}000/M)$ words that hashed to that location, and finally a search of, on the average, about two or three characters per word to determine that we do not have the desired key. We assumed that each character comparison required 3 μsec and that there were 300 words per page, so this scheme would require

$$(1 + (50{,}000/2M) * 2.5) * 3 * 10^{-6} * 300$$

seconds to spell check a page of 300 words. For $M = 100$, this is about 0.6 seconds per page, which is acceptable performance and meets our required specifications. Unfortunately, like the linked list technique we investigated, the chaining scheme has a space rather than a time problem, and we would be overwhelmed by the number of pointers used by the chaining algorithm. The hash table itself requires M pointer variables, the head pointers require two pointer variables each, and the nodes require one pointer per character. The total number of pointers is:

$$M + 2(50{,}000) + (50{,}000 * 5)$$

For $M = 100$, the total number of pointers would be 350,100; at three bytes per pointer, we would need 1.05 Mbytes, exceeding the total memory capacity of our system. There are ways to reduce this number, such as storing more than one character per character node as we did in chapter 8. We will leave this and other techniques for improving the efficiency of hashing in the spelling checker application, as an exercise.

It is interesting to note that in this example, the space demands of hashing outweighed the speed gains that the method provided and hashing did not appear to be the optimal choice. In the next section we will look at an example in which hashing is superior to other techniques for representing search tables and is the preferred method.

9.3 CASE STUDY: SYMBOL TABLES FOR BLOCK-STRUCTURED PROGRAMMING LANGUAGES

A *symbol table* is one of the most important structures created by a compiler during the translation of a language like Pascal, Ada, or Modula-2 to machine code. A symbol table is a data structure that associates the name of a symbol with a collection of *attributes* or characteristics bound to or associated with that name. The specific attributes kept in the table vary with the language being translated, but the table includes the following types of information:

a. The type of object this name represents—procedure, function, data type, variable, or constant
b. For a composite data type such as an array or record, its parameters—for example, array bounds, base type, or number of fields
c. For a simple variable or constant, its data type—for example, real, integer, or Boolean
d. The actual memory location or locations inside the machine that have been assigned to hold the value of this variable

In this case study we will make some simplifying assumptions to keep the example to a manageable length. First, we assume that the only objects stored in our symbol table are simple variables; it will contain no composite variables, procedure or function names, new data types, or constants. Second, the only attributes stored in the symbol table will be the data type of the simple variable and the memory address assigned to it by the memory manager.

If we assume that memory for variables is allocated beginning at memory address 1000 and that each variable occupies two locations, then the following declaration

```
Var
    x : Integer;
    y : Real;
    z : Boolean;
```

would produce the symbol table:

Symbol table

Name	Type	Address
x	Integer	1000
y	Real	1002
z	Boolean	1004
⋮	⋮	⋮

The compiler will use this symbol table during translation in two ways:

1. It checks that we are not incorrectly mixing variables of different data types, as, for example, in the assignment statement

   $y := y + z$

   The type fields of y and z in the symbol table shown above contain Real and Boolean, respectively. These two types are incompatible under the operator +, and we could properly flag this statement as containing a syntax error.
2. It translates references to symbols in a high-level language into the corresponding references to memory locations in machine language. Thus the assignment statement

   $x := 0;$

   would be translated into something like the following machine code

   ```
   MOVE #0, @#1000;   (* Move the constant 0 to the memory address 1000,
                         which is the location of the variable x. *)
   ```

   The memory location 1000 was determined by retrieving the address field value of the symbol table entry for x.

Thus, the primary operations on symbol tables are (1) inserting a new (name, type, address) record in the table when we encounter a **Var** declaration and (2) retrieving a record from the table whenever we reference a symbol within the program. The name and type values for the insert operation come directly from the **Var** declaration. The address value is assigned by the software component called a *memory manager*, which parcels out memory cells and collects them when they are no longer in use. (This program was already discussed in the case study in chapter 4.)

There are several reasons why hashing is an ideal method to use in this particular application:

1. The operations we wish to carry out on the symbol table—insertion and retrieval—are exactly the operations that hashing can do efficiently.
2. Retrieval is by key (the key is the symbol name) rather than by array index. Because this name will be unique within the individual program unit, it can be used as the retrieval key.
3. Space should not be a problem. Unlike the dictionary in chapter 8 with 50,000 words, a program (even a large one) generally does not have more than a few hundred or at most a few thousand symbols. Therefore, leaving at least 20% of the table vacant to improve performance should not be a problem.

Because of these characteristics, hashing is by far the most popular technique for implementing symbol tables within a compiler, and it is the method we will use in this case study.

We must make three important decisions prior to implementing our symbol table package:

1. Choice of the hash function
2. Choice of the collision resolution method
3. Selection of the hash table size

Our hash function *h* must scatter the keys uniformly about the table. One popular method of hashing on keys that are sequences of characters is called *folding*. With folding we do not treat the key as a single primitive element but rather as a collection of elements. We perform randomizing operations on each individual element and then combine these individual values into a final hash value. For example, if our keys had the following structure

```
Const
    Max = . . . ;                  (* Maximum length of symbol names in our
                                      language *)

Var
    Name : Array [1 .. Max] Of Char; (* The symbol *)
    L    : 1 .. Max;                 (* Actual length of the symbol *)
```

then our hash function *h* for a table size of *N* might be

$$h(\text{Name}) = \left[\sum_{i=1}^{L} \text{Ord}(\text{Name}[i])\right] \textbf{ Mod } N + 1$$

in which we sum up the internal ASCII values of each letter in the symbol name. (We assume that the Ord function returns the internal integer value of its character argument.) Other possibilities for hash functions might include:

$$h(\text{Name}) = \left[\sum_{i=1}^{L} W_i * \text{Ord}(\text{Name}[i])\right] \textbf{ Mod } N + 1 \qquad \text{(* } W_i \text{ are constants *)}$$

$$h(\text{Name}) = \left[\prod_{i=1}^{L} \text{Ord}(\text{Name}[i])\right] \textbf{ Mod } N + 1 \qquad \text{(* } \Pi \text{ is the product indicator *)}$$

Determining which of these functions would work best for us requires extensive testing and evaluation. We should implement each function and test it on a large number of typical keys (e.g., names taken from existing programs) and then analyze the results using statistical measures of randomness. We should also measure the time needed to evaluate each function. On most machines, hardware multiplication is significantly slower than addition, usually by a factor of two to five; thus our second and third hash functions, which require L distinct multiplications, might both be prohibitively slow. After analyzing the scattering and timing properties, we would select the hash function that produced the best scattering of keys in the least amount of time. For this case study, we will use the first hash function listed above:

$$h(\text{Name}) = \left[\sum_{i=1}^{L} \text{Ord}(\text{Name}[i])\right] \textbf{ Mod } N + 1$$

Using this function, the variable name XYSum5 would be hashed as follows for a hash table of size $N = 25$:

Letter	*ASCII Value*
X	88
Y	89
S	84
u	109
m	117
5	52

$$\text{Total} = 539$$
$$h(\text{XYSum5}) = (539 \textbf{ Mod } 25) + 1$$
$$= 15$$

and the variable XYSum5 would hash to location 15 in our symbol table. Our second decision involves the collision resolution strategy. The chaining method looks very attractive for our needs because of its characteristic that the total number of keys stored in the table, k, can be greater than N, the table size. With open addressing, the table size is limited. If we used open addressing and a table size of 100, a program with 101 symbols would not compile and would halt with the fatal error called "symbol table overflow." If we made the table size very large, say $N = 2000$, then we would be wasting a good deal of space when we compile small- and medium-sized programs. With a chaining technique and a table size of N, we will have about k/N keys per linked list.

The average number of comparisons needed to retrieve a key from our chained hash table will be $1 + k/2N$. The number needed to insert a new key will be $2 + k/N$. If we know the approximate number of keys we expect to store in our table, we can pick our table size N to give us reasonable behavior. The average number of comparisons needed to retrieve a key from a table containing $k = 100$ keys is graphed in Figure 9–13 as a function of the table size N.

For example, if we will have on the average 100 keys and we want our hash table retrieval method to perform at least twice as fast as binary search (which would require $\log_2 100 \approx 7$ comparisons) then we should create a table of size $N = 25$. This table size will require an average of $1 + 100/(2 * 25) = 3$ comparisons per retrieve.

Figure 9–13
Retrieval Performance of Our Hash Table

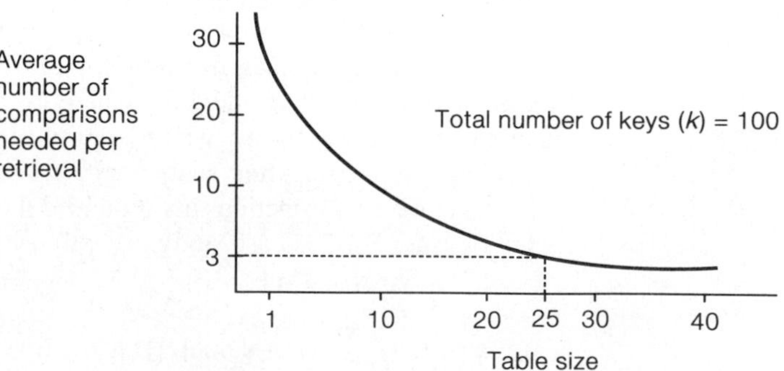

Looking at the memory space requirements, we calculate that the total number of bytes needed to store the hash table plus all of the nodes in the linked list is

$$(N * p) + k\,(\text{Max} + \text{Size(TypeField)} + \text{Size(AddressField)} + p)$$

where N is the hash table size, p is the number of bytes per pointer variable, k is the number of keys stored in our table, Size is a function that returns the number of bytes needed to store a TypeField or an AddressField, and Max is the maximum length of a symbol (in bytes).

For typical values of $p = 3$, $N = 25$, $k = 200$, and Max $= 32$ (and assuming that the TypeField takes one byte and the AddressField takes 3 bytes), the total amount of memory needed is:

$$\begin{aligned}\text{Memory space} &= (25 * 3) + 200\,(32 + 1 + 3 + 6)\\ &= 75 + 8{,}400\\ &= 8{,}475 \text{ bytes}\end{aligned}$$

This amount of memory space is quite small and should, unlike the dictionary of chapter 8, cause no concern.

We are now ready to design and implement a complete symbol table package. We will use the chaining method and a hash table size of $N = 25$. Our hash function will be

$$h(\text{Name}) = \left[\sum_{i=1}^{L} \text{Ord}(\text{Name}[i])\right] \textbf{ Mod } N + 1$$

and we will keep three pieces of information for each symbol:

a. The symbol *name*, in an array of 1 to 15 characters (we assume that symbols can have at most 15 characters).
b. The *type* of the symbol, which is given by the user-defined type

   SymbolType = (Integer, Real, Boolean, Character)

c. The *address* of the symbol. The address is a nonnegative integer value in the range [0 .. AddressMax]. This value is provided by a routine called MemoryManager, which is not specified here.

The three operations in our symbol table package are shown below (T is an object of type SymbolTable):

a. CreateSymbolTable() : T

   This operation creates and initializes an empty symbol table.

b. Insert(T, Symbol, Type) : T

   This operation adds Symbol, its Type, and its address value to the table T using the chaining method. (The address is provided by MemoryManager, which is invoked by Insert.)

c. Retrieve(T, Symbol) : Type, Address, Found

This routine searches the symbol table T to see if the specified Symbol occurs. If it does not, then Found is set to False and Type and Address are undefined. If the Symbol does occur in the symbol table T, then Found is set to True and the Type and Address fields of the symbol are returned.

A complete symbol table package that implements these function is shown in Figure 9–14.

We have one issue left to resolve before we complete this case study—the problem of supporting symbol definitions in block-structured languages like Pascal, Ada, or Modula-2. In languages like these, variables have a *scope*—a region of the program in which they are known and can be referenced. Typically this scope is the block containing the **Var** declarations for that variable plus all blocks properly nested inside that block. For example, let's look at the following nested structure:

```
Procedure X;
    Var A : Integer;
    Procedure Y;
        Var B : Integer;
            •
            •
            •
        Procedure Z;
            Var C : Integer;
                •
                •
                •  ← point 3
        End Z;
            •
            •
            •  ← point 2
    End Y;
        •
        •
        •  ← point 1
End X;
```

At point 1, we can reference only the variable A, since that is the only variable declared in the current block. At point 2 we can access both A and B, B because it was declared in the current block and A because it was declared in an outer block that encloses the current block. At point 3 we can access all three variables, A, B, and C.

To support a block-structured language, we must make some additions to our symbol table package of Figure 9–14. Simply inserting variables into a symbol table is no longer sufficient. We must also be able to *remove* variables declared in a scope

Figure 9–14
Symbol Table Abstract Data Type

```
(* The following module implements a symbol table, as described in the case
      study for chapter 9. It assumes that the memory manager has already
      been initialized, so that calls to Allocate will be meaningful. It also
      assumes that the memory manager will not run out of memory.   *)
Module SymbolTablePackage;

From MemoryManager Import
      AddressType,                (* The data type for memory addresses *)
      Allocate;                   (* Function to allocate a block of memory *)

From ErrorSystem Import
      ErrorHandler;               (* Function to handle error conditions *)

From UserModule Import
      HashSymbol,                 (* Function to return the hash value of a symbol *)
      Length,                     (* Function to return the length of a symbol *)
      SizeOf,                     (* Function to return the amount of memory to
                                        store a data value of a given type *)
      SymbolNameType,             (* The data type for symbol names *)
      SymbolType;                 (* The data type for the type of a symbol *)

Const
   SymTabSize          =          25;        (* The size of the symbol table *)

Type
   SymbolTableType     =          Pointer To SymbolTableRecord;
   SymbolTableRecord   =          Array [1 .. SymTabSize] Of SymbolNodePtr;
   SymbolNodePtr       =          Pointer To SymbolNode;
   SymbolNode          =          Record
                                         Name          : SymbolNameType;
                                         Length        : Integer;
                                         Type          : SymbolType;
                                         Address       : AddressType;
                                         Next          : SymbolNodePtr;
                                  End;

(*  Precondition: None
    Postcondition:     A new, empty symbol table is returned.   *)
Procedure CreateSymbolTable () : SymbolTableType;
Var
   NewTable          : SymbolTableType;
   i                 : Integer;
Begin
   New(NewTable);                 (* Allocate space for the array of head pointers *)

   For i := 1 To SymTabSize Do
      NewTable^[i] := Nil;        (* Set each head pointer to Nil *)
   Endfor;

End CreateSymbolTable;

(*  Precondition: None
    Postcondition:     Symbol is added to Table, with the attribute Type, and
                       some address assigned by the memory manager.   *)
Procedure Insert ( Var Table : SymbolTableType;
                       Symbol : SymbolNameType; Type : SymbolType );
```

(continued)

Figure 9–14 (continued)

```
Var
    h               : Integer;
    type            : SymbolType;
    addr            : AddressType;
    NewNode         : SymbolNodePtr;
Begin

    If (Retrieve(Table, Symbol, type, addr)) Then
        (* If Retrieve succeeds in finding Symbol, then this Symbol
            has previously been inserted into Table, so it is an error. *)
        ErrorHandler();

    Else (* Symbol has not been previously inserted in Table *)
        New(NewNode);                       (* Allocate space for the new symbol *)
        NewNode^.Name := Symbol;            (* And set the fields in the node *)
        NewNode^.Length := Length(Symbol);
        NewNode^.Type := Type;
            (* Allocate space for the value *)
        NewNode^.Address := Allocate(SizeOf(Type));
        h := HashSymbol(Symbol);
            (* Insert new node at the beginning of the list *)
        NewNode^.Next := Table^[h];
        Table^[h] := NewNode;
    Endif;

End Insert;

(*  Precondition: None
    Postcondition:   If Symbol is in Table, Type and Address are set to
                         the type and address associated with Symbol,
                         and True is returned.
                     Otherwise, the values of Type and Address are
                         unchanged,and False is returned.   *)
Procedure Retrieve ( Table : SymbolTableType; Symbol: SymbolNameType;
        Var Type : SymbolType; Var Address : AddressType ) : Boolean;
Var
    Search        : SymbolNodePtr;
Begin
    Search := Table^[HashSymbol(Symbol)];

        (* Search the list with the given hash value for the correct symbol *)
    While (Search <> Nil) And (Search^.Name <> Symbol) Do
        Search := Search^.Next;
    Endwhile;

    If (Search = Nil) Then
        (* Searched the entire list, it wasn't there *)
        Return False;
    Else
        (* Found it, so return the relevant information *)
        Type := Search^.Type;
        Address := Search^.Address;
        Return True;
    Endif;
End Retrieve;

End SymbolTablePackage.
```

block when that block is exited. For example, when we exit procedure Z, the symbol C, along with all its attributes, must be removed from the symbol table because it is no longer accessible.

We must also be able to control the *order* of the search for a symbol in the symbol table. The following declarations

```
Procedure X;
    Var A : Integer;
        •
        •
        •
    Procedure Y;
        Var A : Real;
```

are an example of a *name conflict*, in which two distinct variables share the same name. A name conflict is legal in most languages even though it violates the rule of set structures that says that the search keys in the search table must be unique. In most languages, e.g., Pascal, Ada and Modula-2, a reference to a symbol is always a reference to the innermost definition of that symbol. Therefore, within procedure Y, any reference to A should be interpreted as a reference to the local real variable, not the global integer variable.

Now let's extend our Symbol Table package of Figure 9–14 to support block-structured languages to include the following characteristics:

a. Insertion and removal of symbols as scope units are entered and exited
b. Duplicate keys
c. Controlled order of search from the innermost to the outermost scope unit

We can add these features very simply by taking advantage of the fact that scope units are entered and exited during compilation in a strictly last-in/first-out order. We do not allow overlapping of procedures or blocks as in

```
Procedure X        (* This is illegal. *)
Procedure Y
End X
End Y
```

Therefore, a stack of pointers to separate symbol tables for each scope unit would be an excellent way to manage our block-structured symbol table. Such a stack is usually referred to as a *scope stack*. The symbol table pointed to by the top of the scope stack would be the symbol table for the current scope unit.

When the compiler recognizes a new scope unit, as in

```
Procedure X;
```

it creates a new (empty) symbol table using the routine CreateSymbolTable of Figure 9–14, and it pushes a pointer to this new symbol table on top of the scope stack. When the compiler encounters declarations for new symbols, such as

```
Var
    A,B : Integer;
```

it inserts these symbols into the symbol table pointed to by the top of the stack. This insertion will be made by the Insert routine already provided by our SymbolTable ADT in Figure 9–14. Finally, when the compiler sees the end of a scope unit

```
End X;
```

it pops the scope stack, which effectively discards the current symbol table.

Figure 9–15b shows an example of this scope stack when the compiler has reached point P of the program in Figure 9–15a. Notice that in Figure 9–15 the order of the symbol tables in the scope stack is the reverse order of their nesting structure—Z, X, W. Also notice that there is no symbol table for procedure Y because it has already been exited.

Now, when the compiler encounters a reference to a symbol such as

```
A := C + 1;
```

at point P in Figure 9–15a, it must look up the symbols A and C and return their attributes. It begins the search with the symbol table pointed to by the top of the scope stack (in this case, the table for scope unit Z). It searches that table using the retrieval algorithm given in Figure 9–14. If it finds the symbol (it will find A),

Figure 9–15
A Scope Stack

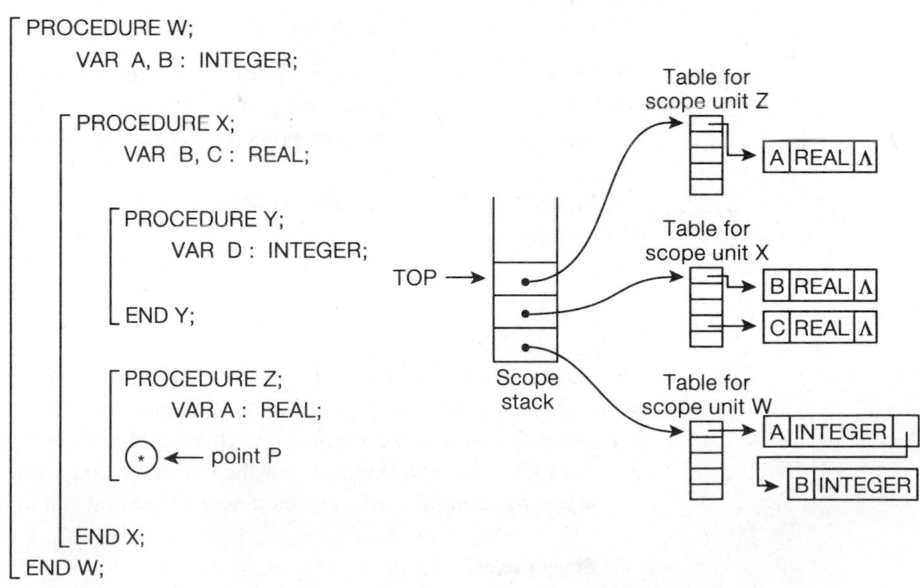

it uses the attributes that it retrieves for that symbol. In this case A will be treated as a local Real variable. No problems are caused by the second declaration of A in the outer block W, because the symbol table containing that declaration was never searched.

When the compiler searches for the symbol C, it does not find it in the topmost symbol table of the stack, so it begins to search the other tables in the order they appear on the stack—Top-1, Top-2, ... This order corresponds to searching the scope units from the innermost to the outermost units, exactly as desired. The declaration for C will be found in the symbol table for scope unit X, and the compiler will retrieve the attributes for that declaration. No problems are caused by referring at point P to a global variable declared in an outer unit.

A complete Scope Stack package that provides the block-structuring capabilities we have just described is shown in Figure 9–16. The package provides four operations to create and manage the scope stack:

a. S := CreateScopeStack() — Create a new scope stack S and initialize it to empty.

b. PushNewTable(S,T) — Push a pointer to the new empty symbol table T on top of scope stack S. This operation essentially opens a new scope.

c. PopTable(S) — Discard the pointer on top of scope stack S and return the space used by the symbol table. This operation closes the current scope.

d. T := RetrieveTable(S,*i*) — Return the symbol table that is *i* positions below the table currently on top of the scope stack; if $i = 0$, the symbol table of the current scope is returned.

Figure 9–16
Scope Stack Package

```
(* The following module contains the implementation of the scope stack
     as described in the case study in chapter 9.  *)
Module ScopeStackPackage;

From SymbolTablePackage Import
          SymbolTableType;

Type
     ScopeStackType          =   Pointer To ScopeStackRecord;
     ScopeStackRecord        =   Record
                                      SymTab      : SymbolTableType;
                                      Next        : ScopeStackType;
                                 End;

(*   Precondition: None
     Postcondition:    A new, empty Scope Stack is returned.  *)
Procedure CreateScopeStack () : ScopeStackType;
Begin
     Return Nil;
End CreateScopeStack;
```

(continued)

Figure 9–16 (continued)

```
(*  Precondition: None
    Postcondition:   The symbol table Table is made the topmost element
                        of scope stack Stack.  *)
Procedure PushNewTable ( Var Stack : ScopeStackType; Table : SymbolTableType );
Var
    NewNode          : ScopeStackType;
Begin
    New(NewNode);                   (* Set up a new scope record *)
    NewNode^.SymTab := Table;
    NewNode^.Next := Stack;         (* And place it on top of the stack *)
    Stack := NewNode;
End PushNewTable;

(*  Precondition: There must be at least one Symbol Table in Stack.
    Postcondition:   If the precondition is met, the topmost Symbol Table
                        is removed from the stack.
                     Otherwise, nothing happens.  *)
Procedure PopTable ( Var Stack : ScopeStackType );
Var
    Temp        : ScopeStackType;
Begin
    If (Stack <> Nil) Then          (* If there are any Symbol Tables in the stack, *)
        Temp := Stack;              (* Remove the first *)
        Stack := Stack^.Next;       (* And make the head pointer point to the next *)
        Dispose(Temp);
    Endif;
End PopTable;

(*  Precondition: Stack contains at least (Index + 1) Symbol Tables
    Postcondition:   If the precondition is met, the Symbol Table which is
                        Index scopes under the current scope is returned.
                        i.e. for the current scope, Index = 0, the immediate
                        enclosing scope, Index = 1, etc.
                     If the precondition is not met, the result is undefined. *)
Procedure RetrieveTable ( Stack : ScopeStackType;
                          Index : Integer ) : SymbolTableType;
Begin
                                (* Locate the correct scope *)
    While ((Stack <> Nil) And (Index > 0) Do
        Index := Index - 1;
        Stack := Stack^.Next;
    Endwhile;

    Return Stack^.SymTab;   (* And return the symbol table associated with it *)
End RetrieveTable;

End ScopeStackPackage.
```

Within an individual symbol table T, we use the symbol table routines Insert and Retrieve provided by the package shown in Figure 9–14.

We can now describe exactly what our compiler must do when it encounters the various types of syntactic constructs found in typical block-structured languages:

1. At the very beginning of compilation:

```
S := CreateScopeStack()          (* Create a new scope stack *)
```

2. When it encounters a **Procedure** declaration:

```
T := CreateSymbolTable();          (* Create an empty symbol table. *)
PushNewTable(S,T)                (* Make this table the current scope. *)
```

3. When it encounters an **End Procedure** statement:

```
PopTable(S)                      (* Close the current scope. *)
```

4. When it encounters a **Var** symbol : type; declaration:

```
T := RetrieveTable(S, 0);          (* Get symbol table for the current scope. *)
Insert(T, symbol, type)            (* Insert this new symbol. *)
```

5. When the program references a symbol:

```
i := 0
Loop
    T := RetrieveTable(S,i)              (* Fetch the next scope table*)
    Found := Retrieve(T,symbol,type,address) (* See if the symbol is in
                                                    that table. *)
    If Found Then Exit                   (*Yes, it is. *)
    i := i + 1                           (*It is not. Go on to next scope table. *)
    If i > StackSize Then Exit           (*Until we reach the outer block. *)
End Loop
```

This technique is used by compilers for existing block-structured languages such as Pascal, Modula-2, and Ada. It demonstraties the Search Table structure of section 9.2 as well as the Stack ADT first introduced in chapter 3.

9.4 CONCLUSION

Along with sorting, searching a table is one of the most common and frequently performed operations in computer science. In this chapter we studied the hash table, a data structure based on the principle of sets and that provides an extremely efficient way to search a collection of values. Under optimal operating conditions, hashing can insert values into a table and retrieve values from a table in O(1) time.

This new representation and the examples of its use demonstrate an important principle in computer science and software development: Specifically, no single data representation is the best in all possible situations. For example, we showed that limitations on available memory space may prevent us from taking advantage of the full power of the hashing method, as happened when we tried to use hashing to store the dictionary for our spelling checker. However, in the symbol table case study, which had a completely different set of characteristics, hashing worked just fine. As another example, consider the sequential search algorithm. In most cases it is horribly inefficient and provides unacceptable performance; however, for small problems, e.g., $N < 100$, it may actually be the best technique available.

These examples illustrate the need for the computer scientist to be familiar with a large number of different data structures and algorithms. Then he or she will be able to evaluate a range of alternative representations and determine which technique will perform best for a given problem.

CHAPTER EXERCISES

1. Assume

   A = {5, 10, 15, 20}
   B = {1, 2, 3, 4, 5}
   C = {6, 8, 10}
   D = {}

   What is the value of:

   a. A ∪ B   g. A–B
   b. A ∪ C   h. B–A
   c. A ∪ D   i. Empty (D)
   d. A ∩ B   j. Member (C,6)
   e. A ∩ D   k. Member (D,0)
   f. B ∩ C   l. Subset (B,A)

2. Define the syntax and semantics of a new set operation $S_1, S_2 \rightarrow S_3$, in which S_3 contains all elements that are in either set S_1 or set S_2 but not in both; that is, ·

   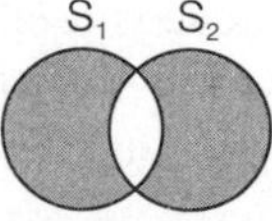

   The shaded portion is S_3. Can this new operation have been defined in terms of the existing set operations described in Figure 9–3?

3. Describe in your own words what each of the nine semantic axioms in Figure 9–2b says about the behavior of the set structure.

4. How would you rewrite the procedure Intersection of Figure 9–4 if the elements of the two sets S_1 and S_2 were integers sorted into ascending order? What would be the time complexity of your procedure?

5. Assume that our sets are stored as a linked list using the following declarations

```
Type
    SetNode = Record
        Data : SetElement;
        Next: SetPointer
              End;
    SetPointer = Pointer To SetNode;
Var
    S1, S2, S3 : SetPointer;
```

   Implement the operation Union (S1, S2, S3) using this linked list representation.
6. Assume we are using a bit vector implementation for sets over the base type [0 .. 10]. Show the internal representation of each of the following sets:
   a. {2, 4, 6, 8, 10}
   b. {0, 1, 2, 3, 4, 6, 7, 8, 9, 10}
   c. {}
7. What would be our mapping function *f* if we wanted to store sets of uppercase characters ['A' . . 'Z'] internally as bit vectors?
8. Using the bit vector implementation of sets of uppercase letter from exercise 7, implement the routine

   Equal (S1,S2)

   which determines if the sets S1 and S2 are identical, that is, if every element that is a member of S1 is a member of S2, and every element that is a member of S2 is a member of S1.
9. Show the internal hardware organization of the bit vector implementation of sets of uppercase characters ['A' .. 'Z']. Assume the word size of your computer is $M = 8$. Give the functions that map a bit vector element S[I] into the correct word W and bit position B in your hardware representation.
10. Is the hardware implementation described in Figure 9–6c the lowest level of abstraction of computer systems? If not, what do you think would be the next level of detail, and what would be the important conceptual points of that level?
11. Express in natural language the meaning of each of the seven axioms specified for the Search Table in Figure 9–7.
12. Write the internal module for the SearchTable ADT shown in Figure 9–8. Use the array-based implementation whose declarations are given in section 9.2.2. Keep the array elements in unordered sequence and use sequential search to locate keys.
13. Translate the open addressing algorithms of Figure 9–11 into a syntactically correct internal module.
14. a. Given a hash table of eight elements (with indices running from 0 to 7), show how the following keys would be stored using hashing, open addressing, and a step size of $c = 1$; that is, if there is a collision, we search sequentially for the next available slot. Assume that the hash function

is just the ordinal position of the letter in the alphabet modulo 8 (i.e., $h(\text{a}) = 0$, $h(\text{b}) = 1, \ldots, h(\text{h}) = 7$, $h(\text{i}) = 0$).

d, e, l, t, g, h, q

b. Repeat the exact same operation, but with a step size $c = 3$.

15. Why must the step size c be relatively prime with the table size N? (Relatively prime means sharing no common factors.) What happens if our table size is 10 (indexed 0 to 9) and our step size is $c = 4$ or $c = 5$?
16. With a table of size $N = 50{,}000$, after how many insertion operations does hashing with open addressing display about the same behavior as binary search? sequential search?
17. One problem with open addressing is the issue of *deletions*. We are not allowed to delete entries in a hash table that uses open addressing for collision resolution. If we had a 10-element hash table that held values in the range [1 .. 100] and used open addressing and the following hash function

    $h(\text{key}) = [\text{key } \textbf{Mod } 10] + 1$

    show exactly what would happen if we executed the following sequence of five operations

    a. Insert (T,10) (* Insert the value 10. *)
    b. Insert (T,20) (* Insert the value 20. *)
    c. Insert (T,30) (* Insert the value 30. *)
    d. Delete (T,20) (* Remove the value 20. *)
    e. Retrieve (T,30) (* Retrieve the value 30, which is still there. *)

    Exactly what happened? Is there any way to solve this problem? If so, describe your solution and implement the Delete operation.
18. Using the data and hash function from exercise 14a, and a table size of $N = 8$, show what the hash table would look like after insertion of those seven letters if we used the chaining technique rather than open addressing.
19. Implement the chaining algorithms shown in Figure 9–12.
20. Assume we are using chaining and want to store approximately 100 keys into our table. About how large should we make our hash table to reduce the average number of comparisons needed for a retrieval operation to four or less? How much space will be required for the table as well as the 100 keys, compared to keeping the 100 keys in an array?
21. Determine whether there is a way to use hashing to implement the dictionary data structure and meet both the time and space specifications given in the problem description in chapter 8.
22. Implement the following hash function:

    $$h(\text{key}) = \left[\sum_{i=1}^{\text{Len(key)}} c_i * \text{Letter}[i]\right] \text{Mod } N + 1$$

    where c_i are constants, Letter(i) is the ASCII value of the ith letter of the key, Len(key) is the length of the key in characters, and N is the table size.

Apply your hash function to a collection of 200 random keys of varying length and a table size $N = 20$. See how well your hash function scatters by applying some statistical test for randomness, such as the Chi-Square Goodness of Fit Test.

23. Implement a variation of the chaining method in which each entry in the hash table is a pointer to the *root* of a binary search tree containing all entries that hashed to that location. The structure of the hash table would look like:

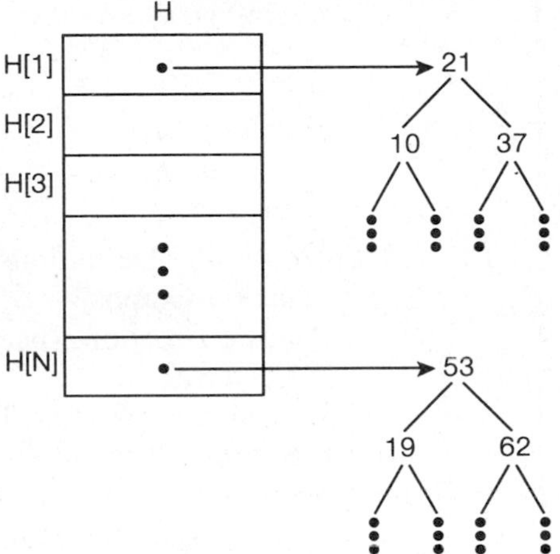

Implement the internal module that uses this method. What is the expected number of comparisons needed to insert and retrieve a value using this representation?

24. Explain how you would modify the symbol table structure of the case study to support
    a. Composite data structures such as arrays
    b. Dynamic variables whose memory addresses are allocated during execution using the New function and released using Dispose

CHAPTER 10

GRAPH STRUCTURES

CHAPTER OUTLINE

10.1 INTRODUCTION AND DEFINITIONS

This chapter will complete our introduction to the four classes of data structures that we first diagrammed in Figure 3–1.

A graph is the most generalized of all data representations. Sets, linear structures, and hierarchical structures can all be treated as specialized graph structures in which the number and nature of the connections between nodes have been restricted in some way.

Formally, a *graph* is a data structure in which the component elements can be structurally related to any arbitrary number of other elements. That is, a graph is a (many : many) data structure in which each component of the graph can have an arbitrary number of successors and an arbitrary number of predecessors. The two fundamental types of graphs are shown in Figure 10–1.

A graph consists of a set of N ($N \geq 1$) information units called *nodes* or *vertices*. In Figure 10–1a and b, the nodes are labeled A, B, C, D, E, and F. The information stored in a node can be of any type and can contain an arbitrary number of fields. For simplicity, we will usually limit the data values in a node to a single character or a single digit, as we did in Figure 10–1. The nodes are connected to each other by a set of arcs called *edges*. An edge connecting node n_i to node n_j will be written as $<n_i, n_j>$, and the set of edges will be referred to as $E = \{<n_i, n_j>, <n_k, n_l>, \ldots\}$. If the edges have a direction associated with them, then the graph is called a *directed graph* or sometimes a *digraph*; an example is shown in Figure 10–1a. If $<n_i, n_j>$ is an edge in a directed graph, then n_i is called the *tail* of the edge and n_j is called the *head* of the edge. We also say that node n_i is *adjacent to* or *incident to* node n_j.

If no direction is associated with an edge, then the structure is called an *undirected graph,* and the presence of an edge implies the existence of an arc in each direction. Such a structure is shown in Figure 10–1b. The following two graphs are equivalent and represent the set of edges $E = \{<A,B>, <B,A>\}$.

However, the two graphs shown on the top of the following page are not equivalent. The one on the left is an undirected graph containing an edge connecting A to B and B to A. The one on the right is a directed graph containing an edge connecting A to B but not B to A.

Figure 10–1
Two Fundamental Types of Graph Structures

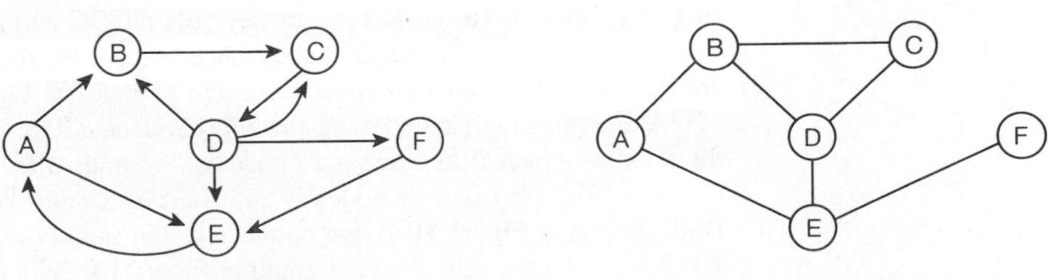

There can be only a single edge between any two nodes in a graph. Structures like the following one, in which there are two or more edges connecting the same nodes, are called *multigraphs*.

Multigraphs are not allowed in traditional graph structures, and they will not be discussed in this chapter.

In addition to being directed or undirected, edges can also be either *weighted* or *unweighted*. A weighted edge has a scalar value W associated with it, and it is written <A, B, W>; the weight is a measure of the *cost* of using this edge to go from node A to node B. For example,

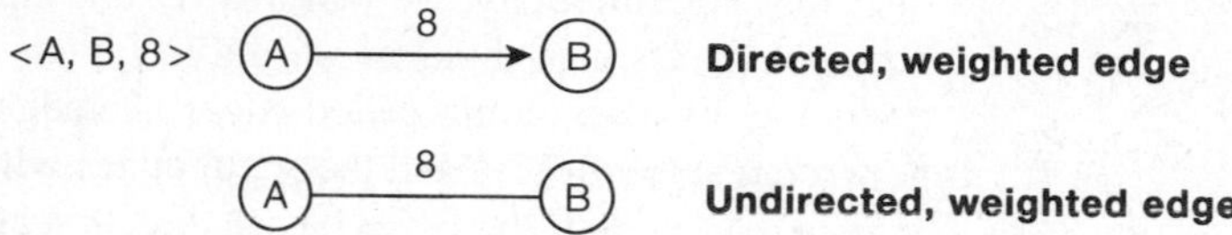

This notation indicates that traveling from A to B along this edge costs eight units. In the undirected case, eight units is also the cost of going from B to A. The weight could represent dollars, time, distance, effort, or any other measure of the consumption of resources. If the edges in a graph are unweighted, the cost of traversing an edge is the same for all edges. Alternatively, an unweighted graph could imply that there is no concept of cost associated with an edge.

A *simple path* through a graph is a sequence of nodes $n_1 n_2 n_3 \ldots n_k$ such that all nodes, except possibly the first and the last, are distinct and each pair of nodes $n_i\, n_{i+1}$, $i = 1, \ldots k - 1$ is connected by an edge. For example, referring to Figure 10–1a, the sequence ABCD is a simple path, so is DEABCD. However, ABE is not, since there is no edge directly connecting nodes B and E. Neither is BCDBC, since not all of the nodes are distinct (the nodes B and C appear twice in the sequence).

One special type of simple path is called a *cycle*. A cycle is a simple path $n_1 n_2 n_3 \ldots n_k$ exactly as defined above, but with the added requirement that $n_1 = n_k$. Informally, a cycle is a path that begins at a node, visits any number of other nodes in the graph exactly once, and then ends up at the node where it began. Again referring to Figure 10–1a, BCDB is a cycle. So are CDC and ABCDFEA. A cycle that visits every node in the graph exactly once (except for the first and the last, which are the same) is called a *Hamiltonian cycle*.

A directed graph is said to be *strongly connected* if for every pair of nodes n_i, n_j, there exists a path from node n_i to node n_j. An undirected graph is said to be *connected* if for every pair of nodes n_i, n_j, there is a path connecting the two nodes. Both graphs in Figure 10–1 are connected, but neither of the structures in Figure 10–2 is connected. The directed graph in Figure 10–2a does not contain paths from B to A, from C to B, or from C to A. The undirected graph in Figure 10–2b contains

Figure 10–2
Examples of Unconnected Graphs

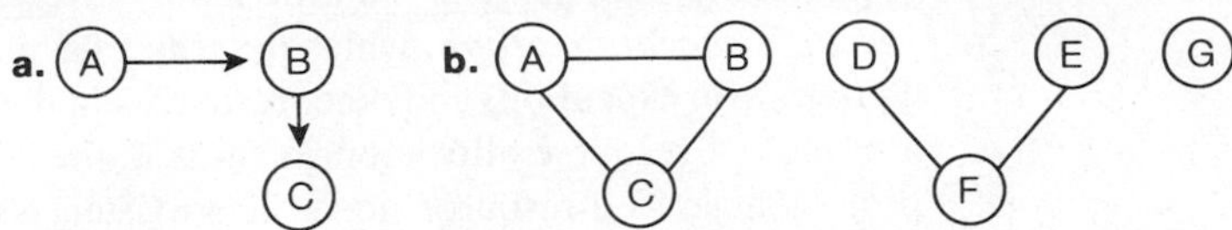

three sets of nodes, {A,B,C}, {D,E,F}, and {G}, that are connected among themselves but are disconnected from each other. These sets of nodes are called *connected subgraphs*. A *subgraph* G′ of a graph G is a graph G′ whose edges and nodes are subsets of the edges and nodes in G.

A tree can also be defined as a connected graph without any cycles (a slightly different definition from the one in chapter 7). Trees can thus be viewed as special types of graph structures.

Graphs occur often in real life, and we encounter them in a number of situations. For example, a road map showing the interstate highway connections between various cities is an excellent example of an undirected graph, since all interstate highways are two-way. We could also add weights to each edge to indicate the distance in miles between the two cities, producing a weighted undirected graph.

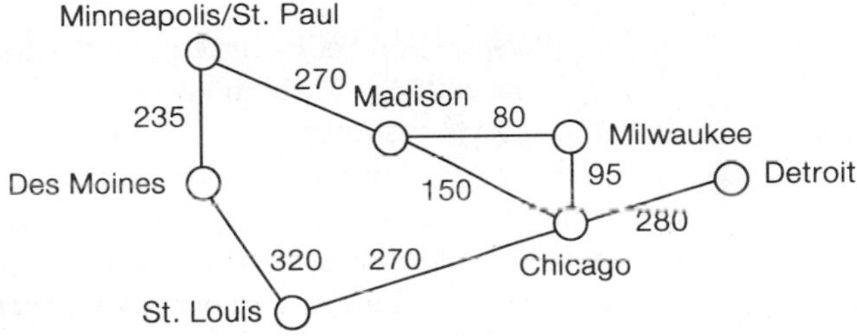

The sequence of courses that one must take to complete a degree in computer science can also be represented as a graph. It is a directed graph in which the direction of the edge implies the specific order in which the courses must be taken.

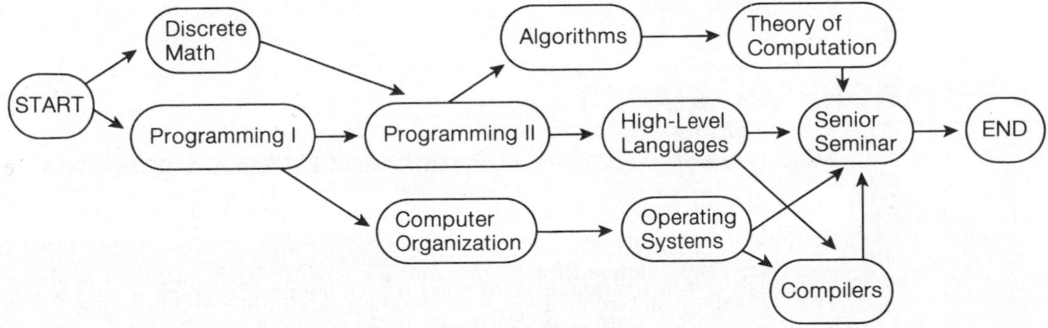

This graph contains no cycles; this type of graph structure is called a *directed acyclic graph* (DAG).

Another example that is a little more closely related to computer science is the *resource allocation graph*, which describes the relationship between a process (i.e., a program in execution) and other resources in the system such as memory, a file, or a printer. A resource allocation graph is a directed graph with edges going from a process node to a resource node. The existence of an edge <P,R> indicates that process P owns resource R.

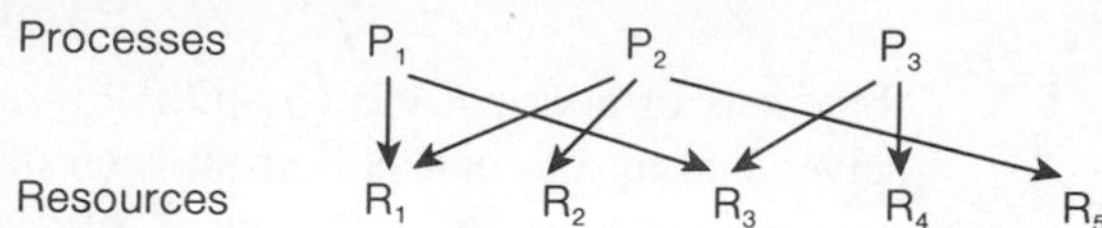

If a resource can be shared among a number of processes, then the graph can be weighted to indicate the number of units of shared resource R_i that have been allocated to process P_j.

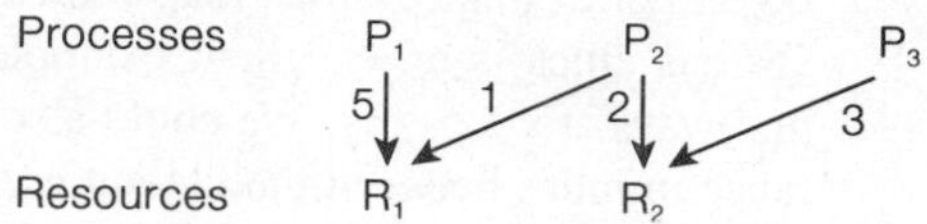

In this example, process P_1 currently holds five units of resource R_1, while process P_2 owns one unit. Similarly, processes P_2 and P_3 own two and three units, respectively, of shared resource R_2. Algorithms exist to take a resource allocation graph like those shown above and determine whether there is any possibility of a *deadlock* occurring; a deadlock is a condition in which processes are waiting to receive resources that will never become available.

A *computer network*, in which computers are interconnected via high speed communication channels such as phone lines, optical cables, microwave relays, or satellites, is another example of the use of graph structures in computer science. We can use a graph-based representation to determine how to route messages from one node to another and to find backup routes in case of node or line outages. We will discuss this particular use of graph structures in more detail in the case study at the end of the chapter.

10.2 OPERATIONS ON GRAPHS

10.2.1 Basic Creation, Insertion, and Deletion Operations

The five basic operations on graphs are graph creation, node insertion, node deletion, edge insertion, and edge deletion. (There are, of course, many other operations that can be defined for graphs, but for now we limit ourselves to these five.) The syntactic structure of these five operations is summarized in Figure 10–3. N is the set of all nodes and E is the set of all edges. Figure 10–3 assumes that the graph is directed and weighted. The description of these five operations for both undirected and unweighted graphs is left as an exercise.

Figure 10–3
The Five Basic Operations on Graphs

a. CreateGraph() : G

Create a new graph G, which is empty; that is, the set of all nodes and the set of all edges are empty.

N = {}, E = {}

b. InsertNode(G, n_i) : G

Add the node n_i to the graph G to produce a new graph G. The set of edges E is unaffected.

$N = N \cup \{n_i\}$

c. InsertEdge(G, n_i, n_j, W) : G

Add a directed edge connecting node n_i to n_j with weight W to the set E. It is assumed that there is currently no edge in E connecting n_i to n_j.

$E = E \cup \{<n_i, n_j, W>\}$

d. DeleteNode(G, n_i) : G

Delete node n_i from graph G, along with all edges that are adjacent to node n_i.

$N = N - \{n_i\}$ $E = E - (\{<n_i, x, W>\}$ and $\{<x, n_i, W>\})$ where x is any node in G.

e. DeleteEdge(G, n_i, n_j) : G

Delete the edge from node n_i to node n_j in Graph G.

$E = E - \{<n_i, n_j, W>\}$

With these five "building block" operations we can construct any arbitrary weighted, directed graph structure. For example, the following sequence of 11 operations

```
G := CreateGraph();
InsertNode (G,A);
InsertNode (G,B);
InsertNode (G,C);
InsertEdge (G,B,C,5)
InsertEdge (G,A,B,2)
InsertNode (G,D)
InsertEdge (G,A,D,6)
InsertEdge (G,B,D,7)
DeleteNode(G,C)
DeleteEdge(G,A,B)
```

would produce the following sequence of graph structures:

1. empty
2.  (A)
3. (A) (B)

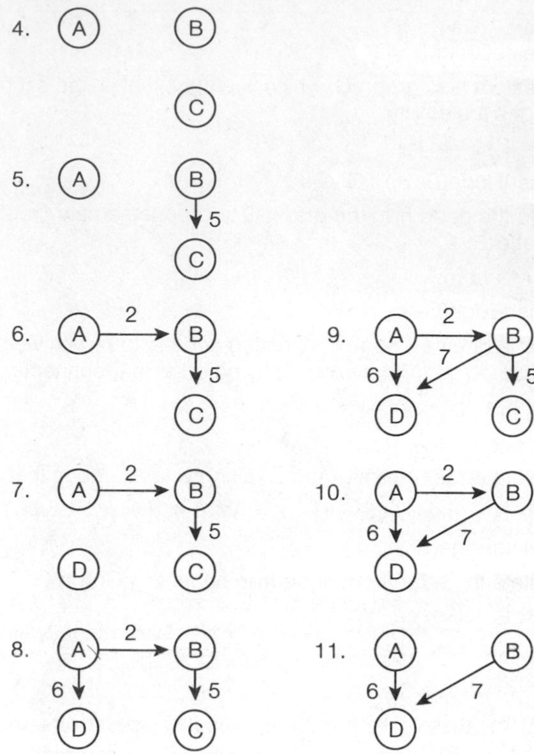

The five operations described in Figure 10–3 are the basic building blocks of the Graph abstract data type. However, the most important operations on graphs are not these simple low-level insertions and deletions, but the more complex, higher level operations that can be constructed from these five building blocks. We will look at some of these higher-level operations in the next three sections.

10.2.2 Traversal

As with trees, the most fundamental high-level operation on a graph is *traversal*, in which we attempt to visit every node in the graph structure exactly once. Graph traversal can form the basis for a number of other operations on graphs, such as searching for a given key or seeing if a graph is connected.

The two basic techniques for traversing a graph are *breadth-first* and *depth-first*. Informally, a breadth-first search means that after visiting node N, we visit all the nodes in the immediate neighborhood of N before moving on to visit nodes that are located further away. That is, we visit a node N and then visit the nodes adjacent to N. The order of the traversal is a series of expanding concentric circles in which we visit the nodes in circle i before moving on to the outer circle $i + 1$.

A depth-first search behaves quite differently. It follows a given path in the graph as far as it will lead. Only when that path has been exhausted (i.e., it dead-ends or cycles back to an earlier node) do we back up and begin to search another path.

Figure 10–4
Types of Graph Traversal

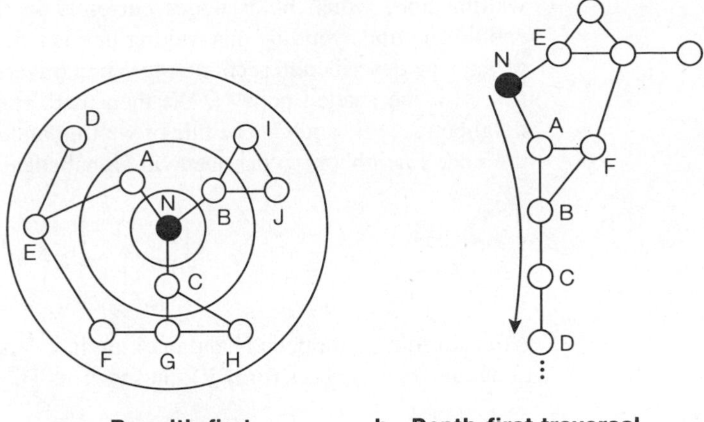

a. Breadth-first traversal **b. Depth-first traversal**

These two approaches are diagrammed in Figure 10–4, where we begin our traversal from the shaded node N in each case. In the breadth-first traversal of Figure 10–4a, we first visit the nodes adjacent to the shaded node, A, B, and C, before moving on to nodes further away such as D, E, F, G, or H. In the depth-first traversal of Figure 10–4b, we continue to follow the path ABCD . . . as far as it leads, even though there are closer nodes such as E or F.

There are two additional concerns that we must address before we can begin to flesh out these traversal algorithms more completely. First, a node N may be the neighbor of two or more nodes, as in

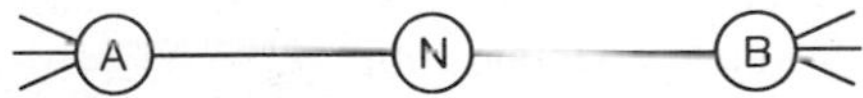

N may first be visited as a neighbor of A. When we visit node B later on, we do not want to visit its neighbor N again. We solve this problem by *marking* a node. Each node N will have a status value called Status(N), which can be one of three values:

Value	*Meaning*
Visited	This node has been visited, and its processing has been completed.
Waiting	A neighbor of this node has been visited, and this node is currently in line waiting to be visited.
Not Visited	Neither this node nor any of its neighbors has yet been visited.

All nodes in the graph originally start out in the Not Visited state. When one of its neighbors is visited, a node goes into the Waiting state, and it is placed in a waiting line. When its turn finally comes, it is processed and marked as being in the Visited state. Simply checking the current value of Status(N) can prevent a node from being visited more than once.

Our second concern is the selection of the proper data structure to use for the waiting line, which holds nodes currently in the waiting state. A little thought should convince you that this waiting line is a first-in/first-out Queue data structure of the type described in section 3.4. When traversing the graph in Figure 10–4a, we first visit the shaded node N. We then mark (as Waiting) and queue up N's three neighbors: A, B, and C. The line of waiting nodes looks like this (assuming we add the node's neighbors to the queue in alphabetical order):

```
        C   B   A
(rear)  ↑       ↑  (front)
```

After finishing with node N and marking it as Visited, we remove the front node A, queue up its neighbors (only E), and visit it. The waiting line now holds

```
        E   C   B
(rear)  ↑       ↑  (front)
```

Notice that the new node E has been placed at the end of the line since we must visit all three neighbors of node N before moving on to their neighbors. We now remove node B from the list, visit it, and queue up its two neighbors I and J.

```
        J   I   E   C
(rear)  ↑           ↑  (front)
```

Each time we visit a node we queue only those neighbor nodes whose status is Not Visited. If the status is Visited, then the node has already been processed. If the status is Waiting, the node is currently in line and there is no need to add it to the queue a second time.

A complete breadth-first graph traversal algorithm utilizing the marking scheme just described is shown in Figure 10–5.

The algorithm of Figure 10–5 applied to the following seven-node graph G

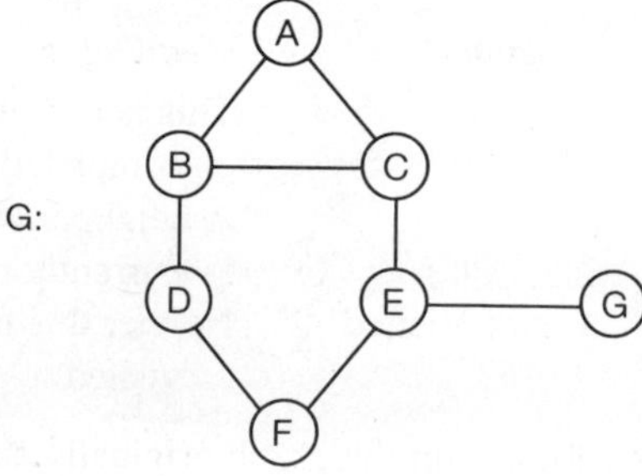

would traverse G, beginning from node A, in the following order

A B C D E F G

Figure 10–5
Breadth-First Graph Traversal Algorithm

```
(* The Breadth First Traversal algorithm visits every node in graph G
   that can be reached from the starting node, X. This algorithm
   is described in the text in section 10.2.2.  *)
BreadthFirstTraversal (G)

   Q := CreateQueue ()

   Set the status of all N nodes in G to Not_Visited
   Pick any node X in G to begin the traversal
   Enqueue (Q, X)
   Set status(X) to Waiting

   Repeat Until Empty (Q)

         (* Visit a node *)
      Dequeue (Q, Y)
      Visit Node Y
      Set status(Y) to Visited

         (* Put its unvisited neighbors in the queue so
            they can be visited. *)
      For all neighbors Z of Y in G Do

         If status(Z) = Not_Visited Then
            Enqueue (Q, Z)
            Set status(Z) to Waiting
         Endif

      Endfor

   Endrepeat

End of BreadthFirstTraversal
```

One of the important applications of breadth-first traversal is to determine whether an undirected graph is or is not *connected*, that is, to determine whether there exists a path from node *i* to node *j* in graph G for all *i* and *j*. If the breadth-first search of Figure 10–5 is applied to a connected graph G, then we will ultimately mark every node in the graph as Visited and G will have been shown to be connected. However, if one or more vertices remain marked as Not Visited after the traversal operation is completed, then the graph is unconnected. We could begin a second traversal operation at any of the unmarked nodes to produce a set of *connected subgraphs*, that is, connected subsets of nodes of graph G. For example, a traversal of the following six-node undirected graph beginning at node A

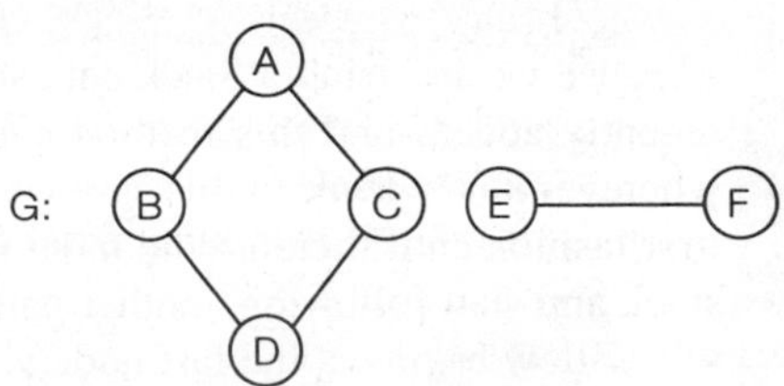

would mark the nodes {A, B, C, D} as Visited, while leaving nodes E and F marked as Not Visited. A second breadth-first traversal beginning at either of the unmarked nodes would produce the set {E, F}. {A, B, C, D} and {E, F} are the two connected subgraphs of the graph G.

A *depth-first graph traversal* is very similar, except that our waiting line now must be a last-in/first-out structure, i.e., a stack. We can see how a depth-first traversal would work using the graph in Figure 10–4b as an example and beginning with the shaded node N. We would first visit node N and then stack up its two neighbors E and A.

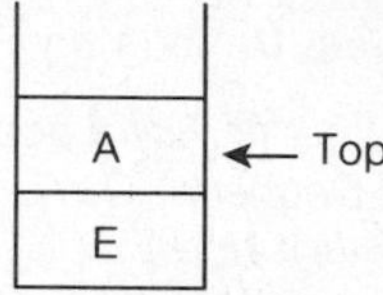

We would now pop the stack, returning node A, visit that node, and then stack the two neighbors of that node, namely F and B. The stack now holds:

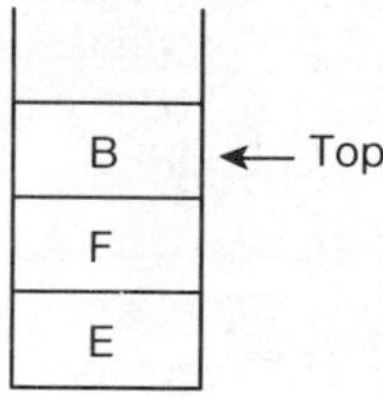

Notice that the most recently added nodes are on top of the stack and will be the ones that are visited next. We now pop node B, visit it, and then stack its neighbor C. (The node F is already in the stack and has been marked as Waiting, so it is not added again.)

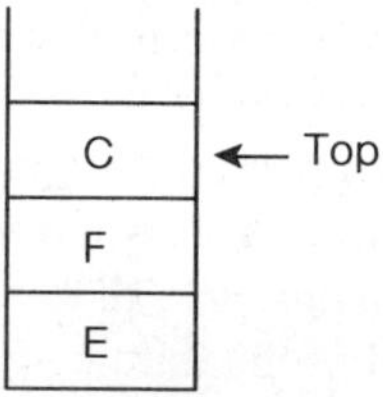

Because we are using a Stack data structure, we first visit the nodes that were most recently added, and this method causes us to continue to follow our current path wherever it may lead. In this case we keep following the path ABCD . . . in a depth-first fashion until there are no more unmarked nodes on that path. Then we pop the stack and start following another path in a depth-first fashion. The new path that we will follow begins at the last node visited in the current path.

Given the following structure:

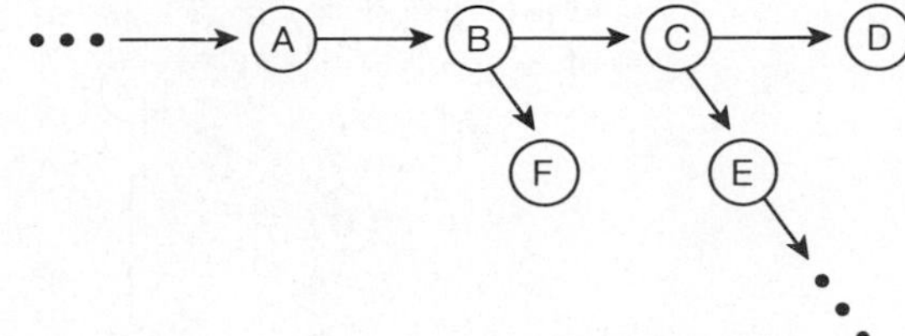

after following the path ABCD and coming to its end at D, we will back up to the previous node C and begin following the path ABCE . . . . When we have reached the end of that path, we will back up to the previous node B and begin following the path ABF . . . .

We leave the implementation of a depth-first graph traversal algorithm as an exercise.

10.2.3 Minimal Spanning Trees

Every connected graph G has a set of edges that connect all of its nodes and form a tree. This tree is called a *spanning tree* of the graph G. Spanning trees are important because they contain thc minimal number of edges, $n - 1$, that still leave the n-node graph in a connected state. We can think of the process of creating a spanning tree as discarding "extraneous" edges from a graph (extraneous only in the sense that a path between these nodes already exists using other edges). Figure 10–6b shows one possible spanning tree T for the graph given in Figure 10–6a. Notice that the graph G contains eight edges and six nodes and is fully connected. The spanning tree T in Figure 10–6b contains the same six nodes but only five edges, and it is still connected.

If the graph is unweighted, as in Figure 10–6 there exists a very simple method for generating a spanning tree. The traversal algorithms of section 10.2.2 visit every node in the graph exactly once. If there is a cycle and we come back to a node a second time via a different edge, we disregard it and do not visit the node a second time. Thus, if we simply save the edges that we use to traverse the graph in either a

Figure 10–6
Sample Spanning Tree

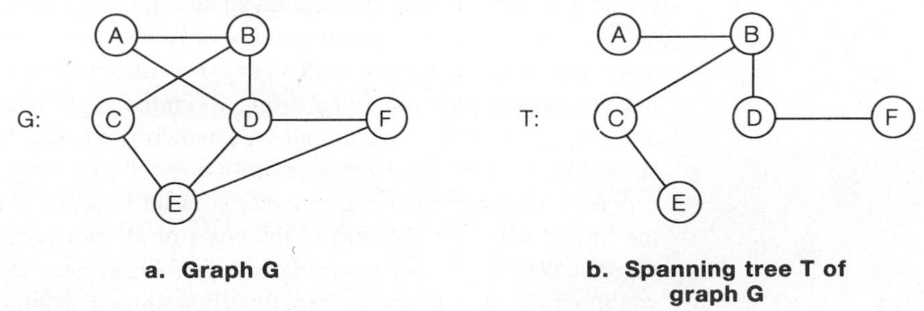

a. Graph G **b. Spanning tree T of graph G**

breadth-first or a depth-first traversal, this set of edges will form a spanning tree of G. For example, given the graph

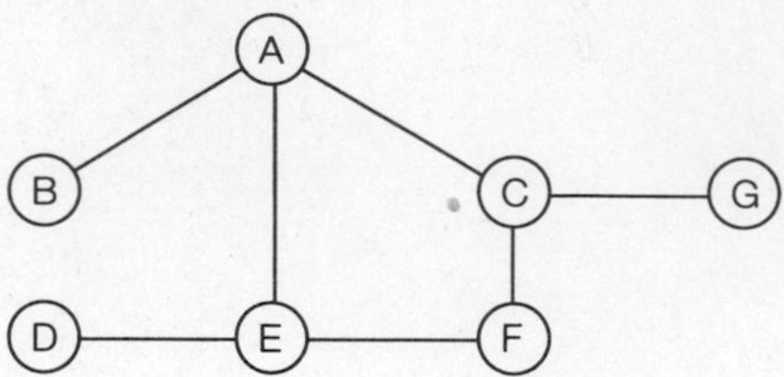

a breadth-first search beginning at node A and queueing nodes in alphabetical order would visit the nodes in the order: ABCEFGD, and it would use the six edges <A,B>, <A,C>, <A,E>, <C,F>, <C,G>, and <D,E>. The spanning tree that results, called a *breadth-first spanning tree* is

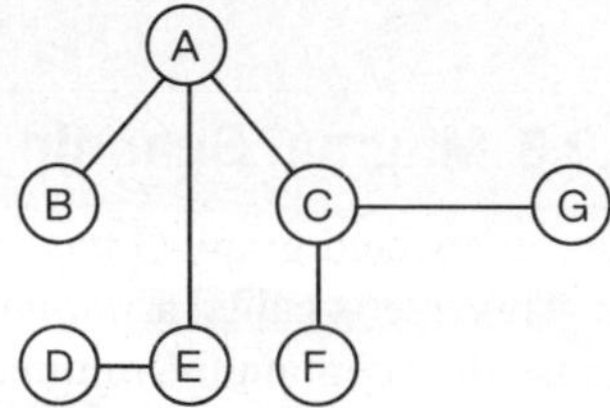

A spanning tree generated by a depth-first traversal is called a *depth-first spanning tree*. For the same graph, a depth-first traversal of G beginning at A would produce the following spanning tree

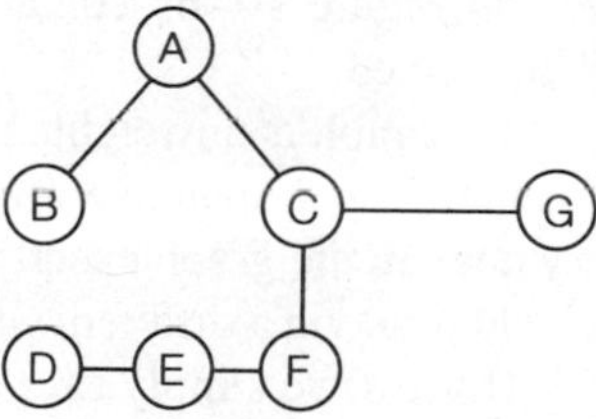

The modification of the breadth-first traversal algorithm of Figure 10–5 to save the edges used and produce the desired spanning tree is shown in Figure 10–7.

The previous two diagrams show only two of the many different breadth-first and depth-first spanning trees that can be constructed from a single graph. The problem becomes a little more interesting when the edges of the graph are weighted. In an unweighted graph, we do not care which particular spanning tree we produce, since they will all have n nodes and $(n - 1)$ edges of equal weight. The case is different for a weighted graph. Now we want to produce the spanning tree that has the lowest value for the sum of the costs of all its edges. This particular spanning tree is called a *minimal spanning tree* (MST). Figure 10–8 shows an example of a weighted graph, a spanning tree, and the minimal spanning tree for that graph.

The most well-known technique for building an MST is called Kruskal's algorithm. It uses what is called a *greedy technique* , in which we always select the

Figure 10–7
Generation of a Breadth-First Spanning Tree

```
(* The Breadth-First Spanning Tree algorithm generates a graph NG from
     another graph G. NG will be a spanning tree of G, created by doing
     a breadth-first traversal of G starting at some node X.   *)
BreadthFirstSpanningTree (G)
     Q := CreateQueue()                    (* NG will be the graph of the spanning
     NG := CreateGraph()                   tree of G *)
     Set the status of all N nodes in G to Not_Visited
     Pick any node X in G to begin the traversal
     Enqueue (Q, X)
     InsertNode (NG, X)                    (* We have to add all vertecies in G to NG *)
     Set status(X) to Waiting
     Repeat Until Empty (Q)
          Dequeue (Q, Y)
          Set status(Y) to Visited
          For all neighbors Z of Y in G Do
               If status(Z) = Not_Visited Then
                    Enqueue (Q, Z)
                    InsertNode (NG, Z)
                    InsertEdge ( NG, Y, Z )    (* The edge from Y to Z is part
                                               of the breadth-first spanning tree.   *)
                    Set status(Z) to Waiting
               Endif
          Endfor
     Endrepeat
End of BreadthFirstSpanningTree
```

Figure 10–8
The Minimal Spanning Tree of a Weighted Graph

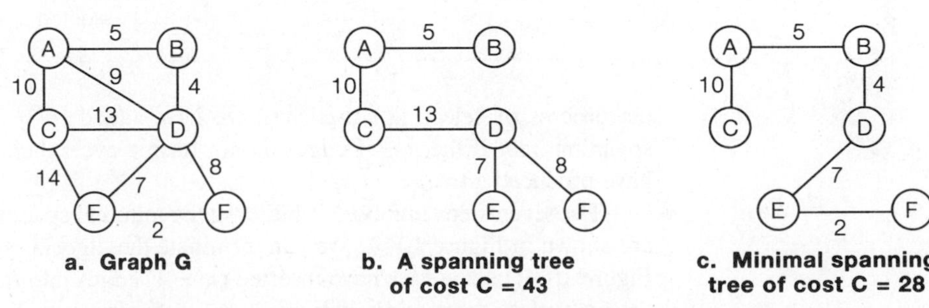

locally optimal choice at each step, regardless of whether it may or may not be the globally optimal choice; that is, we always "grab" the biggest or best object available right now.

With Kruskal's algorithm we keep adding edges to our spanning tree in order of lowest cost. From the set of all edges E, we grab the edge that has the lowest cost. We then keep that edge if it does not create a cycle and reject it if it does. We repeat

Figure 10–9
Using Kruskal's Algorithm to Produce a Minimal Spanning Tree

Edges, Ordered by Cost and Tree Constructed So Far

1. EF, BD, AB, DE, DF, AD, AC, CD, CE
(The underlined edge is the one we are considering adding.)

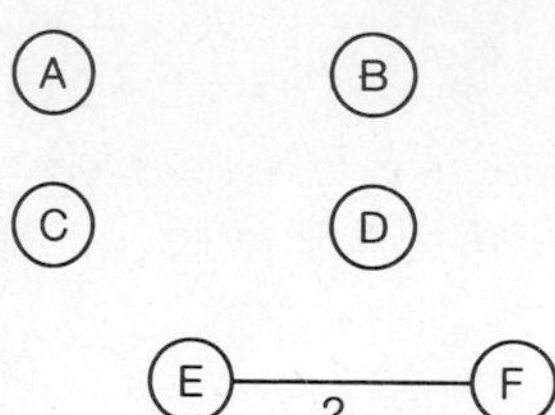

2. BD, AB, DE, DF, AD, AC, CD, CE

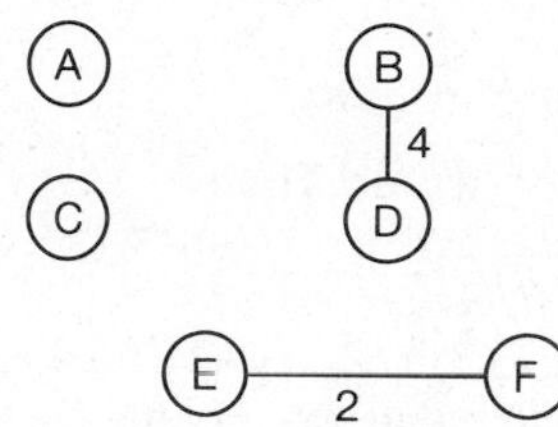

3. AB, DE, DF, AD, AC, CD, CE

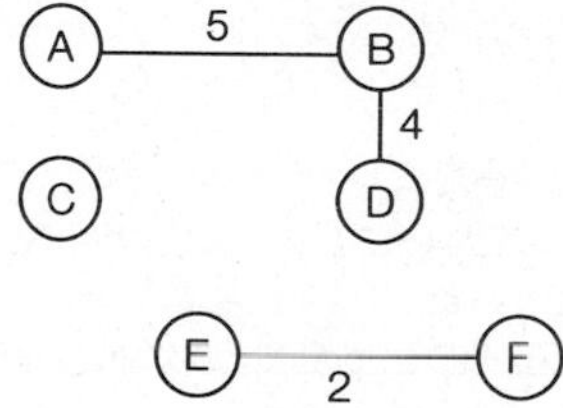

4. DE, DF, AD, AC, CD, CE

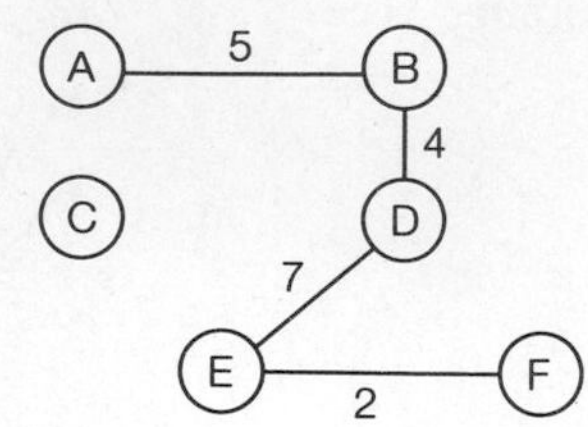

5. DF, AD, AC, CD, CE

Reject DF because it would create a cycle DEFD.

6. AD, AC, CD, CE

Reject AD because it would create a cycle ABDA.

7. AC, CD, CE

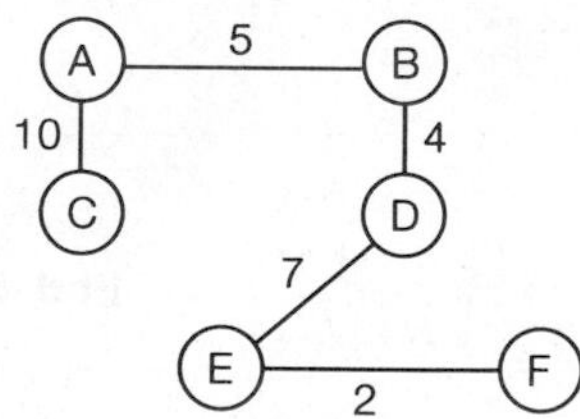

Our task is finished, because we have selected five edges.

the process of selecting edges until we have added ($n - 1$) edges to our n-node spanning tree. If the $n - 1$ edges do not form a cycle then we must, by definition, have produced a tree.

The seven steps involved in building the minimal spanning tree of Figure 10–8c are shown in Figure 10–9. We can terminate the algorithm after the seven steps of Figure 10–9 because we have inserted ($n - 1$) edges into the n-node graph; if there are no cycles, these edges will produce a spanning tree. Since we have always selected the least-cost edge at each decision point, the tree we have produced must have the minimal cost. The outline of Kruskal's algorithm is given in Figure 10–10. We leave the analysis of the time complexity of the algorithm as an exercise.

The real "trick" to implementing Kruskal's algorithm is determining how to efficiently test the Boolean condition specified in the **if** statement, that is, determining whether the addition of an edge to a graph would create a cycle. There is a very elegant way to implement this step using the set data structure discussed in the pre-

Figure 10–10
Kruskal's Algorithm

```
(* Kruskal's algorithm finds the minimal spanning tree of a graph G.
   This algorithm is described in section 10.2.3 in the text. *)
Kruskal's Algorithm
    T := CreateGraph ()
    EdgeCount := 0
    MSTCost := 0

    Repeat Until EdgeCount = (N - 1)
        Select lowest cost edge e = < Ni, Nj, W > in G
        DeleteEdge ( G, Ni, Nj)

        If adding e would not create a cycle in T Then
            InsertEdge ( T, Ni, Nj, W )
            EdgeCount := EdgeCount + 1
            MSTCost := MSTCost + W
        Endif

    Endrepeat
End of Kruskal's Algorithm
```

vious chapter. We simply maintain sets of connected subgraphs; that is, sets of nodes that are connected to each other but not to nodes in other sets.

For example, given the following two sets A = $\{n_1, n_2, \ldots\}$ and B = $\{m_1, m_2, \ldots\}$ the meaning is that all nodes in set A are connected to each other and all nodes in set B are connected to each other, but no node in set A is connected to a node in set B. When we begin the algorithm every node is in its own set, since there are no edges in the graph. If we can maintain this collection of sets of connected components as we insert edges, it is easy to determine if adding an edge would create a cycle. If an edge connects a node in set A to a node in set B, it cannot create a cycle, because these nodes were previously unconnected. Since all the nodes in sets A and B are now connected, we reset A to (A ∪ B), discard set B, and repeat the process until we have a single set containing all the nodes in the graph.

If, on the other hand, we would insert an edge between two nodes in the same set, we would create a cycle. There must already be a path connecting these two nodes because they are already members of the same set. Figure 10–11 shows how this cycle determination would work in building an MST using Kruskal's algorithm.

10.2.4 Shortest Paths

The final graph operation that we will investigate is called the *shortest path* problem. In it we are given a weighted, directed graph G, and any two nodes n_i (the *source node*) and n_j (the *destination node*). We want to determine the shortest path from n_i to n_j, where shortest is defined as having the minimal value for the sum of the costs of each edge in the path. That is, if the path is

$$n_i n_{i+1} n_{i+2} \ldots n_{j-1} n_j$$

Figure 10–11
Using Sets to Detect Cycles in Kruskal's Algorithm

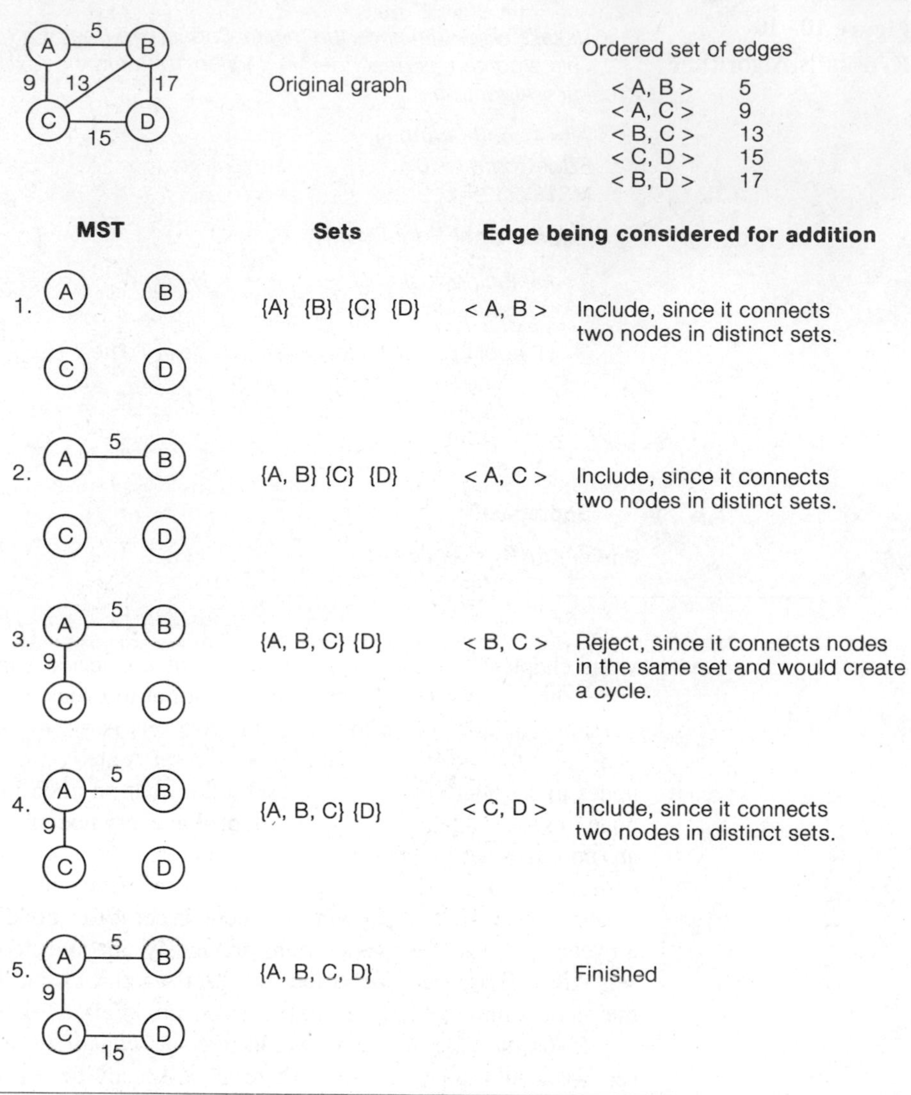

Then the shortest path is defined as the path P having the following property

$$\min \left[\sum_{k=i}^{j-1} \text{Cost } (<n_k, n_{k+1}>) \right]$$

Notice that we are explicitly concerned with finding the shortest path, not simply any path. We can determine a path by building a spanning tree rooted at the source node. If the source and destination nodes are connected, then the destination will be a node in the spanning tree and the path will be the unique path from the root to that node. However, we cannot guarantee that this path will be the shortest possible one. Referring to Figure 10–8a, the shortest path from node C to node F in graph G is

CEF, which has a cost of 16 units (14 + 2). However the minimal spanning tree of Figure 10–8c produces the path CABDEF, which has a total cost of 28 units, almost double the least cost path.

The algorithm that we will use to determine the shortest path between two nodes was first developed by Professor Edsgar Dijkstra and is called, appropriately, Dijkstra's algorithm. Instead of simply determining a shortest path from a single source node n_i to a single destination node n_j, Dijkstra's algorithm determines the shortest path from a single source node n_i to *all* other nodes in the graph.

The algorithm operates by dividing the N nodes of the graph G into two disjoint sets—a set S which contains those nodes for which we have determined the shortest path, and a set U, which contains those nodes for which we have not yet determined the shortest path. These two sets are initialized to the values S = $\{n_i\}$, our source node, and U = {all nodes in G except the source node n_i}. We also must maintain a data structure called the *cost list*, written as C[j], which represents the cost of reaching node j, $j \in$ U, going through only nodes in S. Informally, we can say that C[j] represents the cost of reaching out from the set of shortest path nodes and visiting a node for which we have not yet determined the shortest path. Figure 10–12 shows the relationship between S, U, and C[j]. At the point in the algorithm diagrammed in Figure 10–12, we have determined the shortest path from the source node 1 to nodes 1 and 2 but have not yet determined the shortest path from the source node 1 to nodes 3, 4, or 5. The cost to reach nodes 3, 4, or 5 from node 1, traversing only nodes 1 and/or 2 is C[3], C[4], or C[5], respectively.

The basic idea of Dijkstra's algorithm is to use a greedy technique similar to the approach used in Kruskal's algorithm. At each step in the algorithm we take a single node n_i out of the set U, determine the shortest path to it, and place it in S. We repeat this operation until all nodes of the graph are in set S and the set U is empty.

The node we select at each step is the one that will cost us the least to reach from the current set S. That is, we select the node j in U that has the minimum value of C[j].

Step 1: Determine the minimal value C[k] for $k \in$ U.
Remove node k from the set U.
Place node k in set S.

After completing Step 1 we must update the cost list C, since we have added a new node k to S.

Figure 10–12
The Basic Concepts in Dijkstra's Algorithm

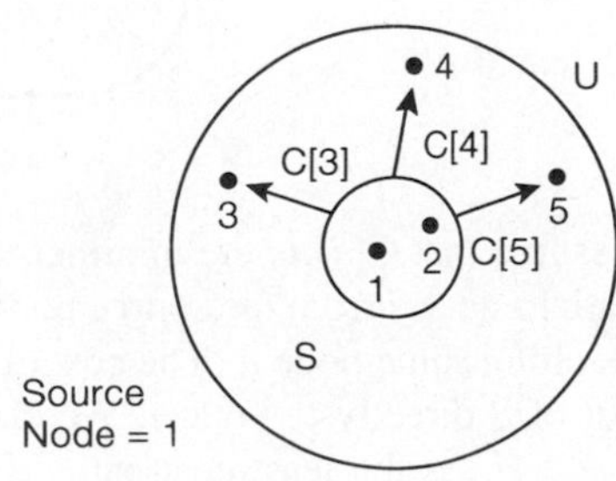

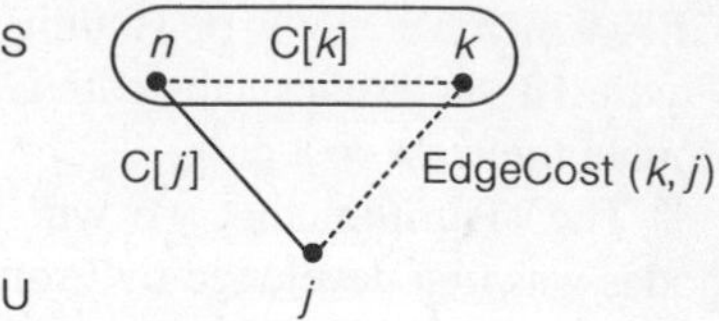

Previously, the cost of reaching a node j, $j \in$ U, from only nodes in S was C[j] (the solid line). Now that we have added node k to S, it may be cheaper to first go from node n to our new node k and then directly out to j (the dotted line). The cost of this new path will be C[k] + EdgeCost (k, j), where EdgeCost (k, j) is the weighted cost of the edge directly connecting nodes k and j, or infinity if no such edge exists. We are essentially determining whether the addition of this new node k to the set S has created a new shortest path to other nodes outside of S.

Step 2: Set C[j] = Min (C[j], C[k] + EdgeCost (k, j)) for all $j \in$ U.

Figure 10–13 shows the application of this updating process to a five-node graph G, using node 1 as the source node.

At the end of the execution of the operations shown in Figure 10–13, we will have determined the cost of the shortest path from the source node 1 to all other nodes. These cost values are simply the most recent values in the cost list C.

Node	*Shortest Path Cost*
2	5
3	6
4	9
5	18

Figure 10–14 shows an algorithm to implement the shortest path method we have just described. Rather than actually determining the shortest path itself, the algorithm in Figure 10–14 determines only the cost of the shortest path from the source node to all other nodes. We leave it as an exercise for you to make the necessary changes so that the algorithm will return a list of the actual nodes contained in the shortest path.

To prove that Dijkstra's algorithm actually does produce the shortest path, we must examine the following diagram

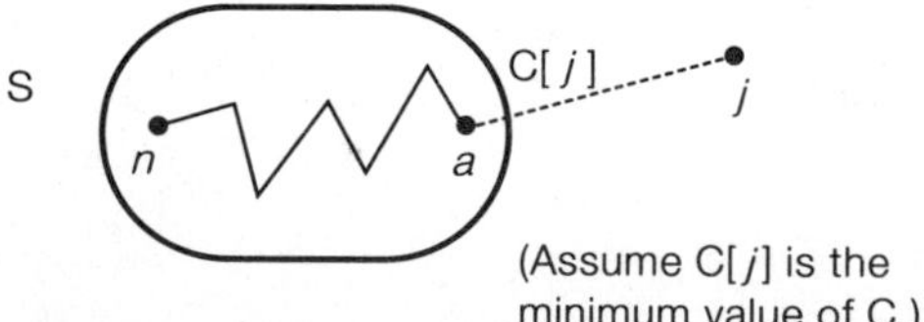

Assume that C[j] is the minimal value in the cost list C. We claim that the shortest path to node j from the source node n will wander around nodes inside S, eventually reaching some node a. The cost of this wandering is C[a]. From there the path goes out of S directly to node j. We claim that this path, which we will write as n . . . a . . . j , is the least-cost path. By definition, it is the lowest cost path containing

Figure 10–13
Example of Dijkstra's Algorithm

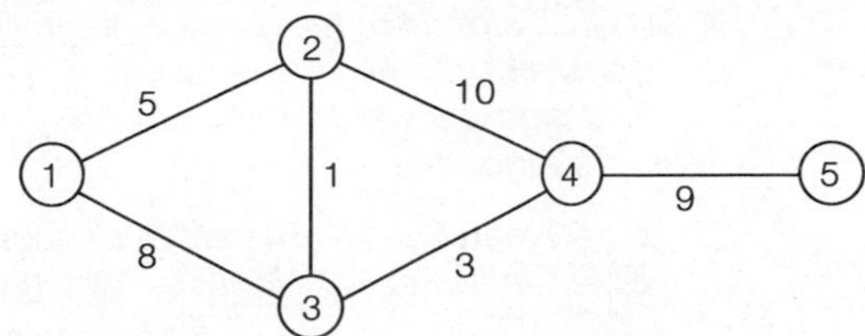

Initial values: $S = \{1\}$ $U = \{2, 3, 4, 5\}$

$C_2 = 5$ $C_3 = 8$ $C_4 = \infty$ $C_5 = \infty$

Phase I:

1. Select the minimal value of C

   $C_2 = 5$ (cost of the shortest path to node 2)

   Move that node into S

   $S = \{1, 2\}$ $U = \{3, 4, 5\}$

2. Recompute C values

   $C_3 = \min(C_3, C_2 + \text{EdgeCost}(2,3))$
   $= \min(8, 5+1)$
   $= 6$ (Notice this has been reduced from 8.)

   $C_4 = \min(\infty, 5+10)$
   $= 15$ (Notice this has been reduced from ∞.)

   $C_5 = \min(\infty, 5+\infty)$
   $= \infty$

Phase II:

1. Select the minimal value of C

   $C_3 = 6$ (cost of the shortest path to node 3)

   Move that node into S

   $S = \{1, 2, 3\}$ $U = \{4, 5\}$

2. Recompute C values

   $C_4 = \min(15, 6+3)$
   $= 9$ (We have lowered it a second time.)

   $C_5 = \min(\infty, 6+\infty)$
   $= \infty$

Phase III:

1. Select the minimal value of C

   $C_4 = 9$ (cost of the shortest path to node 4)

   Move that node into S

   $S = \{1, 2, 3, 4\}$ $U = \{5\}$

2. Recompute C values

   $C_5 = \min(\infty, 9+9)$
   $= 18$ (We have reduced it from infinity.)

Phase IV:

1. Select the minimal value of C

   $C_5 = 18$ (cost of the shortest path to node 5)

   Move that node into S

   $S = \{1, 2, 3, 4, 5\}$ $U = \{\}$

2. U is empty and so we are finished.

Figure 10–14
Dijkstra's Shortest Path Algorithm

```
(* Dijkstra's algorithm takes some graph G and some node X in G, and
     calculates the minimum cost path from X to every other node in G.
     This algorithm is described in the text in section 10.2.4.   *)
Dijkstra's Algorithm

     S := CreateSet() (* The set of all nodes with a known shortest path *)
     U := CreateSet() (* Nodes for which we do not know shortest path *)

     X := source node for path
     Insert (S, X)

     For each node Y in G such that X <> Y Do
          Insert (U, Y)
          C[Y] := EdgeCost (X, Y)
     Endfor

     Repeat Until U is empty

          Choose the vertex Z such that C[Z] is the minimal value in C
          Insert (S, Z)
          Remove (U, Z)

          For each vertex W in U Do
               C[W] := Min ( C[W], (C[Z] + EdgeCost (Z,W)) )
          Endfor

     Endrepeat

End of Dijkstra's Algorithm
```

only nodes in S. If it is not the overall shortest path to *j*, then there would have to be at least one node $b \notin$ S on that other path:

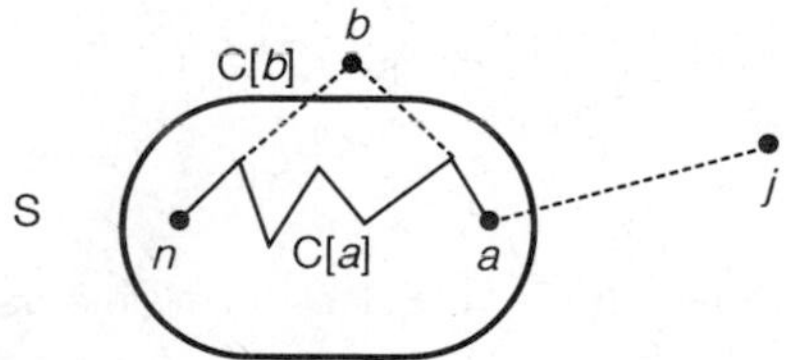

Now the proposed shortest path would wander around nodes in S for a while, but eventually it would have to go outside S to some node $b \in$ U. The cost of going from *n* to *b* via nodes within S is C[*b*]. However, since node $a \in$ S and node $b \notin$ S, we know that C[*a*] < C[*b*] because nodes are being added to S in strictly ascending order of their cost in the cost list C. Therefore the cost of the path *n* . . . *a* must be less than the cost of the path *n* . . . *b* . . . *a*, and the path *n* . . . *a* . . . *j* must be cheaper than the cost of the path *n* . . *b* . . *a* . . *j*. Thus Dijkstra's algorithm does indeed produce the shortest path.

In this section we have surveyed just a few of the many operations that are possible with graph structures: breadth-first and depth-first traversals, spanning trees, minimal spanning trees, and shortest paths. Other interesting graph-based operations that we will not discuss here include:

a. *All-pairs shortest* paths. Determining the shortest path between all possible pairs of nodes in a graph .

b. *Topological ordering* of graphs. Determining whether there exists a linear relationship among the nodes of a directed graph such that each directed edge goes from a node to one of its successors. For example, given the following graph one possible topological ordering is ACBDEF; another is CABDFE.

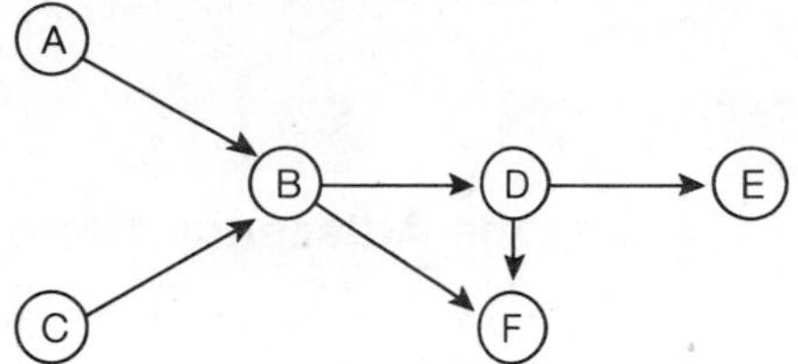

c. Finding *articulation points*. An articulation point is a node whose removal, along with the removal of all edges incident to it, would break the graph into two or more disconnected components. For example, in the following graph

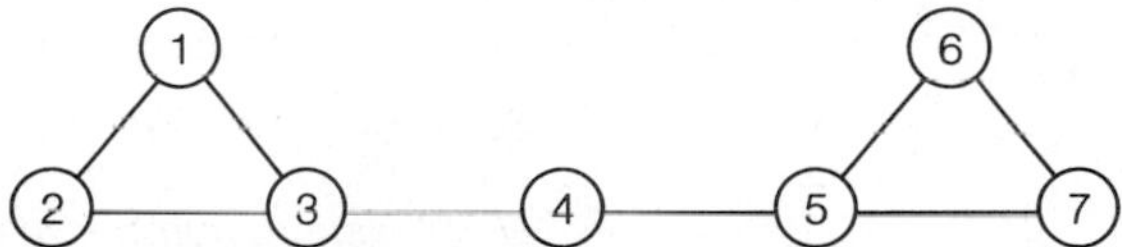

node 4 is an articulation point since its removal would create the disconnected subgraphs {1, 2, 3} and {5, 6, 7}.

d. Determining if a graph G is *bipartite*, that is, if it can be partitioned into two disjoint sets A and B such that no two nodes in A are adjacent in G and no two nodes in B are adjacent in G. The following graph is bipartite:

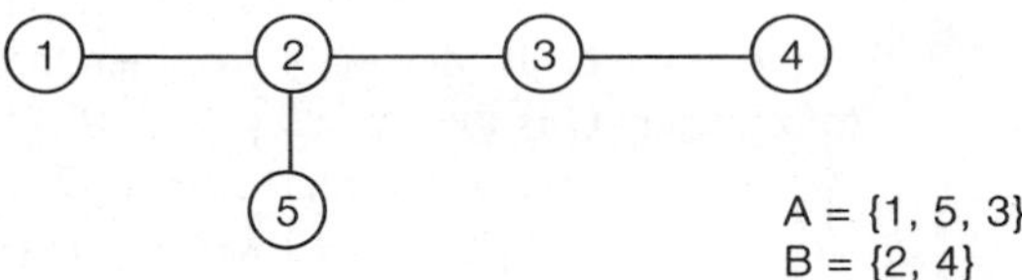

e. Finding a *Hamiltonian cycle*. A Hamiltonian cycle is a cycle of the form $n_1 n_2 \ldots n_k n_1$, which visits every node in the graph exactly once and ends up at the starting vertex.

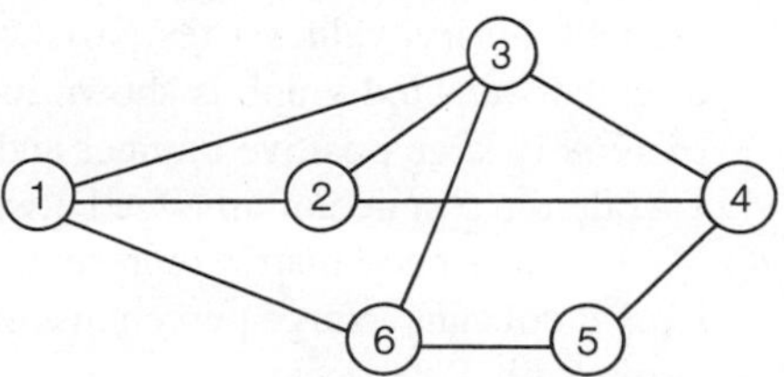

A Hamiltonian cycle for this graph would be 1234561; another is 4321654.

These are just a few of the many interesting operations that can be carried out on graph structures. We will leave them either as exercises at the end of the chapter or as subjects for future classes in such areas as graph theory or discrete mathematics. Now we want to take a look at how we can internally represent the graph structures we have just described and how we can actually implement the operations we have presented.

10.3 IMPLEMENTATION

10.3.1 The Adjacency Matrix Representation

There are two popular approaches to representing graph structures, the *adjacency matrix* and the *adjacency list*. In this section we look at the first of these two techniques.

Assume that the N nodes in a graph G are uniquely numbered 1, . . . , N. (Of course, each node may have a great deal of other data stored in it and be implemented as a complex record structure; however, that other information is not of concern to us here.) An adjacency matrix represents graphs using an $N \times N$ two-dimensional array of binary values that we will refer to as (Yes,No).

```
Const
    Max = . . . ;   (* Maximum number of nodes in the graph *)
Type
    Graph = Array [1 .. Max, 1 .. Max] Of (Yes,No);
Var
    M : Graph;
    N : 1 .. Max;
```

If M(x,y) = Yes, there exists a directed edge from node x to node y, $1 \leq x, y \leq N$ in the graph G. If M(x,y) = No, then there is no edge. The amount of space needed to represent G is $O(N^2)$.

If the graph is undirected, then M(x,y) = M(y,x) for all x,y, and we need to store only the upper or the lower triangular portion of the adjacency matrix, not the entire matrix; and we can thus reduce our space needs to approximately $(N^2/2)$ memory cells. While the space required is still $O(N^2)$, it does cut the number of memory cells approximately in half.

Finally, if the edges in the graph are weighted using real values in the range [0 .. EdgeMax], we simply represent the graph as an $N \times N$ array of reals rather than of binary values (Yes,No). An adjacency matrix representation of an undirected weighted graph is shown in Figure 10–15. (The symbol ∞ stands for some extremely large positive number and represents a virtually infinite cost. It is used to encode the absence of an edge between two nodes.)

An adjacency matrix representation makes sense only if the graph is *dense*, that is, if it contains a large percentage of the N^2 edges that could theoretically exist in a graph with N vertices. However, if the graph is *sparse*, that is, if it contains something closer to the minimum number of edges in a connected graph of N vertices

Figure 10–15 Adjacency Matrix Representation of an Undirected Weighted Graph

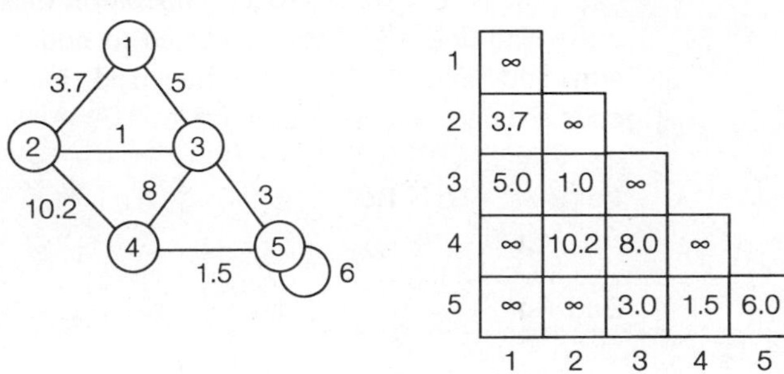

1	∞				
2	3.7	∞			
3	5.0	1.0	∞		
4	∞	10.2	8.0	∞	
5	∞	∞	3.0	1.5	6.0
	1	2	3	4	5

$(N - 1)$ rather than the maximum, the adjacency matrix will be quite empty, with only about $1/N$ of its cells having values other than ∞. For example, if we had a directed graph with 30 vertices, the adjacency matrix representation would require 900 cells; however, the graph could be connected with as few as 29 edges (it would then be a tree), leaving 871 unused cells in the adjacency matrix.

The basic operations of inserting and deleting an edge, which we first introduced in section 10.2.1, are particularly easy to implement using the adjacency matrix representation because of the random access characteristic of arrays. To add an edge from node i to node j, we simply say

M[i,j] := Yes

which is O(1). Deletion is virtually identical

M[i,j] := No

Adding a node can cause a problem because of the static nature of array structures. Once we make the declaration of the size of the matrix

```
Type
    Graph = Array [1 .. Max, 1 .. Max] Of (Yes, No);
```

we can never add more than Max nodes to a graph of this type. An InsertNode operation will fail if N = Max. However, if we have not yet reached the upper limit, adding a node is also easy. It just involves incrementing the count of the current number of nodes in the graph.

```
Var
    NodeCount : 0 .. Max;   (* Current number of nodes in the graph *)
•
•
•
Procedure InsertNode;

    If NodeCount < Max Then
        NodeCount := NodeCount + 1;
```

Finally, the DeleteNode(i) operation must not only mark node i as deleted—it must also find all edges connected to node i, so both row i and column i of the adjacency matrix M must be traversed, looking for any edge that either begins or ends at node i and setting it to No.

```
For k := 1 To N Do
    M(i,k) := No;
    M(k,i) := No;
End For
```

This operation is obviously O(N).

10.3.2 The Adjacency List Representation

The *adjacency list* is a potentially more space-efficient method for representing graphs. With this technique we first create a list of all nodes [1 .. N] in the graph G. This list is called the *node list*. Each element in the node list is the head of a linked list of all neighbors of this node, i.e., a list of the names of all nodes that are physically connected to the node in the node list. These are called the **neighbor lists**. For example, the adjacency list representation of the five-node graph G in Figure 10–15, would be

Node	*Neighbors*
1	2, 3
2	1, 3, 4
3	1, 2, 4, 5
4	2, 3, 5
5	3, 4, 5

The adjacency list can be implemented internally using an array of records, in which each record contains a node identifier and a pointer to another node.

```
Const
    Max = . . . ;   (* Maximum number of nodes in the graph *)
Type
    Graph = Array [1 .. Max] Of NodeRecord;
    NodeRecord = Record
                     NodeName      : [1 .. Max];
                     Next          : Pointer To NodeRecord
                 End;
Var
    M : Graph
```

Using this representation, the directed graph of Figure 10–15 would be stored internally as shown in Figure 10–16.

If we have a graph with N nodes and E edges, there will be one data value and one pointer for each of the N nodes in the node list, and one data value and one pointer for each edge E in the adjacency lists (two if the graph is undirected). If a

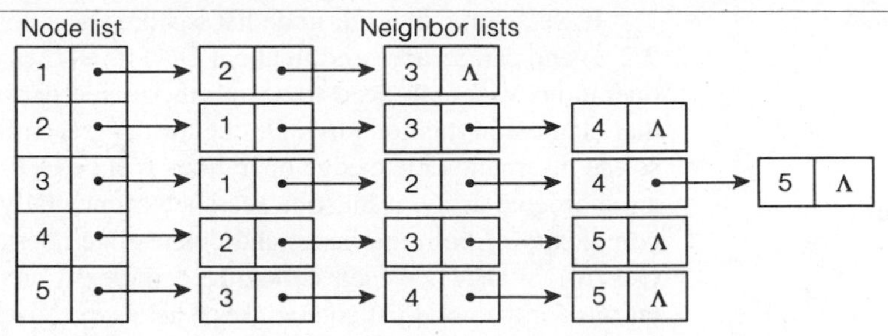

Figure 10–16
Internal Representation of Graphs Using Adjacency Lists

Table 10–1 Comparison of the Space Needs of the Two Graph Representation Techniques

	$N = 20$, $p = 3$ Number of Edges, E	Adjacency List (p=3)	Adjacency Matrix
minimum	19	156	400
	40	240	400
	60	320	400
	80	400	400
	100	480	400
	200	880	400
maximum	400	1680	400

node name requires one memory word and a pointer requires p, then the total amount of space needed for the adjacency list representation of a graph G is :

$$N(1 + p) + E(1 + p)$$
$$= (N + E) + p(N + E)$$
$$= O(N + E)$$

In comparison, the adjacency matrix technique required $O(N^2)$ cells. Table 10–1 shows a comparison of the total memory space needed by the two techniques to represent a twenty-node graph as the number of edges varies from 19 to 400 (the minimum and maximum for a connected graph). The table assumes the number of cells needed to store a pointer variable is three and the number needed to store a node identifier is one.

In this example, the adjacency list is a more efficient technique for graphs with fewer than 80 edges because such graphs are very sparse and the large $N \times N$ matrix is not needed. For the minimum-size connected graph, $E = 19$, the adjacency list gives a space savings of over 60%. However, for denser graphs with more than 80 edges, the adjacency matrix technique becomes superior because we no longer need to allocate space for the large number of pointer variables required by the list-based representation. Although the cut-off points will change for different values of N and p, the basic conclusions on space efficiency will remain the same.

If we assume that our node list is stored as a not very dense hash table (section 9.2.3) and can be accessed in about O(1) time, then the insert edge and delete edge operations will both need to search the linked list of neighbor nodes beginning at that element in the node list. On the average, each linked list will have E/N nodes, so the insert and delete edge operations will be $O(E/N)$. If the node list is stored as an unordered array, it must be searched sequentially, requiring $O(N)$ time, and the complexity of both the insert and delete edge operations will become max $(O(N), O(E/N)) = O(N)$. We leave the time complexity analysis of other internal representations for the node list and neighbor list as exercises.

The time complexity of the high-level operations such as traversal and shortest path depends on which of these two techniques we are using to represent our graphs internally. For example, looking at the breadth-first traversal algorithm of Figure 10–5, we see an outer **Repeat** loop that will be executed N times, since we must visit all N nodes. Within the loop, the critical operation is the **For** loop, where we must locate all the neighbors of a given node y and check their status. If we are using adjacency matrices to represent a graph, this step will require us to look at all N elements in row y of the matrix M, looking for all occurrences of the value Yes.

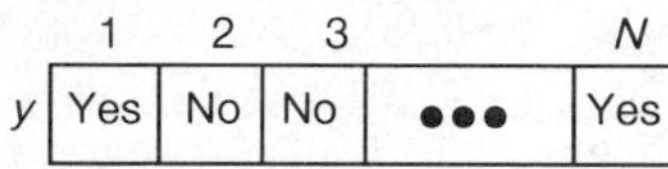

This row search operation takes $O(N)$ time. Coupled with the N repetitions of the outer loop, the complexity of the breadth-first search algorithm implemented with adjacency matrices is $O(N^2)$.

If we are using adjacency lists, the average number of edges contained in each of the N linked lists is E/N. We must search this list each time we execute the **Repeat** loop. If we assume that we can access the node list in constant time, then the average time complexity of the breadth-first search using adjacency lists is $N * (E/N) = O(E)$. If the graph is dense, then $E \approx N^2$, and the two methods take about thc same amount of time. In sparse graphs with few edges, $E \approx N$ and the complexity of breadth-first search using adjacency lists is closer to $O(N)$, a significant improvement.

10.4 CASE STUDY: COMPUTER NETWORKS

One of the most important areas of research and development in computer science is the field of *computer networks* or, to use the more general term, *distributed systems*. A distributed system is a collection of two or more independent processing elements connected by a communications channel. Such systems are able to exchange data, instructions, and messages in order to cooperate in the solving of problems.

Distributed systems come in three types, all of which are very important, but only one of which will be looked at in this case study. These three types are categorized by the distance between the processing elements.

A *multiprocessor* is a single computer system that contains multiple processing elements as an integral part of its machine architecture. Examples of multiprocessors include the Cray Y-MP, with eight processors, up to the Connection Machine (CM), which can have over 64,000. Since these processing elements are within the same system (sometimes even on the same circuit board) the distance between them is typically from only fractions of a meter up to one or two meters.

The second type of distributed system is called a *Local Area Network*, or LAN. Its purpose is to connect independent computer systems and peripherals that are grouped together in a small contiguous geographic area such as a single building or a single campus. These types of systems are typically connected by stringing a high-speed communications channel called a *bus* around the building or campus and letting each system "tap into" that bus and share its communications capability, as shown in Figure 10–17. Typical distances for a LAN are in the range of 100 to 2000 meters.

The third type of distributed system, the one we will focus on in this study, is called a *Wide Area Network*, or WAN. Now we are involved with long-distance communication between geographically distant centers possibly separated by tens of thousands of kilometers.

Even though our case study will focus on the latter system, most real-world distributed systems are actually made up of all three types of networks. For example, a state might have a wide area network whose purpose is to link the branch campuses of a university system located in different cities. Within each campus there will probably be a LAN that ties together the many different academic and administrative computer systems on campus. Finally, one or more of these computer systems may itself be a multiprocessor-based supercomputer. This three-layered hierarchical network structure is shown in Figure 10–18.

Figure 10–17
A Local Area Network

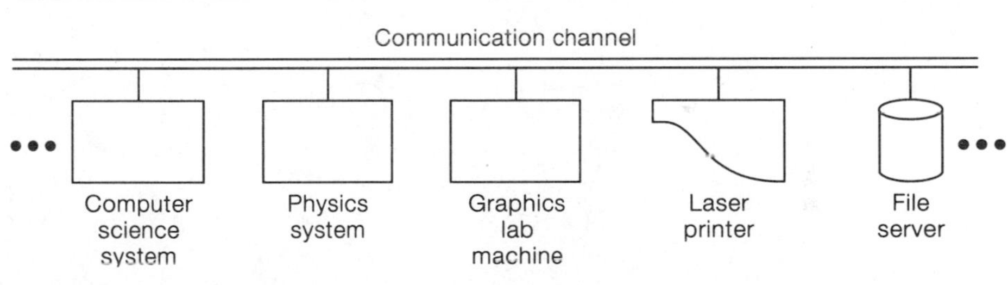

Figure 10–18
Three-Layer Hierarchical Network Structure

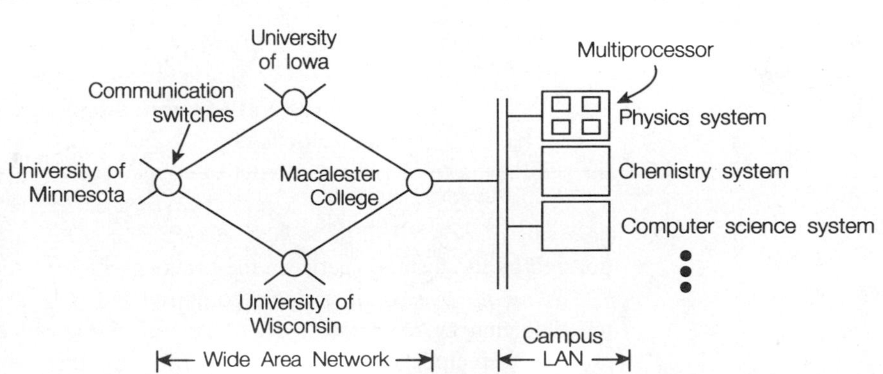

A wide area network is constructed by interconnecting a collection of *communication switches*, as shown in Figure 10–18. These switches are minicomputers that are responsible for implementing the major communication tasks within the network, including

a. *Routing*—getting messages from the source node to the destination node quickly and efficiently.
b. *Flow control*—making sure that the network does not become congested and lose messages.
c. *Error control*—recovering from network failures such as line outages, switch failures, or lost messages.

In addition to providing communication services, the switches act as the connection point into the wide area network for the user's machines or LAN, as shown in Figure 10–18. The switches are interconnected by communication links. These links are usually high-speed telephone lines, microwave channels, optical fibers, or satellite links.

Figure 10–19 shows a portion of the configuration of switches and links in the wide-area network called NSFNet, a well known and widely used WAN that inter-

Figure 10–19
Configuration of NSFNet

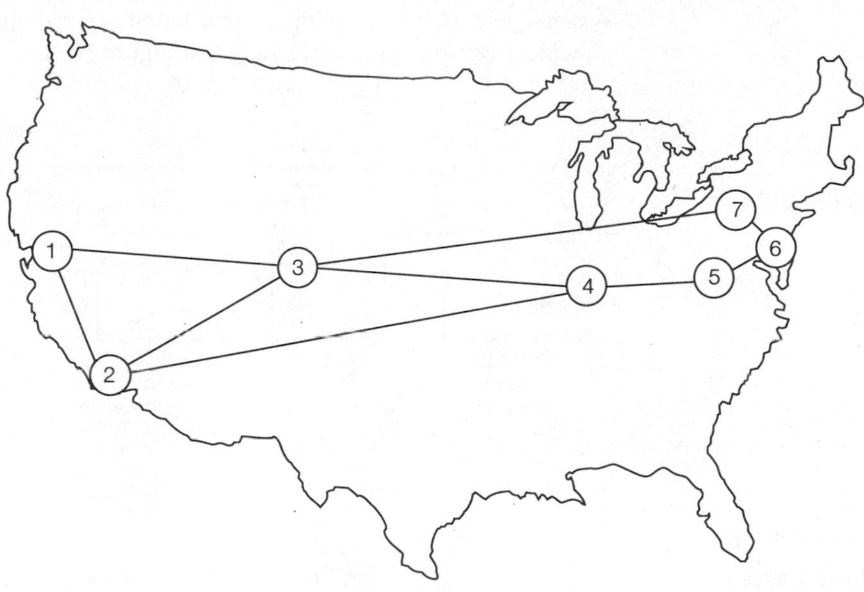

NSFNet Network Sites

Number	Site	Number	Site
1	Stanford University Palo Alto, California	5	Carnegie - Mellon University Pittsburgh, PA
2	University of California San Diego, California	6	Princeton University Princeton, NJ
3	Center for Atmospheric Research Boulder, Colorado	7	Cornell University Ithaca, NY
4	University of Illinois Champaign, Illinois		

connects computer systems located at universities, research centers, and government agencies that are carrying out federally funded scientific research. (That figure shows only a small part of the overall network, the portion known as the *backbone*; the nodes connected by high-speed 1.5 Mbit/second communication links. There are dozens of other sites connected by medium-speed lines and literally hundreds of systems connected by low-speed lines. These nodes have been omitted to keep Figure 10–19 from becoming too cluttered.) Looking at Figure 10–19, we see that a wide area computer network can be viewed as a graph structure in which the communication switches are the nodes of the graphs and the communication links are the edges.

In this case study, we will look at the best way to use graphs to represent a wide area network and see how we can exploit this graph-based representation to provide important network services such as message routing, flow control, and error recovery.

Communication links come in three varieties:

a. *Simplex*—traffic can be sent in only one direction across the link.
b. *Half-duplex*—traffic can be sent in both directions, but in only one direction at a time.
c. *Full-duplex*—traffic can be sent in both direction simultaneously.

The overwhelming majority of communication links in use today are full-duplex, where messages can move in either direction across the link at the same time. Hence our internal representation of a network will use an undirected graph structure to model this simultaneous two-way flow of traffic.

Communication lines also come in a wide range of transmission speeds, measured in bits per second (bps). Slow-speed telephone channels may be able to transmit at only 300–9,600 bps. Medium-speed dedicated lines may range from 10,000–100,000 bps, while high-speed coaxial cable or fiber optic circuits for such applications as digitized voice or graphics may range from 100,000 to as much as 100,000,000 bps (100 Mbps). Obviously, it does not "cost" the same (in terms of time) to transmit a message across a 300 bps line as it does to transmit it over a 50,000 bps link. Sending an 80 $\times$ 25 screen of 8-bit characters at 300 bps requires 53 seconds; at 50,000 bps, only 0.3 seconds; and at 10,000,000 bps, 0.001 seconds. Because of this enormous difference in transmission speeds, an unweighted graph would be an inappropriate representation of a wide area network built from different types of communication links. Instead, we will use a weighted graph in which the cost associated with each edge i is the inverse of the transmission speed of the line i in bits per second:

$$\text{Cost}[i] = 1/\text{Speed}[i]$$

The faster the line, the lower the cost to use that line to transmit a message. (Note that in this example, our use of the word *cost* is not directly related to the dollar cost but is a measure of the time we must spend transmitting.)

Our final decision relates to whether we should use an adjacency matrix or an adjacency list method to internally represent the vertices and edges. If we look at the NSFNet configuration in Figure 10–19, we see that it is quite sparse. Only 9 links are actually used out of the potential number of $(7)^2 = 49$. (The enormous cost of buying communications capacity makes it unrealistic to expect a site to connect to more than one or two other nodes in the network.) This sparsity of links argues strongly for the adjacency list method, as we demonstrated in Table 10–1.

Furthermore, most real-world networks are actually much larger than the one shown in Figure 10–19. For example, BITNET, a wide area computer network used at many colleges and universities, currently has about 1,500 nodes and is growing rapidly. The adjacency matrix technique, which uses $O(N^2)$ cells to represent an N-node graph, would be prohibitively expensive in terms of memory for networks of that size.

This discussion leads us to the conclusion that the best way to represent a typical, real-world wide area computer network would be a weighted, undirected graph structure stored internally using the adjacency list technique of section 10.3.2. (Because we are representing the network as a weighted graph, we have added a field to the record structure of Figure 10–16 to store the line speed.) Figure 10–20 shows the representation of the portion of NSFNet of Figure 10–19 using the method we have selected. It assumes that the speed of all communication channels in the network is 1.5 million bits per second.

How can we use this graph-based representation to provide useful network services? For example, how can we have the network correctly deliver user messages from one city to another? Message routing between nodes in the network is virtually identical to the shortest path problem we discussed in section 10.2.4, because the most efficient route for a message is obviously the least-cost shortest path. One node in the network, called the *routing control center*, could be responsible for determining the best route from node i to node j for all i and j based on the static topology of the network. This situation is equivalent to the *all-pairs shortest path* problem, and one way to implement it is to repeat the single source shortest path algorithm of Figure 10–14 N times, using all N nodes as the source. The only information needed by the routing control center to perform this task is N, the number of nodes, and A, the adjacency list representation of the edges in the graph.

For i := 1 **To** N **Do**
    Determine the shortest path from node i to all other nodes in the network.

Since determining the shortest path for a single source is $O(N^2)$, this routing function is an $O(N^3)$ operation. For large values of N (i.e., big networks) it could be quite

Figure 10–20
Our Internal Representation of NSFNet

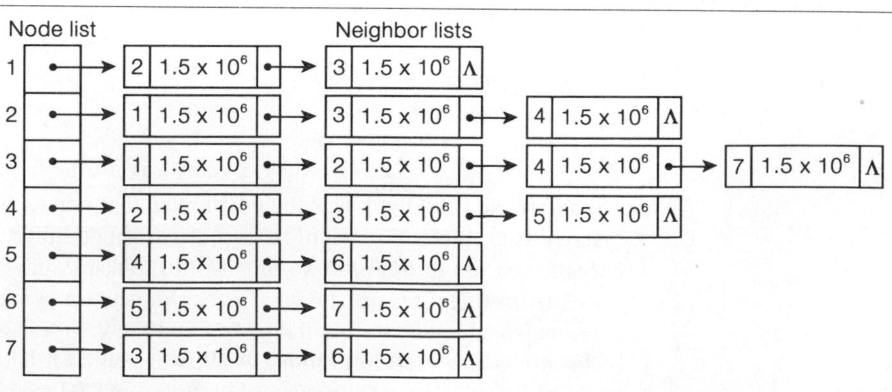

a time-consuming process. However, this algorithm would be tolerable since the determination of optimal routes must be done only when the network is first created and whenever the topology of the network changes, and such changes happen very infrequently.

Once the optimal routes have been determined by the control center, they can be sent out to all nodes in the network. Actually the entire path need not be sent to each node, but only the identification of the next node to which messages must be passed. For example, if we have determined that the shortest path from node 1 to node 5 is

$$1 \rightarrow 8 \rightarrow 2 \rightarrow 7 \rightarrow 15 \rightarrow 5$$

node 2 does not need to know the entire route to node 5. It needs to know only that any traffic it receives from source node 1 to destination 5 is to be routed on to node 7. Therefore a simple three-column array with the following layout

Logical Source	*Logical Destination*	*Next Node (determined by the shortest path algorithm)*
•	•	•
•	•	•
•	•	•
1	5	7
•	•	•
•	•	•
•	•	•

will be adequate to support network routing. This data structure is called a *routing table*, and it is the major data structure for organizing message delivery in wide area computer networks. It guarantees that we will always use the "best" route in terms of the fastest lines and the smallest transmission delays. However, since there are delays involved in sending messages other than just transmission time, e.g., queueing delays and retransmissions due to errors, we cannot guarantee that the route produced by our shortest path algorithm will always produce the minimal overall delay.

What if a line fails (not an unusual phenomenon with computer networks)? (Have you ever picked up your phone and not heard the dial tone? This is an example of a line outage.) Line failure is also handled quite elegantly by our graph representation. All we need to do is reset the cost of the failed link to ∞ (in reality, some large positive number), which corresponds to a line speed of zero. We then rerun the all-pairs shortest path procedure to determine the existence of other routes that do not use the failed line. (Since the cost of using the failed link is infinite, any path including it will cost more than any path containing working lines.) Node outages can be handled in a similar fashion by just resetting to ∞ the cost of all links that are physically adjacent to the failed node and redoing the all-pairs shortest path algorithm.

The primary concern with a line or node failure is determining how the routing center can learn about the failure in the first place so that it will know that it must redo the routing algorithm. We can answer this concern in the design of the *pro-*

tocols, the rules and procedures for exchanging messages across a communication line. When a node A sends a message M to node B

it expects to get an acknowledgement back from B that the message has been correctly received.

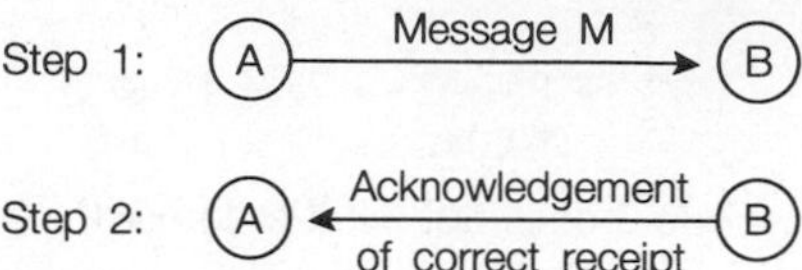

If A does not receive an acknowledgement from B, it retransmits a second copy of the message. However, if node A still has not received a response from node B after a certain number of retransmissions, A will assume that the <A,B> link has failed and send a control message describing this condition to the routing control center. The center will set the weight of the failed link to ∞, redo the routing computations, and forward the information about new routes to all nodes in the network, including A. Node A will now start using an alternative path that avoids the failed link.

When building a network, we want it to be *robust* and *reliable*, i.e., we want it to keep operating reasonably well in the presence of line and node failures. This expectation is no different from the level of service we expect and receive from the telephone company. If a switching center fails, we still want to be able to make both local and long distance calls, even if some calls must take an alternative route.

The best way to guarantee robustness is to provide two or more distinct paths between any two nodes in the network, so that the failure of any one line will not isolate any node in the network. For example, if the AB line in the following network fails,

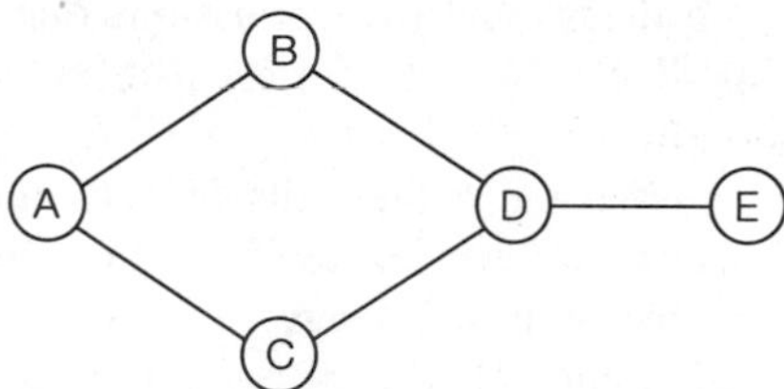

it is not catastrophic to either node A or node B. We can reroute traffic along the ACDB path and still support communication between nodes A and B, even though it may be slightly slower. However, if the DE line fails, it is far more serious. Node E is cut off from any communication with nodes A, B, C, or D, and the graph is disconnected. If this network was connecting worldwide military installations, and node E was a front-line combat center, this condition would be totally unacceptable, even for a short period of time.

To determine whether our proposed network structure is reliable, we could carry out the following operation: We first traverse the graph of the proposed network using the traversal algorithm of Figure 10–5 and see if all of the nodes are marked as visited. This step insures that our original topology does connect all N nodes in the network. We then remove exactly one edge from the graph and repeat the entire traversal process. If all nodes are still marked as visited, then we know that the failure of that communication line will not cause any single node in the network to be disconnected, and thus we have complete redundancy with respect to that edge. We now restore that edge, remove another one, and repeat the entire process for all E edges. On the other hand, if the removal of an edge from the graph leaves one or more nodes marked as not visited, then we know that the existence of this edge is critical to the successful operation of the overall network and its failure will disconnect the graph. We may find this condition unacceptable and decide to purchase redundant links, such as a new communication line to connect nodes B and E in the network shown on the previous page.

The complexity of the traversal algorithm in Figure 10–5 is $O(N^2)$, and it is repeated for each of the E links, so the overall complexity of this process if $O(EN^2)$. This operation can clearly be very time-consuming, but since it needs to be performed only when the network is originally created or when the topology of the network changes (e.g., we add a new node), this situation is probably acceptable.

A switch outage can also be catastrophic in the sense of isolating nodes and disconnecting the graph. In the following graph

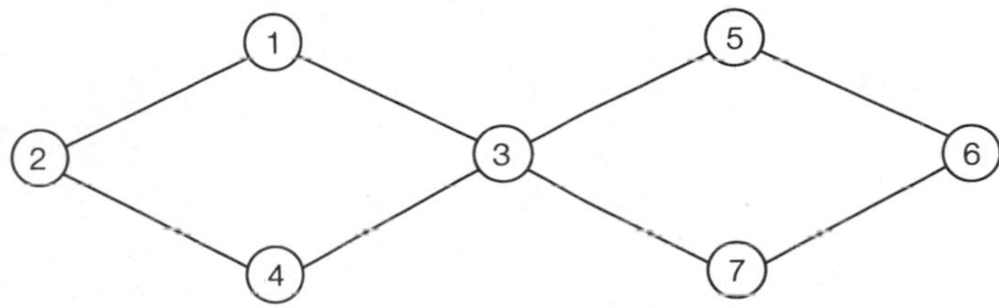

the failure of node 3 disconnects the graph into two subgraphs {1, 2, 4} and {5, 6, 7} that cannot communicate with each other. A node whose deletion, along with the deletion of all edges incident to it, disconnects the graph into two or more nonempty subgraphs is called an *articulation point.* In a reliable and robust communication network, none of the nodes is an articulation point. Such a graph is called *biconnected.*

One way to locate an articulation point is by using its definition, that is, remove a node i and see if the resulting graph is connected. Repeat this for all of the nodes in the graph.

```
ArticulationSet = {}
G' := G
                               (* G is the graph of the network. *)
For i := 1 To N Do
    DeleteNode (G', i)          (* The operation from Figure 10–3 *)
    BreadthFirstTraversal (G')  (* The operation from Figure 10–5 *)
    If any node in G' is marked as Not_Visited Then
        ArticulationSet := ArticulationSet U {i}
    G' := G
End For
Output ArticulationSet
```

For each node i, $i = 1, \ldots, N$, we delete node i from the original graph G, along with all edges incident to i. We now attempt a traversal of G to see if it is possible to visit all nodes. If, after the traversal, one or more nodes is marked Not Visited then the graph has been disconnected and the node we removed is an articulation point whose failure will be catastrophic to the network. We may wish to provide a backup computer system at that site to take over the communication switching responsibilities in the event of a failure in the main system; the backup system will keep the network connected and allow message exchange between all nodes to continue.

This case study showed how a graph data structure can be a good model for the distributed computer system called a wide area network. In addition, it showed how abstract graph operations such as traversals, shortest paths, edge and node insertion, and edge and node deletion can be used to solve real-world network problems and can be helpful in building an efficient and reliable telecommunications system.

10.5 CONCLUSION

We have now completed our study of the four classes of data structures shown in Figure 3–1: sets, linear, hierarchical, and graphs. These structures are categorized by the nature of the successor and predecessor relationships among their components:

Class	*Relationship*	*Example*
1. Set	None	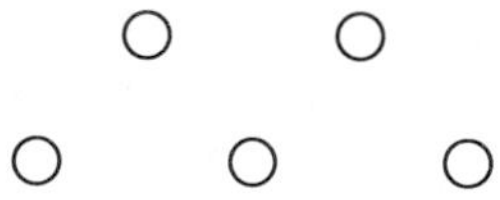
2. Linear	1 : 1	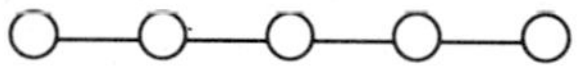
3. Hierarchical	1 : many	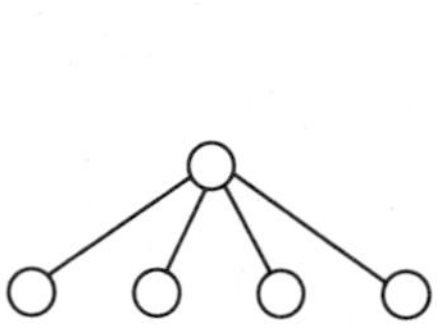
4. Graph	many : many	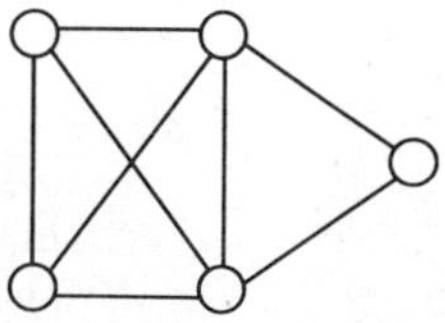

Graphs are the most general and the most powerful of the four structures. All of the structures studied in previous chapters can be viewed as graphs, albeit with certain limitations placed on the number and location of edges. Thus a good Graph ADT package can be used to simulate and support a wide range of other data structures and is a very useful tool.

CHAPTER EXERCISES

1. Given the following directed graph

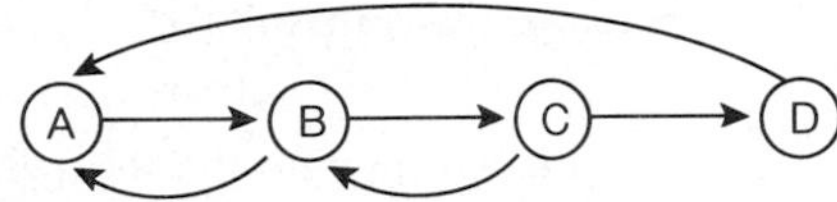

list all its nodes, edges, and cycles.

2. Given the following undirected, weighted graph

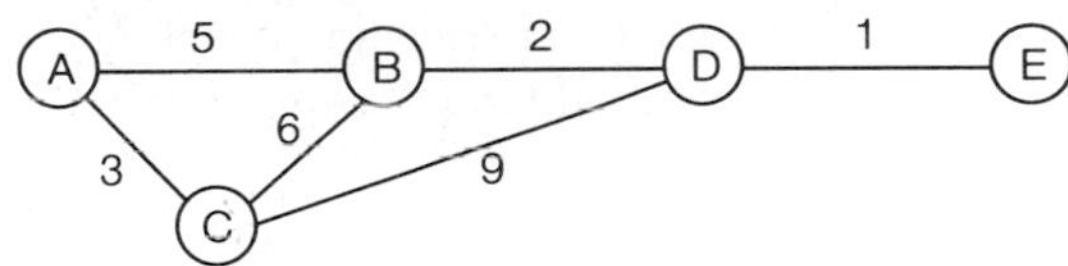

what are the costs of all the simple paths from A to E? Which is the least cost path?

3. Is the following graph connected or disconnected? Explain your answer.

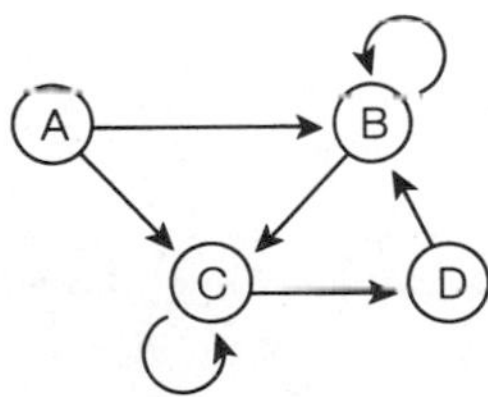

4. Give definitions of sets and linear structures that show them to be simply restricted forms of graphs.
5. Why is a weighted, directed graph the most general-purpose graph representation?
6. Think of some examples of the use of graph structures in everyday life other than the road map and course sequence examples given in section 10.1.
7. Modify the description of the syntax and semantics of the five basic graph operations in Figure 10–3 so that they describe the behavior of
   a. An undirected graph
   b. An unweighted graph
8. Clearly describe what, if any, preconditions would exist for the five operations described in Figure 10–3.

9. What graph structure results from this sequence of operations?

```
G := CreateGraph()
InsertNode (G,A)
InsertNode (G,B)
InsertNode (G,C)
InsertNode (G,D)
InsertEdge (G,A,B,1)
InsertEdge (G,B,C,1)
InsertEdge (G,C,D,2)
DeleteNode (G,B)
```

10. What is wrong with the following pair of operations?

```
InsertEdge(G,A,B,1)
InsertEdge(G,A,B,2)
```

What kind of structure would this represent?

11. How would the following graph

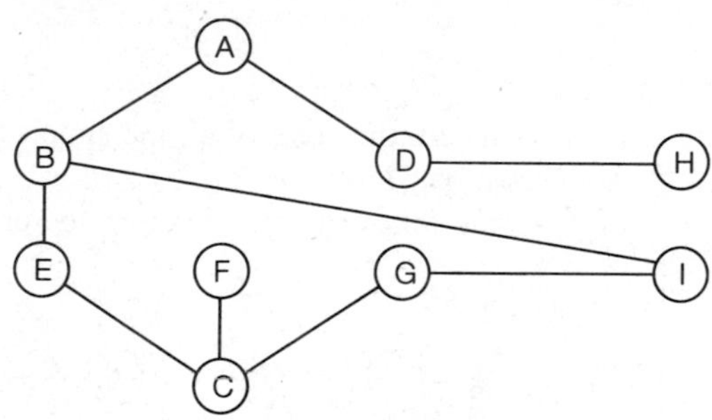

be visited using a breadth-first traversal beginning at node C? at node I? (Assume that nodes are queued in strict alphabetical order.)

12. Write a procedure to determine the number of independent connected subgraphs of a graph G. Given the following three graphs

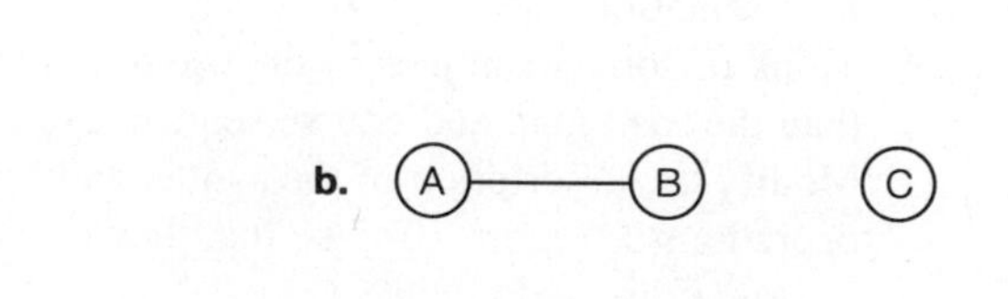

your program would output the values 1, 2, and 3, respectively. You may use the breadth-first traversal algorithm of Figure 10–5.

13. Using the graph structure shown in exercise 11, how would the graph be visited using a depth-first traversal beginning at node A? at node E? (Assume that nodes are stacked in strict alphabetical order with the lowest value on top.)
14. Write an algorithm to implement the depth-first traversal described in section 10.2.2.
15. Using the graph structure of exercise 11, determine the following
    a. a breadth-first spanning tree rooted at node B
    b. a depth-first spanning tree rooted at node C.
16. Given the following weighted undirected graph

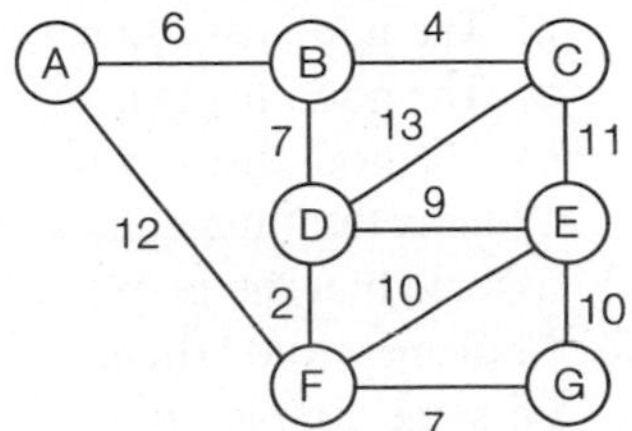

find its minimum spanning tree using Kruskal's algorithm.

17. Write a procedure to implement Kruskal's algorithm of Figure 10–10. Use the set-based technique for locating cycles described in section 10.2.3.
18. What is the time complexity of Kruskal's algorithm of Figure 10–10 in terms of the number of nodes N and the number of edges E?
19. Using the weighted graph of exercise 16, what is the shortest path from node A to node E? from node B to node G? What is the cost of the shortest path from node A to all other nodes using Dijkstra's algorithm of Figure 10–14?
20. Modify Dijkstra's algorithm of Figure 10–14 so that it prints out the edges contained in the shortest path as well as the cost itself.
21. A directed acyclic graph (DAG) is a directed graph that does not contain any cycles, for example,

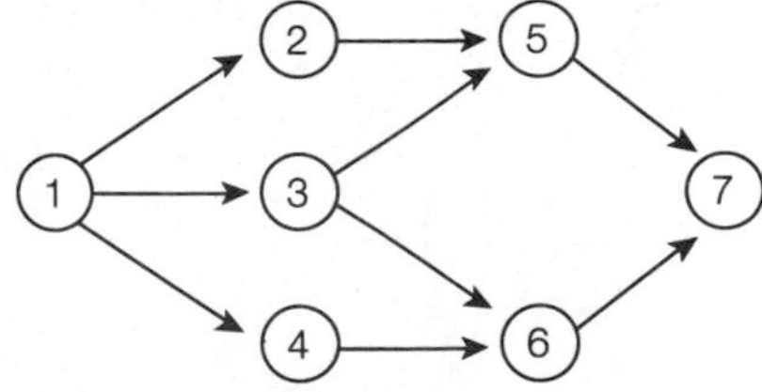

Write a procedure to take a graph G and determine whether it is a DAG.

22. Show the representation of the directed graph in exercise 21 using
    a. An adjacency matrix
    b. An adjacency list

    See how much space each method requires and determine which of the two methods is more space efficient for this particular example. At what point (i.e., how many more or how many fewer edges), would your conclusion about the most efficient representation change?

23. Write the procedure DeleteNode (G,i) which deletes node i in graph G, assuming that G has been represented internally using
    a. An adjacency matrix
    b. An adjacency list
24. Write the procedure InsertEdge (G,i,j,W) which inserts edge $<i,j>$ with weight W in graph G. Assume the graph G is represented using the adjacency list technique described in section 10.3.2.
25. Produce a table giving the complexity of the four basic operations of inserting and deleting nodes and edges, assuming that we are using an adjacency list technique and that the node list and neighbor list are represented as follows:
    a. The node list is a sorted array; the neighbor list is a linked list
    b. The node list is a hash table; the neighbor list is a hash table
    c. The node list is a linked list; the neighbor list is a linked list
26. What is the time complexity of Dijkstra's algorithm in Figure 10–14 if we assume that the graph is represented as an adjacency matrix?
27. Implement the articulation point algorithm shown in the case study and run it on some simple graph structures to locate and print out the articulation points. What is the time complexity of that algorithm?
28. A well known technique for finding a minimum spanning tree is called *Prim's algorithm*. It builds the MST from a graph G edge by edge (as does Kruskal's algorithm), but at each stage in the construction, the set of selected edges forms a tree. It starts with a tree T containing a single node that can be any node in the original graph. It then adds a least cost edge $<n_i, n_j>$ to T so that $T \cup <n_i, n_j>$ is still a tree. In order to guarantee that the structure is still a tree, it must check that either n_i or $n_j \in T$ while the other node is not. This process is repeated until T has exactly $N - 1$ edges.

    Write a procedure to implement Prim's algorithm, and analyze its time complexity if the graph G is stored as an adjacency matrix M.

CHAPTER 11

EXTERNAL SORTING AND SEARCHING

CHAPTER OUTLINE

11.1 INTRODUCTION

The time and space complexity analyses that we have performed throughout this text have been based on two underlying assumptions:

1. The data structure fits entirely into main memory, and every element in that structure is immediately available for processing.
2. All critical operations, whether comparisons, additions, or floating point multiplications, take approximately the same amount of time—on the order of a few microseconds.

Using these assumptions, we are able to compare the relative behavior of different algorithms. For example, when we said that a sequential search is $O(N)$ and a binary search is $O(\log_2 N)$ and that binary search is therefore superior, we used the assumption that the times for the comparisons made in each method take essentially the same amount of time. However, if the processor time needed for one of the ($\log_2 N$) comparisons in the binary search were 3, 4, or 5 orders of magnitude greater than one of the N sequential search comparisons, our analysis would not be so simple and straightforward.

In this chapter we look at algorithms where these two assumptions may no longer be true. We will examine situations in which the amount of data to be processed is so vast that parts of the structure holding that data must be relegated to secondary storage. Before that portion of the data structure can be processed, it must first be moved into main memory. This transfer operation can take from 1,000 to 100,000 times longer than the time needed to process a value already stored in memory. In situations like this one, the critical operation of the algorithm is no longer a memory based operation such as a Boolean comparison or an integer addition; instead, it is the number of times that data records must be moved back and forth between main memory and secondary storage.

Such situations are not just of academic interest or theoretical curiosities. Even though the memory capacities of computer systems are increasing dramatically, and a memory size of 4 to 16 MBytes is not uncommon even for personal workstations, many real-world applications require processing quantities of data that exceed the capacity of virtually all modern machines. We saw one example of such an application in the spelling checker case study of chapter 8. Other common examples of large data structures involve mammoth knowledge bases for artificial intelligence applications, huge commercial data files with millions of transaction records, and the storage of extremely high resolution graphics. In these and similar applications, the memory-resident data structures we have been studying will not suffice, and we need to examine alternative methods.

In this chapter, we will first study how data is stored on external storage devices. Then we will introduce some elementary algorithms for sorting and searching data structures stored on external storage media. These algorithms will not be totally new. Instead, they will be modifications of memory-based techniques that we have already studied—the MergeSort of section 5.4.4 and the binary search tree of section 8.2. The modifications we make to these methods will allow portions of the data structure to reside outside of main memory and will try to limit the number of records that must be transferred in order to maximize efficiency.

11.2 EXTERNAL STORAGE MEDIA

The primary memory of a computer uses an access mechanism called *random access*. (We introduced this term in chapter 3 when we introduced the Array abstract data type, which is a random access data structure.) The two primary characteristics of random-access memory are:

1. All memory cells have a unique address, and all access to those cells is via that address (see Figure 3–6).
2. The time required to fetch or store the contents of a memory cell is independent of the address value and is identical for all cells. (With current technology, main memory access times are typically 50 to 500 nsec, where 1 nsec = 10^{-9} sec.)

In this section we will look at two quite different memory access techniques used in external storage media: *direct access* and *sequential access*.

In a *direct-access storage device*, we eliminate the second characteristic of random access, namely, the characteristic that all data are accessed in exactly the same amount of time. Information is still uniquely addressed and we can go directly to it, but the time required to fetch one piece of information is not a constant value. Instead, the time depends on the location of the information being sought. There are many types of direct-access storage devices (DASDs), for example, floppy disks, hard disks, optical disks, drums, and addressable cassettes. We will discuss data storage on a disk, but the basic principles behind the discussion are valid for any other type of DASD.

Figure 11–1 shows the organization of the surface of a typical disk. The disk surface is coated with ferric oxide, and information is recorded magnetically in concentric circles called *tracks* on the surface of the disk. Each track is divided into the same number of fixed-size units called *sectors*, each of which has a unique address. For example, if our disk has 100 tracks (numbered 00–99) and 500 sectors per track (numbered 000–499), then the sector address 23456 might mean track 23, sector

Figure 11–1
Layout of the Surface of a Disk

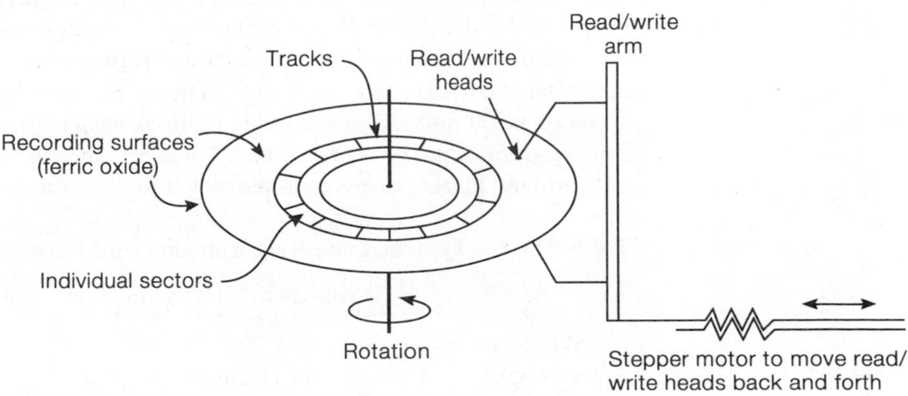

456 from the start of that track. (Each track contains a starting indicator where sector numbering begins.) The layout of an individual disk sector is:

Sector address	Data

The amount of data stored in a sector varies from disk to disk but will typically be about 256, 512, or 1,024 bytes—significantly more than the 1, 2, or 4 bytes of data that can be stored in a single addressable main memory cell. The sector is the addressable unit of a disk and is the unit of information transferred whenever we perform a read or write operation to or from the disk.

Typical disks have many surfaces (not just the single surface shown in Figure 11–1), and each surface may have 100 to 1,000 tracks with 10 to 100 sectors per track. A sector itself may contain 256 to 1,024 individual bytes of information. Therefore, disk capacities vary widely; some small floppy disks may hold as few as a few hundred thousand bytes, while large hard disks or optical disks may store hundreds of millions or even billions of bytes per disk unit.

Fetching a particular sector on a disk involves three steps:

1. Move the read/write head to the correct track (*seek time*).
2. Wait for the correct sector to rotate under the read/write head (*latency time*).
3. Read the entire sector (*transfer time*).

The total disk *access time* required to access any one sector on the disk is therefore:

access time = seek time + latency time + transfer time

Obviously, the total time depends on exactly which sector we are accessing. If it is a sector located on the same track as the current position of the read/write head, then no head movement is necessary and the seek time will be 0. Otherwise, we must move the read/write arm, and the time required will be a function of how far the arm has to travel. Similarly, if we are accessing a sector that is just about to pass under the read/write head, the latency time will be approximately 0. Otherwise we must wait for up to one full rotation. The transfer time is the time that it takes to read the data contained in one sector; it is simply the time required for one sector to rotate completely under the read/write head, so it is the same for all sectors.

Table 11–1 shows some simple best-case/worst-case times for a typical disk, assuming 100 tracks, ½ msec to cross a track, 50 sectors per track, and a rotational speed of 1,200 rpm. All times are in milliseconds (1 msec = 10^{-3} second). As we can see from Table 11–1, the access times for our hypothetical disk are definitely not constant; in fact, in this example they differ by as much as two orders of magni-

Table 11–1 Typical Time Requirements (in Milliseconds) for Disk Access

	Seek time	Latency time	Transfer time	Total time
Best case	0	0	1	1
Worst case	50	50	1	101
Average case	25	25	1	51

Figure 11–2
A Magnetic Drum

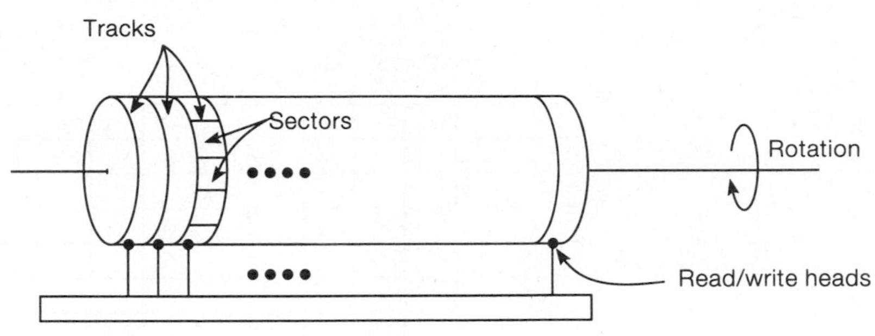

tude, depending on which sector is being accessed. Such variation is a typical characteristic of direct-access storage devices.

Also notice the enormous difference in access times between disk and main memory. Main memory access may require as little as 50 nsec, while the disk of Table 11–1 will require an average of about 50 msec—a difference of six orders of magnitude! This example clearly illustrates why we are so concerned with minimizing disk transfers, rather than internal processor or memory operations.

There are many other types of direct-access storage devices. Figure 11–2 shows a second type called a *drum*. A drum has one read/write head per track, so the seek time on a drum is always 0. Time will still be required for latency and transfer, but because of the elimination of seek time, drums usually have a lower overall access time than disks.

Regardless of the mechanics of the device, however, a DASD always has the following two characteristics:

1. All information is identified by and accessed through a unique address.
2. Access time depends on the location of the information being retrieved, and the difference between the best- and worst-case access times can be significant.

Sequential access is the second basic access mechanism for external storage devices. With sequential access, we dispense with both of the original characteristics of random access. We no longer require that information be accessed through a unique address. Instead, to locate a piece of data, we must search sequentially through all the information stored on the device until we find what we are looking for.

The best known example of a *sequential-access storage device* (SASD) is magnetic tape. Figure 11–3 shows the layout of information on the surface of a tape. Like the surface of a disk, the surface of a tape is coated with ferric oxide; information is magnetically recorded in rows called *channels*. Most modern tapes contain nine channels, allowing the storage of an eight-bit character with one additional bit (called a *parity bit*) used for error checking. The number of characters that can be packed into a specified amount of space is called the *tape density*, and on most current machines it is about 1,600 characters per inch. Since a typical tape is 2,200 feet long, it could theoretically hold about

$$2{,}200 \text{ feet } x \text{ } 12 \text{ inches/foot } x \text{ } 1{,}600 \text{ characters/inch} = 42{,}240{,}000 \text{ characters}$$

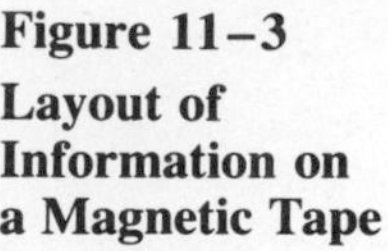

Figure 11–3
Layout of Information on a Magnetic Tape

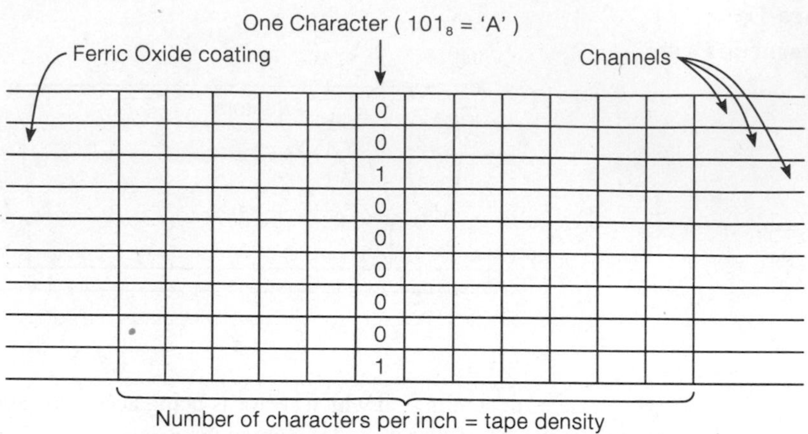

Figure 11–4
Interrecord Gaps on a Magnetic Tape

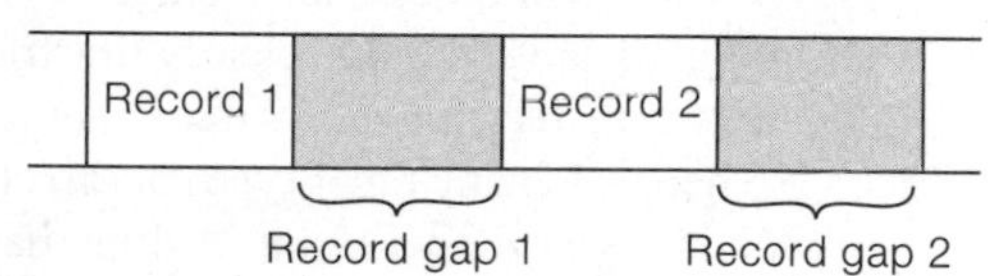

That limit is unattainable, however, because we must allow space for the tape drive to come up to speed and stop. This unused space, called an *interrecord gap* or *tape gap*, is placed between each chunk of data to be read, as shown in Figure 11–4.

Gap 1 in Figure 11–4 allows space for stopping the tape drive after reading record 1 and for starting it up to begin to read record 2. The exact size of these gaps depends on the mechanical characteristics of the particular tape drive, but they can easily occupy 30, 50 or even 70% of the entire tape, reducing the effective storage per reel to 10 to 20 million characters rather than the 42 million characters we computed earlier.

For example, if we stored only one line of 80 characters per tape record (using a 1600 char/inch tape), each record would occupy 80/1600 = 0.05 in. of space on the tape. The average size of an interrecord gap is 0.75 in. If the entire tape had this format, then the fraction of empty space would be 0.75/0.80, or about 94%. The tape would be able to hold only about 2.6 million characters rather than 42 million.

The time required to access data from a magnetic tape depends on exactly where that data is located on the tape. If it is in the very next block, then the access time will be relatively short, perhaps on the order of 1 or 2 msec. However, if the information is at the very end and we are at the beginning of the reel, then we will have to search all 2,200 feet of tape, looking for the desired information one record at a time.

There are a number of other types of SASD, but they all share the characteristic that information is not uniquely addressed. To locate a specific piece of data, we must search sequentially through all items until the desired one is found, a process that may take on the order of seconds or even minutes.

In summary, the following characteristics of external storage media will be important to us in the remainder of the chapter:

1. Information may or may not be accessed directly by address, depending on whether we are using a direct-access or a sequential-access storage device.
2. The capacity of these devices is generally very large, exceeding the capacity of main memory by one or two orders of magnitude.
3. The access time of these devices is slow, usually two to six orders of magnitude slower than main memory.

In the next two sections we shall see how to develop algorithms for processing data stored on devices with these specific characteristics.

11.3 EXTERNAL SORTING USING MERGESORT

In previous chapters of this text we have described several efficient $O(N \log_2 N)$ algorithms for sorting data stored in a computer's memory, for example, HeapSort, QuickSort, and TreeSort. However, the amount of data to be sorted frequently exceeds the capacity of a computer's internal main memory, although it can easily be stored on the machine's secondary storage system (e.g., on a disk). Sorting algorithms that are applied to data on external storage devices are referred to as *external* sorting algorithms, in contrast to the *internal* sorting algorithms we have previously described.

External sorting is extremely important in applications where there are enormous amounts of data to be manipulated. For example, it would not be at all unusual to need to sort a file containing 50,000 customer records, with each customer record containing 200 bytes of data. With any of the internal sorting methods we have studied, this problem would require the allocation of at least 10 Mbytes of primary memory, exceeding the capacity of many machines. However, 10 Mbytes of external storage is quite minimal, and as we showed in the previous section, that amount of disk storage would be available on even the smallest microcomputers or workstations.

We will describe the most popular external sorting technique, which is based on the internal MergeSort algorithm of section 5.4.4; it is called *External MergeSort*.

Assume that the external disk file to be sorted contains the following ten integer values:

7, 29, 2, 11, 3, 170, 1, 55, 349, 41

Obviously, this small amount of data could be sorted using any internal sorting method; we use this small example only to illustrate the operation of the external MergeSort algorithm more easily. Furthermore, the data to be sorted need not be limited to simple scalar values such as integers; they could be large record structures in which the key on which we are sorting is just one field in the record.

The algorithm proceeds in two distinct steps, the *sort phase* and the *merge phase*. First, regions of the input file are individually sorted using any efficient $O(N \log_2 N)$ internal sorting algorithm; a *region* is defined as a subset of data records that fits into the available primary memory. For this example, we will assume that

Table 11–2 First Phase of External MergeSort Algorithm

Region	Original data read into memory	Data sorted in memory	Data written to disk file
1	7 29 2	2 7 29	2 7 29
2	11 3 170	3 11 170	2 7 29 / 3 11 170
3	1 55 349	1 55 349	2 7 29 / 3 11 170 / 1 55 349
4	41	41	2 7 29 / 3 11 170 / 1 55 349 / 41

these regions each contain three elements. The first region of the file is read into memory, sorted using an internal sorting algorithm, and written onto another file stored on the disk. This process of reading, sorting, and appending sorted data onto the output file is continued until all the data from the original file are processed. The results of this first phase for the ten-element file in our example are shown in Table 11–2. (The / indicates the separation between individual regions in the output file.)

The sorted regions of the newly created output file (i.e., the fourth column of Table 11–2) are called *runs*. In this example we have produced four runs. Except for the last run, which contains only one record, the length of each run is three records. The total number of runs, NR, will depend on the value of N, the number of records in the original file, and NM, the number of records that can fit in primary memory. (Note: $\lceil\ \rceil$ is the *ceiling function*. $\lceil i \rceil$ is the smallest integer j such that $j >= i$. $\lfloor\ \rfloor$ is the *floor function*. $\lfloor i \rfloor$ is the largest integer j such that $j <= i$.)

$$\text{NR} = \lceil N/\text{NM} \rceil$$

NM is determined by the amount of memory available and the size in bytes of each data record:

$$\text{NM} = \left\lfloor \frac{\text{bytes of memory available}}{\text{size of data record}} \right\rfloor$$

In this simple cxample, $N = 10$, $\text{NM} = 3$, and $\text{NR} = 4$.

Let's look quickly at another example using more realistic values. If our file to be sorted contained 50,000 customer records, each record holding 200 bytes of data, and we had 64K of primary memory available for our sorting task (64K = 65, 536), then the number of records that could fit in memory at one time would be

$$\text{NM} = \left\lfloor \frac{65536}{200} \right\rfloor = 327 \text{ records}$$

Since $N = 50{,}000$, the total number of distinct runs that we would have produced at the end of the sorting phase would be:

$$\text{NR} = \left\lceil \frac{50{,}000}{327} \right\rceil = 153 \text{ runs}$$

Figure 11–5
Sorting Phase of External MergeSort

```
(* This is an algorithm for the sorting phase of External MergeSort *)
            (* Begin at the first record of Infile *)
Start := 1
            (* Fill in with the number of records in the file *)
N := . . .
            (* Fill in with the amount of memory available for buffer space. *)
MemoryAvailable := . . .
            (* Fill in with the size in bytes of one record. *)
RecordSize := . . .
            (* NM is the number of records that will fit in memory at once. *)
NM := MemoryAvailable Div RecordSize
            (* NR is the number of iterations of read/sort/write we will have to do. *)
NR := Ceiling(N / NM)
For i := 1 To NR Do
            (* End is the number of the last record we must deal with for this iteration. *)
     End := Max(Start + NM − 1, N)
            (* Read the records into memory for this run *)
     Read records of the disk with numbers in the range [Start .. End] from Infile
     and store them in array A
            (* Sort them. This can be done in memory with any internal sorting
            algorithm. *)
     Sort(A)
            (* Write the run to external storage. *)
     Write A to Outfilo
            (* Recalculate the starting record for the next run. *)
     Start := Start + NM
Endfor
```

The algorithm for the sorting phase of External MergeSort is shown in Figure 11–5. The algorithm assumes that the N-record input data is stored in InFile and the sequence of NR sorted runs will be written out to OutFile.

The second phase of the algorithm, the merging phase, takes the runs generated by Phase I and merges them two at a time in a process called a *merge pass*. At the end of one merge pass, we will have reduced the number of runs from NR to NR/2. We now perform another pass, reducing the number of runs from NR/2 to NR/4. After $\log_2$ NR passes, we will have only a single run containing all of the data in sorted sequence. In our example with the simple ten-element file, we began with NR = 4 runs, so we will need $\log_2 4 = 2$ passes to complete the merge phase. The merge process is diagrammed in Figure 11–6.

Now the question is how we can carry out a merge operation like the one shown in Figure 11–6 if the size of the run exceeds the capacity of our memory. In our simple example, we have said that we can store a maximum of three records in memory at once. Yet, referring to Figure 11–6, we see that at the end of Pass 1 we

Figure 11–6
Second Phase of the External MergeSort Algorithm

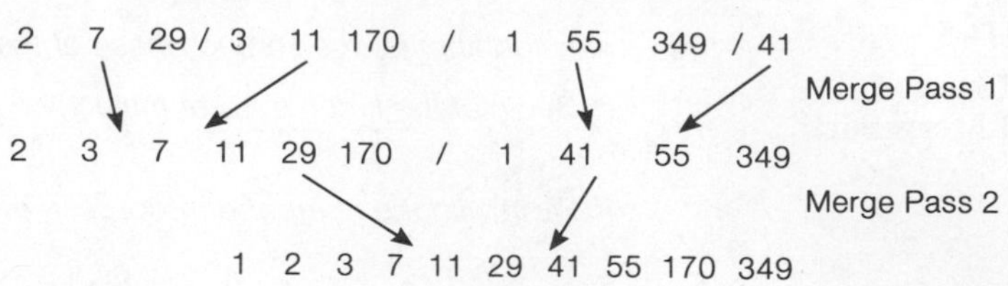

have runs of length 4 and 6, and at the end of Pass 2 we have a run of length 10. Does this violate our assumption about the limits of available memory? If not, how do we accomplish this operation? The answer is that this process is perfectly legal. The trick is to realize that when you are doing a merge operation like the one shown in Figure 11–6, you do not need to have the entire run stored in memory. In fact, you need only the one item from each of the two lists currently being compared. For example, when we start merging the following two runs

	Run 1	*Run 2*	
current →	2	3	← current
	7	11	
	29	170	

the only values we need immediate access to are the smallest values currently contained in each run, 2 and 3 in this case. After the 2 is moved to the merged output file, the only values we need access to are the new smallest values, 3 and 7.

Recall that NM is the total number of records from our data file that can fit in memory. Let us divide the total memory space available for record storage into three distinct memory pools or *buffers*, each of size $\lfloor NM/3 \rfloor$. The three pools will be called In1, In2, and Out. In1 and In2 hold the next $\lfloor NM/3 \rfloor$ records from the two runs being merged. As we select records from either In1 or In2 to be merged, we move them from In1 or In2 into Out. When either In1 or In2 becomes empty, we refill it with the next NM/3 records from the disk file called InFile. After $\lfloor NM/3 \rfloor$ records have been moved to Out, the entire Out buffer is written to OutFile. At no time are there more than NM records in memory, so our memory restrictions are not violated. This merging operation is illustrated in Figure 11–7 for our ten-element example, assuming that the number of records that can fit in memory (NM) is 3. Each of the three separate memory buffers, In1, In2, and Out, will therefore be of size $\lfloor NM/3 \rfloor = 1$ record.

The algorithm for the merging phase of External MergeSort is given in Figure 11–8. The algorithm assumes that the sequence of NR sorted runs is currently in a file called InFile (produced by the algorithm of Figure 11–5) and that the merged runs are to be written to a file called OutFile, which then becomes the input file for the next merge pass. In addition, it assumes the existence of three memory buffers (In1, In2, and Out), each capable of storing $\lfloor NM/3 \rfloor$ records; these three buffers hold the next $\lfloor NM/3 \rfloor$ records of run i, run $i + 1$, and the merged output, respectively.

Figure 11–7
The Merging Phase of External MergeSort

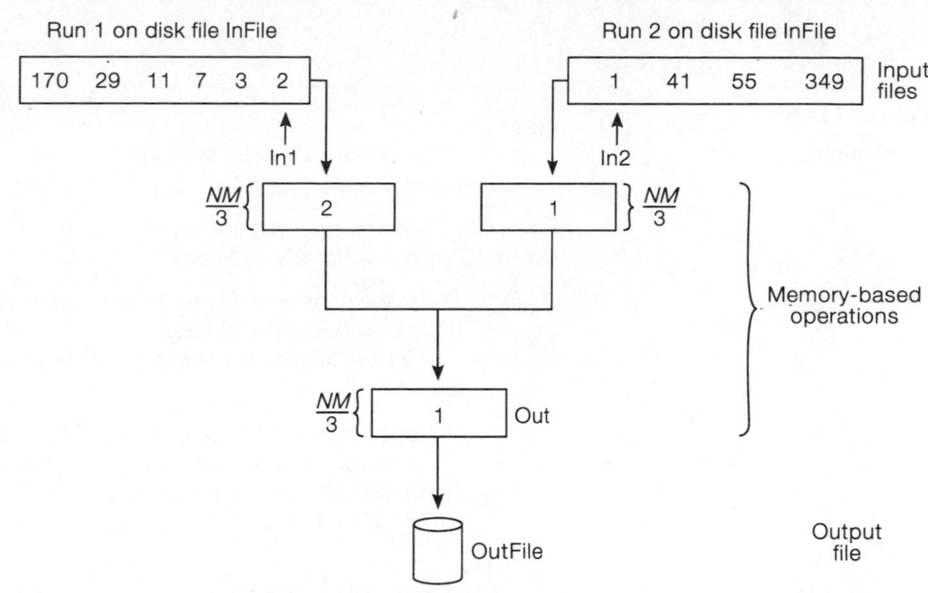

Figure 11–8
Algorithm for the Merge Phase of External MergeSort

```
(* This is the algorithm for the Merge Phase of the External MergeSort algorithm.
The meaning of the variables N, NM, and NR are the same as in the algorithm
describing the Sort Phase, Figure 11.5 *)
For i := 1 To (NR Div 2) Do

        (* Set up buffers and initialize variables *)
    Read first NM Div 3 records of Run (i * 2 - 1) into In1
    Read first NM Div 3 records of Run (i * 2) into In2
    Current1 := 1
    Current2 := 1
    CurrentOut := 1

        (* This loop does the merging of In1 and In2 into Out *)
    Loop
        If (In1[Current1] < In2[Current2]) Then

                (* Select the current value from In1 *)
            Out[CurrentOut] := In1[Current1]

                (* Are we done with the current buffer? *)
            If (Current1 = NM Div 3) Then

                (* Are we done with all the records in this Run? *)
                If done with Run (i * 2 - 1) Then
                    Exit (* Yes, so we're done with this loop *)
                Endif

                (* No, so load up the buffer with the next set of
                    records, and start at the beginning again. *)
                Read next NM Div 3 Records of Run (i * 2 - 1) into In1
                Current1 := 1

            Else (* Not done with buffer, so just move current pointer *)
                Current1 := Current1 + 1
            Endif
```

(continued)

Figure 11–8 (continued)

```
Else
        (* Select current value from In2 *)
    Out[CurrentOut] := In2[Current2]

        (* Are we done with the current buffer? *)
    If (Current2 = NM Div 3) Then

        (* Are we done with all the records in this Run? *)
        If done with Run (i * 2) Then
            Exit (* Yes, so we're done with this loop *)
        Endif

        (* No, so load up the buffer with the next set of
            records, and start at the beginning again. *)
        Read next NM Div 3 Records of Run (i * 2) into In2
        Current2 := 1

    Else
    (* Not done with buffer, so just move current pointer *)
        Current2 := Current2 + 1
    Endif
Endif

    (* Is the output buffer full? *)
If (CurrentOut = NM Div 3) Then
        (* Yes, so write it out. *)
    Write Out to Outfile
    CurrentOut := 1

Else (* No it is not, so just move the current pointer *)
    CurrentOut := CurrentOut + 1
Endif

Endloop

(* When the preceeding loop has been exited, there will always
    be elements left in either Run (i * 2 − 1) or Run (i * 2),
    but never both. Consequently, one of the two following
    loops will be executed (but not both). One of the loops
    transfers the rest of the elements of Run (i * 2 − 1) to
    Out, and the other does the same for Run (i * 2). Note that
    at this point CurrentOut will always be equal to the current
    pointer of the buffer with elements left in it. *)
If (Current1 <= NM Div 3) Then

        (* This loop moves the rest of Run (i * 2 − 1) to Out *)
    Loop
        (* Transfer the elements in the In1 buffer to Out *)
        While (Current1 <= NM Div 3) Do
            Out[CurrentOut] := In1[Current1]
            Current1 := Current1 + 1
            CurrentOut := CurrentOut + 1
        Endwhile

        Write Out to Outfile
        CurrentOut := 1
```

(continued)

Figure 11–8 (continued)

```
                (* Exit the loop if there are no more records in the run *)
                If done with Run (i * 2 - 1) Then
                    Exit
                Endif

                (* There are more records, so read them into the buffer *)
                Read next NM Div 3 Records of Run (i * 2 - 1) into In1
                Current1 := 1
            Endloop
    Else
            (* This loop moves the rest of Run (i * 2) to Out *)
            Loop
                (* Transfer the elements in the In2 buffer to Out *)
                While (Current2 <= NM Div 3) Do
                    Out[CurrentOut] := In1[Current2]
                    Current2 := Current2 + 1
                    CurrentOut := CurrentOut + 1
                Endwhile

                Write Out to Outfile
                CurrentOut := 1

                (* Exit the loop if there are no more records in the run *)
                If done with Run (i * 2) Then
                    Exit
                Endif

                (* There are more records, so read them into the buffer *)
                Read next NM Div 3 Records of Run (i * 2) into In2
                Current2 := 1
            Endloop
    Endif
Endfor
```

Let us determine the total number of disk transfers required by Phase I and Phase II of External MergeSort to sort a file of N records. We will count disk transfers, not comparisons, because, as we mentioned in section 11.1, transfers are the critical operation that will dominate the total time required by the sort operation.

Looking at the sorting algorithm of Figure 11–5, we see that each data record will be read once from InFile and written once to OutFile. If we have a total of N records, the sort phase will require a total of $2N$ disk transfers.

The merge phase of Figure 11–8 requires us to read each record once from InFile into either In1 or In2 and write it once from Out to OutFile. These two operations are done once for each pass, for a total of $2N$ transfers per pass. We have already shown that a file with NR runs needs ($\log_2$ NR) passes, where NR = $\lceil N/\text{NM} \rceil$. Thus the merge phase requires $2N[\log_2(\lceil N/\text{NM} \rceil)]$ disk transfers. The total number of disk transfers needed to sort a file of N records is the sum of the number of disk transfers needed during each phase.

$$\text{total number of disk transfers} = 2N + 2N[\log_2(\lceil N/\text{NM} \rceil)]$$
$$= 2N(1 + \log_2(\lceil N/\text{NM} \rceil))$$

where NM is the number of data records that can fit in memory at once.

For our simple ten-element file where $N = 10$ and NM = 3, the number of disk reads and writes would be:

$$= 2 * 10\ (1 + \log_2 \lceil 10/3 \rceil)$$
$$= 20\ (1 + \log_2 4)$$
$$= 20\ (1+2)$$
$$= 60$$

In our example where $N = 50{,}000$ and NM = 327 (more realistic values), we would need to do

$$2 * 50{,}000\ (1 + \lceil \log_2 153 \rceil)$$
$$\approx 900{,}000 \text{ disk transfers}$$

Using the sample data from Table 11–1, which showed that a typical disk access time is about 51 milliseconds, the total time needed to complete the sort of the 50,000-record file would be

$$= (9.0 \times 10^5 \text{ transfers}) \times (51 \times 10^{-3} \text{ seconds/transfer})$$
$$= 45{,}900 \text{ seconds}$$
$$= 12.7 \text{ hours}$$

a long, long wait! A faster disk, say one with an average time of 10 to 15 msec would help some, but it would still leave us with a sorting time in the range of 2 to 4 hours.

One possible solution to this problem is to use a technique called *blocking*, in which we place more than one data record in each sector of the disk. For example, if our data records are 250 bytes long and a sector holds 1,024 bytes, we could block four records per sector, leaving the final 24 bytes unused.

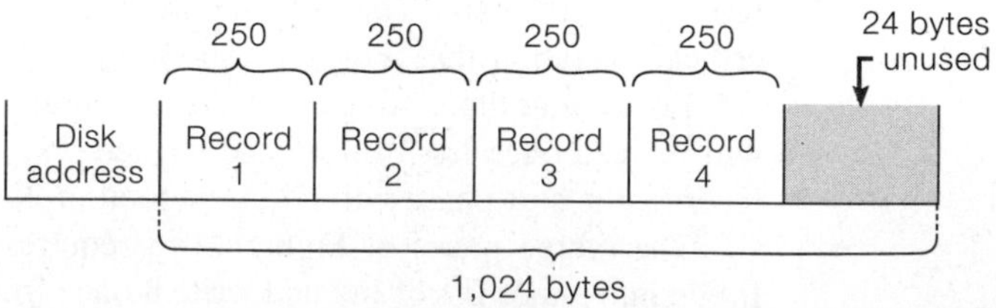

The number of logical records stored in each addressable sector of the disk is called the *blocking factor*, B. In our previous discussion the value of B was 1. In the above diagram the blocking factor is B = 4. When we read a sector containing blocked records from the disk, we get not a single record but B records, all of which are brought into memory. The data record we want is now available, and the next

(B − 1) data records to be read will also come from our memory buffers, not from disk, saving considerable time. There will be similar savings when we write to the disk, since we will transfer blocks of B records instead of just a single record.

The number of disk transfers needed for the sorting phase is now $2N/B$ rather than $2N$, and the number needed by the merge phase is $2N/B(\log_2(\lceil N/NM \rceil))$. With a blocking factor of B = 4, the sorting time for our example would be reduced (assuming the same 51 msec access time) to:

$$(9.0 \times 10^5/4) \times (51 \times 10^{-3})$$
$$= 3.2 \text{ hours}$$

If we also select a faster disk with an average access time of 15 msec rather than 51 msec, we can reduce this time further to about 56 minutes, which is getting close to being reasonable. One final improvement we could make would be to increase the size of our memory buffers so that we can increase the value of NM, the number of data records that can fit in memory at one time. Our earlier example assumed 200 bytes/record (which we will assume is unchangeable) and 64K of available buffer space. If we could afford to buy some additional memory and increase the buffer space available to 256 K ($256K = 2^{18}$), then

$$NM = \lfloor 262{,}144/200 \rfloor = 1{,}310 \text{ records}$$

Now the total time needed for the External MergeSort (using a blocking factor of B = 4 and an average disk access time of 15 msec) would be

$$((2 \times 50{,}000)/4) \times (1 + \log_2 (\lceil 50{,}000/1{,}310 \rceil)) \times 15 \times 10^{-3}$$
$$= 39 \text{ minutes}$$

We have now reduced the time needed to solve our original problem from about 12 hours to about 40 minutes, a reduction of 94%!

The point of this extended discussion has been to illustrate the need to focus on minimizing the number of disk operations in order to produce an efficient solution. By making the following three changes:

1. Blocking four data records per disk sector rather than one
2. Allocating more memory to our buffers so that fewer passes have to be made during the merge phase
3. Buying a faster disk with a lower average access time

we have significantly reduced the time needed to complete our external sorting problem and made the problem computationally feasible.

In contrast, buying a machine with a faster internal processing speed or a lower main memory access time would make virtually no difference in the sorting time. To demonstrate this latter point, let us estimate the number of internal comparison operations needed to complete the sorting phase of External MergeSort, totally disregarding the I/O transfer time. There are NR runs to be sorted, each of length NM. If we use an $O(N \log_2 N)$ sorting technique, e.g., HeapSort, then it will take about ($NM \log_2 NM$) comparisons to sort each run, or a total of about $NR * (NM \log_2 NM)$ comparisons during Phase I. If we use our earlier example, in which NM = 327

records and NR = 153 runs, and assume that a main memory comparison takes 1 μsec (a reasonable value), then the processor time needed for the sorting phase is

$$153 \times (327 \log_2 327) \text{ operations} \times 1 \times 10^{-6} \text{ seconds/operation}$$
$$\approx 0.4 \text{ second}$$

Buying a processor that reduces the sorting time internally by 50% will save us exactly two tenths of a second! Not very much when we realize that disk I/O will require from ½ hour to ½ day. An analysis of the internal processor time spent on the merging phase would show the same results: the processor time is insignificant compared to the I/O transfer delays.

11.4 EXTERNAL SEARCHING

11.4.1 Formal Definition of *m*-Way Search Trees

Just as we did with the External MergeSort sorting algorithm of section 11.3, we want to develop an efficient searching technique that minimizes the number of disk transfers that must be made. The method that we have chosen to discuss in detail in this section is a variation of the binary search tree (BST) technique first described in section 8.2.

For a BST such as the following one,

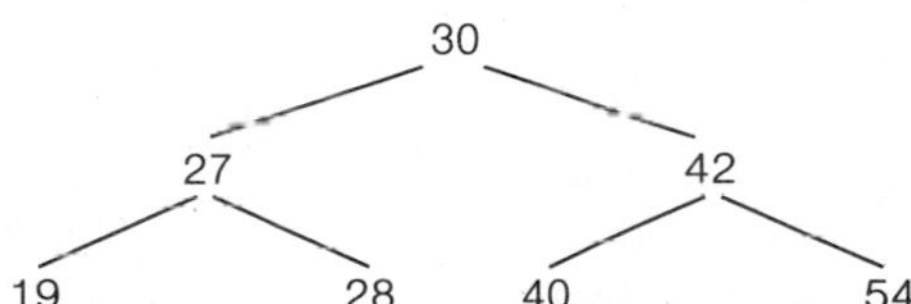

the searching algorithm we developed in chapter 8 led us through the tree, following either the left or the right subtree, until we either found the desired key or we reached a leaf node, in which case we either inserted the key, or stated the key was not contained in the tree (see Figure 8–3). If the tree is relatively balanced, this searching process required $\log_2$ N comparisons. Because this solution is quite efficient, a binary search tree is a popular and widely used data structure for storing and retrieving data.

However, if each of the nodes in a binary search tree is on an external storage device rather than stored in memory, we also must do $\log_2 N$ transfers from disk into memory, and these transfers would be quite time-consuming. If our search tree is balanced and contains 50,000 nodes, then its height $H = (\log_2 50{,}000) \approx 16$. In the worst case, we will need approximately 16 disk accesses to locate an item, with each access taking (for our sample disk) about 51 msec. Thus the total search time would be about one second. If we are working in a high-volume interactive environment (e.g., dozens or hundreds of requests per second), this performance may not be acceptable, especially if the search process is only part of a much larger problem.

One possible solution is to use the technique we introduced in the previous section—*blocking*. We can block B > 1 data values per tree node so that each access to the disk retrieves B values rather than only one. A search tree in which each

node in the tree holds up to $(m - 1)$ data values sorted in increasing order and up to m pointers to other nodes in the tree, as in

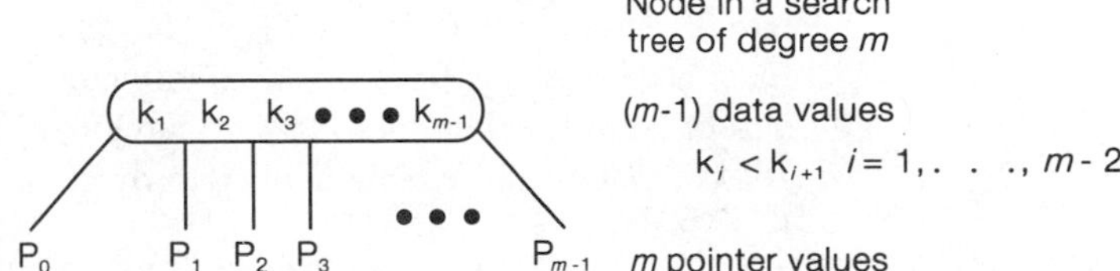

is called an *m-way search tree*. The value m is called the *degree* of the search tree. A binary search tree is just a special case of an m-way search tree with degree $m = 2$.

Let's describe exactly what happens during the search of an m-way search tree. When we access a node from the disk, we get up to $(m - 1)$ values that are now stored in memory. We can search the values $K_1, K_2, \ldots, K_{m-1}$ using the efficient $O(\log_2 N)$ binary search, since the values are in sorted sequence. If any of the K_i is the key we are looking for, then we are finished. If not, we follow one of the m pointers, move on to another node in the tree, read it from the disk, and repeat the process. As m gets larger, that is, as we pack more and more data values into each tree node, we need to spend more time searching each node; this part of the search will take $O(\log_2 m)$ time units rather than $O(1)$. However, we will have fewer tree nodes to examine—$O(\log_2 (N/m))$ rather than $O(\log_2 N)$. Since we have assumed that accessing a new node, which requires a disk transfer, is many times slower than searching the node values stored in memory, it is to our advantage to make m as large as possible, consistent with the size of our records and the size of the disk sectors. If, for example, we could block 8 data values per search tree node, then the search of our 50,000-record customer file could be done with $\log_2 (50{,}000/8) \approx 13$ accesses of the disk rather than 16. However, for each node we must do $(\log_2 8) = 3$ comparisons rather than the one comparison that would be made for a node in a standard binary search tree.

The maximum degree m of an m-way search tree used for external searching is determined by R, the size in bytes of the data values being stored, S, the sector size of the disk, and p, the number of bytes needed to represent a pointer. Since each sector will need to store $(m - 1)$ data values and m pointers, we can determine m as follows:

$$(m - 1)R + mp = S$$

$$m = \lfloor (S + R) / (p + R) \rfloor$$

For example, if our sector size S is 1,024 bytes, our data records R are 80 bytes each, and pointers required $p = 4$ bytes, then m would be:

$$m = \lfloor (1024 + 80) / (4 + 80) \rfloor$$
$$= 13$$

In this case, the highest degree search tree we could construct and store in the sectors of our disk is 13, so we could store 12 data records and 13 pointers in each node of the tree.

Formally, we define an *m*-way search tree as a tree structure in which each node has the following four characteristics

1. Each node contains from 1 to $(m - 1)$ key values $K_1, K_2, \ldots, K_{m-1}$ sorted into ascending order such that $K_i < K_{i+1}$, $i = 1, \ldots, m - 2$.
2. Each node contains from two to m pointers $P_0, P_1, \ldots, P_{m-1}$ which either are null or point to other nodes in the search tree.
3. All key values in the node pointed to by pointer P_i are less than the key value K_{i+1}, $i = 0, \ldots, m - 2$.
4. All key values in the node pointed to by the pointer P_i are greater than the key value K_i, $i = 1, \ldots, m - 1$.

Points 3 and 4 together define what is called the *m-way search tree property*.

Recall from chapter 8 that each node in a binary search tree divides the tree of which it is the root into two subtrees, one containing values that are less than the root value, and one containing values which are greater than the root value. We now generalize that property and say that each node of an *m*-way search tree divides the tree of which it is the root into *m* subtrees. If the keys stored in the node are called $K_1, K_2, \ldots, K_{m-1}$, then the search tree is divided into *m* subtrees, each of which contains values only in the following subranges $[-\infty \,..\, K_1)$, $[K_1, K_2)$, $[K_2, K_3)$, . . . , $[K_{m-2}, K_{m-1})$, $[K_{m-1}, +\infty]$. (Note: The notation [a, b) means that the range includes the value a but does not include the value b. The range [a, b] includes the values of both end-points.) Figure 11–9 shows these subranges for a tree with $m = 4$.

The basic operations on an *m*-way search tree are quite similar to those of a binary search tree, as described in section 8.2. We must be able to create an empty tree, insert new values into the tree in a way which preserves the *m*-way search tree property, and locate values within the tree. The syntax and semantics of these three operations are shown below.

a. CreateMWayTree(*m*) : M

   This operation creates an empty search tree M of degree *m*, $m \geq 2$, on some external storage media.

b. Insert(Key, M) : M

   This operation adds the specified Key to the *m*-way search tree M to produce a new tree M. (We could also have stored a 2-tuple of the form (Key, Value) and inserted the tuple in the tree rather than just the Key. We will omit that level of detail here.) It is assumed that M is stored on some external storage media.

Figure 11–9
Typical Node in a 4-way Search Tree

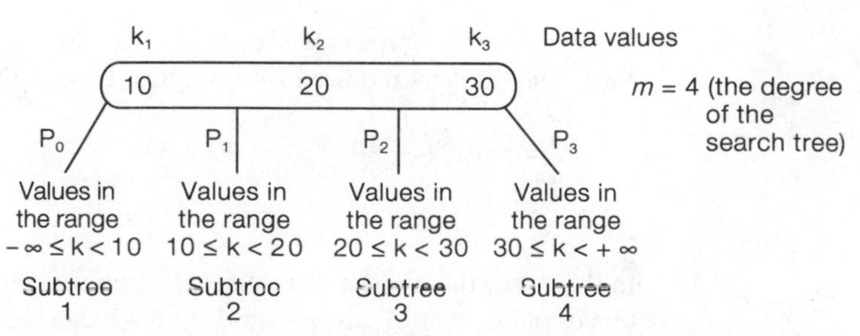

c. Find(Key, M) : Boolean

This operation searches an *m*-way search tree M, stored on some external storage media, to locate the specified Key. If the Key is found, the function returns the value True; otherwise, it returns a False. (If we had stored (Key,Value) pairs, we would return the associated Value.)

The Insert operation must search the tree for the leaf node where the new value is to be inserted in order to guarantee that the addition of the new value maintains the *m*-way search tree property. If that leaf has room for another value, that is, if the number of values currently stored in the node is less than $(m - 1)$, the new key value will be inserted into that leaf node and the values in the node will be sorted into ascending order. If the leaf is full, we must create a new node containing the new value and add that node to the tree as a new leaf. A complete algorithm for *m*-way search tree insertion is shown in Figure 11–10.

Figure 11–10 Insert Algorithm for *m*-Way Search Trees

```
(* This is an algorithm to insert Key into an m-way search tree. *)

Insert (Key, m)

Read the root of the tree from external storage
CurrentNode := root
j := number of keys in CurrentNode

Loop
    Search the j keys in CurrentNode for Key
    If Found Then Exit                    (* Case 1, Key is already there *)

    Elsif (j < m - 1) Then                (* Case 2, there is room in this node *)
        Insert Key in CurrentNode
        j := j + 1
        Sort CurrentNode into ascending order
        Write CurrentNode to external storage
        Exit                              (* Case 2, add Key to existing node *)

    Else                                  (* Case 3, no room in this node *)
        Set i to the value such that k[i] <= Key < k[i+1] in CurrentNode
        If P[i] = Nil Then                (* Do we need to create a new leaf? *)
            (* Yes, so create a node with one value, Key *)
            CreateNode(Key)
            Set P[i] to point to new node
            Update CurrentNode on external storage
            Write the new node to external storage
            Exit                          (* Case 3, Key added to new leaf *)

        Else     (* We have not yet found the insertion point in the tree. *)
        (* Go down one level in tree to try to find correct place for Key *)
            CurrentNode := Node pointed to by P[i]
            Read CurrentNode from external storage
            j := number of keys in CurrentNode
        Endif
    Endif
Endloop
```

There are three cases that must be handled by the Insert process of Figure 11–10. In case 1, the key to be inserted already exists in the tree. Since we do not want to store duplicates, our insertion algorithm will simply return. (If we were storing (Key, Value) pairs, then an alternative approach for duplicate keys would be to update the Value field.)

In case 2, we locate the leaf node where the insertion operation is to be done and find that it has room to hold this new key. For example,

Key = 23 (8 41 75) $m = 5$

Since $m = 5$, each node can hold four values, but this node has only three. We simply add the new key to this node and ensure that all of the values are still in ascending order. The insertion operation thus produces the following node:

(8 23 41 75) $m = 5$

Case 3 occurs when we locate the leaf where the insertion is to be done but discover that it is full, as is now the case with the node shown above. We must first locate the correct subtree in which to place the new key. It will be the subtree pointed at by pointer P_i, where i is a value such that $K_i \le \text{key} < K_{i+1}$. For example, if we want to add the key value 15 to the tree shown above, we must place it in a new node in the subtree pointed to by pointer P_1, since $8 \le 15 < 23$. This step will produce the new tree:

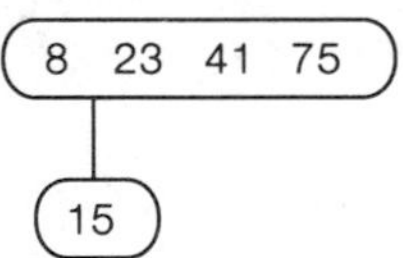

Finally, if none of these three cases applies, then we have not yet arrived at the leaf node where the insertion should be made. In this case we follow the proper pointer to the appropriate subtree and repeat the processes described above. The pointer we follow is P_i, where i is the unique index value such that $K_i \le \text{key} < K_{i+1}$. Figure 11–11 shows the step-by-step construction of an m-way search tree of degree $m = 3$ for the following nine key values

10, 37, 6, 17, 9, 21, 1, 40, 17

The Find operation works in a manner very similar to the insertion process just described, and the specification of the Find algorithm is left as an exercise.

11.4.2 Complexity Analysis of *m*-Way Search Trees

The complexity analysis of the Insertion and Find operations on an m-way search tree must look at the time involved in each of the two distinct phases of the operation, the *tree search* phase, in which we locate the desired node, and the *node search* phase, in which we search the $(m - 1)$ values stored in that node.

Figure 11–11
Insertion Process in an *m*-Way Search Tree

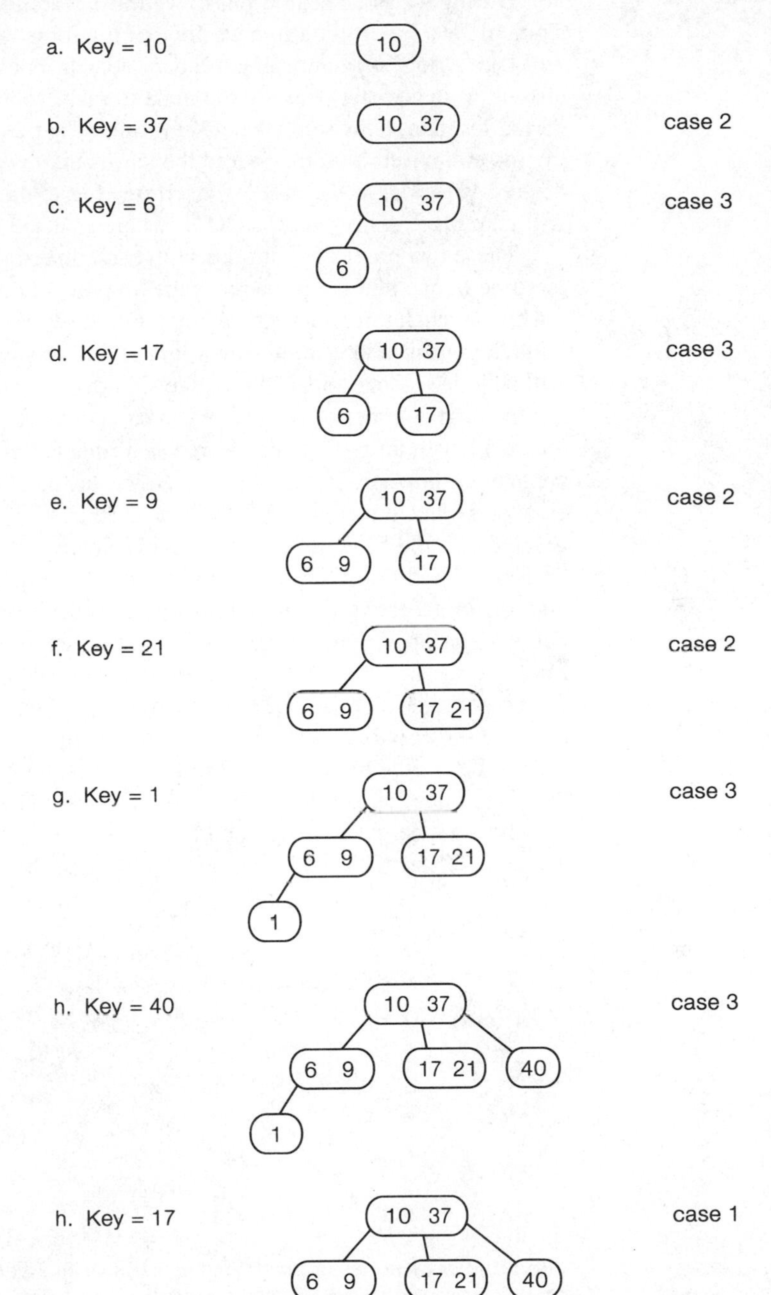

During the node search phase we must search the 1 to $(m - 1)$ keys within a single node to see if the value we are looking for is there. In the worst case, this step will take $O(\log_2 m)$ time using a binary search. For an insertion operation we must also move the existing keys in the node to make room for the new one in the proper sorted location. This step takes $O(m)$ time. The tree search phase involves traversing the entire tree from the root to the leaves until we locate the node containing the desired value or, in the case of insertion, locate the leaf node where the insertion will take place. This phase is $O(H)$, where H is the height of the tree.

These two phases are at odds with each other in the sense that trying to reduce the time of one phase will increase the time of the other. If m is small, then we will not spend much time searching a node, but the search tree will have more nodes and a much greater height, requiring a longer tree traversal. If m is very large, the tree will have few nodes and will be quite shallow, but we will spend more time searching the large number of keys stored in each node. In general, a graph of the time to locate a key in an m-way search tree as a function of m, the degree of the tree, will behave as shown in Figure 11–12. However, our fundamental assumption in this chapter is that the time needed for a disk transfer is many orders of magnitude greater than the time needed for internal processor-based operations such as comparisons or additions. Thus, the tree search phase, which requires the transfer of one disk sector per tree node, will dominate the node search phase, which involves only comparison operations on values stored in memory. The complexity of both the Find and the Insert operations will therefore be completely determined by the tree search phase, which is $O(H)$. Furthermore, the optimal value of m, called m_{opt} in Figure 11–12, will generally be very, very large.

To determine the value of H in terms of N, the total number of values stored in the search tree, and m, the degree of the tree, let us make the assumption that our search tree is height-balanced and full, that is, each node stores its limit of $(m - 1)$ values. We can then determine H by counting the number of key values that are stored in each level of the tree.

	Level	*Number of Values Stored on That Level*
(Root)	0	$(m - 1)$
	1	$(m - 1) \times m$
	2	$(m - 1) \times m^2$
	•	•
	•	•
	•	•
	i	$(m - 1) \times m^i$

The number of nodes at level i is $(m - 1) \times m^i$. Therefore, the maximum number of data values N in a tree of height H is

$$N = \sum_{i=0}^{H} (m - 1) \times m^i$$

$$= m^{H+1} - 1$$

Figure 11–12
Search Time as a Function of *m*, the Degree of the Search Tree

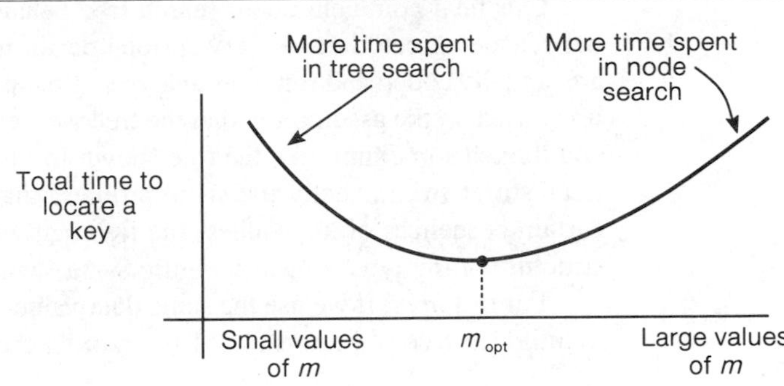

Table 11–3 Height of a Balanced *m*-Way Search Tree as a Function of Its Degree

Degree *m*	Height of an *m*-way search tree for *N* = 50,000
2	16
3	10
4	8
5	7
10	5
25	4
100	3

Solving for H we get:

$$H = \log_m(N + 1) - 1$$
$$H = O(\log_m N)$$

Table 11–3 shows the approximate height of a balanced *m*-way search tree containing 50,000 data values for different values of *m*. By increasing the degree of the tree from 2 to 100, we can reduce from 16 to 3 the number of disk sectors that must, in the worst case, be transferred into memory (assuming, of course, that a disk sector is large enough to hold 99 data values and 100 pointers). This increase in degree saves us 13 I/O operations, which, at 51 msec each (Table 11–1), will potentially reduce the search time by about ⅔ sec. For this decrease in I/O operations, we must pay the price of increasing the number of comparisons per node from $\log_2 2 = 1$ to $\log_2 100 \approx 7$, about 6 additional operations. However, since these comparisons are carried out at the internal high-speed processor rate (approximately 1 μsec/operation), the cost is only 6 μsec extra time per node. With a height of $H = 3$, these extra comparisons will total only 18 μsec = 0.000018 sec extra node search time, which is clearly insignificant compared to the gain of ⅔ sec in tree search time.

The general rule in using *m*-way search trees for external storage and searching is to make *m*, the degree of the tree, as large as possible consistent with the size of the data records and the disk sectors on your computer system.

Our final comment about search tree behavior is that one fundamental flaw in our reasoning could cause very serious performance problems when our programs are actually coded and run. Our analysis of the performance of an m-way search tree was based on the assumption that the tree we were searching was relatively balanced and looked something like the tree shown in Figure 8–5b. However, m-way search trees suffer from exactly the same problem that we introduced in section 8.2: for certain sequences of key values, the tree that we build can degenerate into a linear structure of the type shown in Figure 8–5a, with a height $H = N/(m - 1)$.

For example, if we use the same data values (excepting duplicates) that we used to build the tree of Figure 11–11 but reorder them as follows:

1, 6, 9, 10, 17, 21, 37, 40

then our insertion algorithm would produce the following search tree of degree 3.

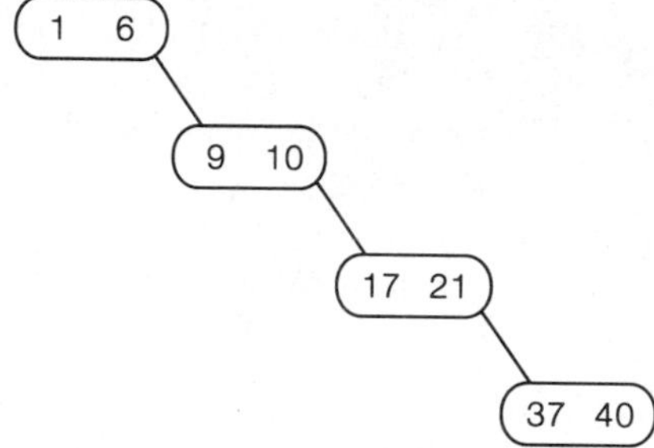

This tree is an example of a *degenerate m-way search tree*. It dramatically increases the number of nodes that must be traversed and consequently the number of disk transfers that must be carried out; it could thus lead to poor performance that does not meet the specifications of the problem. For example, referring to Table 11–3, a balanced tree of degree 25 and $N = 50{,}000$ will have a height $H = 4$. At 51 msec per access, the worst case access time would be $0.051 \times 4 \approx 0.2$ seconds. However, if the tree can become degenerate, the height H could become as large as $(50{,}000/24) = 2{,}083$ and the worst case access time would be $0.051 \times 2083 \approx 1.8$ minutes.

Two solutions to this problem are the use of B-trees and external hashing; both of these solutions will be discussed in the next section.

11.4.3 Other Approaches to External Searching

B-trees

A *B-tree* is an m-way search tree that has the following two structural characteristics:

1. Every leaf node is on the same level, so the tree is balanced with respect to height
2. Every node (except possibly the root) is at least half-full, that is, every node has between $\lfloor m/2 \rfloor$ and $(m - 1)$ children, so the tree is balanced with respect

to node contents. The root is an exception and may have from 1 to $(m - 1)$ values.

The following example shows a two-level B-tree of degree $m = 4$.

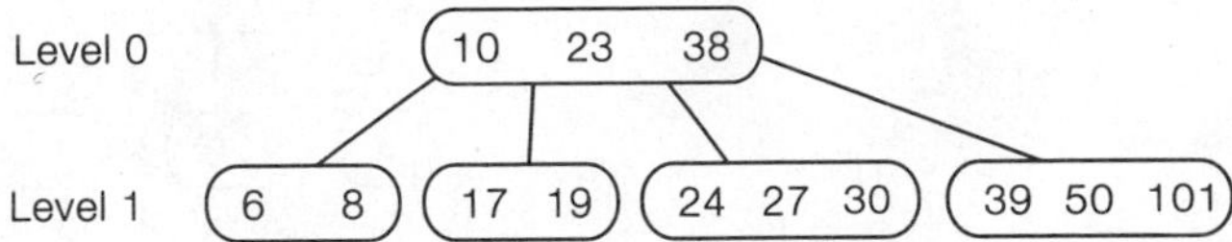

Notice that the four leaf nodes are all located at level 1 of the tree, and each node contains either two or three data values.

The advantage of a B-tree is that we can guarantee (rather than merely hope) that the tree is balanced and that the longest path from the root to a leaf is $O(\log_m N)$, which is always the maximum number of sectors that must be read. With a regular m-way search tree, the height of our tree can range from $O(\log_m N)$ in a balanced tree to $O(N/m)$ in a degenerate one.

The B-tree structure is maintained by rebalancing the search tree (if necessary) after each insertion operation. The rebalancing operations guarantee that the two B-tree properties are always met.

The rebalancing operations are built on the idea of splitting nodes that are full to produce two nodes at the same level, with each node approximately half full. If a node holds $(m - 1)$ values (the limit), adding one more item, produces a node with m values, which is illegal. Therefore, we split the node into two nodes, one containing the smallest $\lfloor m/2 \rfloor$ items and the other the largest $\lceil (m/2) - 1 \rceil$ items—a total of $(m - 1)$ items. The middle item is moved up to the parent to act as the discriminator key for these two new nodes. If the parent node has room for this new value, then rebalancing is complete. If not, we repeat the splitting process. For example, let's add the new key value 4 to the following B-tree of degree $m = 3$

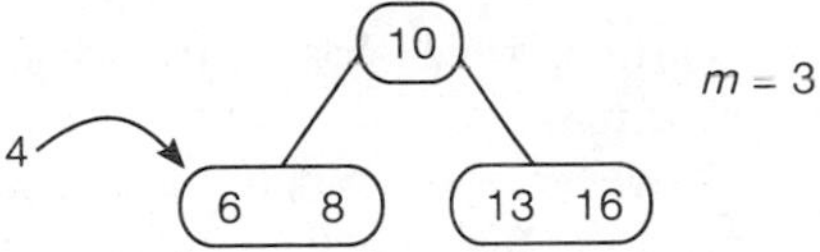

This addition will cause the left child node, which is currently full, to split. The smallest $\lfloor 3/2 \rfloor = 1$ item (the 4) and the largest $\lceil (3/2) - 1 \rceil = 1$ item (the 8) will go into separate nodes, while the middle item (the 6) will move up to the parent, which has room for it. This value will act as the discriminator for the two nodes just created. The result is the B-tree shown below.

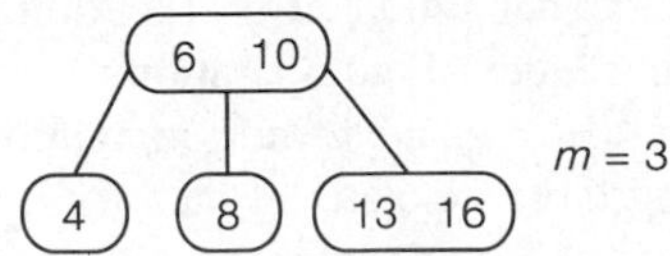

It can be easily verified that this tree still has both B-tree properties. All leaves are still on the same level, and all nodes hold either one or two values.

If we now try to add the value 18 to this B-tree,

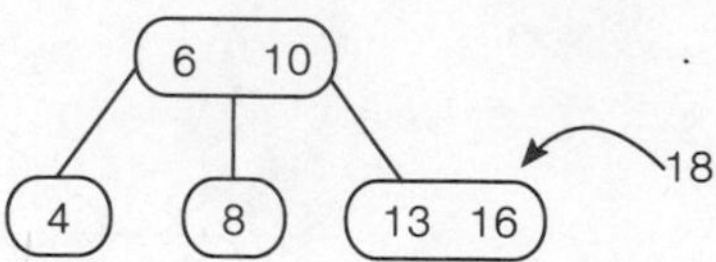

we must again split the existing full node into two new nodes, one holding the value 13, the other holding the value 18. The middle value 16 is passed up to its parent, producing

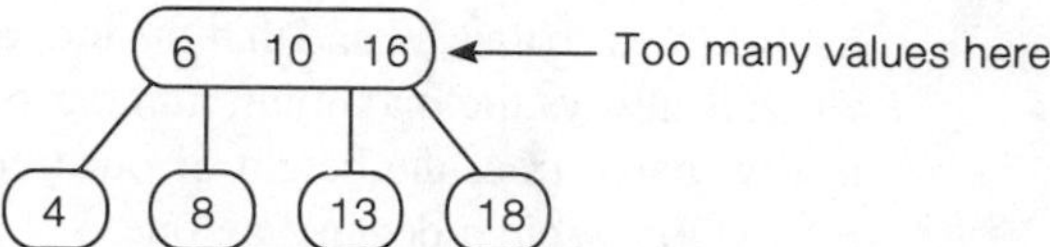

The root node now holds three values, which is illegal, since $m = 3$. We must therefore repeat the splitting operation one more time. We split the root in half with separate new nodes for the values 6 and 16, passing the middle item 10 up to become a new root node. This second splitting operation produces the following tree:

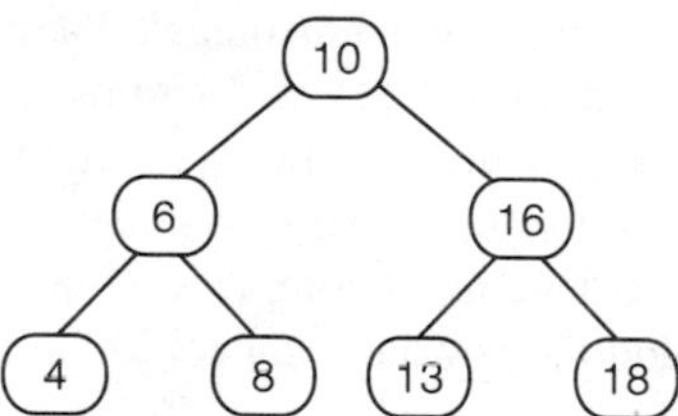

This tree, which has increased in height by one unit, still satisfies both B-tree properties.

We leave the complete specification and coding of the B-tree Insert algorithm as exercises. Note that the Find operation on B-trees is identical to the one presented in section 11.4.1 for m-way search trees, since a B-tree is simply a balanced m-way search tree (the only difference is that in a B-tree we guarantee certain properties about its height and the contents of each node).

One important characteristic of these rebalancing operations is that they can be done in $O(\log_m N)$ time. We can verify this time complexity quite easily by noticing that in the worst case, a splitting operation can propagate only from a leaf node to the root, which is $(H = \log_m N)$ times. This time complexity ensures that we will not expend more effort rebuilding the search tree than we will ultimately gain during subsequent Find operations.

B-trees are a very popular data representation technique for storing and retrieving large amounts of data from an external storage device. For additional information about this interesting data structure, including a full algorithmic description of the insertion, deletion, and find operations, and a description of the related structures called B* and B^+ trees, the reader can refer to the excellent survey article by Doug Comer[1].

Hashing

The second method for searching external files is to discard the search tree approach entirely and use an external variation of the internal hashing technique that we presented in section 9.2.3. This technique is called, appropriately enough, *external hashing*.

Assume that we are using a direct-access (i.e., addressable) storage device to hold our data values and that we have allocated sequential disk sector addresses [Low . . High] to store that data. We must now develop a hash function h of the form

$$h\ (\text{Key}) : [\text{Low} .. \text{High}]$$

that will allow us to map a key value directly into the disk sector address where that key is stored. Since a single sector will probably contain more than one key (i.e., it will be blocked), we need to search the entire sector looking for the desired key. If we do not find the key and the sector is not full, then the key is not in the file (if it were in the file, it would be in this sector). If the sector is full, and we do not find the key we are looking for, then we have a *collision*, just as we had with internal hashing. We now need a collision resolution rule that specifies the exact order in which subsequent disk sectors will be searched. One common system is to search sectors not in order of sequential search addresses but in order of their track position; that is, look at all sectors on the current track before moving on to search other tracks. This approach will minimize seek time, which, as we saw in Table 11–1, is a significant component of overall disk I/O time.

For example, suppose that our disk address were of the form *sttrr*, where s = surface number (0–9), tt = track number (00–99), and rr = sector number (00–99). Suppose that we hash to sector address 30522, which corresponds to surface 3, track 05, sector 22. If we do not locate the desired key after transferring and searching that sector, how will we resolve this collision? It would make sense to first search the remaining 99 sectors on track 05, surface 3, since that operation does not necessitate any arm movement of the disk. Such a collision resolution rule would lead us to search sectors in the following order:

30523, 30524, . . . , 30599, 30500, 30501, . . . , 30521

These are all the sectors on surface 3, track 05, the surface and track on which we are currently located.

If the key is still not found, we should search the same track but on a different surface, rather than move to a different track. Switching surfaces involves only activating a different read/write head of the disk, a procedure that occurs at very high speed, typically on the order of microseconds. However, moving from track to track involves mechanical operations that are orders of magnitude slower and that we want to avoid if possible.

[1] D. Comer, "The Ubiquitous B-tree", *ACM Computing Surveys*, June, 1979.

Thus, with this collision resolution rule, we would now begin searching sectors on track 05 but on a different surface, say surface 4, so we would search the following sectors in the order given:

40522, 40523, 40524, . . . , 40599, 40500, . . . , 40521

If we assume that the hash table stored on the disk is not very dense, then the sector-accessing part of external hashing will be O(1) (i.e., we will usually find what we are looking for in the first sector read). If each sector read holds m values, then the sector search part of external hashing will be $O(m)$ if sequential search is used and $O(\log_2 m)$ if the values are kept in sorted sequence, and we use binary search.

Since external hashing can reduce the number of disk transfers almost to one, it is an extremely popular method of external data retrieval. However, as with internal hashing, we must be sure to allow adequate unused space in our sectors to guarantee that our hashing method does not produce a significant number of collisions and does not degenerate into an inefficient sequential search of a large number of disk sectors.

Figure 11–13 shows an outline of the Find algorithm using external hashing and the collision resolution algorithm just described.

Figure 11–13
Find Algorithm Using External Hashing

```
(* This is an algorithm to find a Key value in an external file using the technique
called External Hashing. *)

Find (Key): Boolean

InitialAddress := Hash(Key) (* Here is where we start the search. *)
DiskAddress := InitialAddress

Loop        (* until we find the Key or we have searched the entire disk *)

    Read the sector at DiskAddress into Buffer
    Search Buffer for the Key
    If Found Then Return True       (* We found the key so we return True. *)
    If Buffer is not full Then      (* We return False because if Key was in the file
        Return False                it would be in this sector, since it is not full. *)

    (* We must keep searching. We first look on the same track. *)
    DiskAddress.Sector := DiskAddress.Sector + 1
    If DiskAddress.Sector = InitialAddress.Sector Then
        (* We have looked at every track. Move to another surface. *)
        DiskAddress.Surface := DiskAddress.Surface + 1
        If DiskAddress.Surface = InitialAddress.Surface Then
            (* Move to a new track only as a last resort. *)
            DiskAddress.Track := DiskAddress.Track + 1
            If DiskAddress.Track = InitialAddress.Track Then
                Return False (* We searched the entire disk. *)
            Endif
        Endif
    Endif

Endloop
```

11.5 CONCLUSION

Computer science is, as we mentioned earlier, both a theoretical and an applied discipline. We are interested in both correct solutions and practical and efficient ones. The time and space analyses of earlier chapters were all based on memory-resident data structures and relatively small amounts of data. These situations can often be highly unrealistic and yield solutions that are either unworkable or inefficient for important real-world problems.

The sorting and searching algorithms described in this chapter have shown how we can modify some of our earlier algorithms to work well under a number of important, practical constraints, such as limited random-access memory or extremely slow input/output operations. These modifications allowed us to create workable algorithms that produce answers in a reasonable amount of time, even under less than ideal conditions.

We must remember that a well-structured, well-designed, and provably correct sorting algorithm that produces its answer in 11.7 hours may be not much better than no solution at all. Although we must always be concerned with the issues of correctness and structure, we must also not lose sight of such other important user-related issues as speed, efficiency, and cost-effectiveness. From the user's point of view, these latter concerns are equally important.

CHAPTER EXERCISES

1. Which of the following are random-access data structures? Explain why or why not.
   a. A Pascal **Record** structure
   b. A singly linked list
   c. A Pascal **File** structure
   d. A three-dimensional array
   e. A hash table with density $\rho = 0.05$
   f. A hash table with density $\rho = 0.90$
2. Assume a disk drive with the following characteristics:

   3 disk platters with 6 recording surfaces
   100 tracks per surface
   100 sectors per track
   512 bytes per sector
   A rotation speed of 1,800 rpm
   A seek time of 0.8 msec per track

   a. What is the capacity of this disk in bytes?
   b. What are the best-case, worst-case, and average-case access times in msec?
3. Assume the device described in exercise 2 were a head-per-track drum like the one in Figure 11-2 rather than a disk. What are the best-case, worst-case, and average-case access times in msec?
4. Assume a tape unit with the following characteristics:

   Recording density of 1,600 characters per inch
   Usable tape length of 2,200 feet

Information recorded in blocks of 132 characters each
An interrecord gap of 1 inch

How much information can be recorded on a single tape reel?

5. The difference between a main memory access time of 500 nsec and a disk access time of 50 msec is five orders of magnitude. This difference is very large, but it is hard for us to fully comprehend because the time units are so small that we have no intuitive concept of them. What length of time is five orders of magnitude larger than one minute? one day? one year?
6. Assume that we have a personnel file containing 14,500 employee records, each record storing 240 bytes of information per employee. We have a 16K memory buffer available for sorting the employee records.
   a. How many employee records will fit in memory at one time?
   b. How many runs will be produced by the sorting phase?
   c. How many merge passes will be required by the merge phase?
7. How many disk transfers will be needed for the problem specified in exercise 6 and assuming our sector size is 512 bytes and the records are unblocked? How many fewer transfers would be required if we blocked the records using a blocking factor of B = 8? How many fewer transfers would there be if we could both block the records and increase the available buffer space to 64K?
8. If the average access time for our disk is 20 msec, what would be the total time needed to sort the file of exercise 6 assuming that the records are blocked with B = 8 and we have 128K of available buffer space.
9. Code the algorithms of Figures 11–5 and 11–8 and debug and test the program on some reasonably large external data files.
10. Find out the average access time for the disk on your computer system. Approximate the time needed to externally sort an N-record file using External MergeSort and the formulas of section 11.3. Now time the program written in exercise 9 on an actual file of N records and compare the predicted and measured values. Explain any difference you observe.
11. The sorting technique that we adapted for external use was a variation on the internal MergeSort method discussed in section 5.4.4. Discuss why you feel that it would or would not be reasonable to adapt the Bubble Sort algorithm of Figure 6–4 for use in external sorting. If you feel that it would be reasonable, describe the algorithm; if not, explain why.
12. Show the m-way search tree that will result from inserting the following twelve values into an empty tree

    103, −8, −7, 50, 60, 70, 55, 45, 35, 0, −103, 5

    Assume $m = 3$. For each insertion, state whether it represents an instance of case 2 or case 3.
13. Repeat the process described in exercise 12 for $m = 5$.
14. If each disk access takes 10 msec and each in-memory comparison operation takes 5 μsec, what is the worst-case time for a Find operation performed on the tree constructed in exercise 12?
15. Assume that a disk access takes 10 msec, each in-memory comparison operation takes 5 μsec, and a node can hold a virtually unlimited number of key and pointer values. What is the optimal number m of keys that should be stored in a node to balance node search times and tree search times?

16. If the following data records

```
Type NameRec = Record
        LastName : Array [1 .. 20] Of Char;
        FirstName : Array [1 .. 20] Of Char;
        Initial : Char;
    End;
```

are stored in an m-way search tree and our disk sector size is 512 bytes, what would be the approximate value of the degree of our search tree?

17. Code and test the m-way search tree Insert algorithm specified in Figure 11–10.
18. Design the algorithm for the Find operation on m-way search trees described in section 11.4.1. Code and test that algorithm.
19. Modify the Insert and Find algorithms of exercises 17 and 18 to accept, store, and retrieve (Key, Value) pairs into the search tree, rather than just keys. Describe the exact syntactic and semantic changes you are making in these two operations.
20. Show the B-tree that would be produced by inserting the following 8 values into a tree of degree 3.

    10, 20, 30, 40, 50, 50, 60, 35

21. What happens when we attempt to insert the value 6 into the following B-tree of degree 3?

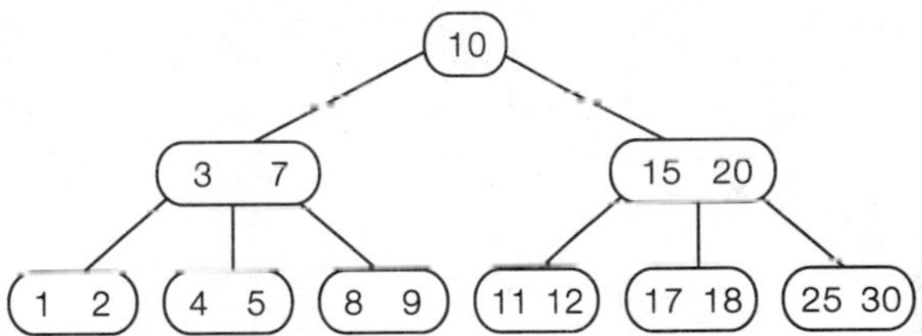

22. Sketch out (informally) an algorithm to insert values into a B-tree of degree m. Handle the following 3 cases:
    a. There is room in the current node for this key.
    b. There is no room in the current node for this key. It must be split into 2 nodes, each holding about half of the original values and with 1 value moving up to its parent.
    c. The node to be split is the root node, which has no parent.
23. Code and test the external hashing algorithm shown in Figure 11–13.

PART II

LARGE-SCALE SOFTWARE DEVELOPMENT AND THE SOFTWARE LIFE CYCLE

We have now completed our discussion of the topic *programming in the small.* By using the ideas and techniques studied in a first computer science course and in Part I of this text, a student should be able to develop correct, elegant, robust, maintainable, and shareable program units. However, what if the software system being built is more than just 500 lines of code containing 20 procedures (typical of what the student has seen is his or her studies so far)? What if it has 50,000 lines with 2,000 procedures or 5,000,000 lines with 200,000 procedures that must be separately implemented and then integrated into a working whole? For undertakings on this massive a scale, we need to be able to manage the overall project, not just the individual pieces. The management of projects of this size is addressed under the topic *programming in the large.*

As an analogy, consider the difference between a home movie and a Hollywood film. Both use the same technology, but that is about the only similarity. A home movie is made by one person for virtually no money, while a Hollywood production involves teams of dozens or hundreds of professionals working for months or years at a cost of tens of millions of dollars. Most people do not enjoy watching home movies (except for their own), but almost all of us will pay to attend professionally made movies because we appreciate and enjoy the high standard of production. This same situation exists with programs. The small program written in an introductory computer science class is the equivalent of a home movie. Very few people would be willing to purchase such programs. The professionally produced programs we use (e.g., Pascal compilers, operating systems, and word processors) are many times larger and more complex, like a Hollywood movie. To design software for the "real world," one must work on this scale.

In Part II of this text we look at issues related to the specification, design, implementation, and verification of large-scale software systems. This topic is extremely complex, and a full treatment would be well beyond the scope of this text. However, it is important that students be introduced to the many problems that can occur when software projects are scaled up from the size of those written in introductory programming classes to programs that are larger by one, two, three, or even four orders of magnitude.

CHAPTER 12

AN OVERVIEW OF THE SOFTWARE LIFE CYCLE

CHAPTER OUTLINE

12.1 INTRODUCTION

In this chapter we begin our study of *software development,* the process of specifying, designing, and implementing correct, maintainable, and cost-efficient software. We will study this topic in its very broadest sense, considering the entire sequence of steps needed to solve a problem on a computer, from the initial rough problem statement to the finished, verified, and documented program. Whereas the first eleven chapters of this text looked at techniques for designing and developing program units, we now want to expand our view. We want to focus on building large real-world projects and getting programs containing hundreds or even thousands of individual pieces of software to become a working and functioning whole. Addressing these concerns is frequently referred to as *programming in the large.*

Too often, beginning students think of the concept of software development in a much narrower sense, as the process of coding in a high-level computer language such as FORTRAN, Pascal, C, Ada, or Modula-2. When given a problem to solve, they want to begin by writing statements and immediately entering them into their workstations. They continue writing and typing until they have a completed program and only then hope that they have produced a valid solution. If their solution is incorrect, their first reaction is to add more statements, hoping to make it correct. Invariably, it is not, and they end up with a logical and structural mess that does not come close to solving their problem.

The error in this approach is that it fails to recognize the enormous amount of preparatory work that must be completed before coding begins. This misunderstanding about programming is somewhat unusual, because with most other tasks we recognize the importance of "laying the groundwork" before beginning implementation. For example, when you are writing a term paper, you would not start with a clean sheet of paper in the typewriter and attempt to produce a finished document. You would precede that step with a good deal of preparatory work researching the topic, developing an outline, and writing one or more rough drafts. Only then would you be ready to produce the final manuscript. Once this preparation is complete, the typing phase should be simple and mechanical. It should be concerned solely with putting on paper, in a correct and visually pleasing format, the creative thoughts and ideas you have already developed.

Similarly, you would not build a house by picking up a hammer, nails, and wood and proceeding directly to erect walls, floors, and ceilings. This approach would lead to chaos. Again, a good deal of preparatory work is needed to ensure the safety and beauty of what you construct. In this case, the preparatory work involves architectural designs, engineering blueprints, and contracting agreements with electricians, plumbers, and masons. When this preparatory work has been done well, construction should be relatively straightforward.

If we recognize the preparatory steps involved in writing term papers and building a house, why do we frequently not see the same needs in the area of software development? Why is the important preparatory work of specifying, designing, planning, and organizing a solution frequently skipped? Why is coding, which is analogous to the mechanical steps of typing a paper or laying the bricks, improperly viewed as the truly creative part of programming?

The answer to these questions is related to the *size* of projects and homework assignments typically solved in introductory programming classes. These programs are extremely (and unrealistically) small. The initial programs that students are

Table 12–1 Size Categories of Software Products

Category	No. of Programmers	Duration	Product Size
Trivial	1	1–4 weeks	<1K lines of code
Small	1–2	1–6 months	1K–5K
Medium	2–5	1–2 years	5K–50K
Large	5–20	2–3 years	50K–100K
Very Large	100–1000	4–5 years	100K–1M
Extremely Large	2000–5000	5–10 years	1M–10M

Source: R. Fairley, Software Engineering Concepts, New York: McGraw-Hill, 1985, p.11

asked to design and write are usually 50 to 100 lines long. Even by the end of a first course, it is still unusual for students to write programs that are more than a few hundred lines in length. However, real-world programs are two, three, or even four orders of magnitude longer. Programs that solve interesting problems contain thousands or tens of thousands of lines of code, and truly large software systems, such as the NASA space-shuttle ground control system, may require the development of more than a million lines of code!

Table 12–1 categorizes software products in terms of their size, the number of professionals needed for their development, and the duration of their implementation. Notice that virtually all programs developed by undergraduate computer science students would be classified as "trivial" (although most students would probably not agree with that categorization, especially when trying to complete a programming assignment the night before it is due!). The independent research projects done by seniors or graduate students would still fall only into the "small" category. However, most software products developed for the marketplace are neither trivial nor small but fall instead into the "medium" or "large" category, occupying a dozen or so programmers for a few years and resulting in tens of thousands of lines of code. The "very large" and "extremely large" categories, typified by such projects as military command and control systems or operating systems for networks of mainframe computers, are some of the largest intellectual enterprises ever undertaken, requiring as much as 5,000 to 50,000 person-years of effort to implement.

It would be impossible to develop correct and maintainable systems of that size without extensive planning, organizing, and design. In fact, for programs on the scale of tens or hundreds of thousands of lines of code, the specification and design phases will require 30 to 40% of the overall effort, whereas coding will typically require less than 20%. (The remaining time is involved with debugging, testing, documentation, etc.) Only for the small problems found in introductory programming classes is it feasible to skip the necessary preparatory work and still get a program working correctly.

The situation is similar for the examples we referred to earlier, writing a paper and building a house. It is not necessary to prepare an outline and write one or two rough drafts to produce a one-paragraph memo and one would not hire an architect to prepare blueprints for a doghouse. Because of their small size, a one-paragraph memo and a doghouse are special cases, and courses in creative writing or architecture do not focus on these unimportant problems—instead, they teach the steps needed to complete a large, complex writing or design project sucessfully.

The same approach should be used in the area of software development. The simple 50- to 100-line programs you write must be considered special cases. The fact that you may be able to pick up pencil and paper and write a correct program for these small projects does not mean that you will be able to repeat the process for bigger problems. In fact, this "coding first" approach quickly collapses when it is applied to a large programming project, e.g., on the order of 1000 or more lines of code.

This inability to manage the development of large software systems is called the *software crisis.* This term refers to the ever-increasing proportion of time and money involved in software development compared to the overall system cost. Programmer productivity, measured by the number of lines of correct code produced per unit time, has not increased significantly in the last ten years. During that time, however, hardware speeds have increased 1000-fold and hardware costs have come down dramatically. In addition, the quality and reliability of most software is lower than the quality and reliability of the hardware on which it runs. When we buy hardware, we generally expect it to operate uninterrupted for weeks or months. When it does fail, we expect it to be repaired quickly and returned to its original level of operation. Unfortunately, the same cannot be said for software. It is not rare to encounter programs that do not do what they say they will, contain numerous bugs, and are inadequately documented. One very popular software package contains the following disclaimer printed in large boldface type on page 1 of its user's manual:

> Company X does not warrant that the functions contained in the software and described in this User's Manual will operate error free or that all software defects will be corrected. Except as set forth in the licensing agreement, there are no warranties, expressed or implied, on any phase of this product.

The company is essentially saying that they are not sure if the package will work and they will not guarantee to fix it if it does not work!

In this and subsequent chapters we introduce and discuss the steps involved in the development of large-scale software. These steps include: the work that must be done *before* coding of the program, such as specification, organization, and design; the work involved *during* coding; and the work that must go on *after* the program is implemented, such as verification, completion of the documentation, and maintenance. Table 12-2 compares the steps involved in writing a term paper to those involved in developing a computer program in order to reinforce the notion of programming and problem solving as a complex series of operations.

12.2 THE STEPS INVOLVED IN SOFTWARE DEVELOPMENT

In this section we will give more specific information on the steps involved in software development and discuss each of these steps in detail.

12.2.1 The Feasibility Study

Too often, people want to use a computer to solve a problem, even if it may not be the appropriate tool for the job. Even though costs of computer hardware are coming down dramatically, computers are still not cheap, typically costing $1000 to $5000

Table 12–2 Comparison of the Steps Involved in Writing a Term Paper and a Computer Program

Writing a Term Paper	Writing a Computer Program
1. Deciding whether it is worth the time and effort to write the paper in the first place	1. Doing the feasibility study
2. Developing a topic and a thesis statement document	2. Developing the problem specification
3. Outlining the paper	3. Developing the program design document
4. Doing library research on the topic and selecting the key points to cover	4. Selecting the best algorithms and data types to solve the problem
5. Writing a rough draft	5. Writing the initial version of the program
6. Reviewing the rough draft and preparing succeeding drafts	6. Debugging the program and preparing new versions, if necessary
7. Sending the manuscript out for review	7. Verifying that the finished program is indeed correct
8. Preparing the final, finished version, including index, bibliography, and cover page	8. Completing the necessary user and technical documentation to support the program
9. Seeing if the instructor is satisfied with the finished product or if it will need some revisions and rewrites	9. Ensuring that the program performs as anticipated by the client or seeing if it need some redesign and recoding

Figure 12–1
Changes in the Relative Cost of Computer System Components

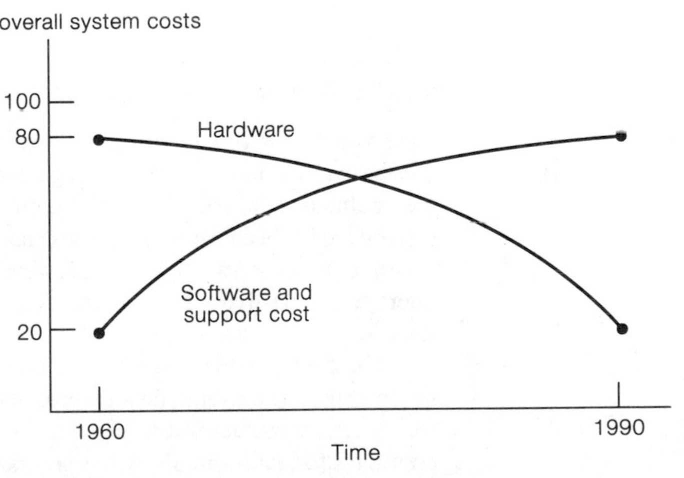

for a small home or business microcomputer system, and \$5000 to \$15,000 for a powerful personal workstation. Larger minicomputer systems capable of supporting 8 to 16 users can easily cost \$25,000 to \$100,000. Added to the purchase price of the hardware are the costs of software and maintenance and the salaries of analysts, consultants, programmers, and data-entry personnel. Typically, these additional costs can be equal to (if not four or five times more than) the original purchase price of the system, as shown in Figure 12–1. Thus, the overall cost of using a computer to solve one's problem can be surprisingly higher than expected and can easily cost more than the value of the information the program provides.

Because of these potentially large costs, the first phase of any programming project should be directed to answering the following critical questions: Is it worth it for me to buy a computer and write or buy software to solve my problem? Is the information that I will get worth the time and the cost? If I do choose to buy a computer, should I purchase existing software or design and build my own? It is important to realize that not every problem you encounter needs a computer system, and for simple problems a sophisticated custom-designed software package may be overkill. Perhaps the best system for storing and retrieving kitchen recipes is not an expensive relational database management system but a box of three-by-five-inch index cards! In addition, there are social costs to consider, including the possible loss of jobs, the retraining of personnel, and the upheaval caused by changes in established procedures.

The *feasibility study,* then, is concerned with evaluating and comparing the costs and benefits of a computer system and its supporting software. The output of this study is a *feasibility document* that recommends whether the user should proceed with the development or purchase of software and any necessary hardware. The creation of this document can be an extremely complex process, because it involves subject matter well beyond computer science, including business principles, management, economics, industrial psychology, and accounting. Thus we will not discuss this topic further in this text. We mention the feasibility study phase to make you realize that a computer is simply a tool, and just as we would for any tool, we first need to decide whether it is the right tool for the job. Only when that question has been answered yes do we continue to the next phase of software development.

12.2.2 Problem Specification

Problem specification, sometimes called *requirements specification* or *requirements analysis,* involves developing a clear, concise, and unambiguous statement of the problem to be solved. It may seem silly to include problem specification as a separate step, because it is obvious that we must know exactly what we are being asked to do before we can do it. However, it is surprising how often software developers begin to solve a problem that is incompletely described, fraught with ambiguities, or even contradictory.

The functionality and performance requirements of a computer program must be described in extreme detail, typically much more detail than is necessary when we describe problems for people. In addition, the specifications must contain enough information to allow the programmer to anticipate and handle all possibilities, not just the expected ones. For example, we probably would not give a payroll clerk specific instructions about what to do if an employee reported a negative number of work hours for a given week. We would expect the clerk to recognize this obvious error and report it to the appropriate people. However, such common sense does not exist in computer software. Unless we state explicitly in our problem specifications that hours worked cannot be a negative quantity, most programs, when told that an employee worked 20 hours and had a pay rate of $10.00/hour, would quite happily produce a paycheck for $-200.00!

Another problem we encounter during problem specification is that natural language (English, in our case) is the most popular notation for expressing user requirements. However, natural language suffers from a number of flaws, the most severe one being its lack of precision. For example, the following specification for an array search problem is highly ambiguous.

> Given a list of integers $A_1, \ldots, A_n$ and a single key value x, determine the location i in the list such that $A_i = x$. *If* x does not occur in the list, determine the location i of the value A_i that is closest to x.

What value should we return if x occurs two or more times in the list? For example, given the following values,

$$A = 5, 8, 13, 7, 8, 1 \qquad x = 8$$

do we return $i = 2$ or $i = 5$? Similarly, what does the English word *closest* mean? It could mean numerically closest. It could also mean lexically closest—the greatest number of similar digits in the same position; with this definition, 899 would be considered closer to 999 (two out of three digits the same) than would 1000 (no digits the same). Finally, what do we do if $n \leq 0$? None of these questions is answered in the above problem statement. Natural language does not provide the precision needed to create clear and unambiguous problem statements that can serve as the basis for the development of correct programs.

Instead of natural language, we could use a more formal and precise notation such as first-order predicate logic. Using this notation, our array search procedure might be expressed as follows:

Given: $(A_1, A_2, A_3, \ldots, A_n)$, $n \geq 1$

Wanted: The unique value of i in the range $[1 \mathinner{..} n]$ that satisfies the following condition:

$$[(A_i = x) \wedge \sim\exists j((A_j = x) \wedge (j < i))] \vee$$
$$[(\forall_j\, (A_j \neq x)) \wedge \forall_j\, ((|A_i - x| \leq |A_j - x|) \wedge (i < j))]$$

Now you may not think that this specification has cleared up anything. (In fact, if you are not familiar with first-order predicate logic, you may think that it has confused the problem beyond recognition!) But this notation can help us immeasurably. It is unambiguous and absolutely precise in its specification of the problem. It states that we are to return the first occurrence of the key in the list, that is, the one with the smallest index. If the key does not occur in the list, it defines the term *closest* to mean the array element for which the absolute value of the difference between it and the key is the smallest. If two array elements are equally close to the key, we return the first value. Finally, it states that if $n \leq 0$, the problem is ill-defined and cannot be solved. Furthermore, it states all these specifications in a very concise and elegant way.

Thus *formal representation techniques* can be helpful in creating and expressing accurate problem specifications. The process of changing the rough problem statement initially posed by a user into a complete, concise, and formal *problem specification document* is the major function of the specification phase of software development.

12.2.3 High-Level Program Design

Any large project, whether in programming or some other area, must first be divided into a collection of smaller and less complex subtasks in order to be managed effectively. Otherwise, the job would be too large and unwieldy to understand and to follow. *High-level program design* involves decomposing the problem specification into a set of modules and data structures that, if they existed, would correctly solve the problem. High-level design is the software development phase where we use the divide-and-conquer problem solving strategy.

For example, a problem to input student test scores, compute the test average, and write out that average may be more easily understood if it is viewed not as a single monolithic task but as an abstract data type called ScoreTable and the following four modules:

1. *Input module:* a program to input test scores, store them in ScoreTable, and signal when all data have been read
2. *Validation module:* a program to check whether the test scores in ScoreTable are correct, or whether one or more of them are out of range
3. *Averaging module:* a program to compute the average of all legal scores in ScoreTable and disregard illegal scores
4. *Report writer module:* a program to print the average in a nice readable format

It should be easier to understand and implement the original problem in terms of these simple modules and an abstract data type than in terms of a single large problem.

The result of this decomposition process will be a *program design document* that contains the following pieces of information:

1. The name of every module in the solution
2. A graphical depiction of the relationship of each module to other modules in the solution
3. The interface specifications of each module
4. The functions carried out by each module
5. The name of all abstract data types in the solution
6. The operations performed on these abstract data types

As we mentioned earlier, most of the programs developed in a first computer science course are small and composed of only one or a small number of modules. For such small problems, the program design phase may not be necessary. Remember, however, that these small programs are special cases and that for most problems, program design is a critically important step. If we look back at Table 12–1, we see that a "large" program contains 50,000 to 100,000 lines of code. Since the average program unit (i.e., a procedure, function, or module) is about 50 lines, the typical large program contains 1,000 to 2,000 separately compilable pieces of software. Without a design document describing these individual pieces, their functions, and how they fit together, the implementation phase would become unimaginably difficult; it would be like trying to build an airplane without the blueprints!

12.2.4 Module Design and ADT Implementation (Low-Level Design)

Once we know exactly what pieces are needed to solve our problem, we can begin to implement the modules contained in our proposed design. We will need to select the method for solving the problem in each module and the internal representations of the abstract data types.

An *algorithm* is a formal step-by-step method for solving problems. It is one of the most important concepts in computer science and one that occupies a central place in any first course. (In fact, one definition of computer science is the study of the design, representation, implementation, and analysis of algorithms.) For some problems, there is only a single technique and the selection is easy, but sometimes the choice of an algorithm is not so obvious because dozens of techniques exist, as is the case with sorting and searching.

One of the issues guiding our selection will be the inherent efficiency of the method. As we learned in chapter 6, the efficiency game is essentially won or lost once the algorithm has been chosen. Therefore, we want to pick an algorithm of the lowest order possible that meets our needs. For example, if we need to sort a list of values we should investigate one of the many good $O(N \log_2 N)$ algorithms such as HeapSort, MergeSort, or QuickSort, rather than an inefficient $O(N^2)$ method like BubbleSort, especially if our list is very large.

In addition to choosing the algorithm to use in implementing a module, we must select internal representations for our abstract data types. For example, the input module referred to earlier must read in test scores. Will these scores be integers (e.g., 0 to 100), decimal quantities (e.g., 0.00 to 100.00), or letter grades (e.g., A, A−, B+, B, . . .)? We also need to decide whether to represent our abstract data type called ScoreTable internally as either a one-dimensional array, a record structure, or a linked list. The topic of abstract data types and their internal realization was a central issue in Part I of the text—we will now see how to use those ideas in the context of the overall problem-solving process.

Once we have selected our algorithms, sketched them in pseudocode, and selected the internal representations for all abstract data types, we have effectively completed the design of an individual module and are ready to begin implementation. Much of what we studied in chapters 2 to 11—abstract data types, data structure design, and the analysis of algorithms—was directed at this specific phase of software development.

12.2.5 Implementation

Implementation (i.e., coding and debugging) is the step that comes to mind when we think of software development, and it is usually the primary topic of discussion in a first programming course. However, as we have shown, much important preparatory work must precede this step. In fact, if this preparatory work has been done well, then coding simply becomes the mechanical translation of an algorithm into the syntax of the appropriate programming language, for example,

> *Algorithm:* Divide the sum of the legal scores by the number of legal scores to determine the average.

```
Modula-2:    Average := Sum/Number
Pascal :     Average := Sum/Number
BASIC :      100 LET A = S/N
FORTRAN :    AVERG = SUM/NUMBR
COBOL :      DIVIDE SUM BY NUMBER GIVING AVERAGE
APL :        average ← sum/number
```

Algorithm: Print out the average.

```
Modula-2:    WriteReal(Average,10);
Pascal :     writeln(Average:10:5);
BASIC :      200 PRINT A
FORTRAN :    WRITE (6,100) AVERG
             100 FORMAT(1X, F10.5)
COBOL :      WRITE AVERAGE
APL :        □ ← average
```

As you can see, there are minor differences in syntax between languages, but conceptually they all carry out the same operation. The most creative part of programming is determining what operations need to be done, not figuring out how to write them.

Table 12–3 lists a number of well-known high-level programming languages. During your career you will probably code in more than one of these languages. It is also likely that some of the languages in Table 12–3 will fall out of favor and into disuse, while new languages will be developed to take their place. (Pascal was virtually unknown 15 years ago; Modula-2 was almost unheard of 5 years ago.) The development and decline of specific languages is not a problem, however, because the key issues in software development, such as problem specification and high-level design, are language-independent. A programming language and its associated syntax, which were so central to the first programming course, are not the critical issue here.

One implementation issue that has become very important in recent years is the concern for building *user-friendly programs,* that is, software that is easy to learn, easy to use, produces easy-to-interpret results, and is forgiving of errors. It is no longer sufficient to implement software that is technically correct. We must also have equal concern for the input/output characteristics and the quality of the interactions between a user and the program.

When the first draft of the code has been finished, we would like to think that implementation is almost complete. Unfortunately, this is not the case. Studies of large software projects show that about 30 to 40% of the time spent on a software project involves correcting, testing, and fixing code after it has been initially written.

As the next step in implementation we must *debug* the program—locate and correct all errors that cause the program to produce incorrect results or perform improper actions. Debugging has always been one of the most frustrating, agonizing, and time-consuming steps in the programming process, usually because, as we have been stressing, insufficient time has been spent on carefully specifying, organizing, and structuring the solution. The resulting program is often a structural mess, with convoluted, hard-to-understand "spaghetti-type" logic. In this type of situation it is easy for bugs to occur and hard to locate and correct them. Always remember:

Table 12–3 A Survey of Some Important High-Level Programming Languages

Language	Approximate Date of Introduction	General Application Areas
FORTRAN	1957	Numerically oriented language; most applicable to scientific, mathematical, and statistical problems; very widely used and very widely available.
ALGOL	1960	Another numerically oriented language but with new language features; more widely used in Europe.
COBOL	1960	The most widely-used business-oriented computer language.
LISP	1961	Special-purpose language developed primarily for list processing and symbolic manipulation; widely used in the area of artificial intelligence.
SNOBOL	1962	Special-purpose language used primarily for character string processing, including applications such as text editors, language processors, and bibliographic work.
BASIC	1965	A simple interactive programming language widely used to teach programming in high schools.
PL/I	1965	An extremely complex, general-purpose language designed to incorporate the numeric capabilities of FORTRAN, the business capabilities of COBOL, and many other features into a single language.
APL	1967	An operator-oriented interactive language that introduced a wide range of new mathematical operations that are built directly into the language.
Pascal	1971	A general-purpose language designed to teach the concepts of structured programming and the efficient implementation of large programs.
C	1972	A popular systems implementation language designed to run under the UNIX operating system
Prolog	1974	A nonprocedural language built on the concepts of first-order predicate logic.
Smalltalk	1980	An object-oriented language that uses objects, inheritance, and message passing to solve problems.
Modula-2	1980	A language that builds on the ideas of Pascal but adds facilities for modularization and data abstraction.
Ada	1981	A systems-implementation language designed and built for the Department of Defense.
C++	1985	An object-oriented extension of C.

> The very best technique for debugging is to *avoid* making mistakes in the first place.

Much of what we will describe about the program specification and design phases in the upcoming chapters is directed at writing the program correct *the first time*, so that the debugging phase is less time-consuming and frustrating.

12.2.6 Testing, Verification, and Benchmarking

Even though a program works correctly on 1, 5, or 1000 data sets, how do we know that it is indeed correct? The testing and verification phase involves demonstrating that the program is correct and will work properly on all data sets, even those that have not been explicitly tested. Two different techniques are used in this phase—*empirical testing* and *formal verification*.

With empirical testing, we carefully select a number of test cases and run the program with these test data. If the program produces correct results for this collection of data, we assert that it will work properly on all data. With verification, we argue in a more formal way to prove that program P will produce the correct output O for all input data I. We treat the program and its individual statements as mathematical entities and prove that they have certain invariant properties. Verification is much more complex than testing, but it allows us to make much stronger claims about the correctness of the program.

In addition to testing the program for correctness, we may also choose to measure the *performance characteristics* of the nearly completed program at this time. How fast does it run? How much memory space does it occupy? Does it perform as required by the user in the specification document? This step is sometimes called *benchmarking* the program. If our measurements indicate that the processing speed (or some other measure of performance) is not up to specifications, then we will have to do some fine-tuning of the code to speed it up. If our run time is way off the mark (i.e., hours versus seconds), fine-tuning will be inadequate, and we may need to redesign entire sections of the program. However, if our program is this far from meeting specifications, it usually indicates that insufficient time was spent on specification, planning, and design.

At the completion of testing and verification, we should have a correct and efficient program. It is important that this phase be done thoroughly and precisely. One of the most important quality characteristics of a program is its *reliability,* or *robustness,* that is, its ability to operate uninterrupted and error free over long periods of time, even in the presence of missing, illegal, or invalid data. An unreliable program will not be used.

12.2.7 Documentation

Programmers are often more comfortable with programming languages like Pascal and Modula-2 than with natural languages such as English. However, a powerful piece of software is worthless if a user does not know how to use it. Documentation involves developing and writing the supporting materials and on-line assistance, that the user will need to understand and use the finished program. Failure to do a good job at this stage can invalidate all the work done to this point. (How often have you become frustrated trying to use something and thrown it away because you could not understand the instruction booklet?) It is not enough for a programmer to be able to communicate with the computer; he or she must also be able to communicate with other people.

Even though we have shown documentation as one of the later steps in the software life cycle, it does not begin when the program is finished. In fact, much of the information needed for documentation is produced during preceeding phases.

- The feasibility document (section 12.2.1)
- The specification document (section 12.2.2)

- The design document (section 12.2.3)
- The algorithms and abstract data type specifications (section 12.2.4)
- Program listings and comments (section 12.2.5)
- Benchmark results and sample output (section 12.2.6)

Now your job is to bring this material together into finished documents that explain how to use the program properly and effectively; this assembly of information is illustrated in Figure 12–2 which shows how documentation occurs throughout the entire life cycle.

A software package has two different types of documentation: system documentation and user documentation.

System documentation, also called *technical documentation,* is the information that another programmer would need to update, correct, enhance or simply understand your program. This material is intended for computer science specialists, not for end users. Therefore, it concentrates on the structural and technical details of the software. The system documentation includes a description of each module in the system as well as a description of all important abstract data types and data structures. It also identifies the author of the program, documents the dates when the program was written and tested, and gives a history of any modifications made to the software since its original release. One of the most important pieces of the technical documentation is the source code listing, especially if the program has a well structured design and uses good programming style.

User documentation is quite different in content. Its purpose is to teach someone how to start up and use the program. Technical details would be highly inappropriate and probably quite confusing. Instead, user documentation concentrates on describing the interactions between the program and the user, that is, it describes the input the user will provide and the results and behavior that he or she should observe. This information is collected into a document called the *user's manual*. However, good quality user documentation is usually much more extensive than just this single manual—it might also include such aids as tutorials, demonstration disks, or on-line assistance, i.e., help that is available from the program as it is executing.

For real world software packages, user documentation is probably the single most important component delivered with the software. Sufficient time should be spent on its preparation to ensure that it has been done well.

12.2.8 Program Maintenance

Programs are not static entities that never change once they are completed. Because of the expense involved in developing software (see Figure 12–1), programs are used for a long time. It is not unusual to see a program in use 5, 10, or 15 years after it was originally written. In fact, the typical life cycle for a medium-to-large software package is 1 to 3 years for development and 5 to 15 years in the marketplace. The cost of maintaining the software over its effective life may exceed the initial cost of development by a factor of two or more. During this long period of use, errors may be uncovered, new hardware may be purchased, user needs may change, and the whims of the marketplace will fluctuate. Thus the original program will need to be modified to meet these changing needs. *Program maintenance* is the process of adapting an existing software product to preserve its accuracy and keep it current with changing specifications and new equipment. If the program has been well organized, well planned, carefully designed as a set of independent modules and abstract data types, well coded, and clearly documented so that we know what it does, then program maintenance will be a much less difficult task. In fact, it would be similar to the job of a TV repairperson who checks the components one by one, locates the defective one, removes it, and snaps in a new one. Much of the purpose of careful planning and design is to ensure that future program maintenance is not a difficult and expensive task.

Maintenance should not really be viewed as a separate step in the software life cycle—it involves only repetition of some or all of the steps that we have previously described. For example, after the program has been completed, we may have to redesign a portion of it to meet an unanticipated need or to add a new feature. After the redesign has been completed, we will need to do implementation, test the new code, and include a description of this new feature in our documentation. Maintenance, then, reflects the fact that the software life cycle is truly a *cycle,* in which we may have to go back and redo earlier phases of development.

The set of steps that we have described in this section and which we have called the software life cycle is diagrammed in Figure 12–2.

Figure 12–2
Model of the Overall Software Life Cycle

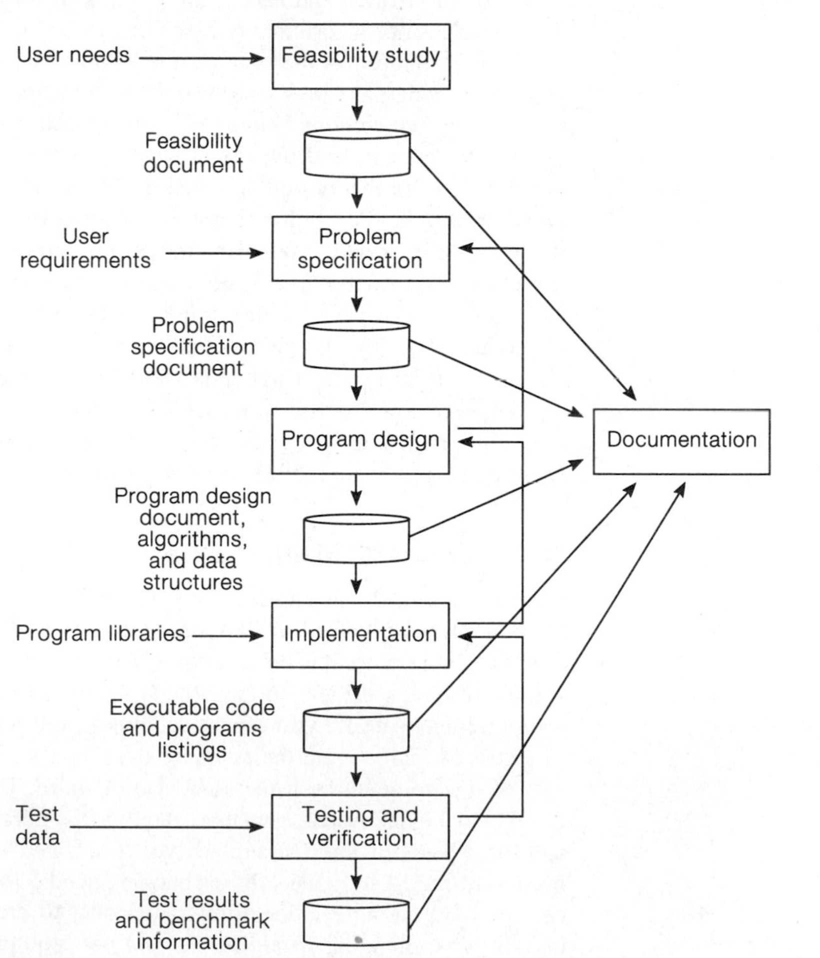

Table 12–4 Approximate Percentage of Time Spent on Each Phase of Programming

Phase	Approximate Percentage of Time
Specification/design/planning	30–40
Implementation	15–20
Testing/reviewing/fixing	30–40
Documenting	10–15

12.3 CONCLUSION

As we have tried to show in this chapter, there is much more to programming than just coding. Recent studies on the time spent by programmers in various stages of initial program development show that a relatively small amount of time is spent on implementation with a much larger percentage spent on the necessary preparatory work. Table 12–4 lists the approximate percentage of time spent on each of the major phases of software development.

Furthermore, Table 12–4 describes only the time allocation for *initial* development. Over the entire 5- to 15-year life of a software package 60% or more of the total time and money spent on a software system will be spent maintaining it after it has been initially released for use.

Software development is an extremely complex task made up of many phases, each of which is important and each of which contributes to the overall solution. Do not equate the topics of software development and implementation. Remember that coding must be preceded by a great deal of preparatory work clarifying, specifying, and designing the solution, and it must be followed by a good deal of testing, verifying, measuring, and documenting to ensure the quality of the finished product. The field of computer science that involves the study and development of methods for managing the systematic implementation of correct, efficient, and reliable software products is called *software engineering*. It is an extremely important area of computer science and an important subject of advanced study.

CHAPTER EXERCISES

1. Go to a computer store and look at the user's manual of any popular software package (e.g., a word processor or educational package). See if there is a warranty disclaimer like the one shown in section 12.1. Why do you feel that it is necessary to put that there? How does it make you feel about using the package?
2. Assume that a new microcomputer and printer could be purchased for two thousand dollars. Try to do an informal feasibility study on whether it would be worthwhile for your school to purchase a computer and write a program that would allow teachers to keep student records on the system—that is, names, test scores, and homework grades, like an electronic grade book. What useful information could the computer give to the teacher? Would it save any time? Do you think it would be worth the cost?

3. The average program written in a first course contains approximately 100 to 200 lines of code. Go to a computer store and talk to a technical specialist to find out the size (in terms of lines of high-level code) of some popular computer programs such as a game, a graphics package, a word processor, or an integrated business software system. Which of the categories of Table 12–1 do they fall into? Discuss the problems that you might have writing programs of this size without adequate planning and organization.
4. A common misconception that people have is that overall computer system costs will decline continuously because hardware costs are dropping. Why does Figure 12–1 refute that argument?
5. Talk to the director of the computer center at your institution and determine the approximate percentage of the overall computer services budget that is allocated to
   a. Hardware purchases, maintenance, and staff
   b. Software development, purchase, and maintenance
   c. User services staff, and documentation

   How do these percentages compare with the values shown in Figure 12–1?
6. Why is it more difficult to specify a problem that will be programmed on a computer than it is to specify a problem that will be given to a person and solved manually?
7. Why is outlining a term paper similar in concept to the program design phase?
8. An algorithm is not simply a concept in computer science. Algorithms occur frequently in everyday life (although they are rarely called that). Describe algorithms that would occur outside the context of computer programs.
9. Looking over the languages listed in Table 12–3, which language do you think you might select for implementing each of the following applications?
   a. A payroll system
   b. A statistics library package such as SPSS (Statistical Package for the Social Sciences)
   c. A Pascal compiler

   Give reasons for your choices.
10. It is well known that poorly planned, poorly organized, and sloppy programs are difficult to get working correctly and difficult to maintain. The following sequence of instructions was intended to try to find which of three given numbers—x, y, z—is the largest and to write out the answer.

Step	*Instruction*
1	if x is bigger than y, then go to step 4
2	if y is bigger than z, then go to step 8
3	go to step 10
4	if x is greater than z, then go to step 6
5	go to step 8
6	set the biggest value to x
7	go to step 11
8	set the biggest value to y
9	go to step 11
10	set the biggest value to z
11	write out the biggest value
12	you are done

Do these instructions do what they are supposed to do? If not, locate and correct the bug. How did the structure of this set of instructions make it difficult to follow? What can you say about the problem of maintaining this type of program? Write out a sequence of instructions that is clearer and easier to follow.

11. Try to find out the release date of the original version of the compiler and operating system used at your institution. What version number are they? How many updates and/or new releases have there been for these software products? What does your answer say about the importance of program maintenance?
12. Talk to a professional programmer and see how much of his or her time is spent on the different programming phases we described in this chapter. Are the responses similar to the values given in Table 12–4? Does he or she perform additional steps that were not described in this chapter?

CHAPTER 13

THE PROBLEM SPECIFICATION PHASE

CHAPTER OUTLINE

13.1 INTRODUCTION

Most problem statements begin as a very rough, incomplete idea that is nowhere near ready to serve as the basis for the design of a large software project. These rough problem statements are the initial thoughts of a user who has an information-based problem but is not sure what needs to be done or how to do it. Such initial problem statements might be made by the teacher who "wants help with recording and averaging student test scores," the scientist who "wants to collect and analyze data from laboratory instruments," and the business person who "wants a program to calculate and print out my 90-day receivables." All these thoughts represent valid applications but none of these statements could, in its present form, serve as the basis for the design and implementation of a complete and finished program.

The *problem specification* phase of software development is concerned with the refinement of an initial problem description, with its omissions, inconsistencies, ambiguities, and uncertainties, into a finished *problem specification document*, which is a complete and unambiguous statement of the exact problem to be solved. The term *problem specification document* is not standard—such names as a *system specification*, a *software requirements document*, and *user-needs inventory* are also used.

What does such a document contain? What information is needed by a programmer to design and implement the program? What information is not yet needed and can be postponed until later? These are the questions we will answer in this chapter.

13.2 CONTENTS OF THE PROBLEM SPECIFICATION DOCUMENT

13.2.1 Input/Output Specifications

A problem specification document is essentially an *input/output* document. It describes what inputs come into the program and what actions or outputs are produced. It says nothing about how the program will transform the inputs into the desired results, that is, it does not describe what algorithms will be used or what data types will be selected. The problem specification document treats the software to be developed as a black box—its only concern is what goes in and what comes out, not what happens inside. The description of these external interfaces is called the *input/output specification* of the problem; it is the first component of the problem specification document. This role of the problem specification document is diagrammed in Figure 13–1. This black-box view is appropriate because users do not care how a program works as long as it produces the desired results in a reasonably

Figure 13–1
Pictorial View of a Problem Specification Document

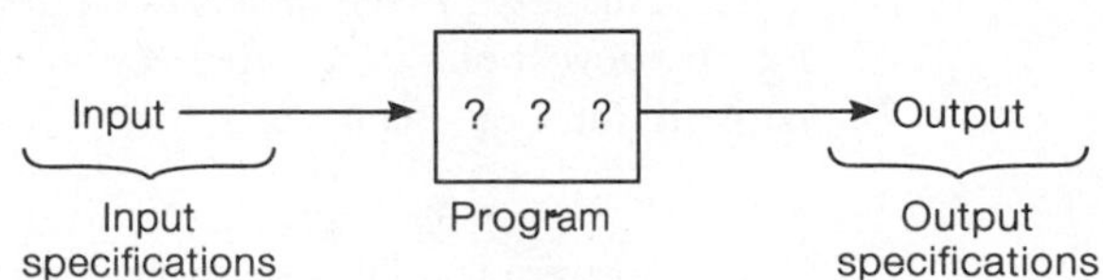

Figure 13–2
Initial Problem Statement for a Test-Scoring Problem

Every student in my Latin class took three tests during the semester. I would like to have a program that would give me the mean and standard deviation for each test.

efficient manner. In fact, including technical details about how the problem will be solved could confuse the user and make the specification document more difficult to read.

To specify the input to the program, the following information is needed:

1. Exactly what values will be provided to the program? In what order will they be provided? The interpretation of these input values must be clear and unambiguous.
2. How many input values will there be? Or, phrased another way, how will we know when there is no more input?
3. What is the format of the input data (including its type, accuracy, and units)?
4. From what input device will these values be provided?
5. Is there a legal range of allowable values for the input? Is there some upper bound on the plausible range of values?

To specify the output of a program, we need to answer the following questions:

1. Exactly what results does the user want the program to produce? The interpretation of these output values must be clear and unambiguous.
2. What layout does the user want for these results (including accuracy, units, spacing, heading, and titles)?
3. On what output device should we display the results?

Together, the input and output specifications represent the major components of the program specification document.

Let us work through a simple example of the development of a problem specification document. Suppose a Latin professor approaches us with the problem shown in Figure 13–2. We have a rough idea of what the professor wants, but this extremely brief problem statement is incomplete[1]. It does not answer any of the following questions:

1. What is the format of the test scores—are they numbers such as 72, 99, or letters such as C+, A−?
2. How many students were in the class?
3. What is the order of the data—are the test 1 scores for the entire class followed by all the test 2 scores, followed by test 3, or, alternatively, are the test 1, test 2, and test 3 scores for each student entered as a 3-tuple?
4. What is the legal range of scores on the test?
5. Exactly how should the output appear? Should the values be printed in alphanumeric form or graphed?

[1] Interestingly, a feasibility study might show that unless the class is large, we probably should not bother to write a program for this problem. Paper and pencil or a hand calculator would probably be cheaper and faster!

6. What accuracy is desired for the mean and the standard deviation?

We must obtain answers to these questions before continuing. Therefore, a key step in the development of a specification document is interviewing the user to determine exactly what he or she wants or needs. It is the job of the software developer to identify what is missing or contradictory in the problem statement and suggest ways to include these missing features. The user can then select the approach that appears best for him or her and that comes closest to providing the desired results.

Sometimes the programmer may be unfamiliar with either the area of application or other specialized subject areas that come up during specification (e.g., statistics). In such a situation, the programmer may need to call in one or more technical specialists in these areas. Then a discussion among the user, the programmer, and these specialists, each contributing ideas and soliciting answers, will be necessary to flesh out a detailed specification.

Let us assume that we interviewed our Latin professor and received answers to all our previous questions. For technical issues where the professor was unsure of what to do (e.g., should we use graphics), we provided sufficient explanation to allow an informed and reasonable decision. Figure 13–3 shows a possible second draft of a specification document for this problem.

After this draft has been written, it is the job of both the software developer and the user to review what has been written and to see if the problem described is exactly what is wanted. It is easy to make changes at this stage in the software development process, since no code has been written. Later, after the design, coding, and testing phases have begun, changes become much more difficult. Software engineering studies have shown that it is approximately 20 times more expensive to make a significant change to a program during the coding stage than during specification. That factor may go as high as 100 for a change made during the final stages of acceptance testing. Last-minute changes to a virtually finished program may require rewriting the specification document, redoing portions of the design, and recoding and debugging selected modules, thus requiring a great deal of effort. The

Figure 13–3
Second Draft of the Problem Specification Document for the Test-Scoring Problem

I have 34 students in my Latin class, each of whom took three tests during the semester. The test scores are whole numbers in the range 0 to 100. I would like a program that would allow me to input test scores in the following order.

T_1, T_2, T_3 (the three test scores of student 1)
T_1, T_2, T_3 (the three test scores of student 2)
• •
• •
• •
T_1, T_2, T_3 (the three test scores of student 34)

After all input has been entered, the program should print the following six lines of output on a hard-copy output device.

The mean of all test 1 scores is *xx.x*.
The mean of all test 2 scores is *xx.x*.
The mean of all test 3 scores is *xx.x*.

The standard deviation on test 1 is *xx.x*.
The standard deviation on test 2 is *xx.x*.
The standard deviation on test 3 is *xx.x*.

Figure 13–4
Relative Cost to Make a Change

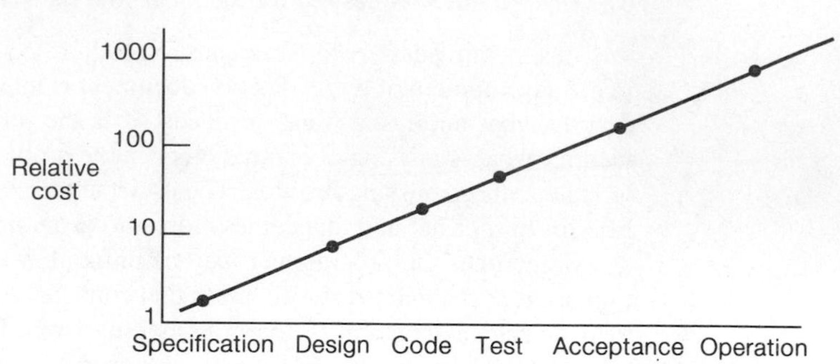

Source: R. Fairley, *Software Engineering Concepts* (New York: McGraw-Hill, 1985) p. 50

moral here is, get it right initially. Figure 13–4 summarizes the relative costs involved in making a change at various points in the software life cycle.

We (the programmers) may decide that the second draft in Figure 13–3 describes an inflexible program without much generality. As it stands, it assumes a fixed class size of exactly 34 students and legal test scores limited to a range of 0 to 100, with no provision for changing these values. Next semester the teacher might have only 28 students or may give 50-point quizzes. We suggest a modification that will allow the program to work for any range of test scores; it would involve having the user enter one additional line of data containing the following three values:

1. The number of students in the class
2. The lowest legal test score
3. The highest legal test score

The program can use these values in all subsequent calculations. Thus, the modified program would work for both a Latin class of 34 taking 100-point tests and a chemistry class of 25 taking a 50-point quiz. This change would greatly improve the generality of the finished program.

Similarly, the professor, after reviewing the previous draft, may decide that it would be easier to input all test 1 scores, followed by all test 2 scores and then all test 3 scores, rather than as described in Figure 13–3. Because the scores on the three tests were recorded on three different pages of the grade book this approach will minimize page flipping and facilitate input. After discussing and accepting these changes, we produce the third draft of the specification document, which is shown in Figure 13–5.

This development process would continue, possibly through a fourth or fifth draft, each time making sure that we are giving the user exactly what he or she needs in the form he or she wants. For example, looking at the third draft of the specification document in Figure 13–5, we might wish to discuss the following issues with the user as possible modifications to the problem:

1. Would you like a program that works for any number of tests, rather than specifically for three? As it now stands, the program lacks complete generality because of its fixed requirement of three tests per student.
2. Would you like the input to come from a data file rather than the keyboard, so that you do not have to reenter the data each time the program is run?

Figure 13–5
Third Draft of the Problem Specification Document for the Test-Scoring Problem

I would like a program that would allow me to input the three examination scores of the students in my class and determine the mean and standard deviation of those scores. All input to the program will be through the keyboard. The first line of input will contain the following three values separated by one or more spaces and entered in this order:

1. The number, N, of students $1 \leq N \leq 500$.
2. The lowest legal test score, LOW.
3. The highest legal test score, HIGH, where HIGH > LOW.

All succeeding input will be test scores, entered one per line in the following order:

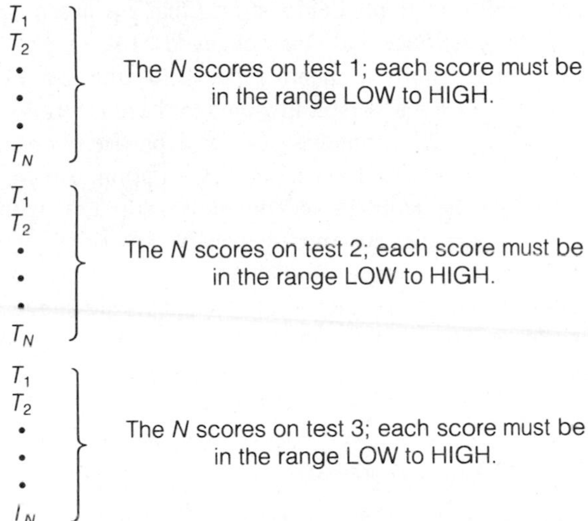

T_1
T_2
•
•
•
T_N
The N scores on test 1; each score must be in the range LOW to HIGH.
T_1
T_2
•
•
•
T_N
The N scores on test 2; each score must be in the range LOW to HIGH.
T_1
T_2
•
•
•
T_N
The N scores on test 3; each score must be in the range LOW to HIGH.

After all input has been entered, the program should print the following seven lines of output on a hard-copy output device.

Number of students = *xx* Range of Test Scores *xxx–xxx*

The mean of all test 1 scores is *xx.x*.
The mean of all test 2 scores is *xx.x*.
The mean of all test 3 scores is *xx.x*.

The standard deviation on test 1 is *xx.x*.
The standard deviation on test 2 is *xx.x*.
The standard deviation on test 3 is *xx.x*.

---

3. Would you like to include the students' names and/or ID numbers on the input as well as their test scores?
4. Would you like to print the examination scores on the output record so that you have a record of the scores?
5. Are there any other statistical measures you would like to have, such as the median, mode, or range?
6. Would you like the scores printed in sorted sequence?
7. Would you like graphical rather than printed output (e.g., bar charts or graphs)?

Depending on the responses to these questions, we may wish to revise the draft shown in Figure 13–5 and incorporate any changes that have been suggested.

In addition to suggesting improvements and enhancements, it is also the job of the programmer to inform the user if he or she requests tasks that would be extremely difficult to do well within the program and that probably should not be part of the specifications. For example, if our Latin professor had asked us to include in the program the ability to determine exactly where a student is weak and have the software plan a set of remedial training exercises, we should point out the complexity of this type of higher-level decision-making and the time and costs that could be involved. It is important to realize that some tasks are better done by people than by programs and probably should not be included in the problem specifications.

This extended example demonstrates that a problem specification document is not something done once and never changed. It is a highly dynamic document that evolves over many drafts as meetings are held, alternatives are discussed, and suggestions are made. Each person involved in these meetings—users, software developers, specialists—contributes his or her expertise to ensure that the system being designed gives the user all necessary information. As we mentioned earlier, it is important to get the problem specification document right initially because future changes will be significantly more expensive and time-consuming. This situation is analogous to making changes in a new house. Changes made during design involve only redrawing blueprints. However, if changes are suggested after the contractors have arrived, dug the foundation, and put up walls, the difficulty and costs increase manyfold.

13.2.2 Exception Handling

If nothing ever went wrong, our discussion would be finished—we could write out the input/output specifications of the software exactly as discussed in the previous section. However, a specification document must describe the actions to take for *every possible input*, including those that are implausible, illegal, or even impossible. This information is included in a second section of the problem specification document. This section, called *exception handling,* describes out-of-the-ordinary events that violate problem constraints, and it specifies the actions the program should take if these events occur. Examples of these special conditions include:

1. Input that falls outside the legal range
2. Too much input
3. Not enough input
4. Input that is in the improper format (e.g., letters instead of digits)
5. Input that would lead to illegal operations (e.g., dividing by 0)

We must anticipate these circumstances and include in our specification document exactly what response to take for each condition. Then our "black-box" program will be able to take meaningful actions under all conditions, not just the expected ones (see Figure 13–6).

The exception-handling section of the specification document is an easy place for a software developer to omit important details, because this type of exception information is frequently not part of instructions given to people. We assume that humans have common sense and will be able to figure out what to do when faced with unanticipated conditions or unexpected circumstances. For example, when writing instructions on how to start a car, we usually do not specify what to do if you

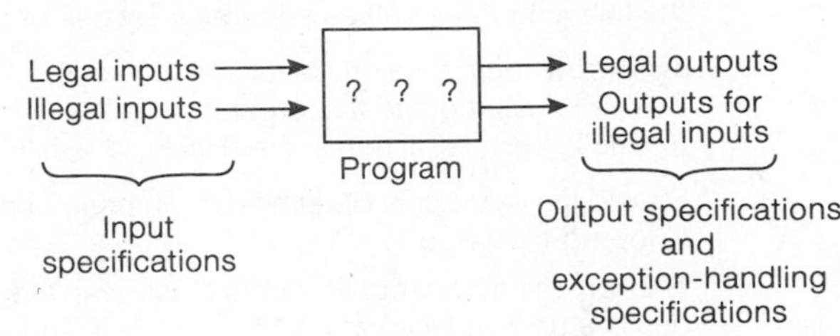

Figure 13–6
Complete Pictorial View of a Program Specification Document

have lost your keys or the car was stolen! We assume that an intelligent adult can determine the appropriate actions to take. However, software systems do not have such common sense. Responses to unexpected events must be planned for, specified, and included in the program. Another example of this point was given in chapter 12: reporting a negative number of work hours. Instructions on how to handle this unusual and unexpected condition must be part of a payroll program specification document.

If we review the third draft of the specification document in Figure 13–5, we see that it does not tell us what to do if any of the following five exception conditions occur:

1. No one took the tests ($N = 0$)
2. Too many people took the tests ($N > 500$), and the program will not be able to store all the data in memory.
3. The test score range is meaningless (LOW $\geq$ HIGH)
4. A test score T is not an integer value
5. A test score T is an integer value, but it is outside the range LOW to HIGH

Again we must talk to the user to find out what he or she would like done for each of these special conditions. Typical ways to deal with erroneous input data include

- Produce a clear, descriptive, and helpful error message and allow the user to reenter correct data
- Automatically enter an on-line assistance service, provide help to the user, and allow the user to reenter the data
- Use a preset default value in place of the illegal one (of course, informing the user that a default value is being used)
- Skip over the incorrect data. Solve the problem using $N - 1$ pieces of data rather than N
- Terminate the program with a clear and helpful error message indicating the reason for termination

After consulting with the user, we must make a decision on how the program should respond to each of the exception conditions listed above and include a description of the selected actions in our specification document. Figure 13–7 shows a fourth draft of the problem specification document for our test-scoring problem; it now contains exception-handling specifications.

Looking over the problem specification in Figure 13–7, we can see how far we have progressed from the original rough problem statement in Figure 13–2 and the succeeding drafts in Figures 13–3 and 13–5. However, because it is so important to

Figure 13–7
Fourth Draft of the Problem Specification Document for the Test-Scoring Problem

I would like a program that would allow me to input the three examination scores of the students in my class and determine the mean and standard deviation of those scores. All input to the program will be through the keyboard. The first line of input will contain the following three values separated by one or more spaces and entered in this order:

1. The number, N, of students $1 \leq N \leq 500$.
2. The lowest legal test score, LOW.
3. The highest legal test score, HIGH, where HIGH > LOW.

Should the value of N be either nonnumeric or outside the range 1 to 500, print the following message:

Error: The number of students must be in the range 1–500. Please reenter the previous line using a legal value.

Should the value for either LOW or HIGH be nonnumeric or should LOW ≥ HIGH, print the following message:

Error: The test score range provided is illegal. The lowest test score cannot equal or exceed the highest test score. Please reenter the previous line using legal values.

If either or both of these messages has been printed, the program should ask the user to reenter a new first line containing all three values. When the first line of input has been entered correctly, the user should input the test scores in the following order:

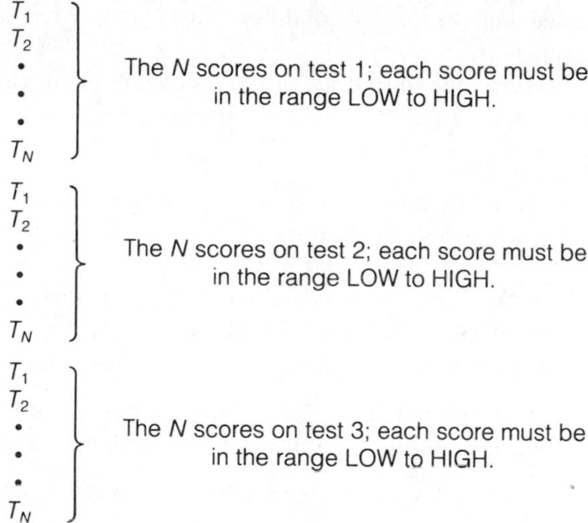
T_1
T_2
•
•
•
T_N
The N scores on test 1; each score must be in the range LOW to HIGH.
T_1
T_2
•
•
•
T_N
The N scores on test 2; each score must be in the range LOW to HIGH.
T_1
T_2
•
•
•
T_N
The N scores on test 3; each score must be in the range LOW to HIGH.

Should any test score T_i be either nonnumeric or outside the range LOW-HIGH, discard it and print the following message:

Error: The test score just entered was not in the range *xxx-xxx*. Please reenter that score.

where *xxx-xxx* represents the range LOW to HIGH. Let the user immediately reenter that test score.

After all input has been legally entered, the program should print the following seven lines of output on a hard-copy output device.

Number of students = *xx*   Range of Test Scores *xxx-xxx*

The mean of all test 1 scores is *xx.x*.
The mean of all test 2 scores is *xx.x*.
The mean of all test 3 scores is *xx.x*.

The standard deviation on test 1 is *xx.x*.
The standard deviation on test 2 is *xx.x*.
The standard deviation on test 3 is *xx.x*.

define the problem accurately, we should not be satisfied with a reasonably good specification. We must work to develop an excellent specification that will minimize future problems. We must carefully review all aspects of the problem to ensure that we have accounted for all possibilities, no matter how unlikely.

For example, if we look in the instructor's grade book, we might notice that some students were excused from one or more tests, and after talking to the professor, we might learn that the missing grades should not be included in the test average. Unless we plan for the possibility of *missing data* right now, here is what might happen when we begin testing the finished program (assume examination scores in the range 1 to 100):

Please enter next test score:

0 (Assume we try to put in a 0 for the missing grade)

Error: The test score just entered was not in the range 1–100. Please reenter.

(Now we try a blank)

Error: The test score just entered was not in the range 1–100. Please reenter.

help

**Error: The test score just entered . . .

Now that we realize our problem, we may have to do a major redesign and recoding of large parts of the program to eliminate this oversight. How much easier it would have been to identify and solve this problem during the problem specification phase. (Exercise 1 at the end of the chapter asks you to modify the specification document in Figure 13–7 to include the possibility of missing examination scores.)

Notice that nowhere in Figure 13–7 did we say anything about how this problem will be solved. Generally, the user does not care about the algorithms or abstract data types we use to solve the problem as long as the program works, is reasonably efficient, and produces the desired result. Thus, we were able to develop the problem specification document even though we might now know exactly how to compute a standard deviation or which data structures we will use for storing test scores.

If the user is satisfied with the description in the current draft, he or she *signs off* on the specification document, that is, he or she certifies that the problem described in that document is what is wanted and agrees not to make any further changes without accepting the delay and expense involved in making those changes. Similarly, the programmer agrees to design and build software that performs as described in the specification document. The problem specification document essentially becomes a contract between user and programmer certifying the work that must be done. The user's initial role in the project is now complete, and the user will not be involved again until the working program is delivered for checkout and acceptance testing.

The input/output specifications of section 13.2.1 and the exception-handling operations described in this section constitute the *functional specifications* of the proposed program. They describe, for every combination of inputs, the behavior (i.e., the functionality) of the finished program. The functional specifications are the most important part of the problem specification document.

In an academic environment, problem specification is generally not done by the student, because it is usually the instructor who thinks up a problem, refines and clarifies it through a number of drafts, and finally prepares a nice, readable document that spells out exactly what problem is to be solved. Thus, in an academic environment the problem specification document is better known as a *homework assignment*! In real life, however, problems rarely start out with such clarity and accuracy. It is up to the programmer to extract from the user adequate information to produce a document of sufficient precision that it can form the basis for the next stage in software development: program design.

13.2.3 Performance Specifications

For some problems the functional specifications of section 13.2.1 and 13.2.2 are all that is needed. However, one additional class of information can be very important in a problem specification document. *Performance specifications* are descriptions of the minimal operating characteristics required of the finished program. Because the specification document is a user-oriented document rather than a technical one, these performance criteria should be expressed in terms that a user can understand, observe, and measure, rather than technical measures understandable only to a software specialist. Therefore, performance criteria such as the following, although they could be appropriate at later stages, might be inappropriate in a specification document:

Execution of at least 10,000 machine-language instructions per second
No more than 100 bus interrupts per second
At least 5000 sector accesses per minute

A better performance specification would be:

The program must be able to process a minimum of 100 customer transactions per second.

This statement gives a performance specification that the user can measure and verify.

Performance metrics, as these specifications are frequently called, should be detailed and quantitative rather than subjective and qualitative. The performance metrics contained in the specification document will be used, along with the functional specifications, to judge the quality and acceptability of the finished program. Subjective measures such as the following are too vague to serve as acceptance criteria:

The program must be extremely quick in processing data.
It must be robust.
It must respond fast enough so that users do not get angry.

(One person may get angry after waiting 3 seconds, whereas another is content to sit for 3 minutes!) Performance criteria must be phrased in measurable quantitative terms such as:

The average response time for all input queries must be less than 2.0 seconds, and no single response must ever require more than 5.0 seconds.

The program must process 90% of the data sets in less than 10 seconds and all data sets in less than 20 seconds.

A user must be able to create a spreadsheet with at least 500 rows and 500 columns.

Performance metrics generally address the following six areas of program performance:

1. *Speed*: how fast the program operates, typically expressed in terms of response time, total time to produce a given result, or worst-case behavior for the largest possible data set.
2. *Throughput*: how much information can be "pushed through" the program in a given amount of time, typically measured in completed data sets/time unit.
3. *Availability*: a measure of the percentage of time the system is up and available for processing; usually a hardware metric but also used to measure the availability and robustness of software products.
4. *Capacity*: a measure of the maximum size data set that can be handled by the program.
5. *Precision*: the accuracy with which the final results can be produced, typically given in terms of significant digits or maximal error bounds.
6. *Equipment needs*: a specification of the resources (e.g., memory or peripherals) that will be needed to run the completed program.

Looking back at the draft of Figure 13–7, we see that it contains two performance metrics: The finished program must be able to handle any number of students up to and including 500, and it must be able to determine the mean and standard deviation to one-decimal-place accuracy. We may wish to add other performance criteria such as

1. The program must be able to accept a 500-element data set and complete all processing of that data set in five seconds or less.
2. The completed program must run on a Macintosh IIfx computer system with 4 Mbyte of memory and a 40-Mbyte hard disk.

The performance criteria serve two important purposes. First, they ensure that the finished product will be not only correct but useful. After all, a correct answer is meaningless if it is not provided quickly enough to be of use or if it requires equipment that the user does not have. Second, these performance measures will be used as standards during *acceptance testing* of the finished program. A program will be considered correct and ready for delivery when it meets both the functional specifications given in the input/output and exception-handling sections and the performance specifications given in the performance metrics section of the problem specification document. Again, we see why completeness, thoroughness, and exactness are important in a specification document. Not only is this document used to describe the problem to be solved, it is also used to determine when the project has been successfully completed.

13.3 FORMAL SPECIFICATION METHODS

Throughout this chapter we have stressed clarity, completeness, and exactness as essential characteristics of a good specification. Every combination of inputs must be anticipated, and there must be no confusion or ambiguity in determining what actions are to be taken. However, we have used a natural language (English in our case) to express these specifications. This choice of notation is poor because natural language suffers from problems of ambiguity, context sensitivity, multiple meanings, and differences in interpretation. Natural languages were never intended to have the clear and precise notational characteristics of mathematics. For example, if I say:

> Sort the list into order by the identification number field.

does "into order" mean to sort the list into ascending or descending order? Similarly, if I say:

> Do not accept any input value that is outside the range 0 to 10,000.

are the end values 0 and 10,000 to be accepted? These uncertainties are typical of the problems that arise when using natural language specifications.

For this reason, a good deal of software engineering research is being carried out in the area of formal representation methods for problem specification documents. These formal notations are not intended to replace natural language documents but are to be used in conjunction with them to help make them more complete and exact. Many different techniques are currently in use. In chapter 12 we gave one example of a technique called first-order predicate calculus. In the next section we will describe two others: *decision tables*, and *finite-state machines*.

13.3.1 Decision Tables

A *decision table* is a two-dimensional matrix structure divided into four quadrants, each of which contains a number of rows and columns. The four quadrants are called the condition statements, condition entries, action statements, and action entries. The columns of the decision table are called *decision rules* and are numbered 1, 2, 3, 4, ... The overall structure of a decision table is shown in Figure 13–8.

Figure 13–8
Structure of a Decision Table

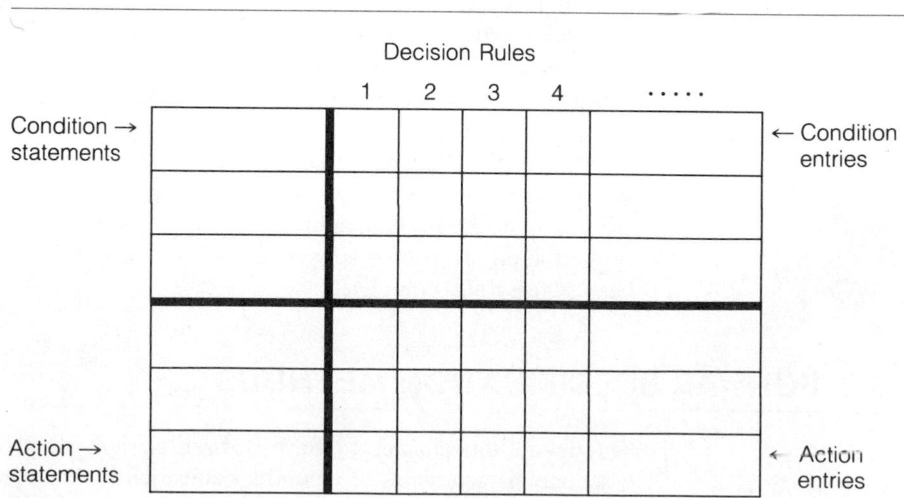

A *condition statement* is a Boolean (i.e., true/false) condition that may or may not be satisfied by a particular data set. Examples of condition statements are:

The value of x is in the range 1 to 100 inclusive.
The size of the data set exceeds 500 elements.
The value for Score is nonnumeric.
There are exactly four numeric items in this data set.

The *condition entries* describe, for a specific decision rule, whether a data set satisfies the Boolean condition described in the condition statement. Generally, the following three symbols are used:

Y = Yes — For this decision rule, the data satisfy the condition given in the condition statement.
N = No — For this decision rule, the data do not satisfy the condition given in the condition statement.
— = Yes or No — For this decision rule, it does not matter whether the data satisfy the condition given in the condition statement (equivalent to writing (Y or N)).

The condition entries will all be set to one of the three values Y, N, or —.

The *action statements* are declarative statements that describe operations to perform, results to compute, or output to be produced by the software. The *action entries* are indicators that specify whether, for this decision rule, we should take this action. We place an X in the box to indicate that this action statement should be carried out and leave it blank if it should not.

The meaning of the entries in a decision table is quite straightforward. If a set of inputs satisfies all the conditions specified in column i of the decision table, then all actions marked by an X in the action entries of column i should be performed. For example, referring to the decision table in Figure 13–9, if we input a data set where $x = 3$, $y = 600$, $z = 1$, then decision rule 2 applies, and we would print out the value of x and then shut down the system in response to this input set. If the

Figure 13–9
Example of a Decision Table

	. . .	2	. . .	4	. . .
x is odd	. . .	Y	. . .	N	. . .
y >= 500	. . .	Y	. . .	N	. . .
$z = 0$		N		—	
Print out the value of x		X			
Find all factors of y				X	
Shut down the system after all output is finished		X			

input were $x = 2$, $y = 400$, and $z = 0$, decision rule 4 would apply and we would proceed to find all factors of y.

The decision rules must satisfy two conditions for a decision table to be valid. First, the rules must be *complete*, that is, every possible combination of (Y,N) values must be accounted for, and every input set must match at least one decision rule. The decision table in Figure 13–10 is incomplete. If both conditions c_1 and c_2 are true, there is no matching decision rule, that is, the table does not specify what actions we are to take. A decision table with k condition statements will require at most 2^k decision rules to be complete (it may require fewer because of the existence of the — entry).

The rules must also be *unambiguous*. An input set must not match more than one decision rule. Otherwise, the actions to be taken by our program would be nondeterministic. The table in Figure 13–11 is ambiguous. If condition c_1 is true and condition c_2 is false, rules 3 and 4 are both satisfied, and we would be unsure whether to take action a_1 or action a_2.

Together, the characteristics of completeness and unambiguousness can be expressed in the following way:

> Every possible set of inputs to the program must match one and only one decision rule. The actions to take in response to that input are all action statements marked by an X in the decision rule that was matched.

Figure 13–10
Incomplete Decision Table

	1	2	3
c_1	N	N	Y
c_2	N	Y	N
	...	...	...

Figure 13–11
Ambiguous Decision Table

	1	2	3	4
c_1	N	N	Y	Y
c_2	N	Y	N	—
a_1	X		X	
a_2		X		X

Figure 13–12
Decision Table for the Prime-Number Problem

	1	2	3	4
The input value *N* is not an integer.	Y	N	N	N
The input value is strictly less than one.	—	Y	N	N
N is legal and prime.	—	—	Y	N
Print out that *N* is prime.			X	
Print out that *N* is not prime.				X
Print out *M* which is a factor of *N*.				X
Print an error message that *N* is illegal.	X	X		
Print the goodbye message.			X	X
Input a new value of *N*.	X	X		
Terminate the program.			X	X

A decision table is a more formalized way to express the input/output characteristics of a program, in contrast to the purely natural language technique we employed in the previous section.

Figure 13–12 shows a decision table specification for the following natural language description of a problem about prime numbers.

> You are to input an integer value, *N*, that is greater than or equal to one, and you are to determine if that number is prime. If it is prime, print out a message that says that the number is prime. If it is not prime, print out a message that says that the number is not prime along with the integer value *M*, where *M* is any factor of *N*. If the value that you read in is illegal, either because it is nonintegral or because it is out of range (that is, strictly less than one), then print out an error message and let the user reenter the data. Repeat the data entry process until you are finally given a single legal value for *N*. When you have solved the problem for that one legal value, your program should indicate that it has completed by printing out an appropriate message, and it should then terminate.

A comparison of this fairly verbose paragraph with the table in Figure 13–12 should clearly demonstrate the conciseness and accuracy of the decision table method. With larger and more complex problems, the savings can be even greater.

13.3.2 Finite State Machines

Decision tables are one of the simplest and easiest but least powerful techniques for formal specification. One variation is a formal representation called a *finite-state automaton*, or a *finite-state machine*.

One of the main problems with the decision table method is that there is only one table. If our input matches decision rule i, then we will always take the same actions, regardless of the previous history of inputs and the current state that we are in. For example, we may be developing a program in which we want the program to print out an error message and let the user reenter the data the first time an input error is made, but we want something different to happen the second time the mistake is made—perhaps the user would automatically enter an on-line help program or a warning message would be flashed on the screen.

A convenient way to specify these two actions would be to use two decision tables. The first one would be used if the user has not yet made an error; the second one would be used if the user has previously made an input error. We would then use the decision table that corresponded to the current state. In addition to specifying what action to take in response to the input, our tables would also contain action entries that specified when to start using the other decision table, as shown in Figure 13–13.

Figure 13–13 shows that the output produced by a program depends not only on its inputs but on the *current state* of the program as well. This situation is exactly what a finite-state machine (FSM) allows us to describe.

An FSM is a collection of states (S_1, S_2, . . .), inputs, (I_1, I_2, . . .), and actions or outputs (A_1, A_2, . . .). The notation shown in Figure 13–14 means that if you are currently in state S_1 and you receive either input I_1, I_2, or . . . , then you are simultaneously to make a transition to state S_2 and perform all actions A_1, A_2, ... A collection of states, inputs, outputs, and transitions is called a *finite-state machine*.

In a sense, each individual state of a state diagram can be thought of as a separate decision table, since each one has a set of inputs and actions to take in response

Figure 13–13
Using Multiple Decision Tables

Input value is correct.	Y	N
Accept value.	X	
Print error message.		X
Reenter value.		X
Start using Decision Table II.		X

a. Decision Table I (no errors)

Input value is correct.	Y	N
Accept value.	X	
Take special action.		X
Go back to using Decision Table I.	X	

b. Decision Table II (one error)

Figure 13–14
Finite-State Machine Notation

S_1 —— $I_1, I_2, \ldots$ / $A_1, A_2, \ldots$ ——→ S_2

Figure 13–15
Finite-State Machine for Specifying How to Handle Input Errors

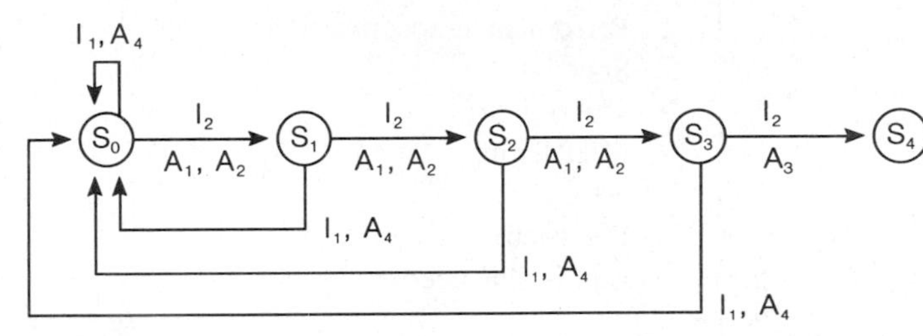

States	Inputs	Actions
S_0: No-error state	I_1: Legal input	A_1: Print error message
S_1: One-error state	I_2: Illegal input	A_2: Get new input
S_2: Two-error state		A_3: Print 'Going into special error state'
S_3: Three-error state		A_4: Perform normal processing operations
S_4: Special "Error State"		

to those inputs. However, by adding the concept of multiple states and state transitions, we have added a *memory* to our decision table technique. We can base the actions that our program should take not only on the current input but on the previous history of inputs.

For example, suppose that we modified the decision table of Figure 13–13 to allow the user to make up to three input errors without penalty. However, if the user makes the same mistake a fourth time, he or she is transferred to a special "error state" where something different happens. This four-step process would be cumbersome to describe using the decision table technique of section 13.3.1. With a finite-state machine, however, it becomes a simple task, as shown in Figure 13–15.

There a number of other formal specification methods in addition to the two described here, including high-level problem specification languages, the first-order predicate logic used in chapter 12, and Petri nets. Future courses in software engineering will expand on this topic at greater length and introduce some of these other formal specification techniques.

13.4 CONCLUSION

This chapter has introduced you to the specification phase and the problem specification document, an important part of software development that ensures that the problem to be solved is clearly understood and unambiguously specified. In addition, the information collected during this phase is used to test and accept the completed software package. The problem specification document is composed of two major sections:

1. Functional specifications
   Input
   Output
   Exception handling
2. Performance specifications
   Speed
   Throughput
   Availability
   Capacity
   Precision
   Equipment needs

In real life, this document may contain other information, such as proposed extensions, budget constraints, delivery-time constraints, or details of the user environment. Most specifications are not as short and simple as the one in Figure 13–7, but are long and highly complicated documents running to dozens or even hundreds of pages and utilizing both formal and informal notation.

Natural language does not offer the precision needed in a specification document. Therefore, our informal English description of a problem will usually be supplemented by formal notation, possibly using one of the methods that we discussed in section 13.3. This formal notation should ensure that we not only get the problem right but also that we solve the right problem!

Even though students rarely develop their own specification document, you should still get in the habit of carefully reviewing any "finished" problem statement that is given to you. Make sure that all input conditions are included, the desired output is clearly described, and all special cases are explicitly addressed. If there are omissions, ambiguities, or discrepancies in the problem statement, get them cleared up before you begin the next phase of software development—program design, which we will discuss in the next chapter.

CHAPTER EXERCISES

1. Write a new draft of the specification document shown in Figure 13–7 adding the following four features:
   a. The program should allow any number of tests per student, rather than exactly three.
   b. The input data will come from a file, rather than the keyboard.
   c. For each test, the teacher wants not only the mean and standard deviation, but also the range, that is, the highest and lowest scores actually received.
   d. The instructor wants to use the value −1 to indicate that a student was legally excused from a test. The computation of means, standard deviations, and ranges should not include excused tests.
2. Write a new draft of the specification document for the prime-number prob-

lem shown in Figure 13–12. The new draft should incorporate the following changes.

a. The program should not terminate after processing one correct input value but should ask the user if he or she wants to input another value. Do not stop until the user explicitly indicates he or she wants to stop.
b. If a number is not prime, print out all factors, not just one.
c. If the user enters a value $N < 0$, determine whether the value $|N|$ (the absolute value of N) is or is not prime, rather than treating that condition as an error.

3. The following specification document describes the problem of evaluating quadratic equations using the quadratic formula. As it stands, it includes only a description of normal input/output—it does not include any exceptions or special circumstances.

   Your program will be given as input three real values, a, b, c, in that order, which correspond to the three coefficients of the following quadratic equations:

   $$ax^2 + bx + c = 0$$

   You should determine the two roots of this quadratic equation using the quadratic formula:

   $$\text{roots} = \frac{-b \pm \sqrt{b^2 - 4ac}}{2a}$$

   Print out the two roots of the quadratic equation in the following format

   The first root is *xxx.xxx*
   The second root is *xxx.xxx*

   and then stop.

   Describe exactly what errors or exception conditions could occur in this problem, and rewrite the specification document to include the responses to each condition.

4. Here is the specification for a table lookup problem:

   You will be given as input a two-column list of names containing from 1 to 80 characters followed by seven-digit phone numbers (*xxx-xxxx*):

   name *phone number*
   name *phone number*
   • •
   • •
   • •
   name *phone number*

   There are about one thousand (name, phone number) pairs. You will then be given a single name as a key. Look up that name in the list of names in the table. When you find the name in the list, produce the following line of output:

The phone number of this person is *xxx-xxxx*.

where *xxx-xxxx* is the corresponding phone number found in the phone number column.

Again, this specification document omits a description of the errors or exception conditions that could occur in this problem. Describe these error conditions and rewrite the specifications so that we know how to handle them. Also, if you feel there is information missing from the functional specifications described above, add it to your new draft.

5. The following list contains very rough initial problem statements. Enlist the aid of the instructor or a fellow student to play the role of the user, and ask the questions you think are needed to produce a clear, unambiguous problem statement. Then write the problem specification document using either natural language or a decision table. Remember to include all the error conditions.
   a. I would like a program to sort a list of N numbers into order.
   b. I would like a program to find roots of equations. That is, if I give it an equation $f(x)$, it will give me all values of x for which $f(x) = 0$.
   c. I would like a program that would tell me how much I would have to pay each month for mortgages of various sizes at different interest rates.
   d. I would like a program that would tell me the day of the week on which my birthday would fall for any year.
   e. I would like a program that would look through some English-language text and locate every occurrence of the character string 'Data Structure'.
   f. I would like a program that would tell me which stock to buy in order to make some money.
6. Closely review the fourth draft of the test-scoring program in Figure 13–7 and see if you feel it is complete and unambiguous. Do you have any suggestions to the user on how the program could be improved or made more flexible? Produce a fifth draft that reflects the improvements you suggested.
7. For each of the following performance metrics, state whether you think it is sufficiently descriptive to be included in a problem specification document.
   a. The finished program should be able to run on a personal computer.
   b. The finished program should be able to run on a Macintosh IIfx.
   c. The program should process most data sets in less than 1 second.
   d. The program should process all data sets in less than 1 second.
   e. The program should process 95% of all data sets in less than 1 second.
   f. The program must successfully sort any table of size up to and including 5,000 elements.
   g. The disk must be large enough to hold 30,000 patient records.
   h. The name field must be large enough to hold the longest patient name without truncation of any characters.
   i. All answers must be accurate to within 0.0001%.
   j. All answers must contain at least three significant digits.
   k. The program must be available 100% of the time.
8. What is wrong with the decision table shown on the next page? What needs to be added or removed to make it correct?

$x > 0$	Y	N	N	Y	Y
$y > 0$	Y	Y	Y	N	N
$z > 0$	—	N	Y	N	Y
Compute r/x.	X			X	X
Compute r/y.	X	X	X		
Compute r/z.			X		X
Print error message.		X	X	X	X

9. Develop a decision table for the following problem:

   You are to read in a part number and an order amount from the keyboard. Look up that part number in an inventory file containing a list of part numbers, along with the amount on hand and the back order amount for that part. If the part number is not found in the file, print an error message that the part number was incorrect and ask the user to reenter it. If the part number is found, check the value of the amount on hand field to determine if it is equal or greater than the order amount. If it is, then process the order, reset the amount-on-hand field by subtracting the order amount from the amount on hand, and update the inventory file. If there is not enough on hand, send out what there is, update the back order amount, and set the amount-on-hand field to zero. Update the inventory file with these new values. In either case, when you finish processing one request, go back and get the next input request. Stop when the part number input is 00000.

   Compare the ease and exactness of developing specifications in a natural language versus a decision table.
10. Develop a decision table specification for the modified quadratic equation program from exercise 3. Your decision table should include the exception-handling conditions that you added to the specification.
11. Develop a decision table specification for the fourth draft of the test-scoring problem contained in Figure 13–7.
12. Using the following finite-state machine

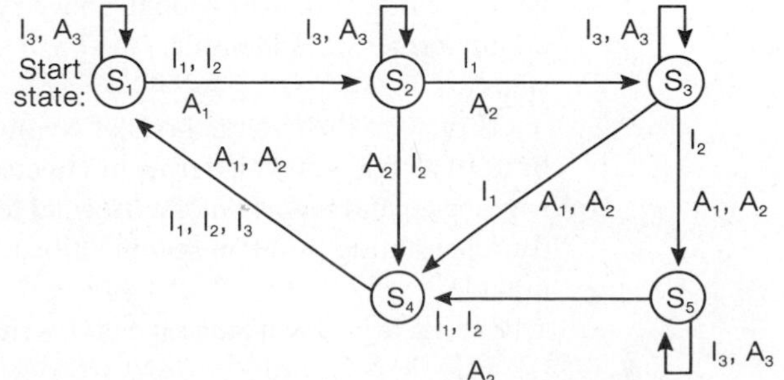

and given the following sequence of inputs:

$I_1, I_3, I_2, I_2, I_2, I_1, I_3$

what state will we end up in if we begin in state S_1? Exactly what sequence of output operations will be performed?

13. Suppose that we are designing a program to input a series of characters that comprise a signed integer value. The syntax of the number is an optional + or − sign, followed by one to four digits in the range 0 to 9, followed by either a blank or a carriage return. Develop a finite-state machine that determines whether a given input meets the specification just described. The FSM should print out one of the following messages:

    Valid number
    Invalid number

    Furthermore, if the syntax is valid, the FSM should take the action of converting that sequence of characters to an integer. Use the notation shown in Figure 13–14.
14. Modify the finite-state machine of exercise 13 so that it treats any number that contains a nonsignificant leading zero as Invalid. That is, numbers like

    −01
    +00387
    000042

    would now cause the output of the "Invalid number" message. (Be careful, though, that you accept the numbers 0, +0, and −0; they are all valid values.)
15. Create a finite-state machine that formally specifies the following natural language description of the syntax of an identifier in a high-level language:

    An identifier is an arbitrarily long string of characters, where the characters are limited to letters (upper- and lower-case), digits, the underscore symbol (_), and a period (.). An identifier must begin with a letter. If an underscore is present in the identifier, it must have at least one letter or digit on either side of it. There cannot be two or more adjacent underscores. If a period is present in the identifier, it must be the last character. The end of the identifier is marked by the presence of either a blank or a carriage return.

    Your finite-state machine will be given a sequence of characters, and it should end up in the "valid identifier" state if the characters that were input form a valid identifier according to the above syntactic specifications; if the characters do not form a valid identifier, the FSM should end up in the "Invalid identifier" state.

    Compare the two methods of writing specifications (natural language and finite-state machines) in terms of conciseness and precision.
16. Investigate and report on other formal techniques not mentioned in this chapter for representing problem specifications. Areas that you may wish to look at include:
    a. Special high-level languages for writing and testing specifications such as

PSL/PSA, an acronym for Problem Specification Language and Problem Specification Analyzer.

b. Petri nets.

c. First order predicate logic.

For the method you select, show examples of specifications and discuss the advantages of this particular technique.

CHAPTER 14

THE PROGRAM DESIGN AND IMPLEMENTATION PHASES

CHAPTER OUTLINE

14.1 INTRODUCTION

We are now at the point in the software development process where we have a clear, concise, and unambiguous problem statement and are ready to design and implement a program to solve that problem. It may seem that our next step would be coding. For example, to implement the grade-book example of the previous chapter, we could select a data structure to store the test scores, choose algorithms to compute the mean and standard deviation, and start writing code.

However, for a real-world programming problem, coding is definitely *not* the next step. There is a very important stage called *program design* that must precede the implementation of our solution. Program design provides the intellectual and administrative techniques for managing the development of a large software project by decomposing a large, complex task into a number of smaller modules and abstract data types.

A design phase is needed in the development of real-world software projects because of their enormous size and complexity. As we saw in Table 12–1, real programs are one hundred to one thousand times larger than those typically given as student assignments. In addition, any realistic program P is composed not of a single logical task but of many interrelated tasks, P_1, P_2, P_3, . . . , that, when integrated into a single software system, will solve the original problem.

For example, even the simple test-scoring program specified in Figure 13–7 would not be implemented as a single monolithic unit but would most likely be subdivided into seven interrelated routines that would handle the following tasks:

- Reading in test scores from the keyboard
- Validating that those scores are numeric and within the legal range
- Processing illegal and out-of-range scores
- Computing a mean
- Computing a standard deviation
- Printing out results
- Creating, storing, and retrieving operations on the ScoreTable abstract data type

The medium and large-sized software projects described in Table 12–1 might be composed of as many as one hundred to one thousand separate pieces, not just seven. Therefore, the next step in the programming process involves taking the problem described in the problem specification document and decomposing it into a collection of interrelated subproblems, each of which is much smaller and much simpler than our original task. This decomposition of the problem is an example of the design technique called *divide and conquer*, which is based on the principle that it is easier to solve many small problems than to solve one extremely large one.

The alternative "design technique," writing code immediately, may work for small programs, but it quickly collapses when applied to longer efforts. The following list contains just some of the problems we would encounter if we attempted to implement a large software project without spending adequate time on design:

1. We would find ourselves totally engulfed in detail. There would be so much to do and remember that we would forget to perform important operations, miss key implementation details, or omit critical sections of code. We would lose track of what has already been done and what still needs to be done.

2. Debugging and testing would become extremely complex. Real-world programs are so large that looking for an error is like searching for the proverbial needle in a haystack.
3. It would be difficult to predict all the ramifications of an early decision. The programs are so large that the effect of a decision may not become evident for days, weeks, or even months. It then may be difficult to undo its effects, and we would be stuck with our first choice, even though it might not be a good one.

Careful planning and a good program design technique can effectively overcome these and other problems and lead to the successful completion of large programs, even those on the scale of the very large and extremely large projects of Table 12–1.

Many different methods and approaches are used in program design, and each one has its adherents. Some of the more well known go by names such as *data flow design*, *object-oriented design*, and *structured analysis and design*. All these approaches are based on the divide-and-conquer concept. They differ only in the criteria they use for decomposition.

The method that we will study in this chapter is by far the simplest to understand and implement, but it will give you a good idea of the issues and problems that must be addressed during the design phase. The technique we will investigate is called *top-down program design*.

14.2 TOP-DOWN PROGRAM DESIGN

Top-down program design involves starting from the broadest and most general description of *what* needs to be done, that is, the problem specification document, and then subdividing the original problem into collections of modules and abstract data types. Each of these lower-level units is smaller and simpler than the original task and is more involved with the details of *how* to solve the problem rather than *what* needs to be done. We proceed from high-level goals to detailed low-level solution methods.

If a program P can be subdivided into three simpler subunits, P_1, P_2, and P_3, we can represent it pictorially as shown in Figure 14–1. This diagram has the familiar tree structure of chapter 7. When a tree is used to show the modules and subprograms needed to solve a problem and the interrelationships between them, it is called a *program development tree*. However, a tree is just one way of representing program designs, and there are a number of other popular representational techniques. The specific pictorial format you choose is not important as long as it clearly

Figure 14–1 Pictorial Representation of the Program Design Method

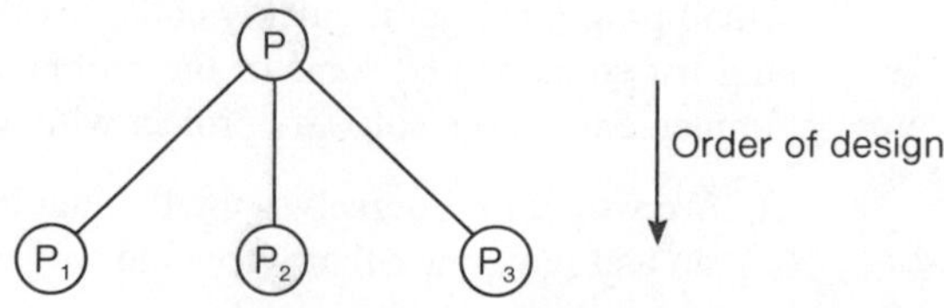

Figure 14–2
Example of a More Realistic Program Design

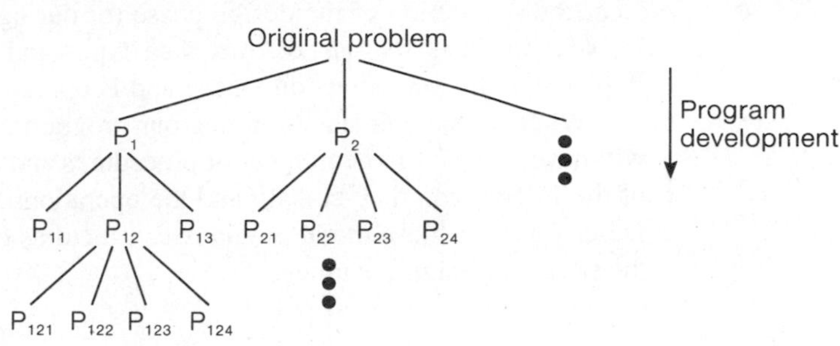

shows the structural relationship between a program unit such as P and the components of that unit, for example, P_1, P_2, and P_3. In this section, we will use the development tree model shown in Figure 14–1 to display the structure of our design. In section 14.3.1 we will discuss the use of other, more formalized notational conventions.

Top-down program design is not the one-step process diagrammed in Figure 14–1. The decomposition and simplification task is performed over and over, first on the original problem and then on successive subunits, until finally we are left with a task that is so elementary it need not be simplified any further. The repeated decomposition and simplification of a task into a collection of simpler subtasks is called *stepwise refinement*; it leads to the more interesting and more realistic program development tree of Figure 14–2. Each of the tasks P_{ijk} in Figure 14–2 represents a separate program unit needed to solve the original problem. A diagram such as Figure 14–2, which shows what program units are needed to solve a problem and how these units are related, is a central component of the *program design document*, which we will discuss in detail in section 14.3.

The data structures needed for the solution are also developed in a top-down fashion as we proceed from general descriptions of abstract data types to operations performed on these data types to their internal implementation. For example, early in a program design we may decide that we need a first-in/first-out queue data structure in which objects called Person are placed at the end of a waiting Line. That level of specification may be enough for us to design some of our early modules.

```
Var
    Line        : Queue;     (* Queue is an abstract data type. *)
    Person      : People;    (* People is an abstract data type. *)
```

Later, we will need to write the external module that describes the syntax and semantics of the operations on objects of type Queue and People, such as:

Initialize(Line)	Sets the initial waiting Line length to 0
LineLength(Line)	Returns the current length of the Line
Enqueue(Person, Line)	Puts the Person at the end of the Line
Dequeue(Person, Line)	Removes the Person at the front of the Line
Cut(Person, Line, i)	Allows a Person to cut into Line at position i

Near the completion of the design phase (or during coding), we will decide on the internal structure for our abstract data types and write the internal module that implements the operations on Queue and People.

When we have finished refining our program units and abstract data types, we will have created a large number of procedures and data structures, defined in terms of the information they contain and the operations that can be performed on them. Descriptions of these modules and data structures constitute a major component of the program design document.

14.3 THE PROGRAM DESIGN DOCUMENT

The *program design document* identifies the individual components of the overall program and specifies the structural relationships between these components. It contains three major sections:

1. The *structure chart*. This pictorial representation shows the structural relationships between the procedures and data structures contained in the design.
2. The *procedure specifications*. For every module, procedure, or other program unit contained in the structure chart, there is a specification that describes the external interface that this program unit presents to the rest of the program.
3. The *data dictionary*. For every major data structure and abstract data type contained in the structure chart, we describe its formal properties, the information in that structure, and the operations that can be performed on that structure.

In the next three sections, we will describe these three components of the program design document.

14.3.1 The Structure Chart

In Figure 14–2, we used a tree structure to diagram the relationships among the individual components of a program. Development trees like Figure 14–2, provide a reasonable pictorial representation, and they are used in program design documents. However, a tree structure suffers from one major problem—not all program designs match the rigidly hierarchical structure of a tree. For example, it is extremely common to have a low-level utility routine such as a random number generator or a sorting routine called by a number of other modules at different levels throughout the system, as shown in Figure 14–3. This diagram violates the one-to-many hierarchical tree structure that we described in chapter 7. For this reason, representation methods other than trees have been developed for displaying the overall structure of a piece of software. These structures are known by such diverse terms as *data flow diagrams*, *bubble charts*, *HIPO* (hierarchy-input-process-output) *charts*, *structure diagrams*, and *flowcharts*.

The technique we will introduce here is similar to a number of these techniques.

Figure 14–3
Example of a Low-Level Routine Called from Many Levels

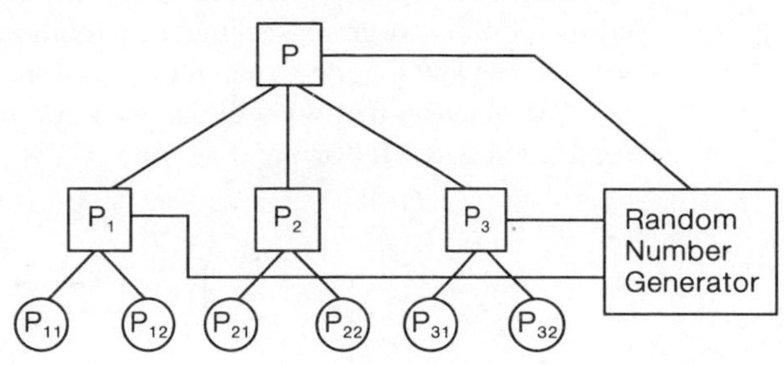

Table 14–1 Notation for Structure Charts in Program Design Documents

Notation	Meaning
M	A program unit M (by convention, the main program unit will be referred to as Main)
M_1 —x→ M_2 ←y- - -	Routine M_1 invokes M_2, passing it the value *x*. Routine M_2 returns the result *y* back to M_1.
←	Input to the program from someone or something outside the scope of the program
→	Output to someone or something outside the scope of the program
D	Data structure D
M —$f(x,y)$→ D	Routine M performs operation *f* on data structure D using parameters *x* and *y*
(A)	Connector to another part of the structure chart

It uses a *directed graph* of the type discussed in chapter 10 to represent the program design pictorially. We will use an unweighted directed graph structure of the form

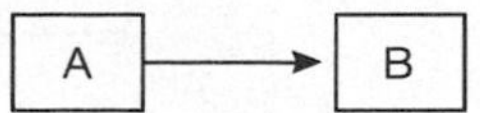

to indicate that program unit A invokes, calls, or performs an action on program unit B. With a directed graph, we are no longer restricted to the rigidly hierarchical relationship imposed by the use of development trees like the one in Figure 14–2. With our directed graph technique, a module may be linked to (i.e., invoke or be invoked by) any other module in the solution, not just its immediate parent or child.

The notation that we will use for our structure chart is shown in Table 14–1. For example, the following diagram

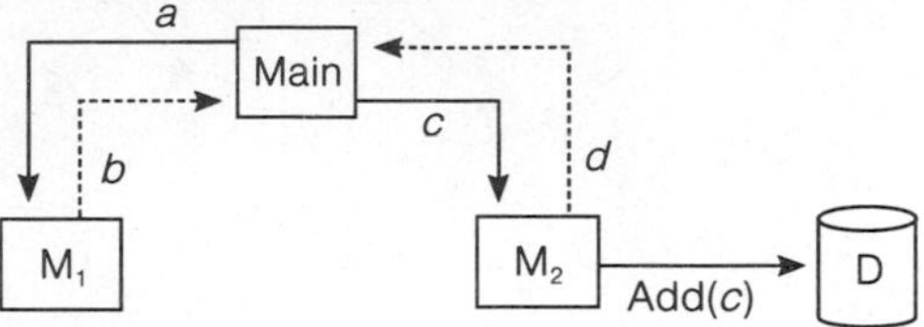

represents the structure of a program containing three units called Main, M_1, and M_2 and one data structure, D. Subprograms M_1 and M_2 are activated by Main and return to it. M_1 is given the value of *a* and returns the result *b*. M_2 is passed the value *c* and returns the result *d*. M_2 performs the operation Add(*c*) to data structure D. Neither Main nor M_1 operate on D, and M_1 and M_2 do not directly invoke each other.

This type of structure chart may seem similar to the *flowcharts* frequently used to represent algorithms in introductory programming courses. However, a structure chart is different in at least two respects. First, it contains neither the looping nor the conditional *control information* found in flowcharts. The notation

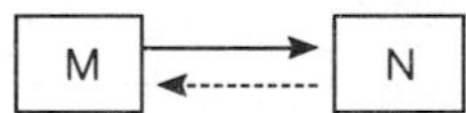

does not imply that routine M will conditionally or unconditionally call N during its execution or that it will call N only once. It simply says that in describing the logic of routine M, a call to unit N will be included somewhere within M. When, if, and exactly how many times N will be called depends on the internal logic of subprogram M, but this logic is not part of the structure chart.

A second difference between a structure chart and flowchart is that a structure chart contains no *temporal information*. It does not imply the order or sequence in which operations will be done. The notation

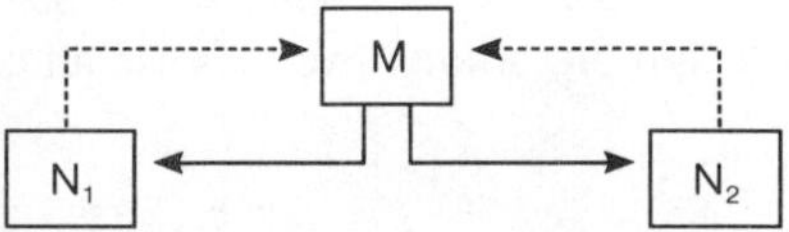

does not imply that routine N_1 will necessarily be invoked before or after routine N_2. It merely says that the design of the logic of procedure M includes the potential activation of both procedures N_1 and N_2. The order in which they are invoked (or,

Figure 14–4
Structure Chart for a Solution to the Test-Scoring Problem

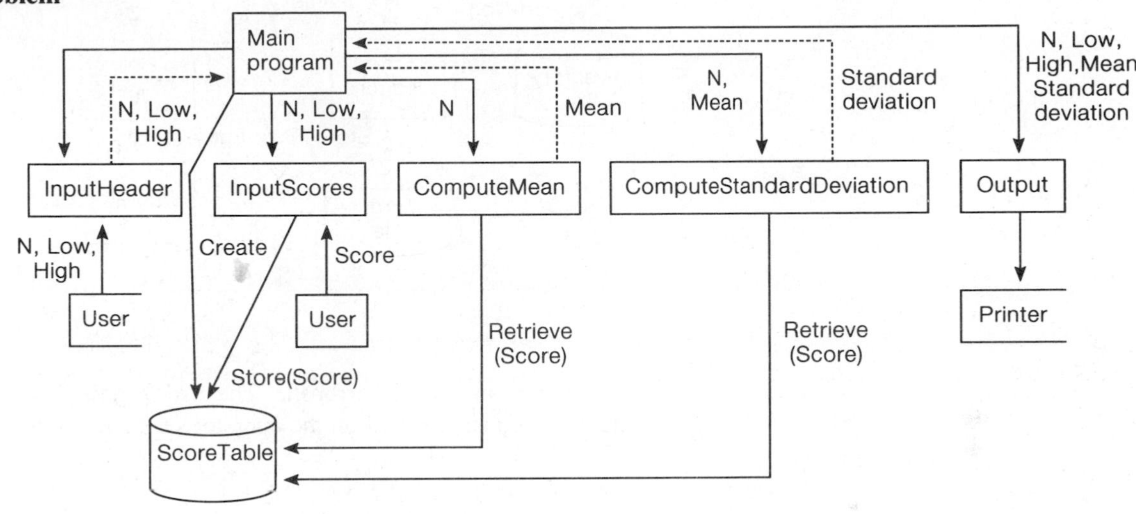

indeed, whether they are invoked at all) will be part of the implementation of M, N_1, and N_2.

Figure 14–4 shows a structure chart for the design of a solution to the test-scoring problem discussed in chapter 13 and shown in Figure 13–7. As we can see, a structure chart for an interesting program can be quite large and contain many, many components. For this reason, structure charts are rarely displayed as a single diagram. Instead, they are usually divided into a number of smaller structure charts spread over many pages and joined by *connector* symbols such as:

As a second example of a structure chart, Figure 14–5 shows a small portion of the design of the software for an inventory control system. The part shown is the PartNumberLookup section. It is assumed that another section of the program (labeled A) has successfully selected a part number. The portion of the structure chart shown in Figure 14–5 invokes a lookup module to find that part number in an inventory file. If the Lookup operation is successful, the module retrieves and returns the complete inventory record for that part. (Notice that the specific lookup algorithm being used is not part of this diagram.) If the Lookup routine cannot find the part number in the file, it activates an error handler, which itself activates a rou-

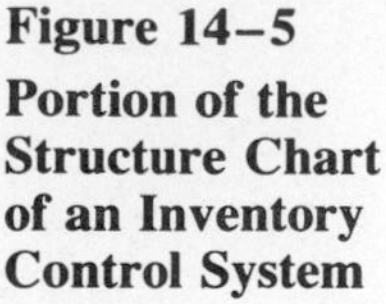
Figure 14–5
Portion of the Structure Chart of an Inventory Control System

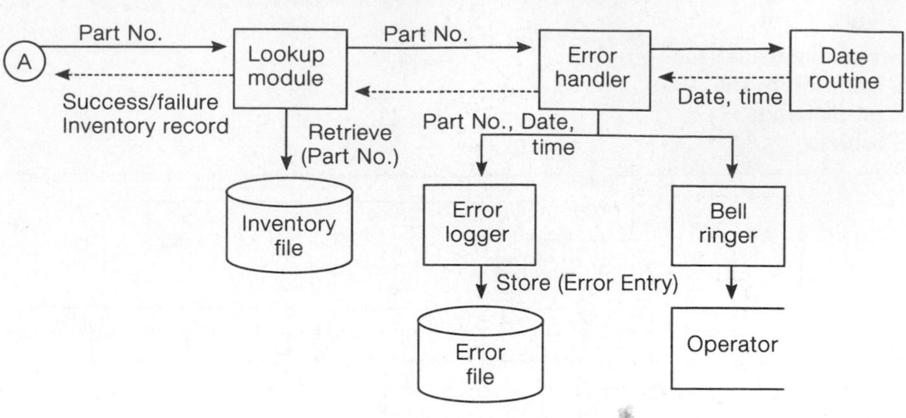

tine to store a time-stamped entry in a special error file. The error handler also activates a bell ringer module, which rings a bell on the operator's console to warn of the error.

A real inventory control program of the type just described might have well over one hundred separate modules and one or two dozen major data structures. A structure chart of its overall design may run to several hundred pages!

The finished structure chart serves a number of important purposes. First, it gives a pictorial overview of the entire solution (the "big picture") and shows the magnitude of the software implementation task ahead. In addition, it is needed for the other two sections of the design document—the procedure specifications and the data dictionary. For every procedure included in the structure chart, we will include a written specification of that unit in the program design document. Similarly, every major data structure shown on the structure chart will have an entry in the data dictionary. Therefore, the structure chart itself need not contain extensive or detailed descriptions of its components; those will come later. The structure chart is simply a pictorial representation of the relationships between components in the proposed solution.

Finally, the structure chart will be quite helpful during implementation. By showing the relationships between segments of the program, we can gather related elements together and implement them as a group. For example, referring to Figure 14–4, if we wanted one programmer to be responsible for all decisions related to I/O, the structure chart shows that we should have him or her code the three routines InputHeader, InputScores, and Output. Similarly, the chart shows that the programmer who selects the internal implementation of the abstract data type, ScoreTable, and codes the operations Create, Store, and Retrieve will work most closely with the people who are implementing the units Main, InputScores, ComputeMean, and ComputeStandardDeviation. This team will be relatively uninvolved with the implementor of the unit called Output. Structure charts can thus show interrelationships, areas of cooperation, and spheres of influence that can be important during the implementation phase. They can help us coordinate the implementation of related routines, facilitate communication between programmers working on common pieces of information, and allocate human resources in the most efficient manner.

14.3.2 Procedure Specifications

When we use the term *procedure* in our discussion of program design documents, we are using it in a generic rather than a technical sense. By *procedure* we mean any independent program unit that satisfies the following four constraints:

1. It is a *named* entity.
2. It can be *activated* or *invoked* by name from other units in the system. At the time of activation, information can be passed into or out of the procedure.
3. When invoked, it can *create* new data objects and/or *perform* executable operations.
4. It can be *compiled* separately from other program units and stored independently in a library.

The most familiar program units that meet all four of these constraints are the well-known functions, subroutines, and procedures of high-level languages such as FORTRAN, BASIC, COBOL, Pascal, C, Ada, and Modula-2. However, the concept is wider than that and includes other program units such as the Modula-2 *module*, the Ada *package*, and the C++ *class* (for describing abstract data types and operations on those data types); the *generic* concept of Ada (models to describe a general class of subprogram); the *task* in Ada, C, and PL/I (program units that execute in parallel with each other); and the *coroutine* (symmetric procedures) of Modula-2. All these fit the definition given above, and we will always use the term *procedure* in this broader sense of any separate, compilable program unit.

There are two parts to the specification of an individual procedure: the *external interface* and the *internal structure*. The external interface of a procedure is always part of the program design document. However, there is disagreement over whether a description of the internal structure should be included, and it may or may not be present. If not, it is postponed until the next phase of programming, the coding stage.

The *external interface* is a complete description of exactly what information is known about this procedure by other procedures in the system. It includes the following:

1. Procedure name
2. Procedure type (e.g., procedure, function, or task)
3. General description of its purpose
4. Calling sequence (how to activate it), including the order and data type of all formal parameters
5. Entry conditions (the state of the procedure and its parameters when it is first activated)
6. Exit conditions (the state of the procedure and its parameters when it has been completed)
7. Side effects (effects on any global objects in the program or the system)
8. Possible error conditions, unusual behavior, or abnormal terminations

Figure 14–6
Design Specification for the Program Unit ComputeMean

1. *Name*: ComputeMean
2. *Type*: Procedure
3. *Purpose*: This program unit computes the arithmetic mean of a series of *N* legal examination scores currently stored in the data structure called ScoreTable.
4. *Calling sequence*: ComputeMean(*N*, ScoreTable, Mean);
5. *Entry conditions*:
   - ScoreTable: Has already been created and initialized. It contains *N* valid test scores (each one in the range Low to High), and they are stored in the first *N* slots of ScoreTable.
   - *N*: Has been defined and validated. It is an integer value in the range 1 to 500 inclusive. *N* specifies exactly how many entries are stored in ScoreTable.
   - Mean: Undefined.
6. *Exit conditions*:
   - ScoreTable: Unchanged by ComputeMean.
   - *N*: Unchanged by ComputeMean.
   - Mean: Has been set to the arithmetic mean of the *N* scores stored in ScoreTable, where the arithmetic mean is a real value defined as follows:

$$\text{Arithmetic Mean} = \frac{\sum_{i=1}^{N} \text{Retrieve (Score, ScoreTable, } i\text{)}}{N}, \quad N \geq 1$$

7. *Side Effects*: None.
8. *Possible error conditions*: None.

In essence, the external interface is what you need to know about a procedure to use it effectively. In addition to this information, designers may choose to add other information that could be of help during implementation, such as the approximate size of the completed routine or the library where it will be stored.

Figure 14–6 shows a design specification for the procedure named Compute Mean from the structure chart of Figure 14–4. This specification includes the eight pieces of information listed above. Notice that the specification of Figure 14–6 describes only the external aspects of the module, that is, those that can be seen by the rest of the system.

The *internal structure* of the module (sometimes called the *internal specifications*, *detailed design*, or *low-level design*) shows how the procedure will solve its subproblem. It describes the algorithm to be used and sketches out, in pseudocode or as a flowchart, the high-level control structure of the module. If we wish to include the internal structure in the design specification, we could add the following pseudocode as section nine after the existing eight sections in the procedure specification of Figure 14–6.

9. *Detailed Module Design*:

```
Initialize Sum to 0
(* We will sum up the elements in the array sequentially. *)
For i = 1 To N Do
    Retrieve(T, ScoreTable, i)
    Sum := Sum + T
End        (* of For loop *)
(* Then we can compute the average. *)
Set Mean to Sum/N
```

Some designers believe that the internal structure of a procedure is more properly part of coding and is inappropriate and too detailed to be included in the program design document. We generally agree with this position and in any future examples will not include the detailed control structure of a procedure in the design specifications, leaving that for the next stage of software development.

14.3.3 The Data Dictionary

The *data dictionary* summarizes the external characteristics of every major data structure included in the structure chart. These characteristics include the following items:

1. Data structure name.
2. General description of that data structure (e.g., linear, hierarchical, random access, direct access, internal, external).
3. Information fields contained within the data structure.
4. Operations that can be performed on the data structure. For each operation, we describe the state of the data structure before and after the operation has been performed.
5. What other modules access this structure; what other modules modify this structure.
6. Limitations or restrictions placed on this data structure.

Basically, the data dictionary describes the external or visible part of the definition of an abstract data type as described in chapter 2. Notice that, just as we did with the procedure specification of section 14.3.2, we do not include a description of the internal implementation of this data structure. Information on the internal implementation is generally not needed during the design phase, so decisions about it can be left to the programmer during the implementation phase, when such technical factors as availability of memory, language features, or the need for efficiency will be considered.

Figure 14–7 shows a sample data dictionary entry for the abstract data type called ScoreTable from the structure chart of Figure 14–4.

Together, these three components, the structure chart, the procedure specifications, and the data dictionary, constitute the essential elements of the program design document.

Once the design document is completed, it will serve as our guide to the next stage of software development, *implementation*. Each of the individual procedure specifications and data structure operations will be given to a programmer to code,

Figure 14–7
Sample Data Dictionary Entry

1. *Data structure name*: ScoreTable.
2. *General description*: A linear, one-dimensional, random-access data structure that holds N examination scores, where $1 \leq N \leq 500$. The slots of ScoreTable are indexed by the values 1, 2, 3, . . . , 500.
3. *Information contained*: ScoreTable holds integer examination scores, each of which is in the range Low to High, where $0 \leq \text{Low} \leq \text{High}$. The examination scores are stored consecutively in the first N slots of ScoreTable.
4. *Operations*:
   a. Create(T) (* T is an object of type ScoreTable. *)
   This operation creates a new object T of type ScoreTable and initializes all of its slots to empty.
   b. Retrieve(Score, ScoreTable, *i*)
   If $1 \leq i \leq N$, then the parameter Score is set to the value contained in the *i*th slot of ScoreTable. If $i < 1$ or $i > N$, then Score is undefined. In addition, if no value has been previously stored in the *i*th slot of ScoreTable, then Score is undefined. Both ScoreTable and *i* are unchanged by this operation.
   c. Store(Score, ScoreTable, *i*)
   If $1 \leq i \leq N$, then the value of the Store operation is a new ScoreTable with the integer value Score stored in the *i*th slot of ScoreTable. Whatever was previously in the *i*th slot of ScoreTable will be overwritten and lost. If $i < 1$ or $i > N$, then the ScoreTable parameter is unchanged. Both *i* and Score are unchanged by this operation.
5. *The names of all modules that create (C), access (A), or modify (M) this data structure*:
   Main (C)
   InputScores (M)
   ComputeMean (A)
   ComputeStandardDeviation (A)
6. *Limitations or restrictions*: ScoreTable must be capable of holding at least 500 examination scores.

debug, and verify. When a component is thoroughly validated and certified to be correct, we integrate it into the overall structure of the developing program, exactly as specified in the structure chart.

14.4 THE ADVANTAGES OF TOP-DOWN PROGRAM DESIGN

As we showed in Table 12–1, an average real-world program can easily be 5,000 to 50,000 lines long and be composed of from 100 to 1,000 separate pieces. Larger programs may be composed of literally thousands of separate program units. For problems of this scale, it would be sheer folly to start writing code immediately. We need a way to manage this welter of detail, this enormous amount of information, and this scale of complexity. We need a way to know what we are currently working on, how it fits into the overall problem, and what will need to be done next.

The top-down program design philosophy described in the previous section brings this needed organization to software development. The problem is solved by working from generalized goals to specific details, so that we are always seeing the "big picture." We always know what we have done and where we are going. We never have to address a detailed, "picky" question until we have first answered all important questions leading up to it. This concept is called *delayed decision making*. For example, if we are trying to decide how to handle some low-level aspect of program unit E in the following design,

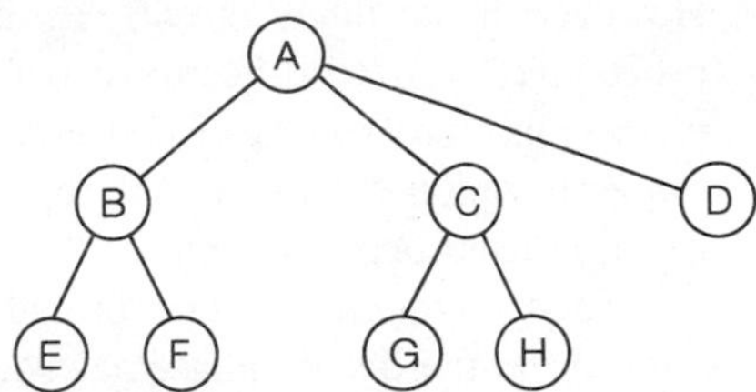

we will have already completed the design and specification of program units A and B, so it should be easier to determine the answers to questions about unit E. If we had started out producing specifications for program unit E, we might have become mired in low-level details in the early stages of program development without knowing how higher-level units would be affected by our decision.

This intellectual manageability has been achieved through two fundamental processes, *abstraction* and *modularization*.

Abstraction

Abstraction, as we mentioned in chapter 2, refers to dealing with an operation from a high-level viewpoint, disregarding its detailed substructure. We can manage the development of large, complex, multimodule programs by disregarding, at first, all lower-level details and concentrating instead on higher-level constructs. Only when we feel that we have a thorough understanding of these points do we begin to flesh out lower-level details that were originally "abstracted away."

Procedural abstraction and data abstraction are the fundamental tools for managing the implementation of large programs; both are used in the top-down design method. With *procedural abstraction* we initially think only about the highest-level functions and procedures needed to solve the problem. The specification of low-level routines is postponed until later. Each successive refinement of the design adds additional detail to the developing solution. With *data abstraction*, we initially view a data structure in terms of the external interface it displays to the user, that is, the operations that can be performed on that structure. Only later do we begin to concern ourselves with the underlying details of the implementation of that data type in a given programming language. (The issue of data abstraction was discussed extensively in chapter 2.)

Modularization

Modularization is the formal term for the *divide-and-conquer* strategy we introduced earlier. It allows us to compartmentalize a large problem into collections of independent program units that address simpler and more coherent subproblems. Modularization also brings with it a number of distinct benefits.

First, it greatly simplifies the task of modifying or adapting a program unit. Since the only part of a procedure visible to the rest of the system is its external interface, a change to the internal structure of a module should have no effect on any other routine. For example, assume that module E in the development tree shown on the previous page was a sorting procedure, and we wished to change its algorithm from InsertionSort to QuickSort for reasons of efficiency. As long as the external interface of unit E remained unchanged, this modification would have no effect on any other unit, other than the fact that the overall program would run more quickly. However, if the three units B, E, and F were implemented as a single monolithic procedure, then modifications to the sorting process could have unplanned side effects on other pieces of code. Modularization allows us to hide the underlying implementation details of one program unit from all other program units and protect it from unauthorized change.

Second, modularization provides us with a way to create an *implementation plan*. After the design phase has been completed, we will be ready to begin implementation. At that point our questions will be What do we do first? What do we do next? How do we create a strategy for writing the tens of thousands of lines of code that we have specified? By modularizing the problem and creating a structure chart that shows the relationships among these units, we have the means to create such an implementation plan.

For example, looking at the preceeding development tree, it would make sense to implement units E and F after coding unit B, in order to get the entire (B, E, F) cluster working properly. Next, we might choose to implement C and then G and H, so that we could get the (C, G, H) cluster working. An alternative approach might be to implement all high-level modules first, leaving the lower-level routines for later. If we choose that strategy, then we might implement the modules in the order A, B, C, D, E, F, ... Or we could choose to go at it in both ways: one group might work on high-level unit A, while another group works on lower-level utility routines E and F.

The important point is that having modularized the problem and developed it in a top-down fashion, we have a choice of ways to approach the implementation. As we work on one unit, we know what unit we should work on next and which ones can be effectively postponed. Without this plan of action, we might write code in some less logical order and thus not have pieces that work together or that can be tested as a unit.

Another advantage of modularization is that we can *verify* each individual program unit for correctness as it is developed, instead of having to wait until the entire program is completely coded. The number of individual statements in a program unit is not the only factor that affects debugging time of that unit—the effects of *interactions* between statements also contribute to debugging time. The time, t, needed to debug a program consisting of n lines thus does not increase at the same rate as n, (i.e., linearly)—it increases *faster*. As program units get larger, debugging time increases dramatically, eventually becoming the dominant step in the entire programming project. Reports show that on large projects with inadequate program management and organization, debugging consumed 40 to 50% of the overall project hours and even then, the programs were not completely free of bugs.

It is definitely to our advantage to debug and test a program as a collection of small units rather than one large one. The top-down design method, which develops a program as a hierarchical set of tasks, defines a natural set of small subunits that can be individually tested, verified, and integrated into the overall solution.

14.5 DESIGN EVALUATION

We have now introduced the concepts of top-down program design and stepwise refinement. At each stage in the design process, we flesh out the details of one program unit and, in the process, may define a number of new lower-level units. The solution develops in the classic downward-growing-tree pattern shown in Figure 14–2. We stressed the importance of using this (or a similar) design methodology when developing large software systems. However, nowhere in our discussion did we talk about methods for the *evaluation* of a given design. Depending on how you view a problem, what you consider a high-level operation, and the order in which you carry out your refinements, you may create a very different design from someone else's. Given the exact same problem specification document, one software designer might end up with seven distinct program units, Main, M_1, M_2, . . . , M_6, structurally grouped into a four-level hierarchy:

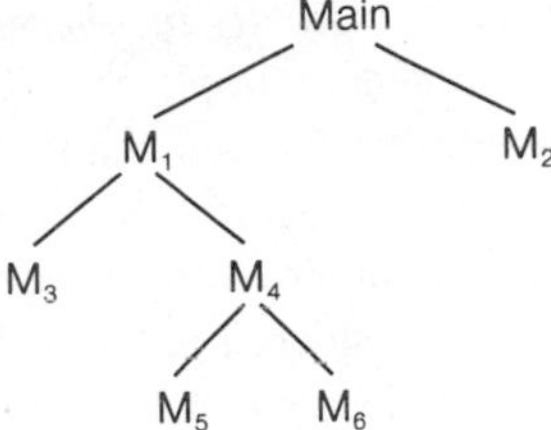

while a second designer may view the identical problem in quite a different way, specifying only four pieces—Main, M_1, M_2, M_3, all of which are larger and which are grouped into a much simper two-level hierarchy:

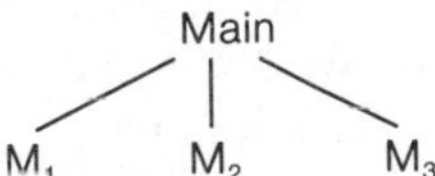

The central question is, do these differences matter? Are these two designs equally good as long as they are correct and solve the original problem? Is there a way to judge the overall quality, goodness, beauty, and elegance of both a design document and a program's structure? The answer to this latter question is a most emphatic yes!

The quality of a design can be evaluated by examining four fundamental characteristics of the individual procedures and abstract data types created by the design and by studying the interrelationships between these components. A good design will display highly desirable behavior with respect to these key design properties. The four design characteristics to be discussed in this section are

1. Logical coherence
2. Independence
3. Connectivity
4. Size

14.5.1 Logical Coherence

A program unit is said to be *logically coherent* (or *cohesive* or *functionally strong*) if it addresses only a single task and if all operations that it performs are very closely related to each other. Informally, we can say that logical coherence means that each individual procedure does only one thing and does it well. Looking back at the design of the test-scoring program in Figure 14–4, we see that all the program units in the design meet this criterion. For example, the program unit InputHeader is responsibile for fetching the three problem parameters (N, Low, High); ComputeMean handles everything related to computing an arithmetic mean and nothing else; Output is responsibile for printing the final report. Within a single unit, all operations are functionally related and highly homogeneous.

The following example illustrates a procedure that is *not* logically coherent:

> Procedure M computes the frequencies of a series of test scores and displays the results on a graphics terminal.

Obviously, the two operations in this procedure—statistically determining frequencies and producing graphical output—are not closely related. We would say that this routine is *logically incoherent* or *functionally weak*.

Another example of a functionally weak program unit would be a single procedure M that takes a matrix A_1, inverts it to produce matrix A_2, and transposes it to produce matrix A_3. Although the operations of matrix inversion and matrix transposition are loosely related by being matrix operations, they would not generally be considered sufficiently related to be placed within a single procedure. We would again say that M is functionally weak. It would be a better design to have two procedures handling the logically separate functions of matrix inversion and matrix transposition.

When attempting to specify logically coherent program units, we must avoid including weakly related tasks from either the same level or different levels within the design. For example, when designing procedure t_{11} in Figure 14–8, we could err in two ways, by including aspects of the peer tasks t_{12} or t_{13} or by including lower-level details from task t_{111} or t_{112}.

It is easy to improperly include operations from distinct peer-level tasks in a single procedure. For example, in Figure 14–8, tasks t_{11} and t_{12} are both required to perform task t_1; therefore, they will be related in some manner. It is incorrect, however, to conclude automatically that two related tasks are one logically coherent operation that should be combined into a single program unit.

For example, the following pairs of tasks are obviously related:

1. Read input. Validate the input for legality.
2. Read a string. Search a string for a specific pattern.
3. Compute the mean. Compute the standard deviation.
4. Sort a list. Merge two sorted lists.

Figure 14–8
Overlapping of Task Responsibility

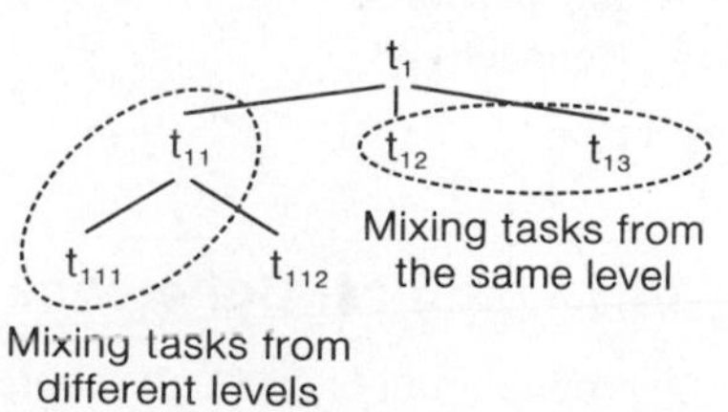

However, in almost all situations these tasks represent two logically distinct operations that should be implemented as separate and independent program units.

The first pair of operations (read, validate) display what is called a *temporal relationship*: the second operation is started immediately after the first one has been completed. (We almost always validate immediately after completing the input.) Another example of a temporal relationship is initialization operations; they are all performed at the very start of program execution.

The second and third pairs of operations display *logical* or *application-oriented relationships*: the two operations address tasks drawn from the same general area of application. The operation in the second pair (read, search) are both string-oriented tasks, as are concatenation, string length, or substring replacement. The third pair (mean, standard deviation) are both statistical computations, along with literally hundreds of other statistical routines.

The fourth pair (sort, merge) display what is called a *shared-data relationship*: both perform tasks on a common data structure, in this case, a list. Other examples of shared data relationships are routines to open and close a file and to enter and remove entries from a stack or queue.

However, neither temporal, logical, or shared-data relationships, in and of themselves, are sufficient to warrant grouping two or more operations together in a single program unit. Grouping should be done only when the operations demonstrate a stronger interaction called a *functional relationship*, where all aspects of the operations are directed at solving functionally related tasks. For example, the following three operations

1. Validate that Low > 0.
2. Validate that High < 100.
3. Validate that High > Low.

display a strong functional relationship because they address the single task of validating the range [Low .. High]. They should, of course, be part of the same program unit. Putting these three operations in their own separate procedures would be inappropriate and, in fact, would create unnecessary complexity.

There are a number of important reasons for keeping program units logically coherent; the most important reason is for ease in *modification* and *program maintenance*. Problem specifications and users' needs change, and implementing these changes usually requires some amount of program modification. To minimize errors during the modification process, we want to change as little of the code as possible. The sections of the code that are unaffected by the new specifications should not be affected by the modification process and they will not be affected if we isolate each indivisible operation into its own separate routine.

For example, assume that we had designed a single procedure that both inputs and sorts data. (Based on our previous discussion, we would say that this routine is functionally weak, since the operations of input and sorting are not functionally related.) Suppose that we now want to rewrite the routine to include a faster sorting algorithm. In the process of rewriting the sorting code, we could introduce an error into the input section, even though the input part of the procedure would ideally be unaffected by the proposed change. (For example, we might accidentally select a variable name in the sorting section that was used in the input section.) If instead we had separate and independent units called Input and Sort, a change to the sorting unit could not in any way affect the input process.

Making a task an independent program unit effectively allows you to put a "wall around it" and protect it from accidental modification. During the design phase, you must ask yourself whether an operation represents a single coherent operation. If the answer is no, then split the routine into two or more separate units. Isolation of responsibility enhances and facilitates change.

Aside from the advantages logical coherence provides during modification, there are also significant benefits during testing. Suppose that we have task A with m distinct control paths and task B with n distinct paths. If we write a procedure that incorporates both tasks into a single program unit, we need at least $(m * n)$ unique data sets to test exhaustively all possible paths through this unit. However, if the two tasks are coded as separate program units, we would need only m cases to test A and n cases to test B—a total of $(m + n)$ data sets. For any $m, n > 2$, $(m + n) < (m * n)$. It is obviously easier to develop and test a program using short, simple procedures. (We will have much more to say about testing program units in chapter 15.)

We have established the importance of maintaining logical coherence between tasks at the same level. Of equal importance is maintaining logical coherence between tasks at *different levels* (see Figure 14–8). Including unnecessary and inappropriate lower-level details in a higher-level routine can obscure the purpose and function of the higher-level program unit.

For example, look at the following program fragment, which reads in a string of characters:

```
i := 0;
While (i < ArrayMax) Do
    i := i + 1;
    Read(Ch);
    If (Ch >= 'a') And (Ch <= 'z') Then
        Ch := Chr(Ord(Ch) - 32)
    End;

    If (Ch = '[') Or (Ch = '{') Then
        Ch := '('
    End;

    If (Ch = ']') Or (Ch = '}') Then
        Ch := ')'
    End;

    If ((Ord(Ch) >= 0) And
        (Ord(Ch) <= 31)) Or
        (Ord(Ch) > 127) Then
            Ch := '?'
    End;

    Text[i] := Ch;
    Write(Ch)
End (* of the While loop *)
```

The logic of the loop is quite simple. It inputs characters coded in ASCII, stores them in an array called Text, and prints them. What makes this simple loop more difficult to interpret is the presence of lower-level detail about how to handle certain special characters. The first **If** statement converts all lowercase characters to uppercase characters, the next two **If** statements map braces and brackets into parentheses, and the last **If** statement converts all nonprinting characters (0–31 and 128–255 in ASCII) into the character '?'. These details are certainly not essential to an understanding of the overall operations, and the entire program fragment would be much more lucid if these items were relegated to a logically separate, lower-level procedure, as in done by the following code:

```
i := 0;
While (i < ArrayMax) Do
    i := i + 1;
    Read(Ch);
    FixUpChar(Ch);          (* Correct certain special characters *)
    Text[i] := Ch;
    Write(Ch)
End (* of the While loop *)
```

By including inappropriate lower-level details in a given program unit, we defeat many of the advantages of abstraction, which we discussed in both the last section and chapter 2. In the first version of this example, we must immediately become aware of and knowledgeable of the low-level rules for character modification. In the second version, the designer has isolated this detail in the abstract entity called FixUpChar. We no longer need to deal with this information until we feel that it is appropriate. In addition, future changes in the rules for character modification can be confined to FixUpChar and will not affect this procedure in any way.

When you design a program unit, ask yourself whether particular details are central to an understanding of the task being performed or whether they are peripheral and may actually complicate an understanding of the logic. If the latter, consider putting them into a separate, lower-level routine whose specification and implementation can be postponed until later.

Naturally, deciding which operations are logically coherent and therefore deserving of their own separate procedures will depend on the specific problem we are trying to solve. However, the general rule still applies: each procedure should do one thing and do it well. If you are unsure about how to decompose a task, err on the side of defining a greater number of shorter procedures; it is much better style to have many short, simple procedures than a few complex and highly interrelated units. The former will usually be easier to work with, understand, test, and modify.

14.5.2 Independence

A program unit is said to be *independent* or *loosely coupled* if it does not need to know about the inner workings of any other program unit in order to perform its job successfully. Specifically, it does not need to know:

- The source of the input passed to it
- The disposition of the output
- Which procedures were activated before it
- Which procedure will be activated after it
- How other procedures are internally implemented

The ideal specification for a program unit would be something like the following:

> I do not know anything about any other units in the program. If you give me value x, I will produce result y and return. Period.

This type of program unit does not depend on knowing where the input parameter x came from, how the result y will be used, or how other routines work. It simply does a task and produces a result. It has no other impact on the behavior of the system.

If we design program units in this manner, we can treat them like circuit boards. We can remove one procedure and "plug in" a different one without affecting the rest of the program, as long as the interface specifications for the two procedures are identical. We use this approach with library routines when we code an assignment statement like the following one:

```
y := sin(theta) − 1.0
```

We do not care what algorithm is used to evaluate the sine function as long as it has the following four characteristics:

1. It accepts one real parameter, x, whose units are radians.
2. It returns a real value, v, such that $v = \sin(x)$ to a high level of accuracy.
3. It returns v in a reasonable amount of time.
4. It has no side effects.

Failure to develop this type of independent routine can result in what is called the *ripple effect*, which occurs when a change to one program unit ripples through the entire system and causes unexpected changes to other units. This effect severely complicates the program modification process, turning minor changes into major undertakings.

For example, suppose that we are asked to design a procedure to compute the root of an equation to eight-decimal-place accuracy, and suppose we know that the output procedure of this program will display the results on a plotter that is not very precise and can draw accurately to only three significant places. We might be tempted to implement a compute routine that (in violation of specifications) stops evaluating when it has produced three significant digits, knowing that this is the limit of precision of our output device and that the additional accuracy requested in the specifications is unnecessary. The program would work. However, we would have a very poor design. If we ever buy a new plotter or switch to another output device, we will not only have to rewrite the output procedure, which we would expect to do, but we will also have to rewrite the compute procedure, which we would not expect to do. Thus, what should have been a simple change has become unexpectedly more difficult because of the dependence of one program unit on the inner workings of another.

A routine should hide what it does internally from all other routines in the system. All that it should see of another unit is what goes in and what comes out. Then, if we change one routine's inner workings, no problems can possibly arise because the other routines could not see these workings in the first place. If we had practiced this principle of *information hiding* in our previous example, then the fact that the output routine requires only three-place accuracy would not be known to any other program unit.

This type of loosely coupled design greatly facilitates the task of program maintenance. Fixing or updating a program designed from independent modules becomes as easy as fixing a TV set. We remove the old program unit and insert the new one, just as the TV repairperson pulls out the failed component and plugs in the new one. However, logical dependencies between separate units of a program are like wires jury-rigged between components in a TV. If they are present, it is no longer easy to insert a new component because of its *ad hoc* relationship to other components. All those interconnecting wires must be unplugged and reconnected in exactly the right order, with a high likelihood of error. This kind of a design, whether it is found in TV sets or computer programs, is not good.

The best design is one in which every procedure is independent of every other procedure in the system to the greatest extent possible. The best way to achieve independence is by

1. Not modifying global variables, thus making the procedure free of undesirable *side effects*
2. Declaring all temporary variables or data structures local to the procedure in which they occur
3. Passing all input parameters by value so that they cannot be accidentally or intentionally modified
4. Making no assumptions whatever about the internal structure or internal logic of other modules
5. Adhering exactly to the calling sequence described in the program design document

Let's look at an example in which these rules are violated. The following procedure finds the location of the largest element in an array A of length *N*:

```
Procedure FindLargest(A : ArrayType; N : Integer; Var Location : Integer);
Var
    i : Integer;
Begin
    For i := 1 To N Do
        If A[i] > Big Then
            Big := A[i];
            Location := i
        End
    End
End FindLargest;
```

This procedure makes a very dangerous and inappropriate assumption, namely, that some other unit in the system will properly initialize the global variable called Big, exactly as follows:

```
Big := -MaxInt;        (* Where -MaxInt is the largest negative number *)
```

If the unit where this initialization is performed is ever changed and this statement is changed or removed, then this procedure may no longer work properly, even though it was not modified in any way. A better way to code this procedure would be to declare Big a local variable and initialize it within FindLargest. Now the existence of the variable Big and its initial value are hidden and cannot be affected by changes made to other units.

Localizing a data structure is another important technique for enhancing program independence. Every data object (integer, array, pointer, etc.) should be declared in the innermost (i.e., most local) program unit possible. For example, suppose that we have the following program structure

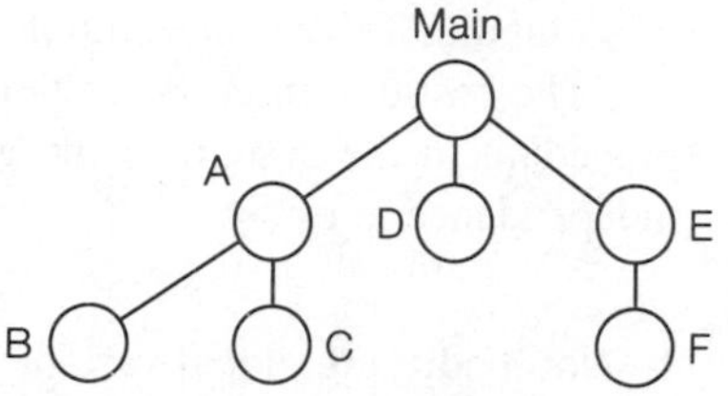

Main
A D E
B C F

and that procedure A creates and manipulates a data structure called DS. B builds DS; C searches DS. Even though no other routine in the program references DS, we could legally declare DS either in Main or in procedure A. However, declaring the data structure DS in Main would also make it available to units D, E, and F, and they could accidentally access and/or modify DS. Placing the declaration of DS in procedure A makes this impossible, since D, E, and F are now outside the scope of the declaration of DS.

This discussion indicates why the powerful scope rules of languages such as Algol, Pascal, Modula-2, and Ada are so important to proper program design. These scope rules allow us to declare a data object at the most appropriate level in the design hierarchy and hide it from program units that should not logically be aware of its existence. The same situation occurs for the abstract data type mechanism, which hides the implementation details of a data type and makes them inaccessible to a user. In a sense, the language itself provides tools that encourage and support the design of independent program units. Languages without these features must rely on a programmer's proper behavior and good intentions to ensure independence.

Our final point about achieving independence is the importance of adhering exactly to the external interface specifications for a procedure as given in the program design document. Ideally, the inner workings of a procedure are hidden from all other units, which see only the standardized interface. If the principles discussed in this section are followed, a change in the internal structure of one routine should have no effect on any other routine. However, a change to the external interface can have drastic consequences.

Suppose, for example, that we were asked to rewrite the library function called Sin and we decided to modify the specifications on our own and add a second output parameter that signaled an error condition. Our new calling sequence would be:

```
Proocdure Sin(x . Real; Var Switch : Boolean) : Real;
```

Now every single program that uses the library function Sin will have to be changed to reflect the new calling sequence—this task could involve literally thousands of program units. Even an apparently small modification such as changing the parameter units could cause massive upheaval: every existing call to the Sin function would need to be preceded by a new assignment statement that converts radians to degrees.

The important point here is that program independence is achieved through agreements on standardized external interfaces. Programmers are free to select the algorithms and data structures to use within a procedure, but they must follow the calling sequences specified in the program design document exactly. Now it is clear why we stressed being so careful in the design of the external module of an abstract data type: any future changes to this external module will necessitate changes in and recompilation of every client module that uses these resources.

14.5.3 Connectivity

Connectivity is another important evaluation criterion of program design. It is a measure of the degree of interconnectedness of the modules in the design. The connectivity of any procedure M, concerns how many other procedures invoke or are invoked by M. Another way to look at connectivity, using the tree terminology of chapter 7, is to ask what is the average number of children for interior nodes in the program development tree?

For example, a design containing ten separate units could be implemented in either of two ways, as shown in Figure 14–9. In Figure 14–9a there is a high degree of connectivity, since the routine labeled Main has direct connections to nine other units labeled $M_1, \ldots, M_9$. In Figure 14–9b there is a lower level of connectivity; Main is connected to only three other units labeled M_1, M_2, and M_3, and each of these modules, in turn, is connected to at most two other third-level routines.

Figure 14–9
Examples of Different Levels of Connectivity

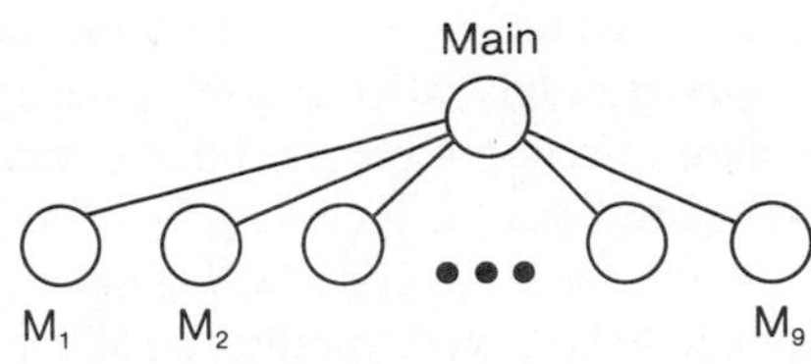

Main
M1
M2
M3
M4
M5
M9

The *high fan-out* structure displayed in Figure 14–9a is generally less desirable than the *low fan-out* structure shown in Figure 14–9b, which makes future maintenance and change much easier. With the structure of Figure 14–9a, a change to the interface of Main would directly affect nine other routines. With the structure of Figure 14–9b, the same change would affect only three other routines. Thus we see again the goals presented throughout this chapter—localizing and isolating changes to the fewest number of program units, so that the effects of an error, a modification, or an update do not propagate throughout the system. If we can localize program units in this way, then we will greatly reduce the time and the cost involved with debugging, testing, and maintaining our programs.

Another advantage of the low fan-out design of Figure 14–9b is that it gives us greater flexibility in where we place our declarations. If a data object needs to be accessed by modules M_4 and M_5, then the declaration of that object would need to be placed in Main if we use the design of Figure 14–9a. However, it would then be available to all nine modules $M_1, M_2, \ldots, M_9$, violating the information-hiding guidelines in the previous section. The design of Figure 14–9b, however, lets us make the declaration of this shared data structure in the intermediate level unit M_1. The data is now available to M_4 and M_5, exactly as we wanted, but it is unavailable to Main, M_2, M_3, or modules M_6 to M_9.

14.5.4 Size

The last property we will discuss—the proper *size* of a program unit—is not an isolated characteristic; instead, it is the direct result of how closely we adhered to the other module guidelines that we have discussed—logical coherence, independence, and low fan-out. If you design your procedures to do only one coherent task and to be independent of other procedures within the system, they will naturally be quite small, and, in programming, small is beautiful. Small program units are easier to debug, easier to verify, and much easier to understand.

The time needed for debugging and testing a program unit does not grow linearly as a function of N, the program length. (Linear growth means that it would be approximately twice as hard to debug a program that is twice as long, three times as hard to debug a program that is three times as long, etc.) In fact, most studies have shown that the total time for debugging a program of size N grows at a rate that is $O(N^k)$, for some constant k greater than one. Therefore, it is always to your advantage to keep your routines small and compact—you will reap an enormous savings in total debugging time.

Although there is no absolute guideline as to what constitutes a small program unit, most software developers adopt the convention that no procedure should be longer than about 50 to 60 lines of code. There is a decidedly nontechnical reason for this value: it is approximately the number of lines that will fit on one page of printed output. Thus, if you use a 50- to 60-line limit, you can see the listing of a module in its entirety without having to flip pages. Some programmers use an upper limit of about 100 lines of code so that they can see the entire procedure on two pages of an open notebook. Others may limit their units to about 25 to 30 lines so that they can see the entire unit displayed at one time on a screen.

Remember that the critical characteristic we are striving for is not smallness per se, but logical coherence. If you find yourself writing program units that are quite large, that is, many hundreds of lines long, you should rethink your design. You are probably performing two or more weakly related operations that should be separated and placed into their own independent units. It is also possible that you are incorporating inappropriate low-level details in a high-level program unit when these details could be "hidden" in their own module and invoked as needed by the higher-level routine.

In this section we presented a set of criteria for evaluating and judging the overall quality of a program design. We have been interested in the characteristics of the software components in the design, that is, how the individual program units of the proposed design communicate, interact, and affect each other. The most important qualitative measures of this interaction are

1. *Logical cohesion*: a measure of the strength of the functional relationships between the tasks carried out within a single program unit.
2. *Independence*: a measure of the dependency of one program unit on the internal structure or implementation details of another.
3. *Connectedness*: a measure of the number of other program units directly connected to a given unit.
4. *Size*: a measure of the average number of lines of code in each program unit.

The best design is one in which, to the greatest extent possible, all components display a high level of cohesion and independence, a low level of connectivity, and contain a small number of lines of code, typically 60 or fewer lines per unit.

14.6 IMPLEMENTATION ISSUES

Following the design phase we are ready to begin the next stage of software development—*implementation*. Implementation is the process of encoding the procedures and abstract data types described in the design document into a high-level programming language, probably one of those listed in Table 12–3. Since this topic was central to both the first course in computer science as well as much of chapters 2–11 of this text, we are not going to spend a great deal of time on it now. In this section we briefly mention two important implementation issues closely related to the topic of program design.

14.6.1 Phased Implementation/Testing

In the design phase, we develop written specifications for all procedures and data structures in the program. We generally complete much or all of the design phase before starting on implementation. However, when implementing the procedures and data structures we have developed, we do not work in the same fashion. We do *not* develop code for all procedures and abstract data types and then begin to debug and test what we have written. Instead, we proceed in *phases*, alternating between coding and testing. We implement a high-level program unit and then test and verify it. Only when it has been shown to be correct do we move to the next level in the design and begin coding those units. For example, consider the following structure chart from our program design document:

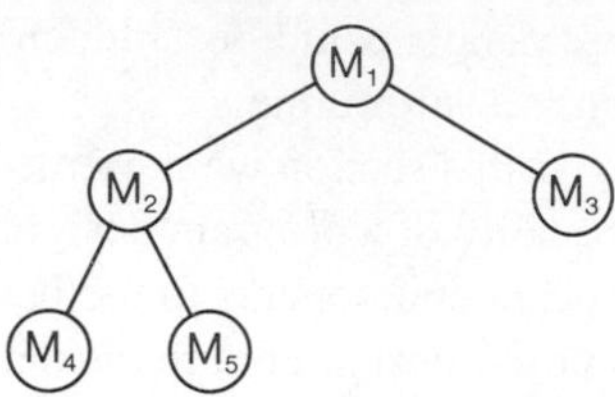

After we have completed the design specifications for each module, we might begin implementation by coding routine M_1. Before coding any additional units, we should thoroughly debug and test M_1. Only when M_1 is correct do we consider coding routines M_2 and/or M_3. We continue implementing the modules in the structure chart in this alternating coding/testing fashion.

There is an important reason for this phased approach to implementation, and it concerns our desire to localize errors. If we were to code all five units (M_1, M_2, . . . , M_5) at once and then begin testing, we would have no idea which unit might be the offending routine when the inevitable error occurred. The error might be anywhere in the system, since none of the procedures has as yet been tested. Our debugging task would be enormous because we would have little or no idea where to begin.

However, if we alternate implementation and testing stages, our job will be considerably easier. Suppose that we have coded and tested M_1 and removed all errors. We now implement both M_2 and M_3, integrate them with M_1, and run them. If an error occurs, we know that the error must be in either M_2 or M_3, or in the M_1–M_2 or M_1–M_3 interface. It should not be in M_1, because that unit has been tested and certified correct.

In general, if program units 1, 2, . . . , $i - 1$ have been written and tested and an error occurs when you add unit i, the error is localized to either (1) unit i itself or (2) the interface between i and some other unit j, $j = 1, \ldots, i - 1$. Phased implementation/testing reduces the area in which we must look for the error and makes the debugging task easier. One should always implement a relatively small number of procedures and then test what has been written before continuing. Writing dozens of modules or hundreds of lines of code and then trying to get it all working correctly is a serious programming error that can increase the time and cost of program development.

This phased approach to implementation has one problem, however. Our top-down program design method always describes a solution in terms of lower-level procedures that are as yet *unwritten*. For example, suppose we are planning to debug and test the following program unit called PrimeChecker which checks to see if a given value N is prime:

```
Procedure PrimeChecker;

Var
    Factor          : Integer;
    Correct         : Boolean;
    N               : Integer;
    PrimeSwitch     : Boolean;

Begin
    GetInput(N);
    Validate(N, Correct);

    If Correct Then
        CheckIfPrime(N, PrimeSwitch, Factor);
        If PrimeSwitch Then
            WriteLn(N, ' is prime')
        Else
            WriteLn(N, ' is not prime');
            WriteLn(Factor, ' is a factor');
        Endif;
    Else
        ErrorHandler();
    Endif;
End PrimeChecker;
```

This procedure has been implemented in terms of four lower-level routines called GetInput, Validate, CheckIfPrime, and ErrorHandler. How is it possible to test PrimeChecker when none or these four routines has yet been written?

We solve this problem by testing our partially written program using *stubs*. A stub is a dummy procedure included in a program unit simply to allow compilation and execution to proceed meaningfully. Stubs do as *little* as possible. They usually carry out only the following three operations:

1. Write out a message that we have reached this procedure to indicate that we are linking to it correctly.
2. Write out the value of any input parameters to ensure that they are being passed into the procedure correctly.
3. If the calling program needs a value defined by the procedure, the stub must also define that value to prevent a run-time error caused by an undefined variable.

In our example, a reasonable stub for GetInput might be

```
(* This is a stub for the procedure called GetInput. *)
Procedure GetInput ( Var N : Integer );
Begin
    Write('We are now in GetInput and would prompt the user for input');
    WriteLn('—not yet completed');
    (* We must give N a value to prevent an error in the calling program. *)
    N := 5
End GetInput;
```

and a reasonable stub for Validate might be

```
(* This is a stub for the procedure Validate. *)
Procedure Validate ( N : Integer; Var Sw : Boolean );
Begin
    Write('Now in Validate and would check for correctness ');
    WriteLn('of the input—not yet completed');
    (* Let's write out the input parameter to make sure it arrived correctly. *)
    WriteLn('The value of N that arrived here is ', N);
    (* Also, we must give Sw a value to prevent an error in the calling program. *)
    Sw := True;
End Validate;
```

Notice that this stub carries out the three operations described above. It prints an informative message, displays the value of the input parameter *N*, and sets the output parameter Sw to True so that we do not get an undefined variable error in the **If** statement of the PrimeChecker unit.

We would continue in this fashion, writing stubs for all lower-level units referenced by the routine being tested. When the stubs are in place, we can begin to test our code. Of course, the program will not operate as described in the problem specification document, but we can compile and test the logic of the code developed so far. For example, the execution of program PrimeChecker (with the two stubs shown and a similar one for CheckIfPrime) would lead to the following output:

> We are now in GetInput and would prompt the user for input—not yet completed
> Now in Validate and would check for correctness of the input—not yet completed
> The value of N that arrived here is 5
> Now in CheckIfPrime to see if value is or is not prime—not yet completed
> 5 is prime

Up to this point, everything seems to be operating properly. When we are satisfied that the logic in the design PrimeChecker is correct, we can proceed to implement the routines at the next level. If, for example, we choose to code GetInput next, we would discard the temporary stub shown above and write the actual code following the specifications given in the design document. One possibility might be

```
Procedure GetInput ( Var N : Integer );
Begin
    Write('Please enter the input value: ');
    Read(N);
    (* Moves cursor back to row 1, col 1 of screen *)
    CursorToHome();
End GetInput;
```

After coding this procedure, we would test our program again.[1] The program now includes the actual code for both PrimeChecker and GetInput, along with the stubs

[1] The refinements we are showing are, of course, unrealistically small. It would not really be necessary to test this three-line module separately!

we used previously for Validate, CheckIfPrime, and ErrorHandler. If the code for GetInput references any new lower-level routines (e.g., the screen-handler program called CursorToHome), we must include stubs for those as well. We are now ready to test this new level of implementation.

One by one, the "do-nothing" stubs are replaced by fully functional program units that perform the operations described in the procedure specification section of the design document. Slowly but surely, the functionality of the program increases and it begins to perform more and more meaningful operations until, when the last piece is put in place, it should ideally perform exactly as described in the problem specification document.

14.6.2 Top-Down versus Bottom-Up Implementation

Program design proceeds in the top-down fashion we described in the first sections of this chapter. The previous section on phased implementation/testing may lead you to believe that implementation also proceeds in the same top-down fashion, always moving from general high-level routines to detailed low-level ones. Although this statement is generally true, it does not tell the whole story.

When developing high-level applications-oriented software, we will almost certainly need to make frequent references to simple, low-level procedures that do everyday housekeeping tasks. These tasks may not be directly related to the application on which we are working; they are simply procedures that perform elementary and universal processing operations, for example, procedures to clear a screen, fetch the current date and time, or change a lowercase character to its uppercase equivalent. Such routines are typically short. All the modules just mentioned would probably be only one or two lines long, so it would be as much trouble to write a stub for these routines as it would be to write the routine itself. Furthermore, without these elementary routines, we have virtually no "bedrock" on which to build our high-level applications, which would be unable to display much useful behavior until the very end, when these basic routines are finally coded.

Therefore, implementation may be not only top-down, but *bottom-up* as well. Before implementation, the program designer identifies a set of essential low-level routines that would be important to have available as early as possible. These procedures, called *utility routines*, would be implemented in parallel with or even preceding the development of the high-level application units. When tested and completed, these utilities are put into a *program development library* and are available as off-the-shelf *programming tools* to all of the professional staff for the duration of the implementation. When the most critical low-level primitives are finished, the designer may identify additional utility routines that would be desirable to have in the library. Thus, implementation usually proceeds in *both* directions, top-down for the development of high-level applications-oriented routines, and bottom-up for the development of utilities and programming tools to support applications development.

It is not possible to give, out of context of a specific application, a list of exactly what tools would need to be developed first. Figure 14–10 is a list of the types of elementary utility routines that are useful to have available in a program development library and might be candidates for early development in a large software project.

Figure 14–10
Typical Utility Routines

Screen Management

Clear a screen
Move the cursor to row *i*, column *j*
Turn on/off the blink field
Turn on/off the reverse video feature
Turn on/off the half-intensity feature

Output

Convert lowercase to uppercase
Convert uppercase to lowercase
Ring the bell
Eject a page
Turn off echo printing
2-D and 3-D graphics routines

File Management

Seek key *i*
Open or close a file
Go to end of file
Return length of file

Numeric/Seminumeric

Random number generator
Sort package
Convert characters to integers
Convert integers to characters
Convert characters to reals
Convert reals to characters

Time/Date Utilities

Convert calendar date to Julian date
Convert regular time to 24-hour time
Interval timers
Get the current time and current date

Application Tools

Create a pull-down menu
Create a window with a scroll bar
Create a window with a resize box
Change the background display
Test if mouse button is up or down
Get the current location of the cursor

14.7 CONCLUSION

In this chapter we have described the program design phase of software development. During this stage we take the problem described in the specification document and divide it into a collection of smaller and simpler program units and data structures that, when combined into a functioning whole, will solve the original problem. We use this divide-and-conquer technique because it is easier to design and implement a large number of small problems than a few very large and complex ones.

This approach is by no means limited to computer science and software development. For example, the general contractor of a large construction project will typically hire a number of subcontractors to manage various parts of the project, such as electrical, heating/cooling, roofing, and masonry work. They in turn may hire additional subcontractors to deliver cement, provide the lumber, or feed the workers. The overall management structure of the construction project begins to look exactly like the program development tree of Figure 14–2. Similarly, the task of writing this book involved dividing up the wealth of material into separate chapters, which were then subdivided into sections and subsections. Divide and conquer is a management approach that is used to handle virtually any large job that is too big to attack directly.

The advantages that can accrue from this type of top-down design strategy include not only the management of complexity but also an improved ability to test, validate, and maintain the software that is ultimately produced. One of the most important ideas to be learned from the previous two chapters is that the program specification and design phases, not implementation, are truly the most creative parts of the software development life cycle.

CHAPTER EXERCISES

1. Comment on whether you would have divided the electronic gradebook program into the six routines shown in Figure 14–4. If not, propose an alternative design.
2. Suppose that we felt the routine called InputHeader in Figure 14–4 was too complex to implement as described. We might propose refining that routine into three simpler units that handle the following jobs separately:
   a. Getting a value for N and validating it.
   b. Getting values for Low and High and validating them.
   c. Handling errors; this routine would be activated if the user made a mistake when entering either N, Low, or High. It would print an appropriate error message to tell the user what mistake was made.

   Do you think this proposed refinement would help or hurt the design of Figure 14–4? Explain your answer.
3. In the design of the electronic gradebook program, we left the data type called ScoreTable unspecified except for the operations called Create, Store, and Retrieve. Discuss the advantages and disadvantages of implementing ScoreTable using
   a. An array of integers
   b. A linked list

   Implement the functions Create, Store, and Retrieve using one of these two internal representations. If we later change our minds about the internal representation of ScoreTable and wish to use the other representation, what effect would that change have on the other modules in the system?
4. Given the following structure chart

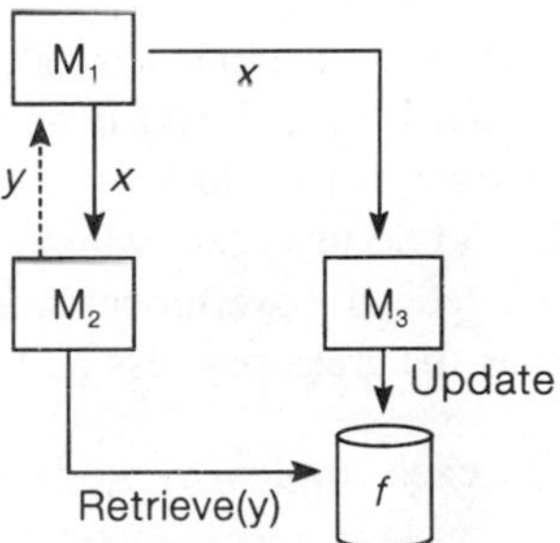

   what (if anything) is wrong with the following statement: M_1 first calls M_2 to retrieve the value y from data structure f and then calls M_3 to update f?
5. Write a procedure specification for the routine entitled InputScores in Figure 14–4. Follow the module specification guidelines given in section 14.3.2.
6. Write a procedure specification for the routine called Lookup on the structure chart of Figure 14–5.
7. Write a data dictionary entry for the Inventory data structure shown in Figure 14–5. Use the guidelines given in section 14.3.3. Assume that the data structure is a direct-access file stored on some external storage medium and that it is made up of part records containing the following information: part num-

ber, part name, amount on hand. Describe the typical operations that would be carried out on this data structure.

8. Write a data dictionary entry for the error file data structure shown in Figure 14–5. Determine for yourself what information it should contain and what operations should be defined for this data structure.
9. The following design specifications is for a procedure called Sort; it was included as part of the program design document. What is poor about it?

   Procedure Sort is given as input a list of 100 integer values. It is the job of this procedure to sort that list of numbers into ascending order using the algorithm called Bubble Sort, in which adjacent values are compared and interchanged if they are out of order. The procedure will keep making passes through the list until no interchanges have been made. It should return, as a result, the list sorted into ascending order.

10. Propose a design for the following problem specification. List what procedures and abstract data types you are including in your design, and write out the specifications for each one.

    You are to write a program to compute the weekly gross pay and net pay for a number of workers. You will receive as input 50 time cards containing names (1 to 20 characters) and hours worked (hours and minutes).

name	*hours*	
name	*hours*	
•	•	50 times cards
•	•	
•	•	
name	hours	

    You are to compute net (take-home) pay in the following manner: The individual is paid $8.00/hour for the first 40 hours and $12.00 for all hours beyond that up to a limit of 60 hours (this is gross pay). Federal tax and Social Security tax, which are computed according to the rules specified by the federal government, are deducted from the gross pay. The net pay is thus the gross pay less all these deductions.

    For each employee, produce the following line of output:

    Name Gross Pay Federal Tax Soc. Sec. Tax Net Pay

    If the hours worked are not in the range 0 to 60 (60 hours is the maximum allowed), print an error message:

    **Error—illegal time card

    and do *not* compute the gross pay.

11. Propose a design for the following problem specification. List what procedures and abstract data types you are including in your design and write out the specifications for each one.

You are to read in values for Low and High, where Low and High are positive decimal real values such that $0 < \text{Low} \le \text{High}$. If Low > High or if either value is negative or zero, then print an error message:

**Error—illegal range provided, please reenter.

and get new values for Low and High.

When you have legal values for Low and High, generate a table of values for x, x^2, and $1/x$ rounded to three-decimal-place accuracy, beginning at Low and proceeding in increments of 0.1 until you have reached (or exceeded) High. For example, if Low is 0.1 and High is 5.0, your program should produce the following output:

	x	x^2	$1/x$
(Low)	0.1	0.010	10.000
	0.2	0.040	5.000
	•	•	•
	•	•	•
	•	•	•
	4.9	24.010	0.204
(High)	5.0	25.000	0.200

12. Propose a design for the following problem specification. Draw the structure chart, and write out the procedure specifications and data dictionary.

You will be given a file of textual material. The file contains a series of words separated from each other by one or more blanks. The words are collected together into lines from 1 to 80 characters in length, with the end of each line marked by a carriage return. The end of all text is denoted by a line whose first character is '$'. You are to design a program to produce a *concordance*—an alphabetized list of every unique word that occurs in the text, along with the number of every line on which that word occurs. Thus, if the text file contained the following lines:

See Spot run.
See Jane run.
See Jane bite Spot.
$

the output from your program would be

Word	*Line Reference*
bite	3
Jane	2, 3
run	1, 2
see	1, 2, 3
Spot	1, 3

Disregard punctuation and differences of case (i.e., See, see). If a word occurs twice on the same line, include only one reference to it.

13. Propose a program design for the following problem specification:

    Assume that we have a file called Dictionary, which contains word pairs separated by one or more blanks. The first word is in English and the second word is its closest Spanish equivalent. The word pairs are sorted alphabetically by the English word in the first column. There are approximately 5,000 pairs of words, and the end of the file is signaled by the character pair "$$". Thus, the file looks like this:

    are esta
    good bueno
    hello hola
    how como
    if si
    then entonces
    you usted
    •
    •
    •
    $$

    Your program should input one line of English text and do a simple word-for-word replacement of each English word by its Spanish equivalent taken from the dictionary. If the English word cannot be found in the dictionary, leave it untranslated. When the entire line has been translated and printed out, request a new English input line. The program should terminate when the input line entered is the character $ followed by a carriage return.

    Examples:

Input:	How are you?
Output:	Como esta usted?
Input:	Who are you?
Output:	Who esta usted?
Input:	If a = b then c := 1
Output:	Si a = b entonces c := 1
Input:	$
	(program terminates)

    Prepare a program design document. Then evaluate each procedure contained in the design using the cohesion, independence, and connectivity criteria proposed in this chapter.

14. Propose a program design for the following problem specification:

    We have a two-dimensional file of diseases and symptoms. For hundreds of diseases d_1, d_2, . . . d_n we have indicated (using a simple yes/no scheme) whether a specific symptom is or is not associated with the disease. Seventeen possible symptoms are maintained in the file.

Disease	*Symptoms*					
	s_1	s_2	s_3	s_4	. . .	s_{17}
d_1	X		X		. . .	
d_2		X		X	. . .	X
d_3		X		X	. . .	
•						
•						
•						
d_n	X	X	X		. . .	

(X = Yes, blank = No)

You are to design a program that takes as input a list of symptoms and produces as output:

a. A list of diseases for which the symptoms marked in the file exactly match the list of input symptoms.
b. A list of diseases for which the symptoms marked in the file match the given list of input symptoms in all places but one. The invalid symptom should be printed.

Example

Input: s_2, s_4
Output: Disease d_3 matches exactly.
Disease d_2 matches except for the presence of symptom s_{17}.
Input: s_1, s_2, s_3, s_4
Disease d_n matches except for the absence of symptom s_4.

Prepare a program design document. Then evaluate each procedure in the design using the cohesion, independence, and connectivity criteria proposed in this chapter.

15. For each of the following pairs of operations, discuss whether they should be placed in the same program module.
    a. Computation of hours worked per week from time cards. Computation of net pay from hours worked, hourly salary, and overtime rules.
    b. The conversion of clock time (e.g., 7:30 A.M., 8:15 P.M.) to a 24-hour-based decimal value (7.5, 20.25). The determination of the fractional interval between two time values (e.g., 7:30 A.M. to 8:15 P.M. is 12.75 hours).
16. Comment on the design of the following procedure:

```
Type
    Deck        = Array [1 .. 52] Of Card;
(* This procedure shuffles a deck using a random number generator. *)
Const
    A           = 16807;
    M           = 2147483647;
    Seed        = 314159;
```

```
Var
    i          : Integer;
    R          : Real;
    Random     : Integer;
    Temp       : Card;
    Z          : Integer;
    D          : Deck;

Begin
    Z := Seed;
    For i := 1 To 52 Do
        Z := (A * Z) Mod M;
        R := Z/M;
        Random := Round (51 * R + 1);

        (* Now interchange the cards at positions i and random *)
        Temp := D[i];
        D[i] := D[Random];
        D[Random] := Temp;
    Endfor;
End Shuffle;
```

If you feel that the design is poor, redesign it.

17. Comment on the design of the following procedure:

```
Procedure CountNegative(L : ListType; Var Count : Integer);

Var
    i     : Integer;

Begin
    (* Count the number of negative values in the list L *)
    For i := 1 To ListSize Do
        If L[i] < 0 Then
            Count := Count + 1;
        Endif;
    Endor;

    WriteLn('Final count is', Count);
End CountNegative;
```

18. Give examples of operations that can cause undesirable dependencies between two or more program units. For each one, list an alternative approach that can eliminate the problem.
19. Some programmers get lazy about scope rules and put every declaration in the outermost block, that is, the main program. Discuss what negative effects this practice could have on a program's design.
20. Get the listing for a major software product that you are using (e.g., a compiler, utility program, or library routine) and measure the average and maximum length of the procedures. Are they within the length guidelines proposed in this chapter? If not, look at some of the longer ones and see if their greater length significantly decreases your ability to comprehend them.

CHAPTER 15

THE TESTING AND VERIFICATION OF SOFTWARE

CHAPTER OUTLINE

15.1 INTRODUCTION

Once the program design phase has been completed and we have implemented code for a few of the modules, we are ready to begin the next stage of software development, in which we attempt to demonstrate the correctness and robustness of the code that we have written.

There are two fundamentally different approaches to demonstrating the correctness of a piece of software: empirical testing and formal verification. In this chapter we will examine these two techniques in detail and compare the strengths and weaknesses of each.

15.2 EMPIRICAL TESTING

Empirical testing is a method of proving correctness by observing the behavior of the program when it is executed with a predetermined collection of test data. It consists of three distinct phases:

1. Unit testing, in which we observe the behavior of the individual program units and make assertions about their correctness
2. System integration, in which we observe the behavior of program units executing as an integrated system and make assertions about the correctness of the entire software package
3. Acceptance testing, in which we observe the behavior of the completed software package in its regular operating environment and in the hands of its regular user community.

We will examine each of these three stages of the empirical testing process in detail.

15.2.1 Unit Testing

Unit testing is the first stage in the testing process. It involves determining the correctness of an individual program unit by running it with a large number of carefully chosen data sets and seeing if it produces correct answers in all cases. If it does, we argue that the likelihood of there being an error in the program after all those tests have been successfully completed is so small that we can assume the program is correct. Of course, this assumption could be wrong. We may have failed to test a section of the program containing an error; there may be two errors that offset each other during testing; or the error may not have been demonstrated by the particular data sets we chose to use. However, if we are extremely careful, systematic, and thorough in our test procedures and our selection of test cases, the overwhelming majority of errors in a program unit will be uncovered and our assumption about correctness will generally be true. Therefore, the most important aspect of unit testing is the careful selection of data sets to use for testing the program unit.

Functional Tests

The first group of test data is designed to test the functionality of the program unit, so we choose legal data values on which the program unit would normally operate and which are within problem specifications. We do not need to choose an enormous number of test cases for functional testing. In fact, too often *quantity* of test data is accepted as a measure of thoroughness in place of *quality*. The mere fact that a program works on 500 test cases means nothing if those 500 sets were not chosen carefully. In fact, if all 500 cases exercised the same section of the program, all we would know is that one specific part works—we could not say anything about the correctness of the remainder of the code.

During this functional phase of testing, our objective will be to select values that cause the execution of all *flow paths* through the program (a flow path is a unique execution-time sequence of statements within a program unit). For example, the following code fragment

```
s1;
If B Then
    s2;
    s3
Else
    s4
End;
s5
```

has two flow paths: s_1, s_2, s_3, s_5 and s_1, s_4, s_5. To execute the former, we must select a test case in which the Boolean expression B is True; to execute the latter, we must select a test case in which B is False. If we had improperly chosen two data sets for which the Boolean variable B was True, then we would never execute statement s_4 and we could not reasonably make any assertions about its correctness.

Every **While**, **Repeat**, **For**, and **If/Then/Else** control statement in a program unit creates two distinct flow paths. A **Case** statement creates *n* unique flow paths, where *n* is the number of alternative branches within the **Case** statement. The creation of these flow paths is diagrammed in Figure 15–1.

The number of flow paths in a program grows exponentially with respect to the number of conditional and iterative statements. In fact, the total number of flow paths through a program unit is approximately 2^k, where k is the number of control statements. For example, to test the following pair of nested **If** statements

```
If B1 Then
    •
    •
    •
    If B2 Then
        •
        •
        •
    Else
        •
        •
        •
Else
    •
    •
    •
```

Figure 15–1
Creation of Alternative Flow Paths by Control Statements

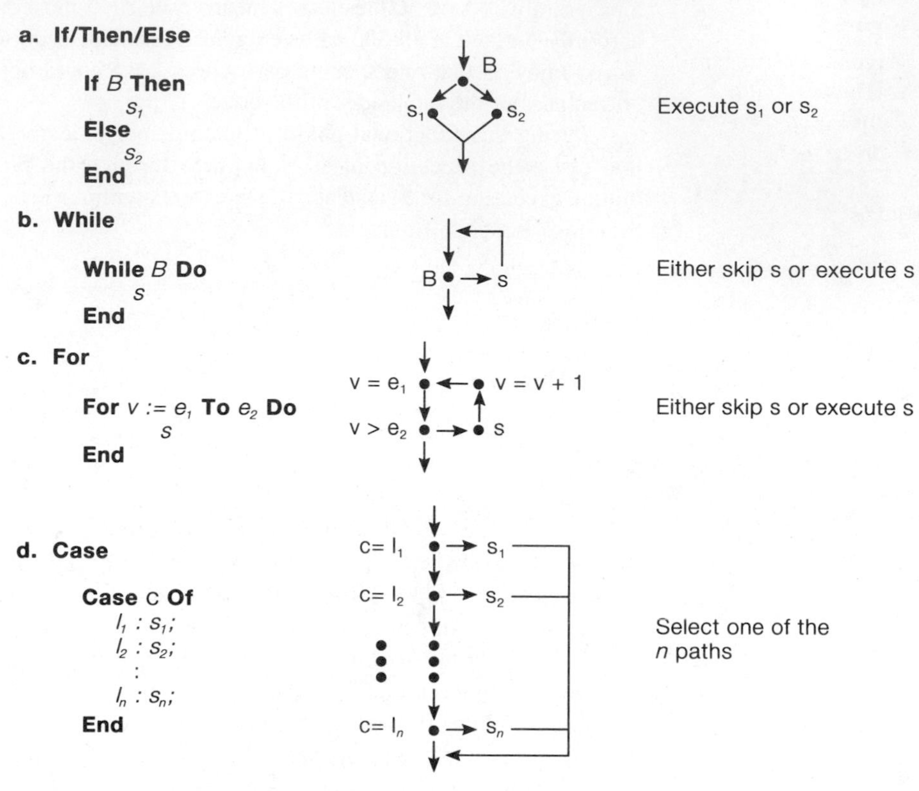

we will require data sets chosen from each of the following four cases:

Case 1: B_1 = True, B_2 = True
Case 2: B_1 = True, B_2 = False
Case 3: B_1 = False, B_2 = True
Case 4: B_1 = False, B_2 = False

If we had three **If/Then/Else** statements we would require 8 (2^3) distinct test cases. For small values of k such as 3, 4, or 5 the number of distinct flow paths remains manageable (about 8, 16, or 32) and it is feasible to select data sets to test each path. However, in very large procedures with a great deal of decision logic, the number of control statements may grow to 10 or 15, and we would need thousands of pieces of data to test every possible flow path. We probably would not be able to test the program unit adequately, and undetected bugs might be present in the finished product. The requirements of functional testing present another reason for keeping program units short and testing each one as it is developed rather than attempting to test a large program all at once.

Thus our first group of test data is directed at testing every expected flow path in the program, preferably testing each path a number of times. We will illustrate functional testing using the procedure in Figure 15–2, which computes a worker's pay based on the number of hours worked, the hourly pay rate, and an overtime bonus of

Figure 15–2
Paycheck Program to Demonstrate Functional Testing Procedures

```
(* Program used to illustrate the principles of empirical testing. *)
Procedure PayCheck( Hours: Real; PayRate: Real; Var Pay: Real;
                    Var Error: Boolean );
Begin
    If (Hours < 0.00) Or (PayRate < 3.75) Then
        Error := True;
    Else
        Error := False;
        If Hours <= 40.0 Then
            (* There is no overtime. *)
            Pay := Hours * PayRate;
        Else
            If Hours <= 58 Then
                (* There is between 0 and 18 hours of overtime. *)
                Pay := (40.0 * PayRate) + (Hours - 40.0) * PayRate * 1.5;
            Else
                (* There is excessive overtime. *)
                Write('Excessive overtime hours, ');
                WriteLn('will only be paid for 18');
                Pay := (40.0 * PayRate) + (18.0 * PayRate * 1.5);
            Endif;
        Endif;
    Endif;
End PayCheck;
```

50% for all hours above 40. No workers may work more than 18 hours of overtime; if they do, they are paid for only 18 hours.

During functional testing we must select a number of data sets from each of the following three cases:

Case 1: Hours worked $\leq$ 40 (no overtime)
Case 2: 40 $<$ hours worked $<$ 58 (overtime)
Case 3: 58 $<$ hours worked (excessive overtime)

Choosing sets from each of these three cases will ensure that every statement in the **Else** clause of the first **If** statement will be executed at least once.

As a second example, the functional testing phase of the binary search algorithm of Figure 6–3 will need data sets from each of the following cases:

Case 1: A data set where the key is not found
Case 2: A data set where the key is found on the first look (so no recursion is done)
Case 3: A data set where the key is found after k looks, where $k > 1$, so that at least one recursive call is made

These examples show that thorough functional testing does not require thousands upon thousands of test sets to be done correctly. If a procedure is small and well structured, a relatively small number of carefully chosen data sets should suffice to test all normal functions; as we have said, the amount of data is not as critical as how well it was selected.

Boundary Tests

One particular subset of data is so critical that testing it should be carried out as a separate, identifiable stage. This subset is composed of data sets that fall at the limits of a range of legal values or at a crossover point between two distinct classes of test cases. These data sets are called *extremal cases* or *boundary cases*, and this phase of testing is usually called *boundary testing*.

One of the most common errors in programming is the *off-by-one* error, in which boundary or termination conditions are not handled correctly. Whenever your program includes statements of the following form:

```
While (i <= Limit) Do . . .
If (x > 0.0) Or (x < 10) Then . . .
Repeat . . . Until (Count = MaxCount)
```

it is important to test your program with boundary values such as:

i = Limit
x = 0.0
x = 10.0
Count = MaxCount

Other examples of extremal testing include such operations as:

1. Storing a value into the first or last element of a linear data structure or the root or leaves of a hierarchical structure
2. Retrieving a value from the first or last position of a linear data structure or from the root or leaves of a hierarchical structure
3. Filling a data structure exactly to its maximum declared capacity
4. Testing a procedure using the largest or smallest legal values of its parameters
5. Executing a loop the allowed minimum and maximum number of times

For a specific example, let's look again at the paycheck program of Figure 15–2. We should include one or more test data sets selected from each of the following four boundary cases:

Case 4: Hours = 0.0 (the lower boundary for legal hours)
Case 5: Pay rate = 3.75 (the lower boundary for a legal pay rate)
Case 6: Hours = 40.0 (the crossover point between overtime/no overtime)
Case 7: Hours = 58.0 (the upper limit for overtime hours)

To test our binary search program, we should select data sets that attempt to locate keys stored in the first and last positions of the array. We will also want to test the program with an array that holds the maximum number of elements as well as an array that holds only one.

A related aspect of extremal testing is testing your program on the *null case*. Make sure that your program works correctly for the degenerate case where the program has nothing to do. Where appropriate, check your program with test cases such as an empty file, an empty table, an array of length 0, or a pointer value of **Nil**.

For example, we should test the binary search program by attempting to retrieve a key from an empty array.

Error Tests

The goal of the first two phases of our unit test operations is to ensure that the program functions properly on legal and expected data. The third aspect of testing moves into the area of *illegal data*. We must ensure that our program takes meaningful action in the presence of improper or illegal input. A program that has this characteristic is said to be *robust*.

Illegal data items can fall into four categories, each of which should be included in this phase of testing:

1. Data that violate the specifications given in the problem specification document
2. Data that violate physical or real-world constraints (e.g., 25 hours per day, 8 days per week)
3. Data that violate the restrictions imposed on a value by the **Type** declarations (e.g., a Boolean value of 'Maybe'; an integer value of 2.561)
4. Data that is missing or not provided by the user

For all illegal cases, no matter how pathological, your program should do something meaningful and not terminate abnormally. If possible, try to carry on with program execution. If that is impossible, produce an instructive error message and allow the user to correct the entry. A program that checks for errors and handles them in a way that allows meaningful processing to continue is said to exhibit *graceful degradation*. A program with this characteristic is obviously more user-friendly than one that terminates abnormally whenever an error occurs.

With our paycheck program, we would include the following two test cases to see how the program handles values that fall outside specifications:

Case 8: Hours < 0.0 or Hours > 168.0 (an illegal value for Hours)
Case 9: Pay rate < 3.75 (an illegal value for Pay Rate)

We should also check to see what would happen if the input values violate the syntax of the real data type:

Case 10: Hours nonreal (e.g., 'Forty')
Case 11: Pay rate nonreal (e.g., '$5.00')

In all these cases, the program should detect the error, provide useful information to the user about the cause of the error, and allow the user to recover by reentering correct values, as in the following dialogue.

```
> $5.50        (* The user incorrectly includes a '$' character in the pay
                  rate field. *)
** Incorrect value for pay rate. The character '$' is not allowed, please
reenter. **
>
```

Failure to adequately test error detection and correction can lead to a very unforgiving and "user-unfriendly" program. Under normal operating conditions such programs work properly; however, when the user makes an error (e.g., by striking the wrong key or misunderstanding the type of input requested), the program behaves erratically and/or terminates abnormally.

Volume Tests

The last set of unit test cases is used for *volume testing*. Volume testing is generally not carried out on small student assignments because of time and cost constraints, but it is an important aspect of testing in the real world. During volume testing, we test the program's behavior under the stress of extreme conditions either in its operating environment or in the quantity of data. We test the program under such conditions as

1. Excessive amounts of input data
2. Large amounts of data entered in a very short period of time
3. A large number of simultaneous input operations
4. A large number of persons using the program at the same time
5. Running the program on a heavily overloaded computer system

The last set of test cases is included because some flow paths in a program are designed to handle the rarest of circumstances—those that occur under the most extreme conditions. Only if we correctly simulate these extreme operating conditions can we force the execution of those flow paths and be sure the program will work properly when faced with this situation in real life. To force these conditions to occur, we must typically stress the program with excessive amounts and rates of data.

For example, a program may have a block of code that deals with the situation in which the system is completely out of available memory (e.g., the memory manager of chapter 4 cannot satisfy the request New(X)). This situation is rare and would not be observed under normal working conditions. We may have to set up a test case that simulates the occurrence of thousands of simultaneous requests for memory to force this condition to exist.

As a second example, you may have a 5,000-element array that holds values to be sorted and an error-handler that is activated only when the array overflows. You will need at least one test case with 5,001 or more data values to force the invocation of this procedure.

Volume testing is the most time-consuming testing to perform because it may be difficult to set up test data that forces a special condition to occur or an unusual flow path to be executed. However, it is important that volume testing be done. If a particular flow path is never executed during testing, we can never really be sure of the execution-time behavior of that sequence of code.

The importance of testing programs in short, compact units becomes clear when we look back at our selection of test cases for the procedure PayCheck in Figure 15–2. This procedure is quite short, only about 20 lines in length, but thorough and complete testing of that unit required us to carefully select a number of data sets from 11 distinct classes. As program units grow in size to 100, 200, or more lines, the number of cases needed to test them grows impossibly large, and soon it is no longer feasible to apply the systematic procedures presented here. Untested program statements are likely to have undetected bugs, and the result is an incorrect program. Without testing, a bug may not be detected until a user supplies a data set that activates the bug and causes the program to "bomb out."

15.2.2 System Integration

We have just described the testing procedures that apply to an individual program unit. However, the fact that each separate unit works properly does not guarantee that the complete software package will work correctly. Errors may exist in the interface between two procedures, and these errors might not be apparent until the separate units are linked and tested as a complete system. Therefore, additional testing of the overall program is essential for determining whether the individual pieces fit together properly. This second phase of testing is typically called *system testing* or *system integration*.

System integration typically proceeds in stages. Units are tested in small clusters that in turn are integrated with other clusters until the entire package has been completely assembled. For example, given the program development tree of Figure 15-3, we might first carry out unit testing on program units M_1, M_2, M_3, and M_4 to make sure they are correct. We might then choose to link and test the (M_2, M_3, M_4) cluster. Similarly, we might do unit testing on M_5, M_6, and M_7 followed by system testing on the (M_5, M_6, M_7) cluster. After both clusters have been thoroughly tested, we would integrate and test all seven units operating as a complete system.

The following three types of error would be discovered during system testing and would not be discovered during unit testing:

1. Errors in the interface between two program units
2. Errors or misunderstandings in interpreting the specifications of a program unit
3. Errors caused by side effects in the execution of a program unit

Let's look at an example of this last class of errors. Suppose we are asked to develop a procedure to update some records in a disk file. The procedure should lock the desired records, update them, and then unlock them so that other program units can access the new value. If our procedure incorrectly fails to unlock the records when it is finished, we might not detect that error during unit testing, since our only concern at that time is whether the procedure is doing its job of updating the record. The disastrous side effect of leaving part of the file in a locked state might not be discovered until other procedures try unsuccessfully to access the new value following the update.

However, this class of errors (those caused by side effects), should not occur in any well-written program; they are evidence of violation of the independence guidelines laid down in section 14.5.2, where we specified that procedures should not modify global variables or have unexpected side effects on any other part of the program. If these principles are followed, only errors of type 1 or 2—interface problems or a misunderstanding of specifications—should be uncovered during sys-

Figure 15–3
Program Development Tree

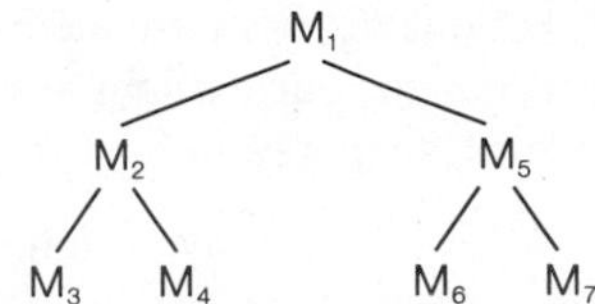

tem testing. Thse two types of errors are really quite similar and might be regarded as two variations of the same problem.

Interface errors are syntactic or semantic inconsistencies between the invocation of a program unit and its declarations, and they generally fall into one of the following categories:

1. Incorrect number of parameters
2. Incorrect order of parameters
3. Incorrect data type for one or more parameters
4. Improper parameter passing mechanism (i.e., value, reference)
5. Improper unit type (e.g., function, procedure)
6. Mismatched program unit name

Some languages let these errors pass undetected during unit testing, so they will need to be caught during system testing. In other languages, especially strongly typed languages such as Pascal, Modula-2, or Ada, the compiler will catch some of these interface inconsistencies at compile time and they will be flagged as syntax errors. Even in strongly-typed languages, however, it is possible to have interface errors when using independently compiled library routines stored as relocatable object modules. Thus, the first phase of system testing is directed at simply making sure the program units will link together properly.

Even if the interfaces are in order, problems can still arise from a misunderstanding about how to interpret the value of an input or output parameter. Such an error is called an *interface specification error*. For example, the person writing a function to evaluate some complex trigonometric formula might assume the result is to be returned as a real number whose units are radians. The person invoking this function may assume that the result is real and the units are degrees. Each will test his or her own unit under his or her own (possibly incorrect) assumption and determine that it is correct. Only when these two routines are put together will the incompatibility be detected. However, specification errors will be minimized if we have a clearly written program design document and if each programmer adheres exactly to the calling sequence described in that document.

Thus, if we implement our individual units exactly as described in the procedure specification section of the program design document and we adhere to the guidelines of independence and logical coherence, the difficulty of carrying out system-level testing should be greatly reduced.

15.2.3 Acceptance Testing

The last phase of testing is called *acceptance testing*. At this point we determine whether the program is finished and can be released for general use. Acceptance testing differs from unit testing and system testing in two very important ways:

1. It is typically done by the end-user, not the programmer.
2. It is carried out without any knowledge of the internal structure and organization of the program.

The users last involvment in the project was helping to develop the problem specification document, which we described in chapter 13. Since that point, the design, implementation, unit testing, and system testing phases have been carried out by the software development team without direct user assistance. It is now time for the user to become involved in acceptance testing to determine whether the software product is correct as it stands.

The user brings an important, nontechnical perspective to the testing operation. In selecting data to use in checking the program, users can draw on their specialized knowledge of the applications area, the environment in which it will operate, and the characteristics and habits of the user community. Special situations or conditions that were ignored by the technical staff but that are important to the users will be anticipated and more thoroughly tested. Thus, acceptance testing is not simply more testing but testing from a different perspective—that of a user, not a developer. In addition, acceptance testing is more concerned with user-related issues such as user-friendliness, ease of use, and on-line assistance.

The second major difference is that acceptance testing is carried out in ignorance of the internal structure of the program. Unit and system-level testing is called *white-box testing*—it is carried out with complete knowledge of the internal design of the program. We typically choose a piece of data to test a specific flow path, procedure, or module. Our test data act like probes, examining the correctness of individual components of the program. Acceptance testing, however, is *black-box testing*, because the user is totally unaware of the program's internal structure. In fact, the user may be totally naive about programming and computers. All he or she has available is the original problem specification document, which describes what the program is supposed to do and shows what test cases should be tried during acceptance testing. Alternatively, users may select their own test cases based on their knowledge of the application. The users are not concerned about testing every flow path or module; they simply want to make sure the program operates according to specifications.

When the program has passed acceptance testing, it is deemed correct and released for general use. By the standards of empirical testing, it is correct. Of course, there could still be errors in the program that were not uncovered, even if the testing guidelines laid out in this section were followed precisely. However, following these guidelines is the best that we can do using empirical testing methods. To do better than this and to be able to make stronger claims about correctness, we must use an entirely different technique, called *formal verification*.

15.3 FORMAL VERIFICATION

What can we say about our program after we have completed the empirical testing procedures described in section 15.2? As we mentioned at the beginning of that section, we cannot say that the program is correct. Testing can only detect the presence of errors; it can never prove their absence. All we can say about the program is that for a wide range of very carefully chosen data cases, it has worked properly and produced the correct results. From this experience, we extrapolate to the statement that the program will work correctly under all circumstances, even for those test cases not explicitly tested. This extrapolation is really a "leap of faith" that is not based on either mathematical formalities or physical laws but on empirical observation and human judgment.

Thus empirical testing establishes only a weak form of correctness, quite different from the idea of proof in such classical disciplines as mathematics or logic. If a mathematician wished to study the formal properties of a function, he or she would

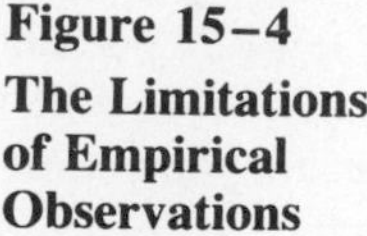

Figure 15–4
The Limitations of Empirical Observations

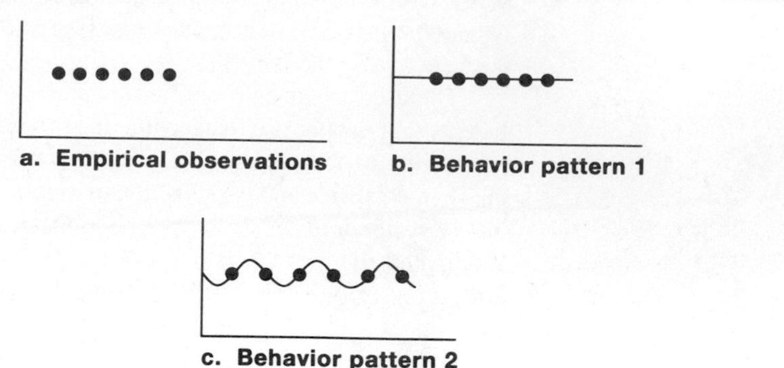

not do it by empirically observing the value of that function at a few carefully selected points $(x_0, y_0), (x_1, y_1), (x_2, y_2), \ldots$, as shown in Figure 15–4a. A mathematician knows that it would not be possible to make formal assertions about the function's behavior at points not explicitly observed. The function could demonstrate very different and unanticipated characteristics at the unobserved points, as shown in Figure 15–4b and c. Because of the limitation on what can be asserted based on empirical observations, the mathematician would instead attempt to express the function in a form that describes its continuous behavior over the entire range of its definition: $y = f(x)$. This form would allow the mathematician to make provable assertions about the formal properties of the function f.

Computer scientists are trying to demonstrate that software development can utilize the same principles. Just as mathematicians can prove that a theorem is correct, so can programmers prove that a program is correct. A program, P, could be treated like a function with inputs $x_1, x_2, \ldots, x_n$. We could then make assertions about y, the output of program P, for any arbitrary input, that is, $y = P(x_1, x_2, \ldots, x_n)$. Of course, the most important assertion is that y is the output described in the specification document for input $x_1, x_2, \ldots, x_n$. Developing assertions about the logical and mathematical properties of program units is called *formal verification* of programs.

This formal approach to correctness allows us to make much stronger claims about the behavior of a program. Instead of observing its instantaneous behavior at a few selected points, as in Figure 15–4a, we assert its correctness over the entire range of defined inputs. These assertions have the highest level of reliability and essentially allow us to make the claim that the program is provably correct.

Program verification is a complicated and somewhat controversial technique, but recent developments are simplifying this process. New programming languages designed with program verification in mind include special features and formalized semantics that make the verification process easier. Theoretical computer scientists believe that correctness should be an integral part of a program's design. This constructive approach to verification is promising, especially for programs in which computations are executed in parallel as opposed to sequential execution (e.g., the parallel sorting algorithm developed in Section 6.6).

The technique of formal verification is based on describing, for every statement S in a programming language, what conditions we know to be true before S is executed (the *preconditions*) and what conditions we know to be true after S has been executed (the *postconditions*). The relation between the preconditions, the postconditions, and the statement is usually written

{P} S {Q}

where

{P} are Boolean preconditions
{Q} are Boolean postconditions
S is the statement in the language

Together, {P} and {Q} are called *assertions*, because they assert that a given condition is true at a given point in a program. Our goal, however, is not to make an assertion about the behavior of a single statement but to study the behavior of entire programs. We can proceed from the behavior of a single statement to the behavior of sequences of statements by using the *composition laws* of symbolic logic, which say that

{P} S_1 {Q} and {Q} S_2 {R} implies
{P} S_1; S_2 {R}

Thus, by knowing the preconditions and postconditions associated with individual statements, we can make assertions about what happens when sequences of statements are executed, that is, when we run a program. In the above example, if we know that the Boolean predicate {P} is initially true, then we know that postcondition {R} will be true after executing the "program" S_1; S_2.

For example, if we had the assignment statement a := b + 5 and we knew that the variable b was positive when we reached this statement, then we would know (by the formal semantics of the assignment statement) that the variable a would be greater than 5 and b would be unchanged after the assignment operation was completed. We could write this assertion as:

```
{b > 0}
a := b + 5
{b unchanged and a > 5}
```

In general, though, we are interested in going in the reverse order: usually we know what we want to end up with, and we must determine what initial conditions need to be asserted to achieve this result.

Given the assignment statement v := e and some postcondition {Q}, how do we go about determining the necessary precondition {P} so the {P} v := e {Q}? If we think about the semantics of the assignment operation, we realize that it makes e and v "equivalent" in the sense that after the assignment statement is executed, the value of the expression e is stored in the location associated with the variable v. Therefore, if {Q} is true using the value v after execution of v := e, then it must have been true using the value of the expression e before execution. Thus, the precondition {P} can be derived from {Q} by simply replacing every occurrence of v in {Q} with e. The precondition that results is called the *weakest precondition* of {Q}. For example, the weakest precondition for

```
{P}
Disc := (b * b) − (4.0 * a * c)
{b = 10 and Disc > 0}
```

would be determined by replacing Disc by $b^2 - 4ac$ in the given postcondition, resulting in

$$(b^2 - 4ac) > 0$$

We also know that $b = 10$, and this condition will not be affected by the assignment operation. Therefore, the above expression becomes

$$100 - 4ac > 0$$

or

$$ac < 25$$

and the desired precondition P is

```
{b = 10 and ac < 25}
Disc := b * b − 4.0 * a * c
{b = 10 and Disc > 0)
```

Next, let us look at the formal properties of the **If/Then/Else** statement.

{*P*} **If** *B* **Then** S_1 **Else** S_2 **End** {*Q*}

The formal semantics of the **If** statement say that if B is true, we execute statement S_1, otherwise, we execute statement S_2. If we write the above statement as

{*P*} **If** *B* **Then** {P_1} S_1 {Q_1} **Else** {P_2} S_2 {Q_2} **End** {*Q*}

then we can say that when we have completed execution of the statement, the following postcondition {Q} must be true:

$$\{Q\} = (B \text{ and } \{Q_1\}) \text{ or } (\text{not } B \text{ and } \{Q_2\})$$

For example, consider a simple conditional statement which we claim determines the absolute value of a variable x:

```
If x >= 0 Then
    y := x
Else
    y := -x
End
```

The empirical testing method of section 15.2 would use a set of test data (with one value of x >= 0, and one value where x < 0) to "prove" our claim. The precondition P for this conditional statement is that the variable x has been defined. From the semantics of the **If** statement, we can easily derive the preconditions for the **Then** and **Else** clauses.

```
{x has been defined}
If x >= 0 Then
    {x >= 0} →
    y := x
Else
    {not (x >=0)}
    y := −x
End
```

The postconditions are derived using the techniques discussed earlier for assignment statements.

```
{x has been defined}
If x >= 0 Then
    {x >= 0}
    y := x
    {(x >= 0) and (y = x)}
Else
    {not (x >= 0)}
    y := −x
    {not (x >= 0) and (y = −x)}
End
```

The postcondition for the complete **If** statement is obtained by noting that only one branch of the **If** is ever executed. Therefore one of the two postconditions must be true. The final postcondition becomes

{Q} = {[(x >= 0) and (y = x)] or [not (x >= 0) and (y = −x)]}
{Q} = {[(x >= 0) and (y = x)] or [(x < 0) and (y = −x)]}

which is mathematically equivalent to

y = abs(x)

We have formally verified that if the precondition {x has been defined} is true, the **If** statement shown above correctly determines the absolute value of x and assigns that value to y.

Finally, we come to looping statements of the language, and we will show how verification works on the **While** statement.

{P} **While** B **Do** S **End** {Q}

The behavior of the **Repeat** and **For** are very similar.

Looping statements are the most difficult statements about which to make assertions, for two reasons:

1. Because we do not know how many times the loop will execute, the postcondition {Q} must be independent of how many times we go through the loop. Specifically, it must be true on loop entry (since the loop may execute zero times), and it must be true whenever we exit the loop. Because of these requirements, postconditions on loops are frequently called *loop invariants*.
2. It is not enough to simply say that the postcondition {Q} will be true on loop exit. We must also prove that the loop will actually terminate in finite time. For example, look at the following statement:

   {a > 0} **While** True **Do** a := a + 1 **End** {a > 0}

   The postcondition is true, but that is immaterial, since the loop is infinite and will never terminate.

Probably the most important aspect of formal program verification is determining the proper loop invariant for each loop in the program. For example, suppose we are given the following program fragment to find the largest element in an array X[1], . . . , X[N].

```
{N >=1 and X1, . . . , XN are defined}
i := 1;
Big := X[1];
While i < N Do
    i := i + 1;
    If Big < X[i] Then
        Big := X[i]
    End
End
```

A careful study of the loop shows that when i has any value in the range [1 . . N], the variable Big contains the largest of the first i values in the array X. This condition is true upon loop entry since i = 1 and Big = X[1]. It also remains true on every iteration through the loop. Thus, the loop invariant can be expressed as

```
{N >=1 and X1, . . . , XN are defined}
i := 1;
Big := X[1];
{Big = Max[X1, . . . , Xi], 1 <= i <= N}
While i < N Do
    I := i + 1;
    If Big < X[i] Then
        Big := X[i]
        {Big = Max[X1, . . . , Xi], 1 <= i <= N}
    End
End
```

In addition to determining the loop invariant, we must also show that the loop terminates—a fairly easy task in this case. We rely on the fact that between any two finite integers i and j there can be only a finite number of other integers. We begin at the integer value $i = 1$ and continue adding 1 until we exceed the integer value N, which we know is greater than or equal to 1 because of the preconditions. Therefore, this operation must terminate after a finite number of additions.

From the semantics of the **While** loop, we know that when the loop terminates, the Boolean condition (not B) must be true. Since we have just shown that the preceding loop must terminate, we know that the negation of the boolean condition $i < N$ will be true upon completion. The negation of $i < N$ is $i \geq N$.

At this point we have determined a loop invariant that we know to be true for every pass through the loop, we have shown that the loop will terminate, and finally, we have stated the condition that must be true upon loop termination. Combining this information, we get:

$$\{Q\} = \{\underbrace{(i \geq N)}_{\text{Loop termination condition}} \text{ and } \underbrace{(1 \leq i \leq N, \text{Big} = \text{Max}[X_1, \ldots X_i])}_{\text{Loop invariant}}\}$$

Together, the two clauses $(i \geq N)$ and $(1 \leq i \leq N)$ imply that $i = N$, and therefore

$$\{Q\} = \{\text{Big} = \text{Max}[X_1, \ldots, X_N]\}$$

Thus, the code fragment to find the biggest element in an array has been proven correct.

A proof of this type is the strongest possible form of correctness. We have not merely examined the behavior of the code for a few selected cases but are stating that for *any* data set for which the precondition $\{N \geq 1$ and $X_1, \ldots, X_N$ are defined$\}$ is true, the program will end with the desired postcondition $\{\text{Big} = \text{Max}[X_1, \ldots, X_N]\}$.

Verification is a complex technique. To be done properly, it requires mathematical sophistication in such areas as symbolic logic, predicate calculus, mathematical induction, and axiomatic semantics. If you look through the literature, you will see that the overwhelming majority of proofs have been carried out on simple 10- to 30-line "toy" programs that find the sum of *N* numbers, the greatest common divisor, or (as we did here) the biggest of *N* numbers. The reason is quite obvious: proofs of program correctness can be quite long, frequently longer than the program itself! Proofs of more interesting and more realistic programs can run to dozens of pages and can be difficult to follow. This complexity is one of the main arguments people use against the future of verification as a realistic programming tool. They feel that the proofs are so long and complicated that there is as much likelihood of an error in the proof as there is of an error in the original program.

Although this argument appears to be an attractive and somewhat convincing, it is not completely true. A number of developments in this area could make it more likely that formal verification will ultimately become an important and usable tool.

The first is the development of languages whose structure is designed to facilitate the verification process. Early languages such as FORTRAN and COBOL, with their **goto** statements, common variables, equivalence statements, side effects, and weak typing rules made proof development virtually impossible. Newer procedural languages such as Pascal, Ada, and Modula-2, with their improved control structure, reduced side effects, and rigidly enforced scope rules, have eased this task somewhat. Functional languages like LISP or nonprocedural languages such as Prolog, which are based entirely on the principles of symbolic logic, could simplify verification even further.

Even more helpful would be the development of automated program verifiers—programs that would attempt to carry out mechanically the proof that we did manually. The input to a program verifier would be the program to be verified and some formalized representation of the specification document that describes what the program is supposed to do, perhaps in the form of a decision table or a finite-state machine, as described in chapter 13. The output of a verifier would be a statement that the program is or is not correct according to the given specifications.[1]

No reliable, general-purpose program verifiers are currently available, but research work in this area is being carried out, and the development of such programs would make formal verification a realistic goal. Since verification will probably become a more important tool in the near future, programmers will need to have the necessary mathematical background in logic, discrete mathematics, and predicate calculus and will need to be familiar with the basic concepts of verification, such as preconditions, postconditions, and loop invariants.

15.4 INFORMAL VERIFICATION

Until formal verification of every program unit becomes a practical reality, there is one other thing that programmers can learn from these techniques and use in their own programs—the idea of *informal verification*. Informal verification means that you argue and rationalize the correctness of your program as it is being written (just as with formal methods) but without necessarily using the mathematical notation and proof techniques of formal verification. Instead, you use natural language to argue and convince yourself of the correctness of what you have written. Informal verification represents a middle ground between the difficulties of the complex verification methods discussed earlier and avoiding the problem altogether.

Too often, programmers do not even bother to think about their programs as they are being written. They assume that if they make a mistake, it will be caught and corrected during testing (so why worry now?). This approach increases the time and difficulty of the debugging and testing task. (Remember our earlier comment—the easiest bug to correct is the one that *did not* get into the code!) For example, suppose that we are writing the following fragment to compute the sum of the first N elements in an array X:

[1] As an interesting aside, we note that this problem cannot be solved for any arbitrary program P. There will always exist some programs for which the verifier will not be able to decide the question of correctness. This important result comes from the area of computability theory.

```
i := 1;
Sum := 0;
While i ? N Do (* Not sure which relational operator to use here *)
    Sum := Sum + X[i];
    i := i + 1
End
```

If we are not completely sure whether the test condition in the loop should be $i < N$ or $i \leq N$, a lazy solution would be simply to write out whichever operator we think is correct, knowing that boundary testing should detect the error if we choose the wrong one. That may be true, but if this practice occurs often enough, it is possible for a large number of bugs to creep into the program, and some of them may be overlooked. Certainly this laziness will add greatly to the time spent in debugging and testing.

The discussion on verification in the previous section has shown that it is possible to reason logically about the behavior of programs. We can use this form of logical reasoning to argue the correctness of our code, even if we do not use the formal notation of symbolic or Boolean logic. For our preceeding code fragment, the reasoning might go something like this:

> When we initially enter the loop, the value of i is 1. Within the loop we add X[1] to Sum, set i to 2, and end this first iteration. After one pass, we have added one item from X to Sum and i is 2. After two passes, we have added two items from X to Sum and i is 3. Continuing this process, I can see that after k passes through the loop, we will have added X[1], . . . , X[k] to Sum and i will have the value k + 1. Thus, if I want to exit the loop after I have computed the sum X[1] + . . . + X[N], I will want to continue iterating while i has the values 1, 2, . . . , N and I will want to terminate the loop when i has the value N + 1. Based on this line of reasoning, the correct Boolean condition to write in the **While** loop must be **While** i <– N.

Even though our argument has been expressed in natural language rather than mathematical notation, this type of informal reasoning can be a powerful tool in helping you write correct programs. Every time you write out a loop or other control structure, stop and reason through the code you have just written. Convince yourself of the correctness of the logic by trying to explain its behavior in terms of the state of the computation. A good habit to get into is to include your *assertions* about the behavior of the program as comments in the code, as shown in Figure 15–5.

These assertions, even if they are informally stated and not part of an explicit proof, can be an important component of the finished program. They are a written statement describing the programmer's thoughts about the program's behavior. The assertions can be checked later, by the programmer or someone else, to verify that the reasoning is sound and that all the stated claims are indeed true. Some languages (e.g., Ada) contain language facilities that allow you to check your assertions during execution and interrupt the program if any are shown to be false.

Another important verification technique that has been developed recently is the "formalization" of the process of checking the informal assertions about program

Figure 15–5
Including Assertions as Comments in the Code

```
i := 1;
Sum := 0;

(* Assertion: The following loop will work correctly if N >= 1 and the elements
X[1], . . . , X[N] have been previously defined. *)
While i <= N Do
    Sum := Sum + X[i];
    i := i + 1
    (* Assertion: At this point Sum will contain X[1] + . . . + X[k] and i =
    k + 1, where k is the number of completed loop iterations. *)
End;
(* Assertion: At this point Sum will contain X[1] + . . . + X[N] and the
problem has been correctly solved. *)
```

correctness. Instead of reasoning logically only to themselves, many programmers now make a much more formal oral presentation to a group of their peers and fellow team members. Such a presentation is called a *structured walkthrough*.[2]

In this presentation, the programmer tries to argue and convince the listeners of the correctness of his or her work. The arguments follow a form very similar to the one we gave earlier and should be based on the principles of logic and mathematics, rather than on intuition or common sense. The audience acts as a devil's advocate, trying to find flaws in the reasoning and uncover errors or inconsistencies in the logic. They pick and probe until they are satisfied that the basic design is sound and that the assertions about the program's behavior are indeed correct.

Thus, even though formal verification may not yet be a completely feasible tool for widespread use, there are still a number of realistic steps that can be taken to minimize the number of bugs that get into the code:

1. Reason logically about the behavior of your code as it is being written. Convince yourself of its correctness immediately, rather than waiting until testing.
2. Include comments in the code to list your assertions about the program's behavior and the reasoning you used to justify the correctness of the code.
3. Show these assertions to one or more professional computer scientists and try to convince them, by reviewing your arguments, that your assertions are indeed correct.

These steps, along with a well-organized empirical testing scheme, will go a long way toward eliminating bugs before they occur, quickly removing the few that are present, and ensuring the correctness of the finished software product.

15.5 CONCLUSION

This chapter completes our all too brief discussion of programming in the large and the software life cycle (Figure 12–2). Our purpose here has been to introduce you to

[2] This type of presentation technique need not be limited to the correctness of code. It is also used to argue the correctness of both problem specifications and program design.

the wealth of important concepts, issues, and decisions that go into the creation of correct, efficient, cost-effective, and maintainable software.

As we mentioned in the very first chapter of this text, students often have the mistaken idea that software development is equivalent to implementation. In addition, they sometimes believe that coding is the most important and intellectually challenging aspect of problem solving. We hope that part II of the text has introduced you to some of the important and highly creative tasks (in addition to implementation) that must be successfully completed to ensure the success of a software development project.

The difference between coding and software development is like the difference between a study of grammar and creative writing. A knowledge of the former will allow you to write correctly, but a knowledge of both will allow you to write elegantly. The issues addressed in part II of the text are directed at teaching you how to create both correct and elegant software.

CHAPTER EXERCISES

1. Discuss exactly what test data you would use to unit test the Memory Manager program shown in section 4.6.
2. Repeat exercise 1 using the MergeSort program of section 5.4.4.
3. Repeat exercise 1 using the Symbol Table package of section 9.3.
4. Discuss what type of volume testing should be done on the hash table/open addressing procedure shown in Figure 9–11. Is volume testing needed or appropriate for the chaining method of collision resolution? Explain why or why not.
5. How many unique flow paths are there in the following skeletal outline of a program unit (where S_i are legal noncontrol statements)? List each one.

```
If B1 Then
    S1
Else
    If B2 Then
        S2
    Else
        While B3 Do
            S3
        End;
        S4
    End
End;
S5;
If B4 Then
    S6
End
```

6. Here is the skeletal outline of a program.

```
While B1 Do
    S1;
    If B2 Then
        S2
    Elseif B3 Then
        S3
    Else
        While B4 Do
            S4
        End
    End
End
```

   Identify the complete set of test cases that would have to be tested to ensure that every flow path would be checked. Identify the test cases by specifying the truth or falsehood of the Boolean expressions $B_1, \ldots, B_4$.
7. Do you think the program called PayCheck in Figure 15–2 has the characteristic called graceful degradation? Justify your answer.
8. In the following code fragment, identify the boundary tests that should be conducted.

```
Var
    a : Array [1 .. 100] Of Integer;
        •
        •
        •
    Read(i);
    Read(x);
    If (i < 1) Or (i > 100) Then
        Write("Error")
    Else
        If i <= 50 Then
            a[i] := x
        Else
            Repeat
                x := x + delta;
                i := i + 1
            Until i >= 90
        End
    End
```

9. The following program fragment implements integer division by repeated subtraction:

```
(* Computes a/n by repeated subtraction to get quotient q and remainder r. a
   >= 0 and n > 0 *)
q := 0;
r := 0;
While a >= n Do
      q := q + 1;
      a := a - n
End;
r := a
```

Prove formally that this code is correct if the necessary preconditions are met.

10. What is the loop invariant in the previous exercise?

INDEX

S

T